# Price Index Concepts and Measurement

Studies in Income and Wealth
Volume 70

National Bureau of Economic Research
Conference on Research in Income and Wealth

# Price Index Concepts and Measurement

Edited by **W. Erwin Diewert, John Greenlees, and Charles Hulten**

**The University of Chicago Press**

Chicago and London

W. Erwin Diewert is professor of economics at the University of British Columbia and a research associate of the National Bureau of Economic Research. John Greenlees is a research economist in the Division of Price and Index Number Research at the Bureau of Labor Statistics. Charles Hulten is professor of economics at the University of Maryland, chairman of the executive committee of the Conference on Research in Income and Wealth, and a research associate of the National Bureau of Economic Research.

The University of Chicago Press, Chicago 60637
The University of Chicago Press, Ltd., London

Printed in the United States of America

18 17 16 15 14 13 12 11 10 09   1 2 3 4 5
ISBN-13: 978-0-226-14855-7 (cloth)
ISBN-10: 0-226-14855-6 (cloth)

Library of Congress Cataloging-in-Publication Data

Price index concepts and measurement / edited by W. Erwin Diewert, John Greenlees, and Charles Hulten.
p. cm. — (Studies in income and wealth ; v. 70)
Includes bibliographical references and indexes.
ISBN-13: 978-0-226-14855-7 (alk. paper)
ISBN-10: 0-226-14855-6 (alk. paper)
1. Indexation (Economics)—Congresses. 2. Inflation (Finance)—Congresses. 3. Price indexes—Congresses. I. Diewert, W. E. (W. Erwin) II. Greenlees, John Shearer. III. Hulten, Charles R. IV. Conference on Research in Income and Wealth. V. Series: Studies in income and wealth ; v. 70.
HC106.3.C714 vol. 70
[HG229.5]
338.5'28—dc22

2009017691

♾ The paper used in this publication meets the minimum requirements of the American National Standard for Information Sciences—Permanence of Paper for Printed Library Materials, ANSI Z39.48-1992.

## Relation of the Directors to the Work and Publications of the National Bureau of Economic Research

1. The object of the NBER is to ascertain and present to the economics profession, and to the public more generally, important economic facts and their interpretation in a scientific manner without policy recommendations. The Board of Directors is charged with the responsibility of ensuring that the work of the NBER is carried on in strict conformity with this object.

2. The President shall establish an internal review process to ensure that book manuscripts proposed for publication DO NOT contain policy recommendations. This shall apply both to the proceedings of conferences and to manuscripts by a single author or by one or more co-authors but shall not apply to authors of comments at NBER conferences who are not NBER affiliates.

3. No book manuscript reporting research shall be published by the NBER until the President has sent to each member of the Board a notice that a manuscript is recommended for publication and that in the President's opinion it is suitable for publication in accordance with the above principles of the NBER. Such notification will include a table of contents and an abstract or summary of the manuscript's content, a list of contributors if applicable, and a response form for use by Directors who desire a copy of the manuscript for review. Each manuscript shall contain a summary drawing attention to the nature and treatment of the problem studied and the main conclusions reached.

4. No volume shall be published until forty-five days have elapsed from the above notification of intention to publish it. During this period a copy shall be sent to any Director requesting it, and if any Director objects to publication on the grounds that the manuscript contains policy recommendations, the objection will be presented to the author(s) or editor(s). In case of dispute, all members of the Board shall be notified, and the President shall appoint an ad hoc committee of the Board to decide the matter; thirty days additional shall be granted for this purpose.

5. The President shall present annually to the Board a report describing the internal manuscript review process, any objections made by Directors before publication or by anyone after publication, any disputes about such matters, and how they were handled.

6. Publications of the NBER issued for informational purposes concerning the work of the Bureau, or issued to inform the public of the activities at the Bureau, including but not limited to the NBER Digest and Reporter, shall be consistent with the object stated in paragraph 1. They shall contain a specific disclaimer noting that they have not passed through the review procedures required in this resolution. The Executive Committee of the Board is charged with the review of all such publications from time to time.

7. NBER working papers and manuscripts distributed on the Bureau's web site are not deemed to be publications for the purpose of this resolution, but they shall be consistent with the object stated in paragraph 1. Working papers shall contain a specific disclaimer noting that they have not passed through the review procedures required in this resolution. The NBER's web site shall contain a similar disclaimer. The President shall establish an internal review process to ensure that the working papers and the web site do not contain policy recommendations, and shall report annually to the Board on this process and any concerns raised in connection with it.

8. Unless otherwise determined by the Board or exempted by the terms of paragraphs 6 and 7, a copy of this resolution shall be printed in each NBER publication as described in paragraph 2 above.

# Contents

# Prefatory Note

This volume contains revised versions of most of the papers and discussions presented at the Conference on Research in Income and Wealth entitled "Price Index Concepts and Measurement," held in Vancouver, British Columbia on June 28–29, 2004.

Funds for the Conference on Research in Income and Wealth are supplied by the Bureau of Economic Analysis, the Bureau of Labor Statistics, the Census Bureau, the Federal Reserve Board, the Internal Revenue Service, and Statistics Canada. We are indebted to these organizations for their support.

We thank Erwin Diewert, John Greenlees, and Charles Hulten, who served as conference organizers and editors of the volume.

# Introduction
## What are the Issues?

W. Erwin Diewert, John Greenlees, and Charles Hulten

The report of the National Research Council (NRC) Panel on Conceptual, Measurement, and Other Statistical Issues in Developing Cost-of-Living Indexes, under the chairmanship of Charles Schultze, addresses virtually all the fundamental issues in consumer price measurement that have long been the subject of debate.[1] Underlying many of these issues is the concept of the Cost-of-Living Index or COLI, or other methodological alternatives to it. The role of the COLI as the methodological foundation for a Consumer Price Index (CPI) was examined and advocated in two previous reviews of the CPI, the 1961 Stigler Report[2] and the 1996 Boskin Report.[3] The NRC panel took a different, and somewhat controversial, position by suggesting a Cost-of-Goods Index (COGI) as a potential alternative theoretical foundation for the CPI. This COGI methodology would differ sharply from the COLI in several ways by, for example, justifying a Laspeyres-type index formula.

The conference on Price Index Concepts and Measurement held in Vancouver in June 2004 provided an opportunity to review the state of understanding of the issues raised by the NRC panel. In this introduction we

W. Erwin Diewert is a professor of economics at the University of British Columbia and a research associate of the National Bureau of Economic Research. John Greenlees is a research economist in the Division of Price and Index Number Research at the Bureau of Labor Statistics. Charles Hulten is a professor of economics at the University of Maryland, chairman of the executive committee of the Conference on Research in Income and Wealth, and a research associate of the National Bureau of Economic Research.

The authors thank Susanto Basu, Dennis Fixler, Alice Nakamura, Mick Silver, Christina Wang, and two anonymous reviewers for their helpful comments.

1. See Schultze and Mackie (2002).
2. See Stigler (1961).
3. See Boskin et al. (1996).

provide a brief overview of the papers presented on those issues, in the context of three fundamental topics—the COLI concept, quality change and new goods, and index scope—which have been central issues in almost all previous reviews of the CPI. We use these topics to organize the discussion of the papers, which appear in the conference volume as chapters 1 through 12. We conclude our overview with a description of the new international manuals on price index construction and with a list of important issues remaining for further research.

## The Cost-of-Living Concept

The most easily recognized distinction between the CPI and a COLI is the fact that the CPI is constructed in part using a Laspeyres-type fixed weight index formula that does not reflect the potential for consumer substitution in response to relative price changes.[4] The role of the COLI concept and its relation to fixed-weight indexes have been central to the debate over the CPI for more than four decades. Support for the COLI concept was one of the broad themes of the Stigler Committee report, which was prepared for the U.S. Government by the National Bureau of Economic Research. The report stated that "A constant-utility index is the appropriate index for the main purposes for which the Consumer Price Index is used" and followed with a series of recommendations designed "to modify the CPI in the direction of a welfare index."[5]

The initial reaction of the Bureau of Labor Statistics (BLS) to the Stigler Committee's COLI recommendation was negative, based on the difficulty of estimating a COLI.[6] However, later statements about the CPI by BLS officials combine references to the COLI as a measurement objective with caveats noting the obstacles to achieving that objective. Using language essentially unchanged since 1984, the current *BLS Handbook of Methods* states:[7]

> A unifying framework for dealing with practical questions that arise in construction of the CPI is provided by the concept of the cost-of-living (COL) index . . . However, the concept is difficult to implement operationally because it holds the standard of living constant, and the living standard must be estimated in some way.
>
> The CPI uses a fixed market basket to hold the base-period living standard constant . . . The CPI provides an approximation to a COL index as a measure of consumption costs.

4. The new international *Consumer Price Index Manual* notes that the usual formula employed by statistical agencies should be termed more precisely a Lowe (1823) index, since the reference periods for the base period quantities and base period prices typically do not coincide as they should in order for an index to be a true Laspeyres index; see ILO et al. (2004, 270–74). The COLI theory has been developed by Pollak (1989), Diewert (1976, 2001, 2002) and others.
5. Stigler (1961, 52–55).
6. Some of the following discussion is taken from Greenlees (2001).
7. Bureau of Labor Statistics (1997, 170).

The Boskin Commission strongly advocated the COLI framework. Its first and fundamental recommendation was that the BLS should adopt the COLI objective, and it also urged the BLS to employ formulas to approximate a COLI as closely as possible. Subsequently, statements by the BLS were somewhat more explicit in indicating the Bureau's acceptance of the cost-of-living objective.

In contrast to the Stigler Committee, the Boskin Commission, and the BLS, the NRC report did not advocate the COLI as the sole appropriate basis for construction of the CPI.[8] As previously noted, the NRC panel provided renewed support for the Laspeyres view of price indexing as an alternative to the COLI framework by proposing the COGI, which they defined as "the change in expenditures required by a household to purchase a fixed-weight basket of goods and services when prices change between some initial reference period and a subsequent comparison period."[9] They argued that neither the COLI nor COGI frameworks alone could handle all of the operational problems associated with the CPI.

This argument is examined by Marshall Reinsdorf and Jack Triplett in chapter 1 of this volume. They provide a detailed history of the evolution of the CPI, and a comprehensive review of the various commissions formed to study it. This review reveals the long-standing nature of many CPI issues that are still controversial today. In addition to giving a detailed summary of the various CPI reviews, Reinsdorf and Triplett present their views on the alternative methodological foundations for a consumer price index and, in particular, they debate the merits of the economic or COLI approach versus the COGI. They also note the political economy dimension of the debate. Finally, Reinsdorf and Triplett also contrast the COLI approach to the test or axiomatic approach to the CPI. They argue that the COLI approach to CPI index construction is superior to either the COGI or test approaches, but note that the test approach can be useful on occasion as a supplement to the economic approach to index construction.

Many of the chapters in this volume apply the theory underlying the COLI framework to address difficult measurement issues, issues for which the fixed-weight, fixed basket COGI approach often is silent (for example, the treatment of quality change and the new goods problem). On the other hand, few statistical agencies around the world have accepted the COLI con-

8. At higher levels of aggregation, the Boskin Commission recommended the use of a superlative index number formula and at the lowest level of aggregation (the elementary level), endorsed the use of a geometric mean of price relatives (the Jevons formula) over an arithmetic mean (the Carli formula). These recommendations were also endorsed by the *Consumer Price Index Manual;* see ILO et al. (2004). The NRC Panel, however, paid relatively little attention to formula issues, particularly at the elementary level.

9. The panel did not seem to object to the use of the Jevons formula at the elementary level of aggregation (see Schultze and Mackie (2002, 279). At higher levels of aggregation, the panel was split between COLI and COGI proponents, with COLI proponents favoring the use of a superlative formula while COGI proponents favored a Laspeyres or Lowe type index (see Schultze and Mackie [2002, 1 and 73]).

ceptual objective. Those agencies, nevertheless, have often employed measurement techniques—such as adjustments for quality differences between products, and frequent updating of product samples and weights—that are consistent with COLI theory. This ambiguity is mirrored in the NRC panel, which could not agree on the COLI-COGI issue but achieved unanimity on all the specific recommendations in its report.

## Quality Adjustment and Hedonic Indexes

Quality adjustment long has been recognized as the most important and difficult issue in the construction of price indexes. In recent decades, hedonic models increasingly have been seen as the preferred tool for solving the quality adjustment problem. The Stigler Committee led the way in this regard, with Zvi Griliches' (1971) path-breaking paper on hedonic models for automobiles as a supporting staff paper. That committee stated, "This method of estimating quality change deserves extensive exploration and application."[10]

In the Boskin Report, issues in quality adjustment played a prominent role because the Boskin Commission attributed much of their estimated upward bias in the CPI to the index's failure to adequately deal with improvements in product quality over time. The commission members believed that the BLS should be more aggressive in making quality adjustments, but while they considered hedonics to be a valuable tool, an expansion in hedonic modeling was not one of the specific recommendations in the Boskin Report.

The NRC panel devoted considerable effort to explaining how quality adjustment fits within the COLI and COGI contexts. It also made eight recommendations concerning hedonic methods, some of which have been controversial. Although the panel agreed that "Hedonics currently offers the most promising technique for explicitly adjusting observed prices to account for changing product quality," they also recommended that the BLS should be cautious in further expanding the use of hedonically adjusted price change estimates into the CPI (Recommendation 4-3).[11] Other recommendations involved the types of hedonic model and index that the NRC panel considered most appropriate and promising. For example, the hedonic approach currently used by the BLS is termed by the panel the "indirect method," because regression coefficients are not used directly in index calculation (instead, individual coefficients associated with quality variables are

10. Stigler (1961, 36).

11. Schultze and Mackie (2002, 122). Hedonic models were employed in the CPI shelter indexes (to adjust for aging of the rent sample) beginning in the 1980s, and in the apparel indexes beginning in the early 1990s. Between 1998 and 2000, however, the BLS extended the CPI's use of hedonic quality adjustment to computers, televisions, and several other products. Recommendation 4-3 was made in that context. See, for example, Abraham, Greenlees, and Moulton (1998, 31), for the BLS view with respect to this issue.

used to adjust the price differences between disappearing product versions and the models that replace them in the CPI sample). The NRC panel recommends that, while the BLS should continue to study the indirect method, it should also experiment with the "direct characteristics method," in which the index change between two periods is computed using separate hedonic functions estimated for each period. The panel recommends against the approach of estimating index change from the coefficient on a time dummy in a pooled regression.

Highlighting the importance and timeliness of these concerns, three chapters in this volume explore how hedonic methods can be used to develop more accurate price indexes. In chapter 2, Robert Gordon compares hedonic and matched-model indexes for apparel prices in the United States using Sears catalogue data over the period 1914 to 1993, and compares the resulting indexes with the corresponding BLS apparel index over the same period. Gordon finds that the Sears matched-model indexes do not exhibit a consistent negative or positive drift relative to their BLS CPI counterparts. However, he also finds that the hedonic price index for women's apparel always increases more rapidly than the corresponding matched-model index. Gordon sums up his results as follows:

> To the extent that the Sears hedonic and matched model indexes are based on the same data, so that systematic differences between catalog market shares and pricing policies are not relevant, the results provided here may offer a nice complement to past research on computer prices, which also found that price changes were contemporaneous with model changes. Just as hedonic price indexes for computers almost always drop faster than matched model indexes for computers, we have found the opposite relationship for apparel prices, although presumably for the same reason.

Thus, new computers come into the marketplace at *lower* prices once they are adjusted for quality changes, whereas items of apparel (a fashion good) come in at a *higher* price once they are adjusted for quality change. Gordon interprets his new results as casting some light on what he calls the "Hulten paradox," which he explains as follows:

> In an important and influential example, Nordhaus (1997) speculated that, when plausible rates of upward price index bias are extrapolated backwards for two centuries, the increase in real wages from 1800 to 1992, which in the official data is by a factor of 13 to 18, might have been by a factor of 40 with a low estimate of price index bias (0.5 percent per year) or by a factor of 190 with a higher estimate of bias (1.4 percent per year).

In commenting on the Nordhaus results, Hulten (1997) notes that these extrapolations imply an implausibly low real income for U.S. families in 1800. Gordon suggests that this implies that the large Nordhaus upward bias must have been smaller or perhaps even negative at some point in the past, and that his own results for downward bias in apparel should be interpreted in light of this possibility.

In chapter 3, Robert Feenstra and Christopher Knittel suggest a new reason why conventional hedonic methods may overstate the price decline of personal computers. They model computers as a durable good and assume that as software changes over time, this influences the efficiency of a computer. Anticipating future increases in software, purchasers may "overbuy" characteristics, in the sense that the purchased bundle of characteristics is not fully utilized in the first months or year that a computer is owned. If this is the case, Feenstra and Knittel argue that hedonic procedures do not provide valid bounds on the true price of computer services at the time the machine is purchased with the concurrent level of software.

The authors develop a theoretical model along these lines, estimate it econometrically, and obtain results that in some cases differ sharply from the hedonic price index constructed with BLS methods. Over the first half of their 1997 to 2001 study period, the hedonic price index declines at an average annual rate of 51 percent, compared to rates of decline of 14 percent and 38 percent for the two indexes based on the authors' production function approach. This overstatement of the fall in computer prices is largely reversed in the second half of their study period, in which the hedonic index falls much more slowly than the production function indexes. Another important result in the Feenstra and Knittel chapter is the establishment of useful bounds on a *nonseparable hedonic price index* for computer services. The usual theory for a hedonic price index is based on a separability assumption; that is, the constant quality price of a model depends only on the characteristics of the model and not on what quantities of other inputs or outputs that purchasers are using.[12] However, Feenstra and Knittel develop a model in which the production function for the services of a personal computer depends not only on its vector of characteristics but also on a vector of other (complementary) inputs, and they develop bounds on a constant quality price index that do not depend on being able to observe the vector of complementary inputs. This is an important methodological innovation.

Chapter 4, by W. Erwin Diewert, Saeed Heravi, and Mick Silver, deals with the "direct characteristics method" approach mentioned previously, in which the index change between two periods is computed using separate hedonic functions estimated for each period. The authors compare this method (which they call the "hedonic imputation method") to the usual time dummy approach to hedonic regressions, and derive the exact conditions under which the two approaches to hedonic regressions will give the same

12. See Diewert (2003) for an outline of the usual separable approach to hedonic price indexes.

results. They consider both weighted and unweighted hedonic regressions and find exact algebraic expressions that explain the difference between the hedonic imputation and time dummy hedonic regression models.

**New Goods and New Outlets**

The arrival of new goods in the marketplace poses difficult problems for price measurement. These problems can be addressed from two operational perspectives, although they reflect the same conceptual issue. One perspective is the need for statistical agencies to incorporate these goods into their samples in as timely a fashion as possible. On this first point there seems to be little disagreement, and the only issues surround the expense and operational difficulties of selecting and employing timely samples. The other problem is to incorporate the new goods in a way that reflects the welfare gains arising from the innovations embodied in the new types of products or in the new methods of distributing these goods.[13]

The U.S. CPI, unlike most CPIs around the world, accepts the COLI framework and, in principle, would adjust for the gain in consumer surplus achieved when new goods expand the consumer choice set (or the welfare loss when goods disappear). At this time it is largely a theoretical point, however, because the BLS has argued that the techniques for estimating consumer surplus gains—notably those proposed by Jerry Hausman (1997, 1999)—". . . are in their infancy, and may never be adaptable for implementation in a large, ongoing price measurement program like the CPI."[14] This position is consistent with another somewhat controversial Conclusion 5-1 of the NRC panel, that virtual price reductions associated with the introduction of new goods should not be imputed for use in the CPI.

The panel's conclusion is controversial because all economists would agree that if the appearance of new goods makes it possible for some, if not all, consumers to reduce the expenditure required to achieve a given utility level, a properly designed COLI should reflect this fall. Moreover, from a conceptual point of view, the idea of reflecting the welfare gains from the introduction of a distinctly new good like e-mail is no different from the idea of reflecting the welfare gains from the introduction of a slightly enhanced model of television, which the CPI already attempts to do through its quality adjustment processes. Indeed, the boundary between quality adjustment and new goods can depend on the level of aggregation: at the level of "personal motor vehicles," the advent of the sport utility vehicle may be treated as an enhancement in quality through an increase in quantity of

13. Hicks (1940, 114) developed a suitable methodology and Hausman (1997, 1999) implemented this methodology. For some potentially useful techniques that could be used to quantify estimates of bias in a COLI, see Diewert (1998) and Hausman (2003).

14. Abraham, Greenlees, and Moulton (1998, 33).

some hedonic characteristics, but when viewed from the standpoint of the market for transportation services, it appears as a new good. The NRC panel's qualified endorsement of price hedonics but failure to endorse a new goods adjustment are difficult to reconcile, highlighting the difficult and controversial nature of the new goods issue. Unfortunately, it appears that the importance of the issue will only increase with time. In today's economy the rate of introduction of wholly new goods is accelerating, breaking down the barriers between product categories and presenting many new challenges for calculation of a COLI-based CPI.

The new goods controversy is, to some extent, a debate over issues of implementation. The BLS and the NRC panel are in agreement that there are reliable operational (e.g., price hedonic) methods for comparing the effectiveness of different *models* in providing the services of a television or computer. They also agree with each other (although not with all economists) that similarly reliable methods do not yet exist for comparing the effectiveness of new methods of interpersonal communication—such as cellular telephones, text messages, and e-mail—or for valuing the benefits to consumers of a wider array of product choices in markets like breakfast cereal.

The phenomenon of new outlet types parallels that of new products. In chapter 5, Jerry Hausman and Ephraim Leibtag focus on the fact that the CPI does not compare the prices charged for the same items at different outlets. In effect, the BLS assumes that any price differences can be explained by differences in outlet characteristics valued by consumers, such as locational convenience or customer service. It therefore may fail to incorporate the gains to consumers from the continuing growth in sales at Wal-Mart and other low-price, high-volume superstores. The authors employ the A.C. Nielsen Homescan consumer panel data to identify the price differentials for twenty food product categories between supercenters, mass merchandisers, and club stores (SMCs) and other outlets. These differentials, combined with the SMCs' increasing market share, lead Hausman and Leibtag to conclude that CPI food at home inflation is too high by about 0.32 to 0.42 percentage points annually.

## Index Scope and the Conditional COLI

The NRC panel gave considerable attention to the question of the appropriate scope of a COLI. Conceptually, a COLI can be unconditional, in the sense that it reflects changes in life expectancy, future income, air quality, indeed, all other factors affecting consumer welfare beyond the direct consumption of goods and services. These indirect factors are hard to capture in a price index and make the index hard to interpret when they are captured (do we want the CPI to show a change during a period of constant prices because air quality has changed?). As an alternative, a variant of the COLI can be defined that is conditional on some or all of those "environmental" factors.[15]

This distinction was not a major emphasis in the Stigler or Boskin reports, although the latter did include recommendations for research on quality of life factors, crime, and other factors. In contrast, Conclusions 2-1, 2-2, and 3-1 of the NRC panel report argued that the unconditional COLI is unsuitable for the CPI, and that within either the COLI or COGI framework the appropriate index concept should be restricted to private goods and services. Like the Boskin Commission, the NRC panel did also recommend that the BLS undertake research on more comprehensive price measures on an experimental basis, jointly with other federal statistical agencies.

As the panel noted, the U.S. CPI is designed to approximate a conditional COLI. The conceptual view taken by the BLS was laid out by Robert Gillingham (1974), based on the theory of conditional COLI subindexes as presented by Robert Pollak.[16] It should be noted, however, that even having established that the CPI is designed to approximate the conditional COLI, there still may be problems or ambiguities in specifying the precise nature of what is held constant as a conditioning variable.

Chapters 6 through 11 in this volume examine (directly or indirectly) issues concerning the scope of a COLI. Two of these involve measurement of the cost of financial services. The U.S. CPI excludes most financial services because it regards these services as costs of moving consumption from one period to another period and hence regards the costs as being out of scope. However, in chapter 6, Dennis Fixler makes a case for including these transactions costs in a CPI, and he presents a user cost model for the treatment of financial services, in which the prices of loan and deposit services are represented by the difference between the corresponding interest rates and a risk-free reference rate. He constructs various alternative household financial services price indexes using quarterly data from the Bureau of Economic Analysis (BEA) over the period 1987 to 2003. Two controversial components in Fixler's experimental indexes are (a) the reference rate(s) of return used to calculate the nominal user costs of household bank deposits and household bank loans and (b) the deflator(s) used to convert nominal financial service flows into real flows.

In chapter 7, Christina Wang, Susanto Basu, and John Fernald present a general equilibrium approach to measuring bank output, an approach that turns out to be quite different from Fixler's in some important respects. In contrast to deflating nominal asset holdings by a user cost price index,

15. Schultze and Mackie (2002, 86–87). Diewert (2001) developed the theory of the conditional COLI in some detail and suggested that if the chain principle is used, then an aggregate conditional COLI can usually be reasonably well approximated by an appropriate Fisher ideal index. Caves, Christensen, and Diewert (1982, 1409–11) also have a useful exact result for a conditional COLI for a single consumer who has translog conditional preferences.

16. Pollak (1989), chapter 2.

Wang, Basu, and Fernald suggest that *direct measures* of the services rendered by consuming financial services be constructed and then the nominal service flows deflated by these direct measures. In resolving this controversy, the devil is in the details; that is, a detailed model developed by user cost advocates such as Fixler can be compared to the detailed model developed by Wang and her coworkers, and users can decide which framework seems more reasonable.

Another scope issue has to do with the pricing of medical services. One chapter of the NRC Report and three specific recommendations are devoted to the problem of medical care pricing. The Stigler Committee did not specifically address medical care, and the Boskin Commission discussed it only in the context of estimating upward bias in the CPI medical care indexes and as part of its broad recommendation to expand the CPI framework. We include medical care in this section because it highlights the issue of what prices should be used in the CPI. Traditionally, the U.S. CPI collected prices on the goods and services used as *inputs* to health care: prescription drugs, office visits, surgical procedures, and so on. This would appear to be consistent with a COGI framework. During the 1990s, a shift was made in the CPI Hospital Services component to pricing patterns of treatment for specific conditions, rather than the individual inputs. Ideally, a COLI would be based on pricing *outcomes,* with "health" as the argument in the consumer's utility function. Chapter 8 by Xue Song, William Marder, Robert Houchens, Jonathan Conklin, and Ralph Bradley looks at some of the issues involved in implementing such an approach. Comparing disease-based indexes to indexes simulated using current CPI methodology for New York, Philadelphia, and Boston, Song and colleagues suggest that the disease-based indexes may be superior, but that given the large standard errors the differences among indexes were not significantly different in many cases.

Extension of price measurement to the difficult area of government-provided education services is the subject of chapter 9, by Barbara Fraumeni, Marshall Reinsdorf, Brooks Robinson, and Matthew Williams. This market presents the usual problems of services price measurement; in addition, education services are provided without explicit charge to consumers, their production involves significant nonmarket inputs, the contribution of providers is difficult to isolate, and the benefits of education are complex and difficult to value.

The authors begin their chapter with a careful review of the literature on measuring education output in the United States and elsewhere. They then develop and compare alternative quality-adjusted and unadjusted measures of the price and real output of U.S. primary and secondary education services, using three dimensions of quality: teaching staff composition, the pupil-teacher ratio, and the high-school dropout rate. For their entire 1980 to 2001 period of study, the use of their preferred method of quality adjustment raises the estimated annual growth rate of real output by 0.18 percent. This study is part of the ongoing efforts by the BEA to improve the valuation of government output in the U.S. national accounts.

Kam Yu's chapter 10 presents a novel approach to pricing gambling services, using data on the Canadian lottery system. Like Statistics Canada and most statistical agencies, the BLS excludes gambling from the scope of the CPI, partly because it is difficult to determine exactly what is the appropriate pricing concept and partly because the complexity of making adjustments for "quality" improvements seems to be incredibly complex.[17] The quality adjustment problem arises from the fact that, if a lottery increases the odds of winning the lottery, then it appears that a positive increase in "quality" has occurred. Classical expected utility theory could be applied to provide answers to this quality adjustment problem but, as Yu notes, this theory does not work satisfactorily in the gambling context. Yu's chapter does specify an appropriate concept but its theoretical complexity and empirical volatility may prevent statistical agencies from adopting his concept.

Chapter 11 by T. Peter Hill discusses another aspect of the CPI scope problem—the implications of expanding coverage of the CPI to include nonmarket household production. Hill notes that a major problem with the traditional theory of the CPI is that households do not *directly* consume most of the goods and services recorded under consumer expenditures. Estimates for the United States in 1992 suggest that only 12 percent of the goods and services recorded as final consumer expenditures are directly consumed by households without further processing.

Meals prepared at home are a case in point. The household purchases groceries and combines them with household labor and capital to produce the meals on the table. By implication, the CPI is *not* an index of the cost of consumption (the usual interpretation), but is instead largely a price index of the intermediate goods used by households to produce consumption goods.

Hill cites estimates by Landefeld and McCulla (2000) that suggest that the inclusion of household production in the U.S. national accounts increases GDP by 43 percent in 1946 and by 24 percent in 1997. However, he also notes that the inclusion of household production in the CPI will lead to many imputations in the resulting index and hence

> a price index that is calculated mainly from imputed prices would not be acceptable to most users. A CPI is key statistic for policy purposes which can have important financial implications as it is widely used for indexation purposes. It has to be objective, transparent, reliable and credible.

Hill does not speculate whether the CPI is a reasonable proxy for the "true" price index of household consumption, nor whether "policy and indexation

17. In the production accounts of most countries, the output of the lottery sector is measured by the inputs used.

purposes" are better served by the "true" index of the CPI, but he does raise the following question: if a cost-of-living adjustment is to be based on the compensating variations of utility theory (a point debated by the NRC panel), the implication of this chapter is that the CPI is on rather shaky theoretical ground.

The last chapter in this volume deals with issues of durable goods and rental equivalence. The treatment of durable goods, in particular of residential housing, was a major issue in the Stigler Report, and statistical agencies around the world continue to differ widely on their treatment of homeownership costs. The Stigler Committee argued that because a true cost-of-living index or "constant-utility index" is the appropriate index for the CPI, and because the welfare of consumers depends upon the flow of services from durable goods, not upon the stocks acquired in a given period, successful development of a rental equivalence series would offer the basis for an improved CPI. Agencies that reject the COLI framework either exclude homeownership from the CPI or measure homeowner costs using prices of housing assets; agencies like the BLS that accept the COLI tend to employ the rental equivalence approach.

The problem of homeownership is one aspect of the broader household consumption problem. Both the Boskin Commission and the NRC panel accepted the Stigler Committee's view that a flow-of-services measure of consumption is the conceptually correct concept for homeownership. The NRC report concludes that the prices of durable goods ideally should be converted to user costs before being aggregated into a price index, whether a basket price index (COGI) or a COLI.[18] Recognizing a wide range of conceptual and practical difficulties, however, the panel did not examine durable goods pricing in detail.[19]

In chapter 12, Erwin Diewert provides a detailed review of alternative treatments of homeownership in a CPI, discussing the advantages and disadvantages of several approaches to measuring homeowner costs: the acquisition price of housing units, per-period homeowner spending for mortgage interest and other periodic payments, user cost, and rental equivalence. The latter two techniques are alternative flow-of-services approaches. Diewert notes that a major difficulty associated with forming *any* housing price index is that units are unique and they also depreciate (or are augmented by renovations) over time, making it difficult to construct price indexes using a matched-model methodology, and discusses various methods for overcoming this difficulty. He suggests that the "right" price for housing services is the maximum of its rental equivalence price and its user cost.

18. Schultze and Mackie (2002, 72).
19. Schultze and Mackie (2002, 35).

## Discussants' Comments

Our brief synopsis of the chapters has not included a summary of the discussant comments. We highly recommend that they be read jointly with the corresponding chapter, since many offer critical comments and alternative views.

## The New CPI and PPI Manuals

Shortly after the NRC panel report appeared, two new international manuals on price measurement problems appeared in 2004: the *Consumer Price Index Manual: Theory and Practice,* edited by T. Peter Hill, and the *Producer Price Index Manual: Theory and Practice,* edited by Paul Armknecht; see the International Labour Organization (ILO 2004) and the International Monetary Fund (IMF 2004), respectively. These new international agency manuals replaced an older ILO CPI Manual that was published in 1989 and an even older United Nations (UN) Producer Price Index (PPI) Manual that was published in 1979. The sponsoring international agencies for these two manuals were Eurostat, the ILO, the IMF, the Organization for Economic Cooperation and Development (OECD), the World Bank, and the UN.

The new price manuals were quite different from previous international manuals, which tended to prescribe "best practices" but did not have much discussion on what led up to the chosen procedures. In contrast, the new manuals were much less prescriptive and instead tried to present the alternatives in a more or less unbiased way. However, this new less dogmatic approach actually proved to be very productive. In particular, statistical agencies on both sides of the Atlantic were able to agree that no matter what approach one took to index number theory, a superlative index seemed to be a reasonable target index to aim for in practice.[20] Thus, the new manuals tried to present reasonable principles rather than specific rules. The two manuals also tried to harmonize their contents so that they would not contradict each other.

Some of the important topics that these new manuals considered in more detail than the older manuals were:

- Quality adjustment methods, including extensive discussions about hedonic regression methods.
- Approaches to seasonal adjustment.

20. European price statisticians tended to favor the fixed basket, test, or stochastic approaches to index number theory while North American price statisticians tended to favor the economic approach. The new Manuals showed that all of these approaches led to either the Fisher ideal, the Törnqvist-Theil, or the Walsh indexes and since these indexes closely approximated each other numerically, it was not worth arguing over which approach was the "right" one.

- A detailed treatment of the Lowe index.[21]
- The usefulness of producing indexes for different classes of users; that is, statistical agencies should produce not only "standard" indexes but also "analytical" indexes that meet the needs of specialized users.

Following on the success of these two new manuals, the international agencies who are concerned with economic price and quantity measurement problems are sponsoring a new effort: an XMPI (Export Import Price Index) Manual, with the IMF taking the lead in organizing and publishing the manual.

## Outstanding Issues in the Construction of a Consumer Price Index

We conclude with a few of the outstanding issues in the construction of a CPI that need to be resolved. Most of the questions in the partial list below were raised by the chapters in this volume. Answers will probably not be forthcoming in the immediate future, but these are important questions that require either further research or discussion that would lead to a consensus on the issues:

- How should the value of service-sector outputs like banking, educational, medical, gambling, and insurance services be measured, and can they reliably be separated into price and quantity components?
- How can satellite accounts for the household production sector be constructed in current and constant prices?
- How should the welfare gains from new goods be incorporated into the price index? How does the classical "new goods" problem differ from the price hedonic problem of measuring quality change in a continuum of "improved" goods?
- If scanner data are being used at the elementary (lower) level of the CPI, then how much time aggregation is desirable as unit values are aggregated over time? One could also ask the same question with respect to aggregation over outlets.
- What is the "right" index number formula to use at the elementary (lower) level of index aggregation if weight information is or is not available?
- How can we deal with outlet bias in an objective manner?
- What is the "best" way for a statistical agency to employ hedonic regressions in official CPIs, and should the regressions be run with or without weights?

21. The Lowe price index is one that uses (annual) weights from one reference period and base period (monthly) prices from another reference period, as well as current period (monthly) prices, which is in fact how most CPIs are constructed. Somewhat surprisingly, the academic literature on index numbers never considered the properties of such an index.

- Should price measurement be harmonized with the System of National Accounts or should it proceed in a more or less independent manner?
- What is the "right" concept to price the services of owner-occupied housing?

## References


Abraham, K. G., J. S. Greenlees, and B. R. Moulton. 1998. Working to improve the Consumer Price Index. *Journal of Economic Perspectives* 12 (1): 27–36.

Boskin (Chair), M. J., E. R. Dulberger, R. J. Gordon, Z. Griliches, and D. W. Jorgenson. 1996. *Final report of the Commission to Study the Consumer Price Index.* U.S. Senate, Committee on Finance, Washington DC: GPO.

Bureau of Labor Statistics. 1997. *BLS handbook of methods, Bulletin 2490.* Washington, DC: GPO.

Caves, D. W., L. R. Christensen, and W. E. Diewert. 1982. The economic theory of index numbers and the measurement of input, output, and productivity, *Econometrica* 50 (6): 1393–1414.

Diewert, W. E. 1976. Exact and superlative index numbers. *Journal of Econometrics* 4 (2): 114–45.

———. 1998. Index number issues in the Consumer Price Index. *The Journal of Economic Perspectives* 12 (1): 47–58.

———. 2001. The Consumer Price Index and index number purpose. *Journal of Economic and Social Measurement* 27: 167–248.

———. 2002. Harmonized indexes of consumer prices: Their conceptual foundations. *Swiss Journal of Economics and Statistics* 138 (4): 547–637.

———. 2003. Hedonic regressions: A consumer theory approach. In *Scanner data and price indexes,* Studies in Income and Wealth vol. 64, ed. R. C. Feenstra and M. D. Shapiro. 317–47. Chicago: University of Chicago Press.

Gillingham, R. 1974. A conceptual framework for the Consumer Price Index. *Proceedings of the American Statistical Association 1974 Business and Economic Statistics Section.* Washington, DC: American Statistical Association.

Greenlees, J. S. 2001. The U.S. CPI and the cost-of-living objective. Paper prepared for the Joint ECE/ILO Meeting on Consumer Price Indices. 2 November, Geneva, Switzerland.

Griliches, Z. 1971. Hedonic price indexes for automobiles: An econometric analysis of quality change. In *Price indexes and quality change,* ed. Zvi Griliches, 55–87. Cambridge, MA: Harvard University Press.

Hausman, J. A. 1997. Valuation of new goods under perfect and imperfect competition. In *The economics of new goods,* Studies in Income and Wealth 58, ed. T. F. Bresnahan and R. J. Gordon, 209–37. Chicago: University of Chicago Press.

———. 1999. Cellular telephone, new products, and the CPI. *Journal of Business and Economic Statistics* 17 (2): 188–94.

———. 2003. Sources of bias and solutions to bias in the CPI. *The Journal of Economic Perspectives* 17 (1): 23–44.

Hicks, J. R. 1940. On the valuation of the social income. *Economica* 7 (February): 105–24.

Hulten, C. R. 1997. Comment. In *The economics of new goods,* Studies in Income and Wealth vol. 58, ed. T. F. Bresnahan and R. J. Gordon, 66–70. Chicago: University of Chicago Press.

International Labour Organization (ILO), Eurostat, IMF, OECD, World Bank, and the UN. 2004. *Consumer Price Index manual: Theory and practice,* ed. Peter Hill. Geneva: International Labour Organization. Available at: http://www.ilo.org/public/english/bureau/stat/guides/cpi/index.htm.

Landefeld, J. S., and S. H. McCulla. 2000. Accounting for nonmarket household production within a national accounts framework. *Review of Income and Wealth* 46 (3): 289–307.

Lowe, J. 1823. *The present state of England in regard to agriculture, trade and finance,* 2nd edition. London: Longman, Hurst, Rees, Orme, and Brown.

Nordhaus, W. D. 1997. Do real output and real wage measures capture reality? The history of lighting suggests not. In *The economics of new goods,* Studies in Income and Wealth vol. 58, ed. T. F. Bresnahan and R. J. Gordon, 29–66. Chicago: University of Chicago Press.

Pollak, R. A. 1989. *The theory of the cost-of-living index.* New York: Oxford University Press.

Schultze, C. I., and C. Mackie, eds. 2002. *At what price? Conceptualizing and measuring cost-of-living and price indexes.* Committee on National Statistics, Washington DC: National Academy Press.

Stigler, G. J. (Chairman). 1961. *The price statistics of the federal government.* New York: National Bureau of Economic Research.

1

# A Review of Reviews
## Ninety Years of Professional Thinking About the Consumer Price Index

Marshall Reinsdorf and Jack E. Triplett

It is not often that a price index, a tool of statisticians, becomes an object of political debate.
—Ostrander 1944, 849

The theory of price indexes is usually left to specialists, but when a suspicion that something has gone wrong is coupled with the possibility of large political and fiscal benefits from fixing it, the topic can move into the limelight.
—Deaton 1998, 37

### 1.1 Introduction

The U.S. Bureau of Labor Statistics (BLS) first published an index of consumer prices for food at home in 1903, with continuous publication uninterrupted by budget shortfalls beginning in 1911 (Goldberg and Moye 1985, 37). The next milestone in the development of the index now known as the U.S. Consumer Price Index (CPI) came in 1914, when methods were improved and the index basket was expanded to include cloth and

Marshall Reinsdorf is Chief, Economic Analysis and Research Group, National Economic Accounts, at the U.S. Department of Commerce, Bureau of Economic Analysis. Jack E. Triplett is a nonresident senior fellow at the Brookings Institution.

We appreciate comments from the editors, John Greenlees and Charles Hulten, and also from Bert Balk, Michael Boskin, Angus Deaton, Erwin Diewert, and Charles Schultze. The usual disclaimer disassociating some or all of those who made comments from the content of the chapter applies. The views expressed should not be attributed to the Bureau of Economic Analysis, or to the Brookings Institution, as they are solely those of the authors. This original version of the chapter was presented at the NBER-CRIW conference on price indexes, Vancouver, B.C., June 2004.

clothing. The result was the earliest version of the CPI that is still available from BLS.

A decision during World War I by the Shipbuilding Labor Adjustment Board to escalate wages by a price index led to the development of BLS's first comprehensive index of consumer prices. The existing index, composed almost entirely of fast-rising food prices (which were strongly affected by the war), was obviously unrepresentative of consumer prices in general, so a consumer expenditure survey was conducted to develop a broader index basket. Initially this survey included just the shipbuilding cities, but in June of 1918 its scope was expanded to include other cities. Publication of a national index of consumer prices with weights reflecting survey data on purchasing patterns began in 1919 (Goldberg and Moye 1985, 105).

The U.K. Retail Price Index began, similarly, as a wage escalator during the same war (Roe and Fenwick 2004), as did the Canadian CPI (Statistics Canada 1995, 9–10; Urquhart and Buckley 1965, 287–89). The Swedish index began a little earlier (Dalen 2001). Indexes in all four countries were originally called Cost-of-Living Indexes, but new names were introduced in all four cases after World War II.

The history of economists' analysis of BLS price indexes begins with the assistance of Irving Fisher and Wesley Mitchell, with the food index improvements of 1914 (Goldberg and Moye 1985, 91–92). Here Fisher's hand seems evident in the abandonment by BLS of a method that he often criticized, the averaging of price relatives. A year later, Mitchell increased awareness in the United States of the distinction between consumer prices and what we now call the Producer Price Index (PPI) in a review of what was then called the Wholesale Price Index, or WPI, (Mitchell [1915] 1921; summarized by Banzhaf [2001]). Distinguishing consumer prices from wholesale or producer prices may seem obvious now. But as we point out in section 1.2, Mitchell's distinction was not considered in most index number writing before that time.

Over the years, reviews by committees and panels have critically influenced the development of the U.S. CPI. Moreover, the long record of the debate over CPI concepts and methods preserved in their reports provides important background for understanding the current state of the discussion of CPI methods. This chapter examines the treatment of two questions, one conceptual and one methodological, in officially sanctioned reviews of the CPI.

The conceptual question is, what measurement objective is the appropriate one for the CPI? A modern statement (Schultze and Mackie 2002) presents the alternatives as COLI versus COGI (Cost-of-Living Index versus Cost-of-Goods Index). The conceptual question concerns not just the index number "formula," as it is often called, but essential questions about what components are included in the index, and how the components are to be measured. This question is the subject of our section 1.2.

The methods question is, what sampling procedures and formulas should be used to construct the lowest level, detailed component indexes, or elementary aggregates of the CPI? We discuss the methods question in section 1.3.

Though our topic begins in 1914, the formal reviews that we consider begin with the World War II era reviews of what was then called the Cost-of-Living Index.[1] Four reviews were produced as part of the same investigation; this set of reviews marks a major milestone in the history of thinking about CPI measurement issues.

The second formal review is the 1961 report by the "Price Statistics Review Committee" chaired by George Stigler (Stigler et al. 1961). The World War II criticisms of the procedures used to construct the detailed component indexes of the CPI laid the foundation for the reforms in sampling procedures recommended by the Stigler Committee and later adopted by BLS, and also for the Stigler Committee's concern for the problems posed by quality change. In turn, the Stigler Committee's report influenced the third formal review by the widely-discussed Boskin Commission. Finally, the BLS funded the fourth formal report by a panel selected by the Committee on National Statistics (CNSTAT), largely as a response to the Boskin Commission review. Continuity in the reviewers' recommendations is echoed in continuity among the reviewers, as the Stigler Committee and Boskin Commission included participants in the preceding reviews.

In the following sections, we review each of our topics chronologically.

## 1.2 Recommendations Concerning the Measurement Concept for the Index

The first BLS measure of consumer prices was influenced by Mitchell's review of the Wholesale Price Index, which he called "The Making and Use of Index Numbers" (Mitchell 1915).[2] As the title suggests, this report was more than just a review of the WPI.

1. We restrict our attention to reviews of the U.S. CPI, for lack of resources to conduct a broader investigation. A noteworthy wartime review of the Swedish CPI is described in Dalen (2001), as are several subsequent external reviews. The equivalent index in the U.K., known historically as the Retail Price Index, has been reviewed a number of times by committees established by the relevant Parliamentary Secretary; Roe and Fenwick (2004, appendix A) provide a list of these reviews and a summary of their recommendations. Melser and Hill (2005) present excerpts from Revision Advisory Committees on the New Zealand CPI. In Canada, a Price Measurement Advisory Committee to Statistics Canada meets on a regular schedule. Other similar bodies no doubt exist.

2. After a long period of neglect, Mitchell's contributions to price index history have recently been resurrected in an insightful paper by Banzhaf (2001). Mitchell made the connection between the design of an index number and its purpose so much a part of his approach to price indexes that it was repeated as a mantra by others years after. He was also perhaps the first to focus on measuring the components of the CPI, as opposed to the methods for aggregating them. This focus may partly explain the neglect of Mitchell: index number researchers are often more interested in the problems of higher-level aggregation than in the methods used for the lowest-level aggregates, even though that latter are probably more important empirically.

At the time of this report, consumer price indexes were often constructed by weighting WPI components by family expenditure data. Mitchell excoriated this practice: "To pretend that wholesale price index numbers when weighted on the basis of family expenditures show fluctuation in the cost of living is to overtax the credulity of those who know and to abuse the confidence of those who do not" (Mitchell [1915] 1921, 63). Partly as a result of Mitchell's review, when the comprehensive household inflation measure was launched in 1919, it was based on retail prices. The 1919 index was named the "Cost-of-Living Index" because it covered consumers' entire budgets with weights that reflected their purchasing patterns.[3]

So far as we know, the first professional review of the U.S. price index for households was conducted in 1933 and 1934 by an Advisory Committee appointed by the American Statistical Association. Its recommendations were practical, not conceptual, and concerned surveys to improve the weights for combining items and cities in the "all-items" index, data collection, and the use of imputations for items not priced directly (Hogg 1934; BLS 1966). The Committee suggested that even the cities in the index were not representative, since shipbuilding cities remained overrepresented.

Yet the interwar period was not devoid of thinking about conceptual questions related to the CPI—quite the contrary. The appendix reviews interwar price index research as background for the remainder of the chapter; in the next section, we provide a summary.

### 1.2.1 Interwar Price Index Research

Major developments in the 1920s influenced professional thinking about CPIs and were absorbed into the intellectual tradition that influenced subsequent reviews of the CPI. The first, the "test approach," had its origins in nineteenth century discussions of index number properties and in a 1901 book by Correa Walsh, but its major development came in the work of Irving Fisher. Fisher's (1911) exposition of this approach was focused on finding the $P$ and $T$ terms of the equation of exchange $MV = PT$. In Fisher (1922), the approach was applied to all kinds of index numbers. There is no evidence that Fisher thought much about a specific application to the measurement of consumer inflation.[4]

The second development was Konüs' (1924) theory of the Cost-of-Living Index (COLI). In contrast with Fisher and his forebears, Konüs' contribution was uniquely a contribution to the measurement of consumer prices, inspired, no doubt, by the new "Cost-of-Living Indexes" in the United States, Canada, the United Kingdom, and other countries.[5]

3. Meeker (1919). By 1943, its full name was: "Index of the Cost of Living of Wage Earners and Lower-Salaried Workers in Large Cities." See Ostrander (1944).

4. Diewert (1993, 34) cites Joseph Lowe, who wrote much earlier, as the "father of the consumer price index." Lowe explored a number of problems, including indexes for different demographic groups.

5. See Diewert (1983). A third development from this period, the Divisia index, is discussed in Balk (2005), and used by Hulten (1973).

The appendix sets out our position on test (or axiomatic) and COLI (or economic) approaches to the CPI. In summary, we emphasize three points:

1. It is sometimes said that test and economic approaches converge because each leads to one of the superlative indexes, especially the Fisher index. However, as applied by the advocates of this approach, the tests are an arbitrarily chosen set of index number properties. *The test approach does not yield the Fisher index, unless the tests are chosen to get this result.*

2. The favored index number properties include some that are objectionable on economic grounds. Moreover, advocates of the test approach invariably exclude some other properties (for example, additivity and consistency in aggregation—see the appendix) that are desired by some index number users. The arbitrariness of the set of index number properties traditionally included in the tests means that some other set of properties would yield, not the Fisher index, but some other index. Moreover, the absence of criteria for selecting the tests is matched by the absence of criteria for ranking the importance of the various tests, except by arbitrarily ranking all tests equally (contending, for example, that the Fisher index, or some other index, passes more tests than other indexes). The value of any index number property depends on the index number purpose, so no system of discriminating among tests, including equal weighting, has universal applicability.

3. The economic approach to index numbers is much more than a framework for determining how index number components should be aggregated (the index number formula). It provides a framework that can be used to analyze the domain of the index (the components that are included) and to analyze how index components should be measured. The test approach is completely silent on these essential matters.

Although the test approach was not used in some of the professional reviews of the CPI, we include it in this section and in the appendix because it has come back into vogue in recent years and because we think its limitations are not always understood.

### 1.2.2 Wartime Committees: Clarifying the Meaning of the BLS "Cost-of-Living" Index

In 1942, the National War Labor Board, in what was known as the "Little Steel Agreement," permitted wage increases that matched increases in the BLS Cost-of-Living Index, as it was still then called (citation to the decision is given in Ostrander [1944, 850]). The Labor Board's action repeated the escalation use of a BLS index in the previous war. Very soon thereafter, the labor unions attacked the index as a flawed measure—indeed, an understated measure—of the change in cost of the workers' living standard.

The unions' complaints ultimately led to the preparation of four different reviews of the index. The Labor Department initiated the first, conducted by a special committee of the American Statistical Association chaired by

Frederick Mills, but this review did little to assuage the unions.[6] Almost immediately thereafter (within a month), President Roosevelt set up a "tri-partite" (that is, having labor, management, and government members) Presidential Committee on the Cost of Living, chaired by War Labor Board chairman William Davis, to investigate the matter. The Davis Committee also failed to bring about consensus. Instead, it generated a minority report issued by its labor members, George Meany of the American Federation of Labor (AFL) and R. J. Thomas of the Congress of Industrial Organizations (CIO) (the Meany-Thomas report), a business report issued by the National Industrial Conference Board,[7] and finally, a report by a "Technical Committee," which was chaired by Wesley Mitchell. The staff and members of the Mills and Mitchell Committees make up a veritable list of prominent economists and statisticians of the time.[8]

The wartime dispute is unique among political discussions of consumer prices in three respects: (a) the topic was alleged understatement of inflation, not overstatement, as was true of all subsequent reviews; (b) the unions appeared (though the language is not precise) to support the concept of the COLI, unlike their position subsequently; (c) the professional reviews chaired by Mills and Mitchell supported (sometimes, we suspect, too uncritically) BLS methodology—subsequent professional reviews of the CPI range from mildly to overwhelmingly critical.

Examining the period from January 1941 to December 1943, Meany and Thomas (1944) estimated that the true rise in the cost of living was 43.5 percent, compared with only 23.4 percent reported by the BLS—see figure 1.1. The unions gathered some of their own data; the report's empirical sections are considered in part 1.3.

Among many alleged sources of downward bias in the Cost-of-Living Index that the Meany-Thomas report identified, some reflect the authors' views on what the index should have measured. In particular, Meany and Thomas contended that consumers were often forced to substitute more expensive varieties or goods for ones that had disappeared from the marketplace because of wartime shortages or "product line upgrading." They also alleged that consumers were often forced into more expensive dwellings than

6. *Washington Post* editorial, 14 February, 1946. See also Goldberg and Moye (1985, 154), Banzhaf (2001, 354), Mills et al. (1943), and Ostrander (1944).

7. Now the Conference Board. At the time and long thereafter, the organization published its own Cost-of-Living Index.

8. In addition to its chairman, the Mills Committee consisted of E. Wight Bakke, Reavis Cox, Margaret Reid, Theodore W. Schultz, and Samuel Stratton, with staff consisting of Dorothy Brady and Solomon Fabricant. The Mitchell Committee consisted of Mitchell, Reid, and Simon Kuznets, with Fabricant again on the staff. Reid, a prominent academic researcher on the subject of consumer behavior, was at the time on the staff of the Office of Statistical Standards in what is now the Office of Management and Budget (OMB), and Brady, also a prominent researcher on the same topic, was a member of the BLS staff in the 1930s, and again after the war. Reid subsequently returned to the University of Chicago and Brady joined the faculty of the University of Pennsylvania.

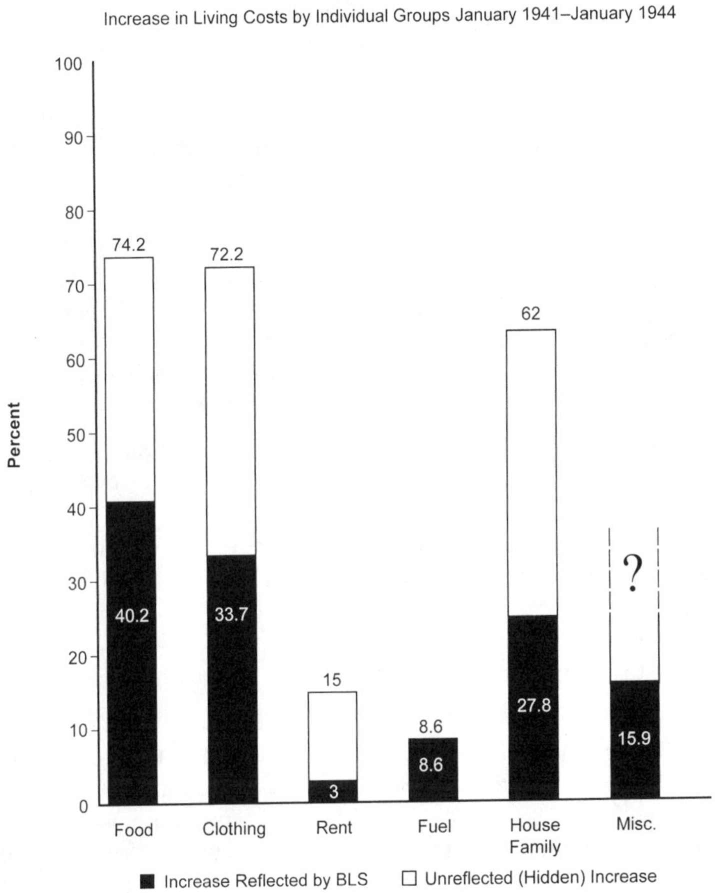


**Fig. 1.1 Illustration from the Meany-Thomas Report**

they wanted because of shortages of affordable housing. These involuntary substitutions raised consumers' cost of living in ways that the BLS index missed. In addition, lower-quality varieties often replaced higher-quality ones in the marketplace, which occurred when manufacturers relabeled a lower grade item as a higher grade one. The index, they contended, took no account of the quality decline. Finally, Meany and Thomas argued for the inclusion of extra expenses necessitated by lifestyle changes, such as increased consumption of restaurant meals due to meat rationing and the entrance of women into the labor force, and extra costs from migration between cities to fill wartime jobs.[9] In their report they did not treat effects

9. Accounting for the value of home production that was lost was overlooked: their only concern was the increased (monetary) costs of substituting market commodities for home production.

of rising standards of living as additional costs to be included in the Cost-of-Living Index, but—judging from rebuttals by their opponents—they were so interpreted.

The BLS vigorously disputed the Meany-Thomas report's contention that the Cost-of-Living Index understated inflation by almost half. The BLS's positions were largely supported by the outside experts on the Mitchell Committee.

An important part of the Mitchell Committee's response to the Meany-Thomas report was a clarification of the conceptual goal of the BLS Cost-of-Living Index. Though the concept of the COLI was known among economists (see section 1.2.1), the term "Cost-of-Living Index" did not always have the same meaning in 1944 that it does today. As Banzhaf (2001) points out, the term was then used, or interpreted, in at least three different ways.

- The now-standard meaning—a price index that holds constant the standard of living. The Mitchell Committee referred to this as a measure of the "real price."
- A fixed basket index that covered the entire family budget, which is what the BLS was in fact producing under the "Cost-of-Living Index" name.
- The cost of attaining the standard of living deemed appropriate, compared to the cost of a possibly lower standard of living in some previous period.

In its discussion of item substitutions involving a change in quality, the Mitchell Committee introduced consumer theory in a limited way as a basis for thinking about the design of the Cost-of-Living Index. When an item disappearance was thought to reflect voluntary substitution behavior by consumers, BLS usually introduced a replacement item into the index via overlap price linking. The Mitchell Committee argued that this procedure was justifiable under the assumption that the relative utility of different qualities varied directly with the ratio of their prices, which requires consumers to be informed about quality and supplies to be freely available (Mitchell, Kuznets, and Reid 1944, 11–12). If, for example, the replacement variety had a lower price, the larger quantity that could now be purchased with the same expenditure might be expected to yield the same utility as the smaller quantity of the higher-priced variety, whose quality was presumably higher.

However, in a passage with a slightly different problem in mind (forced substitution to lower qualities), the Mitchell Committee seemed skeptical about the existence of "a satisfactory way of measuring changes in 'real' prices—that is the price of a given quantity of utility, usefulness or service . . . when poorer qualities are priced" (19). Indeed, the Committee wrote: "To mix in additional factors with price changes would make the meaning of [BLS's] index even harder to determine than war conditions have already made it" (14). The Meany-Thomas "life style changes" were not to be considered. In the Committee's view, the Cost-of-Living Index ought to measure only the influence of prices on the cost of living, not the influence of other factors such as lifestyle changes, changes in taxes and government-provided services, or obviously, consumption increases that were in response to rising income.[10]

To clarify that nonprice influences on welfare were out of scope, and to avoid confusing the BLS index with one that included some changes in the standard of living, the Mitchell Committee recommended that BLS change the name of its index (20).[11] This recommendation was not intended to mark a change in the measurement goal of the index, which index experts had always understood to be limited to direct effects of prices. In particular, at the time of the name change, the term "Cost-of-Living Index" lacked the economic connotations that it now has, so the change in name should be interpreted as a statement about the domain of the CPI, and about public confusion between a price index and a standard of living index, not as a statement about today's debate over the Cost-of-Living Index concept.[12]

With respect to the other issues, the Mitchell Committee (Mitchell, Kuznets, and Reid 1944) concluded that the effects cited in the Meany-Thomas report were much smaller than claimed or that they were absent. The Committee anticipated the Boskin Commission of fifty years later in performing a "guesstimate" of the probable size of CPI error. It said that the combined effect of the all sources of bias mentioned by Meany and Thomas might be 3 to 5 percentage points over the three year long period, with an additional one-half point possible from the omission of smaller cities from the index, which implies an average rate of roughly 1.0 to 1.8 index points per year.[13] The largest part of the estimate concerned undetected, negative quality changes, set at 2 to 3 points. Scant attention was paid to possible upward biases that might offset the sources of downward bias, presumably because quality improvements were not thought to be of much importance in wartime, and because the Committee thought it infeasible to estimate substitution bias.

Though Meany and Thomas were not disinterested price collectors and their evidence was anecdotal, some of their exhibits were intriguing. For ex-

10. Some of the commentary on the debate considered whether the evidence suggested that workers' real consumption levels had declined. See Ostrander (1944).

11. The BLS did so in September of 1945 following the departure of Labor Secretary Frances Perkins, who had been opposed. The press release stated that the name change to "Consumers' Price Index for Moderate Income Families in Large Cities . . . should end the confusion and controversy caused by the misunderstanding of what the index is designed to measure and by the use of the index for purposes for which it is not adapted."

12. In the much later debate over the Boskin Commission (Boskin et al. 1996) recommendations, certain BLS statements about the 1946 change in name revealed misunderstanding of the episode. The inadequate discussion in Goldberg and Moye (1985) may have contributed to this confusion.

13. Ostrander (1944, 854) says that the 3 to 5 point range was subsequently lowered to 3 to 4.5 points.

ample, they presented menus from cafeterias showing increases in standard meals, which seemed substantially greater than the comparable restaurant component of the index. They documented (graphically, with a drawing) the deterioration in materials and workmanship in shoes, along with an estimate of the shortened lifetime of the shoes that would result. They pointed out that the items in the BLS sample (judgmental, in that era) were disproportionately the ones under price controls or subsidies, and that similar items with higher price changes were omitted from the index. From the vantage point of sixty years later, it is hard to avoid some sense that their evidence was dismissed too readily.[14] Indeed, the unions' complaints retained sufficient credence so that, when the Korean War broke out, BLS felt compelled to rush into production an "interim" revised CPI to avoid a repeat of some of the World War II criticisms (Goldberg and Moye 1985, 193). The CPI was nevertheless attacked in 1951 by the Union of Electrical Radio and Machine Workers (known as "UE," a union that was expelled from the CIO for being Communist dominated) and by the Soviet delegation to the UN Economic and Social Council in Geneva.

### 1.2.3 The Stigler Committee: A Welfare Index as the Measurement Concept for the CPI

In 1957 the Joint Economic Committee (JEC) undertook an investigation of "employment, growth and price levels," which inevitably raised questions about the price-making process and the measurement of prices. The need for reliable price statistics emerged as a minor theme in the subsequent hearings. Notable was a paper by Kenneth Arrow (1958), who argued for a Cost-of-Living Index objective for the CPI because of the importance of commodity substitution behavior (in U.S. Congress Joint Economic Committee [1958, 11]).

Subsequently, the U.S. Bureau of the Budget (now Office of Management and Budget) contracted with the National Bureau of Economic Research, which appointed a "Price Statistics Review Committee" chaired by George Stigler. The Stigler Committee included Dorothy Brady, who had participated in the Mitchell Committee investigation fifteen years earlier.[15] The Committee's report (Stigler et al. [1961]; hereafter, "Stigler Commit-

14. The *American Economic Review* article on the matter describes the Meany-Thomas report in language that is sometimes disparaging: "On the basis of the Meany-Thomas report, *assuming there were any substance to it,* the increased consumer expenditures by the end of 1943 would have been more than absorbed by price increases . . ." (Ostrander 1944, 853; emphasis added).

15. The other members of the Committee were: Edward Denison, Irving Kravis, Albert Rees, Richard Ruggles, Boris Swerling, and Philip McCarthy. Authors of staff papers included with the report were: Philip McCarthy, Victor Zarnowitz, Harry McAllister, Eleanor Snyder, John Flueck, Peter Steiner, Albert Rees, Zvi Griliches, Walter Oi, Geoffrey Shepherd, Earl Swanson, and Reuben Kessel.

tee report"), accompanied by twelve "staff papers," was transmitted to the Bureau of the Budget late in 1960.[16]

The Stigler Committee report made no explicit mention of the Mitchell Committee, but it did refer to the consensus by the participants in the World War II era debate that the CPI ought, in principle, to reflect the effects of substitution:

> In periods of wartime . . . price quotations on the virtually unobtainable commodities may not show much increase, or even be rigidly fixed by price controls. Consumers are driven to available substitutes, which are more expensive relative to desired performance (forced uptrading) or rise rapidly in response to expanding demands. Few economists or consumers come to the defense of the rigidly fixed market basket approach under these circumstances. This suggests strongly that what is in fact being measured is not the cost of a fixed set of consumer goods and services, but rather the cost of maintaining a constant level of utility. (51)

However, the Stigler Committee went beyond the Mitchell Committee in stating unequivocally that the measurement concept for the CPI ought to be the cost of staying on an indifference curve: "A constant-utility index is the appropriate index for the main purposes for which the CPI is used" (Stigler et al. 1961, 52).[17] Furthermore, whereas neither the Meany and Thomas report nor the Mitchell Committee report discussed *voluntary* substitutions by consumers as a source of bias in the official Cost-of-Living Index, the Stigler Committee (52) wrote:

> Since consumers will substitute those goods whose prices rise less or fall more for those whose prices rise more or fall less—and within limits they can do this without reducing their levels of real consumption—the fixed-weight base CPI overstates rises in the cost of equivalent market baskets.

What had changed since the Mitchell review? Partly, professional economists had grown more accepting of economic theory as a guide to practical economics. The contrast between the careers of the two chairmen is illustrative (though both were associated with the National Bureau of Economic Research).

16. The Stigler Committee report can be hard to locate. The report and staff papers were published in January 1961 as Part I of the record of the JEC hearings (Stigler et al. 1961). Subsequent hearings (U.S. Congress, Joint Economic Committee 1961, Part II) elaborated on a number of aspects of the report's findings, including comments by BLS as well as others, and are an important part of the record of the Committee's work, its recommendations, and its impact. The report and staff papers (but not the hearings) were also published by the NBER (Price Statistics Review Committee, NBER 1961).

17. The Stigler Committee also used the term "welfare index," defined as an index that tracks the cost of maintaining a constant level of utility. Interestingly, it never used the term "Cost-of-Living Index," perhaps in response to the wartime confusion over that name. However, in response to a question at the JEC hearing, a member of the Stigler Committee referred to "what Commissioner Clague calls a Cost-of-Living Index."

Secondly, regarding the aggregation part of COLI theory, no proposal for estimating commodity substitution behavior existed in 1944, as the Mitchell Committee noted. Indeed, in a 1942 study on "The Empirical Derivation of Indifference Functions," W. Allen Wallis and Milton Friedman concluded, "We doubt that [the indifference function] has any material value for the organization of empirical data."[18]

But shortly after the Mitchell Committee report, an empirical estimate of bounds for substitution bias was published. In ten comparisons of Laspeyres and Paasche indexes, Ulmer (1946) found that all the differences were less than 1.5 percentage points. He argued that the maximum of the observed Laspeyres-Paasche differentials estimated the maximum possible value for the substitution bias of the Laspeyres index.[19]

Ulmer's bounds study was followed by a proposal for estimating consumer demand functions from which commodity substitution effects in a COLI could be derived—Klein and Rubin's (1947–1948) "linear expenditure system." By 1960, the linear expenditure system (also known as the "Stone-Geary" system) had been employed for empirical work on consumer demand (see Stone [1954]), though no actual COLI estimates existed. In contrast to the situation in 1945, by the time the Stigler Committee wrote its report estimates of substitution effects needed for a Konüs index seemed within reach.

Nevertheless, the Stigler Committee refrained from recommending that the BLS estimate a COLI econometrically. It recommended only that the BLS periodically estimate a Paasche index version of the CPI to gauge the potential size of the bias from substitution, and "possibly" update the weights more frequently to reduce the size of the bias.[20] It did not consider changing the Laspeyres index formula—though at the hearings on the report, Senator Douglas asked BLS to experiment with the use of the Fisher formula (U.S. Congress 1961, 566).

Commodity substitution was not the only question that the Stigler Committee viewed in the COLI framework. As we noted in section 1.2.1, the COLI framework influences many parts of the price index and many decisions that must be made in compiling it. Notable among the Stigler Committee's examples of COLI applications were the effects of changes in quality,

18. Quoted by BLS in a submission to the Joint Economic Committee Hearings; see U.S. Congress (1961, 580).

19. We now know that these are bounds for a common COLI only in the homothetic case; otherwise, they are bounds for two different COLI estimates, one using the initial indifference curve (Laspeyres perspective COLI), the other using the comparison period indifference curve (Paasche perspective COLI). It is thus possible in principle for the substitution bias in the Laspeyres index to be larger than the Paasche-Laspeyres difference, but all empirical COLI estimates lie between Paasche and Laspeyres indexes.

20. In 1960, the BLS was still using 1951 to 1952 weights and those were from an "interim" revision of the weights from the consumer expenditure survey of 1948. The Committee's recommendation seems timid, from today's perspective.

the treatment of consumer durables, and the effects of new products. For example, consumer preferences were the key to evaluating the effects of new products:

> If these new commodities are additional options open to the consumer, he will adopt them only if he prefers them (at their current prices) to goods previously available. (52)

To minimize the bias from new products, the Committee recommended their early introduction into the CPI with weights adjusted to reflect growth in their sales. The Committee thought that "typically" a successful new good enters with a high price and a low quantity sold, but then experiences a rapid decline in price and a rapid growth in quantity. By introducing the product early in its life cycle, tracing out the price decline that accompanied the rise in demand as the price fell, at least part of the welfare gain from the new good would be incorporated into the index.[21]

The problem of quality changes in existing goods had no simple, general solution. The Stigler Committee observed that if a quality increase was accompanied by a decline in price, the CPI should at least reflect the decline in price as a reduction in the cost of living.[22] In response to a question from Senator Douglas, Stigler suggested that instead of pricing the cost of a hospital room and physician's services, the CPI might take account of the more rapid recovery and shorter hospital stay required to treat a condition such as appendicitis (U.S. Congress 1961, 533).[23] Also, one of the report's staff papers, by Griliches (1961), investigated the use of hedonic functions for quality adjustment purposes, a method the Committee viewed as quite promising. Griliches' paper proved to be the most widely cited contribution of the report.

Last, for durable goods, the Stigler Committee noted that consumers' welfare depends on the flow of services from the durable, not on its value at the time of acquisition. Therefore, the cost of the use of the good is theoretically the correct concept for consumer price measurement. As a practical measure, the Stigler Committee recommended that BLS investigate the rental equivalence approach for measuring shelter costs for homeowners.

When asked by Senator Douglas what the Committee's proposal to move the CPI "toward" a Cost-of-Living Index entailed, Stigler gave the following list:

21. The objection that this stereotypical product cycle might not portray the pattern for all goods was raised at the time. On this, see Pakes (2003), who points to low "introductory" prices for new goods, followed by rising prices as knowledge spreads about them and demand increases. Very little empirical information exists on which pattern of price changes predominates for new varieties of goods.

22. The BLS procedures, at least in recent years, are consistent with this recommendation (see Triplett and Bosworth 2004) and were probably consistent in 1960.

23. Stigler noted a study, though he cited no source. Evidently, the Committee was apprised of a preliminary version of the work of Scitovsky (1964).

- "More objective" procedures for handling quality change.
- The same for new products.
- Treating durable goods as the consumption of the flow of services they provided.
- Substituting the average mortgage interest rate for the current rate in the owner-occupied housing measure.[24]
- "Perhaps" more frequent weight changes in the CPI.

Stigler was asked in the JEC hearings to make an estimate of the amount by which the CPI differed from a COLI, but, explaining that the Committee did not know enough to make such an estimate, he refused. In this, the Stigler Committee differed from the Mitchell Committee and the later Boskin Commission, both of which made guesstimates of CPI bias. Richard Ruggles, however, inserted a footnote into the report, which implied an annual bias estimate of 3 percentage points, but this was neither endorsed by the rest of the Committee, nor by Stigler himself.[25]

The initial reaction of the BLS to the Stigler Committee's COLI recommendation was quite negative, based partly on the lack of research showing how to estimate a COLI, and partly on doubts about the suitability of the COLI for the purposes of the CPI.[26] Commissioner Ewan Clague testified to a subcommittee of the Joint Economic Committee in 1961 that:

> There is one very important recommendation [in the report] with which the Bureau of Labor Statistics cannot agree, even with modifications. This is the recommendation that the Consumer Price Index be reoriented gradually toward a "welfare" or "constant utility" index. We would see some value in having a "true cost-of-living" or constant utility index if techniques can be developed for defining such an index, and then for compiling it objectively . . . We must emphasize, however, that this is a long-range goal that is now unattainable, may always be unattainable, and at best could be fully attained only after considerable further theoretical and statistical exploration. (U.S. Congress 1961, 560)

Later in the same hearings, BLS elaborated its position:

> Any partial movement toward a cost-of-living index, before the theoretical frame and operational structure is fully developed, could only lead to ambiguity and subjectivity. Based partly on price index principles and partly on cost-of-living index principles, such an index could not evoke the confidence of its users in its objectivity. (U.S. Congress 1961, 582)

24. A curious recommendation, since the Committee favored the rental equivalence measure of owner-occupied housing that BLS subsequently (in 1983) adopted. Stigler's testimony is also more guarded than the Committee report itself on increasing the frequency of weight updating.

25. Private communication by one of us with Stigler, who wrote that he had never quoted any estimate of the bias.

26. Some of the following discussion parallels Greenlees (2001).

Comments by others at the hearings on the Stigler Committee's report were also skeptical. Even Senator Douglas (a coinventor, after all, of the Cobb-Douglas model of producer substitution behavior, which Klein and Rubin [1947–1948] extended to the consumer case) expressed doubt about the feasibility of valuing quality changes by the amount that would hold utility constant. "I remember those lines of Browning," he remarked at the hearings: "'all, the world's coarse thumb and finger fail to plumb.' I always thought that there was always a large part of satisfaction that could not be plumbed by figures" (U.S. Congress 1961, 572).[27]

Despite BLS's initial opposition to the COLI concept, the tide changed in the 1960s. Part of the reason for the change in BLS's position was a change in its organization and staff. The Stigler Committee recommended that BLS set up a research unit within the BLS Office of Prices and Living Conditions. Funding for that was provided, and after some initial false starts a real research unit was established. It led to a more favorable view of the Stigler Committee's recommendations. As early as 1966, Commissioner Arthur Ross described to the Joint Economic Committee many restrictions on the applicability of economic theory for cost-of-living measurement but noted, "It is the only theory available, and if used with a proper understanding of its limitations does provide some guidance in the operation of a consumer price index" (Ross 1966).

Later statements about the CPI by BLS officials continued to combine references to the COLI measurement objective with caveats about the obstacles to achieving that objective. Statements that the CPI was not a COLI appeared in the *BLS Handbook of Methods* until its 1974 edition. However, a 1974 paper by BLS economist Robert Gillingham laid out the conceptual framework that was adopted for the 1978 revision to the CPI.[28] That paper, which focused on Pollak's concepts of partial and conditional cost-of-living subindexes, states that BLS "assumed that the primary purpose of the [CPI] is to approximate changes in the cost of living of consumers" (Gillingham 1974, 246). Moreover, using language that has been virtually unchanged since at least 1984, the 1997 *BLS Handbook of Methods* states:[29]

27. The Browning line is from "Rabbi Ben Ezra," in *Dramatis Personae.* As set by the Government Printing Office, a crucial comma is omitted, corrected in the above. The sense of the lines preceding the one quoted (stanza 24) is that things "that took the eye and had the price" are readily valued, "But all" (that is, the total of one's work in the eyes of God) is not. We thank Pimone Triplett for providing this reference.

28. Gillingham was a member of the CPI revision staff, and also of the Research Division. The manager of the 1978 CPI revision was John Layng, who became head of the BLS Office of Prices and Living Conditions. Administratively, then, the line officials in charge were closely identified with accepting the COLI framework. Indeed, little or no opposition to this framework was heard inside the BLS from around the mid-1970s until the mid-1990s (see the subsequent section on the Boskin Commission). See also Greenlees (2001) for a similar account.

29. Bureau of Labor Statistics (1997b, 170).

> A unifying framework for dealing with practical questions that arise in construction of the CPI is provided by the concept of the cost-of-living (COL) index [. . .] However, the concept is difficult to implement operationally because it holds the standard of living constant, and the living standard must be estimated in some way.
>
> The CPI uses a fixed market basket to hold the base-period living standard constant [. . .] The CPI provides an approximation to a COL index as a measure of consumption costs.

Thus, despite its initial skeptical reaction to the Stigler Committee's recommendation on the COLI, the BLS position eventually became (a) the COLI objective provides the framework for the CPI, but (b) the CPI cannot be called a COLI because of limitations of scope, failure to reflect all consumer substitution, and other problems.

The BLS implemented many recommendations of the Stigler Committee. Most notably, it instituted a system of probability sampling and, after a long public battle, it changed the index for owner-occupied housing to a rental equivalence measure.

Yet when the subsequent Boskin Commission was appointed twenty-five years later, BLS had still not implemented other Stigler Committee recommendations aimed at bringing the CPI into closer alignment with a COLI, or enabling the CPI to be compared to a COLI retrospectively. For example, the CPI weights were not updated frequently, new goods that did not fit into the existing item structure of the CPI were not introduced early, and a retrospective index that provided direct evidence on substitution bias in the CPI was not published until 1993. In addition, use of hedonic indexes was limited; for example, as late as 1991, when BLS began working on price indexes for computer equipment, its work plan specified that hedonic methods would be used only if all other methods failed. Nevertheless, considerable research on hedonic indexes was conducted within BLS starting in the late 1960s, which continues to this day. (Triplett [1990] reviews the early BLS hedonic research, and Fixler et al. [1999] review the research in the 1990s on the use of hedonics in the CPI.)

### 1.2.4 BLS Empirical Research on Estimating Substitution Bias

The BLS objected to the Stigler Committee's COLI recommendation in part because little research existed on estimating a COLI. Even on the relatively tractable problem of substitution effects in the estimation of a COLI, the Stigler Committee's report contained little beyond calculating a Paasche-type index to obtain bounds. None of the report's twelve staff papers estimated substitution bias or suggested how to do it, and Klein and Rubin (1947–1948) was not in the references. For the BLS staff, it must have seemed as if they were being told to do the impossible.

Subsequently, however, BLS undertook an extensive program of theoretical and empirical work on substitution bias under the auspices of the price research unit that the Stigler Committee had recommended. This unit became fully operational in 1968 under the direction of Joel Popkin. Part of its budget was used to fund academic visitors such as Robert Pollak. Pollak's papers for BLS (which form the chapters in Pollak [1989]) resulted in the major advances in cost of living index theory of the 1970s, along with Erwin Diewert's (1976) paper, and the work of Franklin Fisher and Karl Shell (1972).

*Substitution Bias Estimates*

For empirical work, BLS research strategy followed the Klein-Rubin (1948) lead. Improved computer capability finally made estimates of the Klein-Rubin system practical, one of the earliest estimates being Goldberger and Gameletsos (1970).

The BLS developed or adapted improved specifications for systems of consumer demand functions that were less restrictive than the Klein-Rubin system (Brown and Heien 1972; Heien 1973; Christensen and Manser 1976; Braithwait 1980), and that could be used to explore the sensitivity of estimated COLIs to the demand system specification. The BLS empirical estimates of the substitution bias using systems of demand equations include: Christensen and Manser (1976), Manser (1975, 1976)—who studied detailed food categories, and Braithwait (1980), who treated food as an aggregate but included fifty-two other commodity groups, using data from the National Accounts. Taken together, these studies covered consumers' budgets at approximately a sixty-three commodity level of detail. This is a far greater level of detail than was found in previous research: BLS researchers estimated substitution among categories such as "beef, poultry, pork and fish," whereas the previous studies used aggregates like durables, nondurables, and services. Of course, even sixty-three commodity groupings may be too coarse to capture some important substitution behavior, and the use of aggregate data ignores the problem of aggregating over households, which amounts to assuming away one of the major problems with COLI theory.

Nevertheless, the early BLS studies produced two remarkable results. First, substitution bias, at around 0.1 to 0.2 points per year, was discovered to be much smaller than most economists had expected; guesstimates of upwards of 1 percentage point per year, or even more, prevailed in textbooks and informal discussions among economists. Substitution among CPI categories was indeed substantial, as was expected (Braithwait's unpublished BLS working paper has the most exhaustive elasticity estimates), but it did not result in the expected large bias in the index.[30]

Second, BLS researchers found that econometric estimates of substitu-

30. These studies did not consider substitution within CPI basic components; they estimated bias at the CPI level at which weights were held fixed in the Laspeyres formula, or actually, at a somewhat higher level. The question of bias within components emerged later on—see section 1.3.

tion bias in the price index were remarkably robust across different specifications of consumer demand systems. This finding of insensitivity of substitution bias estimates to utility function specifications was surprising because estimates of demand elasticities *are* sensitive to demand specifications. It is true that the roughly eight to ten utility specifications employed in the BLS studies covered only a limited range of possibilities (the studies employed all of the major demand systems that existed at the time, with one major exception that was developed too late for inclusion in the research design).[31] But their results are consistent enough to conclude that substitution bias estimates are empirically robust to model specification choices, contrary to the presumption made in some subsequent discussions of substitution bias.

In the middle of the BLS research project on estimating substitution bias, another development fundamentally changed researchers' perspectives. Diewert (1976), who drew on Byushgens (1925) and Konüs and Byushgens (1926), showed that one could obtain a good approximation to the substitution bias using "superlative" index numbers. Specifically, superlative indexes provide exact COLIs for "flexible" (homothetic) indirect utility functions that have enough free parameters to provide a second-order approximation for an arbitrary twice-differentiable indirect utility function (the "true" function). The approximating function is thus homothetic, but the function being approximated need not be. Superlative indexes include the Fisher index and the Törnqvist index.

One of the flexible functions considered by Diewert, the homothetic translog indirect utility function of Christensen, Jorgenson, and Lau (1975), had already been estimated by Christensen and Manser (1976). Diewert showed that the homothetic translog estimate could be expected to be close to the COLI estimates from any utility function, and Christensen and Manser showed that this was true, empirically, for the ones they estimated. Further experimentation with alternative consumer demand systems seemed unnecessary. Indeed, econometric estimation of a demand system was itself unnecessary, because the COLI could be estimated directly using one of the superlative indexes.

Manser and McDonald (1988) used Diewert's superlative indexes for point estimates of the substitution bias in a Laspeyres index of consumer prices. They supplemented the point estimates with nonparametric bounds derived from revealed preference theory by Afriat (1967) and exposited and advanced by Diewert (1973) and by Varian (1982, 1983). For the period that they studied, the Afriat-Varian method bounds showed that the approximation was very good. The substitution bias estimate averaged 0.18 percent per year.[32]

31. The exception was the "Almost Ideal Demand System." See Deaton and Muellbauer (1980).

32. Blow and Crawford (2001) used an extended version of the procedures in Manser and McDonald to estimate substitution bias in the U.K. index. Also, Balk (1990) estimated the substitution error in the Dutch index.

Finally, Aizcorbe and Jackman (1993) estimated substitution bias using superlative index numbers at a greater level of commodity detail than had been done previously, and unlike earlier studies their database *was* from the CPI. Their estimate, at roughly 0.15 index points per year, was consistent with earlier research. Because it was done on a larger number of commodities, it supplemented the earlier research, which mostly was conducted at a higher level of commodity detail (sixty-three commodities for the combined demand system results of Braithwait and of Manser, and roughly twice that number for Manser and McDonald).

Recently, BLS has begun to publish a "Chained CPI" that uses the Törnqvist index. As Boskin (2005) and Gordon (2006) note, this index differs from the official Laspeyres CPI by more than the 0.1 to 0.2 estimates of earlier studies. (The initial year difference was 0.8 percent, but this has come down to 0.3 percent per year in recent years.) The bias discussed by the Stigler Commission from failure to bring in new products promptly is part of the explanation for the unexpectedly large divergence between the Chained CPI and the ordinary CPI: Shoemaker (2004) traces some of it to higher weights for cell phone service in the Chained CPI. Cage, Greenlees, and Jackman (2003) also point to larger changes in relative prices in the period covered by the Chained CPI than some in earlier years, giving as specific examples rising natural gas prices and falling computer prices. The kind of behavioral response that would convert these relative price changes into significant substitution bias in a Laspeyres index seems more plausible in the case of computers than in the case of the inelastically-demanded natural gas.

### *The Empirical Effects of Assuming Homotheticity on COLI Estimates*

Homotheticity is the bête noire of demand analysis. Homotheticity is the condition that Engle curves are straight lines that pass through the origin, so that for any set of relative prices households at all income levels consume commodities in the same proportions. It is well-known that empirical demand curves that are derived from homothetic utility functions are not only unrealistic, but can lead to biased estimates of demand elasticities.

From what is known from the analysis of consumer behavior, use of a homothetic function to estimate a COLI is on its face suspect. The CNSTAT report, discussed following, emphasizes this point. However, the question is not the validity of homotheticity as a specification of consumer behavior, nor is it the impact of maintaining homotheticity on estimates of demand elasticities; the question is the empirical impact of maintaining homotheticity on the size of the estimated substitution bias.

In a notable finding, BLS researchers discovered that an assumption of homotheticity, though a poor specification of consumer demand behavior, does not much influence econometric estimates of substitution bias. Christensen and Manser's (1976, 434–35) estimates of "branch" COLI's for meat are an example of this. They estimated five different nonhomothetic utility functions, which gave "branch" COLI estimates for 1971 (using 1958 preferences as the base and 1958 = 1.000) that ranged from 1.228 and 1.231; their three homothetic functions produced estimates between 1.228 and 1.233. Thus, over the thirteen-year period 1958 to 1971 as a whole, the maximum difference among all the estimates was only 0.005 index points, and the mean difference between homothetic and nonhomothetic estimates was nil. Using the whole period covered by their data (1947 to 1971), the results were similar: with 1947 = 1.000, the indexes for nonhomothetic forms ranged from 1.437 to 1.440 in 1971, homothetic ones from 1.441 to 1.444. In this case, the homothetic estimates are outside the range of the nonhomothetic ones, but the difference in average annual rates of change of the homothetic and nonhomothetic indexes is again exceedingly small. Yet Christensen and Manser's estimated demand elasticities were sensitive to whether a homothetic system was estimated, in line with previous research.

How could it be true that demand estimates are sensitive to maintaining homotheticity, yet COLI estimates are not? Consider figure 1.2, which shows a nonhomothetic indifference map. For simplicity in drawing the diagram (*only*) the true (nonhomothetic) Engel curve is drawn linear (labeled "A"), and a (counterfactual) homothetic Engel curve is labeled "B."

It is well-known that demand has both income and substitution effects; as figure 1.2 suggests, both would be misestimated if homotheticity were imposed on the data. But for estimating the substitution bias for a COLI, only the substitution term is relevant, and only around the initial (base) period's tangency and the comparison period's tangency. We may thus ask: how much error will be introduced from incorrectly maintaining homotheticity, in effect estimating the substitution term around the tangencies represented by BB, instead of along AA?

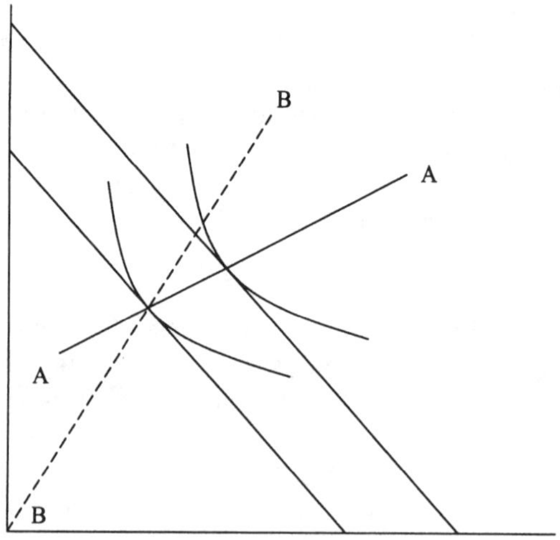


**Fig. 1.2 A change in income with nonhomothetic indifference curves**

The curvature of the implied indifference curves along BB and along AA may well differ. However, for small differences in income levels and barring extreme curvatures of the indifference curves, the curvatures along AA and BB will differ only slightly, so the *estimated* substitution biases can be similar. The Christensen-Manser substitution bias estimates cited in the previous paragraph suggest that something like figure 1.2 represents the data. Estimates of the substitution bias when homotheticity is imposed do indeed differ from substitution bias estimates when it is not, but not by much. Manser-McDonald's bounds on the approximating error of the superlative index indicate the same thing: their assumption of homotheticity does not keep superlative indexes from providing a close bound on the substitution bias, just as the use of homothetic demand systems does not create much of an error in econometric COLI estimates.

The CNSTAT Panel argued that Diewert's superlative index method implied homotheticity, which is an unsupportable assumption about consumer preferences.[33] The panel made a valid, albeit well-known, theoretical point. Yet it overlooked the empirical literature that would have provided perspective on the empirical importance of their criticism—the empirical estimates that exist, cited in the previous paragraphs, show that the effect of imposing homotheticity in COLI estimation is negligible. Further discussion of this question follows in the section on the panel's report.

### 1.2.5 The Boskin Commission: Further Developments in the Cost-of-Living Index Approach

At the 1993 Allied Social Science Associations (ASSA) meetings in Anaheim, Reinsdorf presented a paper documenting upward bias in CPI component indexes for food and gasoline (published in revised form as Reinsdorf [1998]). Partly as a result of the attention drawn to Reinsdorf's results by Erwin Diewert (who, as the paper's discussant, called it "the measurement paper of the decade") and by Robert Gordon, CPI bias became a topic of much discussion. After a remark on upward bias in the CPI in testimony by Federal Reserve Chairman Alan Greenspan (Berry 1995), the Senate Finance Committee appointed an "Advisory Commission to Study the Consumer Price Index." The Commission became known as the Boskin Commission, after its chair, Michael Boskin. Like earlier review panels, the Boskin Commission had one carryover from the Stigler Committee: Zvi Griliches (who had contributed a staff paper on hedonic indexes).

Like the Stigler Committee, the Boskin Commission recommended that BLS adopt the Cost-of-Living Index as the measurement concept for the CPI (Boskin et al. 1995). Indeed, the Boskin Commission took the appro-

33. Actually Diewert's (1976) results included a demonstration that the Törnqvist index is exact for a nonhomothetic translog model if the COLI is evaluated at an intermediate level of utility. This is a less satisfactory measurement concept than either a COLI evaluated at the initial level of utility or a COLI evaluated at the final level of utility.

priateness of the COLI objective for the CPI as almost self-evident, presenting no alternatives and laying out no specifics as to how the COLI should be defined. The COLI factors identified by the Stigler Committee, including substitution induced by changes in relative prices, new products, and changes in quality of existing products, figured prominently in the Boskin Commission's report.

As we noted in an earlier section, BLS had initially been disinclined to accept the COLI recommendation of the Stigler Committee. Even in the run up to the naming of the Boskin Commission, statements from BLS that the CPI is not a COLI had occasionally seemed to disclaim the COLI even as an objective for the CPI.[34] In light of BLS's long-standing acceptance of the COLI concept, these BLS statements were surprising, and they contributed to a perception that the Boskin Commission's COLI recommendation was one that BLS professional staff opposed. In turn, this COLI misunderstanding (if that is what it was) inflamed contentions over the rest of the Commission's findings, some of which were indeed flawed. All manner of political speculations clouded the debate over the Commission's report, ranging from the Senate Committee's motivation in selecting the panel members (reducing the rate of increase in the CPI would reduce expenditure growth on government indexed programs) to whether the independence of a statistical agency was threatened.

Along with its call to embrace the COLI as the measurement objective, the Boskin Commission urged BLS to use superlative or similar index number formulas to approximate a COLI, and here its recommendation constituted a genuine change. Specifically, the Boskin Commission urged BLS to use a superlative index number formula for a retrospective annual index, and to use a geometric mean formula (which is not superlative, but would not require unavailable data on current expenditure patterns) for the monthly CPI. Research results that had become available since the time of the Stigler Committee made these recommendations possible, as noted in section 1.2.4.

The Boskin Commission discussed sources of CPI-COLI difference beyond those that Stigler Committee had considered. One of these was "lower-level substitution bias." The estimates described in section 1.2.4 pertain to what the Boskin Commission called "upper level substitution bias," the bias that occurs *among* the basic components of the index, the levels at which the weights are held fixed (roughly 200 commodity groups in the index structure that was in place at the time). Lower level substitution bias—to be discussed more fully in section 1.3 of this chapter—occurs among the detailed items

34. Baker (1998, 131) interprets the 1995 BLS report to the House Budget Committee as taking this position, and others formed the same interpretation. Moreover, based on personal conversations one of us had with Boskin Commission members at the time, we believe that they also interpreted BLS statements as indicating that the BLS was opposed to the COLI concept.

and varieties that are aggregated to construct the 207 item group indexes in the CPI (that is, *within* the basic components). The problem of aggregating price quotations into basic components had been discussed previously (Carruthers, Sellwood, and Ward 1960; Szulc 1983). However, its importance was little appreciated until the empirical results on the topic that appeared in the early 1990s showed the surprising magnitude of these aggregation effects (Schultz 1994; Reinsdorf 1993; Moulton 1993; Reinsdorf and Moulton 1995; Diewert 1995; Reinsdorf 1998).

The Boskin commission also called attention to the related problem of the unmeasured reduction in the cost of living from substitution to outlets offering lower prices, such as Wal-Mart. We discuss this problem in section 1.3 because it affects the construction of the detailed component indexes.

Like the Mitchell Committee, but unlike the Stigler Committee, the Boskin Commission estimated biases in the CPI. Their 0.15 percentage points per year from upper level substitution was based on the empirical estimates discussed in section 1.2.4, but likely more on the latest of those estimates (Aizcorbe and Jackman 1993) than the earlier ones. The Commission also estimated 0.25 percentage points per year from lower level substitution (this was based on Reinsdorf and Moulton [1995]; Reinsdorf [1998]), 0.6 points from new products and quality change in existing products, and 0.1 points from outlet substitution. The Boskin Commission acknowledged that in some cases the available evidence to make these estimates was not strong, and some reviewers chided the Commission for its lack of objectiveness in indulging in guestimates. Some of the quality change estimates were marred by faulty understanding.[35]

The Boskin Commission also revisited a question that had received little attention since the discussion in the Mitchell Committee's 1944 report: to what extent should developments beyond market price changes that affect the cost of living be reflected in the CPI? Here the Boskin Commission raised some worthwhile questions concerning inconsistencies that can arise from consideration of price effects in isolation from nonprice effects. For example, is it sensible to show a decline in the COLI when the cost of treating AIDS drops because of medical advances if no increase in the COLI was shown for the appearance of this previously unknown disease?

35. For example, its guestimate of upward bias in rental housing (which was based on introspective estimates about the extent that quality of housing had improved) ignored results in Randolph (1988) that showed that the BLS linking procedure for bringing improved housing units into the sample imparted a downward—not upward—bias. An additional downward bias, caused by censored reporting of rents during vacancies, was discovered by Crone, Nakamura, and Voith (2004). These downward biases were replicated by Gordon and van Goethem (2003). Randolph's result was replicated by Gordon and van Goethem (2007) over a longer historical period, and Gordon (2006) revised the Commission's guestimate on housing. Additional discussion of these matters (which are beyond the scope of the present chapter) are in a 2006 symposium on the Boskin Commission report. See, in addition to Gordon (2006), Berndt (2006), Baily (2006), Greenlees (2006), and Triplett (2006).

However, in its discussion of the effects of broader changes in the environment on the cost of living, the Commission failed to make the distinction between the "conditional" COLI and the "unconditional" COLI. Gillingham (1974) and Pollak (1989, chapter 2) contended that the CPI can be interpreted as an approximation to a conditional COLI, for which environmental effects—though appropriate for some broader measures—are out of scope. By discussing environmental effects without providing the appropriate context, the Boskin Commission report implicitly suggested that they might be in scope, creating confusion.[36] This contrasts with the Mitchell Committee's consideration of the need to restrict the domain of the index in its response to the Meany-Thomas report, as well as with the extensive discussion of the domain question in the subsequent CNSTAT report.

The BLS agreed with some, but not all, of the Boskin Commission's recommendations and findings. Regarding its recommendation that the CPI establish a COLI objective, the BLS paper, "Measurement Issues in the Consumer Price Index," indicated:

> The BLS has for many years used the concept of the cost-of-living index as a framework for making decisions about the CPI and accepts the COLI as the measurement objective for the index . . . The cost-of-living index approximated by the CPI is a subindex of the all-encompassing cost-of-living concept. (Bureau of Labor Statistics [1997a, 4]; see also Abraham, Greenlees, and Moulton [1998, 27].)

The Boskin Commission report has been very influential, not just in the U.S., but also worldwide (Diewert 1998). But the basis for its influence, ironically, was its estimates of CPI bias, not its endorsement of the concept of COLI. Indeed, many countries reject the COLI framework, and a number of them initially contended that the Boskin Commission's bias estimates did not apply to their CPI's because their indexes were not intended as approximations to a COLI. Subsequently, however, the discussions the Commission generated resulted in increased efforts to improve CPI measurements, worldwide (Ducharme [1997]; Abraham [2003]; Hausman [2003]; Triplett [2006] and the items cited there).

### 1.2.6 The CNSTAT Panel: Second Thoughts about the Cost-of-Living Index

The Boskin Commission had limited resources and it operated in a politically charged environment. Critics of the Commission's report argued that its treatment of CPI biases lacked balance, and that the membership of the Commission excluded alternative points of view. Robert Pollak—echoing a suggestion made earlier by Boskin Commission member Zvi Griliches—therefore recommended that the technical issues related to the

36. However, two members of the Boskin Commission stated elsewhere that these nonprice effects do not belong in the CPI—see Gordon and Griliches (1997, 87).

CPI be examined by a committee of technical experts under the auspices of an organization such as the National Academy of Sciences (Pollak 1998, 76). Consistent with this proposal, BLS asked the Committee on National Statistics of the National Academy of Sciences to convene a panel to investigate "issues in the development of cost-of-living indexes" (Schultze and Mackie 2002, 17).

In contrast to all previous review panels, the CNSTAT Panel was not composed primarily of scholars with expertise on the CPI: despite the technical nature of the question that the panel was charged with investigating, the goal seemed to be to make sure that a broad range of perspectives was represented. The panel included economists whose primary expertise was in other areas of economics, as well as representatives of disciplines such as statistics, psychology, and marketing. Among the economists on the panel, some had not participated in the debate over the issues discussed by the Boskin Commission, and some were known to differ with the views from the Boskin Commission. The only carryover was Griliches, who had also provided the bridge from Stigler to Boskin, but he died before the panel got very far into its work.[37]

If the goal was to obtain a diversity of perspectives, that is certainly what BLS got. In particular, the view that the COLI is the appropriate measurement concept for the CPI, which had broad support from most economists for half a century,[38] proved so contentious that the panel was unable to reach a consensus on this fundamental issue.

### *The COLI versus the COGI*

Rather than measuring the cost of maintaining a constant standard of living, some members of the CNSTAT Panel believed that the conceptual objective of the CPI ought to be measurement of the change in the cost of purchasing a fixed basket of goods and services, or what the panel called a "cost of goods index" or COGI (Schultze and Mackie 2002, 15). In principle, the fixed basket could be based on the initial (or "reference") period consumption pattern, the final (or "comparison") period's consumption pattern, or even some point in between (Schultze and Mackie 2002, 16). However, the report's subsequent discussion of the COGI often suggested its

37. The other members of the CNSTAT panel were its chairman Charles Schultze, Ernst Berndt, Angus Deaton, Erwin Diewert, Claudia Goldin, Christopher Jencks, Albert Madansky, Van Doorn Ooms, Robert Pollak, Richard Schmalensee, Nobert Schwartz, and Kirk Wolter.

38. For example, panel member Robert Pollak (1989, vii) wrote that at BLS in 1968 to 1969 he approached problems in the CPI "with the conviction that a well-developed theory of the cost-of-living index could provide practical solutions." In addition, substitution bias in the CPI had long been a staple of textbooks for principles of economics classes, which is again evidence of a wide consensus that the COLI was the correct concept for the CPI. On the other hand, the economists who were named to the CNSTAT panel were divided on the applicability of the COLI.

equivalence to a Laspeyres index, which uses the initial period's expenditure pattern (see, for example, the report's page 112).

The proponents of the COGI supported their view with three contentions. First, they argued that the COLI concept was unsuitable for the CPI. Second, they pointed to problems in the theory of the COLI. Third, they cited the arbitrariness of any definition for the domain of the conditional COLI, which they thought implied that the concept was unworkable as a guide to index procedures.

*COLI Unsuitable for the CPI*

The COGI proponents who found the COLI concept unsuitable for the CPI accepted that a fixed-basket index overcompensates for price increases because of substitution bias. However, they believed that the CPI should measure the "price level" rather than the level of compensation needed to hold welfare constant (Schultze and Mackie 2002, 58). The COGI advocates apparently viewed the price index in a way that coincides with the views of Fisher—some price level exists, like the level of water in a lake, and the index is a device to find it.

Mitchell's (1921) comment that the notion of the price level is inherently ill-defined (see the appendix) still seems apt in considering this aspect of the CNSTAT 2002 Panel's report. The charge that the domain of the "price level" is undefined might be answered by COGI advocates by saying that Mitchell's critique has less force in the case of consumer prices because the content of consumer expenditures defines the domain. On the other hand, the CNSTAT panel thought that the domain should be defined on the services of durable goods, not on the purchases of durables themselves (thus agreeing with the COLI point of view). In this case, the price index domain is not defined by the observable content of consumer expenditures, but rather by recourse to the theory of consumption.

Leaving aside the flow of services problem, the concept of a "price level" suffers from a more fundamental problem. Given the domain, in principle one could observe all the transactions that take place at a given date and compute the average level of their prices. Different commodities would be weighted, in this system, by their transactions. In this sense, a price level might exist, for a point in time.

Taking another date, the computation could be repeated. The transactions on the second date would differ from those on the first, and again, a price level exists in this sense for the second period. Taking the ratio of the two price levels amounts to a unit value index, whose weights differ between the numerator and denominator. The *average* price of a transaction on each date depends arbitrarily on such factors as the lumpiness of transactions, and the commodity and quality mix. In some sense, this change is a change in the price level (in the sense that, for example, it influences the demand for money). But it is hardly what one wants from a price index.

Even though price indexes are often said to measure the change in the price level, this is just careless or imprecise language, for they do not actually do that at all. As price indexes are actually computed, they are based on samples chosen to measure price change, not the price level. Consider all the apparatus that is put in place in the CPI to hold constant the retail outlet, product characteristics, and so forth. This apparatus is intended to assure that price change is measured without contamination, not that the price level is measured accurately. Though Fisher spoke of "the price level," and of a price index as a device for measuring it (comparable to measuring the level of water in a lake), he also discussed the need to make the price index independent of the units of measurement (his "commensurability axiom"), which ruled out the averaging of prices and the use of unit value indexes.[39]

Rather than addressing specifically what the seemingly vague price level notion means, the report provides only an example of what it does not mean—the treatment of new goods. Recall that the Stigler Committee included the welfare gains associated with new goods in the concept that the CPI should try to measure, and hence advised bringing new goods in early to minimize the bias. Hausman (1997) proposed a method to include all the welfare gains in the CPI by extrapolating the demand curve for a new good out to a Hicksian virtual price (Hicks 1940), at which the good's sales would fall to zero (the virtual price provides the price for the period before the new product was introduced). Some members of the CNSTAT Panel argued against the Hicks-Hausman technique because they contended that gains from the invention or introduction of new goods were not part of the change in the price level (Schultze and Mackie 2002, 160–1). Without a precise definition of the price level, whether their contention is correct is unclear.

*Problems with COLI*

The second argument for the COGI approach was a negative case against the COLI, built from problems with the concept of the COLI, rather than a positive case for the COGI. The "not COLI" position pointed to the need for unrealistic assumptions in some forms of the theory of the COLI (the panel dwelt especially on homotheticity, constant tastes, constant environmental conditions, and the difficulty of aggregating over individual consumer's behavioral functions). Some members also contended that the standard of living (held constant in the COLI) cannot be defined, which provides a counterpart to the assertion of COGI detractors that the price level is not definable.

39. In his (1911) discussion of the equation of exchange $MV = PT$, he defined the quantity units in $T$ as "a dollar's worth in the base period," and found that this implied that $P$ was a Paasche price index, not a ratio of averages.

The COLI for the base-period standard of living is bounded from above by the Laspeyres index and the COLI for the comparison period standard of living is bounded from below by the Paasche index, but these are different COLI indexes if preferences are nonhomothetic. Similarly, the conventional assumption that the COLI of a "representative consumer" who has the aggregate demand patterns summarizes (or "averages") the COLIs of individual households is not justified without unrealistic assumptions about the nature of preferences. Therefore, estimation of an aggregate COLI involves difficult distributional issues, as Pollak (1989, chapters 6 and 7) showed. On the other hand, similar taste and distributional issues affect the COGI (e.g., the Laspeyres COGI will differ from the Paasche COGI), but this seemingly was not regarded as a problem.

*Domain of the Conditional COLI*

Within the context of the COLI approach, the panel agreed that the appropriate version of the COLI for the CPI was a *conditional* COLI that covers private market goods and services and holds the broader environmental factors constant (Schultze and Mackie 2002, 73). The immediate intellectual roots of the concept of the conditional COLI are found in Pollak (1989, chapter 2), though the domain question can also be linked historically to the position that the Mitchell Committee took nearly sixty years earlier, when it recommended that BLS change the name of its "Cost-of-Living Index" to avoid confusion about the breadth of effects that the index covered.

Some members of the CNSTAT panel viewed the need to restrict the domain of the COLI as an argument for the COGI approach because in deciding on how to condition the COLI, arbitrariness and inconsistency can be hard to avoid. One must condition the COLI on some new technologies, the panel asserts, but not on others. For example, the CNSTAT Panel favored diagnostic-based measures of medical care rather than input-based measures whenever possible (188), which implies that the CPI should decline when a new pharmaceutical makes treatment of a diagnosis cheaper. Nevertheless, most of the panelists did not think that the invention of Viagra should cause a decline in the CPI (Schultze and Mackie 2002, 67).[40]

Of course, the COGI must also have a domain. Choosing the domain of the COGI appears to present the same kind of problem as choosing the domain of the conditional COLI. As Schultze (2003, 11) put it in summarizing the debate within the panel: "According to the supporters of the cost-of-living concept, the fact that the basis for . . . domain decisions cannot be provided from within the general theory underlying that concept is not a

40. This appears to be an arbitrary judgment about what medical conditions are appropriately included in the treatments priced for the CPI. This kind of arbitrariness could be considered a powerful argument against the COGI approach, because it lacks any theoretical framework for determining what goods are to be included and how they are to be measured.

reason to preclude using the conditional cost-of-living index as the framework for the design and construction of the Consumer Price Index."

### 1.2.7 Assessment of the Debate over the Conceptual Basis for the CPI

At one level, the COLI-COGI debate involves competing charges of "immeasurable" or "undefined" hurled like spears at the opponents' concept. Detractors of COGI point out that the price level is undefined, as is the COGI domain. The COGI advocates answer that the key concepts of the utility level and the standard of living in the COLI approach are undefined or immeasurable. Observers who are users of the CPI but belong to neither camp might view the competing charges as a draw, and decide that what matters is staying out of spear range.

A more specific criticism of the COLI in the CNSTAT report is the one that has been current in statistical agency circles seemingly forever: the theory rests on questionable behavioral assumptions that do not describe how consumers actually behave and (at a somewhat more sophisticated level) the topics on which the theory is inchoate dominate the topics on which firm conclusions can be drawn. Deaton (1998, 37–38 and 42) summarizes this criticism with his usual eloquence:

> That the Bureau of Labor Statistics should establish a cost-of-living index as its objective in measuring consumer prices, taken by them [the Boskin Commission] as essentially obvious, is a contentious proposition that requires serious argument. In fact, it is unclear that a quality-corrected cost-of-living index in a world with many heterogeneous agents is an operational concept.
>
> We know rather little about whether consumers maximize utility at all, let alone whether they do so instantaneously or take time to adapt to price changes. We do know that there are many consumers, not one, and that, even if each behaves as we like to suppose, we cannot represent their behavior or their welfare by that of a single representative agent.

We emphasize that we do not dispute Deaton's critique of the COLI, nor the elaboration of parallel matters in the CNSTAT report's sections ("The Theory of Price Indexes and Its Critics" and "Two Perspectives," pages 43–72). These shortcomings of COLI theory have long been recognized. (Indeed, Jorgenson [1990] and Jorgenson and Slesnick [1983] proposed a generalization of COLI theory that avoids the use of the single representative agent to represent a society of heterogeneous consumers.) What separates adherents of the COLI view (where we place ourselves) and those of the COGI *is not so much disagreement about the shortcomings or ambiguities of the theory on which the COLI is based as it is disagreement about the shortcomings of the alternatives to COLI, such as COGI.*

A conceptual framework for the CPI must address a broader range of questions than just the scheme for aggregating the basic component indexes. Passages in the CNSTAT Panel report suggest agreement: "Quality adjustment is possibly the area in which the COLI has the greatest advantage over the COGI approach" (Schultze and Mackie 2002, 62).[41] Overall, however, when the panel discusses these "other" questions, the overwhelming weight of its discussion falls on problems, or supposed problems, with the COLI. The COGI "wins" this debate by default.[42]

In constructing the CPI, hundreds of decisions must be made, and many of them involve the question, "What do we want to measure?" (Triplett 2001, 315). An explicit underlying conceptual motivation is needed to provide a unifying framework for consistent decision making in index design and to provide a clear interpretation of the index. A conditional COLI has long served this purpose in the U.S. CPI, and satisfactory alternatives have not been developed.

A fixed basket index as the objective leaves the question of the underlying conceptual motivation largely inchoate. The motivations offered for the COGI—to track "the prices of the things that people buy" or "the price level"—provide little analytic insight into questions such as what items belong in the basket,[43] what price concept to use in cases where the definition of the price is ambiguous, what to do about quality change, how to treat voluntary or involuntary substitution, how to treat product introductions and disappearances, and so forth.

In contrast, the COLI approach provides guidance about how to handle problems such as what to do when items in the index disappear, or what to do when new goods or new quality levels appear, or (when an immediate conclusion is not obvious) it provides a vehicle for thinking about them in a consistent and coherent manner. It can also help to resolve methodological ambiguities and it can aid in the discovery of improvements by making the

41. On the other hand, speaking of the COLI framework, some members of the Panel expressed themselves as "concerned about the BLS adopting a conceptual framework that is not always well defined in the presence of quality change" (Schultze and Mackie 2002, 73). By default, this means adopting the COGI framework (which one can contend is even less adequate), though the Panel also expressed the opinion that with respect to quality change "the distinctions between the two approaches are blurred" (63).

42. One example of this fault is the Panel's discussion of "Using Indexes for Compensation," which is a subsection of its "Two Perspectives." The section contains an excellent discussion of how escalating a *portion* of income with a COLI does not leave the recipient at the same standard of living (as pointed out in Triplett [1983]; see also Triplett [2001]), but it concludes, "Even in the area for which it seems best suited—compensation—the cost-of-living index is not as obvious a choice as at first appears." Because the section in which this conclusion is found is one that purports to be comparing the advantages of COLI and COGI, one would not be amiss in interpreting the Panel as saying that the COGI is immune from the fault, and for this reason should be preferred. The Panel missed the chance to say something meaningful about escalation practices, choosing instead to look for arguments against the COLI. In this, the Panel's report lacks balance.

43. The "domain" of the index. "Prices of things that people buy" provides no guidance: People buy apartment buildings and other investments. The theory of consumption guides, explicitly or implicitly, the domain of the CPI. Some proposals for including some kinds of investments in the CPI appeal to COLI theory for justification (for example, Goodhart [2001]).

index's shortcomings identifiable.[44] An underlying conceptual objective such as a COLI can provide an analytic framework to reason about such basic questions of what price concept should be used in situations where this is not obvious; for example, what to do when a two-part or multipart tariff replaces a simple price, or how to measure complex commodities like insurance.

Using insurance as an example, Beelen (2004, 6) discusses the price concept for insurance in the CPI. When a household purchases an insurance policy, is the service the absorption of risk by the insurance company? If so, the price concept is the risk-adjusted premium. Or is it the administration of the insurance pool on the behalf of the policyholders? In this case, the service is a management service by the insurance company, and the price is the price of the management service (usually measured by premiums minus claims). The European Harmonized Indexes of Consumer Prices (HICP), which operate under a "not COLI" concept, have adopted the latter.[45]

How does one resolve such questions? Though one might contend that COLI theory by itself does not fully answer them without more development, the COLI framework permits development of the theory, just as any problem in economics is typically addressed by developing the relevant theory. The alternative is an ambiguous framework where the decision itself *and the framework for discussing it* are both arbitrary.

Finally, as Blow and Crawford (2001, F359) point out, many uses of the CPI require an interpretation as an approximation to a COLI. As illustrated by the union complaints in the World War II era, users' complaints about the CPI have often reflected a desire for a Cost-of-Living Index, and political debates regarding indexation often refer to adjusting benefits for the "cost of living." The CNSTAT Panel believed that the concepts of the COLI are difficult for noneconomists to understand; newspaper discussions of the Boskin Commission report attest to the contrary—many of them were quite clear and perceptive about the COLI and its objectives, and how the COLI differed from the CPI in its treatment of substitution. In any event, most applied economic research on topics such as tax analysis or benefit-cost analysis also use the same of kind of theoretical measures as the COLI, so an estimate of a COLI is usable in a great many economic analyses with no conceptual inconsistency. Nothing comparable can be said about a "cost of goods" framework.

We also believe that the theoretical problems of the COLI are of less practical importance than is commonly supposed. The CNSTAT report makes much of the implausibility of the assumptions needed for a single

44. Greenlees (2001, 12–14) provides examples of design improvements in the CPI guided by the COLI concept.

45. The HICP strove for compatibility with national accounts, so its decision on insurance was influence by the 1993 System of National Accounts. On measuring insurance in national accounts and CPI, see chapter 6 in Triplett and Bosworth (2004).

representative agent to represent the welfare of a group of households. Yet as the CNSTAT 2002 report (51–52) also observes, these extreme theoretical assumptions are not needed for the aggregate Laspeyres index to be an upper bound for a social Cost-of-Living Index concept known as the "Scitovsky-Laspeyres" index. This index concept, introduced by Pollak (1980, 1981), tracks the cost of keeping every household at its initial standard of living, holding constant its tastes and endowment of environmental factors. A parallel result from Diewert (2001, 172–3) shows that the aggregate Paasche index is a lower bound for an analogous "Scitovsky-Paasche" index, which tracks the cost of keeping every household at its final standard of living, given its final endowment of tastes and environmental factors under similarly weak assumptions.

The empirical literature on estimated COLIs shows that some other criticisms of the COLI are theoretical niceties with less empirical importance. Chapter 2 of the CNSTAT report explains the theoretical significance of homotheticity to consumer demand analysis (not in doubt) and demonstrates that it *might* have an impact on empirical estimates of a COLI (again, not in doubt).

Yet surely the issue for the panel's report is, how much does homotheticity matter empirically for COLI estimates? The CNSTAT Panel made no attempt to distill the empirical literature on estimated COLIs—or any of the empirical evidence in economics—that had a bearing on its COLI-COGI deliberations.

We reviewed the existing empirical COLI research in section 1.2.4. We noted that estimated COLIs based on homothetic indirect utility functions differ trivially from COLIs computed from nonhomothetic indirect utility functions. Empirically, homotheticity matters far less than the CNSTAT panel report implied. One might contend that the existing empirical COLI research amounts to a small number of studies, using a limited number of demand specifications. Nevertheless, a professional review panel has an obligation to consider all the relevant research.

Another way to assess homotheticity is to evaluate the effects of changing the reference base. It is well-known that the value of a COLI is independent of the reference base (the base indifference curve) only with homotheticity. Christensen and Manser (1976, 434–7) found that changing the reference standard of living from the 1947 to the 1967 level (that is, moving it by twenty years) raised their *nonhomothetic* cost-of-living subindexes for meat over this period by about 2 percentage points and lowered their cost-of-living subindexes for produce by about 1.5 percentage points over the whole period—trivial effects given the large change in the reference utility level (see the additional discussion in section 1.2.4), and more trivial still for a normal measurement time horizon. The problem that so occupied the CNSTAT panel—the dependence of the COLI on the reference indifference curve—is correct in theory, but does not have much empirical significance.

Furthermore, in many studies Laspeyres indexes have been found to be above Paasche indexes by an amount that could be expected from substitution effects (the earliest estimate of this kind that we know is Ulmer [1946]). If the other kinds of effects emphasized by the panel had a major role, we would presumably observe many instances where the Paasche index lies above the Laspeyres index or where Paasche-Laspeyres index differences exhibit wide swings.[46]

These empirical results do not, of course, imply that violations of COLI assumptions can never cause distortions large enough to be a practical concern. For example, in a country that is experiencing a severe economic crisis, changes in the standard of living would presumably be large enough for nonhomotheticity to matter, and even in the United States this may occur over long intervals of time. Similarly, a substantial distortion from changing tastes is possible in a long-run index for a good that requires repeated quality adjustments. If each adjustment reflects the tastes of the time when it is made, the cumulative value of many adjustments may not be right for any single configuration of tastes.[47] In the special cases where the potential for important effects from violations of COLI assumptions is high, this possibility should be taken into account. But the solution is not to discard the entire COLI approach, especially when the potential shortcomings of the COGI alternative have not been adequately weighed.

## 1.3 Recommendations Concerning Detailed Component Indexes and Sampling

Sampling theory was not well developed when BLS first began to estimate a price index for consumers. Mitchell recommended judgmental sampling, which the BLS largely followed until 1978. Some improvements in sampling procedures were recommended by an ASA committee in 1933 to 1934 (Hogg 1934).

### 1.3.1 Wartime Committees: The Problem of Unrepresentative Samples of Varieties and Forced Substitution

Among the biases in the BLS Cost-of-Living Index discussed in the Meany-Thomas Report were three that occurred in constructing its detailed component indexes. One of these was caused by failure to collect prices on weekends, when sales were common. The Mitchell Committee conceded

46. The panel noted that "an assessment of the ability of a superlative index to approximate a measure of the [COLI] depends on a judgment about the extent to which changes in the pattern of quantities purchased are driven by changes in income and tastes or by substitution responses to relative prices" (Schultze and Mackie 2002). This is an empirical proposition that is readily explored (and has been).

47. This is a special application of the well-known principle that a chain index may not give the same measure after several links as an index that directly compares first and last periods.

that this bias was present because weekend sales had become less prevalent, forcing some consumers to pay higher prices. However, their guesstimate for the size of this bias was only half a percent over three years.

A second source of bias identified by Meany and Thomas arose from forced substitution to more expensive varieties or outlets. Inexpensive varieties tended to disappear or to be differentially affected by shortages, resulting in forced "trading up." The Mitchell Committee observed that this likely affected the poorest families more than it did the "average" family (wage earners and salaried clerical workers) tracked by BLS's index. In addition, the Committee noted that some shift to higher-priced outlets (from chain stores to higher-priced independents) could be expected because long hours of work, gasoline rationing, and reduced car ownership made visiting lower-priced outlets inconvenient (II-4). Finally, because of quality deterioration in product lines, consumers were also forced to buy more expensive varieties simply to keep quality constant.[48] After noting the difficulty in valuing quality deterioration ("who is to say how much the real price of shorts has gone up because they have ties rather than elastic sides?") the Mitchell Committee made an educated guess that the downward bias between January 1941 and December 1943 from forced trading up and quality deterioration was 1 to 3 percent for the food index, 4 to 5 percent for the clothing index, and 8 to 11 percent for the house furnishings index.[49]

The third problem identified by Meany and Thomas highlights the vulnerability of judgmental sampling to error or manipulation that can damage the credibility of detailed component indexes. Meany and Thomas argued that samples were unrepresentative and that the varieties (or varieties priced for the detailed component indexes) were causing a large downward bias in the Cost-of-Living Index.[50] Usually one or two tightly specified varieties ("items" in BLS terminology) were selected to represent a commodity category, facilitating use of "specification pricing" as had been recommended many years earlier in Mitchell's report on the Bureau of Labor's Wholesale Price Index. Since the same variety or quality level was priced in many outlets, city level averages for the price could be meaningfully calculated. Thus, the first step in calculating the CPI was to calculate the average price of, say, refrigerators or white bread, in each of the CPI cities, where the averages were always computed for matched samples of varieties and outlets. These city averages could be compared over time to form basic component indexes for commodities or narrowly defined groups of commodities. This

48. Meany and Thomas also alleged that unmeasured quality deterioration was an important cause of downward bias in the Cost-of-Living Index.

49. Note the interesting parallel with the Boskin Commission, which also prepared guestimates of bias on a component-by-component basis.

50. An unrepresentative geographic sample and an unrepresentative market basket of goods and services were also sources of bias alleged by Meany and Thomas. We do not discuss these because our focus is on problems in the construction of the basic component indexes.

simplicity came at a cost, however. The risk that the small, judgmentally selected samples of varieties would fail to represent their commodity group was high.[51]

The errors introduced by the sampling of varieties might, of course, average out to about zero, implying very little bias at the aggregate level. Meany and Thomas claimed, however, that the sampling errors in the component indexes were systematic, biasing the index downward. According to tables 3 and 4 in their report, 77.3 percent of the food index was based on varieties with price subsidies, but of thirty-seven varieties with rising price control ceilings, only eleven were in BLS's index. To illustrate the problem, Meany and Thomas discussed many cases of the inclusion in the CPI of particular varieties subject to subsidies or price rollbacks. For example, subsidized apples represented deciduous fruits; other deciduous fruits not in the sample were unsubsidized (86). Oranges, which had a 25 percent rollback in their price control ceiling, represented citrus fruits; other citrus fruits (not in the CPI) had no price rollback (86). Shortening was used to represent fats and oils; subsidies were about to expire for all fats and oils except shortening (87), so even though most fats and oils prices would rise, the index would not.

To respond to Meany and Thomas's charge that foods not priced by BLS went up twice as fast as those priced, BLS collected a special sample of foods not in the official index (apparently, a retrospective price collection). It found that their weighted average inflation rate between August 1939 and January 1944 was 33.4 percent, compared with 37 percent for the foods used to represent them in the official index (A-9 to A-12). On balance, therefore, the Mitchell Committee concluded that no bias had been caused by the selection of varieties for use in the index. The Committee did, however, recommend pricing broader ranges of items in the future (II-39).

Although the BLS evidence did carry significant weight, it is hard not to be impressed that Meany and Thomas produced actual data to support their position. They were not disinterested samplers, it is true. Although the Mitchell Committee essentially opted for a "not proven" verdict on the points that Meany and Thomas raised, a potential for bias clearly did exist.

### 1.3.2 The Stigler Committee: Representative Samples for Detailed Component Indexes

The Stigler Committee recommended the use of probability sampling to estimate the detailed component indexes used to calculate the CPI.[52] Though the Committee cited technical papers by K. S. Banerjee (1959) and Irma

51. Additionally, such data are subject to error from differences over space in store amenities and services, so interarea indexes might not be so simple to compute as supposed.

52. It also recommended that the CPI be extended to cover all households. This was done in the 1978 Revision (CPI-U), but an index with weights corresponding to the old household definition was published separately (CPI-W).

Adelman (1958) as background, the wartime controversy was implicitly also part of the background of this proposal.[53] Of the Committee's recommendations, this was the one that had the most important effect on the CPI.

In addition to avoiding risk of a repeat of the wartime charges of manipulation of BLS's samples, probability sampling had a number of advantages. It made possible reliable estimates of index variances via the technique of comparing index values from replicated samples calculated using well-defined procedures to ensure consistency of methods (Stigler et al. 1961, 40).[54] Another benefit identified by the Committee was that the attempt to make sampling conform to a probability model would force the index designers to think explicitly about problems of definition and estimation that are easily ignored with judgmental procedures (42). Finally, probability sampling was the only way to guard against biases due to an unrepresentative selection of outlets and varieties (42). For example, types of retail establishments or outlets of growing importance were underrepresented, but use of "sampling frames showing the distribution of consumer expenditures for particular goods and services by market area and type of retail establishment" seemed a promising solution (58).

At the time, the specifications of the items to be priced were still determined centrally. The Stigler Committee thought that centralized specification of what was to be priced risked instructing field agents to price items that were unrepresentative of the sales in the particular retail outlets chosen, or even unavailable in those outlets. Probability selection of items in retail outlets meant that the items selected could indeed be found there, and assured that the full range of product specifications could be represented in the index in proportion to their sales.

One of the "Staff Papers" included with the Stigler Committee's report elaborated on the technical problems involved in probability sampling for estimation of the basic component indexes of the CPI. In this paper McCarthy (1961) discussed the sampling of commodities under the assumptions that the base year weights, base year prices, and comparison year prices were known without error for specified-in-detail commodities, and that the goal was to estimate a Laspeyres index (McCarthy 1961, 209). Following Adelman (1958), within any stratum, price relatives could be sampled with probability proportion to their base period expenditure. In an ideal situation, the sample estimator of the Laspeyres index for the stratum could then be calculated as a simple average of the sampled price relatives (McCarthy

53. Though the Stigler Committee report makes no explicit connection between probability sampling and the wartime controversy, John Marcoot, who was at BLS at the time of the Stigler Committee, cited in discussions with one of the authors the unions' criticisms as a reason for the adoption of probability sampling of outlets and varieties.

54. Assume, for example, availability of two index estimates for a commodity in a city based on two independent samples, selected by identical procedures. The difference between the estimates can be squared and divided by four to obtain an unbiased estimate of the variance of a "best" index estimate, based on a pooled sample.

1961, 213). McCarthy recommended selection by probability sampling of smaller cities, of detailed items within 150 commodity categories, and of outlets (227–9).

A witness at the hearings held to discuss the Stigler Commission's report made a noteworthy observation concerning the detailed component indexes that was not in the Committee's report. Arant (1961, 696) claimed that "[m]ost of the reductions in consumer prices brought about by the growth of mass distribution . . . have not been measured by the Consumer Price Index." Arant argued that the linking procedure used to bring new outlets into the CPI removed the effects of the lower price levels at chain supermarkets compared with the small independent stores that they were replacing.

Hoover and Stotz (1964) investigated Arant's claim and found that had BLS not linked new outlets into the CPI, the food component of the CPI would have dropped by 0.7 percentage points more than it did (their estimate was based on the difference between the weights for chains and independents in 1948 and weights implied by 1958 data). Note, however, that BLS did not ignore the growing importance of chain stores; it linked in interim adjustments to reflect this growing importance on four occasions in between the benchmarking of the weights to the 1948 and 1958 Censuses. Reinsdorf (1998, 184) found that after one of these interim adjustments, which reflected seven years of change in purchasing patterns, the average price series for foods dropped 0.7 percent compared with the official CPI.

Seemingly nothing has been done about the Hoover-Stotz finding, even though Hoover went on to be head of the CPI and Stotz went on to head the PPI. The issue lay quiet until the study by Reinsdorf (1993).

### 1.3.3 The Boskin Commission: Geometric Means as Basic Component Indexes

The Boskin Commission identified four sources of bias in the basic component indexes of the CPI. We leave the discussion of one of these, quality change, to a later paper. Here we will consider formula bias, lower level substitution bias, and outlet substitution bias.[55]

Formula bias was a focus of the Boskin Commission's "interim report," dated September 1995, because it had a substantial effect on the CPI and, unlike most index problems, which are far easier to recognize than to resolve, it was amenable to a quick solution. The Boskin Commission's final estimate of the size of this effect was about 0.5 percent per year. This estimate is consistent with research in Reinsdorf (1998, 185), indicating that formula bias in the commodities and services portion of the CPI may have had an effect on the all-items CPI of around 0.4 percent per year, and that a similar bias in the

55. The Boskin Commission's discussion of bias from new products is not included here because new products are discussed in the sections on the measurement concept. Also, new products are not specifically a problem affecting detailed component indexes since they may not fit into an existing item stratum.

owners' equivalent rent component of the CPI may have had an additional effect of around 0.1 percent per year.[56] The effect of formula bias on the CPI, was, therefore, more than twice as large as the Manser-McDonald estimate of commodity substitution bias of under 0.2 percent per year. Moreover, because important segments of the CPI, such as tenant-occupied shelter, were unaffected, a bias of 0.5 percent per year in the aggregate index implies quite a large bias for many of the affected individual components. For example, for two very homogeneous CPI components indexes—fresh whole chicken and bananas—a reasonable estimate of the combined effect of formula bias and outlet substitution bias can be made by comparing the growth rate of the CPI component index with the growth rate of a weighted average price in the CPI sample. Over an interval from 1980 to 1992, appropriately weighted averages of the prices in the CPI sample grew 1.1 percent per year faster than the CPI component indexes calculated from virtually the same set of prices (Reinsdorf 1998, 192). Comparisons of price levels between outlet samples in Reinsdorf (1993) suggested a typical value of about 0.25 percent per year for outlet substitution bias, leaving a residual not far below 1 percent per year for formula bias.

Formula bias was caused by procedures adopted in the 1978 revision of the CPI to implement probability sampling for selecting varieties and outlets as recommended by the Stigler Committee.[57] Notwithstanding this problem, probability sampling was an important step forward with many benefits. The CPI was less susceptible to bias from unrepresentative samples of varieties or qualities or from manipulation, as Meany and Thomas had alleged. Furthermore, BLS could estimate realistic variances for the CPI, something not possible when a single variety and quality level was chosen judgmentally to represent an entire commodity class.[58] Finally, estimates of variance components could be used to design efficient samples aimed at maximizing the precision of the CPI subject to the budget constraint.

Although one member of the Boskin Commission was heard to remark that the formula bias problem showed that BLS did not understand logarithms, the procedures in question came from papers by distinguished academics (Adelman 1958; McCarthy 1961) and from the Stigler Committee's report. To understand the genesis of the problem, note that random sampling of varieties and quality levels precluded continued use of averages of

56. Subsequently, experimental CPI's showed an average effect on the all-item CPI of about 0.24 percent per year, not counting the effect from owner's equivalent rent or the effect of lower-level substitution bias as measured by geometric mean indexes. See the *Economic Report of the President* (President's Council of Economic Advisors 1999, 94).

57. Probability sampling of outlets, but not varieties, began with the 1964 revision of the CPI with the assistance of Phillip McCarthy. (See U.S. BLS 1966, 26).

58. However, BLS publishes CPI variances only in places like the *CPI Detailed Report* and ASA Proceedings volumes, but not, as yet, on its website. Thus, an important benefit of the substantial expense of probability sampling is not easily available to users of the index.

prices, since prices of dissimilar items cannot meaningfully be averaged.[59] Constructing the refrigerator price index for city A as the ratio of average prices for average quality refrigerators sold in city A in two periods had been sensible, but trying to calculate an average price for musical instruments in a sample that contained guitar picks and pianos (an example used by Moses and Moulton [1997]) would not be. This suggested a change in computation for the basic component indexes from ratios of average prices (used before 1978) to averages of price ratios (used thereafter). The simple average of price ratios discussed by McCarthy was an unbiased sample estimator of a Laspeyres price index *if* the specific items priced were selected with probabilities proportional to expenditures in the base period and price collection began in the base period.

Neither McCarthy nor Adelman (nor Westat, the statistical consulting firm brought in to design the BLS move to probability sampling) considered a problem that arose in practical application. The BLS estimated sampling probabilities as well as possible (a new "Point of Purchase survey" was instituted to collect information on outlets, and item selection was done by probability methods within each retail outlet). Nevertheless, the perfect measurement of base period expenditures and prices assumed by McCarthy is far from achievable in practice. The base period for measuring expenditures was usually long enough to encompass one or more price changes, and additional price changes were likely to occur in the interval between the period of measurement of expenditures and the initial collection of price data. In addition, the estimates of expenditure shares of outlets and varieties within outlets were subject to sampling error.[60] Even if Cobb-Douglas substitution behavior by consumers kept expenditure shares invariant over time, the desired quantities for the Laspeyres index were from the time period when the expenditure shares were measured, and prices in that time period would not be the same as the prices in the period when price sampling began. Consequently, ratios of sampling probabilities to prices were not proportional to the desired quantities for a Laspeyres index.

59. Before 1978, the (unweighted) formula for a CPI basic component was: $(\Sigma p_{i,t+1}/n)/(\Sigma p_{it}/n)$, where $t$ is the last price observation (month for monthly pricing) and $t + 1$ the current month, and the calculation was done separately for each city. In words, then, the initial calculation for, say, refrigerators in the San Francisco area was the change in the average price of a matched sample of refrigerators in this city in the two months, and this calculation became the basic component for that item in the city index for San Francisco.

60. The estimates of expenditures for probability-proportional-to-size sampling of outlets came from surveys of consumers. Once the sample of outlets was known, to select detailed varieties and quality levels within sampled outlets BLS usually calculated sample selection probabilities based on approximate revenue breakdowns furnished by store managers or estimated from a proxy for revenue, such as shelf space. The time period for the outlet expenditures was earlier than the time period for the expenditures on varieties and quality levels within outlets, which was, in turn, earlier than the time of initial collection of price data in a newly selected sample.

Of course, by redefining the desired base period for the Laspeyres index to the time of initial price collection, one could show that the procedure yielded an unbiased estimator of a Laspeyres index objective given a Cobb-Douglas behavioral assumption, but, at the same time, this behavioral assumption would imply that the Laspeyres index with time of initial price data collection as its base period is a particularly poor objective. In comparison with a COLI-like objective, Cobb-Douglas behavior would imply great susceptibility to substitution bias.

What is more, given the "price bouncing" behavior that is typically observed at the lowest level of aggregation, Cobb-Douglas behavior would equally imply upward bias in a statistical sense in comparison with the objective that the index designers had in mind, a Laspeyres index with the time period furnishing the expenditure shares as its base. This bias is present because a downward transitory shock to an initial period price simultaneously implies an upward error in its implicit quantity weight and an upward shock to the change in the price. Since transitory price shocks are common for many types of items, the errors in the weights were positively correlated with the price changes, resulting in an upward bias.

For example, let item 1 and item 2 be represented in a component index, and let the prices for these two items in any month be either ($1, $2) or ($2, $1), with either configuration equally likely. With probabilities of selection based on historical averages of expenditure shares, the probability of selection of the item priced at $1 would be one-half, resulting in an expected value for the estimator of the component index used by BLS of (1/2)($2/$1) + (1/2)($1/$2) = 1.25.

Does any simple set of assumptions exist that would justify this estimator for the index? Two possibilities are shown in table 1.1. Suppose, first, that consumers always buy equal quantities of the items, a Leontief behavioral assumption. Equal quantities imply an expenditure share of one-third if the price is $1, so the item with an initial price of $1 should have a one-third probability of selection for the index sample. The sample estimator implied by this assumption therefore has an expected value of (1/3)($2/$1) + (2/3)($1/$2) = 1, which agrees with the value of 1 for the theoretical index shown at the bottom of the Leontief assumption portion of table 1.1.

Next, consider the assumption of Cobb-Douglas behavior, with consumers always spending equal amounts on the two items. Now the expenditure shares will indeed equal one-half, but the prices observed in the initial or reference period for the index will be of no value in estimating the quantities consumed in the earlier base period for the Laspeyres index basket. The expected values of the reference period prices are uniform. As is shown in the last row of table 1.1, if we estimate the base period quantities as inversely proportional to these uniform expected prices, the implied Laspeyres index again equals 1.

**Table 1.1 Component index objectives under two possible assumptions**

| Time period | Price of item 1 and item 2 | Base period quantities of items 1 and 2 | Cost of base period quantity of item 1 | Cost of base period quantity of item 2 |
|---|---|---|---|---|
| | | *Leontief behavioral assumption* | | |
| Reference period for index | (1,2) | (1,1) | 1 | 2 |
| Comparison period for index | (2,1) | (1,1) | 2 | 1 |
| Base period for index basket | (1,2) or (2,1) equally likely | (1,1) | (1,2) or (2,1) equally likely | |
| | | *Cobb-Douglas behavioral assumption* | | |
| Reference period for index | (1,2) | (1,2) or (2,1) equally likely | 1 or 2 equally likely | 4 or 2 equally likely |
| Comparison period for index | (2,1) | (1,2) or (2,1) equally likely | 2 or 4 equally likely | 2 or 1 equally likely |
| Base period for index basket | (1,2) or (2,1) equally likely | (2,1) or (1,2) | 2 | 2 |

Implied indexes

| Index description | Behavioral assumption | Index value |
|---|---|---|
| True Laspeyres | Leontief | (1 + 2)/(2 + 1) |
| True Laspeyres, based on realized market basket | Cobb-Douglas | (4 + 1)/(2 + 2) or (2 + 2)/(4 + 1) |
| True Laspeyres, based on expected value market basket | Cobb-Douglas | (1.5 + 3)/(3 + 1.5) |
| Estimator adopted in 1978 | n.a. | (1/2)(2/1) + (1/2)(1/2) |

*Note:* n.a. = not available.

Finally, continuing to assume Cobb-Douglas behavior, we could fill in the missing prices from the base period for the Laspeyres index with the two equally likely cases of (a) ($1, $2) and (b) ($2, $1). In case (a), applying the formula for the updating of expenditure weights (needed to calculate the change in a Laspeyres index starting in a period later than its base period; BLS calls these adjusted expenditure shares "relative importances") yields an adjusted expenditure weight (and sampling probability) of 4/5 for item 1 whenever its initial price in the index is $2, and an unchanged expenditure weight of 1/2 whenever its price is back at its base period value of $1. In case (b), the relative importance of item 1 equals 1/5 when its price is $1 and 1/2 when its price is back at the base period value of $2. The two possible outcomes for the change in the correctly based Laspeyres index are therefore (1/2)2 + (1/2)0.5 = 5/4 and (1/5)2 + (4/5)0.5 = 4/5. Thus, under this approach to defining the objective for estimation, the expected value for the Laspeyres index objective, given the information that is available, again approximately equals 1.[61]

In January 1995, shortly before the naming of the Boskin Commission, BLS introduced the method of "seasoning" as a way to remove the correlation between the price changes and the measurement errors in the item weights that caused the problem of formula bias in the component index estimator adopted in 1978. The initial price data from a new sample was used to calculate the implicit quantity weights, then the sample was allowed to season for several months before its price changes were used in index calculations. Doing this converted the new average-of-ratios formula back into a ratio-of-averages formula; for example, a seasoned index from June to July might be an average of ratios of July prices to January prices divided by an average of ratios of June prices to January prices. Prompted by the interim report of the Boskin Commission, in June 1996 BLS extended the method of "seasoning" to nearly all items other than shelter.

The Boskin Commission was not satisfied with this solution. It regarded seasoning as only a partial cure for the formula-related problems of the basic component indexes, so its final report identified a remaining problem of "lower level substitution bias." This bias could be avoided by using geometric mean of price relatives as the formula for most component indexes in the CPI.

Whereas formula bias exists even with Leontief behavior, a substitution bias is, by definition, caused by substitution behavior. With some exceptions, consumers are likely to regard the varieties and outlets in a component index as highly substitutable. The Boskin Commission (19), citing a rationale in Shapiro and Wilcox (1996, 1997) (for which those authors had, in turn, cited a draft of Reinsdorf [1998]), argued that use of geometric means to average price relatives would result in unbiased estimation of basic component indexes for the COLI objective. Based on estimates of the effect on the CPI of the use of geometric means for basic component indexes, the Boskin Commission therefore estimated that the lower-level substitution bias was one-quarter percent per year.

Finally, the Boskin Commission discussed the effect of "new outlet substitution bias" on the basic component indexes of the CPI. This bias occurred when the entry of outlets offering lower prices, such as Wal-Mart, allowed consumers to save money by changing where they shopped. The effect on the cost of living of substitution between outlets with different price levels had, of course, been identified as an important problem in the Meany-Thomas report—though in the opposite context of involuntary substitu-

61. The reason the expected value is not exactly equal to 1 has to do with the behavior of expected values of nonlinear transformations, such as the division operation in calculating a price index. For larger sample sizes, the expected value would differ from 1 by a negligible amount. This exposition oversimplifies the BLS procedures to make the exposition of the root problem clearer.

tions to higher prices!—and BLS had acknowledged the possibility that price differentials between outlets could cause bias in its index as early as 1964.[62] Nevertheless, the issue was largely forgotten until a paper by Reinsdorf (1993). Multiplying the estimated 40 percent share of the CPI subject to this effect by Reinsdorf's (1993) upper bound estimate of 0.25 percent per year for the food and gasoline components of the CPI, the Boskin Commission estimated this bias at 0.1 percent per year. Subsequent research has shown similar outlet substitution problems in CPIs elsewhere—see, for example, the study by Saglio (1994) on chocolate bars in the French CPI.

### 1.3.4 The CNSTAT Panel: Guarded Agreement with the Boskin Commission

The BLS adopted geometric means for most basic component indexes in the CPI in 1999. This change made seasoning unnecessary, because the geometric mean formula is not subject to the kind of bias that seasoning corrects. The CNSTAT Panel gave qualified support to the change to geometric means. It observed that high substitutability between the product varieties in component indexes was generally plausible, with exceptions for some items such as prescription drugs. Hence, even though the specific behavioral assumption underlying the geometric mean formula—a unitary elasticity of substitution—was unlikely to be exactly true, the formula change was probably an improvement. Nevertheless, it was unclear to the panel that the geometric mean index would always be superior to the seasoned Laspeyres index. The CNSTAT Panel also remarked that this change marked "BLS's first attempt to build substitution effects into the CPI itself," and a "change in perspective from a COGI conceptual basis (informed by COLI considerations) to an explicit COLI basis" (Schultze and Mackie 2002, 62).

On the question of new outlet substitution bias, the CNSTAT Panel noted that the empirical evidence available to the Boskin Commission for its estimate of 0.1 percent per year was limited, and that Reinsdorf had viewed his estimates as upper bounds because price reductions might be accompanied by quality reductions (Schultze and Mackie 2002, 173). The panel's review of the available evidence suggested that outlet substitution bias was significant enough to be a matter of concern, but they doubted whether researchers would be able to produce sensible, reproducible estimates for adjusting for quality differences between outlets (175). They therefore concluded that BLS had little choice but to continue its present practice of linking in new outlets (176). They did, however, recommend continued research on the effects of outlet characteristics on prices.

62. Hoover and Stotz (1964) investigated outlet substitution effects. Consistent with their findings, Jaffee (1984) wrote: "This procedure [fixed samples of outlets] may in fact result in failure of the index to reflect real change in the prices paid by consumers which result from new outlets" (923).

### 1.3.5 Assessment of the Debate over Component Indexes

We have nothing to add to the CNSTAT Panel's treatment of new outlet substitution bias. However, the discussions of the geometric mean indexes in the reports of the Boskin Commission and the CNSTAT Panel raise two important issues.

First, in many cases the standard model of commodity substitution (which justifies the geometric mean, given Cobb-Douglas behavior) is not the appropriate model of the consumer choice process; rather, in cases where the varieties and outlets in a component index are virtually interchangeable, a model of consumer search with costly and imperfect information would be more appropriate, as Pollak (1998), Feenstra and Shapiro (2003), and Triplett (2003) point out. The CNSTAT Panel recognized this issue, and recommended further research on it.

Second, even granting the assumptions that (a) the standard commodity substitution model applies to component indexes and (b) the elasticities of substitution are near unity, the panels' discussion of substitution bias as the reason to adopt geometric means fails to consider the implications of lack of information on expenditure patterns within a component index. If the weights on the items in the component index reflect the purchasing patterns at the initial prices, geometric means are indeed a good way to adjust the weights for the changes in purchasing patterns brought about by price changes. But often what is needed is a theory applicable to situations where the weights do not necessarily reflect initial purchasing patterns. The solution in many of these situations is, again, a geometric mean index, but the logic that supports that solution is not the same as the logic used by the panel.

*Shopping Behavior versus Substitution Behavior*

Economists have sometimes interpreted the difference between arithmetic mean (Laspeyres-type) and geometric mean aggregators for basic components as just the classic substitution bias paradigm drawn from Konüs (1924), only applied one level down. This seems to be the interpretation of the Boskin Commission, which followed Diewert (1995).

Commodity substitution behavior is clearly a relevant concern for basic components. Part of the shift in the composition of musical instrument expenditures is accounted for by changes in relative prices (though it is also hard to maintain the constant tastes assumption for empirical work for such a category), and many other index components are made up from samples of substitutable commodities.

A theory of basic components, however, must be applicable to all basic components. It must explain differences between arithmetic and geometric means for components such as the CPI banana price index, which is as close to a homogeneous product (in the United States, at any rate) as can be found.

An even more challenging example is Schultz (1994), who found enormous formula differences in Canadian CPI data for a single size bottle of a single brand of soft drink—surely there is no room for commodity substitution within a single size and brand of one product.

To apply to index number formulas at this level, a theory of consumer behavior must model consumers' choices across sellers of a homogeneous commodity, as well as choice behavior across different (substitutable) commodities. Pollak (1998) put it well:

> I argue against the view of the Boskin Commission and Diewert (1995) that the "elementary aggregate" problem, which the Commission calls "lower level substitution bias," is primarily a problem of choosing an appropriate formula for combining the prices of items (71).
>
> At least when discussing price indexes . . . economists almost always proceed as if the "law of one price" holds so that the price distribution facing the consumer collapses to a point. With very few exceptions—the published literature appears to consist of three papers: Baye (1985), Anglin and Baye (1987) and Reinsdorf (1994)—economists have ignored the implications of price dispersion and search for the cost-of-living index (73).

Or as Pollak (1998) also put it, in a heading: "Why Shop?" The theory that is relevant to the basic component problem includes consumer shopping behavior, search behavior, inventory, and storage behavior. When soft drinks go on sale, consumers do not necessarily consume more of them (as the theory of commodity substitution has it); they stock up and store the soft drinks. Search, storage, and so forth are not necessarily modeled adequately at all by simply switching to a superlative index or a geometric index, since the theory that lies behind those indexes is not the theory that explains the consumer behavior that motivates consumer purchases.

Indeed, Triplett (2003, 156) presents a simple numerical example to show that with an imputation for search costs, no standard formula applied to prices collected from matched retail outlets will measure the COLI of households who shop. Feenstra and Shapiro (2003) develop a model for analyzing storage behavior (their application was canned tuna, using scanner data), and suggest that when this type of behavior is important the definition of a time period in the index should be as long as the intervals over which consumers plan their purchases. Hendel and Nevo (2002) show that neglect of consumer storage and shopping behavior results in an overestimate of ordinary demand elasticities, surely a fatal problem if one proposes to model index number substitution bias at the component level with a simple Konüs system.

In some cases characterized by shopping behavior, use of a unit value index might be justifiable. The usual objection to this simple method is that the unit value average of prices may change solely because of a change in the distribution of quantities over sellers, so that the unit value index may be outside not only the Laspeyres-Paasche bounds, but bounds equal to the maximum and minimum price relatives. However, if the average price paid drops because information has become easier to obtain, so that consumers are better able to find the lowest prices, the COLI approach indicates that a drop in the price index is acceptable even though no price has changed.[63] The Laspeyres and Paasche indexes of the prices *from different sellers* are not necessarily bounds on the index needed for a COLI in the presence of costly information.[64]

The CNSTAT Panel (5, 24) addressed the question of consumer search: "Further research should be conducted on consumer shopping and substitution behavior with an eye to improving knowledge of the appropriate application of geometric means at the lower level of index construction" (5). Also: "Consumer responses to price differences may reflect something other than substitution behavior: for example, a consumer stocks up on particular items when sales occur but does not change the amount of those items purchased per month or per year" (24).

We agree that more research on these "nonstandard" problems is the proper future direction for understanding how to measure basic components in price indexes. Attempts to fit the basic component problem into the standard Konüs commodity substitution model lack insight into the nature of the problem and risk yielding misleading conclusions.

*Why Use Geometric Means?*

The property of simultaneously being an average of price relatives and ratio of average price levels makes the geometric mean index well-suited for handling the heterogeneity in varieties and qualities found in probability samples. However, the CNSTAT Panel report implies that the main purpose of the geometric mean formula is to account for substitution effects in component indexes that contain closely substitutable varieties, or closely substitutable outlets.

Assume—as is sometimes the case—that the standard model of commodity substitution is applicable to the items in the component index. Under the assumption that the expenditure shares are measured correctly, the geomet-

63. A BLS memorandum from 1963 summarizing expert advice from Edward Denison stated that the average price paid should ideally be used in the index, although Denison acknowledged the impracticality of collection of data on prices paid from households.

64. Note that costly information is probably immaterial for modeling choices over commodities even if it is important for modeling choices among competing sellers. Sellers' prices for the same commodity are likely to be characterized by high-frequency noise around a common trend, which is harder to learn about than the divergent trends and seasonal cycles that are likely to characterize different commodity prices. Also, as averages, the component price indexes for commodities (or commodity groups) and the weights used to aggregate these indexes into the all-items CPI are likely to be affected only slightly by the randomness associated with costly information. In contrast, the constituents of a single component index are individual prices, not averages.

ric mean index is indeed the formula for a COLI if the elasticity of substitution equals 1 (i.e., inverse movements of relative prices and relative quantities keep expenditure shares constant). Yet the relevant question is: what to do if the expenditure shares are unknown or measured poorly?

Consider first the case when the expenditure shares are unknown. In this case, we cannot measure a COLI with any precision, and to pretend otherwise is to deceive ourselves. With no knowledge of expenditures, the principle of symmetric treatment for items about which one has identical information implies an assumption of uniform expenditures in both the initial and the final period if the index includes dissimilar items. This assumption implies a geometric mean index.[65] Or, to assume explicitly that the elasticity of substitution is zero while avoiding the assumption of uniform quantities because the items are far apart in value, two alternative versions of the Leontief assumption must be treated as equally likely. One is that initial period expenditures are uniform while final period expenditures are directly proportional to the price relatives; the other is that final period expenditures are uniform while initial period expenditures are inversely proportional to the price relatives. An average of the two Laspeyres indexes implied by these equally plausible assumptions virtually equals a geometric mean index. (The equality is exact if the component index contains two items and the Laspeyres indexes are averaged geometrically.) Therefore, if expenditure patterns are unknown, it is a fallacy to infer from the fact that the items in the index are not substitutable that a geometric mean index will be downward biased.

The CNSTAT Panel's presumption of a link between the geometric mean formula and Cobb-Douglas substitution behavior led them to recommend against its use in compiling component indexes for items that are not substitutable (e.g., prescription drugs that treat different conditions). However, few indexes exclusively contain nonsubstitutable items (even a prescription drug index may have some substitutable items, such as generics from different makers or identical drugs from different outlets), so the right question is how to handle a mixture of substitutable and nonsubstitutable items.

Usually the information on expenditures shares of the outlets and varieties covered by a component index is somewhere in between perfect measurement and perfect ignorance, so a plausible assumption is that the expenditure shares reflected in the component index sample approximately equal the shares at the start of price data collection. When substitutes are available for the items with unusually high or low price relatives and the weights reflected in the index approximate the true weights, the geometric mean index for-

65. If the index covers homogeneous items, the symmetric assumption is one of uniform quantities in both time periods. This assumption implies a ratio of average prices for the index formula. But when pianos and guitar picks are in the same component index (an example from Moulton and Moses [1997]), a uniform distribution of quantities implies wildly unequal expenditures.

mula provides a good measure of the component index for the COLI. In the short run, these conditions are plausible, even for a component index containing many nonsubstitutable items. Yet in the long run, a geometric mean component index containing nonsubstitutable items may tend to be biased downward because prices of the nonsubstitutable items in the index often follow divergent trends, but not the substitutable items. If every item that could be substituted follows the same price trend, but items that cannot be substituted follow divergent trends, opportunities for substitution will be limited in the long run. This provides some support for the CNSTAT Panel's recommendation to avoid the geometric mean for component indexes covering nonsubstitutable items.

## 1.4 Conclusion

The history of reviews of BLS price index programs begins almost as early as the impressively long history of those programs. These reviews, and the parallel professional literature on price measurement that influenced them, provide a record of how the interplay between intellectual progress in the disciplines of economics and statistics on the one hand, and the need to address public and professional perceptions of shortcomings in existing procedures on the other, shaped the evolution of the methods used to measure the CPI.

Two of the most distinctive features of the U.S. CPI compared to its counterparts in many other countries are its use of probability sampling to select outlets and product varieties for the basic component indexes and the use of the Konüs Cost-of-Living Index as the measurement concept. Both these features can be traced to the Stigler Committee, whose recommendations were influenced by the World War II era controversy over the charges contained in the Meany-Thomas report. In turn, one of them (the Cost-of-Living Index) played a key role in the subsequent review of the CPI by the Boskin Commission, and a memorable role in the recent deliberations of the CNSTAT Panel.

We also link the Boskin Commission with the component index recommendation. The original implementation of probability sampling gave rise to formula bias in the basic component indexes. The emerging evidence of this problem—which was discovered by BLS researchers—played a key role in the events leading up to the naming of the Boskin Commission. The recommendation of the Boskin Commission that had the greatest practical effect on the CPI was to construct most basic component indexes using a geometric mean index formula that is well-suited for probability samples of outlets and varieties.

The CNSTAT review of the CPI is most memorable for its partial retreat from the Stigler Committee's recommendation of the use of the COLI as the measurement concept for the CPI. Some of the skepticism about the

COLI is the result of people on both sides of the debate taking language too literally—statements about substituting commodities in ways that yield equal amounts of "satisfaction" or "utility" are, at bottom, statements about economic value, not psychological states of mind. The criticisms of the COLI measurement concept in CNSTAT Panel's report provide valuable illumination of the limited domain of this theory, and a valuable reminder that the effects of violations of the underlying assumptions can be important enough to be a practical concern in some situations, such as attempts to adjust the CPI for the effect on the COLI of new kinds of goods.

Yet despite its defects, the COLI offers some unique and critical advantages. No other approach provides an identifiable abstract objective to guide our thinking and to unify our treatment of the broad range of questions that arise in designing and using the CPI. Moreover, many of the assumptions that affect the COLI also affect the alternatives to the COLI, but only in the COLI framework are we able to rigorously analyze their implications for the measure of price change.

## Appendix

### *Economic and Test Approaches to Index Numbers*

Three major developments in the 1920s influenced professional thinking about CPIs and were therefore absorbed into the intellectual tradition that influenced subsequent reviews of the CPI.[66] In the first, Fisher (1911, 1922) elaborated the "test approach" and extended a way of thinking about index numbers that carried over from the nineteenth century (see also Walsh [1901]). Fisher's approach was not specific to consumer price indexes; it applied to all types of index numbers.

The second development was Konüs' (1924) theory of the Cost-of-Living Index (COLI). In contrast with Fisher and his forebears, Konüs' contribution was uniquely a contribution to the measurement of consumer prices, inspired, probably, by the new "Cost-of-Living Indexes" in the United States, Canada, the United Kingdom, and other countries. Konüs' COLI concept resembles one introduced earlier by Pigou (1920). Pigou was interested primarily in what is now called the standard of living index, a quantity index that represents movement from one indifference curve to another. However, he recognized that a price index was needed as a deflator.[67] The

66. This appendix is based largely on Reinsdorf (2007) and unpublished materials by Triplett. It also draws on Balk (1995, 1996), whose views among the contributors to this topic are closest to our own, and on Diewert (1992, 1993).

67. Whether Pigou should get the credit for the invention of the Cost-of-Living Index has been debated. Pigou (1912; 1920; 1932, 59–65) showed that the Laspeyres and Paasche indexes

third development, the Divisia index, is unrelated to current questions about measurement of the CPI, so we ignore it here.[68]

Test and COLI approaches have been reviewed previously. Because ours is not always the standard interpretation, a clarification of our interpretation is important background for the chapter. And because this is an appendix to an already long chapter, it is appropriate to present at the outset how we come out.

We favor the COLI approach over the test approach. It is easy to point to problems with the application of COLI theory to actual index number problems (Schultze and Mackie [2002] present a most comprehensive treatment of that set of problems). However, the problems surrounding the application of the test approach, *as it has been presented in the literature,* are far more daunting, and are less well documented and therefore less well appreciated.

We do think there is some role for pragmatic review of index number properties in particular settings. However, we relegate that role primarily to choosing among index numbers with equally good economic properties.

As an example, a GDP system requires a price index and a quantity index that together exhaust the change in current price GDP between two periods, what Stone and Prais (1952) called a "compatible index number system." A Fisher index number system for national accounts has the convenient property that the product of a Fisher price index and a Fisher quantity index equals the change in current price expenditure between the two periods; thus, both the "change in real GDP" and the associated implicit price deflator can be written as explicit and straightforward index numbers.[69] This convenient property of Fisher indexes led the U.S. Bureau of Economic Analysis to choose, several years ago, a Fisher index number system for both its measures of price change (the implicit deflator, a price index) and of constant price GDP (a quantity index).

The BEA chose the Fisher system only after the options were narrowed to index numbers with equally-appealing economic properties. Diewert (1976)

were upper and lower bounds for his index concept, so Staehle (1934) contended that Pigou's theory contained the essential elements of Konüs' contribution. Frisch (1936, 22), however, disagreed, arguing that only Konüs had really used indifference concepts to define the index. Other early discussions of Laspeyres-Paasche bounds were in von Bortkiewicz (1923), Gini (1924), Haberler (1927), Bowley (1928), and Keynes (1930). Even earlier discussions that did not include the bounds were an 1898 discussion by Wicksell of an index number concept that held well-being constant (see Frisch 1936, 11) and a 1707 discussion of an index number objective of "same Ease and Comfort" used by the Bishop of Ely in 1707 (see Samuelson and Swamy 1974, 567).

68. On the connection between the Divisia index and the COLI, see Hulten (1973) and Balk (2005).

69. The deflator corresponding to a Tornqvist quantity index is the change in expenditure divided by the Tornqvist quantity index. It cannot be reduced to a simpler expression that can be easily manipulated and analyzed. Hence, using a Tornqvist index to measure constant price GDP would make the analysis of inflation awkward and difficult.

showed that such indexes include the Törnqvist and the Walsh index numbers, as well as the Fisher. The Fisher index was not chosen from among all the candidate index numbers by applying tests.

Indeed, as we explain in this appendix, the test approach does not yield the Fisher index as the "best" index number, *unless one selects the tests to yield the Fisher index as a result,* which Fisher (and others who have followed him) have done. The test approach, as it has been applied in the literature from Fisher (1922) to the present, includes some properties that are questionable. It also arbitrarily excludes appealing (to some users) properties that would have yielded a different index number as "best." Additivity (of the numerator) and consistency in aggregation are the most notable properties that are omitted in the traditional test literature. Consideration of these properties, particularly if high weight is placed on them, would have tilted the test results toward the Laspeyres index.

In short, the properties that have traditionally been included (and excluded) in the test approach, as it has appeared in its own literature, are disputable. The approach contains no criteria to explain why properties are included or excluded. Lacking an analytical framework, it substitutes instead notions of "appealing" index number properties. Yet different index number users have different views about which index number properties are appealing (perhaps because of different index number settings). To those index number users who endorse a different set of properties, a user of the test approach can only say: "I do not share your views."

Without ignoring its problems (though we think they have often been exaggerated), the COLI approach offers an analytical framework for thinking about index number construction. The COLI's analytical framework extends far beyond the simple problem of choosing an index number formula (the only problem for which the test approach has been developed). It provides a framework for reasoning about the myriad other problems that arise in practical index number construction.

**Fisher and Konüs**

For Fisher (1911), the purpose of price index measurement was to obtain a $P$ for the quantity theory expression $MV = PT$, the equation of exchange. The quantity theory was, at the time, the only well-specified economic theory for which a price index was relevant—though it is the price *level* that is directly relevant.

Mitchell (1921, 1923) disagreed with Fisher. Mitchell criticized the equation of exchange as a foundation for a price index. "To 'measure variations in the exchange value or purchasing power of money' is not a clearly defined aim. . . . What does 'the purchasing power of money' include? Merely the standardized wares of the wholesale markets which are sampled with varying thoroughness in the current index numbers? Or does it include also commodities at retail, stocks, bonds, labor of all sorts, farm lands and town lots, loans, transportation, insurance, advertising space, and all the other classes of goods that are bought and sold? [. . .] To insist that this problem has but one meaning and therefore one 'best' solution [he refers here to Fisher and to Walsh] obstructs progress" (Mitchell 1921, 23).[70] In this passage, Mitchell raises, possibly for the first time, the question of "domain" of the index number, and the basis for choosing the domain.

As the quantity theory implies, Fisher regarded the price level as an entity in itself. Banzhaf (2001) points to Fisher's use of physical analogies: to measure the level of water in a lake, one ignores the ripples and waves; alternatively, the change in the price level is like an exploding shell where one ignores the paths of the fragments to obtain the true trajectory. The best form of the index number is determined by "tests" on the "reasonableness" of the measured index, which Fisher conceived as a problem that is parallel with measuring the level of the lake or the trajectory of the shell. References to such physical analogies show that Fisher was influenced by the older literature on the stochastic approach to index numbers, which contained many analogies of this type.[71]

Fisher's view of price indexes encompassed neither an economic concept nor an explicit theory of aggregation over commodities.[72] In contrast, Konüs' COLI theory is not only an economic concept, it is also *explicitly a theory of aggregation.* In COLI theory, the index tracks changes in the cost of attaining a specified utility level. To accomplish this requires an aggregating function that is derived from the form of the utility function (strictly, the form of the indirect utility function). Pollak (1983, 1989) and Diewert (1983) provide surveys.

Unlike Fisher, for whom the movements of the individual prices indexes were simply noise (the fragments of a bursting shell or the ripples in the pond), in Konüs' approach the deviations of the individual basic components—in particular, the relative prices—were the essence of the measurement. This roots the theory in the individual prices. Individual prices are real and observable. The aggregate index, on the other hand, is an economic

70. The inclusion of asset prices in the Consumer Price Index has a modern counterpart, but in the COLI context. See Goodhart (2001) and Cecchetti et al. (2000).

71. The stochastic approach sought to estimate statistically the central tendency of the price changes in the economy and generally made no attempt to weight items in the index to reflect expenditure patterns. It was used by Jevons, Edgeworth, and others, but abandoned, at least in its original form, following Keynes' (1930, 85) criticism of it as "root-and-branch erroneous." Keynes credits Fisher, Mitchell, and Walsh for avoiding this mistaken approach.

72. Dimand (2005) pointed out that Fisher's ignoring the potential of consumer theory for a consumer price index (as he did as well for some of his other research) was peculiar, in view of his pioneering nineteenth century work on utility theory. He goes on to attribute this to Fisher's contracting tuberculosis. After his illness, he seems to have belittled pleasure as a guideline for social welfare, and perhaps as well had become agnostic about the rationality of individual choice (Fisher devoted a great amount of energy after his illness toward changing behavior in more healthy directions). If the latter is true, he was a precusor to recent reconsideration by economists of their models of individual and household behavior.

abstraction, useful for economic analysis but hardly analogous to a directly observable quantity like the level of water in a lake. The Konüs view of things implies that the price index is not some physical or metaphysical entity that is "out there," waiting to be captured by an appropriate measuring rod. Instead, it is an invention by economists and statisticians for the purposes of economic analysis.

Fisher thought his ideal index (the geometric mean of Paasche and Laspeyres indexes) provided the true measure of price change between the Laspeyres-Paasche bounds introduced by Pigou for his welfare index deflator. Keynes (1930, 112–113) found Fisher's logic unconvincing:

> Then, as we have seen above, the true measure of comparison—assuming that tastes, etc. are constant and that only relative prices are changed—between the price levels in the two positions necessarily lies somewhere *between p* [the Laspeyres index] and *q* [the Paasche index]. Professor Fisher (amongst others) concludes from this that there must be some mathematical function of *p* and *q* which will afford us the best possible estimate of whereabouts between *p* and *q* the true value lies. Setting out on these lines, he has proposed and examined a great variety of formulae with the object of getting the best possible approximation to the true intermediate position. [. . .] I see no real substance in Professor Fisher's long discussion, by which, after examining a vast number of formulae, he arrives at the conclusion that $\sqrt{pq}$ . . . is theoretically ideal—if, that is to say, he means by this that it is likely to be arithmetically nearer to the truth than other formulae. This conclusion is the result of applying a number of tests. [. . .] All these tests, however, are directed to showing not that it is correct in itself, but that it is open to fewer objections than the alternative *a priori* formulae. They do not prove that any one of the formulae has a leg to stand on, regarded as a probable approximation.

Ironically, a demonstration of the approximation property of the Fisher index that Keynes found lacking in Fisher already existed when Keynes wrote these words.

In papers written in Russian that were little known until Diewert (1976) revived them, Byushgens (1925) and Konüs and Byushgens (1926) showed that the homogeneous quadratic indirect utility function yields a COLI that corresponds to Fisher's "ideal" index.[73] Later, Diewert (1976) showed that this utility function provides a second order approximation to the unknown true function; thus, the Fisher index can be used to approximate the COLI index. The exposition of this point in the Committee on National Statistics Panel report (Schultze and Mackie 2002, 84) is worth quoting:

> The remarkable thing about this [Byushgens (1925)] result is not that it is possible to find a cost function and a set of demand functions that justify a given price index, but the fact that the result is so general. [. . .] The Fisher ideal index is therefore *exact* for a set of preferences and demand

73. Because neither of us reads Russian, we follow Diewert's 1976 exposition of these two articles, supplemented by his personal communication on our chapter.

functions that do not restrict *substitution* behavior in ways beyond that required for the theory. It therefore permits a way of computing a general cost-of-living index without having to estimate the demand functions.

## Comparison of COLI and Test Approaches

Both Fisher (1922) and Konüs and Byushgens (1926) justified the same formula. For this reason, it is sometimes said that test and COLI approaches converge: COLI theory shows that the Fisher index is a good approximation to the true index, which merges with Fisher's conclusions on the basis of his tests. However, the conclusion is too superficial, for two reasons.

First, it implies that the Fisher index clearly emerges from the test approach. In fact, *results from the test approach depend on the subjective process of selecting the tests.* We elaborate on this in the following numbered section, "Selection of Tests."

Second, the notion that test and economic approaches converge presumes that the only thing that matters is the index number formula, and that the implications of the COLI approach are limited to the choice of an aggregator. In fact, the COLI framework is more than a guide to aggregation (that is, to the choice of index number formula). *It is also a way to think about what should be included in the price index and how to measure the price index components.* The test approach is completely silent on these matters, leaving vital portions of CPI construction without a guiding framework.

Again, Mitchell was insightful: "The first step, framing a clear idea of the ultimate use of the results, is most important, since it affords the clue to guide the compiler through the labyrinth of subsequent choices. It is, however, the step most frequently omitted" (Mitchell 1921, 23). He points to Fisher and Walsh as examples of researchers who ignored this principle. It has also been ignored by nearly all of the subsequent followers of Fisher and the test approach.

## 1. Selection of Tests

Fisher discussed numerous index number tests, though he explicitly applied the term "test" only to those he found especially noteworthy. Some of these he dismissed (the circularity test, which involves a kind of transitivity property, came in for particular criticism). Selection among the tests was necessary because, as Frisch (1930) later showed, no index number formula satisfies all reasonable tests.

Fisher treated two tests as particularly important. One of these was the time reversal test, which requires that the index number for the change from period 0 to period $t$, $P_{0t}$, equal the reciprocal of $P_{t0}$. The other was the "factor reversal" test, which requires that the price index and the quantity index have the same functional form. He identified as superior the formula that is now known as the "Fisher Ideal" index because it satisfied these two tests, and because it also had some additional, less critical, advantages.

Fisher's test approach is subject to three criticisms: First, the index properties included in the tests are arbitrary; little basis is given in the test literature for why the properties that are included are there. Second, as suggested by the first criticism, the approach invariably omits index number properties that some users of National Accounts and the CPI contend are critically important—notably additivity and consistency in aggregation. Third, though some index number properties included in the tests must be more important than others for particular uses, advocates of the test approach usually favor a metric where each test is of equal importance.

## Properties Included

Fisher presented no theory to explain why the particular price index properties he selected provide the relevant tests. Indeed, on economic grounds some authors have rejected some of these tests.

Notably, the factor reversal test was dismissed by Samuelson and Swamy (1974, 575) with the colorful remark, "A man and his wife should be properly matched, but that does not mean I should marry my identical twin!" Because the form of the COLI depends on the form of the indirect utility function, and the form of the associated standard of living index depends on the direct utility function,[74] Fisher's factor reversal test thus implies that direct and indirect utility functions should have the same form. This property is known as "self-dual" in the demand literature. Most demand specifications used empirically do not have this characteristic (for example, Deaton and Muellbauer's [1980] "Almost Ideal Demand System" is not self-dual). There is no reason to specify the self-dual property as some sort of theoretical ideal.

The time reversal test can also be criticized as inconsistent with the economic approach to index numbers. If the indifference curve used to evaluate the COLI is predetermined, the COLI indeed has the time-reversal property. However, the usual convention is to use either the starting or the ending period to define the reference indifference curve. That is, one can frame the cost-of-living question as: what is the minimum expenditure necessary currently to achieve the base period's standard of living?[75] Alternatively: what is the expenditure necessary in the base period to consume the current period's standard of living? Adopting either of these conventions makes the COLI fail the time reversal test, except in the special case of homotheticity. Beginning at one point, passing to another, and then returning to the first (the essence of the time reversal test) involves passing through two utility levels; it is not the same thing at all as remaining at the initial point. The two

74. See Samuelson and Swamy (1974) and Pollak (1989).

75. The index uses the answer to the question as the numerator and the actual base period's expenditure as the denominator.

utility levels have equal influence on the (three-period) result and with non-homotheticity, the time-reversal test will (*appropriately*) fail. Fisher's time reversal test is seemingly plausible, but he and others who have endorsed it failed to recognize the equally-important role of the two consumption levels that are involved in it.

Thus, Fisher's tests include some that are insupportable from the standpoints of economic theory and empirical work on consumer demand. This is our first criticism of the test approach.

Properties Omitted

Many users of national accounts (in the United States and elsewhere) have maintained that additivity of the index number is an essential property because it enables the users of the accounts to add up the component measures of constant price output (real output, in U.S. macroeconomics usage) to get, for example, constant price investment expenditure, or the level of constant price GDP. Users desire that GDP $= C + I + G$, in real or constant price terms, as well as in current price terms, and that one can add constant price expenditures on structures, equipment, and inventories to get constant price investment. A similar contention has been made for the CPI. The Laspeyres index is additive in the sense desired, nearly all other index numbers are not.[76]

The test approach provides no basis for evaluating the position that additivity is or is not an important "axiom" for an index number, so one must either arbitrarily accept it or arbitrarily reject it. The Fisher index number, which is among the preferred index numbers under the economic approach and also the index number that Fisher thought the best, fails the additivity test. If one regards additivity as important—even more if additivity is thought to be the most important property of index numbers—one might contend that the Fisher index has worse test properties than index formulas (such as the Laspeyres index, or the Edgeworth-Marshall index) that do satisfy this test. (This, for example, is Baldwin's [2009] conclusion.[77])

Consistency in aggregation is another desirable property of index numbers for many purposes. This property means that the index can be calculated in stages, with the intermediate stage aggregates treated as if they were price relatives at the next higher stage of aggregation. For example, the aggregate Laspeyres CPI can be calculated from its component indexes for food, clothing, housing, appliances, services, and so forth.[78] The Fisher index, as one

76. To avoid confusion, what is wanted is additivity in the levels (the components of the numerator of the index number), not additivity in the index changes. The Walsh index is also additive in the levels under certain circumstances. An index that is additive in the levels will also be consistent in aggregation.

77. To be clear, we are not advocating additivity as a property of either the CPI or of national accounts. But that is because we accept the economic approach to index numbers, which does not support imposing additivity.

78. Balk (1996) presents a more precise definition of consistency in aggregation and a discussion of a family of indexes that have this property.

example, is not consistent in aggregation—a Fisher index of Fisher indexes is not a Fisher index (indeed, the Bureau of Economic Analysis publishes estimates of the error from combining component Fisher indexes).[79] An index number that is additive is also consistent in aggregation, but nonadditive indexes may also be consistent in aggregation.

When BEA adopted Fisher indexes to measure price and quantity change in the U.S. national accounts, users complained that Fisher indexes were not additive and not consistent in aggregation. Yet the literature on the test approach is almost entirely silent about these two desirable properties (the previously cited items by Balk are exceptions). In consequence, the supposedly pragmatic test approach to index numbers has nothing to say about some of the major—and most controversial—pragmatic issues of index number construction that have arisen in recent years.

### No Rationale for Determining Which Properties Are Included in the Tests

No index number formula satisfies all of Fisher's tests, so a decision must be made about which to select as valid. Some tests appear trivial, others as we noted previously, objectionable. Often the tests that are selected are justified as "reasonable." Reasonableness, however, is defined differently by different people (as experience richly shows), and reasonableness may also depend on the purpose of the index number.[80] The economic approach has been used to pare down the list of valid tests, but not in a thorough and comprehensive way.

### No Rationale for Weighting the Index Properties

In the most common application of the test approach, one simply counts the number of the arbitrary tests that are passed by a particular index number formula. The formula that passes the most tests "wins." This amounts to weighting all tests equally. Why should they get equal weight? And, most importantly, why should all the tests get the same weighting, equal or not, for every index number problem?

### Summary

The particular tests that Fisher (and others who have followed him) chose included some that are debatable and excluded others that some index users regard as essential. Had different index number properties been included in the tests, a different index number formula would have emerged as "best,"

79. The error of approximation is fairly small and so empirically supports Diewert's (1978) analytical result that all superlative indexes are approximately consistent in aggregation. Nevertheless, critics have not been satisfied with approximate consistency when other index number systems (Laspeyres) give *exact* consistency in aggregation.

80. We are aware of the counterargument that says that if the test approach rests on "axioms," the COLI approach also rests on an "axiom" (utility maximization). We regard this point as semantic manipulation. The "axiom" of utility maximization is a testable hypothesis, on which a great amount of economic literature exists. It is hardly comparable to index number "tests" such as time reversal and so forth, which are simple index number properties.

especially if one gives up the notion that all tests should be weighted equally. In an extreme case, perhaps, some users of index numbers have contended that additivity and consistency in aggregation should receive all the weight (they prefer, naturally, the Laspeyres index number); the test approach itself has no basis for excluding this view other than arbitrary rejection of it. Accordingly, the test approach does not yield the Fisher index number, *unless one selects the tests in order to get it.* Index number properties have a role for choosing among index number formulas, but that role is primarily to choose among index numbers with good economic properties.

## 2. Measurement of Index Components

The economic and the test approaches to index numbers differ in a more fundamental dimension because the theory of the COLI has two parts. One part, as noted, is a theory of aggregation—that is, selecting the index number "formula." The second part concerns (a) which components are to go into the index—the domain of the index—and (b) how components of the index are to be measured.

The COLI provides the answer to a question, for example: "What is the cost at today's prices of obtaining the standard of living of the base period?" This is not, we emphasize, the same thing as the question: "What index number formula do we choose?" The COLI question is much broader and much more comprehensive. It directs attention to the standard of living, and invites us to ask how the standard of living should be measured.

As an example, faced by at least one of the reviews covered in this chapter, a forced substitution (for example, a regulatory change that removes some variety of a product from the market) and a voluntary substitution induced by changes in relative prices are both changes in the "market basket." Should these be handled in the same way in the price index? Or not? The COLI theory forces us to confront those questions, and suggests some answers, at least in qualitative terms. The test approach is wholly silent.

Another example comes from a current controversy in CPI measurement around the world: is the standard of living defined on the consumption of housing services? Or is it defined on the purchase of houses? Does the consumption of housing or the purchase of houses belong in the domain of the CPI?

The COLI approach has universally been interpreted as implying that housing services are the appropriate concept for the index.[81] On the other

81. The CNSTAT report (Schultze and Mackie 2002) points out that one could use the flow of services approach to owner-occupied housing (which is derived from the theory of consumption) in an index that does not use the theory of consumption for aggregation. That is, the flow of services from durables could be combined with what the CNSTAT committee called the COGI approach. Though the position is logically sustainable, around the world

hand, no "test" on the reasonableness of an index supports any particular treatment of housing in the CPI. Consequently, a great variety of approaches to owner-occupied housing (Diewert [2004] reviews them) have emerged in countries that do not subscribe to the COLI framework. Various strategies (an "acquisitions" index, a "payments" index, and so forth) have been devised to try to provide a non-COLI framework for designing CPI components. None, in our view, succeeds.[82]

## Conclusion

We have contended that the test approach to index numbers cannot be used for guidance about aggregating the basic components (see paragraph section 1). The tests included and excluded from the tests are arbitrary and the index number that emerges as "best" is very sensitive to the arbitrary choice of tests. In particular, the test approach does not, despite so many assurances to the contrary over many years, favor the Fisher index, unless the set of tests is chosen to produce the Fisher.

Secondly, the test approach has nothing to say about which components should be included in a consumption index; it cannot be used to define the index domain. It also says nothing about how those components should be measured. Those are essential points in constructing an index—likely more essential than the choice of index number formula, important as that is—and they are points for which the economic approach has much to say.

Significantly, no U.S. review, with the exception of some passages in the CNSTAT Panel's report, puts any weight on test approaches. This was undoubtedly because, as Reinsdorf (2006) remarks, the economic approach to index numbers dominated the test approach through most of the twentieth century. More recently, the test approach has become popular in Europe, especially in academic circles, while the economic approach remains popular in the United States—a curious trans-Atlantic reversal of roles since the early developers of the economic approach were all European, while main developers of the test approach were the Americans Fisher and Walsh.

no one inhabits this particular "intellectual house." When statistical agencies reject the flow of services approach to owner-occupied housing, they also reject the COLI approach as the conceptual guide for their index, and they frequently reject the COLI *because* they do not wish to implement a flow of services approach to owner-occupied housing.

82. Melser and Hill (2005) suggest that the "use" approach sometimes proposed in these non-COLI frameworks is compatible with the economic approach to index numbers.

## References


Abraham, K. G. 2003. Toward a cost-of-living index: Progress and prospects. *Journal of Economic Perspectives* 17 (11): 45–58.

Abraham, K. G., J. S. Greenlees, and B. R. Moulton. 1998. Working to improve the Consumer Price Index. *Journal of Economic Perspectives* 12 (1): 27–36.

Adelman, I. 1958. A new approach to the construction of index numbers. *Review of Economics and Statistics* 40 (3): 240–9.

Advisory Commission to Study the Consumer Price Index. 1996. See Boskin et al. 1996.

Afriat, S. N. 1967. The construction of utility functions from expenditure data. *International Economic Review* 8 (February): 67–77.

Aizcorbe, A. M., and P. C. Jackman. 1993. The commodity substitution effect in CPI data, 1982–91: Anatomy of price change. *Monthly Labor Review* 116 (12): 25–33.

Anglin, P. M., and M. R. Baye. 1987. Information, multiperiod search, and cost-of-living index theory. *Journal of Political Economy* 95 (6): 1179–95.

Arant, W. D. 1961. Statement. In *U.S. Congress, Joint Economic Committee (1961): Government price statistics, hearings, part 1, May 1, 2, 3, 4, and 5, 1961.* Washington, DC: GPO.

Arrow, K. J. 1958. The measurement of price changes. In *The relationship of prices to economic stability and growth: Compendium of papers submitted by panelists appearing before the Joint Economic Committee.* Joint Economic Committee Print, March 31. Washington, DC: GPO.

Baily, M. N. 2006. Implications of the Boskin Commission Report. *International Productivity Monitor* 12 (Spring): 74–83.

Baker, D. 1998. *Getting prices right.* Washington, DC: M. E. Sharpe.

Baldwin, A. 2009. Chain price and volume aggregates for the System of National Accounts. *Price and Productivity Measurement* 6:241–78.

Balk, B. M. 1990. On calculating cost-of-living index numbers for arbitrary income levels. *Econometrica* 58 (1): 75–92.

———. 1995. Axiomatic price index theory: A survey. *International Statistical Review* 63 (1): 69–93.

———. 1996. Consistency-in-aggregation and Stuvel indices. *Review of Income and Wealth* Series 42 3 (September): 353–63.

———. 2005. Divisia price and quantity indices: 80 years after. *Statistica Neerlandica* 59 (2): 119–58.

Banerjee, K. S. 1959. Precision in the construction of cost-of-living index numbers. *Sankhya* 21 (3/4): 393–400.

Banzhaf, H. S. 2001. Quantifying the qualitative: Quality-adjusted price indexes in the United States, 1915–61. *History of Political Economy* 33 (suppl. 1): 345–70.

Baye, M. R. 1985. Price dispersion and functional price indices. *Econometrica* 53 (1): 213–23.

Beelen, G. 2004. Vehicle, homeowners', and tenants' insurance in the Canadian CPI. Paper presented to the Statistics Canada Price Advisory Committee. April, Tunney's Pasture, Ottawa, Canada.

Berndt, E. R. 2006. The Boskin Commission report after a decade: After-life or requiem? *International Productivity Monitor* 12 (Spring): 61–73.

Berry, J. M. 1995. Agencies debate changes to Consumer Price Index: Billions in cost-of-living changes at stake. *Washington Post,* January 27.

Blow, L., and I. Crawford. 2001. Should the cost-of-living index provide the conceptual framework for the Consumer Price Index? *The Economic Journal* 111 (472): F357–F382.

Boskin Commission. 1996. See Boskin et al. 1996.

Boskin, M. J. 2005. Causes and consequences of bias in the Consumer Price Index as a measure of the cost of living. *Atlantic Economic Journal* 33 (1): 1–13.

Boskin, M. J., E. R. Dulberger, R. J. Gordon, Z. Griliches, and D. Jorgenson. 1995. Toward a more accurate measure of the cost of living: Interim report to the Senate Finance Committee from the Advisory Commission to Study the Consumer Price Index. Washington, DC: Senate Finance Committee.

Boskin, M. J., E. R. Dulberger, R. J. Gordon, Z. Griliches, and D. Jorgenson. 1996. Toward a more accurate measure of the cost of living: Final Report to the U.S. Senate Finance Committee. In *U.S. Senate Finance Committee. Senate Print 104-72, December, 104th Congress, 2nd Session.* Washington, DC: GPO.

Bowley, A. L. 1928. Notes on index numbers. *The Economic Journal* 38 (150): 216–37.

Braithwait, S. D. 1980. The substitution bias of the Laspeyres Price Index: An analysis using estimated cost-of-living indexes. *The American Economic Review* 70 (1): 64–77.

Brown, M., and D. Heien. 1972. The s-branch utility tree: A generalization of the linear expenditure system. *Econometrica* 40 (4): 737–47.

Buyshgens, S. S. 1925. Sur une classe des hypersurfaces: A propos de l'index ideal de M. Irving Fischer. *Mathematischkii Sbornik* 32:625–31.

Cage, R., J. Greenlees, and P. Jackman. 2003. Introducing the chained Consumer Price Index. Paper presented at the Seventh Meeting of the International Working Group on Price Indices. May, Paris, France.

Carruthers, A. G., D. J. Sellwood, and P. W. Ward. 1980. Recent developments in the retail prices index. *The Statistician* 29 (1): 1–32.

Cecchetti, S. G., H. Genburg, J. Lipsky, and S. Wadhwani. 2000. Asset prices and Central Bank Policy. Paper presented to ICMB International Center for Monetary and Banking Studies and Centre for Economic Policy Research. July, Geneva.

Christensen, L. R., D. W. Jorgenson, and L. J. Lau. 1975. Transcendental logarithmic utility functions. *The American Economic Review* 65 (3): 367–83.

Christensen, L. R., and M. E. Manser. 1976. Cost-of-living indexes and price indexes for U.S. meat and produce. In *Household production and consumption,* studies in income and wealth vol. 40, ed. N. Terleckyj, 399–446. New York: Columbia University Press.

Committee on National Statistics. 2002. See Schultze and Mackie, eds.

Crone, T. M., L. I. Nakamura, and R. Voith. 2004. Measuring American rents: Regression-based estimates. Federal Reserve Bank of Philadelphia Working Paper no. 04-22.

Dalen, J. 2001. *The Swedish Consumer Price Index: A handbook of methods.* Stockholm: Statistics Sweden.

Deaton, A. 1998. Getting prices right: What should be done? *Journal of Economic Perspectives* 12 (1): 37–46.

Deaton, A., and J. Muellbauer. 1980. *Economics and consumer behaviour.* Cambridge: Cambridge University Press.

Diewert, W. E. 1973. Afriat and revealed preference theory. *Review of Economic Studies* 40 (3): 419–26.

———. 1976. Exact and superlative index numbers. *Journal of Econometrics* 4 (2): 115–45.

———. 1978. Superlative index numbers and consistency in aggregation. *Econometrica* 46 (4): 883–900.

———. 1983. The theory of the cost-of-living index and the measurement of welfare changes. In *Price level measurement,* ed. W. E. Diewert and C. Montmarquette, 163–233. Ottawa, Canada: Minister of Supply and Services.
———. 1992. Fisher ideal output, input and productivity indexes revisited. *Journal of Productivity Analysis* 3 (3): 211–48.
———. 1993. The early history of price index research. In *Essays in index number theory,* vol. 1, ed. W. E. Diewert and A. O. Nakamura, 33–66. New York: North Holland.
———. 1995. Axiomatic and economic approaches to elementary price indices. Discussion Paper no. 95-01. Vancouver, Canada: University of British Columbia, Department of Economics.
———. 1998. Index number issues in the Consumer Price Index. *Journal of Economic Perspectives* 12 (1): 47–58.
———. 2001. The Consumer Price Index and index number purpose. *Journal of Economic and Social Measurement* 27: 167–248.
———. 2004. Index number theory and measurement economics. University of British Columbia. Unpublished Manuscript.
Dimand, R. W. 2005. Comments on William D. Nordhaus's "Irving Fisher and the contribution of improved longevity to living standards." *American Journal of Economics and Sociology* 64 (1): 393–97. January.
Ducharme, L. M. 1997. *Bias in the CPI: Experiences from five OECD countries.* Statistics Canada, Prices Division, Analytic Series No. 10. (catalogue No. 62F0014MPB). Ottawa, Canada: Statistics Canada.
Feenstra, R. C., and M. D. Shapiro. 2003. High-frequency substitution and the measurement of price indexes. In *Scanner data and price indexes,* National Bureau of Economic Research studies in income and wealth vol. 64, ed. R. C. Feenstra and M. D. Shapiro, 123–46. Chicago: The University of Chicago Press.
Fisher, I. 1911. *The purchasing power of money.* New York: MacMillan.
———. 1922. *The making of index numbers.* Boston: Houghton Mifflin.
Fisher, F., and K. Shell. 1972. *The economic theory of price indices: Two essays on the effects of taste, quality, and technological change.* New York: Academic Press.
Fixler, D., C. Fortuna, J. Greenlees, and W. Lane. 1999. The use of hedonic regressions to handle quality change: The experience in the US CPI. Paper presented at the fifth meeting of the International Working Group on Price Indices. 25–27 August, Reykjavik, Iceland. Available at: http://www.ottawagroup.org/pdf/bls.pdf.
Frisch, R. 1930. Necessary and sufficient conditions regarding the form of an index number which shall meet certain of Fisher's tests. *Journal of the American Statistical Association* 25 (December): 397–406.
———. 1936. Annual survey of general economic theory: The problem of index numbers. *Econometrica* 4 (January): 1–39.
Gillingham, R. 1974. A conceptual framework for the CPI. In *Proceedings of the American Statistical Association, Proceedings of the Survey Research Methods System.* Alexandria, VA: American Statistical Association.
Gini, C. 1924. Quelques considérations au sujet de la construction des nombres indices des prix et des questions analogues. *Metron* 4 (July): 3–162.
Goldberg, J. P., and W. T. Moye. 1985. *The first hundred years of the Bureau of Labor Statistics.* Washington, DC: GPO.
Goldberger, A. S., and T. Gamelestos. 1970. A cross-country comparison of consumer expenditure patterns. *European Economic Review* 1 (3): 357–400.
Goodhart, C. A. E. 2001. What weight should be given to asset prices in the measurement of inflation? *The Economic Journal* 111 (472): F335–F356.

Gordon, R. J. 2006. The Boskin Commission report: A retrospective one decade later. *International Productivity Monitor* 12 (Spring): 7–22.

Gordon, R. J., and T. van Goethem. 2007. Downward bias in the most important CPI component: The case of rental shelter, 1914–2003. In *Hard-to-measure goods and services: Essays in Honor of Zvi Griliches,* ed. E. R. Berndt and C. R. Hulten, 153–95. Chicago: University of Chicago Press.

Gordon, R. J., and Z. Griliches. 1997. Quality change and new products. *The American Economic Review* 87 (2): 84–88.

Greenlees, J. S. 2001. The U.S. CPI and the cost-of-living objective. Paper presented at the Conference of European Statisticians Joint ECE/ILO Meeting on Consumer Price Indices. 2 November, Washington, DC.

———. 2006. The BLS response to the Boskin Commission report. *International Productivity Monitor* 12 (Spring): 23–41.

Griliches, Z. 1961. Hedonic price indexes for automobiles: An econometric analysis of quality change. Staff Paper no. 3 in U.S. Congress, Joint Economic Committee. *Government Price Statistics, Hearings, Part 2, May 1, 2, 3, 4, and 5, 1961.* Washington, DC: GPO.

Hausman, J. A. 1997. Valuation of new goods under perfect and imperfect competition. In *The economics of new goods,* studies in income and wealth vol. 58, ed. T. F. Bresnahan and R. J. Gordon, 209–48. Chicago: University of Chicago Press.

———. 2003. Sources of bias and solutions to bias in the Consumer Price Index. *Journal of Economic Perspectives* 17 (1): 23–44.

Heien, D. M. 1973. Some further results on the estimation of the s-branch utility tree. Working Paper no. 10. Washington, DC: Bureau of Labor Statistics.

Hendel, I., and A. Nevo. 2002. Sales and consumer inventory. NBER Working Paper no. 9048. Cambridge, MA: National Bureau of Economic Research, July.

Hicks, J. R. 1940. The valuation of the social income. *Economica* 7 (May): 105–24.

Hogg, M. H. 1934. Revising the wage earners' cost-of-living index. *Journal of the American Statistical Association* 29 (March): 120–4.

Hoover, E. D., and M. S. Stotz. 1964. Food distribution changes and the CPI. *Monthly Labor Review* 87 (January): 58–64.

Hulten, C. R. 1973. Divisia index numbers. *Econometrica* 41 (6): 1017–25.

Jaffee, S. A. 1984. The statistical structure of the revised CPI. *Monthly Labor Review* 87 (August): 916–24.

Jorgenson, D. W. 1990. Aggregate consumer behavior and the measurement of social behavior. *Econometrica* 58 (5): 1007–40.

Jorgenson, D. W., and D. T. Slesnick. 1983. Individual and cost-of-living indexes. In *Price level measurement: Proceedings from a conference sponsored by Statistics Canada,* ed. W. E. Diewert and C. Montmarquette, 864–75. Ottawa: Minister of Supply and Services Canada.

Keynes, J. M. 1930. *A treatise on money.* New York: Harcourt, Brace.

Klein, L. R., and H. Rubin. 1947–1948. A constant utility index of the cost-of-living. *Review of Economic Studies* 15 (2): 84–87.

Konüs, A. A. 1924. The problem of the true index of the cost of living. Published in translation in *Econometrica* 7 (January, 1939): 10–29.

Konüs, A. A., and S. S. Byushgens. 1926. On the problem of the purchasing power of money (in Russian). *Voprosi Konyunkturi* II (1): 151–72.

Manser, M. E. 1975. A note on cost-of-living indexes for U.S. food consumption. BLS Working Paper no. 57. Washington, DC: Bureau of Labor Statistics.

———. 1976. Elasticities of demand for food: an analysis using non-additive utility functions allowing for habit formation. *Southern Economic Journal* 43 (July): 879–91.

Manser, M., and R. MacDonald. 1988. An analysis of substitution bias in measuring inflation, 1959–85. *Econometrica* 46 (4): 909–30.
McCarthy, P. J. 1961. Sampling considerations in the construction of price indexes with particular reference to the United States Consumer Price Index. Staff paper no. 4 in U.S. Congress, Joint Economic Committee. *Government Price Statistics, Hearings, Part 2, May 1, 2, 3, 4, and 5, 1961.* Washington, DC: GPO.
Meany, G., and R. J. Thomas, 1944. U.S. Commerce Department Library. *Recommended report for the Presidential Committee on the cost of living index.* Washington, DC: CIO.
Meeker, R. 1919. The possibility of compiling an index of the cost of living. *American Economic Review,* Papers and Proceedings of the Thirty-First Annual Meeting of the American Economic Association 9 (1): 108–17.
Melser, D., and R. Hill. 2005. Developing a methodology for constructing spatial cost of living indexes: A report prepared for Statistics New Zealand. University of New South Wales, Sydney, Australia. Unpublished Manuscript, August.
Mills, F. C., E. W. Bakke, R. Cox, M. G. Reid, T. W. Schultz, and S. S. Stratton. (Special Committee of the American Statistical Association.) 1943. An appraisal of the U.S. Bureau of Labor Statistics cost of living index. *Journal of the American Statistical Association* 38 (December): 387–405.
Mitchell, W. C. 1915. The making and using of index numbers. Part I of *Index numbers of wholesale prices in the United States and foreign countries,* Bulletin of the U.S. Bureau of Labor Statistics, no. 173 (July): 5–114. Washington, DC: GPO.
———. [1915] 1921. The making and using of index numbers. Part I of *Index numbers of wholesale prices in the United States and foreign countries,* Bulletin of the U.S. Bureau of Labor Statistics, no. 284: 7–114. (Revised ed.) Washington, DC: GPO.
Mitchell, W. C., S. Kuznets, and M. G. Reid. 1944. U.S. Commerce Department Library. Prices and the cost of living in wartime—An appraisal of the Bureau of Labor Statistics index of the cost of living in 1941–1944: Report of the technical committee appointed by the Chairman of the President's Committee on the Cost of Living, June 15. Reprinted in *Report of the President's Committee on the Cost of Living.* Washington, DC: GPO.
Moses, K., and B. Moulton. 1997. Addressing the quality change issue in the consumer price index. *Brookings Papers on Economic Activity,* Issue no. 1: 305–49. Washington, DC: Brookings Institution.
Moulton, B. R. 1993. Basic components of the CPI: Estimation of price changes. *Monthly Labor Review* 116 (12): 13–24.
National Research Council. 2002. See Committee on National Statistics 2002.
Ostrander, F. T. 1944. The Mitchell Committee's report on the cost-of-living index: Comments. *The American Economic Review* 34 (4): 849–56.
Pakes, A. 2003. A reconsideration of hedonic price indexes with an application to PCs. *American Economic Review* 93 (5): 1578–96.
Pigou, A. C. 1912. *Wealth and welfare.* London: Macmillan.
———. 1932. *The economics of welfare,* 4th edition. (1st edition: 1920). London: Macmillan.
Pollak, R. A. 1980. Group cost-of-living indexes. *American Economic Review* 70 (2): 273–8.
———. 1981. The social cost-of-living index. *Journal of Public Economics* 15 (2): 311–36.
———. 1983. The theory of the cost-of-living index. In *Price level measurement: Proceedings from a conference sponsored by Statistics Canada,* ed. W. E. Dei-

wert and C. Montmarquette, 87–162. Ottawa: Minister of Supply and Services Canada.

———. 1989. *The theory of the cost-of-living index.* New York: Oxford University Press.

———. 1998. The Consumer Price Index: A research agenda and three proposals. *Journal of Economic Perspectives* 12 (1): 69–78.

President's Council of Economic Advisors. 1999. *Economic Report of the President.* Washington, DC: GPO.

Price Statistics Review Committee. 1961. See Stigler et al. 1961.

Randolph, W. C. 1988. Housing depreciation and aging bias in the Consumer Price Index. *Journal of Business and Economic Statistics* 6 (3): 359–72.

Reinsdorf, M. B. 1993. The effect of outlet price differentials on the U.S. Consumer Price Index. In *Price measurements and their uses,* studies in income and wealth vol. 57, ed. M. Foss, M. Manser, and A. Young, 227–60. Chicago: University of Chicago Press.

———. 1994. The effect of price dispersion on cost of living indexes. *International Economic Review* 35 (1): 137–49.

———. 1998. Formula bias and within-stratum substitution bias in the U.S. CPI. *Review of Economics and Statistics* 80 (2): 175–87.

———. 2006. Axiomatic price index theory. Washington D.C., Bureau of Economic Analysis. Unpublished Manuscript, May.

———. 2007. Axiomatic price index theory. In *Measurement in economics: A handbook,* ed. M. Boumans, 153–88. Amsterdam: Elsevier.

Reinsdorf, M. B., and B. R. Moulton. 1995. The construction of basic components of cost of living indexes. In *The economics of new goods,* ed. T. F. Bresnahan and R. J. Gordon, 397–423. Chicago: University of Chicago Press.

Roe, D., and D. Fenwick. 2004. The new inflation target: The statistical perspective. *Economic Trends* (January): 24–46.

Ross, A. M. 1966. Prepared statement for hearings of the Joint Economic Committee. In U.S. Congress, Joint Economic Committee. Hearings before the Subcommittee on Economic Statistics of the Joint Economic Committee, Congress of the United States. Eighty-Ninth Congress, second session. May 24, 25, and 25. Washington, DC: GPO.

Saglio, A. 1994. Comparative changes in average price and a price index: Two case studies. In *Papers and final report of the first meeting of the International Working Group on Price Indices,* ed. L. M. Ducharme, 197–270. Ottawa: Statistics Canada.

Samuelson, P. A., and S. Swamy. 1974. Invariant economic index numbers and canonical duality: Survey and synthesis. *The American Economic Review* 64 (4): 566–93.

Schultz (Szulc), B. 1994. Choice of price index formula at the micro-aggregation level: Issue, and a Canadian empirical evidence. In *Papers and final report of the first meeting of the International Working Group on Price Indices,* ed. L. M. Ducharme, 93–128. Ottawa: Statistics Canada.

Schultze, C. 2003. The Consumer Price Index: Conceptual issues and practical suggestions. *Journal of economic perspectives* 17 (1): 3–22.

Schultze, C., and C. Mackie, eds. 2002. *At what price? Conceptualizing and measuring cost-of-living and price indexes.* Washington, DC: Panel on Conceptual, Measurement, and Other Statistical Issues in Developing Cost-of-Living Indexes.

Scitovsky, A. A. 1964. An index of the cost of medical care—a proposed new approach. In *The economics of health and medical care,* ed. S. J. Axelrod: 128–42. Ann Arbor: Bureau of Public Health Economics, University of Michigan.

Shapiro, M., and D. Wilcox. 1996. Mismeasurement in the Consumer Price Index: An evaluation. *NBER Macroeconomics Annual,* ed. B. S. Bernanke and J. Rotemberg, 93. Cambridge, MA: MIT Press.

———. 1997. Alternative strategies for aggregating prices in the CPI. *The Federal Reserve Bank of St. Louis Review* 79 (3): 113–25.

Shoemaker, O. J. 2004. Analysis of divergence between chained CPI-U and regular CPI-U for the all-US all-items indexes (2000–2002). BLS Statistical Survey Working Paper. U.S. Department of Labor, Bureau of Labor Statistics.

Staehle, H. 1934. *International comparisons of food costs.* International Labour Office Report, Series N, no. 20.

Statistics Canada. 1995. *The Consumer Price Index reference paper.* Ottawa: Minister of Industry.

Stigler, G., D. S. Brady, E. Denison, I. B. Kravis, P. J. McCarthy, A. Rees, R. Ruggles, and B. C. Swerling. 1961. *The price statistics of the federal government.* In U.S. Congress, Joint Economic Committee. *Government Price Statistics, Hearings, Part 1, May 1, 2, 3, 4, and 5, 1961.* Washington, DC: GPO.

Stone, J. R. N. 1954. *The measurement of consumers' expenditure and behaviour in the United Kingdom, 1920–1938.* London: Cambridge University Press.

Stone, R., and S. J. Prais. 1952. Systems of aggregative index numbers and their compatibility. *The Economic Journal* 62 (247): 565–83.

Szulc [Schultz], B. J. 1983. Linking price index numbers. In *Price level measurement: Proceedings sponsored by Statistics Canada,* ed. W. E. Diewert and C. Montmarquette, 537–66. Ottawa: Minister of Supply and Services Canada.

Triplett, J. E. 1983. Escalation measures: What is the answer? What is the question? In *Price level measurement: Proceedings from a conference sponsored by Statistics Canada,* ed. W. E. Diewert and C. Montmarquette, 457–82. Ottawa: Minister of Supply and Services Canada.

———. 1990. Hedonic methods in statistical agency environments: An intellectual biopsy. In *Fifty years of economic measurement: The jubilee of the Conference on Research in Income and Wealth,* studies in income and wealth vol. 54, ed. E. R. Berndt and J. E. Triplett, 207–33. Chicago: University of Chicago Press.

———. 2001. Should the cost-of-living index provide the conceptual framework for a Consumer Price Index? *The Economic Journal* 111 (472): F311–F334.

———. 2003. Using scanner data in the Consumer Price Indexes: Some neglected conceptual considerations. In *Scanner data and price indexes,* studies in income and wealth vol. 64, ed. R. C. Feenstra and M. D. Shapiro, 151–62. Chicago: University of Chicago Press.

———. 2006. The Boskin Commission report after a decade. *International Productivity Monitor* 12 (Spring): 42–60.

Triplett, J. E., and B. P. Bosworth. 2004. *Services productivity in the United States: New sources of economic growth.* Washington, DC: Brookings Institution Press.

Ulmer, M. J. 1946. On the economic theory of Cost-of-Living Index numbers. *Journal of the American Statistical Association* (December): 530–42.

Urquhart, M. C., and K. A. H. Buckley. 1965. *Historical indexes of Canada.* Toronto: McMillan.

U.S. Congress, Joint Economic Committee. 1958. *The relationship of prices to economic stability and growth: Compendium of papers submitted by panelists appearing before the Joint Economic Committee.* Joint Committee Print, March 31. Washington, DC: GPO.

———. 1961. *Government price statistics: Hearings before the Joint Economic Committee, Congress of the United States.* Eighty-seventh Congress, first session pursuant to Section 5(a) of Public Law 304 (709th Congress). Part 2. Washington, DC: United States Congress (May 1, 2, 3, 4, and 5).

U.S. Department of Labor, Bureau of Labor Statistics. 1966. The Consumer Price Index: History and techniques. Bulletin no. 1517. Washington, DC: GPO.

———. 1997a. Measurement Issues in the Consumer Price Index. *Response to the U.S. Congress,* Joint Economic Committee, June. Washington, DC: GPO.

———. 1997b. The Consumer Price Index. *BLS Handbook for Methods for Surveys and Studies* (April): 167–202.

Varian, H. R. 1982. The nonparametric approach to demand analysis. *Econometrica* 50 (4): 945–74.

———. 1983. Non-parametric tests of consumer behaviour. *The Review of Economic Studies* 50 (1): 99–110.

von Bortkiewicz, L. 1923. Zweck und Struktur einer preisindexzahl. *Nordisk Statistiek Tidschrift* 2:3–4.

von Haberler, G. 1927. *The meaning of index numbers.* Munich: J. C. B. Mohr.

Walsh, C. M. 1901. *The measurement of general exchange value.* New York: Macmillan.

*Washington Post.* 1946. Editorial. February 14.

2

# Apparel Prices 1914–1993 and the Hulten/Bruegel Paradox

Robert J. Gordon

## 2.1 Introduction

So much evidence has been produced over the years demonstrating an upward bias in the Consumer Price Index (CPI) and National Income and Product Account (NIPA) deflators, especially for consumer and producer durable goods of relatively recent invention, that it requires a sharp adjustment in one's mind-set to contemplate the opposite: that for major consumption components over long intervals, the CPI may have incorporated a significant *downward* bias. Yet the Hulten-Bruegel paradox as interpreted here makes a convincing logical case that at some point in the past there *must have been* a downward bias in the CPI for several major components. This chapter demonstrates that one of these components is apparel, one of the three "necessities" (along with food and shelter), and a companion paper (Gordon and VanGoethem 2007) reaches the same conclusion for rental shelter. Both are unique in covering most of the twentieth century; 1914 to 1993 in this chapter on apparel and 1914 to 2003 in the companion paper on shelter.

Viewed as a contribution to the price index literature, this chapter joins others that have explored differences in hedonic and matched-model (MM)

Robert J. Gordon is Stanley G. Harris Professor in the Social Sciences at Northwestern University and a research associate of the National Bureau of Economic Research.

This research has been supported by the National Science Foundation. The Sears catalog prices for the matched-model indexes were collected by a succession of Northwestern undergraduates, in chronological order: Hannah Lipman, Stephanie Glenn, Katrina Katzenberger, Eileen Altman, Laura Veldkamp, Tho Kutty, Gabe Plotkin, Philip Ordway, and Jayun Kim. The data for the hedonic regression study were collected and analyzed by Philip Ordway, Jayun Kim, Jungyun Kim, and Ian Dew-Becker. I am particularly grateful to Ian Dew-Becker for bringing the loose ends of this project together both before and after the Vancouver conference. Helpful comments were provided by participants in the 2000 NBER Summer Institute.

indexes developed from the same data. Several previous studies have found that computer prices tend to be reduced upon the introduction of new models, leading hedonic price indexes to exhibit more rapid rates of price decline than matched-model indexes from the same data.[1] The matching process appears to exclude price declines when new computer models are introduced. There has long been a suspicion in the apparel price literature that price *increases* occur with changes in models or styles and are missed by the matched-model procedures of the CPI, and this chapter is perhaps the first study to demonstrate this systematic difference between hedonic and matched-model indexes from a uniform data set for apparel over a long historical period of time.[2] A striking corollary of the results is that quality change in apparel over the long period 1914 to 1993 has been negligible, in the sense that the new hedonic index tracks raw unadjusted price change relatively closely, while changes in the implied index of average quality are relatively minor.

This chapter represents the fulfillment of a long-standing goal to extract from the Sears catalog a new history of apparel prices over the entire history between the beginning of the CPI in 1914 and the final year of the Sears catalog in 1993 (the catalog itself began in 1893, two decades after the Montgomery Ward catalog's initiation in 1872).[3] Initially the goal of this project was to duplicate the CPI matched-model methodology with catalog data and compare CPI apparel subcomponents with the corresponding Sears matched-model indexes. Subsequently it became apparent that the same Sears data could be used to develop hedonic price indexes for at least one product—womens' dresses—where an ample number of data observations are available in the catalogs. The resulting differences in the hedonic and matched-model indexes for womens' dresses provide convincing evidence that the matched-model technique misses a significant portion of price increases that occur when styles and models change.

### 2.1.1 The Hulten-Bruegel Paradox

Numerous economists have speculated about the implications for estimates of long-term economic growth of bias in official price indexes. In an

1. Among studies that examine differences between matched-model and hedonic indexes for personal computers and/or software are Berndt, Griliches, and Rappaport (1995); Berndt and Rappaport (2003); Doms, Aizcorbe, and Corrado (2003); and Triplett (2004).

2. For history buffs, the time period of this study, dictated solely by the starting date of the CPI and the termination date of the Sears catalog, echoes dates signifying the start and end of the most terrible events of the twentieth century. In the words of Eric Hobsbawm (1994, 3), the interval 1914 to 1991 marks the "short twentieth century" bookmarked by the start of World War I and the final collapse of the Soviet Union.

3. Sears catalog data for 1893 to 1914 were previously analyzed by Rees (1961b), as discussed further following. A history of the Sears Roebuck and other mail-order catalogs and further references can be found in Gordon (1990, 419–23).

important and influential example, Nordhaus (1997) speculated that when plausible rates of upward price index bias are extrapolated backwards for two centuries, the increase in real wages from 1800 to 1992 (which in the official data is by a factor of 13 to 18) might have been by a factor of 40 with a low estimate of price index bias (0.5 percent per year) or by a factor of 190 with a higher estimate of bias (1.4 percent per year).

Nordhaus' conference discussant, Charles Hulten, pointed out the implausibility of this thought experiment; the high bias estimate implies (in my own numerical example that makes Hulten's point with different numbers than his) that median household income in the year 1800 was $143 in 1992 prices, or $0.39 per day: enough to buy a mere 1.3 pounds of potatoes per day for the household, with nothing left over for shelter, clothing, or anything else.[4]

But why stop there? The "Hulten paradox" should be renamed the "Bruegel paradox," after the landmark painter Pieter Bruegel the Elder (1525–1569). Even if we assume that the then-unavailable official estimates would register no increase in the real wage from 1569 to 1800, when we extrapolate Nordhaus' high bias estimate back to the last year of Bruegel's life, we find the implication that the real wage should have increased from 1569 to 1992 by a factor of 5,482, making median *annual* household income in the earlier year equal to $5.59, enough to buy exactly 0.8 ounces of potatoes per day, with nothing left over for food or shelter.[5] Yet the happy burghers in Bruegel paintings often look overfed, content, well-clothed, and with solid-looking houses in the background.

### 2.1.2 The Application to Apparel

In setting a research agenda to look for the possibility of negative CPI bias, one looks first to the three traditional consumer necessities—food, apparel, and shelter—these are the "big three" items of consumer expenditure and have a sufficient weight to "matter" in arriving at an eventual resolution of the Hulten/Bruegel paradox. While there might be some long-term bias in the CPI for food, I have sidelined that category to the back burner for lack of an obvious data source that would incorporate developments over time in the increased degree of processing of food (canned food, frozen food, delis in the supermarket, etc.) Instead, the research payoff looks more promising for the remaining two necessities, apparel and shelter, for two reasons. First,

4. The 1992 current-dollar median household income was $30,786 and the 1992 price of a pound of white potatoes was $0.31 (U.S. Bureau of the Census 1994, tables 707 and 763, respectively). Extrapolating backwards a growth rate of real wages of 2.8 percent per year yields a ratio of real wages in 1992 divided by the year 1800 of 216 ($30,786/216 = $142.50).

5. The factor of 5,482 equals the factor of 216 implied by the high-bias estimate (a bias of 1.4 percent per year added to the official growth rate of real wages of 1.4 percent per year), multiplied by an additional factor of 25.3 to take account of a 1.4 percent bias in the 231 years from 1569 to 1800.

there is prima-facie evidence, reviewed following for apparel (and equally true for structures) that raw (non-quality-adjusted) price data for a given type of apparel sold in mail-order catalogs increase far more over the 1914 to 1993 period than the CPI. Second, apparel is one of the three main areas where critics have suggested that the CPI may incorporate a downward bias (the others being housing and autos, see Wynne and Sigalla [1994, 10–11]).

Among the reasons suggested for the downward bias in apparel is the strong seasonal pattern in clothing styles and prices, leading to possible inaccuracy in linking prices for old styles sold at low closeout prices with new styles sold at high initial prices. In suggesting that "style" goods are a source of the bias problem, Wynne-Sigalla cite the difference between the 1967 to 1987 CPI inflation rate of 6.0 percent for infants' and toddlers' apparel with those for men's and boys' apparel (3.4 percent) and women's and girls' apparel (2.9 percent). A much more comprehensive study of "style" and "fashion" goods is provided by Pashigian and coauthors (Pashigian 1988; Pashigian and Bowen 1991; Pashigian, Bowen, and Gould 1995) and indicates that seasonal fluctuations in the prices of women's apparel are greater than for men's apparel, and that prices of women's apparel start high because of uncertainty by retailers about what styles will be popular and prices later decline as "sales" are necessary to clear out inventories of unpopular merchandise. Without extreme care in linking old styles last year to new styles this year, any price index based on linking is subject to major errors.

### 2.1.3 Plan of the Chapter

Our review of the evidence begins with comparisons over the long 1914 to 1993 period between changes in the CPI and in raw price changes for selected items from the Sears catalog; the much faster increase in the Sears prices could be reconciled by a rapid quality change, by an atypical rate of Sears increase relative to economy-wide apparel prices, or by a downward bias in the CPI. To address the representativeness of Sears catalog prices, we then turn to a consideration of advantages and disadvantages of the catalog as a data source.

The rest of the chapter develops the matched-model (MM) for numerous apparel product categories and the hedonic index for womens' dresses. The MM indexes are based on more than 10,000 data observations, and the hedonic index on roughly 6,500 observations. The discussion of the MM indexes and a comparison with the CPI is followed by a detailed presentation of the hedonic results. The case for a downward bias in the CPI rests primarily on the hedonic regression study of women's dresses, which exhibits a much faster rate of price increase than either the Sears MM index for women's dresses or the CPI for womens' dresses. The negligible rate of quality improvement for women's dresses is extrapolated to other types of apparel to reach the general conclusion of downward bias in the CPI not just for women's dresses but for all apparel.

## 2.2 Further Motivation for a Study of Apparel Prices

Between 1914 and 1993 the CPI implies that apparel prices on average rose by a factor of 7.6 (an average annual growth rate of 2.6 percent per annum). However, a quick glance at any Sears catalog in the era prior to World War I reveals prices that seem much too low relative to 1993 to be consistent with the CPI. In 1914 cotton percale house dresses, trimmed with braid and ruffles, could be purchased for $0.98 and a taffeta silk jacket for $6.75. Men's all-wool pants were $1.35, an all-wool suit was $4.50, and an all-wool overcoat was $7.00.

The impression that the catalog prices have increased far more than the 1993/1914 price ratio of 7.6 for the CPI can be quantified. Taking the median dresses (ranked from most to least expensive) sold by Sears in 1993 and the median sold in 1914, the 1993/1914 price ratio is 32.7. For the two most expensive dresses in each year the ratio is 27.4, while for the two least expensive dresses the ratio is 59.5. It might seem easy to dismiss this discrepancy between the CPI increase and the median increase in catalog dress prices by arguing that quality has increased commensurately, but in fact an inspection of the photos and specifications in the catalogs suggests that, if anything, quality was higher in the earlier era, with higher quality fabrics (silk, cashmere) and more decorative elements (ruffles, braids, etc.).

Experts at the Bureau of Labor Statistics (BLS) have long suspected that the CPI for apparel, at least prior to 1988, might incorporate a downward bias.[6] Both the CPI and Sears MM indexes may understate the true rate of quality-adjusted price increase. If our hedonic regression results consistently display a faster rate of price increase than the MM indexes from the same catalog data, then this would support the view based on the raw (quality-unadjusted) comparisons previously cited that the CPI may understate secular inflation in apparel prices, thus helping to explain the Hulten/Bruegel paradox.

### 2.2.1 Other Aspects of This Research

Part of the goal of this research is to determine if for important product groups like apparel and shelter that there is any case to be made for a downward bias in the CPI over any significant period of time. Another goal is simpler and more direct, to create a complementary study of price changes to that of Rees (1961b), who carried out detailed studies of apparel prices from catalogs as well as for other products (e.g., shelter prices from newspaper advertisements). Rees covered the period 1890 to 1914; that is, the years between the establishment of the Wholesale Price Index (WPI) and of

6. Further discussion of possible bias in the CPI for apparel is contained in Armknecht and Weyback (1989) and Liegey (1993). Recent experiments with hedonic price indexes for apparel are described in Liegey (1994).

the CPI. The coverage in this chapter of apparel prices for the period after 1914 complements the study by Rees and sheds new light on his results, since his study was based entirely on matched-model methodology and did not make any use of hedonic regression techniques.

The research in this chapter is based on much more evidence on MM indexes than on hedonic indexes. Matched-model indexes have been created for most types of apparel covered by the CPI over the entire period 1914 to 1993. Our hedonic study is of necessity limited to women's dresses, because of inadequate sample sizes for other types of apparel.

### 2.2.2 Advantages and Disadvantages of Catalog Price Data

In my past work on price measurement (Gordon 1990), an important preliminary step has been to discuss advantages and disadvantages of using mail-order catalogs as a supplementary source of price index numbers to be compared with official price indexes like the CPI. This comparison of advantages and disadvantages needs to be put in perspective by two sets of factors. First, for many durable goods examined in my book (Gordon 1990), price indexes based on *Consumer Reports* were so clearly superior in the extent of industry coverage and attention to the collection of true transaction prices that, whenever available, *Consumer Reports* indexes were used in preference to catalog indexes. For this study of apparel, the first consideration is irrelevant, since *Consumer Reports* has never compiled ratings, quality evaluations, or prices of apparel. Second, the emphasis in this chapter is more on differences in methodology to extract alternative matched model versus hedonic indexes from the same data than it is on differences in implied price changes between catalog indexes and the official CPI. Thus, differences in the validity of catalogs versus the official CPI are less important. Nevertheless, it is worthwhile to review the advantages and disadvantages of catalog data, especially for this study of apparel that goes back to 1914.

### 2.2.3 Advantages of Catalog Price Data

Among the most important advantages of catalog price indexes are the following:

1. Most important, specifications and illustrations published in catalogs allow closer control for changes in quality than in the official price indexes. The continuity of item codes from one catalog to the next is often helpful in following a particular item, and there is usually a long list of specifications that can be checked to insure that the models being compared are absolutely identical. In the CPI exact specifications are not available and accessible over any kind of long historical period. The consistency of specification listings in catalogs also makes them preferable to newspaper advertisements as a data source.

2. The matched-model methodology used to compare catalog items over time insures that price comparisons are included only for items that are absolutely identical in every dimension reported in the catalog specification. In

contrast, since 1978 the CPI has not been based on published specifications, and even before 1978—the time period most relevant for this study—the CPI made direct comparisons between nonidentical goods if both fell within the same specification description.[7]

3. Related to the first two advantages is the fact that catalog price indexes can in principle be replicated by anyone with access to a library containing historical catalog volumes or microfilms. In contrast, there is no way that CPI indexes at either the lower or upper level can be replicated by anyone except BLS employees. As a practical matter, for historical periods several decades in the past, original source data for the CPI may not be available at all.

4. The selection of products and individual models sold in catalogs responds automatically to the needs of the marketplace. It has always been true that "space to items always has been allotted on the basis of sales" (Hendrickson 1979, 249). This gives catalog price indexes two inherent advantages over the CPI, especially prior to the introduction of the current CPI sampling framework in 1978. First, for products sold in a large number of models or varieties, "it seems reasonable to assume that the number of different detailed varieties in the catalog will be greatest where the volume of sales is greatest, so that we probably weight the major varieties of an item in rough proportion to their importance" (Rees 1961a, 141). There is no such assurance that product indexes are sales weighted across models within a product category in the CPI, at least prior to 1978.

Also, products tend to be introduced into the catalogs soon after they become marketable, in contrast to the CPI, which often has introduced new products many years after they become commercially important. This factor, which is crucial for durable goods like room air conditioners (introduced into the Sears catalog in 1952 but not in the CPI until 1964), is presumably less important for apparel. Prior to 1978 the CPI adhered to fixed specifications over a long period of time, which could lead to a disproportionate weight for obsolete items.[8]

5. Prices printed in the catalogs are actual transaction prices. If retail and wholesale outlets that compete with catalog firms price items at varying discounts, catalog houses must adjust their published prices to remain com-

7. This statement about the CPI comes from Rees (1961a), who states "the BLS makes direct comparisons between nonidentical goods if both fall within the same specification." Triplett (1971, 186, table 6.1) quotes a study showing that for nonfood items in the CPI in April 1966, more than half of all product substitutions were handled by direct comparison of prices of the old and new model, and well under 1 percent were handled by an "explicit size or quality adjustment."

8. As reported by Rees (1961a, 141–2), ". . . it seems probable to us that the selection of specified-in-detail items for the CPI is often at too low a quality level for the index population, probably because the index population moved up to better qualities after the item was specified. In a number of cases we were unable to find any variety of an item in the catalogs . . . whose quality was as low as that specified by the BLS." Rees further reports (142) that rigid adherence to BLS specifications would require excluding a large fraction of the observations that can be collected from the catalogs, in one case reducing the sample by a factor of ten.

petitive (occasionally in the past few decades specialty catalogs for particular products advertising sale prices would be mailed between the issuance of the biannual catalogs—since these interim sale catalogs are not collected by libraries, we cannot use them in this research).

6. Since postage and shipping costs, credit charges, and taxes (except for Federal excise taxes when applicable) are not included in the published catalog prices, the services provided with each item are held constant. In contrast, the CPI may reflect a changing mix of services (e.g., some full-service department stores eliminated free delivery in the 1970s under pressure from discount-store competition). The CPI and catalog indexes can differ due to the inclusion in the CPI of state and local sales taxes.

### 2.2.4 Disadvantages of Catalog Price Data

The case against catalog price indexes takes two forms. First, there are clear disadvantages of relying on catalogs. Second, criticisms can be offered of the already listed advantages.

1. The most serious problem in the use of catalog prices is the possibility of a systematic difference in the secular growth rates in prices of the same product sold by catalog and noncatalog outlets, due, for instance, to differential growth in the efficiency of catalog operations or changes in pricing policies. Regarding efficiency, for any comparison with the CPI catalog prices include payment for warehouse and distribution services and would have a slower secular rate of increase than prices of retail competitors if the growth of efficiency in the provision of these services by catalog houses had been relatively rapid compared to the services provided by retail stores. It is hard to believe that such a bias could be important, since innovations in warehouse technology are likely to have been adopted by noncatalog competitors, and indeed Wal-Mart has outpaced Sears in warehouse and distribution efficiency over the past several decades.

In fact, it seems to be the catalog merchants who were more efficient than standard retailers in the early decades of the twentieth century and less efficient in the later decades. In my book (Gordon 1990, 422–23), model-by-model price comparisons for consumer appliances between the Sears catalog and *Consumer Reports* indicated that the catalog models tended to be at the lower end of the price range in the early postwar period but drifted toward the middle of the price range over time. Such behavior is consistent with a change in pricing strategy by Sears in the late 1960s and early 1970s ("we're selling last year's goods at next year's prices"). This evidence, if applicable to apparel as well as to consumer appliances, would predict that Sears catalog price indexes for apparel would drift upwards relative to the "true" universe of prices that should be compared with the CPI. Any difference between the representativeness of the Sears data and the CPI is not relevant to our comparison of MM and hedonic indexes for women's dresses, which is based on an identical database from the Sears catalog.

2. Another criticism of the preceding section on advantages of catalog price indexes concerns reproducability, where we need to distinguish two issues. First, an unambiguous advantage of a catalog price index is that *in principle* it can reproduced by anyone with access to the same catalogues. Second, we would not claim that any such reproduction would necessarily yield an identical index, because subjective decisions must inevitably be made in situations where models change without an overlap period, or when only a subset of available information is used in order to economize on research time. The methods used to develop the catalog indexes were, however, designed to minimize subjective decisions, since the actual data collection was carried out by a succession of research assistants.

### 2.2.5 Weighing the Advantages and Disadvantages

In the goal of finding alternative sources of price data to compare with official price indexes, particularly for earlier decades when the official methodology was not as refined as it is today, catalog price indexes are no panacea. Even if catalog prices are fully corrected for quality change, they may not accurately reflect the unobserved true quality-corrected price index for all suppliers, because of differences between catalog firms and all firms in the growth of efficiency or in the evolution of pricing policies. In comparisons of catalog prices with the CPI for apparel, there is the problem that the selection of models or types of apparel sold through catalogs may be different from those sold by other outlets (e.g., if catalogs typically sell more items that are small or lightweight in order to minimize shipping costs). We might also expect that the product mix sold in catalogs would be more heavily weighted to standard utilitarian items and less heavily to fashion goods. This difference could make the catalog indexes behave differently than the closest comparable CPI strata indexes, although there is no presumption for the direction of the drift.

Further, catalog prices may not adequately control for all types of quality change. Some changes may be introduced without being explicitly acknowledged in the printed catalog descriptions. Indeed, catalog indexes based on the matched-model method are as vulnerable as the CPI to deleting price change that occurs when new models are introduced. Matched-model indexes based on catalog prices or in the CPI may be biased downward if the timing of price increases typically coincides with the introduction of new models (in the apparel case) or biased upward if improvements in performance-price ratios coincides with the introduction of new models (as for computers and other electronic goods).

## 2.3 The Methodology of the Matched-Model Research

A close analog to this study is the catalog price index for thirty-six clothing items developed by Rees (1961b) for the period 1890 to 1914. Rees' study differs from the approach taken here, not only that he was comparing with the WPI since the CPI did not yet exist, but also in that he did not attempt to match catalog price indexes with WPI indexes on an item-by-item basis, but rather used catalog prices and expenditure survey weights to construct a completely new index that might be compared with the overall WPI for clothing and for home furnishings. Because Rees made no attempt to compare identical items, his index might differ from the WPI due to a different selection of items and the earlier introduction of new items. In contrast, the drift in the catalog/CPI ratios recorded in this chapter relates to identical items within the limits of feasibility in matching catalog products with CPI strata indexes for apparel.

For any given investment of research resources, there is a trade-off between the number of different catalogs consulted for a given product and the number of separate products that can be included. An initial decision (in Gordon [1990] and carried over to this chapter) was made to limit this study only to Sears, the largest catalog house, and thus to allow time to copy data for additional varieties and products. This procedure is supported by Rees' conclusion (1961a) that the Sears and Ward catalogs gave similar results in his research. Sears' catalog sales in the 1970s were triple Ward's and equal to Ward's sales and the sales of the next three catalogs combined. To allow time to copy prices for more products, prices were copied only from one catalog per year (spring-summer), even though catalogs were published biannually. This decision has the disadvantage that the resulting indexes may understate the degree of short-run flexibility in the catalog prices.

### 2.3.1 Timing

Because the primary purpose of this study is a comparison of the catalog prices with CPI indexes for the same apparel products and time periods, a decision was required on the choice of time periods for that comparison. The catalog data in this study were collected from the Chicago-area edition of the Sears, Roebuck spring-summer general catalog. According to a Sears official, however, prices are set long in advance of catalog distribution. Since the spring-summer catalog went to press in October of the previous year, and final price decisions were made in October, the most closely comparable CPI indexes would be those for October of the year previous to the date printed on the catalog. However, another interpretation is that the correct BLS index is that of the following spring, contemporaneous with the period during which the catalog prices are in effect, because aspects of Sears' pricing strategy were forward-looking. For instance, in some past periods, Sears purchased futures in goods like cotton and rubber to cover anticipated sales in the following six months. They also owned parts of corporations supplying them with products and arranged to buy forward at a price established for conditions of the following six months.

While in some early stages of the research on the 1990 book, BLS prices in year $t-1$ were compared with prices in the spring-summer catalog for year $t$, in the end, both were compared in year $t$. It might have been preferable to use monthly BLS indexes for, say, September or October of the year prior to the date on the catalog, but monthly data for BLS commodity indexes were not as complete as for annual data. This choice to adopt contemporaneous pricing is made partly because it is probably more accurate and also to simplify the presentation of the results. Slight inaccuracies may be introduced on the timing of major cyclical movements in prices, such as those in the Great Depression, but there is unlikely to be any effect on the measured rate of change of the Sears/CPI ratios over periods of a decade or more.

## 2.4 Matched-Model Catalog Indexes for Apparel, 1914 to 1993

Which products are chosen for study? For the apparel matched-model (MM) indexes the approach is straightforward. Historical CPI strata indexes are available for broad groupings (e.g., "women's separates and sportswear"). We turned to the Sears catalog and selected virtually every category of apparel that corresponded to each CPI stratum description. Table 2.1 lists the thirty-nine separate apparel categories for which Sears catalog matched-model indexes were constructed, the average number of annual price comparisons carried out for each category, and the CPI strata with which groups of categories were compared. The table is divided into three sections, corresponding to the three intervals of the 1914 to 1993 period for which research was carried out at separate stages.

### 2.4.1 Method of Comparison

Price comparisons for each pair of years are facilitated by Sears' policy of carrying several models in each product category. Changes in specifications usually affect only a subset of models in any one year, so for almost every product at least a few identical models are available for a price comparison between a pair of years. Because model changes occur at irregular intervals, the number of price comparisons of identical models for any given product may be on the order of seven for a series of years and then collapse to two or three in a year of substantial model changes. Price changes for models that are discontinued, newly introduced, or subject to quality change are imputed to the price changes of models that remain completely unchanged in a given comparison of prices in years $t$ and $t-1$. In the subsequent comparison of prices in $t+1$ and $t+2$, a different set of models is covered, perhaps including one or more models newly introduced in year $t+1$ and excluded in the previous comparison of $t$ with $t+1$.

Thus, each pair of years is treated separately and the list of models is allowed to change annually. This approach allows much more frequent model changes than in the CPI as it was constructed prior to 1978, when CPI field agents were required to find prices for models according to a detailed

**Table 2.1 Sears products and corresponding CPI products**

| Sears product | Years excluded | CPI products | Comparisons per year |
|---|---|---|---|
| | | *A Apparel 1914–1947* | |
| Women's apparel | | Women's and girl's apparel | 26.0 |
| Coats | — | Wool apparel | 1.7 |
| Skirts | — | | 1.3 |
| Dresses | — | Rayon and silk apparel | 1.2 |
| Slips | 1926–1947 | | 1.6 |
| Panties | — | | 0.8 |
| Hosiery | — | | 1.0 |
| Pajamas | 1914–1929 | | 1.0 |
| Dresses | — | Cotton apparel | 0.9 |
| Housedresses | — | | 1.5 |
| Nightgowns | — | | 0.6 |
| Unionsuits | — | | 1.6 |
| Hosiery | — | | 1.0 |
| Bloomers | 1927–1947 | | 0.4 |
| Slips | — | | 0.6 |
| Hats, wool | — | Other apparel | 1.9 |
| Gloves | — | | 1.8 |
| Girdles | — | | 1.6 |
| Brassieres | — | | 1.8 |
| Rubbers | — | Footwear | 1.8 |
| Street shoes | — | | 1.9 |
| Men's apparel | | Men's and boy's apparel | 26.1 |
| Suits | — | Wool apparel | 2.0 |
| Trousers | — | | 1.8 |
| Sweaters | 1914–1922 | | 1.4 |
| Overcoats | 1931–1946 | | 0.5 |
| Socks | — | Rayon apparel | 0.9 |
| Overcoats | — | Cotton apparel | 1.7 |
| Overalls | 1946–1947 | | 1.6 |
| Shirts, work | — | | 0.9 |
| Shirts, business | — | | 1.0 |
| Pajamas | 1946–1947 | | 1.6 |
| Unionsuits | — | | 2.1 |
| Socks | — | | 1.0 |
| Hats, wool | — | Other apparel | 2.1 |
| Neckties | — | | 1.8 |
| Rubbers | — | Footwear | 1.9 |
| Street shoes | — | | 1.9 |
| Work shoes | — | | 1.9 |
| | | *B Apparel (1947–1964)* | |
| Women's apparel | — | Women's apparel | 99.4 |
| Bathrobes | 1947–1948, 1963–1964 | Underwear, nightwear, hosiery, and accessories | 3.9 |
| Brassieres | — | | 19.8 |
| Camisoles | 1947–1949, 1950–1952, 1963–1965 | | 2 |

**Table 2.1** (continued)

| Sears product | Years excluded | CPI products | Comparisons per year |
|---|---|---|---|
| Hosiery | — | | 13.2 |
| Panties | — | | 29.9 |
| Slips | 1947–1948 | | 9.5 |
| Jackets | 1947–1948 | Coats and jackets | 4.4 |
| Jeans | 1953–1954 | Separates and sportswear | 5.3 |
| Pants | — | | 5.9 |
| Skirts | 1947–1949 | | 2.4 |
| Dresses | 1948–1949, 1960–1961, 1963–1964 | Dresses | 3.1 |
| Men's apparel | | Men's apparel | 146.8 |
| Bathrobes | 1960–1961 | Furnishings and special clothing | 2.3 |
| Belts | — | | 5.8 |
| Coveralls | — | | 3.7 |
| Pajamas | 1947–1948 | | 3.4 |
| Shorts | 1947–1955 | | 1.4 |
| Socks | 1964–1965 | | 16.5 |
| Swimming trunks | 1947–1948, 1949–1950, 1953–1955 | | 2.4 |
| Undershirt | — | | 10.6 |
| Underwear | 1947–1948 | | 20.1 |
| Jeans | 1947–1948 | Dungarees, jeans, and trousers | 10.3 |
| Pants | — | | 12.4 |
| Dress shirts | — | Shirts | 11.1 |
| Shirts | — | | 13.4 |
| Blazers | 1962–1963 | Suits, sport coats, coats, and jackets | 1.8 |
| Jackets | — | | 10.7 |
| Rainwear | — | | 12.6 |
| Suits | 1947–1948, 1962–1964 | | 8.1 |

| Sears products | CPI products | Comparison per year |
|---|---|---|
| | *C Apparel 1965–1993* | |
| Women's apparel | Women's apparel | 57.9 |
| Bathrobes | Underwear, nightwear, hosiery, and accessories | 3.3 |
| Bras | | 9.3 |
| Camisoles | | 2.4 |
| Hosiery | | 7.7 |
| Panties | | 9.3 |
| Slips | | 6.1 |
| Jackets | Coats and jackets | 4.7 |
| Jeans | Separates and sportswear | 4.4 |
| Pants | | 4.1 |

*(continued)*

**Table 2.1** (continued)

| Sears products | CPI products | Comparison per year |
|---|---|---|
| Skirts | | 3.4 |
| Dresses | Dresses | 3.3 |
| Men's apparel | Men's apparel | 93.3 |
| Bathrobes | Furnishings and special clothing | 3.1 |
| Belts | | 4.8 |
| Coveralls | | 5.2 |
| Pajamas | | 5 |
| Jumpsuits | | 3.2 |
| Shorts | | 3.1 |
| Socks | | 8.3 |
| Swimming trunks | | 2.4 |
| Undershirts | | 8.1 |
| Underwear | | 10.8 |
| Jeans | Dungarees, jeans, and trousers | 7.5 |
| Pants | | 5.7 |
| Dress shirts | Shirts | 4.4 |
| Shirts | | 7.8 |
| Blazers | Suits, sport coats, coats, and jackets | 3.7 |
| Jackets | | 6.8 |
| Rainwear | | 4.5 |

*Note:* Dashed cells in panels A and B indicate that no years were excluded.

description that might well have become obsolete. Extra models can be included that appear and disappear between major CPI revisions. Ideally, this approach should lead to the inclusion of more models per product than in the CPI.

The matched-model indexes were developed by comparing all identical models in every pair of adjacent years. For a comparison to be made, the adjacent-year observations had to have the same serial number (subject to the following qualifications), the photo or drawing depicting the model must have been identical, and the description of the model must have been identical. Identical catalog numbers do not always ensure that two models are identical, just as dissimilar catalog numbers do not necessarily signify differences between models. Therefore the determining criterion for the direct comparison of models relied heavily on the match of product descriptions. Nevertheless, the model numbers are very useful for quickly spotting models that are likely to be identical or for spotting changes in characteristics in the set of models available for two adjacent years.

Figure 2.1 presents a schematic diagram of the method of matching models for the important example of women's dresses. This method was carried out not only for women's dresses but for all apparel types in developing all the indexes reported in tables 2.2 through 2.7. The criteria for matching are very tight and the resulting MM price indexes are surely representative of apparel "models" that have almost exactly the same quality. The defect of the

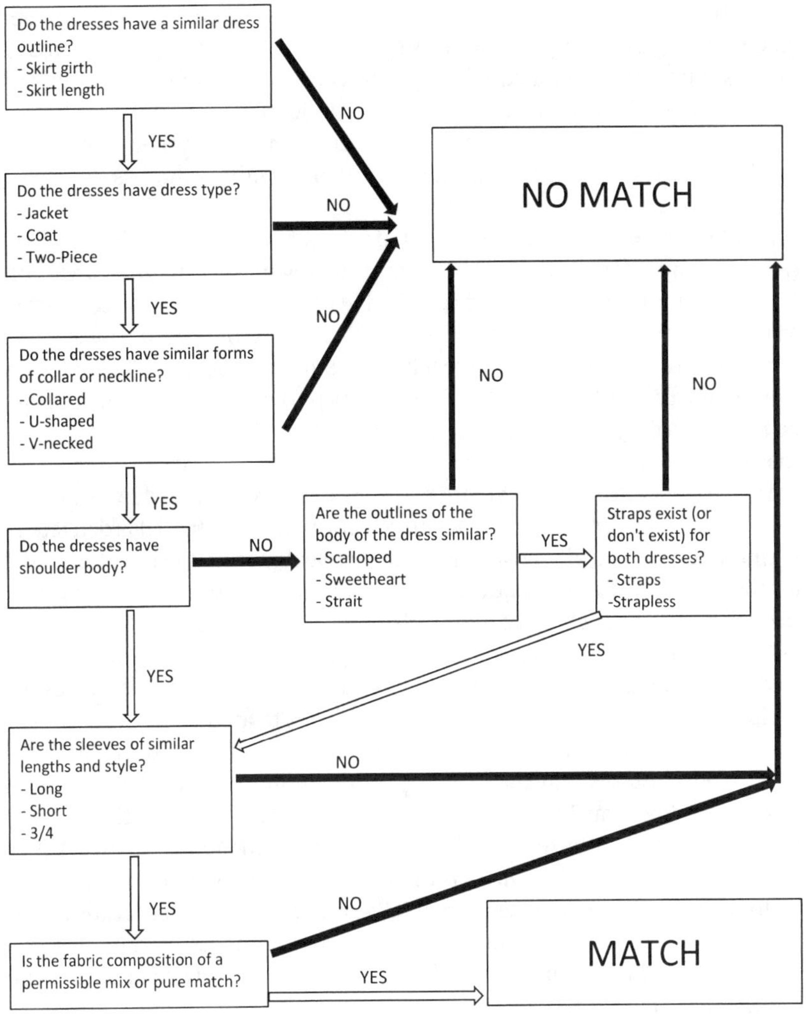


**Fig. 2.1 Matched-model flowchart**

MM method is that these tight criteria often exclude models that change in minor ways but for which prices increase much more than for the models that are matched. The irony of the MM method is that it can control completely for changes in quality without providing an accurate measure of changes in price, a phenomenon that only becomes evident when comparing the MM indexes with hedonic indexes for the same products.

The lowest-level observation for the catalog matched-model price indexes is the log change in price between two adjacent years for a given model that has been determined by the process previously described to have remained identical across the two years. Then these price changes are aggregated. Log price changes (e.g., for an identical dress in two adjacent years) are aggregated into log product price changes for a product category (e.g., "women's dresses") by applying an equal weight to each model in any given pair of adjacent years. The absence of model-by-model sales data necessitates the use of equal weights for each model of a given product. Some response to market sales is incorporated to the extent that the mix of models that Sears carries for a given product responds to the relative volume of sales.

Product price changes are aggregated into subgroup price indexes, where the subgroup refers to the lowest level of aggregation available in the CPI. Equal weights are applied to each product in forming subgroup price indexes. Then subgroup price indexes are aggregated into groups and totals, using the appropriate CPI weights for each subgroup. The indexes created in this chapter have the advantage that they are open to public inspection and can be reproduced by anyone with access to a library that holds back issues of the Sears catalog. As stated previously, the catalog indexes are subject to the same problem as any MM index, including those compiled by BLS. Any price change that occurs upon the introduction of a new model is deleted. If manufacturers typically postpone price increases during the life of a model for the occasion of a new model introduction, then deletion causes the exclusion of major price changes and leads to a downward secular bias in price indexes. If, on the other hand, quality improvements in new models tend to be introduced with no change in price, the deletion technique causes the exclusion of reductions in "true price" and leads to an upward secular bias. We learn subsequently in the comparisons of the hedonic and MM indexes for women's dresses that the former phenomenon dominates and causes a significant downward bias. As we will point out in discussing the hedonic index for women's dresses, a striking aspect of the MM indexes is that they are based on *so few observations.* In contrast, for many pairs of years the hedonic sample size is more than 300, or more than 150 observations per year for just a single product. This reflects the tightness of the matching criterion used in developing the MM indexes; that is, how hard it is to find exactly the same item in the catalogs for two successive years.

The new MM price indexes for apparel cover thirty-nine types of women's, men's, girls', and boys' apparel over part or all of the period 1914 to 1993, covering the years from the beginning of the CPI in 1914 to the date when Sears discontinued publication of its general catalog in 1993. Details on the types of apparel are shown separately for 1914 to 1947, 1947 to 1965, and 1965 to 1993 in table 2.1. The sum of matched-model comparisons in these tables is 10,385, an average of fifty-two per year during 1914 to 1947 (for a total of 1,719), an average of 146 per year during 1947 to 1965 (for a total of 4,432), and 151 per year during 1965 to 1993 (for a total of 4,234).

### 2.4.2 Matched-Model Results, 1914 to 1993

Separate catalog MM price indexes and comparisons with the CPI are displayed in tables 2.2 and 2.3 for women's and men's apparel; the

Table 2.2 **Matched-model apparel price indexes (1958 = 100), 1914–1993 (Women's Apparel)**

| Year | Sears | CPI | Sears/CPI | Observations |
|---|---|---|---|---|
| 1914 | 75.8 | 38.3 | 1.98 | 27 |
| 1915 | 79.0 | 39.0 | 2.02 | 30 |
| 1916 | 116.1 | 42.9 | 2.70 | 28 |
| 1917 | 133.7 | 51.4 | 2.60 | 28 |
| 1918 | 167.3 | 69.7 | 2.40 | 30 |
| 1919 | 214.9 | 92.3 | 2.33 | 31 |
| 1920 | 283.0 | 109.9 | 2.58 | 30 |
| 1921 | 179.4 | 84.7 | 2.12 | 28 |
| 1922 | 152.0 | 68.8 | 2.21 | 27 |
| 1923 | 140.9 | 69.2 | 2.04 | 28 |
| 1924 | 137.6 | 68.3 | 2.01 | 23 |
| 1925 | 134.4 | 67.1 | 2.00 | 31 |
| 1926 | 129.9 | 66.1 | 1.97 | 31 |
| 1927 | 121.9 | 64.6 | 1.89 | 29 |
| 1928 | 116.1 | 63.7 | 1.82 | 31 |
| 1929 | 109.3 | 63.0 | 1.73 | 28 |
| 1930 | 109.1 | 61.7 | 1.77 | 30 |
| 1931 | 101.5 | 56.0 | 1.81 | 27 |
| 1932 | 82.7 | 49.7 | 1.66 | 30 |
| 1933 | 79.2 | 47.9 | 1.66 | 28 |
| 1934 | 93.9 | 52.5 | 1.79 | 28 |
| 1935 | 74.9 | 53.0 | 1.41 | 26 |
| 1936 | 77.5 | 53.7 | 1.44 | 25 |
| 1937 | 77.2 | 56.2 | 1.37 | 26 |
| 1938 | 75.6 | 55.9 | 1.35 | 24 |
| 1939 | 75.8 | 55.2 | 1.37 | 23 |
| 1940 | 80.8 | 55.5 | 1.46 | 26 |
| 1941 | 83.0 | 58.1 | 1.43 | 27 |
| 1942 | 95.8 | 67.1 | 1.43 | 24 |
| 1943 | 97.2 | 66.6 | 1.46 | 26 |
| 1944 | 107.5 | 75.5 | 1.43 | 22 |
| 1945 | 108.9 | 79.6 | 1.37 | 26 |
| 1946 | 117.9 | 85.5 | 1.38 | 23 |
| 1947 | 131.9 | 99.0 | 1.33 | 23 |
| 1948 | 126.7 | 104.9 | 1.21 | 57 |
| 1949 | 125.7 | 99.1 | 1.27 | 85 |
| 1950 | 117.3 | 95.7 | 1.22 | 83 |
| 1951 | 126.0 | 103.1 | 1.22 | 95 |
| 1952 | 122.6 | 101.9 | 1.20 | 90 |
| 1953 | 104.8 | 100.7 | 1.04 | 89 |
| 1954 | 107.5 | 99.8 | 1.08 | 114 |
| 1955 | 103.5 | 99.0 | 1.05 | 106 |
| 1956 | 103.8 | 99.7 | 1.04 | 101 |
| 1957 | 100.0 | 100.2 | 1.00 | 109 |
| 1958 | 100.0 | 100.0 | 1.00 | 127 |
| 1959 | 99.1 | 100.5 | 0.99 | 135 |
| 1960 | 99.9 | 101.0 | 0.99 | 118 |
| 1961 | 98.3 | 101.4 | 0.97 | 142 |

(*continued*)

**Table 2.2** (continued)

| Year | Sears | CPI | Sears/CPI | Observations |
|---|---|---|---|---|
| 1962 | 98.5 | 101.2 | 0.97 | 79 |
| 1963 | 95.5 | 102.0 | 0.94 | 101 |
| 1964 | 93.8 | 102.6 | 0.91 | 82 |
| 1965 | 94.9 | 103.4 | 0.92 | 91 |
| 1966 | 95.2 | 105.5 | 0.90 | 100 |
| 1967 | 100.6 | 110.2 | 0.91 | 89 |
| 1968 | 103.2 | 116.9 | 0.88 | 87 |
| 1969 | 106.1 | 123.2 | 0.86 | 88 |
| 1970 | 106.5 | 127.8 | 0.83 | 91 |
| 1971 | 106.7 | 132.5 | 0.80 | 58 |
| 1972 | 107.3 | 135.6 | 0.79 | 58 |
| 1973 | 110.4 | 140.2 | 0.79 | 46 |
| 1974 | 119.3 | 148.7 | 0.80 | 47 |
| 1975 | 124.4 | 152.3 | 0.82 | 47 |
| 1976 | 116.3 | 156.6 | 0.74 | 48 |
| 1977 | 125.0 | 161.3 | 0.77 | 42 |
| 1978 | 131.2 | 164.6 | 0.80 | 61 |
| 1979 | 139.9 | 167.5 | 0.84 | 43 |
| 1980 | 145.1 | 170.4 | 0.85 | 44 |
| 1981 | 155.7 | 172.6 | 0.90 | 50 |
| 1982 | 169.5 | 174.4 | 0.97 | 39 |
| 1983 | 179.8 | 177.7 | 1.01 | 48 |
| 1984 | 187.5 | 180.1 | 1.04 | 59 |
| 1985 | 195.1 | 186.9 | 1.04 | 72 |
| 1986 | 193.5 | 185.3 | 1.04 | 77 |
| 1987 | 195.8 | 196.8 | 1.00 | 32 |
| 1988 | 199.0 | 204.6 | 0.97 | 32 |
| 1990 | 180.6 | 218.1 | 0.83 | 37 |
| 1991 | 172.3 | 226.4 | 0.76 | 34 |
| 1992 | 185.2 | 230.8 | 0.80 | 44 |
| 1993 | 187.2 | 235.4 | 0.80 | |

comparison for each is with the total CPI apparel index before 1935, since the CPI began to break out separate aggregates for women's and men's apparel only in that year. Tables 2.4 and 2.5 exhibit results in the same format for girls' and boys' apparel for the much shorter period 1978 to 1993. Table 2.6 provides the most important results of the research—the comparison of the catalog MM and CPI indexes for all apparel—and table 2.7 breaks out the Sears/CPI ratios separately for women's, men's, and all apparel. Graphical displays of the results are also presented, with figures 2.2 and 2.3 corresponding to tables 2.2 and 2.3; figure 2.4 corresponding to table 2.6, and figure 2.5 corresponding to table 2.7.

Table 2.8 summarizes the results by providing growth rates of the Sears catalog indexes, corresponding CPI, and the Sears/CPI ratios for four

Table 2.3 **Matched-model apparel price indexes (1958 = 100), 1914–1993 (Men's Apparel)**

| Year | Sears | CPI | Sears/CPI | Observations |
|---|---|---|---|---|
| 1914 | 58.27338129 | 32.2519084 | 1.81 | 28 |
| 1915 | 58.27338129 | 33.01526718 | 1.77 | 27 |
| 1916 | 69.78417266 | 36.25954198 | 1.92 | 26 |
| 1917 | 78.89688249 | 43.51145038 | 1.81 | 29 |
| 1918 | 102.3980815 | 58.77862595 | 1.74 | 26 |
| 1919 | 128.2973621 | 78.05343511 | 1.64 | 25 |
| 1920 | 152.9976019 | 92.9389313 | 1.65 | 23 |
| 1921 | 113.4292566 | 71.5648855 | 1.58 | 21 |
| 1922 | 109.8321343 | 58.20610687 | 1.89 | 26 |
| 1923 | 99.28057554 | 58.39694656 | 1.70 | 28 |
| 1924 | 102.1582734 | 57.82442748 | 1.77 | 27 |
| 1925 | 98.32134293 | 56.67938931 | 1.73 | 28 |
| 1926 | 94.48441247 | 55.72519084 | 1.70 | 26 |
| 1927 | 89.6882494 | 54.58015267 | 1.64 | 25 |
| 1928 | 96.16306954 | 53.81679389 | 1.79 | 22 |
| 1929 | 94.48441247 | 53.24427481 | 1.77 | 27 |
| 1930 | 96.882494 | 52.09923664 | 1.86 | 30 |
| 1931 | 88.96882494 | 47.32824427 | 1.88 | 27 |
| 1932 | 69.78417266 | 41.98473282 | 1.66 | 29 |
| 1933 | 67.14628297 | 40.45801527 | 1.66 | 30 |
| 1934 | 78.65707434 | 44.46564885 | 1.77 | 30 |
| 1935 | 56.59472422 | 44.84732824 | 1.26 | 27 |
| 1936 | 58.7529976 | 45.41984733 | 1.29 | 27 |
| 1937 | 59.95203837 | 47.90076336 | 1.25 | 28 |
| 1938 | 56.11510791 | 47.70992366 | 1.18 | 28 |
| 1939 | 56.59472422 | 46.75572519 | 1.21 | 29 |
| 1940 | 65.94724221 | 47.70992366 | 1.38 | 29 |
| 1941 | 61.39088729 | 50 | 1.23 | 26 |
| 1942 | 70.50359712 | 58.20610687 | 1.21 | 22 |
| 1943 | 74.34052758 | 61.06870229 | 1.22 | 25 |
| 1944 | 75.29976019 | 63.93129771 | 1.18 | 24 |
| 1945 | 75.29976019 | 66.60305344 | 1.13 | 21 |
| 1946 | 78.41726619 | 75.57251908 | 1.04 | 22 |
| 1947 | 103.5971223 | 89.69465649 | 1.15 | 52 |
| 1948 | 100.2398082 | 94.65648855 | 1.06 | 95 |
| 1949 | 99.28057554 | 91.98473282 | 1.08 | 95 |
| 1950 | 96.16306954 | 91.60305344 | 1.05 | 118 |
| 1951 | 106.7146283 | 99.04580153 | 1.08 | 126 |
| 1952 | 103.3573141 | 99.61832061 | 1.04 | 121 |
| 1953 | 102.6378897 | 98.85496183 | 1.04 | 132 |
| 1954 | 102.6378897 | 98.28244275 | 1.04 | 130 |
| 1955 | 97.60191847 | 97.13740458 | 1.00 | 131 |
| 1956 | 98.56115108 | 98.85496183 | 1.00 | 141 |
| 1957 | 98.32134293 | 100.3816794 | 0.98 | 137 |
| 1958 | 100 | 100 | 1.00 | 138 |
| 1959 | 103.5971223 | 99.80916031 | 1.04 | 133 |
| 1960 | 105.2757794 | 101.7175573 | 1.03 | 141 |
| 1961 | 105.9952038 | 102.8625954 | 1.03 | 127 |
| 1962 | 108.1534772 | 103.4351145 | 1.05 | 121 |
| 1963 | 108.6330935 | 104.7709924 | 1.04 | 128 |

(*continued*)

**Table 2.3** (continued)

| Year | Sears | CPI | Sears/CPI | Observations |
|---|---|---|---|---|
| 1964 | 108.8729017 | 106.2977099 | 1.02 | 126 |
| 1965 | 107.6738609 | 107.4427481 | 1.00 | 135 |
| 1966 | 110.0719424 | 110.3053435 | 1.00 | 177 |
| 1967 | 116.7865707 | 114.5038168 | 1.02 | 152 |
| 1968 | 123.501199 | 120.8015267 | 1.02 | 118 |
| 1969 | 131.8944844 | 128.6259542 | 1.03 | 128 |
| 1970 | 135.0119904 | 133.9694656 | 1.01 | 118 |
| 1971 | 139.8081535 | 137.7862595 | 1.01 | 102 |
| 1972 | 144.1247002 | 139.5038168 | 1.03 | 90 |
| 1973 | 153.4772182 | 144.6564885 | 1.06 | 77 |
| 1974 | 168.5851319 | 156.1068702 | 1.08 | 73 |
| 1975 | 191.6067146 | 162.7862595 | 1.18 | 69 |
| 1976 | 188.0095923 | 168.3206107 | 1.12 | 82 |
| 1977 | 208.8729017 | 176.1450382 | 1.19 | 88 |
| 1978 | 215.58753 | 179.9618321 | 1.20 | 92 |
| 1979 | 221.3429257 | 182.6335878 | 1.21 | 78 |
| 1980 | 239.8081535 | 190.8396947 | 1.26 | 86 |
| 1981 | 263.0695444 | 201.1450382 | 1.31 | 86 |
| 1982 | 289.4484412 | 208.9694656 | 1.39 | 82 |
| 1983 | 302.8776978 | 214.1221374 | 1.41 | 62 |
| 1984 | 317.0263789 | 218.129771 | 1.45 | 91 |
| 1985 | 326.1390887 | 224.6183206 | 1.45 | 110 |
| 1986 | 322.7817746 | 227.2900763 | 1.42 | 106 |
| 1987 | 315.3477218 | 235.8778626 | 1.34 | 51 |
| 1988 | 322.3021583 | 245.610687 | 1.31 | 60 |
| 1990 | 341.0071942 | 262.9770992 | 1.30 | 70 |
| 1991 | 341.0071942 | 271.3740458 | 1.26 | 63 |
| 1992 | 372.6618705 | 275.9541985 | 1.35 | 72 |
| 1993 | 367.3860911 | 277.480916 | 1.32 | |

**Table 2.4** **Matched-model apparel price indexes (1980 = 100), 1978–1993 (Girl's Apparel)**

| Year | Sears | CPI | Sears/CPI | Observations |
|---|---|---|---|---|
| 1978 | 88.8 | 95.3 | 0.93 | 21 |
| 1979 | 95.9 | 96.6 | 0.99 | 22 |
| 1980 | 100.0 | 100.0 | 1.00 | 24 |
| 1981 | 107.5 | 103.6 | 1.04 | 18 |
| 1982 | 116.5 | 103.6 | 1.12 | 18 |
| 1983 | 129.4 | 104.6 | 1.24 | 19 |
| 1984 | 134.3 | 104.6 | 1.28 | 21 |
| 1985 | 141.8 | 107.6 | 1.32 | 22 |
| 1986 | 145.2 | 106.4 | 1.37 | 21 |
| 1987 | 141.2 | 112.2 | 1.26 | 12 |
| 1988 | 151.7 | 117.4 | 1.29 | 6 |
| 1990 | 126.7 | 125.9 | 1.01 | 14 |
| 1991 | 139.0 | 133.3 | 1.04 | 16 |
| 1992 | 153.2 | 138.0 | 1.11 | 15 |
| 1993 | 157.9 | 137.5 | 1.15 | |

**Table 2.5** **Matched-model apparel price indexes (1980 = 100), 1978–1993 (Boy's Apparel)**

| Year | Sears | CPI | Sears/CPI | Observations |
|---|---|---|---|---|
| 1978 | 87.1 | 90.1 | 0.97 | 29 |
| 1979 | 95.2 | 94.2 | 1.01 | 30 |
| 1980 | 100.0 | 100.0 | 1.00 | 27 |
| 1981 | 106.8 | 105.0 | 1.02 | 29 |
| 1982 | 116.8 | 108.1 | 1.08 | 25 |
| 1983 | 120.1 | 112.0 | 1.07 | 19 |
| 1984 | 121.5 | 113.9 | 1.07 | 29 |
| 1985 | 123.3 | 116.7 | 1.06 | 28 |
| 1986 | 125.1 | 117.1 | 1.07 | 27 |
| 1987 | 127.0 | 115.7 | 1.10 | 8 |
| 1988 | 127.8 | 119.2 | 1.07 | 2 |
| 1990 | 128.3 | 121.4 | 1.06 | 20 |
| 1991 | 131.8 | 125.4 | 1.05 | 17 |
| 1992 | 140.9 | 129.0 | 1.09 | 19 |
| 1993 | 138.5 | 131.0 | 1.06 | |

**Table 2.6** **Matched-model apparel price indexes (1958 = 100), 1914–1993 (All Apparel)**

| Year | Sears | CPI | Sears/CPI | Observations |
|---|---|---|---|---|
| 1914 | 66.5 | 30.6 | 2.17 | 55 |
| 1915 | 68.0 | 31.2 | 2.18 | 57 |
| 1916 | 90.9 | 34.3 | 2.65 | 54 |
| 1917 | 103.8 | 41.2 | 2.52 | 57 |
| 1918 | 132.0 | 55.7 | 2.37 | 56 |
| 1919 | 167.6 | 73.8 | 2.27 | 56 |
| 1920 | 212.0 | 87.9 | 2.41 | 53 |
| 1921 | 143.6 | 67.7 | 2.12 | 49 |
| 1922 | 129.5 | 55.1 | 2.35 | 53 |
| 1923 | 118.5 | 55.3 | 2.14 | 56 |
| 1924 | 118.7 | 54.7 | 2.17 | 50 |
| 1925 | 104.5 | 53.6 | 1.95 | 59 |
| 1926 | 110.9 | 52.9 | 2.10 | 57 |
| 1927 | 104.5 | 51.6 | 2.03 | 54 |
| 1928 | 105.6 | 51.0 | 2.07 | 53 |
| 1929 | 101.8 | 50.5 | 2.02 | 55 |
| 1930 | 102.9 | 49.4 | 2.09 | 60 |
| 1931 | 95.1 | 44.9 | 2.12 | 54 |
| 1932 | 76.2 | 39.9 | 1.91 | 59 |
| 1933 | 72.9 | 38.4 | 1.90 | 58 |
| 1934 | 86.0 | 42.1 | 2.04 | 58 |
| 1935 | 65.3 | 42.5 | 1.54 | 53 |
| 1936 | 67.6 | 42.9 | 1.58 | 52 |
| 1937 | 68.0 | 44.9 | 1.51 | 54 |
| 1938 | 65.3 | 44.7 | 1.46 | 52 |
| 1939 | 65.5 | 44.2 | 1.48 | 52 |
| 1940 | 73.1 | 44.5 | 1.64 | 55 |
| 1941 | 71.3 | 46.6 | 1.53 | 53 |

(*continued*)

**Table 2.6** (continued)

| Year | Sears | CPI | Sears/CPI | Observations |
|---|---|---|---|---|
| 1942 | 82.2 | 54.5 | 1.51 | 46 |
| 1943 | 85.1 | 56.8 | 1.50 | 51 |
| 1944 | 90.2 | 60.9 | 1.48 | 46 |
| 1945 | 90.7 | 64.0 | 1.42 | 47 |
| 1946 | 96.4 | 70.1 | 1.37 | 45 |
| 1947 | 116.9 | 95.0 | 1.23 | 75 |
| 1948 | 112.4 | 100.7 | 1.12 | 152 |
| 1949 | 111.6 | 95.9 | 1.16 | 180 |
| 1950 | 106.2 | 94.2 | 1.13 | 201 |
| 1951 | 116.4 | 101.7 | 1.14 | 221 |
| 1952 | 112.7 | 100.9 | 1.12 | 211 |
| 1953 | 104.0 | 100.0 | 1.04 | 221 |
| 1954 | 105.3 | 99.1 | 1.06 | 244 |
| 1955 | 100.5 | 98.3 | 1.02 | 237 |
| 1956 | 100.9 | 99.3 | 1.02 | 242 |
| 1957 | 98.9 | 100.2 | 0.99 | 246 |
| 1958 | 100.0 | 100.0 | 1.00 | 265 |
| 1959 | 101.1 | 100.2 | 1.01 | 268 |
| 1960 | 102.9 | 101.1 | 1.02 | 259 |
| 1961 | 103.5 | 101.7 | 1.02 | 269 |
| 1962 | 104.7 | 101.9 | 1.03 | 200 |
| 1963 | 103.6 | 103.0 | 1.01 | 229 |
| 1964 | 103.1 | 103.7 | 0.99 | 208 |
| 1965 | 103.1 | 104.5 | 0.99 | 226 |
| 1966 | 104.4 | 106.3 | 0.98 | 277 |
| 1967 | 110.5 | 110.6 | 1.00 | 241 |
| 1968 | 115.5 | 116.9 | 0.99 | 205 |
| 1969 | 121.6 | 123.7 | 0.98 | 216 |
| 1970 | 123.5 | 128.8 | 0.96 | 209 |
| 1971 | 126.2 | 132.7 | 0.95 | 160 |
| 1972 | 128.9 | 135.3 | 0.95 | 148 |
| 1973 | 135.1 | 139.9 | 0.97 | 123 |
| 1974 | 147.6 | 150.1 | 0.98 | 120 |
| 1975 | 162.5 | 155.7 | 1.04 | 116 |
| 1976 | 156.7 | 160.1 | 0.98 | 130 |
| 1977 | 156.7 | 166.6 | 0.94 | 130 |
| 1978 | 162.7 | 170.5 | 0.95 | 153 |
| 1979 | 171.8 | 175.3 | 0.98 | 121 |
| 1980 | 181.8 | 185.5 | 0.98 | 130 |
| 1981 | 196.9 | 192.6 | 1.02 | 136 |
| 1982 | 215.3 | 195.7 | 1.10 | 121 |
| 1983 | 227.6 | 199.8 | 1.14 | 110 |
| 1984 | 236.4 | 202.6 | 1.17 | 150 |
| 1985 | 247.6 | 208.2 | 1.19 | 182 |
| 1986 | 246.5 | 208.9 | 1.18 | 183 |
| 1987 | 244.5 | 218.6 | 1.12 | 83 |
| 1988 | 250.7 | 228.2 | 1.10 | 92 |
| 1990 | 237.8 | 244.9 | 0.97 | 107 |
| 1991 | 249.5 | 254.2 | 0.98 | 97 |
| 1992 | 266.7 | 259.7 | 1.03 | 116 |
| 1993 | 268.4 | 263.1 | 1.02 | |

*Note:* n.a. = not available.

Table 2.7 Comparison of Sears/CPI ratio (1958 = 1.0)

| Year | Women's Apparel | Men's Apparel | All Apparel |
|---|---|---|---|
| 1914 | 1.98 | 1.81 | 2.17 |
| 1915 | 2.02 | 1.77 | 2.18 |
| 1916 | 2.70 | 1.92 | 2.65 |
| 1917 | 2.60 | 1.81 | 2.52 |
| 1918 | 2.40 | 1.74 | 2.37 |
| 1919 | 2.33 | 1.64 | 2.27 |
| 1920 | 2.58 | 1.65 | 2.41 |
| 1921 | 2.12 | 1.58 | 2.12 |
| 1922 | 2.21 | 1.89 | 2.35 |
| 1923 | 2.04 | 1.70 | 2.14 |
| 1924 | 2.01 | 1.77 | 2.17 |
| 1925 | 2.00 | 1.73 | 1.95 |
| 1926 | 1.97 | 1.70 | 2.10 |
| 1927 | 1.89 | 1.64 | 2.03 |
| 1928 | 1.82 | 1.79 | 2.07 |
| 1929 | 1.73 | 1.77 | 2.02 |
| 1930 | 1.77 | 1.86 | 2.09 |
| 1931 | 1.81 | 1.88 | 2.12 |
| 1932 | 1.66 | 1.66 | 1.91 |
| 1933 | 1.66 | 1.66 | 1.90 |
| 1934 | 1.79 | 1.77 | 2.04 |
| 1935 | 1.41 | 1.26 | 1.54 |
| 1936 | 1.44 | 1.29 | 1.58 |
| 1937 | 1.37 | 1.25 | 1.51 |
| 1938 | 1.35 | 1.18 | 1.46 |
| 1939 | 1.37 | 1.21 | 1.48 |
| 1940 | 1.46 | 1.38 | 1.64 |
| 1941 | 1.43 | 1.23 | 1.53 |
| 1942 | 1.43 | 1.21 | 1.51 |
| 1943 | 1.46 | 1.22 | 1.50 |
| 1944 | 1.43 | 1.18 | 1.48 |
| 1945 | 1.37 | 1.13 | 1.42 |
| 1946 | 1.38 | 1.04 | 1.37 |
| 1947 | 1.33 | 1.15 | 1.23 |
| 1948 | 1.21 | 1.06 | 1.12 |
| 1949 | 1.27 | 1.08 | 1.16 |
| 1950 | 1.22 | 1.05 | 1.13 |
| 1951 | 1.22 | 1.08 | 1.14 |
| 1952 | 1.20 | 1.04 | 1.12 |
| 1953 | 1.04 | 1.04 | 1.04 |
| 1954 | 1.08 | 1.04 | 1.06 |
| 1955 | 1.05 | 1.00 | 1.02 |
| 1956 | 1.04 | 1.00 | 1.02 |
| 1957 | 1.00 | 0.98 | 0.99 |
| 1958 | 1.00 | 1.00 | 1.00 |
| 1959 | 0.99 | 1.04 | 1.01 |
| 1960 | 0.99 | 1.03 | 1.02 |
| 1961 | 0.97 | 1.03 | 1.02 |
| 1962 | 0.97 | 1.05 | 1.03 |
| 1963 | 0.94 | 1.04 | 1.01 |
| 1964 | 0.91 | 1.02 | 0.99 |
| 1965 | 0.92 | 1.00 | 0.99 |

(*continued*)

**Table 2.7** (continued)

| Year | Women's apparel | Men's apparel | All apparel |
|---|---|---|---|
| 1966 | 0.90 | 1.00 | 0.98 |
| 1967 | 0.91 | 1.02 | 1.00 |
| 1968 | 0.88 | 1.02 | 0.99 |
| 1969 | 0.86 | 1.03 | 0.98 |
| 1970 | 0.83 | 1.01 | 0.96 |
| 1971 | 0.80 | 1.01 | 0.95 |
| 1972 | 0.79 | 1.03 | 0.95 |
| 1973 | 0.79 | 1.06 | 0.97 |
| 1974 | 0.80 | 1.08 | 0.98 |
| 1975 | 0.82 | 1.18 | 1.04 |
| 1976 | 0.74 | 1.12 | 0.98 |
| 1977 | 0.77 | 1.19 | 0.94 |
| 1978 | 0.80 | 1.20 | 0.95 |
| 1979 | 0.84 | 1.21 | 0.98 |
| 1980 | 0.85 | 1.26 | 0.98 |
| 1981 | 0.90 | 1.31 | 1.02 |
| 1982 | 0.97 | 1.39 | 1.10 |
| 1983 | 1.01 | 1.41 | 1.14 |
| 1984 | 1.04 | 1.45 | 1.17 |
| 1985 | 1.04 | 1.45 | 1.19 |
| 1986 | 1.04 | 1.42 | 1.18 |
| 1987 | 1.00 | 1.34 | 1.12 |
| 1988 | 0.97 | 1.31 | 1.10 |
| 1990 | 0.83 | 1.30 | 0.97 |
| 1991 | 0.76 | 1.26 | 0.98 |
| 1992 | 0.80 | 1.35 | 1.03 |
| 1993 | 0.80 | 1.32 | 1.02 |

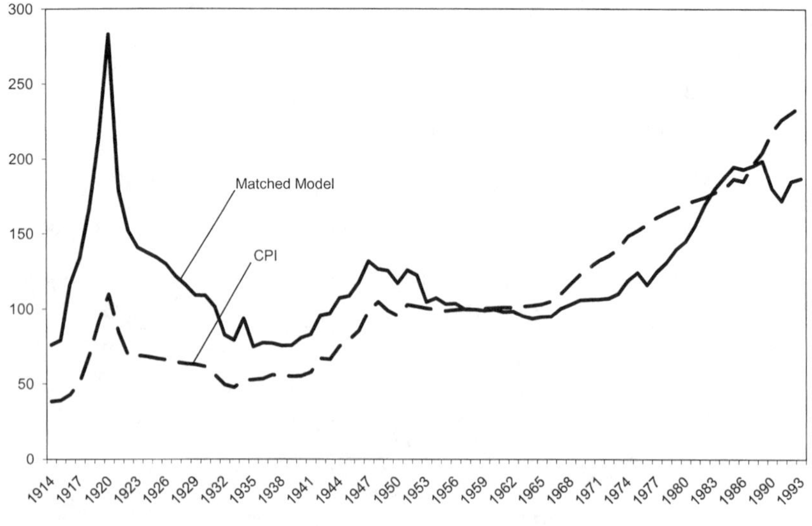


**Fig. 2.2 Sears matched-model index vs. CPI for women's apparel (1958 = 100), 1914–1993**

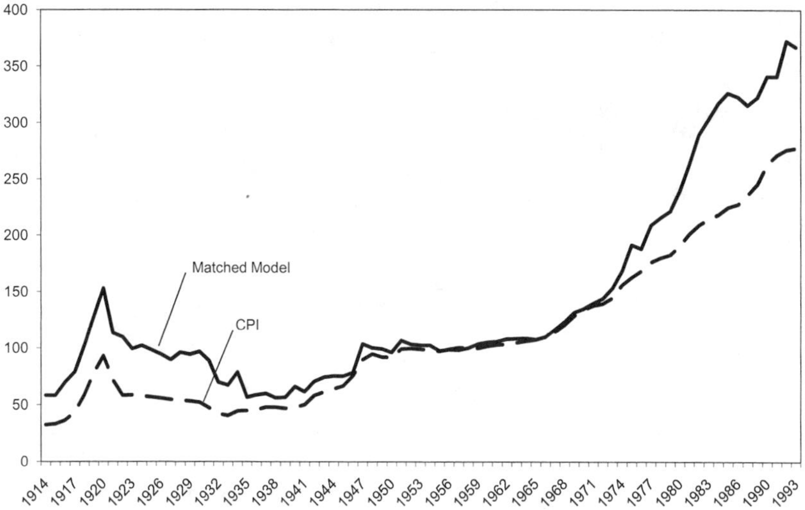


**Fig. 2.3 Sears matched-model index vs. CPI for men's apparel (1958 = 100), 1914–1993**

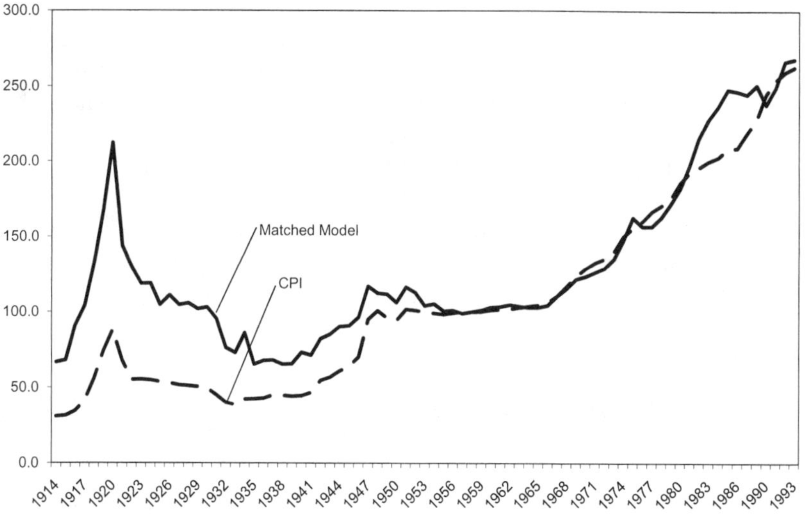


**Fig. 2.4 Sears matched-model index vs. CPI for all apparel (1958 = 100), 1914–1993**

selected subperiods of the 1914 to 1993 interval and for the entire interval as well.

As shown in table 2.8, for women's apparel the 1914 to 1947 annual growth rate of the Sears matched-model index is 1.68 percent per year, considerably slower than the CPI increase of 2.87 percent per year, implying growth rate of the Sears/CPI ratio of –1.19 percent per year. The difference is similar for

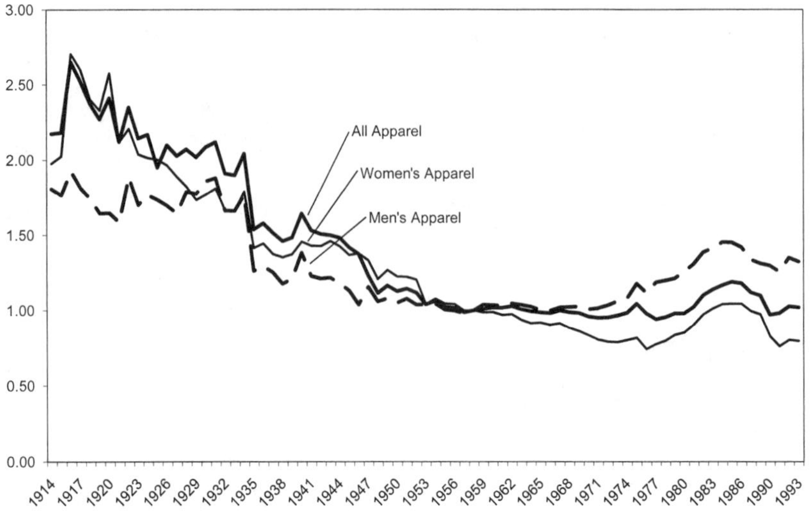


**Fig. 2.5 Ratio of Sears matched-model index to CPI for women's, men's and all apparel (1958 = 100), 1914–1993**

men's apparel, 1.74 percent per year for Sears versus 3.10 percent for the CPI, implying a growth rate of the Sears/CPI ratio of –1.36 percent per year.

A striking aspect of the results is that much of the decline in the Sears/CPI ratio occurs during a single pair of years, 1934 to 1935; this is particularly evident in figure 2.5, which plots the Sears/CPI ratios. The most obvious explanation would be a major mistake in transcribing the Sears prices, so we have double-checked and triple-checked the 1934 to 1935 comparisons. Here are some sample prices for this pair of years for particular clothing items classified as identical by our matched-model procedure.

| | *1934* | *1935* |
|---|---|---|
| Men's suits | 13.50 | 11.95 |
| Men's union suits | 0.79 | 0.59 |
| Men's work socks | 0.17 | 0.12 |
| Men's wool pants | 4.85 | 4.45 |
| Men's "Chieftan" overalls | 0.88 | 0.77 |
| Women's silk slips | 1.98 | 1.69 |
| Women's cotton hosiery | 0.33 | 0.25 |
| Women's washfast house dresses | 0.95 | 0.49 |
| Women's rayon gloves | 0.98 | 0.59 |
| Women's rayon pajamas | 1.00 | 0.59 |

It is possible that Sears changed its pricing policy relative to the rest of the marketplace in 1935, but it is also possible that the CPI missed a shift in the availability of discount outlets during the Great Depression—perhaps an early example of "outlet substitution bias."

**Table 2.8** **Growth rates of Sears matched-model (MM) indexes compared with the CPI, alternative intervals, 1914–1993**

| | 1914–1947 | 1947–1965 | 1965–1978 | 1978–1993 | 1914–1993 |
|---|---|---|---|---|---|
| Women's apparel | | | | | |
| Sears MM | 1.68 | –1.83 | 2.49 | 2.37 | 1.15 |
| CPI | 2.87 | 0.24 | 3.57 | 2.39 | 2.30 |
| Sears/CPI | –1.19 | –2.07 | –1.08 | –0.02 | –1.15 |
| Men's apparel | | | | | |
| Sears MM | 1.74 | 0.21 | 5.34 | 3.55 | 2.33 |
| CPI | 3.10 | 1.00 | 3.97 | 2.89 | 2.72 |
| Sears/CPI | –1.36 | –0.79 | 1.37 | 0.67 | –0.39 |
| All apparel | | | | | |
| Sears MM | 1.71 | –0.70 | 3.51 | 3.34 | 1.77 |
| CPI | 3.43 | 0.53 | 3.77 | 2.89 | 2.72 |
| Sears/CPI | –1.72 | –1.22 | –0.25 | 0.44 | –0.95 |

When we look more broadly at the full 1914 to 1993, we notice several interesting patterns. First, there is a consistent downward drift in the Sears/CPI ratio for women's apparel in all periods but the last, 1978 to 1993. Second, there is a distinct turnaround in the drift of the Sears/CPI ratio for men's apparel from negative over 1914 to 1965 to positive during 1965 to 1993, with a small overall negative drift over the entire period. Third, there is a consistent tendency for the inflation rate in women's apparel to be a smaller positive rate or larger negative rate than for men's apparel, and this difference is more pronounced for the Sears indexes than for the CPI. This finding is consistent with the view that matched-model indexes "link out" more quality change for women's apparel, which are subject to more frequent changes in styles. Averaging together women's and men's apparel for 1914 to 1993 with girls' and boys' apparel for 1978 to 1993, the Sears indexes increase less than the CPI during 1914 to 1978 and by more during 1978 to 1993, and the overall drift in the Sears/CPI ratio for the entire period is roughly –1.0 percent per year. Note in the bottom line of table 2.8 that the Sears/CPI drift shifts progressively from a large negative rate of –1.72 percent per year in 1914 to 1947, to smaller negative rates in 1947 to 1965 and 1965 to 1978, and finally to a positive drift in the final period 1978 to 1993. This is consistent with the hypothesis that in the early years Sears was an innovative low-price market leader, analogous to today's Wal-Mart, but gradually over the years lost its competitive edge and found its relative price position rising from the bottom toward the middle or upper-middle.

## 2.5 Hedonic Price Indexes for Women's Dresses

This section discusses the application of hedonic regression techniques to apparel. In this study we have chosen to do an intensive investigation of a single type of apparel, women's dresses, because the available data allows much larger sample sizes in the regressions than for any other apparel product. The choice of variables is limited to those provided in the catalogs, which differ from year to year. Women's dresses are complex products and many of their features are visible only in photos (e.g., decorative items, pockets, belts, etc.). Thus, the large data set used in this hedonic regression study was custom-built by several research assistants who examined the photos as well as the detailed specifications as published in the catalog to assign values to the quality characteristics entered into the regressions.[9]

### 2.5.1 Determination of Explanatory Variables and Their Mean Values

The list of variables is displayed in table 2.9. Of these, the most important is weight, which proxies the quality of fabric, amount of fabric, complexity of construction, presence of linings, and so forth, and would be expected to have a positive coefficient. In addition, several dummy variables are included to indicate the presence or absence of higher-quality "organic" fabrics, knit or woven fabrics, and other quality characteristics that should raise price and thus have a positive coefficient in the regressions, including the presence of lace, sequins, embroidery, belt, jacket, bow, tie, zipper, and the need for dry cleaning. There is also a dummy variable for imported dresses (when they are identified as such in the catalog), and no presumption whether the coefficient should be positive or negative.

The hedonic regression study for women's dresses is carried out for sixty of the seventy-nine possible pairs of adjacent years between 1914 and 1993. The exceptions are the years of rapid inflation during World War I and its aftermath (1915 to 1920 are excluded), the years of World War II price controls (1942 to 1945 are excluded), and the years when the catalog for unknown reasons temporarily suspended publication of weight data for each item (1929 to 1933). For a subset of fifteen of the included years table 2.10 displays the number of observations in that particular year, the average weight, and the percentage of dresses having the various quality attributes designated by the zero, one dummy variables.

The sample sizes for the hedonic study of women's dresses are much larger than the sample on which the matched-model indexes for dresses is based (only 0.9 matches during 1914 to 1947 and only 3.3 matches during 1965 to 1993). The number of observations shown in table 2.9 are as high as 183 per year for 1936 and as low as forty-two per year for 1980. The number of observations diminishes markedly after 1988, and for this reason the hedonic study terminates in 1988 rather than 1993.

Table 2.10 exhibits the mean values of price and weight through 1993 and of the other explanatory variables through 1988. The mean price jumps

9. I am particularly grateful to Jayun Kim for her understanding of the nuances of women's dresses and acknowledge that she designed the final form of the hedonic project, including the choice of the quality characteristics and their description.

**Table 2.9** **Characteristics of hedonic index dresses**

| Variable name | Coding | Description |
|---|---|---|
| LN weight | LN WT | The weight of a dress (in ounces), indicates the amount of fabric utilized to construct the dress and is a proxy for its overall quality. |
| Organic | ORG | Organic fabrics include wool, silk, linen, and cotton derivatives such as velvet. These type of fabrics are considered high grade material and contributes to the perceived quality of apparel. |
| Imported | IMP | Apparel that were imported from a foreign country and advertised as such, could add or subtract from perceived quality. |
| Lace/Sequins/ Embroidery | LSE | Manufacturing cost for items of apparel with either lace, sequins, or embroideries tend to be priced higher than those without these qualities. |
| Belt | BLT | Presence of a belt. |
| Two-Piece | 2-PC | Two-piece dresses require more fabric as well as sewing to produce. |
| Dry Clean | DRY | Indicates whether or not the apparel required dry cleaning or any other special care for laundering. |
| Jacket | JCK | Indicates the inclusion of a jacket or blazer, generally of heavier fabric and higher quality than the top of a two-piece dress (see "2PC" above). |
| Bow/Tie | BOW/TIE | Items of apparel with either a bow or a tie were considered to have extra trimmings and contributed to its cost. |
| KNIT or woven | KWV | Indicates that the fabric was knit or woven. |
| Zipper | ZIP | Indicates presence of a zipper. |

around from year to year but on average in 1993 was 13.3 times the average in 1914 ($63.52 versus $4.75). Recall that the ratio for the median price was 32.7, indicating that the mean of the 1914 distribution was skewed upward by relatively expensive dresses. The mean value of weight was by coincidence almost exactly the same in 1914 and 1993 at about 1.5 pounds, but there were "long waves" in the behavior of the mean weight. During the entire 1928 to 1948 period, weight was at 3.0 pounds or higher, and weight fell to as low as 0.9 pounds in 1983 to 1984. A ten-year moving average of the mean weight from the hedonic sample is displayed in figure 2.6. To the extent that weight is the most important explanatory variable and contributes positively to quality, then there was no appreciable change in quality between 1914 and 1993, and substantial fluctuations in quality in the intervening years.

For the other quality variables as summarized in table 2.10, a surprise is the lack of consistent trends. In the early years (1914 to 1930) Sears sold numerous elaborate dresses made of silk and/or velvet, and this shows up in the relatively high value of the "Organic" variable in table 2.10. Similarly,

**Table 2.10** **Percentage of dresses with various quality attributes**

| Year | Observations per year | Price | Weight | ORG | IMP | LSE | BLT | 2-PC | DRY | JCK | BOW/TIE | KWV | ZIP |
|---|---|---|---|---|---|---|---|---|---|---|---|---|---|
| 1914 | 60 | 4.0 | 18.8 | 15.0 | 1.7 | 73.3 | 23.3 | 5.0 | 0.0 | 1.7 | 51.7 | 1.7 | 0.0 |
| 1921 | 77 | 8.0 | 25.7 | 18.2 | 0.0 | 37.7 | 20.8 | 2.6 | 0.0 | 1.3 | 61.0 | 0.0 | 0.0 |
| 1926 | 71 | 8.3 | 26.0 | 46.5 | 4.2 | 33.8 | 11.3 | 11.3 | 0.0 | 0.0 | 80.3 | 1.4 | 0.0 |
| 1936 | 183 | 3.0 | 18.9 | 0.5 | 5.5 | 31.7 | 28.4 | 79.8 | 0.0 | 23.0 | 33.3 | 13.1 | 0.0 |
| 1941 | 148 | 3.1 | 20.0 | 2.0 | 0.0 | 23.0 | 6.8 | 16.9 | 23.0 | 18.9 | 14.9 | 32.4 | 11.5 |
| 1946 | 96 | 4.9 | 21.6 | 0.0 | 0.0 | 18.8 | 13.5 | 39.6 | 67.7 | 0.0 | 6.3 | 57.3 | 19.8 |
| 1950 | 157 | 6.1 | 23.6 | 0.6 | 0.0 | 10.8 | 21.0 | 8.9 | 66.9 | 10.2 | 4.5 | 61.1 | 31.8 |
| 1955 | 155 | 7.0 | 22.1 | 0.0 | 0.6 | 8.4 | 12.3 | 6.5 | 43.9 | 9.7 | 18.7 | 37.4 | 26.0 |
| 1960 | 150 | 9.5 | 17.9 | 5.3 | 6.0 | 21.3 | 10.7 | 5.3 | 60.7 | 6.7 | 10.7 | 43.3 | 0.0 |
| 1965 | 149 | 10.2 | 16.2 | 2.7 | 0.0 | 5.4 | 0.0 | 22.8 | 58.4 | 8.1 | 4.7 | 84.6 | 0.0 |
| 1970 | 97 | 13.9 | 21.7 | 1.0 | 1.0 | 6.2 | 13.4 | 9.3 | 53.6 | 8.2 | 12.4 | 97.9 | 0.0 |
| 1975 | 78 | 18.8 | 19.1 | 0.0 | 0.0 | 14.1 | 14.1 | 9.0 | 2.6 | 17.9 | 1.3 | 94.9 | 0.0 |
| 1980 | 42 | 20.8 | 14.8 | 2.4 | 0.0 | 0.0 | 21.4 | 14.3 | 0.0 | 19.0 | 7.1 | 90.5 | 0.0 |
| 1985 | 100 | 42.7 | 14.6 | 6.0 | 3.0 | 15.0 | 45.0 | 16.0 | 16.0 | 9.0 | 10.0 | 78.0 | 0.0 |
| 1988 | 80 | 49.5 | 30.0 | 6.3 | 7.5 | 28.8 | 47.5 | 15.0 | 16.3 | 10.0 | 7.5 | 15.0 | 0.0 |
| 1993 | n.a. | 63.5 | 22.2 | n.a. | n.a. | n.a. | n.a. | n.a. | n.a. | n.a. | n.a. | n.a. | n.a. |

*Note:* n.a. = not available.

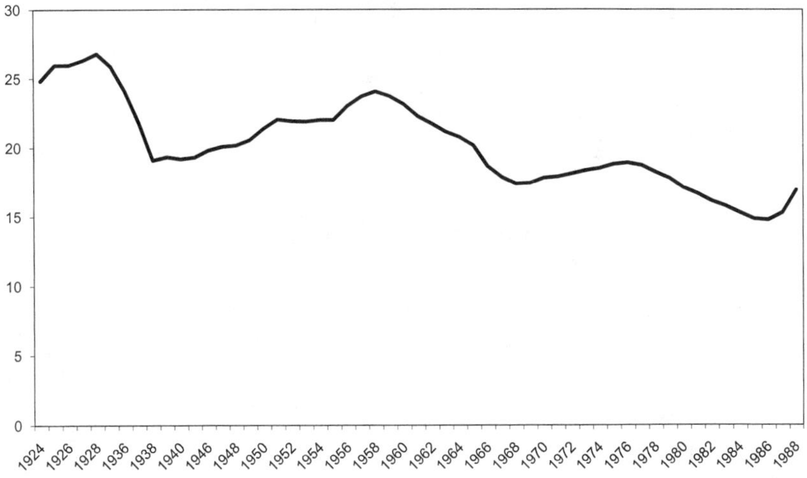


**Fig. 2.6 Ten-year backward moving average of the weight of dresses in the hedonic sample, 1914–1988**

through 1940 there were relatively large values for the "LSE" (lace, sequins, embroidery) variable. The mix of dresses then shifts in the postwar period to a very large fraction of knit and/or woven ("KWV"). A peculiar aspect of table 2.9 is that the "DRY" (dry cleaning) variable was at a high value between the late 1940s and mid-1970s and then dropped off to almost nothing. This could indicate a change in the catalog policy of explicitly listing the need for dry cleaning.

### 2.5.2 Hedonic Regression Results

There is always a trade-off between two extremes in running hedonic price regressions on a long time-series of data. One extreme would be to run separate regressions on every pair of years. This has the advantage of allowing the regression coefficients on characteristics like weight to shift as market and production conditions change, and the disadvantage that it minimizes sample size. The opposite extreme would be to run a single regression on all the data for all the years. This has the advantage of maximizing sample size and the disadvantage that it forces coefficients on characteristics to remain the same over a sample period of seventy-nine years.

In the case of apparel, there is the additional consideration that fabrics changed over time—silk disappeared and synthetics appeared, and so an approach that allowed for changing coefficients seemed essential. There were sufficient data to base the estimated coefficients on each successive pair of years, an abundance of data that allowed us to escape the many compromises required in a previous study of mainframe computers (Gordon 1989, 1990). Looking at the regression coefficients as displayed in table 2.11, those on

**Table 2.11 Coefficients from hedonic regressions of women's dresses**

| Years | YEAR | LN WT | ORG | IMP | LSE | BLT | 2-PC | DRY | JCK | BOW/ TIE | KWV | ZIP | Adjusted $R^2$ | SEE | OBS |
|---|---|---|---|---|---|---|---|---|---|---|---|---|---|---|---|
| 1914–1921 | 0.553** | 0.444 | 1.259** | 0.066 | 0.397** | 0.060 | –0.168 | n.a. | –0.057 | 0.198* | 0.296 | n.a. | 0.70 | 0.44 | 137 |
| 1921–1922 | –0.490** | 0.436* | 1.182** | 0.020 | 0.312** | –0.205* | 0.102 | n.a. | –0.315 | 0.039 | –0.361 | n.a. | 0.69 | 0.42 | 168 |
| 1922–1923 | 0.178** | 0.351 | 1.119** | 0.116 | 0.227** | –0.021 | –0.071 | n.a. | 0.001 | 0.127 | 0.100 | n.a. | 0.74 | 0.37 | 151 |
| 1923–1924 | 0.183** | 0.651** | 0.899** | 0.221** | –0.011 | 0.013 | 0.103 | n.a. | 0.231 | 0.067 | –0.082 | n.a. | 0.68 | 0.31 | 133 |
| 1924–1925 | –0.117 | 1.060** | 0.915** | 0.286** | 0.030 | 0.058 | 0.379* | n.a. | –0.032 | 0.003 | –0.032 | n.a. | 0.57 | 0.40 | 163 |
| 1925–1926 | 0.071 | 0.616* | 0.957** | 0.276* | 0.088 | 0.140 | 0.447** | n.a. | –0.223 | –0.121 | 0.112 | n.a. | 0.59 | 0.44 | 161 |
| 1926–1927 | –0.177* | 0.355* | 0.941** | –0.263 | 0.149 | 0.068 | 0.411** | n.a. | n.a. | 0.096 | 0.235 | n.a. | 0.57 | 0.38 | 153 |
| 1927–1928 | –0.168** | 0.545** | 0.963** | 0.145 | 0.123 | 0.102 | 0.357** | n.a. | 0.182 | n.a. | 0.247 | 0.228** | 0.58 | 0.40 | 178 |
| 1928–1934 | 0.209* | 1.116** | 0.679** | –0.030 | 0.172* | 0.167** | 0.275* | n.a. | n.a. | –0.383* | 0.261 | 0.188** | 0.70 | 0.46 | 192 |
| 1934–1935 | –0.301** | 1.118** | 0.490** | 0.034 | 0.188** | 0.238** | –0.003 | n.a. | –0.075 | 0.235** | 0.026 | 0.137 | 0.67 | 0.40 | 228 |
| 1935–1936 | 0.219** | 1.294** | 0.489** | n.a. | 0.031 | 0.027 | 0.092 | 0.055 | 0.004 | 0.206** | 0.186** | 0.084 | 0.70 | 0.34 | 316 |
| 1936–1937 | –0.022 | 1.481** | –0.036 | n.a. | –0.018 | 0.096 | –0.029 | –0.040 | 0.034 | 0.142** | 0.185** | 0.386 | 0.76 | 0.30 | 329 |
| 1937–1938 | 0.093** | 1.612** | –0.415* | n.a. | –0.077 | –0.184* | –0.002 | –0.058 | 0.089 | 0.105** | 0.148** | 0.233** | 0.79 | 0.27 | 299 |
| 1938–1939 | –0.127* | 1.570** | 0.103 | n.a. | –0.057 | 0.062 | –0.065 | –0.004 | 0.060 | 0.123* | 0.100 | 0.154** | 0.65 | 0.39 | 336 |
| 1939–1940 | 0.059 | 1.471** | 0.230* | n.a. | 0.148** | –0.006 | 0.123* | n.a. | 0.084 | 0.062 | 0.140** | 0.111* | 0.69 | 0.37 | 335 |
| 1940–1941 | –0.173** | 1.635** | 0.052 | n.a. | 0.248** | –0.042 | 0.100* | 0.033 | 0.089 | 0.002 | 0.145** | 0.095* | 0.83 | 0.28 | 300 |
| 1941–1946 | 0.354** | 1.600** | 0.117 | n.a. | 0.132** | 0.029 | 0.041 | 0.041 | 0.088 | 0.081 | 0.239** | 0.160** | 0.82 | 0.29 | 244 |
| 1946–1947 | 0.337** | 1.015** | n.a. | n.a. | 0.066 | 0.174** | 0.028 | 0.134* | n.a. | 0.189* | 0.261** | 0.253** | 0.70 | 0.26 | 174 |
| 1947–1948 | 0.199** | 1.104** | 0.887** | n.a. | 0.161** | 0.050 | 0.154** | 0.128* | 0.251** | 0.009 | 0.182** | 0.137** | 0.80 | 0.22 | 202 |
| 1948–1949 | –0.081** | 0.912** | 0.892** | n.a. | 0.029 | –0.025 | 0.155** | 0.203** | 0.179** | –0.061 | 0.184** | 0.062 | 0.81 | 0.20 | 289 |
| 1949–1950 | –0.310** | 0.974** | 0.731** | n.a. | 0.045 | 0.062 | 0.077 | 0.144** | 0.108* | –0.060 | 0.154** | 0.000 | 0.71 | 0.23 | 323 |
| 1950–1951 | 0.106** | 1.094** | 0.730** | n.a. | 0.119** | 0.083* | 0.001 | 0.111 | 0.090 | 0.054 | 0.071* | –0.023 | 0.67 | 0.26 | 292 |
| 1951–1952 | 0.098** | 0.669** | 0.759** | n.a. | 0.168** | 0.000 | 0.027 | 0.334** | 0.150** | 0.110 | 0.063 | –0.029 | 0.64 | 0.28 | 276 |
| 1952–1953 | –0.036 | 0.498** | 0.638** | n.a. | 0.159** | –0.020 | 0.135 | 0.372** | 0.189** | 0.166** | –0.006 | –0.135** | 0.59 | 0.30 | 286 |
| 1953–1954 | 0.101** | 0.540** | 0.421* | n.a. | 0.106 | –0.027 | 0.137* | 0.337** | 0.037 | 0.150** | –0.062 | –0.174** | 0.51 | 0.30 | 286 |
| 1954–1955 | –0.021 | 0.625** | 0.487* | 0.094 | 0.118* | –0.029 | –0.049 | 0.222** | –0.008 | 0.096* | –0.025 | –0.184** | 0.46 | 0.28 | 296 |
| 1955–1956 | –0.253** | 0.765** | 0.787** | 0.169 | 0.221** | 0.027 | 0.017 | 0.325** | 0.086 | 0.029 | 0.040 | 0.028 | 0.63 | 0.28 | 332 |
| 1956–1957 | 0.218** | 0.786** | 0.902** | n.a. | 0.321** | –0.144** | 0.043 | 0.365** | 0.099* | –0.015 | 0.039 | 0.063 | 0.70 | 0.29 | 367 |
| 1957–1958 | 0.103** | 0.760** | 0.792** | n.a. | 0.253** | –0.140** | –0.020 | 0.340** | 0.143* | 0.070 | 0.024 | 0.037 | 0.68 | 0.30 | 342 |

| | | | | | | | | | | | | | | | |
|---|---|---|---|---|---|---|---|---|---|---|---|---|---|---|---|
| 1958–1959 | 0.186** | 0.829** | 0.672** | n.a. | 0.153** | 0.017 | 0.001 | 0.305** | 0.197** | 0.038 | –0.050 | n.a. | 0.67 | 0.30 | 345 |
| 1959–1960 | 0.096** | 0.849** | 0.623** | 0.074 | 0.181** | 0.039 | 0.008 | 0.255** | 0.105 | 0.016 | –0.047 | n.a. | 0.72 | 0.29 | 333 |
| 1960–1961 | 0.092* | 0.846** | 0.494** | 0.167* | 0.156** | 0.215** | 0.025 | 0.285** | 0.027 | 0.134* | –0.037 | n.a. | 0.78 | 0.27 | 253 |
| 1961–1962 | 0.066 | 0.840** | 0.560** | 0.271* | 0.056 | 0.215** | –0.118 | 0.412** | 0.115 | 0.049 | –0.008 | n.a. | 0.73 | 0.30 | 217 |
| 1962–1963 | 0.007 | 0.625** | 0.488** | 0.312* | 0.109* | 0.299** | –0.125 | 0.584** | 0.160 | 0.249* | 0.040 | n.a. | 0.68 | 0.33 | 237 |
| 1963–1964 | 0.023 | 0.629** | 0.381** | –0.180 | 0.170** | 0.266** | –0.036 | 0.532** | 0.107 | 0.190 | 0.082* | n.a. | 0.7 | 0.32 | 290 |
| 1964–1965 | 0.020 | 0.635** | 0.437** | –0.386 | 0.219** | 0.241** | 0.062 | 0.474** | 0.043 | 0.162 | 0.135** | n.a. | 0.74 | 0.29 | 316 |
| 1965–1966 | 0.043 | 0.467** | 0.416** | n.a. | 0.294** | 0.345* | 0.166** | 0.524** | 0.148* | 0.194* | 0.107* | n.a. | 0.67 | 0.30 | 308 |
| 1966–1967 | 0.068 | 0.430** | n.a. | n.a. | 0.268** | 0.266* | 0.122* | 0.380** | 0.156* | 0.117 | 0.052 | n.a. | 0.62 | 0.30 | 288 |
| 1967–1968 | –0.024 | 0.738** | n.a. | n.a. | 0.123** | 0.142 | –0.040 | 0.170** | 0.044 | 0.116 | 0.129* | n.a. | 0.69 | 0.27 | 273 |
| 1968–1969 | 0.066* | 0.849** | 0.623* | n.a. | 0.080* | 0.070 | –0.062 | 0.130** | 0.046 | 0.137 | 0.158 | n.a. | 0.78 | 0.25 | 258 |
| 1969–1970 | 0.007 | 0.865** | 0.602* | –0.239 | 0.043 | 0.007 | –0.001 | 0.083* | 0.033 | 0.050 | 0.117 | n.a. | 0.8 | 0.22 | 211 |
| 1970–1971 | 0.162** | 0.703** | 0.462 | n.a. | –0.112 | 0.096 | 0.029 | 0.131** | 0.247** | 0.100 | 0.121 | n.a. | 0.71 | 0.23 | 197 |
| 1971–1972 | –0.019 | 0.721** | n.a. | n.a. | –0.016 | 0.171* | 0.014 | 0.194** | 0.317** | 0.138 | 0.061 | n.a. | 0.63 | 0.26 | 200 |
| 1972–1973 | 0.230** | 0.621** | n.a. | n.a. | 0.069 | 0.081 | 0.056 | 0.330** | 0.139 | 0.126 | 0.046 | n.a. | 0.62 | 0.26 | 201 |
| 1973–1974 | 0.093** | 0.486** | n.a. | n.a. | 0.071 | 0.045 | 0.180** | 0.313** | 0.221** | 0.206* | 0.038 | n.a. | 0.6 | 0.23 | 192 |
| 1974–1975 | 0.063 | 0.443** | n.a. | n.a. | 0.074 | 0.025 | 0.142* | 0.157 | 0.216** | 0.208 | –0.107 | n.a. | 0.56 | 0.23 | 169 |
| 1975–1976 | –0.027 | 0.420** | n.a. | n.a. | 0.117* | 0.050 | 0.133* | –0.054 | 0.071 | 0.224** | –0.101 | n.a. | 0.51 | 0.22 | 166 |
| 1976–1977 | 0.023 | 0.314** | n.a. | n.a. | 0.155** | 0.157** | 0.128* | | 0.179** | 0.280** | 0.139 | n.a. | 0.53 | 0.22 | 155 |
| 1977–1978 | 0.093* | 0.192* | n.a. | n.a. | 0.145 | 0.149* | 0.171* | 0.549** | 0.305** | 0.367** | –0.098 | n.a. | 0.44 | 0.25 | 138 |
| 1978–1979 | 0.272** | 0.186* | –0.109 | n.a. | 0.206* | 0.099 | 0.127 | 0.500** | 0.202* | 0.121 | –0.067 | n.a. | 0.47 | 0.24 | 116 |
| 1979–1980 | –0.187** | 0.085 | 0.027 | n.a. | 0.260* | 0.147** | 0.087 | 0.468* | 0.181** | 0.125 | 0.155* | n.a. | 0.48 | 0.19 | 87 |
| 1980–1981 | 0.110** | 0.087 | n.a. | n.a. | 0.068 | 0.114** | 0.079 | | 0.174** | 0.231** | 0.362** | n.a. | 0.57 | 0.16 | 83 |
| 1981–1982 | 0.095** | 0.232** | 0.660** | n.a. | 0.117* | 0.076* | 0.150* | 0.306 | 0.177** | 0.129* | 0.037 | n.a. | 0.51 | 0.20 | 115 |
| 1982–1983 | 0.299** | –0.225* | 0.262 | 0.187 | –0.024 | –0.172** | 0.092 | –0.673** | 0.132 | –0.010 | 0.006 | n.a. | 0.32 | 0.35 | 170 |
| 1983–1984 | –0.006 | –0.054 | 0.611** | 0.788** | –0.077 | –0.097 | 0.094 | –0.467** | 0.090 | 0.063 | 0.164 | n.a. | 0.18 | 0.40 | 204 |
| 1984–1985 | 0.160** | 0.557** | 0.006 | 0.137 | 0.136* | 0.046 | 0.092* | 0.427** | –0.014 | 0.067 | –0.063 | n.a. | 0.64 | 0.23 | 208 |
| 1985–1986 | 0.023 | 0.497** | –0.086 | 0.266** | 0.195** | 0.041 | 0.146** | 0.472** | 0.056 | 0.018 | –0.047 | n.a. | 0.67 | 0.21 | 169 |
| 1986–1987 | –0.154** | 0.387** | 0.045 | 0.176* | 0.084 | 0.000 | 0.079 | 0.464** | –0.017 | 0.054 | 0.030 | n.a. | 0.71 | 0.19 | 150 |
| 1987–1988 | 0.014 | 0.411** | 0.168* | 0.049 | 0.137** | 0.009 | –0.041 | 0.354** | 0.030 | –0.001 | 0.077 | n.a. | 0.69 | 0.18 | 161 |

*Note:* n.a. = not available.

**Significant at the 5 percent level.

*Significant at the 10 percent level.

weight are almost always highly significant, with an average estimated elasticity of 0.71. The weight elasticity is much higher in the 1928 to 1948 period (1.0 or above) and lower at the beginning and end. Several of the other quality variables are highly significant with the expected positive coefficient and a plausible magnitude of coefficients, particularly the "organic fabric" variable, as well as the "LSE" (lace, sequins, embroidery) and "DRY" (dry cleaning) variables.

The implied hedonic price index for women's dresses is compared with the CPI for women's dresses and the Sears MM index for women's dresses. These are displayed in table 2.12 and in figures 2.7 and 2.8, along with the median price and the implicit hedonic quality index (i.e., median price divided by the hedonic price index). Table 2.13 summarizes the growth rates of these five indexes for women's dresses over key intervals. Except for the negligible difference during 1914 to 1947, the huge positive differences between the annual growth rates of the hedonic and MM indexes for women's dresses from absolutely the same data set are remarkable. The introduction of this chapter provided a context for the "Hulten-Bruegel" paradox based on long-term annual rates of bias of 0.5 or 1.5 percent. Here we have a long-term difference in the Sears hedonic versus MM index of 2.90 percent per year.

An important aspect of these results is that the Sears/MM difference in growth rates is so much larger in the postwar era than between 1914 and 1947. While this is a puzzle, it may be related to the very different quality of dresses sold by Sears in the early part of the sample period—silk and velvet during 1914 to 1930, compared to pedestrian working-class dresses in the later parts of the sample (e.g., 1975 to 1993). A paradox that is not resolved by this chapter is the hedonic/MM difference increases in annual growth rates in the later years of the postwar era just when Sears is becoming more "pedestrian" and "less fashionable."

### 2.5.3 A Closer Look at Particular Pairs of Years

Are any generalizations possible about the periods when the Sears hedonic price increased so much more than the Sears MM index? To answer this question, a closer look was taken at three pairs of adjacent years with the greatest difference in growth rates between the two price indexes; as shown in the first three columns of table 2.14, these were 1972 to 1973, 1978 to 1979, and 1982 to 1983. The fourth column looks at the five-year interval (1978 to 1983) that had the greatest discrepancy. For contrast, three other pairs of years were chosen with only negligible differences between the growth rates of the two indexes; these pairs (1960 to 1961, 1966 to 1967, and 1977 to 1978) are displayed in the three right-hand columns of table 2.14.

The first three lines of table 2.14 records the annual growth rates of the two price indexes in each pair of years. The greatest difference was in 1982 to 1983, with a 30 percent increase in the hedonic index versus zero for the MM index. The next greatest difference was in 1978 to 1979, with respective

**Table 2.12** **Comparison of price indices for women's dresses**

| Year | Sears median price | CPI | Sears matched-model index | Sears hedonic price index | Sears implicit quality index |
|---|---|---|---|---|---|
| 1914 | 45.34 | 43.87 | 84.16 | 44.71 | 101.42 |
| 1915 | n.a. | 44.74 | 87.68 | *48.38* | n.a. |
| 1916 | n.a. | 49.13 | 129.03 | *52.36* | n.a. |
| 1917 | n.a. | 59.07 | 148.53 | *56.67* | n.a. |
| 1918 | n.a. | 79.83 | 186.22 | *61.32* | n.a. |
| 1919 | n.a. | 105.86 | 239.00 | *66.37* | n.a. |
| 1920 | n.a. | 126.04 | 314.81 | *71.82* | n.a. |
| 1921 | 90.01 | 97.09 | 199.56 | 77.72 | 115.81 |
| 1922 | 67.90 | 78.96 | 169.06 | 47.62 | 142.60 |
| 1923 | 84.85 | 79.25 | 156.74 | 56.89 | 149.14 |
| 1924 | 86.42 | 78.37 | 153.08 | 68.32 | 126.50 |
| 1925 | 94.16 | 76.91 | 149.41 | 60.77 | 154.94 |
| 1926 | 92.82 | 75.74 | 144.43 | 65.25 | 142.26 |
| 1927 | 37.04 | 73.99 | 135.48 | 54.66 | 67.76 |
| 1928 | 88.44 | 73.11 | 129.03 | 46.21 | 191.39 |
| 1929 | n.a. | 72.23 | 121.55 | *47.85* | n.a. |
| 1930 | n.a. | 70.77 | 121.26 | *49.54* | n.a. |
| 1931 | n.a. | 64.34 | 112.76 | *51.29* | n.a. |
| 1932 | n.a. | 57.02 | 91.94 | *53.11* | n.a. |
| 1933 | n.a. | 54.98 | 88.12 | *54.99* | n.a. |
| 1934 | 42.42 | 60.24 | 104.40 | 56.95 | 74.49 |
| 1935 | 33.33 | 60.53 | 83.28 | 42.15 | 79.09 |
| 1936 | 33.56 | 60.74 | 86.07 | 52.47 | 63.96 |
| 1937 | 33.11 | 62.58 | 85.78 | 51.32 | 64.51 |
| 1938 | 38.16 | 61.35 | 84.02 | 56.33 | 67.75 |
| 1939 | 40.97 | 61.55 | 84.16 | 49.61 | 82.58 |
| 1940 | 35.02 | 61.55 | 89.88 | 52.62 | 66.54 |
| 1941 | 34.90 | 63.60 | 92.23 | 44.26 | 78.86 |
| 1942 | n.a. | 76.48 | 106.45 | *47.51* | n.a. |
| 1943 | n.a. | 79.75 | 108.06 | *51.00* | n.a. |
| 1944 | n.a. | 87.32 | 119.50 | *54.74* | n.a. |
| 1945 | n.a. | 92.02 | 120.97 | *58.75* | n.a. |
| 1946 | 55.56 | 93.87 | 130.94 | 63.07 | 88.09 |
| 1947 | 73.51 | 107.16 | 150.88 | 88.34 | 83.22 |
| 1948 | 87.43 | 115.95 | 146.63 | 107.79 | 81.11 |
| 1949 | 87.65 | 99.80 | 148.24 | 99.40 | 88.18 |
| 1950 | 68.91 | 90.18 | 128.30 | 72.91 | 94.52 |
| 1951 | 79.24 | 96.93 | 122.58 | 81.06 | 97.75 |
| 1952 | 78.34 | 97.03 | 120.82 | 89.40 | 87.62 |
| 1953 | 74.64 | 97.14 | 117.45 | 86.24 | 86.54 |
| 1954 | 83.73 | 97.34 | 111.73 | 95.41 | 87.76 |
| 1955 | 79.12 | 97.96 | 107.48 | 93.43 | 84.69 |
| 1956 | 89.67 | 98.77 | 119.79 | 72.54 | 123.62 |
| 1957 | 103.48 | 99.39 | 107.04 | 90.21 | 114.71 |
| 1958 | 100.00 | 100.00 | 100.00 | 100.00 | 100.00 |
| 1959 | 101.46 | 102.45 | 94.72 | 120.44 | 84.24 |
| 1960 | 106.29 | 102.86 | 90.47 | 132.58 | 80.17 |

*(continued)*

**Table 2.12** (continued)

| Year | Sears median price | CPI | Sears matched-model index | Sears hedonic price index | Sears implicit quality index |
|---|---|---|---|---|---|
| 1961 | 109.43 | 103.07 | 98.68 | 145.35 | 75.28 |
| 1962 | 112.68 | 103.48 | 78.89 | 155.27 | 72.57 |
| 1963 | 116.27 | 104.29 | 78.15 | 156.36 | 74.36 |
| 1964 | 128.84 | 106.34 | 82.70 | 160.00 | 80.53 |
| 1965 | 114.48 | 108.18 | 87.98 | 163.23 | 70.13 |
| 1966 | 123.01 | 113.50 | 87.98 | 170.40 | 72.19 |
| 1967 | 133.22 | 123.31 | 94.87 | 182.39 | 73.04 |
| 1968 | 130.86 | 137.83 | 95.75 | 178.07 | 73.49 |
| 1969 | 143.55 | 151.33 | 81.23 | 190.22 | 75.46 |
| 1970 | 156.57 | 159.51 | 103.81 | 191.55 | 81.73 |
| 1971 | 141.86 | 157.26 | 103.81 | 225.24 | 62.98 |
| 1972 | 145.68 | 160.33 | 103.81 | 221.00 | 65.92 |
| 1973 | 176.54 | 167.48 | 106.45 | 278.15 | 63.47 |
| 1974 | 206.06 | 173.62 | 111.44 | 305.26 | 67.50 |
| 1975 | 211.22 | 177.71 | 115.69 | 325.11 | 64.97 |
| 1976 | 203.70 | 184.05 | 121.70 | 316.45 | 64.37 |
| 1977 | 220.99 | 190.80 | 127.86 | 323.81 | 68.25 |
| 1978 | 210.21 | 195.30 | 140.18 | 355.37 | 59.15 |
| 1979 | 288.33 | 202.25 | 146.63 | 466.46 | 61.81 |
| 1980 | 233.33 | 202.25 | 146.63 | 386.90 | 60.31 |
| 1981 | 252.08 | 202.45 | 146.63 | 431.89 | 58.37 |
| 1982 | 307.63 | 196.93 | 147.95 | 474.93 | 64.77 |
| 1983 | 409.99 | 203.68 | 147.95 | 640.45 | 64.02 |
| 1984 | 410.89 | 213.09 | 157.18 | 636.62 | 64.54 |
| 1985 | 478.79 | 217.38 | 174.19 | 747.08 | 64.09 |
| 1986 | 549.61 | 214.72 | 174.19 | 764.46 | 71.89 |
| 1987 | 498.32 | 238.45 | 145.60 | 655.35 | 76.04 |
| 1988 | 555.56 | 252.56 | 147.07 | 664.59 | 83.59 |
| 1989 | n.a. | 252.54 | 148.53 | n.a. | n.a. |
| 1990 | n.a. | 263.68 | 148.53 | n.a. | n.a. |
| 1991 | n.a. | 273.75 | 169.21 | n.a. | n.a. |
| 1992 | n.a. | 273.2 | 169.21 | n.a. | n.a. |
| 1993 | n.a. | 278.35 | 150.88 | n.a. | n.a. |

*Note:* Italics indicate that the Sears hedonic price index is interpolated for these years. n.a. = not available.

increases of 27.2 and 4.5 percent. We note from table 2.11 that the hedonic regressions for 1978 to 1979 and 1982 to 1983 were based on 116 and 170 observations, respectively, whereas the MM indexes are based on only four observations in each year-pair. Even this small number of comparisons overstates the representativeness of the MM index, since in 1978 and 1979 the "two" models in each year are actually a single dress, with the two models differing only as to whether they are available in half-sizes (with a slightly higher price).

The remaining lines of table 2.4 stratify the dresses in the hedonic sample

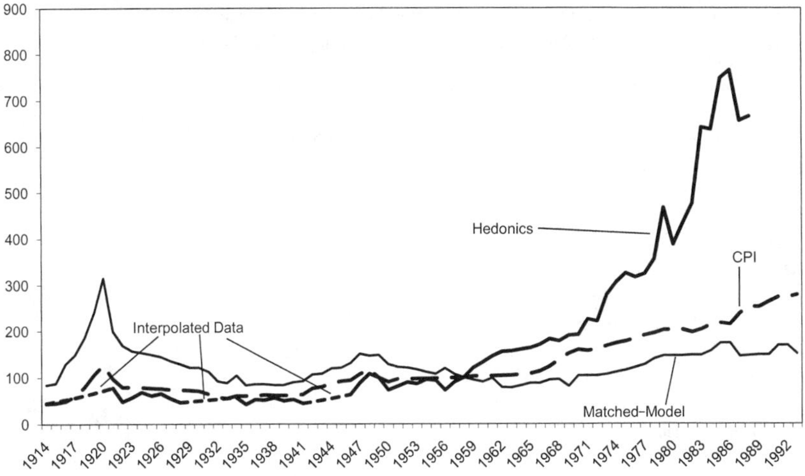


**Fig. 2.7 Alternative price indexes for women's dresses: Sears hedonic, Sears MM, and CPI (1958 = 100), 1914–1993**

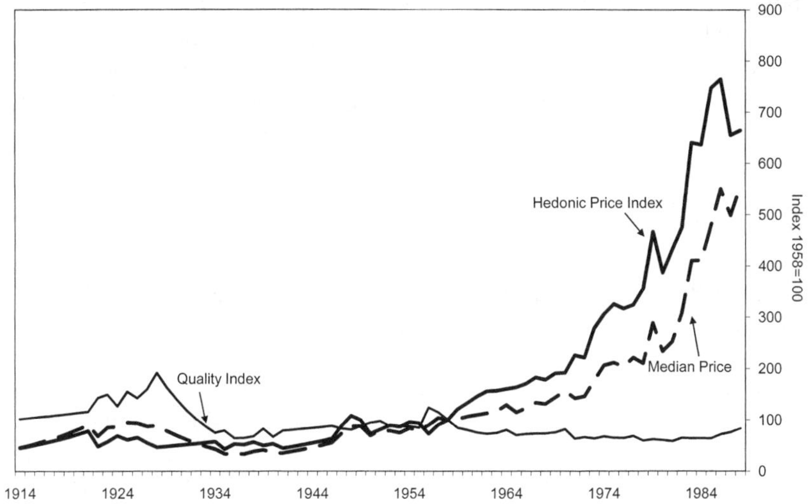


**Fig. 2.8 Median price, hedonic, and implicit quality index**

in each year by weight. The top section shows raw price change in each weight quartile in each pair of years; this number was obtained by regressing the price on a constant and a dummy variable for the second year in each pair. The second section shows the coefficient on a time dummy in hedonic regressions run separately for each weight quartile. Because the sample sizes were smaller by a factor of four, degrees of freedom were economized by deleting any quality variable (among those listed in table 2.8) that was not

**Table 2.13** **Growth rates of Sears matched-model (MM) and hedonic indexes compared with the CPI, the median price, and the implicit quality index, alternative intervals, 1914–1988**

| | 1914–1947 | 1947–1965 | 1965–1978 | 1978–1988 | 1914–1988 |
|---|---|---|---|---|---|
| Sears median price | 1.46 | 2.46 | 4.67 | 9.72 | 3.39 |
| CPI | 2.71 | 0.05 | 4.54 | 2.57 | 2.37 |
| Sears MM index | 1.77 | –3.00 | 3.58 | 0.48 | 0.75 |
| Sears hedonic index | 2.06 | 3.41 | 5.98 | 6.26 | 3.65 |
| Median price – CPI | –1.25 | 2.41 | 0.13 | 7.15 | 1.02 |
| CPI – Sears MM index | 0.94 | 3.05 | 0.96 | 2.09 | 1.62 |
| CPI – Sears hedonic index | 0.65 | –3.36 | –1.44 | –3.69 | –1.28 |
| Sears MM index – Sears hedonic index | –0.29 | –6.41 | –2.40 | –5.78 | –2.90 |
| Implicit quality index = Median price – Sears hedonic index | –0.60 | –0.95 | –1.31 | 3.46 | –0.26 |

significant in a particular regression at the 10 percent level. The third section subtracts the numbers in each cell in the second section (hedonic price change) from the corresponding cell in the first section (raw price change), resulting in the change in the implicit hedonic quality index. For instance, in the second column for 1978 to 1979, the raw price change is 34 percent, the hedonic price change is 29 percent, and the implicit improvement in quality is 5 percent.

In the first four columns there is a consistent pattern that the lighter dresses (first two weight quartiles) exhibit a substantially faster rate of raw price change and hedonic price change than the two heavier quartiles, especially the heaviest. There was no such difference across the lower two and higher two weight quartiles in the final three columns, showing three pairs of adjacent years when the hedonic and MM price indexes increased by about the same amount. Given the large samples in the hedonic regressions, this result is consistent with the hypothesis that the MM technique, with its sample sizes that of necessity are severely truncated, misses large price increases associated with model changes. Looking at the bottom section of table 2.14, there does not appear to be any significant tendency for lighter dresses to decline in quality relative to the heavier dresses. In several columns, the change in quality across weight quartiles has a zig-zag pattern, alternating between positive and negative.

Several other experiments were run on the data for these pairs of years. Each of the subset of significant quality variables was interacted with the year dummy to look for changes in the coefficients of quality characteristics over time. However, none of these interaction terms was significant at the 10 percent level. The absence of time interaction effects, and the stability of the subset of coefficients that are significant in table 2.11, attests to the

**Table 2.14** **Comparison of years when Sears hedonic index grew much faster than Sears MM index with years when the two indexes grew at the same rate, annual growth rates in percent**

| | Hedonic >> MM | | | | Hedonic ≈ MM | | |
|---|---|---|---|---|---|---|---|
| | 1972–1973 | 1978–1979 | 1982–1983 | 1978–1983 | 1960–1961 | 1966–1967 | 1977–1978 |
| Hedonic price index | 23.0 | 27.2 | 29.9 | 11.8 | 9.2 | 6.8 | 9.3 |
| Matched-model price index | 2.5 | 4.5 | 0.0 | –0.6 | 8.7 | 7.5 | 9.2 |
| Hedonic–MM | 20.5 | 22.7 | 29.9 | 12.4 | 0.5 | –0.7 | 0.1 |
| Raw price change | 22.0 | 34.0 | 20.0 | 11.8 | 1.0 | 9.0 | –4.0 |
| First weight quartile | 37.0 | 38.0 | 34.0 | 16.9 | –1.0 | 0.0 | 8.0 |
| Second weight quartile | 28.0 | 40.0 | 50.0 | 18.7 | 9.0 | 1.0 | –12.0 |
| Third weight quartile | 16.0 | 34.0 | 19.0 | 10.0 | 9.0 | 27.0 | –5.0 |
| Fourth weight quartile | 9.0 | 22.0 | –24.0 | 1.1 | –3.0 | 10.0 | –8.0 |
| Hedonic price index by weight quartile | 24.0 | 29.0 | 32.0 | 11.8 | 9.0 | 8.0 | 10.0 |
| First | 32.0 | 44.0 | 48.0 | 14.2 | 0.0 | 23.0 | 10.0 |
| Second | 35.0 | 40.0 | 53.0 | 20.1 | 17.0 | 7.0 | 5.0 |
| Third | 14.0 | 13.6 | 26.0 | –1.0 | –5.0 | 26.0 | 26.0 |
| Fourth | 13.0 | 24.0 | –10.0 | 13.6 | 14.0 | 5.0 | –1.0 |
| Implicit quality change by weight quartile | –2.0 | 5.0 | –12.0 | 0.0 | –8.0 | 1.0 | –14.0 |
| First | 5.0 | –6.0 | –14.0 | 2.7 | –1.0 | –23.0 | –2.0 |
| Second | –7.0 | 0.0 | –3.0 | –1.4 | –8.0 | –6.0 | –17.0 |
| Third | 2.0 | 20.4 | –7.0 | 11.0 | 14.0 | 1.0 | –31.0 |
| Fourth | –4.0 | –2.0 | –14.0 | –12.5 | –17.0 | 5.0 | –7.0 |

robustness of the hedonic regression results. Another experiment was to stratify the sample for these years by the DRY variable (0 or 1 depending on the need for dry cleaning), but price changes in this stratification appeared to differ randomly across the DRY = 0 and DRY = 1 subsets of the sample. The last experiment was to identify subsets of dresses with identical quality characteristics across two adjacent years. This amounts to trying to "mimic" the MM technique within the subset of variables available for the hedonic regression, without requiring (as does the MM technique) that the models are absolutely identical. The result is that within these constant-quality subsets, price increases in adjacent-year pairs were mostly higher rather than lower than the basic hedonic time coefficient in those same year-pairs.

As a last step to understand the phenomenon of rapid price increases in the hedonic regressions for these pairs of years, I visited the pair of microfilm machines displaying the 1978 and 1979 Sears catalogs (after years of relying on research assistants to collect the data). I checked the MM models to make sure they were identical, and they were in both the photo, the available colors, and the specifications:

> Fabric: polyester-cotton blend. Tuck-stitching at sides, front placket opening, pointed collar, should yoke in front, yoke and shirring in back, one side-seam pocket, short sleeves, self-tie belt.

This standard dress in standard sizes increased in price from $11.44 to $11.99, and in available half sizes increased from $12.44 to $12.99. These price increases calculated in logs are 4.7 and 4.3 percent, respectively, yielding the 4.5 percent increase in the MM index shown in table 2.14, line 2, for 1978 to 1979.

Then I looked for 1979 dresses that were "closely comparable" to their 1978 counterparts, and it immediately became apparent why the sample sizes in the MM indexes are so small. I found a poly-rayon blend "cap-sleeve" one-piece dress in 1978 that in its photo looked just like a cap-sleeve one-piece dress in 1979. But upon closer inspection of the specifications, they were not identical at all. The 1979 dress was poly-cotton rather than poly-rayon, its weight was thirteen ounces instead of nine ounces, it had no collar instead of a pointed collar, and it had one pocket instead of two (the price increased from $18 to $25). A two-piece dress comparison was more promising, since both the 1978 and 1979 version had a poly-cotton fabric.

Both had a pointed collar, placket opening, and a skirt with a "slightly flared style." However, the 1978 dress had a zipper in back while the 1979 style was "pullover," the 1979 dress had an elastic waistband that was not mentioned in 1978, and the 1978 dress had "attached tabs with D-ring closure" that was not mentioned in 1979. Despite a decline in weight from fifteen to ten ounces, the price went up from $20 to $24. Similarly, a floral print one-piece dress increased in weight from six to seven ounces but increased in price from $19 to $27. Again, they looked similar in photos but upon closer inspection one had a square neck, the other a "band neckline," one had 3/4 length sleeves, the other elbow-length sleeves, and the 1979 skirt was "three-tiered."

Overall, the mind boggles at the difference between price research on women's dresses and on the many types of durable goods studied in my previous book (Gordon 1990). In durable goods quality improves steadily, if not from year to year then from decade to decade. Engines become more powerful, quieter, and more fuel efficient. Electric and electronic products become more capable at the same time as they become smaller. The difference with women's dresses could not be more profound. The many small changes from year to year in women's dresses that prevent a researcher from "matching a model" do not correspond to our standard notions of "quality." A pocket is moved from the top to the side, a zipper is replaced by buttons or vice versa, a square neck is replaced by a scooped neck. Immersion in the catalogs for a year-pair like 1978 to 1979 leaves the overwhelming impression that the isolated model that was "matched" was actually a freak, and that the large sample of dresses with as many as ten dimensions of quality controlled make the hedonic regression results greatly superior to the MM indexes.

Many types of apparel, from men's suits to work clothes to underwear to children's clothes, exhibit far fewer dimensions of style change than women's dresses. But our overall finding of minimal quality change between 1914 and 1993 should carry over to these apparel products as well, if there is any communality of production techniques used across different types of apparel. One may speculate that an index of the raw price change for the Sears sample of these more homogeneous types of apparel would be closer to the truth than the corresponding MM indexes displayed in tables 2.2 through 2.7.

## 2.5 Conclusion

This chapter develops new price indexes for apparel based on data from the Sears catalog for the entire period 1914 to 1993, beginning in the first year of the CPI and ending in the last year of the general Sears catalog. The research, which is based on roughly 10,000 exact comparisons for the matched-model (MM) index and another 6,500 observations on the prices and quality characteristics of women's dresses, leads to several conclusions and numerous questions for further research.

The Sears matched-model indexes do not exhibit a consistent negative or positive drift relative to the CPI. For women's apparel the drift is always negative but for men's apparel there is a turnaround, from negative before 1965 to positive thereafter. Both the matched-model indexes and the CPI rise less rapidly for women's apparel than for men's apparel, which would be consistent with the hypothesis that price changes accompanying model changes are more frequent for women's apparel, since models change more frequently.

The hedonic price index for women's dresses increases much faster than the matched-model index from the same data over the entire postwar period, although not in the earlier 1914 to 1947 period. Likewise, the hedonic index also increases faster than the CPI over the entire postwar period but also not during 1914 to 1947 (when the CPI-hedonic difference is a relatively minor 0.65 percent per year). To the extent that the Sears hedonic and matched-model indexes are based on the same data, so that systematic differences between catalog market shares and pricing policies are not relevant, the results provided here offer a nice complement to past research on computer prices, which also found that price changes were contemporaneous with model changes. Just as hedonic price indexes for computers almost always drop faster than matched-model indexes for computers, we have found the opposite relationship for apparel prices, presumably for the same reason.

Despite the large amount of data examined in this chapter, it leaves open the answer to the basic question that motivated the research—what is the overall bias in the CPI for apparel from 1914 to 1993? One answer is a downward bias of 1.28 percent per year, the difference between the CPI and hedonic indexes for women's dresses over the 1914 to 1988 period for which the hedonic index was compiled. As shown in table 2.13, the figure of 1.28 is misleading, since the difference was actually in the opposite direction before 1947, and the 1947 to 1988 difference implies a much higher downward bias of –2.83 percent per year for that period.

In extrapolating this difference from women's dresses sold by Sears to all apparel sold by all retail outlets, two factors suggest scaling down the –2.83 difference for the postwar period to a smaller number, say –1.5 percent. First, as discussed, the market position changed over the years from the lowest-priced vendor to somewhere in the middle. The fact that the catalog was eventually shut down in 1993 suggests the growing importance of lower-priced merchants like Target and Wal-Mart. Second, the underlying diagnosis of the MM-hedonic price difference as being due to frequent style changes would apply less to men's and children's apparel than to women's dresses, suggesting that the CPI may have done a better job in these other categories. However, the annual rate of increase in the CPI for men's apparel over the 1947 to 1993 period was only 0.57 percent per year faster than that for women's apparel, indicating that the style-fashion source of bias for women's versus men's apparel is only a fraction of the overall difference between the CPI for women's dresses and Sears hedonic for women's dresses established in this chapter. Our final conclusion is that the downward bias in the CPI for the postwar period, at least through 1988, is roughly in the range of –1.5 to –2.0 percent, with no evidence of bias in the 1914 to 1947 period.

The implications of this chapter go beyond the limited empirical application of Sears catalog data for women's dresses. Perhaps the most important conclusion of this chapter is one that economizes enormously on future research resources. Quality change in women's dresses over the full 1914 to

1993 period was negligible. If this can be extended to other types of apparel, this creates a radical breakthrough for historical research. However sophisticated the modern CPI in measuring price changes for apparel in the twenty-first century, significant information may be contained in raw price changes of individual apparel products for most of the twentieth century.

## References

Armknecht, P. A., and D. Weyback. 1989. Adjustments for quality change in the U.S. Consumer Price Index. *Journal of Official Statistics* 5 (2): 107–23.

Berndt, E. R., Z. Griliches, and N. Rappaport. 1995. Econometric estimates of price indexes for personal computers in the 1990s. NBER Working Paper no. 4549. Cambridge, MA: National Bureau of Economic Research, August.

Berndt, E. R., and N. Rappaport. 2003. Hedonics for personal computers: A reexamination of selected econometric issues. MIT Sloan School Draft Manuscript, August.

Doms, M., A. Aizcorbe, and C. Corrado. 2003. When do matched-model and hedonic techniques yield similar measures? Federal Reserve Bank of San Francisco, Working Papers in Applied Economic Theory 2003-14.

Gordon, R. J. 1989. The postwar evolution of computer prices. In *Technology and capital formation,* ed. Dale W. Jorgenson and Ralph Landau, 77–125. Cambridge, MA: MIT Press.

———. 1990. *The measurement of durable goods prices.* Chicago: University of Chicago Press.

Gordon, R. J., and T. vanGoethem. 2007. A century of downward bias in the most important component of the CPI: The case of rental shelter, 1914–2003. In *Hard-to-measure goods and services,* Conference on Research in Income and Wealth, ed. E. Berndt and C. Hulten, 153–95. Chicago: University of Chicago Press.

Hendrickson, R. 1979. *The grand emporiums: The illustrated history of America's great department stores.* New York: Stein and Day.

Hobsbawm, E. 1994. *The age of extremes: A history of the world, 1914–91.* New York: Pantheon.

Liegey, P. F., Jr. 1993. Adjusting apparel indexes in the Consumer Price Index for quality differences. In *Price measurements and their uses,* ed. M. F. Foss, M. E. Manser, and A. H. Young, 209–26. Chicago: University of Chicago Press.

———. 1994. Apparel price indexes: Effects of hedonic adjustment. *Monthly Labor Review* 117 (5): 38–45.

Nordhaus, W. D. 1997. Do real-output and real wage measures capture reality? In *The economics of new goods, Conference on Research in Income and Wealth,* ed. T. F. Bresnahan and R. J. Gordon, 29–66. Chicago: University of Chicago Press.

Pashigian, B. P. 1988. Demand uncertainty and sales: A study of fashion and markdown pricing. *American Economic Review* 78 (5): 936–53.

Pashigian, B. P., and B. Bowen. 1991. Why are products sold on sale?: Explanations of pricing regularities. *Quarterly Journal of Economics* 106 (4): 1015–38.

Pashigian, B. P., B. Bowen, and E. Gould. 1995. Fashion, styling, and the within-season decline in automobile prices. *Journal of Law and Economics* 38 (2): 281–309.

Rees, A. 1961a. Alternative retail price indexes for selected nondurable goods, 1947–59. In *The price statistics of the federal government,* General Series 73, ed. Price

Statistics Review Committee, 137–72. New York: National Bureau of Economic Research.

Rees, Albert (1961b). *Real Wages in Manufacturing, 1890–1914.* Princeton, N.J.: Princeton University Press for NBER.

Triplett, J. 1971. Determining the effects of quality change on the CPI. *Monthly Labor Review* 94 (May): 27–32.

———. 2004. *Handbook on hedonic indexes and quality adjustments in price indexes: Special application to information technology products.* Paris: Organization for Economic Cooperation and Development (OECD), Directorate for Science, Technology, and Industry.

U.S. Bureau of the Census. 1994. *Statistical abstract of the United States 1994.* Austin, TX: Hoover's Books.

Wynne, M. A., and F. D. Sigalla. 1994. The Consumer Price Index. *Federal Reserve Bank of Dallas Review* (second quarter): 1–22.

3

# Reassessing the U.S. Quality Adjustment to Computer Prices
## The Role of Durability and Changing Software

Robert C. Feenstra and Christopher R. Knittel

### 3.1 Introduction

In the second half of the 1990s, the positive impact of information technology (IT) on productivity growth for the United States became apparent (Jorgenson and Stiroh 2000; Oliner and Sichel 2000). The measurement of this productivity improvement depends on hedonic procedures adopted by the Bureau of Labor Statistics (BLS) and Bureau of Economic Analysis (BEA). These procedures include the hedonic adjustment of prices for mainframes and peripherals since 1985 (Cole et al. 1986; Cartwright 1986), for personal computers (PCs) since 1991 (Holdway 2001), and for semiconductors since 1996 (Grimm 1998).[1] The rapid price declines of these products means that their production and use accounts for a sizable portion of recent U.S. productivity gains.

It is sometimes suggested that the price declines in IT products may be overstated due to the use of hedonic techniques, though this belief has not been confirmed. Triplett (1999), for example, critiques a number of suggested reasons why the hedonic techniques might overstate the price decline of IT products, but he generally finds that these reasons are not persuasive.

Robert C. Feenstra is the C. Bryan Cameron Distinguished Chair in International Economics and professor of economics at the University of California, Davis, and a research associate of the National Bureau of Economic Research. Christopher R. Knittel is an associate professor of economics at the University of California, Davis, and a research associate of the National Bureau of Economic Research.

Prepared for the CRIW conference "Index Theory & Measurement of Price and Productivity," June 28–29, 2004, Vancouver, B.C. We thank Bert Balk and the participants of the CRIW conference for helpful comments. We thank Roger Butters and Konstantinos Metaxoglou for research assistance. We benefited greatly from discussions with Lanier Benkard at an early stage of the research, who also provided data, for which we are grateful.

1. See Moulton (2001) who details the use of hedonic methods in U.S. statistical agencies.

Empirically, Landefeld and Grimm (2000) show that the hedonic adjustments used in official statistics closely match those recommended by academic studies, such as Berndt and Rappaport (2001), so there is no presumption of a downward bias in the official calculations. But concern about this potential bias will no doubt continue.[2]

In this chapter we suggest a new reason why conventional hedonic methods may overstate the price decline of personal computers, which are treated here as a durable good. We suppose that software changes over time, which influences the efficiency of a computer. Anticipating the future increases in software, purchasers may "overbuy" characteristics, in the sense that the purchased bundle of characteristics is not fully utilized in the first months or year that a computer is owned. Forward-looking buyers will equate the marginal benefits of characteristics over the *lifetime* of a machine to the marginal cost at the time of purchase. This means that the marginal costs are equated to marginal benefits evaluated at *future* levels of software. In this case, we argue that hedonic procedures do not provide valid bounds on the true price of computer services at the time the machine is purchased with the concurrent level of software.

There are two ways that this concern might influence calculations of total factor productivity (TFP). Following Oliner and Sichel (2000), let us make the distinction between the *use* of Information Technology (IT) capital and the *production* of IT capital. The use of IT capital will influence TFP calculations through the measurement of the IT capital stock. This will require depreciation rates for computer equipment, and if changes in software influence the efficiency of a machine then depreciation rates should reflect this. We do not attempt to solve that problem here, though our framework could likely be adapted to address it.[3] Rather, we focus on the production of IT capital, and in particular, on the hedonic price index constructed for personal computers, as in Holdway (2001). This hedonic index can be used to construct dual TFP for personal computers; that is, as the difference between weighted growth in factor prices within that sector and the growth in the hedonic output price. If the hedonic output price is intended to reflect the efficiency of new machines to users at the *current* level of software, then we argue that conventional hedonic methods may well overstate this price decline.

2. For semiconductors, Aizcorbe (2004) argues that falling price-cost margins by selling firms may accentuate the price decline. Gordon (2000) presents a different reason why the TFP contribution of IT capital may be overstated. He argues that the increase in TFP during the second half of the 1990s is a cyclical rather than trend increase, and by focusing only on the trend, the contribution of IT capital to productivity is smaller. Conversely, Benkard and Bajari (2003) argue that standard hedonic index can be upward biased due to unobserved characteristics.

3. Overviews of the measurement of capital and depreciation rates are provided by Diewert (1980), Harper, Berndt, and Wood (1989), and Hulten (1990), though only Diewert (1980, 503–06) includes a discussion of hedonics. Specific discussion of depreciation for computers is in Oliner (1993) and Harper (2000).

We begin the analysis in section 3.2 by describing a case where the conventional hedonic adjustment provides a valid measure for the true services price of computers, similar to Rosen (1974) or Pakes (2003), though we allow for purchases of multiple units. In that section, it is assumed that the computers being purchased are nondurable, which is the assumption made by those authors and also Diewert (2003, 2009).

In section 3.3 we analyze the case where computers are durable and software is changing over time. We find that conventional hedonic methods do not provide valid bounds to the true price of computer services (evaluated with current levels of software). The extent to which the true services price deviates from the conventional hedonic index will depend on the *interaction* between software and characteristics in the services that buyers' obtain from the machine. If software and characteristics are complements, in the sense that anticipated increases in software will lead the buyer to purchase more characteristics today, then it is more likely that the conventional hedonic methods will overstate the true price decline.

To assess these theoretical results, in sections 3.4 and 3.5 we estimate the model using a two-step procedure. First, monthly hedonic regressions are run over a sample of desktop PCs, from August 1997 to September 2001. Second, we utilize a data set of all purchases of PCs at the University of California, Davis, over similar dates. In the second step, the estimated hedonic coefficients are regressed on the characteristics actually purchased each month and a weighted average of software quality over the lifetime of the machine. The coefficients obtained in this second step reveal the users' "production functions" by which characteristics and software are transformed into computer services. Therefore, we can use these coefficients to obtain the true services price for users, and compare this with the bounds obtained from conventional hedonic methods.

It turns out that our results differ in the first and second halves of our sample. Before 2000, we generally find that the hedonic price index constructed with BLS methods overstates the fall in computer prices, as compared to the true price index constructed using the estimated production functions for users. This accords with our theoretical results. Furthermore, we find that the true services price falls *faster* when it is evaluated with *future* rather than *current* levels of software. This corresponds to our intuition that characteristics may be overbought, so their value with current software is less than with future software, and the true price index with current software is above the price index with future software.

After 2000, however, the BLS hedonic index falls more slowly, reflecting the reduced marginal cost of acquiring (and therefore marginal benefit to users) of characteristics such as RAM, hard disk space, or speed. Depending on the starting month, by the end of 2001 it turns out that the BLS index matches quite closely the true production function index constructed with *current* software. In this sense, the overstatement of the price decline by BLS methods has been ameliorated in the later years of our sample. The production function index constructed with *future* software falls faster than either of the other two indexes, however, which is explained by the pending release of Windows XP and 2003 after the end of our sample, with its large hardware requirements. Additional conclusions are provided in section 3.6.

## 3.2 Buyer's Problem with Nondurable Capital

In his classic treatment, Rosen (1974) considers the problem of buyers and sellers who purchase and produce differentiated goods. Under his assumptions (perfect competition and many varieties) this results in an equilibrium price schedule $p_t = h^t(\mathbf{x}_t)$, where $\mathbf{x}_t \in R^M$ is the vector of characteristics and $p_t$ is the price in period $t$. We will take this price schedule as given and reexamine the buyer's problem, introducing one important difference from Rosen: we shall allow the buyer to purchase *multiple units* of the differentiated good (i.e., multiple computers). The reason for allowing this will become clear shortly. Since this assumption is more realistic for firms than for consumers, we will use that language to describe our model, but much of the same results would hold for a consumer purchasing multiple units.

In addition to computers, the firm uses other inputs denoted by the vector $\mathbf{y}_t$. The services obtained in year $t = 1, \ldots, T$ from a computer of characteristics with $\mathbf{x}_t$ is $f(\mathbf{x}_t, \mathbf{s}_t)$, where the vector $\mathbf{s}_t$ denotes the state of software. We will sometimes refer to $f(\mathbf{x}_t, \mathbf{s}_t)$ as the "production function" for the firm, and it shows how computer characteristics and software combine to create computing services. Treating the computer as a nondurable good, the firm purchases $n_t$ identical units in year $t$.[4] The computers, purchased along with other inputs $\mathbf{y}_t$, yields per-period revenue $G[\mathbf{y}_t, n_t f(\mathbf{x}_t, \mathbf{s}_t)]$ for the firm. Then the maximization problem is to choose $n$, $\mathbf{x}$, and $\mathbf{y}$ in year $t$ to:

$$(1) \qquad \max_{n,x,y} G[\mathbf{y}, nf(\mathbf{x}, \mathbf{s}_t)] - nh^t(\mathbf{x}) - \mathbf{q}_t\mathbf{y},$$

where $p = h^t(\mathbf{x})$ is the price of a computer, $q_t$ is the price of the other inputs $\mathbf{y}$, and we denote the solution to (1) by $n_t$, $\mathbf{x}_t$, and $\mathbf{y}_t$. We assume that $f(\mathbf{x}, \mathbf{s})$ and $h^t(x)$ are positive and continuous functions of $\mathbf{x}$ and $\mathbf{s}$, where we are allowing for a continuous choice of characteristics (i.e., there are enough models of computers available that we treat the choice of $x$ as continuous).[5]

We will let $K_t \equiv n_t f(\mathbf{x}_t, \mathbf{s}_t)$ denote the capital stock of computers, measured in efficiency units. To compare our results with Rosen and other authors, suppose first that the number of computers purchased $n_t$ cannot be varied (for example, $n_t = 1$). Then the first-order conditions for problem (1) are:

4. We could generalize the problem to allow the firm to choose several types of computers, each in multiple units, by giving it several service functions $f(\mathbf{x}_t, \mathbf{s}_t)$ (e.g., for desktops, laptops, etc.).

5. We also treat the number of computers purchased, $n$, as a continuous variable.

$$G_y[\mathbf{y}_t, n_t f(\mathbf{x}_t, \mathbf{s}_t)] = q_t, \tag{2}$$

$$G_K[\mathbf{y}_t, n_t f(\mathbf{x}_t, \mathbf{s}_t)]\, n_t f_x(\mathbf{x}_t, \mathbf{s}_t) = n_t \mathbf{h}^t_x(\mathbf{x}_t), \tag{3}$$

where $\mathbf{h}^t_x(\mathbf{x}_t)$ denotes the vector of derivatives $(\partial h^t/\partial x_{1t}, \ldots, \partial h^t/\partial x_{Mt})$ for the $M$ characteristics. Canceling $n_t$ from the left- and right-hand side of (3), the first-order condition is interpreted as the marginal benefit of each characteristic $(G_K f_x)$ equaling its marginal cost $(\mathbf{h}^t_x)$. A difficulty that arises is that the marginal benefit depends on the quantity of other inputs purchased via $G_K[\mathbf{y}_t, n_t f(\mathbf{x}_t, \mathbf{s}_t)]$, or implicitly, on their prices $q_t$. This complicates the empirical application of hedonic methods, and several approaches have been taken to simplify the problem.

First, we could suppose that the revenue function is additively separable, so that $G[\mathbf{y}_t, n_t f(\mathbf{x}_t, \mathbf{s}_t)] = g(\mathbf{y}_t) + n_t f(\mathbf{x}_t, \mathbf{s}_t)$. In that case, the maximization of firm profits in equation (1) implies the subproblem of choosing characteristics $\mathbf{x}_t$ to:

$$\max_x f(\mathbf{x}, \mathbf{s}_t) - h^t(\mathbf{x}), \tag{4}$$

for which the first-order condition is simply $f_x(\mathbf{x}_t, \mathbf{s}_t) = \mathbf{h}^t_x(\mathbf{x}_t)$. This formulation of the problem is implicitly used by Pakes (2003), for example. Second, we could reformulate the buyer's problem in terms of its dual, and carry along the prices $\mathbf{q}_t$ of the other goods in the first-order conditions. Diewert (2003) takes this approach and shows how an aggregate of the prices $\mathbf{q}_t$ affects the hedonic price surface.

Third, the approach we shall take is to allow the firm to optimally choose the number of computers $n_t$. This implies the additional first-order condition:

$$G_K[\mathbf{y}_t, n_t f(\mathbf{x}_t, \mathbf{s}_t)]\, f(\mathbf{x}_t, \mathbf{s}_t) = \mathbf{h}^t(\mathbf{x}_t). \tag{5}$$

Combining (3) and (5) we readily obtain:

$$\frac{\mathbf{h}^t_x(\mathbf{x}_t)}{\mathbf{h}_t(\mathbf{x}_t)} = \frac{f_x(\mathbf{x}_t, \mathbf{s}_t)}{f(\mathbf{x}_t, \mathbf{s}_t)}. \tag{6}$$

This shows the equality of the marginal price of characteristics with their marginal value to the user when the number of units are also chosen. It is analogous to the first-order condition derived by Rosen (1974), and has the benefit that the price or quantity of other goods purchased do not appear.

The simplicity of the first-order condition (6) will be useful empirically, but also allows a reformulation of the theoretical problem. Again, letting $K_t \equiv n_t f(\mathbf{x}_t, \mathbf{s}_t)$ denote the capital stock of computers so that $n_t = K_t / f(\mathbf{x}_t, \mathbf{s}_t)$, problem (1) can be rewritten as:

$$\max_{K,x,y} G(\mathbf{y}, K) - K\left[\frac{h^t(\mathbf{x})}{f(\mathbf{x}, \mathbf{s}_t)}\right] - \mathbf{q}_t \mathbf{y}. \tag{1'}$$

For the choice of characteristics $\mathbf{x}_t$, it is evident that to maximize (1′), the buyer must solve the subproblem:

$$\min_{x} \frac{h^t(\mathbf{x})}{f(\mathbf{x}, \mathbf{s}_t)}. \tag{7}$$

Notice the difference between this subproblem and that in equation (4): both are correct, but are obtained under slightly different assumptions. The formulation in (1′) and (7) makes it clear that the *price of computer services* is $p_t/f(\mathbf{x}_t, \mathbf{s}_t) = h^t(\mathbf{x}_t)/f(\mathbf{x}_t, \mathbf{s}_t)$; that is, the *ratio* of the nominal price to benefits rather than their *difference* in equation (4). We will presume that the goal of a price index is to measure the change over time in the "true" services price $p_t/f(\mathbf{x}_t, \mathbf{s}_t)$.

The first-order conditions for (7) are just (6), and the simple statement of the problem also allows the second-order conditions to be easily examined. Minimizing equation (7) is equivalent to minimizing its natural log, and a necessary second-order condition for a local minimum is that the following matrix be positive semi-definite around $\mathbf{x}_t$:

$$\left[\frac{\partial^2 \ln \mathbf{h}_t(\mathbf{x}_t)}{\partial \mathbf{x}_t^2} - \frac{\partial^2 \ln f(\mathbf{x}_t, \mathbf{s}_t)}{\partial \mathbf{x}_t^2}\right] \tag{8}$$

$$= \left[\frac{\mathbf{h}^t_{xx}(\mathbf{x}_t)}{\mathbf{h}^t(\mathbf{x}_t)} - \frac{\mathbf{h}^t_x(\mathbf{x}_t)\mathbf{h}^t_x(\mathbf{x}_t)'}{\mathbf{h}^t(\mathbf{x}_t)^2} - \frac{f_{xx}(\mathbf{x}_t, \mathbf{s}_t)}{f(\mathbf{x}_t, \mathbf{s}_t)} + \frac{f_x(\mathbf{x}_t, \mathbf{s}_t)f_x(\mathbf{x}_t, \mathbf{s}_t)'}{f(\mathbf{x}_t, \mathbf{s}_t)^2}\right]$$

$$= \left[\frac{\mathbf{h}^t_{xx}(\mathbf{x}_t)}{\mathbf{h}^t(\mathbf{x}_t)} - \frac{f_{xx}(\mathbf{x}_t, \mathbf{s}_t)}{f(\mathbf{x}_t, \mathbf{s}_t)}\right],$$

where the equality follows using the first-order conditions (6).

Consider the case where the price function for computers, $h_t(x_t)$, takes on the semi-log form, $\ln p_t = \ln \mathbf{h}^t(\mathbf{x}_t) = \alpha_t + \beta_t'\mathbf{x}_t$. Then equation (8) is positive semi-definite if and only if $\ln f(\mathbf{x}, \mathbf{s}_t)$ is concave in a neighborhood around $x_t$, which gives our first set of assumptions.

ASSUMPTION 1. *(a) $h^t(\mathbf{x})$ is semi-log in* $\mathbf{x}$, $\ln p_t = \ln h^t(\mathbf{x}) = \alpha_t + \beta_t'\mathbf{x}$, $t = 1, \ldots, T$; *(b)* $\ln f(\mathbf{x}, \mathbf{s})$ *is concave in x in an open convex region that includes* $(\mathbf{x}_t, \mathbf{s}_t)$, $t = 1, \ldots, T$.

Note that by letting $\mathbf{x}_t = \ln \mathbf{z}_t$ for underlying characteristics $\mathbf{z}_t$, then assumption 1 can also be used for the log-log hedonic price function.

Clearly, parts (a) and (b) of assumption 1 go together: with other assumptions on the functional form of the hedonic regression $h^t(\mathbf{x})$, there would be alternative properties for $f(\mathbf{x}, \mathbf{s}_t)$ implied by the second-order conditions. For example, suppose that we treated $h^t(\mathbf{x})$ as linear in $\mathbf{x}$ rather than semi-log. Then the matrix $\mathbf{h}^t_{xx}(\mathbf{x}_t)$ in equation (8) vanishes, and we see that the second-order necessary condition is satisfied if and only if $f(\mathbf{x}, \mathbf{s}_t)$ is concave in a neighborhood around $\mathbf{x}_t$, which gives our second, alternative set of assumptions.

ASSUMPTION 2. *(a)* $h_t(\mathbf{x})$ *is linear in* $\mathbf{x}$, $p_t = h^t(\mathbf{x}) = \alpha_t + \beta_t'\mathbf{x}$, $t = 1, \ldots, T$; *(b)* $f(\mathbf{x}, \mathbf{s})$ *is concave in* $\mathbf{x}$ *in an open convex region that includes* $(\mathbf{x}_t, \mathbf{s}_t)$, $t = 1, \ldots, T$.

The BLS actually uses a linear hedonic regression (Holdway 2001), but we will derive results that hold under either assumptions 1 or 2.[6]

The BLS makes a hedonic adjustment to computer prices to deflate the output of the computer sector within the producer price index. This price index then becomes an input price to sectors using computers, where we expect the hedonically-adjusted price index to reflect the cost of services obtained. To describe this in terms of problem (1′), the "true" price of computer services is $p_t/f(\mathbf{x}_t, \mathbf{s}_t)$, or the nominal price deflated by the services obtained from a machine. Let $P^0(p_{t-1}, p_t, \mathbf{x}_{t-1}, \mathbf{x}_t)$ and $P^1(p_{t-1}, p_t, \mathbf{x}_{t-1}, \mathbf{x}_t)$ denote two alternative measures of a constant-quality price ratio for a computer model between years $t-1$ and $t$ (i.e., with *constant* characteristics). We wish to use these measures to obtain bounds on the true services price $p_t/f(\mathbf{x}_t, \mathbf{s}_t)$, such that:

$$P^0(p_{t-1}, p_t, \mathbf{x}_{t-1}, \mathbf{x}_t) \geq \frac{p_t/f(\mathbf{x}_t, \mathbf{s}_t)}{p_{t-1}/f(\mathbf{x}_{t-1}, \mathbf{s}_t)}, \tag{9a}$$

and,

$$P^1(p_{t-1}, p_t, \mathbf{x}_{t-1}, \mathbf{x}_t) \leq \frac{p_t/f(\mathbf{x}_t, \mathbf{s}_{t-1})}{p_{t-1}/f(\mathbf{x}_{t-1}, \mathbf{s}_{t-1})}. \tag{9b}$$

The right side of equation (9) is the ratio of the price of computers services, but measured at a *constant* level of software ($\mathbf{s}_t$ or $\mathbf{s}_{t-1}$). If the inequalities in equation (9) hold, then we have obtained bounds on the change in the true services price, using the constant-quality price ratios $P^0$ and $P^1$. (Additional bounds will be obtained after the statement of proposition 1.)

In practice, BLS constructs the producer price index for personal computers as follows (Holdway 2001). Let $p_t = \mathbf{h}^t(\mathbf{x}_t) = \alpha_t + \beta_t'\mathbf{x}_t$ denote the linear hedonic regression, $t = 1, \ldots, T$. Then $\mathbf{h}^t(\mathbf{x}_{t-1}) = p_t - \beta_t'(\mathbf{x}_t - \mathbf{x}_{t-1})$ measures the price in year $t$ *minus* an adjustment for the changed characteristics between the two years. Triplett (1986) refers to this as making an "explicit hedonic adjustment" to the period $t$ price. The ratio of prices in year $t$ and $t-1$ with constant characteristics is:

$$P^0(p_{t-1}, p_t, \mathbf{x}_{t-1}, \mathbf{x}_t) \equiv \frac{\mathbf{h}^t(\mathbf{x}_{t-1})}{p_{t-1}} = \frac{[p_t - \beta_t'(\mathbf{x}_t - \mathbf{x}_{t-1})]}{p_{t-1}}. \tag{10a}$$

6. While assumptions 1 or 2 ensure that the second-order necessary conditions for (7) hold, we will further assume that (7) gives a unique solution for the characteristics.

While equation (10) is the method used by BLS, it is straightforward to consider alternative ways to make the hedonic adjustment. In particular, rather than adjusting the period $t$ price in (10a), we could instead adjust the period $t-1$ price, obtaining:

$$\text{(10b)} \qquad P^1(p_{t-1}, p_t, \mathbf{x}_{t-1}, \mathbf{x}_t) \equiv \frac{p_t}{\mathbf{h}^{t-1}(\mathbf{x}_t)} = \frac{p_t}{[p_{t-1} + \beta'_{t-1}(\mathbf{x}_t - \mathbf{x}_{t-1})]}.$$

We would expect the indexes $P^0$ and $P^1$ to be quite close in practice, provided that the price surface $\mathbf{h}^t(\mathbf{x}_t)$ is not changing too rapidly over time.

The particular form for the hedonic correction used in equation (10) depends on the functional form of $\mathbf{h}^t(\mathbf{x}_t)$. If instead we suppose that $\ln p_t = \ln \mathbf{h}^t(\mathbf{x}_t) = \alpha_t + \beta'_t\mathbf{x}_t$ is semi-log, $t = 1, \ldots, T$, then the constant-quality price ratios are:

$$\text{(11a)} \qquad P^0(p_{t-1}, p_t, \mathbf{x}_{t-1}, \mathbf{x}_t) \equiv \frac{\mathbf{h}^t(\mathbf{x}_{t-1})}{p_{t-1}} = \frac{p_t \exp[-\beta'_t(\mathbf{x}_t - \mathbf{x}_{t-1})]}{p_{t-1}},$$

and,

$$\text{(11b)} \qquad P^1(p_{t-1}, p_t, \mathbf{x}_{t-1}, \mathbf{x}_t) \equiv \frac{p_t}{\mathbf{h}^{t-1}(\mathbf{x}_t)} = \frac{p_t}{p_{t-1}\exp[\beta'_{t-1}(\mathbf{x}_t - \mathbf{x}_{t-1})]}.$$

Following Berndt and Rappaport (2001, 270), we define the hedonic Laspeyres and Paasche prices indexes, respectively, as equations (11a) and (11b), evaluated using the *mean value* of characteristics over the models available each period. The mean value of characteristics are *also* used to evaluate the expected prices, $\bar{p}_t \equiv \mathbf{h}^t(\bar{\mathbf{x}}_t)$, $t = 1, \ldots, T$. Notice that the hedonic Laspeyres index is then $P^0 = \mathbf{h}^t(\bar{\mathbf{x}}_{t-1})/\mathbf{h}^{t-1}(\bar{\mathbf{x}}_{t-1})$, which uses last-period characteristics, while the hedonic Paasche index is $P^1 = \mathbf{h}^t(\bar{\mathbf{x}}_t)/\mathbf{h}^{t-1}(\bar{\mathbf{x}}_t)$, which uses present-period characteristics.[7]

We will use equation (11) as the constant-quality price ratio corresponding to assumption 1, and those in equation (10) for assumption 2. The question is whether either of these provide valid bounds to the true price of computer services. The following result shows that this is indeed the case.

PROPOSITION 1. *Suppose that characteristics are chosen optimally as in (6). Then under assumption 1 (or 2), the constant-quality price ratios defined in (11) (or 10, respectively) provide bounds to the change in the true price of computers services, so that (9) is satisfied.*

The proof of proposition 1 is in the appendix, and follows from exploiting the concavity of $f(\mathbf{x}_t, \mathbf{s}_t)$ or $\ln f(\mathbf{x}_t, \mathbf{s}_t)$. Note that if the one-sided bounds in

7. Of course, the usual Laspeyres and Paasche price indexes use last-period and present-period *quantity weights,* respectively. We will not have the quantities available in our data set, so our definition of these terms in the hedonic context refers to the use of last-period and present-period characteristics. Feenstra (1995) argues that the Laspeyres and Paasche hedonic indexes provides bounds on the change in consumer welfare, analogous to proposition 1.

equations (9a) and (9b) hold, then we can also obtain two-sided bounds by following a technique due to Diewert (1983, 173) and Diewert (2001, 173 and 242), and originally due to Konüs (1939, 20–21). Define $s(\lambda) \equiv \lambda \mathbf{s}_{t-1} + (1-\lambda)\mathbf{s}_t$ for $0 \leq \lambda \leq 1$, and let $R(\lambda) \equiv \{p_t/f[\mathbf{x}_t, s(\lambda)]\}/\{p_{t-1}/f[\mathbf{x}_{t-1}, s(\lambda)]\}$ denote the ratio appearing on the right of equation (9). Since we have assumed that $f(x, s)$ is positive and continuous in $s$, then $R(\lambda)$ is continuous in $\lambda$. With this notation, the inequality in (9a) is $P^0 \geq R(0)$, and the inequality in (9b) is $R(1) \geq P^1$. In general, we might find that $P^0$ is above or below $P^1$, so we do not obtain two–sided bounds on either $R(0)$ or $R(1)$. But by using the Diewert-Konüs technique, we can establish two-sided bounds on $R(\lambda^*)$, for $\lambda^* \in (0,1)$, as follows.

COROLLARY 1. *Under the hypotheses of proposition 1, there exists* $\lambda^* \in [0,1]$ *and* $\mathbf{s}^* \equiv \lambda^*\mathbf{s}_{t-1} + (1-\lambda^*)\mathbf{s}_t$ *such that:*

$$\text{(12a)} \qquad P^0(p_{t-1}, p_t, \mathbf{x}_{t-1}, \mathbf{x}_t) \geq \frac{p_t/f(\mathbf{x}_t, \mathbf{s}^*)}{p_{t-1}/f(\mathbf{x}_{t-1}, \mathbf{s}^*)} \geq P^1(p_{t-1}, p_t, \mathbf{x}_{t-1}, \mathbf{x}_t),$$

*or,*

$$\text{(12b)} \qquad P^0(p_{t-1}, p_t, \mathbf{x}_{t-1}, \mathbf{x}_t) \leq \frac{p_t/f(\mathbf{x}_t, \mathbf{s}^*)}{p_{t-1}/f(\mathbf{x}_{t-1}, \mathbf{s}^*)} \leq P^1(p_{t-1}, p_t, \mathbf{x}_{t-1}, \mathbf{x}_t),$$

*depending on which of* $P^0(p_{t-1}, p_t, \mathbf{x}_{t-1}, \mathbf{x}_t)$ *and* $P^1(p_{t-1}, p_t, \mathbf{x}_{t-1}, \mathbf{x}_t)$ *is larger.*

Provided the two bounds $P^0(p_{t-1}, p_t, \mathbf{x}_{t-1}, \mathbf{x}_t)$ and $P^1(p_{t-1}, p_t, \mathbf{x}_{t-1}, \mathbf{x}_t)$ are reasonably close to each other, we conclude from equation (12) that the use of either one provides a good measure of the change in the services price for that computer, evaluated at an intermediate level of software. Proposition 1 and corollary 1 give us some confidence in the hedonic adjustment made by BLS, but it obtained by ignoring issues of dynamics. The durability of computers, along with changing software, is introduced in the next section.

### 3.3 Dynamic Problem with Changing Software

We now suppose that a computer purchased lasts for a number of periods. The services received in period $t$ for a computer purchased in $t-\tau$ with characteristics $\mathbf{x}_{t-\tau}$, is $f(\mathbf{x}_{t-\tau}, \mathbf{s}_t)$. We adopt the convention that if $f(\mathbf{x}_{t-\tau}, \mathbf{s}_t)$ ever becomes negative (i.e., the computer is dysfunctional), then we redefine the value of this function at zero. The firm will continue to use this computer so long as $f(\mathbf{x}_{t-\tau}, \mathbf{s}_t) > 0$. Let $\overline{T}$ be the longest period that any computer is held. Then the buyer solves the dynamic problem:

$$\text{(13)} \qquad \max_{y_t, n_t, x_t} \sum_{t=\overline{T}}^{\infty} \beta^{t-\overline{T}} G\left[y_t, \sum_{\tau=0}^{\overline{T}} n_{t-\tau} f(\mathbf{x}_{t-\tau}, \mathbf{s}_t)\right] - n_t \mathbf{h}^t(\mathbf{x}_t) - q_t \mathbf{y}_t,$$

where $p_t = \mathbf{h}^t(\mathbf{x}_t)$ is again the price of a computer, $K_t \equiv \sum_{\tau=0}^{\bar{T}} n_{t-\tau} f(\mathbf{x}_{t-\tau}, \mathbf{s}_t)$ is the capital stock measured in efficiency units, $\beta$ is a constant discount rate between 0 and 1, and the values of $n_t$ and $\mathbf{x}_t$ for $t < \bar{T}$ are taken as given. Note that for simplicity we have treated the future state of software $\mathbf{s}_t$ as known with perfect foresight.

The first-order conditions for equation (13) are:

$$G_y(\mathbf{y}_t, K_t) = q_t, \tag{14a}$$

$$\sum_{\tau=0}^{\bar{T}} \beta^\tau G_K(\mathbf{y}_{t+\tau}, K_{t+\tau}) f(\mathbf{x}_t, \mathbf{s}_{t+\tau}) = h^t(\mathbf{x}_t), \tag{14b}$$

$$\sum_{\tau=0}^{\bar{T}} \beta^\tau G_K(\mathbf{y}_{t+\tau}, K_{t+\tau}) n_t f_x(\mathbf{x}_t, \mathbf{s}_{t+\tau}) = n_t \mathbf{h}_x^t(\mathbf{x}_t). \tag{14c}$$

Dividing equation (14c) by (14b), we obtain:

$$\frac{\sum_{\tau=0}^{\bar{T}} \beta^\tau G_K(\mathbf{y}_{t+\tau}, K_{t+\tau}) f_x(\mathbf{x}_t, \mathbf{s}_{t+\tau})}{\sum_{\tau=0}^{\bar{T}} \beta^\tau G_K(\mathbf{y}_{t+\tau}, K_{t+\tau}) f(\mathbf{x}_t, \mathbf{s}_{t+\tau})} = \frac{\mathbf{h}_x^t(\mathbf{x}_t)}{\mathbf{h}^t(\mathbf{x}_t)}, \tag{15}$$

as the first-order condition that defines the choice of characteristics $\mathbf{x}_t$ for the computer(s) purchased in period $t$.

This first-order condition is *forward-looking,* in that the firm will be evaluating the marginal productivity of characteristics over the lifetime of the machine. To make this explicit, note that equation (15) can be rewritten as:

$$\sum_{\tau=0}^{\bar{T}} \theta_{t,\tau} \frac{f_x(\mathbf{x}_t, \mathbf{s}_{t+\tau})}{f(\mathbf{x}_t, \mathbf{s}_{t+\tau})} = \frac{\mathbf{h}_x^t(\mathbf{x}_t)}{\mathbf{h}^t(\mathbf{x}_t)} \tag{16a}$$

with the weights,

$$\theta_{t,\tau} \equiv \frac{\beta^\tau G_K(\mathbf{y}_{t+\tau}, K_{t+\tau}) f(\mathbf{x}_t, \mathbf{s}_{t+\tau})}{\sum_{\tau=0}^{\bar{T}} \beta^\tau G_K(\mathbf{y}_{t+\tau}, K_{t+\tau}) f(\mathbf{x}_t, \mathbf{s}_{t+\tau})}, \tag{16b}$$

where $\sum_{\tau=0}^{\bar{T}} \theta_{\tau,t} = 1$.

To simplify this first-order condition, it is convenient to adopt a specific functional form for the production function $f(\mathbf{x}, \mathbf{s})$. In particular, we shall adopt the translog form:

$$\ln f^\ell(\mathbf{x}, \mathbf{s}) = a_\ell' \mathbf{x} + \frac{1}{2}\mathbf{x}' A \mathbf{x} + b' \mathbf{s} + \frac{1}{2}\mathbf{s}' B \mathbf{s} + \mathbf{x}' \Gamma \mathbf{s}, \tag{17}$$

where $\ell = 1, \ldots, L$ denotes different buyers. The parameters $(A, b, B, \Gamma)$ are constant across buyers, while we allow the marginal benefits to vary across users by the coefficients $a_\ell$. To satisfy Assumption 1(b) the matrix **A** must be negative semi-definite, and we shall consider some restrictions on the matrix $\mathbf{\Gamma}$ following.

Notice that the marginal value of characteristics, $f_x^\ell / f^\ell$, is linear in the software **s**. It follows that by substituting equation (17) into (16), we can rewrite the first-order condition as:

(18a)
$$\frac{f^{\ell}(\mathbf{x}_t, \tilde{\mathbf{s}}_t)}{f^{\ell}(\mathbf{x}_{t-1}, \tilde{\mathbf{s}}_t)} = \frac{\mathbf{h}^t_x(\mathbf{x}_t)}{\mathbf{h}^t(\mathbf{x}_t)},$$

where

(18b)
$$\tilde{\mathbf{s}}_t \equiv \sum_{\tau=0}^{\bar{T}} \theta_{t,\tau} \mathbf{s}_{t+\tau}.$$

That is, the marginal value of characteristics, evaluated with the *average future state of software* $\tilde{\mathbf{s}}_t$, equals the marginal cost of characteristics today. This first-order condition (18) takes the place of equation (9), as obtained with a nondurable computer, and shows that the characteristics $\mathbf{x}_t$ chosen at time $t$ are *optimal for the future state of software* $\tilde{\mathbf{s}}_t$.

Turning to the hedonic adjustment of computer prices, we continue to assume that the goal of the constant-quality price ratios $P^0(p_{t-1}, p_t, \mathbf{x}_{t-1}, \mathbf{x}_t)$ and $P^1(p_{t-1}, p_t, \mathbf{x}_{t-1}, \mathbf{x}_t)$ is to satisfy the inequalities in equation (9). However, now we need to ask: at what level of software are the efficiency of the new and old computers compared? In equation (9), we considered the software available at either $\mathbf{s}_{t-1}$ or $\mathbf{s}_t$. In the dynamic model, however, the characteristics chosen in equation (18) are optimal for the future level of software $\tilde{\mathbf{s}}_t$. This can be expected to impact the form of the inequalities in equation (9), as is confirmed by the following result:

PROPOSITION 2. *Suppose that computer services are given by the translog function (17) and characteristics are chosen optimally as in (18). Then under Assumption 1 (or 2), the constant-quality price ratios defined in (11) (or 10, respectively) provide the bounds:*

(19a)
$$P^0(p_{t-1}, p_t, \mathbf{x}_{t-1}, \mathbf{x}_t) \geq \frac{p_t / f^{\ell}(\mathbf{x}_t, \tilde{\mathbf{s}}_t)}{p_{t-1} / f^{\ell}(\mathbf{x}_{t-1}, \tilde{\mathbf{s}}_t)},$$

*and,*

(19b)
$$P^1(p_{t-1}, p_t, \mathbf{x}_{t-1}, \mathbf{x}_t) \leq \frac{p_t / f^{\ell}(\mathbf{x}_t, \tilde{\mathbf{s}}_{t-1})}{p_{t-1} / f^{\ell}(\mathbf{x}_{t-1}, \tilde{\mathbf{s}}_{t-1})}$$

The constant-quality price ratios $P^0$ and $P^1$ appearing on the left of equation (19) are similar to current BLS practice, while the expressions on the right of (19) are the true change in the price of computer services. So this result shows that BLS methods provides valid bound to the true change in the price of computer services when period $t-1$ and $t$ machines *are both evaluated at the same average future level of software.* It is worth stressing that these bounds (like those in proposition 1) are an economic property, and depend on optimizing behavior; that is, on the first-order condition (18) as well as the concavity properties in assumption 1 or 2. In our empirical work we shall evaluate these bounds by computing the quality-adjusted price ratios on the left of (19) and estimating the production function $f^{\ell}(\mathbf{x}_t, \tilde{\mathbf{s}}_t)$ that appears on the right. We will find periods in the sample where the bounds do not hold, which can arise due to nonoptimizing behavior or due to mismeasurement of the production function.

Setting aside the empirical validity of the bounds in equation (19), however, there is another question we can ask about proposition 2, and that concerns the level of software used to evaluate true ratio of services price on the right of (19). Suppose that instead of evaluating the firms' production functions $f^{\ell}(\mathbf{x}_t, \tilde{\mathbf{s}}_t)$ with *future* software as in (19), our goal instead is to evaluate it with *current* software ($\mathbf{s}_t$ or $\mathbf{s}_{t-1}$), as on the right of equation (9). Thus, when the BLS producer price index for computers is used to deflate computer input purchases by firms, we are assuming that the price index accurately reflects cost of purchasing services at the current level of software. Therefore, we are interested in knowing whether BLS procedures—like the construction of the constant-quality price ratios $P^0$ and $P^1$—provide bounds to the true services price ratio at current levels of software.

To answer this question, we introduce additional restrictions on the production function $f^{\ell}(x, s)$. In particular, suppose that characteristics and software are *complements* in the sense that $\partial^2 \ln f^{\ell}/\partial x \partial s = \Gamma > 0$, so that an increase in software raises the marginal product of characteristics. With this assumption we have the following extension of proposition 2:

COROLLARY 2. *If* $\Gamma > 0$ *and software is rising over time,* $\mathbf{s}_{t-1} \leq \mathbf{s}_t$, *then the bounds in (19) become:*

$$\text{(20a)} \qquad P^0(p_{t-1}, p_t, \mathbf{x}_{t-1}, \mathbf{x}_t) \geq \frac{p_t/f^{\ell}(\mathbf{x}_t, \tilde{\mathbf{s}}_t)}{p_{t-1}/f^{\ell}(\mathbf{x}_{t-1}, \tilde{\mathbf{s}}_t)} \leq \frac{p_t/f^{\ell}(\mathbf{x}_t, \mathbf{s}_t)}{p_{t-1}/f^{\ell}(\mathbf{x}_{t-1}, \mathbf{s}_t)},$$

*and,*

$$\text{(20b)} \qquad P^1(p_{t-1}, p_t, \mathbf{x}_{t-1}, \mathbf{x}_t) \leq \frac{p_t/f^{\ell}(\mathbf{x}_t, \tilde{\mathbf{s}}_{t-1})}{p_{t-1}/f^{\ell}(\mathbf{x}_{t-1}, \tilde{\mathbf{s}}_{t-1})} \leq \frac{p_t/f^{\ell}(\mathbf{x}_t, \mathbf{s}_{t-1})}{p_{t-1}/f^{\ell}(\mathbf{x}_{t-1}, \mathbf{s}_{t-1})}.$$

*Conversely, if* $\Gamma < 0$ *and software is rising over time, then the second inequalities appearing in (20a) and (20b) are reversed.*

The first inequalities appearing in equation (20) are identical to those in (19), of course, so the new results in the corollary are the second inequalities. From (20), it is evident that BLS procedures do not provide bounds to the true services price ratio evaluated at *the current (period t – 1 or t) fixed level of software.* When $\Gamma > 0$, the constant-quality price ratio $P^0$ on the left of (20a) is no longer an upper bound for the change in the price of services on the right. While the price ratio $P^1$ on the left of (20b) is a lower bound for the change in the price of services, there is nothing that guarantees that this bound will be tight: it could be significantly less than the true change in the prices of computer services.[8] When $\Gamma < 0$ then the second inequalities in (20) are reversed, and with mixed signs within $\Gamma$ we will generally have to evaluate the production functions $f^{\ell}(\mathbf{x}_t, \tilde{\mathbf{s}}_t)$ and $f^{\ell}(\mathbf{x}_t, \mathbf{s}_t)$ to know how the true ratio of services price compares at the future and current levels of software.[9]

As noted in the previous section, when we evaluate the quality-adjusted price ratios $P^0$ and $P^1$ at the *mean* level of characteristics each year (and corresponding expected price), we obtain the hedonic Laspeyres and Paasche indexes, respectively. These are the bounds on the left of (20), and the Laspeyres index is currently constructed by the BLS. Likewise, we can evaluate the production functions appearing in (20) at the mean level of characteristics each year to obtain indexes of the true price of computer services. As in (20), these indexes can be constructed with either future levels of software ($\tilde{\mathbf{s}}_{t-1}$ or $\tilde{\mathbf{s}}_t$) or current levels of software ($\mathbf{s}_{t-1}$ or $\mathbf{s}_t$). The precise construction of these indexes is discussed in the next section.

## 3.4 Measurement of Computer Price Indexes

Our interest is in estimating $\Gamma$ and other parameters of the translog services function (17), and to use these to construct the true price ratio of computer services, measured with constant software $\mathbf{s}_{t-1}$ or $\mathbf{s}_t$ as on the right of equation (20). These time-series of true services prices can then be compared to the constant-quality price ratios $P^0$ and $P^1$ in equation (11). If there is a significant difference between the change in the true price ratio and these constant-quality price ratios, this will indicate the potential bias in current BLS procedures.

The estimation will rely on a two-step procedure. In the first step we estimate conventional hedonic regressions on desktop PCs from monthly data. The data are from the *PC Data Retail Hardware Monthly Report* and report quantities, average monthly prices, and a number of machine characteristics for desktop computers. These data run from August 1997 to December 1999.[10] We augment these data with desktop computer ads from *PC Maga-*

8. This problem also arises for the bound in (9b), which might not be tight. However, the derivation in (10) shows that provided the indexes $P^0(p_{t-1}, p_t, \mathbf{x}_{t-1}, \mathbf{x}_t)$ and $P^1(p_{t-1}, p_t, \mathbf{x}_{t-1}, \mathbf{x}_t)$ and are reasonably close to each other, then we do obtain a tight bound for the "true" index $R(s^*)$ evaluated at an intermediate level of software $s^*$. Using (19) and the same argument as in (10), we could obtain two-sided bounds for the "true" index $R(\tilde{s}^*)$ at an intermediate level of *forward-looking* software $\tilde{s}^*$. But what corollary 2 shows is that we *do not* obtain the two-sided bounds for the "true" index evaluated at any intermediate level of *current* software $s^*$, lying in-between $\mathbf{s}_{t-1}$ and $\mathbf{s}_t$.

9. Note that the second inequalities appearing in (20) are numerical rather than economic properties: once the sign pattern of $\Gamma$ is established by estimation, if it has mostly positive elements then the true price index with current software should exceed that with future software.

10. We thank Lanier Benkard for providing these data.

*zine;* these data cover April 1999 to September 2001, but have fewer observations per month. Following Benkard and Bajari (2003), for each machine in our data, we collected processor benchmark data from *The CPU Scorecard.* The benchmark data reduce the complex interaction between a processor's type and speed to a single index measuring performance. In addition to the processor benchmark, we include the amount of memory, the size of the hard drive, and a number of indicator variables in the hedonic regressions. These indicator variables are: whether the computer has a CD player, sound card, Zip drive, network card, LCD monitor, and whether it has SCSI hard drives. In addition, we treat the computer's factory-installed operating system as a characteristic in the hedonic regressions. The summary statistics for prices and computer characteristics are reported in table 3.1, while table 3.2 reports the correlation matrix for the variables.

In the first step, we estimate the semi-log form:

$$\text{(21)} \qquad \ln p_{it} = \alpha_t + \beta_t' \mathbf{x}_{it} + \varepsilon_{it}, \qquad i = 1, \ldots, N; t = 1, \ldots, T,$$

where $i = 1, \ldots, N$ denotes individual personal computers (not necessarily available each period), and $t = 1, \ldots, T$ denotes months from August 1997 to September 2001. Using these monthly hedonic regressions, we construct the change in constant-quality prices from equation (11) as:

$$\text{(22a)} \qquad \ln P_i^0 = \ln p_{it} - \ln p_{it-1} - \hat{\beta}_t'(\mathbf{x}_{it} - \mathbf{x}_{it-1}),$$

$$\text{(22b)} \qquad \ln P_i^1 = \ln p_{it} - \ln p_{it-1} - \hat{\beta}_{t-1}'(\mathbf{x}_{it} - \mathbf{x}_{it-1}).$$

As discussed in section 3.3, we follow Berndt and Rappaport (2001, 270) and construct the hedonic Laspeyres and Paasche price indexes by evaluating (22a) and (22b) using the mean value of characteristics over the models

**Table 3.1** **Aggregate summary statistics**

| Variable | Mean | Median | Standard deviation | Min | Max |
|---|---|---|---|---|---|
| Price | 1,197.52 | 1,088.91 | 5,999.20 | 400 | 9,430 |
| Processor speed | 851.971 | 777 | 622.98 | 55 | 7,768 |
| Ram (megabytes) | 52.505 | 32 | 45.15 | 0 | 1,128 |
| HD size (gigabytes) | 5.731 | 4.30 | 5.88 | 0 | 200 |
| Have CD? | 0.681 | 1 | — | 0 | 1 |
| SCSI? | 0.004 | 0 | — | 0 | 1 |
| Zip drive? | 0.034 | 0 | — | 0 | 1 |
| NIC? | 0.215 | 0 | — | 0 | 1 |
| Sound card? | 0.397 | 0 | — | 0 | 1 |
| LCD? | 0.063 | 0 | — | 0 | 1 |
| Sample Size: 32,406 | | | | | |

*Note:* Dashed cells indicate standard deviation not calculated.

**Table 3.2 Correlation matrix of computer characteristics**

| | Price | Processor speed | RAM | HD size | Have CD? | SCSI? | Zip drive? | NIC? | Sound card? | LCD? |
|---|---|---|---|---|---|---|---|---|---|---|
| Price | 1.00 | | | | | | | | | |
| Processor speed | 0.21 | 1.00 | | | | | | | | |
| Ram (megabytes) | 0.31 | 0.66 | 1.00 | | | | | | | |
| HD Size (gigabytes) | 0.21 | 0.83 | 0.66 | 1.00 | | | | | | |
| Have CD? | –0.02 | –0.01 | –0.00 | –0.00 | 1.00 | | | | | |
| SCSI? | 0.10 | 0.01 | 0.00 | –0.01 | 0.03 | 1.00 | | | | |
| Zip drive? | 0.08 | 0.10 | 0.17 | 0.15 | –0.01 | –0.01 | 1.00 | | | |
| NIC? | 0.11 | 0.25 | 0.11 | 0.14 | 0.03 | 0.10 | –0.02 | 1.00 | | |
| Sound card? | 0.14 | 0.51 | 0.29 | 0.50 | –0.01 | –0.01 | 0.05 | 0.07 | 1.00 | |
| LCD? | 0.07 | 0.12 | 0.09 | 0.14 | 0.03 | 0.00 | –0.01 | 0.02 | 0.10 | 1.00 |

available each period, $\overline{\mathbf{x}}_{t-1}$ and $\overline{\mathbf{x}}_t$, and the prices $\ln \overline{p}_t \equiv \hat{\alpha}_t + \hat{\beta}_t'\overline{\mathbf{x}}_t$, $t = 1, \ldots, T$. Substituting these into equation (22), we obtain:

(23a) Change in hedonic Laspeyres index $= [\hat{\alpha}_t - \hat{\alpha}_{t-1} + (\hat{\beta}_t - \hat{\beta}_{t-1})'\overline{\mathbf{x}}_{t-1}]$,

(23b) Change in hedonic Paasche index $= [\hat{\alpha}_t - \hat{\alpha}_{t-1} + (\hat{\beta}_t - \hat{\beta}_{t-1})'\overline{\mathbf{x}}_t]$.

The average of these is:

(24) Change in hedonic Fisher index

$$= [\hat{\alpha}_t - \hat{\alpha}_{t-1} + \frac{1}{2}(\hat{\beta}_t - \hat{\beta}_{t-1})'(\overline{\mathbf{x}}_t + \overline{\mathbf{x}}_{t-1})]$$

These log changes can be cumulated to obtain the levels of each index.

In the second step, we make use of actual purchases of desktop PCs by each academic or administrative department at the University of California, Davis, which we index by $\ell = 1, \ldots, L$. These data cover July 1997 through September of 2001 and report the machine characteristics for all purchases by each academic and administrative department. Table 3.3 reports the summary statistics for these data.[11] The UC Davis data are used to estimate the parameters of the translog production function (17), by using the first-order condition (18). Using (17) and (21), (18) then becomes:

(25)
$$\hat{\beta}_t = a_\ell + Ax_{i\ell t} + \sum_{\tau=0}^{\overline{T}} \theta_{t,\tau}\Gamma s_{t+\tau} + \mathbf{u}_{it},$$
$$i = 1, \ldots, N; \ell = 1, \ldots, L; t = 1, \ldots, T.$$

11. We do not use the purchase price for the UC Davis data set because it includes peripheral equipment, but we report this price in table 3.3 for completeness.

**Table 3.3** **Aggregate summary statistics for University of California, Davis, purchasing data**

| Variable | Mean | Median | Standard deviation | Min | Max |
|---|---|---|---|---|---|
| Price | 2,488.72 | 2,344.00 | 991.34 | 824 | 18,340 |
| Processor speed | 1,809.78 | 1,650 | 858.04 | 272 | 4,519 |
| Ram (megabytes) | 162.874 | 128 | 131.36 | 0 | 4,096 |
| HD size (gigabytes) | 13.878 | 10 | 12.877 | 0 | 180 |
| Have CD? | 0.720 | 1 | — | 0 | 1 |
| SCSI? | 0.068 | 0 | — | 0 | 1 |
| Zip drive? | 0.389 | 0 | — | 0 | 1 |
| NIC? | 0.704 | 1 | — | 0 | 1 |
| Sound card? | 0.503 | 1 | — | 0 | 1 |
| LCD? | 0.182 | 0 | — | 0 | 1 |
| Sample Size: 3,718 | | | | | |

*Note:* Dashed cells indicate standard deviation not calculated.

In this notation, $x_{i\ell t}$ denotes a computer of type $i$ purchased by department $\ell$ in month $t$, and $\mathbf{u}_{it}$ is a vector of residuals arising from regressing the *estimated* first-stage coefficients $\hat{\beta}_t$ on the observed purchases $x_{i\ell t}$ by each department and future software $\mathbf{s}_{t+\tau}$.[12] Notice that (25) is a vector of equations, one for each characteristic. From (17b), the weights $\theta_{t,\tau}$ sum to unity over $\tau = 0,1,..,\overline{T}$, where $\overline{T}$ is the numbers of periods that a machine purchased at time $t$ is used. For simplicity in the estimation we set $\overline{T}$ at three years.

Having obtained the estimates of $A$ and $\Gamma$ from (25), we can use these to construct the true change in computer services price, using the software at date $t-1$:

$$(26)\quad \ln\left[\frac{p_{it}/f^{\ell}(x_{it}, \mathbf{s}_{t-1})}{p_{it-1}/f^{\ell}(x_{it-1}, \mathbf{s}_{t-1})}\right]$$

$$= \ln p_{it} - \left(\hat{a}_{\ell}'x_{it} + \frac{1}{2}x_{it}'\hat{A}x_{it} + x_{it}'\hat{\Gamma}\mathbf{s}_{t-1}\right) - \ln p_{it-1}$$

$$+ \left(\hat{a}_{\ell}'x_{it-1} + \frac{1}{2}x_{it-1}'\hat{A}x_{it-1} + x_{it-1}'\hat{\Gamma}\mathbf{s}_{t-1}\right),$$

which follows from (17). To simplify (26), we can use the Quadratic Identity of Diewert (1976, 118), which states that the difference between the quadratic functions $\ln f^{\ell}(x_{it}, s_{it-1})$ and $\ln f^{\ell}(x_{it-1}, s_{it-1})$ equals:

12. The observed purchases $x_{i\ell t}$ are endogenous, but we do not attempt to control for that in the estimation of (25).

$$(27)\quad \ln f^{\ell}(\mathbf{x}_{it}, \mathbf{s}_{it-1}) - \ln f^{\ell}(\mathbf{x}_{it-1}, \mathbf{s}_{it-1}) = \frac{1}{2}\left[\frac{\partial \ln f^{\ell}}{\partial x_{it}} + \frac{\partial \ln f^{\ell}}{\partial x_{it-1}}\right]'(\mathbf{x}_{it} - \mathbf{x}_{it-1}),$$

where both derivatives are evaluated at $\mathbf{s}_{it-1}$. Let us denote the estimates of these derivatives by:

$$(28)\quad \hat{\hat{\beta}}^{\ell}_{t-1} \equiv \frac{1}{2}\left[\frac{\partial \ln f^{\ell}}{\partial x_{it}} + \frac{\partial \ln f^{\ell}}{\partial x_{it-1}}\right] = \hat{a}_{\ell} + \frac{1}{2}\hat{A}(\mathbf{x}_{it} + \mathbf{x}_{it-1}) + \hat{\Gamma}\mathbf{s}_{it-1},$$

which follows from the definition of the translog function in (17).

Then substituting (28) and (29) into (26), we can alternatively express the true change in services price, using the firms' production functions, as:

$$(26')\quad \ln\left[\frac{p_{it}/f^{\ell}(\mathbf{x}_{it}, \mathbf{s}_{t-1})}{p_{it-1}/f^{\ell}(\mathbf{x}_{it-1}, \mathbf{s}_{t-1})}\right] = [\ln p_{it} - \ln p_{it-1} - \hat{\hat{\beta}}^{\ell\prime}_{t-1}(\mathbf{x}_{it} - \mathbf{x}_{it-1})].$$

This formula applies to a single machine. To obtain an index of the true services price we evaluate (26′) at the mean value of characteristics in each period. We also use these mean characteristics to evaluate $\hat{\hat{\beta}}^{\ell}_{t-1}$ in (28), and to evaluate the prices $\ln \bar{p}_t \equiv \hat{\alpha}_t + \hat{\beta}_t'\bar{\mathbf{x}}_t$, also using the mean $a_\ell$ across departments. This gives us the index of the true change in services price:

$$(29)\quad \text{Change in true services price with software } s_{t-1}$$
$$= [\alpha_t + \hat{\beta}'_{it}\bar{\mathbf{x}}_t - \alpha_{t-1} - \hat{\beta}'_{it-1}\bar{\mathbf{x}}_{t-1} - \hat{\hat{\beta}}^{\ell\prime}_{t-1}(\bar{\mathbf{x}}_t - \bar{\mathbf{x}}_{t-1})].$$

Similarly, we can construct the true index using software at date $t$. Let $\hat{\hat{\beta}}^{\ell}_t$ denote exactly the same expression as in (28) but using $\mathbf{s}_t$ rather than $\mathbf{s}_{t-1}$.[13] Then taking the average of (29) evaluated with $\hat{\hat{\beta}}^{\ell}_{t-1}$ and $\hat{\hat{\beta}}^{\ell}_t$, we obtain a Fisher-type true index:

$$(30)\quad \text{Change in true services price with current software } \frac{1}{2}(\mathbf{s}_{t-1} + \mathbf{s}_t)$$
$$= [\alpha_t + \hat{\beta}'_{it}\bar{\mathbf{x}}_t - \alpha_{t-1} - \hat{\beta}'_{it-1}\bar{\mathbf{x}}_{t-1} - \frac{1}{2}(\hat{\hat{\beta}}^{\ell}_{t-1} + \hat{\hat{\beta}}^{\ell}_t)'(\bar{\mathbf{x}}_t - \bar{\mathbf{x}}_{t-1})].$$

Finally, we can evaluate the firms' production functions using future software $\tilde{\mathbf{s}}_t$, defined in (18b), rather than current software $\mathbf{s}_t$. Let $\tilde{\beta}^{\ell}_{t-1}$ denote exactly the same expression as in (28) but using $\tilde{\mathbf{s}}_{t-1}$ rather than $\mathbf{s}_{t-1}$, while $\tilde{\beta}^{\ell}_t$ uses $\tilde{\mathbf{s}}_t$. Then the Fisher-type true index using the future levels of software is:

$$(31)\quad \text{Change in true services price with future software } \frac{1}{2}(\tilde{\mathbf{s}}_{t-1} + \tilde{\mathbf{s}}_t)$$
$$= [\alpha_t + \hat{\beta}'_{it}\bar{\mathbf{x}}_t - \alpha_{t-1} - \hat{\beta}'_{it-1}\bar{\mathbf{x}}_{t-1} - \frac{1}{2}(\tilde{\beta}^{\ell}_t - 1 + \tilde{\beta}^{\ell}_t)'(\bar{\mathbf{x}}_t - \bar{\mathbf{x}}_{t-1})].$$

13. Again, we evaluate $\hat{\hat{\beta}}^{\ell}_t$ at the mean level of characteristics and the mean level of $a_\ell$ across departments.

We can compare these true service price indexes, obtained from the firms' production functions, to the Laspeyres and Paasche bounds from (23) or the hedonic Fisher index in (24). Notice that the difference between the change in the true services price using current software in (30) and the hedonic Fisher index in (24) can be simplified as:

(32) Change in true services price with current software – hedonic Fisher index

$$= \sum_{i=1}^{N} \frac{1}{2} [(\hat{\beta}_{t-1} + \hat{\beta}_t) - (\hat{\hat{\beta}}^{\ell}_{t-1} + \hat{\hat{\beta}}^{\ell}_t)]'(\overline{\mathbf{x}}_t - \overline{\mathbf{x}}_{t-1}).$$

Likewise, the difference between equations (31) and (24) has the same form as (32), but using $\tilde{\beta}_{t-1}$ and $\tilde{\beta}_t$ rather than $\hat{\hat{\beta}}_{t-1}$ and $\hat{\hat{\beta}}_t$. With characteristics growing over time, expression (32) will be *positive* provided that $(1/2)(\hat{\beta}_{t-1} + \hat{\beta}_t) > (1/2)(\hat{\hat{\beta}}^{\ell}_{t-1} + \hat{\hat{\beta}}^{\ell}_{t-1})$. This condition states that the typically estimated hedonic coefficients, $\hat{\beta}_{t-1}$ and $\hat{\beta}_t$, exceed the true value of these characteristics to the user with software at time $t-1$ and $t$, $\hat{\hat{\beta}}^{\ell}_{t-1}$, and $\hat{\hat{\beta}}^{\ell}_t$. This corresponds to our intuition that users may "overbuy" characteristics such as RAM and hard disk space because they will become more valuable at future states of software.

## 3.5 Empirical Results

### 3.5.1 Hedonic Regressions

To conserve on space, we do not report each of the coefficients from the monthly hedonic equations, but table 3.4 summarizes the coefficients for the included characteristics. The typical $R^2$ from the hedonic regression is roughly 0.60, but ranges from 0.13 to 0.90. It is important to note that the value of the characteristics captured by indicator variables may not be identified in a given month, since in some months all of the computers in

**Table 3.4** **Summary statistics for hedonic coefficients, semi-log model**

| Variable | Mean | Standard deviation | Min | Max | N |
|---|---|---|---|---|---|
| Processor speed | 0.0007 | 0.0003 | 0.0003 | 0.0016 | 50 |
| Ram | 0.0024 | 0.0015 | –0.0012 | 0.0068 | 50 |
| HD size | 0.0050 | 0.0138 | –0.0219 | 0.0416 | 50 |
| Have CD? | –0.0218 | 0.0746 | –0.1973 | 0.1941 | 49 |
| SCSI? | 0.2239 | 0.1249 | –0.0231 | 0.5398 | 29 |
| Zip drive? | 0.0283 | 0.1047 | –0.2288 | 0.2631 | 36 |
| NIC? | 0.0567 | 0.0899 | –0.2304 | 0.1905 | 50 |
| Sound card? | –0.0384 | 0.3867 | –0.9108 | 0.4198 | 29 |
| LCD? | 0.3309 | 0.3623 | –0.7544 | 0.9122 | 31 |

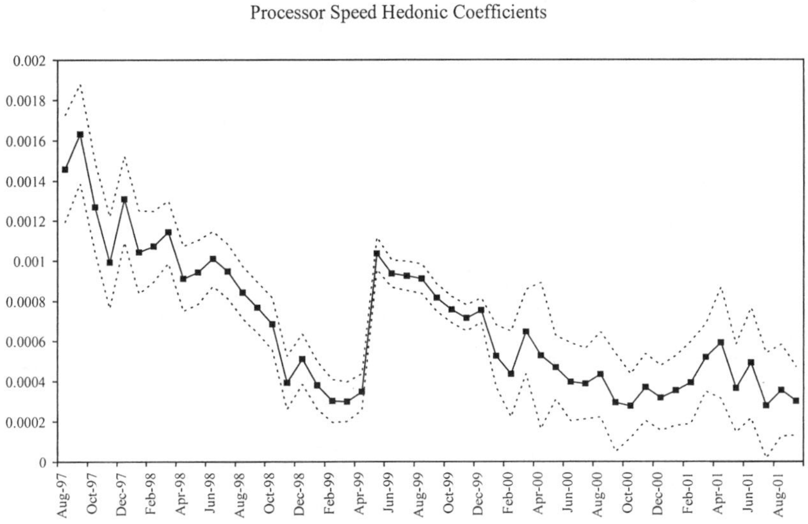


**Fig. 3.1 Plot of the monthly processor speed hedonic coefficients for semi-log model**

the sample have or do not have the given characteristic. In general, the mean coefficient for each of the characteristics is positive. The exceptions are the indicator variables for whether the computer has a CD or a sound card; the coefficients associated with these characteristics are quite noisy.

Figures 3.1 through 3.3 track the monthly hedonic coefficients for the processor speed, RAM and hard drive size variables and provide 95 percent confidence intervals for the point estimates. We focus on these three characteristics because their coefficients are identified in every month and they are the main determinants of a computer's price.[14] Each of the coefficients display a general downward trend as characteristic prices fell during our sample; a regression of the coefficient on a linear time confirms this and yields negative and significant coefficients for each of the variables. The processor speed coefficient displays a sharp increase between May 1999 and June 1999. We have verified with www.cpuscorecard.com that this is not due to a change in the benchmark definition. In addition, the hard drive coefficient exhibits a sharp decline between August 1997 and August 1998. Finally, the processor speed and RAM coefficients display a reduction in precision later in the sample. This is due to smaller sample sizes for the *PC Magazine* price data compared to the *PC Data Retail Hardware Monthly Report* data.[15]

14. These three variables alone account for, on average, over 80 percent of the *explained* variation from the hedonic regressions.

15. In our second stage regressions, we report heteroskedastic consistent standard errors to account for this.

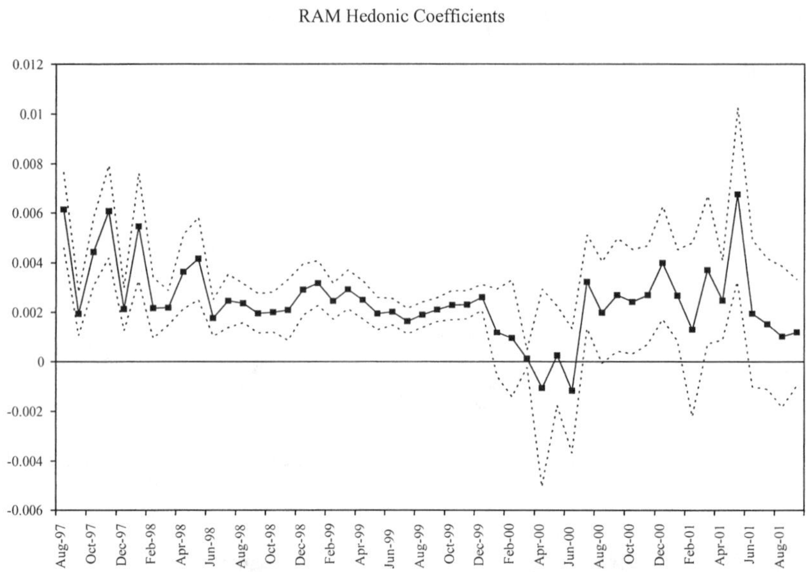


**Fig. 3.2 Plot of the monthly RAM hedonic coefficients for semi-log model**

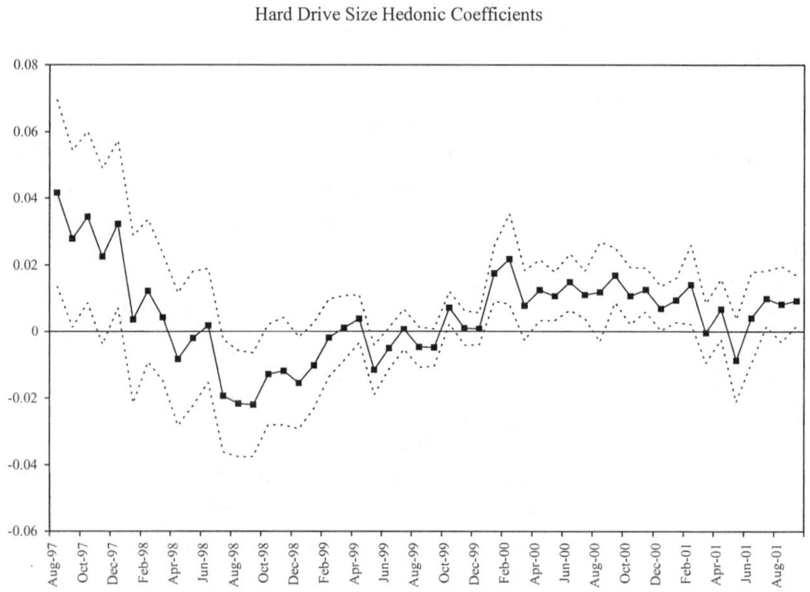


**Fig. 3.3 Plot of the monthly hard drive hedonic coefficients for semi-log model**

### 3.5.2 Departmental Production Functions

A key component for the decision process of the consumer or firm is the expected software quality; admittedly, this is difficult to quantify. We discussed a number of potential measures of quality with software programmers and settled on the *recommended hard drive space* for both Microsoft Windows and Microsoft Word. Increases in software require additional hard-drive capacity and will be reflected in the recommended hard drive capacities of the programs.[16] This measure displays a general upward trend as both Office and Windows have added features. As with the dependent variable in the second stage, our software quality measure exhibits time series variation and is identified from the change in the average characteristics of purchased computers over time.

Estimating equation (25) requires including the *expected* movements in software quality over the lifetime of the machine. Rather than modeling the primitives of these expectations, we include the actual movements of our software quality measure. To capture the uncertainty associated with these expectations, we assume an artificially high discount rate, 2 percent per month, in equation (18b). This implies that departments place more weight on the expectations of software quality during the earlier months of a computer's lifetime. The high discount rate suggests they do so because there is less uncertainty regarding quality early in the lifetime of the machine.

We focus on the first-order condition (25) for three characteristics: processor speed, hard drive size, and RAM. We estimate the three first-order conditions simultaneously via least squares and impose symmetry in the matrix A of the production function.[17] The results from the second-stage regressions are reported in table 3.5. The results with respect to the quadratic portion of the production function (the A matrix) are largely consistent with our economic intuition. The diagonal elements are negative suggesting decreasing returns to speed, hard drive capacity, and memory. Two of the three off-diagonals are positive, the exception being the cross-derivative of RAM and hard drive capacity.

The results with respect to the software measures are somewhat puzzling. On the one hand, increases in the hard disk requirements of Microsoft Office tend to *increase* the marginal product of the computer characteristics ($\Gamma_{\text{Office}} > 0$ in two out of three columns of table 3.5). This means that Office and the hardware characteristics are complements, in the sense that increases in Office requirements lead to *higher* purchases of speed, RAM, and hard disk size. In other words, departments "over purchase" the characteristics

16. The required memory was also a candidate. However, the programmers that we spoke to were under the impression that software engineers now "waste" more memory than in previous periods, whereas this is not the case for hard drive space. Including the recommended RAM levels does not qualitatively change the results.

17. Individual tests on the symmetry of the off-diagonals fail to reject equality.

**Table 3.5** **Second stage production function estimates**

| | $\beta_{Speed}$ | $\beta_{RAM}$ | $\beta_{HDSize}$ |
|---|---|---|---|
| Speed | $-5.92 \times 10^{-8***}$ | — | — |
| | $(1.01 \times 10^{-8})$ | | |
| RAM | $2.06 \times 10^{-8}$ | $-1.27 \times 10^{-7}$ | — |
| | $(2.43 \times 10^{-8})$ | $(1.87 \times 10^{-6})$ | |
| HD size | $2.47 \times 10^{-6***}$ | $-2.20 \times 10^{-6*}$ | $-6.96 \times 10^{-5***}$ |
| | $(2.61 \times 10^{-7})$ | $(1.26 \times 10^{-6})$ | $(1.68 \times 10^{-5})$ |
| Have CD? | $1.06 \times 10^{-6}$ | $4.20 \times 10^{-5}$ | $-7.33 \times 10^{-3*}$ |
| | $(7.21 \times 10^{-6})$ | $(5.28 \times 10^{-5})$ | $(4.28 \times 10^{-3})$ |
| SCSI? | $-5.93 \times 10^{-6}$ | $1.29 \times 10^{-4}$ | $-6.78 \times 10^{-4}$ |
| | $(1.21 \times 10^{-5})$ | $(8.90 \times 10^{-5})$ | $(7.19 \times 10^{-4})$ |
| Zip drive? | $-1.63 \times 10^{-5**}$ | $8.93 \times 10^{-5*}$ | $-7.66 \times 10^{-5*}$ |
| | $(6.64 \times 10^{-6})$ | $(4.87 \times 10^{-6})$ | $(3.95 \times 10^{-5})$ |
| NIC? | $4.76 \times 10^{-6}$ | $9.04 \times 10^{-6}$ | $-1.78 \times 10^{-3***}$ |
| | $(6.87 \times 10^{-6})$ | $(5.04 \times 10^{-5})$ | $(4.09 \times 10^{-4})$ |
| Sound card? | $-6.88 \times 10^{-6}$ | $-1.02 \times 10^{-4**}$ | $-5.96 \times 10^{-4}$ |
| | $(6.64 \times 10^{-6})$ | $(4.86 \times 10^{-5})$ | $(3.95 \times 10^{-4})$ |
| LCD? | $5.45 \times 10^{-5***}$ | $5.76 \times 10^{-5}$ | $1.28 \times 10^{-3**}$ |
| | $(9.51 \times 10^{-6})$ | $(6.70 \times 10^{-5})$ | $(5.51 \times 10^{-4})$ |
| $\Gamma_{Office}$ | $1.62 \times 10^{-3***}$ | $-5.10 \times 10^{-4***}$ | $8.25 \times 10^{-4}$ |
| | $(1.51 \times 10^{-4})$ | $(1.27 \times 10^{-4})$ | $(3.04 \times 10^{-4})$ |
| $\Gamma_{Windows}$ | $-8.35 \times 10^{-5**}$ | $4.96 \times 10^{-4***}$ | $-8.29 \times 10^{-6}$ |
| | $(4.11 \times 10^{-5})$ | $(4.27 \times 10^{-5})$ | $(5.04 \times 10^{-6})$ |

$N = 3{,}931$.

*Notes:* In this table, we report the results from estimating $\beta_t = a_k + Ax_{kt} + \Sigma\theta_{t,\tau}\,\Gamma s_{t+\tau} + u_{kt}$ using data from UC Davis departmental computer purchases from July 1997 to September 2001 using the first stage hedonic pricing coefficients for processor speed, RAM, and hard-drive size; the parameter estimates represent the parameters of the production function. The θ's are not separately identifiable from the Γ's. Instead, we define the θ's by assuming a monthly interest rate of 2 percent and that departmental output is constant over the three years. The measure of software quality is the recommended hard drive space for Microsoft Office and Windows. We assume that each department has an idiosyncratic constant term, $a_k$, but departments have the same $A$, θ, and Γ. White's heteroskedastic consistent standard errors in parentheses. An $F$-test marginally rejects symmetry between the processor speed and hard drive equations ($p$-value equal to 0.126). Equality between the processor speed and RAM equations and the hard drive and RAM equations cannot be rejected ($p$-values equal to 0.617 and 0.402, respectively). The results with respect to software quality remain qualitatively unchanged if symmetry is not imposed. Including a time trend that also left the results qualitatively unchanged. Dashed cells indicate coefficients not estimated.

***Significant at the 1 percent level.

**Significant at the 5 percent level.

*Significant at the 10 percent level.

in the current period to compensate for future increases in Office software requirements; this is consistent with our priors. On the other hand, the coefficients associated with Windows hard disk requirements tend to be negative ($\Gamma_{Windows} < 0$ in two out of three columns), which suggests that departments *reduce* their demand for hardware characteristics in response to an increase in Windows hard disk requirements.

One possible explanation for this finding is that departments do not increase the characteristics of a computer purchase in response to expected changes in Windows, but instead shorten the time period in which the computer is held. That is, if departments expect increases in Windows quality in the near future, they reduce the characteristics of the current purchase in expectation of buying a computer when the new version of Windows was released. This is consistent with anecdotal evidence that suggests that consumers do not upgrade Windows as much as Office, instead implicitly "upgrading" by purchasing a new machine, and that quality changes of Windows appear to be more discrete than quality changes of Office. Behavior of this type is outside our model, however, because the time a computer is held is taken as exogenous. An alternative, statistical explanation for $\Gamma_{\text{Windows}} < 0$ is that it is capturing the overall negative trend in the hedonic coefficients, which are the dependent variable in equation (25).

### 3.5.3 Price Indexes

Given the estimates from the second stage, we calculate five price indexes. The first three are the hedonic Laspeyres, Paasche, and Fisher, in equations (23) through (24); the fourth is the true services price with current software $(1/2)(\mathbf{s}_{t-1} + \mathbf{s}_t)$ in (28), which we refer to as the "production function, current software;" and the fifth is the true services price with future software $(1/2)(\tilde{\mathbf{s}}_{t-1} + \tilde{\mathbf{s}}_t)$, which we refer to as the "production function, future software." The five price indexes are graphed in figures 3.4 through 3.7 and display a number of interesting points.

First, the production function method that uses current software levels is consistently higher than the hedonic Fisher index in figure 3.4, which is itself bounded quite tightly by the Laspeyres and Paasche indexes. A close examination of that figure shows that the indexes diverge immediately in the first months of our sample, however, so to control for this possibly erratic behavior, in figure 3.5 we show the same five indexes but normalized at 100 in May 1998 rather than August 1997. In this case the production function index with current software is still above the hedonic Fisher index, but by the end of the sample the indexes are about equal. This means that the slower decline of the production function index in the early years (1998 to 1999) is offset by a faster decline of this index in later years (2000 to 2001), as compared to the hedonic Fisher index.

This difference in the growth rates over the two halves of our sample can also be seen from figures 3.6 and 3.7, where we graph the five indexes from August 1997 to July 1999 and August 1999 to September 2001, respectively. In figure 3.6, the faster decline of the hedonic indexes from the production function indexes are readily apparent. This is also seen from the average annual growth rates (AAGR) reported in table 3.6, where the hedonic Fisher declines at a 51 percent AAGR during the first half of the sample, as compared to 14 percent and 38 percent for the production function with current

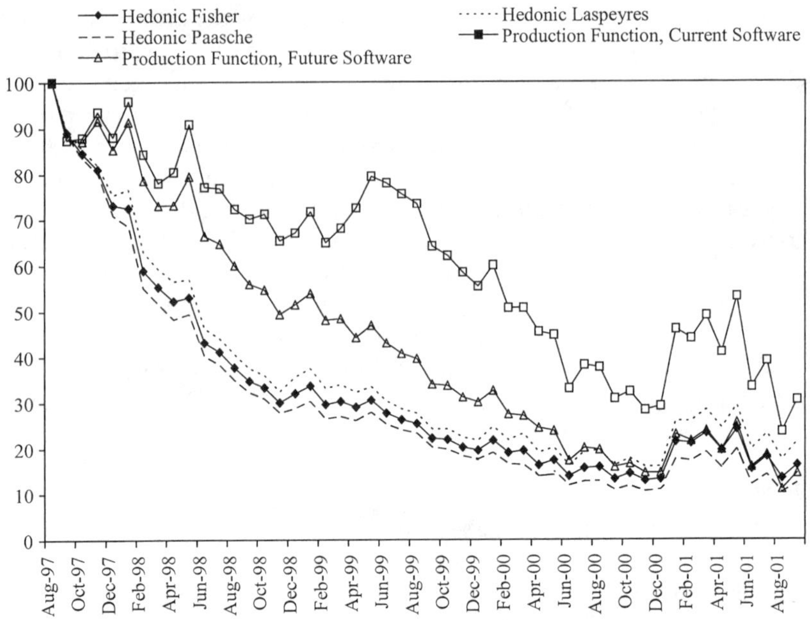


**Fig. 3.4 Price index calculations**

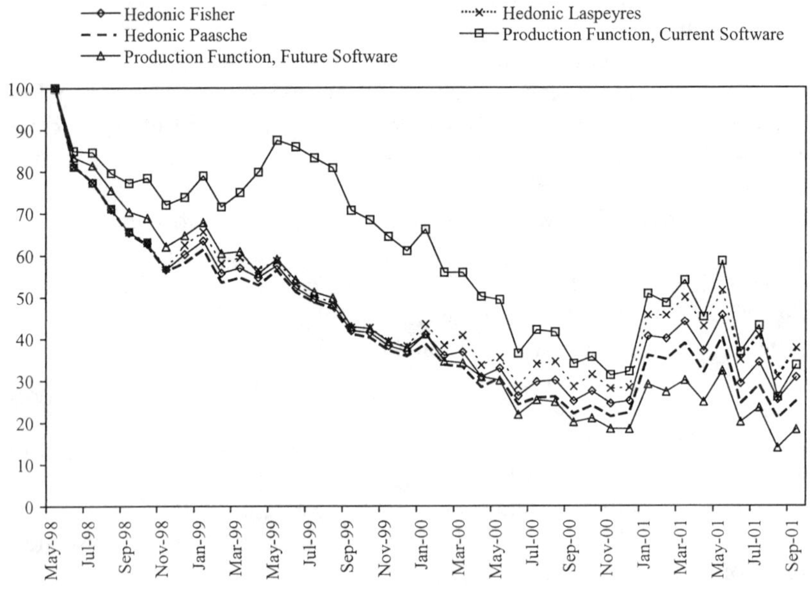


**Fig. 3.5 Price indexes beginning in May of 1998**

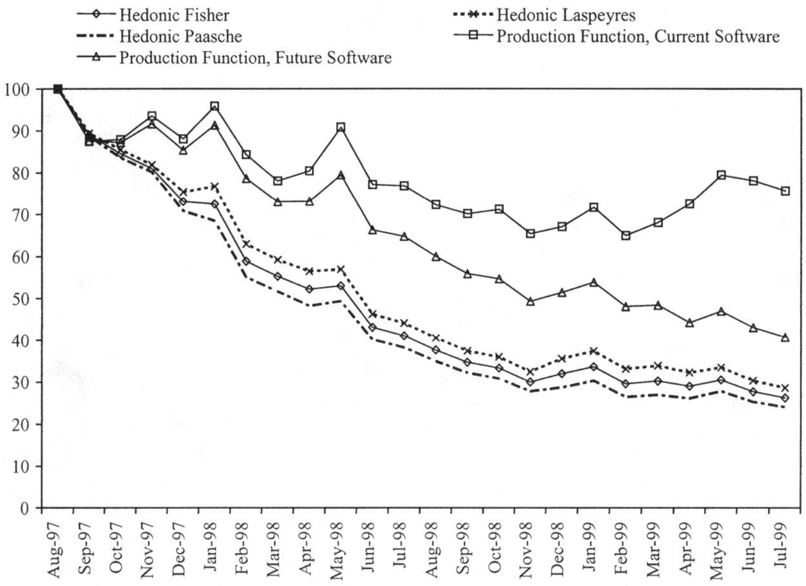


**Fig. 3.6 Price indexes during first half of the sample**

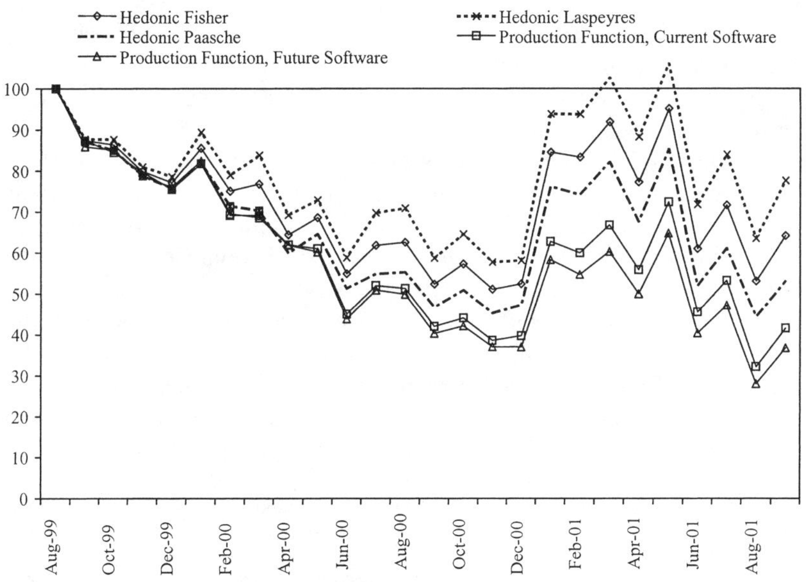


**Fig. 3.7 Price indexes during second half of the sample**

Table 3.6 Average annual growth rates of price indexes

| | Hedonic Fisher index | Production function, current software | Production function, future software |
|---|---|---|---|
| Entire sample[a] | –36.4 | –25.5 | –38.2 |
| First half | –51.3 | –13.6 | –38.0 |
| Second half | –19.9 | –34.7 | –38.3 |
| 1997 | –62.4 | –32.1 | –38.3 |
| 1998 | –57.6 | –24.1 | –40.4 |
| 1999 | –39.3 | –17.4 | –42.2 |
| 2000 | –32.5 | –48.3 | –52.4 |
| 2001 | 30.6 | –6.3 | 0.7 |

*Notes:* As in figures 3.6 and 3.7, the first half of the sample is defined as August 1997 to July 1999, while the second half is defined as August 1999 to September 2001.

[a]If the average annual growth rates are instead computed from May 1998 to September 2001, which excludes the first nine months of the sample, then we obtain –30.2 for the hedonic Fisher index, –28.2 for the production function with current software, and –40.5 for the production function with future software.

and future software, respectively.[18] If the sample for this study had stopped in 1999, the evidence in figure 3.6 and table 3.6 would have led to the conclusion that the hedonic method (either the Fisher, Laspeyres, or Paasche) was substantially overstating the true decline in prices as measured by the production function method with current software. This is consistent with the results of corollary 2 when $\Gamma > 0$, so that software requirements and hardware are complements.[19]

However, this overstatement is reversed in the second half of the sample, as shown in figure 3.7 and the third row of table 3.6, where the hedonic Fisher index falls at a 20 percent AAGR, as compared to 35 percent and 38 percent for the production function with current and future software, respectively. Evidently, both of the production function indexes are being pulled down by factors that do not influence the hedonic indexes. In 2001, the AAGR of the production function index with future software is actually above that with current software, which from corollary 2 can occur if and only if some of the $\Gamma$ coefficients are negative. Recall that these coefficients are negative for Windows software in two of the three regressions shown in table 3.5, meaning that the Windows quality is a substitute rather than a complement with hardware characteristics. This puzzling finding seems

18. In comparison, Berndt and Rappaport (2001, 271) report an AAGR for the hedonic Laspeyres and Paasche indexes of –40 percent and –42 percent, respectively, over 1994 to 1999, for desktop PCs.

19. The fact that the hedonic indexes are also overstating the decline in the production function index with future software is not consistent with the inequality (19a) in proposition 2. But notice that if we exclude the first nine months of the sample, as in figure 3.6, then the hedonic indexes closely track the production function index with future software, at least through the first half of the sample.

to affect the production function indexes in the second half of our sample, possibly because of the especially large hard disk requirements of Windows XP and 2003. We have already suggested that the negative Γ coefficients on Windows may be due to our assumption of a fixed lifetime of a machine (three years). We conclude by suggesting two other reasons for the slower growth rate of the hedonic indexes in the second half of our sample, as compared to the production function method.

First, we mention again that our sample used to estimate the hedonic regressions is much smaller after 2000, because it is collected from advertisements in *PC Magazine* rather than the *PC Data Retail Hardware Monthly Report* data. The somewhat erratic behavior of the hedonic coefficients after 2000, and the fact that the hedonic indexes actually *increase* in 2001, suggest that a large sample of computer prices and characteristics would be desirable in the second half of our sample. This might affect our results.

Setting aside this statistical concern, there is the conceptual possibility that technological improvements in the production of RAM, hard disk space, and speed of machines means that these are no longer the limiting features of a computer. Rather, some computer scientists have suggested that it is the *functionality* of software that limit users, and not the hardware. In this case the slowdown in the fall of the hedonic computer price would be a real phenomena, and the overstatement of the "true" decline in the price of computer services would be history. Under this scenario, the benefits to users would need to be evaluated using *both* hardware and software. While we have incorporated software in this chapter, it has been more as a complement (or substitute) for hardware, but not as an independent feature affecting the functionality of machines. Assessing this aspect of software is one important area for future research.

## 3.6 Conclusions

In this chapter we show that conventional hedonic methods may overstate the price decline of personal computers, which are treated here as a durable good. Optimizing agents that anticipate increases in software quality will "overbuy" the characteristics of a computer, in the sense that the purchased bundle of characteristics is not fully utilized in the first months or year that a computer is owned. Forward-looking buyers equate the marginal benefit of characteristics over the *lifetime* of a machine to the marginal cost at the time of purchase. In this case, hedonic procedures may not provide valid bounds on the true price of computer services at the time when the new machine is purchased, with the concurrent level of software. While we focus on personal computers, our results may also apply to any durable good in which the quality of a complementary product changes over time. For example, if there are switching costs associated with bank accounts, then a consumer will establish a deposit account based on expected changes in the size of banks' ATM networks, ATMs being a strong complementary product to a deposit account.[20]

Our empirical application confirms the theoretical results in the first half of our sample. Using data from UC Davis computer purchase behavior, we find that the hedonic price index constructed with BLS methods typically overstates the fall in computer prices, as compared to the true price index constructed using the users' estimated production function. Furthermore, we find that the true services prices falls *faster* when it is evaluated with *future* rather than *current* levels of software. However, in the second half of the sample this bias has been ameliorated and even reversed so that, depending on the starting month, the overall decline in the hedonic indexes is not that different from the true indexes that result from estimating the firms' production functions over computer characteristics. This provides some empirical justification for the hedonic methods now used by BLS and BEA, despite the fact that their theoretical properties are called into question when computers are treated as a durable good and software changes.

We have suggested that one area for further research is to directly evaluate the usefulness of software in enhancing consumer benefits of personal computers. White et al. (2004) provide evidence on the price declines of these software over 1984 to 2000, and note that price declines are generally greater in the later years of their sample. Conversely, Ellison and Fudenberg (2000) argue theoretically that the backwards connectivity of software packages, as well as network effects, can lead firms to develop *too many* upgrades, resulting in a loss in social welfare. So a full evaluation of the costs and benefits of software is evidently complicated. But perhaps we have reached a point where more attention needs to be paid to software and its characteristics, and not to the declining costs of extra megahertz or gigabytes, in evaluating the productivity and welfare impact of personal computers.

## Appendix

Proof of Proposition 1. First, suppose that assumption 2 holds. The efficiency of a computer purchased in year $t$ relative to that in year $t-1$, with both using the software in $t$, is:

$$\frac{f(\mathbf{x}_t, \mathbf{s}_t)}{f(\mathbf{x}_{t-1}, \mathbf{s}_t)} \geq \frac{f(\mathbf{x}_{t-1},\mathbf{s}_t) + f_x(\mathbf{x}_t,\mathbf{s}_t)'(\mathbf{x}_t - \mathbf{x}_{t-1})}{f(\mathbf{x}_{t-1},\mathbf{s}_t)}$$

$$= \frac{f(\mathbf{x}_{t-1},\mathbf{s}_t)+[f(\mathbf{x}_t,\mathbf{s}_t)/h_t(\mathbf{x}_t)]\beta_t'(\mathbf{x}_t - \mathbf{x}_{t-1})}{f(\mathbf{x}_{t-1},\mathbf{s}_t)},$$

20. For example, Knittel and Stango (2004) estimate hedonic price regressions for banking services and find that ATM network sizes have a significant impact on prices, as does the compatibility between deposit accounts of one bank and the ATMs of another.

where the first line follows from concavity of $f(\mathbf{x}_t, \mathbf{s}_t)$, and the second line from equation (6) and the definition of $\beta_t \equiv h_t'(\mathbf{x}_t)$. Multiplying through by $[h_t(\mathbf{x}_t)/f(\mathbf{x}_t, \mathbf{s}_t)]$ and rearranging terms, we obtain $[h_t(\mathbf{x}_t) - \beta_t'(\mathbf{x}_t - \mathbf{x}_{t-1})]/f(\mathbf{x}_{t-1}, \mathbf{s}_t) \geq h_t(\mathbf{x}_t)/f(\mathbf{x}_t, \mathbf{s}_t)$. Then dividing by $[h_{t-1}(\mathbf{x}_{t-1})/f(\mathbf{x}_{t-1}, \mathbf{s}_t)]$ and using the definition of $P^0$ in equation (10a), we readily obtain (9a).

The efficiency of a computer purchased in year $t$ relative to $t-1$, using software in $t-1$, is:

$$\frac{f(\mathbf{x}_t, \mathbf{s}_{t-1})}{f(\mathbf{x}_{t-1}, \mathbf{s}_{t-1})} \leq \frac{f(\mathbf{x}_t, \mathbf{s}_{t-1})}{f(\mathbf{x}_t, \mathbf{s}_{t-1}) - f_x(\mathbf{x}_{t-1}, \mathbf{s}_{t-1})(\mathbf{x}_t - \mathbf{x}_{t-1})}$$

$$= \frac{f(\mathbf{x}_t, \mathbf{s}_{t-1})}{f(\mathbf{x}_t, \mathbf{s}_{t-1}) - [f(\mathbf{x}_{t-1}, \mathbf{s}_{t-1}) / h_{t-1}(\mathbf{x}_{t-1})]\beta_{t-1}'(\mathbf{x}_t - \mathbf{x}_{t-1})},$$

where the first line follows from concavity of $f$, and the second line from (6) with $\beta_{t-1} \equiv h_{t-1}'(\mathbf{x}_{t-1})$. Inverting this expression, multiplying by $[h_{t-1}(\mathbf{x}_{t-1})/f(\mathbf{x}_{t-1}, \mathbf{s}_{t-1})]$ and rearranging terms, we obtain $[h_{t-1}(\mathbf{x}_{t-1}) + \beta_{t-1}'(\mathbf{x}_t - \mathbf{x}_{t-1})]/f(\mathbf{x}_t, \mathbf{s}_{t-1}) \geq h_{t-1}(\mathbf{x}_{t-1})/f(\mathbf{x}_{t-1}, \mathbf{s}_{t-1})$. Then dividing by $[h_t(\mathbf{x}_{t-1})/f(\mathbf{x}_t, \mathbf{s}_{t-1})]$, using the definition of $P^1$ in (10b), and inverting again we readily obtain (9b).

Now suppose that assumption 1 holds. The log-efficiency of a computer purchased in year $t$ relative to that in year $t-1$, with both using the software in $t$, is:

$$\ln f(\mathbf{x}_t, \mathbf{s}_t) - \ln f(\mathbf{x}_{t-1}, \mathbf{s}_t) \geq \beta_t'(\mathbf{x}_t - \mathbf{x}_{t-1}),$$

which follows from concavity of $\ln f(\mathbf{x}_t, \mathbf{s}_t)$, and (6) with $\beta_t \equiv h_t'(\mathbf{x}_t)/h_t(\mathbf{x}_t)$. Taking exponents and inverting we obtain $f(\mathbf{x}_{t-1}, \mathbf{s}_t)/f(\mathbf{x}_t, \mathbf{s}_t) \leq \exp[-\beta_t'(\mathbf{x}_t - \mathbf{x}_{t-1})]$. Then it follows from the definition of $P^0$ in (11a) that (9a) holds.

The log-efficiency of a computer purchased in year $t$ relative to that in year $t-1$, with both using the software in $t-1$, is:

$$\ln f(\mathbf{x}_t, \mathbf{s}_{t-1}) - \ln f(\mathbf{x}_{t-1}, \mathbf{s}_{t-1}) \leq \beta_{t-1}'(\mathbf{x}_t - \mathbf{x}_{t-1}),$$

using the concavity of $\ln f(x_t, \mathbf{s}_{t-1})$, and (6) with $\beta_{t-1} \equiv h_{t-1}'(\mathbf{x}_{t-1})/h_{t-1}(\mathbf{x}_{t-1})$. Taking exponents and inverting we obtain $f(\mathbf{x}_{t-1}, \mathbf{s}_{t-1})/f(\mathbf{x}_t, \mathbf{s}_{t-1}) \geq \exp[-\beta_{t-1}'(\mathbf{x}_t - \mathbf{x}_{t-1})]$. Then it follows from the definition of $P^1$ in (11b) that (9b) holds. QED.

Proof of Corollary 1. Suppose initially that $P^0 \geq P^1$. Using the notation introduced in the text, there are four possible ways that the inequalities in (9) can hold: (i) $P^0 \geq R(0) \geq R(1) \geq P^1$; (ii) $R(1) \geq P^0 \geq P^1 \geq R(0)$; (iii) $P^0 \geq R(1) \geq P^1 \geq R(0)$; or (iv) $R(1) \geq P^0 \geq R(0) \geq P^1$. In all of these cases, it can be seen that the interval between $R(0)$ and $R(1)$ overlaps with the interval between $P^0$ and $P^1$. Let $P^*$ denote a point in the intersection of these two intervals. Then by the intermediate value theorem, there exists $\lambda^* \in [0,1]$ such that $R(\lambda^*) = P^*$. Since $P^*$ is in the interval in-between $P^0$ and $P^1$, and $P^0 \geq P^1$ by assumption, it follows that the inequalities in (12a) hold.

If instead we start with $P^0 \leq P^1$, then we again have four ways that the inequalities in (9) can hold, and in all of these cases the interval between $R(0)$ and $R(1)$ overlaps with the interval between $P^0$ and $P^1$. So in that case the inequalities in (12b) hold. QED.

PROOF OF PROPOSITION 2. The proof of this result is identical to that of proposition 1, where we just replace $\mathbf{s}_{t-1}$ with $\tilde{\mathbf{s}}_{t-1}$ and $\mathbf{s}_t$ with $\tilde{\mathbf{s}}_t$, and make use of (18a) rather than (9).

PROOF OF THE COROLLARY 2. The first inequalities in (20a) and (20b) are identical to those in (19a) and (19b). Taking natural logs of the second inequality in (20a), and multiplying by –1, we obtain:

$$\ln f(\mathbf{x}_t, \tilde{\mathbf{s}}_{t-1}) - \ln f(\mathbf{x}_{t-1}, \tilde{\mathbf{s}}_{t-1}) \geq \ln f(\mathbf{x}_t, \mathbf{s}_{t-1}) - \ln f(\mathbf{x}_{t-1}, \mathbf{s}_{t-1}),$$

which can be rewritten as:

$$\int_{\mathbf{x}_{t-1}}^{\mathbf{x}_t} [\partial \ln f(z, \tilde{\mathbf{s}}_{t-1})/\partial z - \partial \ln f(z, \mathbf{s}_{t-1})/\partial z]dz \geq 0.$$

By the mean value theorem, the integrand can be written as $[\partial^2 \ln f(z, \mathbf{s})/\partial z \partial s]'(\tilde{\mathbf{s}}_{t-1} - \mathbf{s}_{t-1})$ for some value of $s$ between $s_{t-1}$ and $\tilde{s}_{t-1}$. This expression is nonnegative because (i) $\Gamma = \partial^2 \ln f/\partial x \partial s > 0$ by hypothesis, and (ii) $\tilde{\mathbf{s}}_{t-1} \geq \mathbf{s}_{t-1}$ from (18b) and because software is growing over time by hypothesis. Therefore, the second inequality in (20a) holds. A similar proof applies to the second inequality in (20b), and to the converse case where $\Gamma = \partial^2 \ln f/\partial x \partial s < 0$. QED.

## References

Aizcorbe, A. 2004. Semiconductor prices in the mid-1990s: Can mismeasurement explain the faster rates of price decline? Paper presented at the American Economic Association. January, San Diego.

Benkard, C. L., and P. Bajari. 2003. Hedonic price indexes with unobserved product characteristics, and application to PC's. NBER Working Paper no. 9980. Cambridge, MA: National Bureau of Economic Research, September.

Berndt, E. R., and N. J. Rappaport. 2001. Price and quality of desktop and mobile personal computers: A quarter century historical review. *American Economic Review* 91(2): 268–73.

Cartwright, D. W. 1986. Improved deflation of purchases of computers. *Survey of Current Business* 66 (March): 7–10.

Cole, R., Y. C. Chen, J. A. Barquin-Stolleman, E. Dulberger, N. Helvacian, and J. H. Hodge. 1986. Quality adjusted price indexes for computers processors and selected peripheral equipment. *Survey of Current Business* 66 (January): 41–50.

Diewert, W. E. 1976. Exact and superlative price indexes. *Journal of Econometrics* 4 (2): 115–45.

———. 1980. Aggregation problems in the measurement of capital. In *The measurement of capital,* ed. D. Usher, 433–528. Chicago: University of Chicago Press.

———. 1983. The theory of the cost-of-living index and the measurement of welfare change. In *Price level measurement,* ed. W. E. Diewert and C. Montmarquette, 163–233. Ottawa: Statistics Canada.

———. 2001. The Consumer Price Index and index number purpose. *Journal of Economic and Social Measurement* 27:167–248.

———. 2003. Hedonic regressions: A consumer theory approach. In *Scanner data and price indexes,* ed. R. C. Feenstra and M. D. Shapiro, 317–47. Chicago: University of Chicago Press.

———. 2009. Hedonic producer price indexes and quality adjustment. In *Price and productivity measurement: Volume 5, hedonic methods,* ed. W. E. Diewert, B. M. Balk, D. Fixler, K. J. Fox, and A. O. Nakamura, 21–29. United Kingdom: Trafford Press.

Ellison, G., and D. Fudenberg. 2000. The neo-luddite's lament: Excessive upgrades in the software industry. *Rand Journal of Economics* 31 (2): 253–72.

Feenstra, R. C. 1995. Exact hedonic price indexes. *Review of Economics and Statistics* 78 (9): 634–53.

Gordon, R. J. 2000. Does the "New Economy" measure up to the great inventions of the past? *Journal of Economic Perspectives* 14 (4): 49–74.

Grimm, B. T. 1998. Price indexes for selected semiconductors. *Survey of Current Business* 78 (February): 8–24.

Harper, M. J. 2000. Obsolescence and the use of prices to measure inputs of high tech capital. Bureau of Labor Statistics, Unpublished Manuscript.

Harper, M. J., E. R. Berndt, and D. O. Wood. 1989. Rates of return and capital aggregation using alternative rental prices. In *Technology and capital formation,* ed. D. W. Jorgenson and R. Landau, 331–72. Cambridge, MA: MIT Press.

Holdway, M. 2001. Quality-adjusting computer prices in the producer price index: An overview. Bureau of Labor Statistics, Washington, DC. Available at: http://www.bls.gov/ppi/ppicomqa.htm.

Hulten, C. 1990. The measurement of capital. In *Fifty years of economic measurement,* ed. E. R. Berndt and J. E. Triplett, 119–52. Chicago: University of Chicago Press.

Jorgenson, D. W., and K. J. Stiroh. 2000. Raising the speed limit: U.S. economic growth in the information age. *Brookings Papers on Economic Activity* 31 (1): 125–236. Washington, DC: Brookings Institution.

Knittel, C. R., and V. Stango. 2004. Compatibility and pricing with indirect network effects: Evidence from ATMs. NBER working paper no. 10774. Cambridge, MA: National Bureau of Economic Research, September.

Konüs, A. A. 1939. The problem of the true index of the cost of living. Trans. J. Bronfenbrenner. *Econometrica* 7:10–29.

Landefeld, J. S., and B. T. Grimm. 2000. A note on the impact of hedonics and computers on real GDP. *Survey of Current Business* 80 (December): 17–22.

Moulton, B. R. 2001. The expanding role of hedonic methods in the official statistics of the United States. BEA Papers no. 0014. Bureau of Economic Analysis, U.S. Department of Commerce.

Oliner, S. D. 1993. Constant-quality price change, depreciation, and retirement of mainframe computers. In *Price measurements and their uses,* ed. M. F. Foss, M. E. Manser, and A. H. Young, 19–61. Chicago: University of Chicago Press.

Oliner, S. D., and D. E. Sichel. 2000. The resurgence of growth in the late 1990s: Is information technology the story? *Journal of Economic Perspectives* 14 (4): 3–22.

Pakes, A. 2003. A reconsideration of hedonic price indexes with an application to PC's. *American Economic Review* 93 (December): 1578–96.

Rosen, S. 1974. Hedonic prices and implicit markets: Product differentiation in pure competition. *Journal of Political Economy* 82 (1): 34–55.
Triplett, J. E. 1986. The economic interpretation of hedonic methods. *Survey of Current Business* 66 (January): 49–52.
———. 1999. The Solow computer paradox: What do computers do to productivity? *Canadian Journal of Economics* 32 (2): 309–34.
White, A. G., J. R. Abel, E. R. Berndt, and C. W. Monroe. 2004. Hedonic price indexes for personal computer operating systems and productivity suites. NBER working paper no. 10427. Cambridge, MA: National Bureau of Economic Research, April.

4

# Hedonic Imputation versus Time Dummy Hedonic Indexes

W. Erwin Diewert, Saeed Heravi, and Mick Silver

## 4.1 Introduction

The purpose of this chapter is to compare two main and quite distinct approaches to the measurement of hedonic price indexes: time dummy hedonic indexes and hedonic imputation indexes. Both approaches not only correct price changes for changes in the quality of items purchased, but also allow the indexes to incorporate matched and unmatched models. They provide a means by which price change can be measured in product markets where there is a rapid turnover of differentiated models. However, they can yield quite different results. This chapter provides a formal exposition of the factors underlying such differences and the implications for choice of method. We consider both weighted and unweighted hedonic regression models. Unweighted hedonic regression models will be considered in sections 4.2 and 4.3. These models are of course useful in a sampling context where information on the quantity or value of sales (or purchases) is unavailable. Weighted hedonic regression models are considered in sections 4.4 and 4.5. The weighting is chosen so that if we are actually in a matched model situation for the two periods being considered, then the resulting hedonic regression measures of price change resemble standard superlative index number formulae.

The standard way price changes are measured by national statistical offices

W. Erwin Diewert is a professor of economics at the University of British Columbia and a research associate of the National Bureau of Economic Research. Saeed Heravi is a Reader in Quantitative Methods at Cardiff Business School. Mick Silver is a senior economist in the Statistics Department of the International Monetary Fund.

Our thanks to Ernst Berndt, John Greenlees, Jan de Haan, Alice Nakamura, and Jack Triplett for helpful comments. The authors are at the University of British Columbia, the University of Cardiff, and the International Monetary Fund, respectively.

is through the use of a matched models methodology. Using this methodology, the details and prices of a representative selection of items are collected in a base reference period and their matched prices collected in successive periods so that the prices of "like" are compared with "like." However, if there is a rapid turnover of available models, then the sample of product prices used to measure price changes becomes unrepresentative of the category as a whole. This is as a result of both new unmatched models being introduced (but not included in the sample), and older unmatched models being retired (and thus dropping out of the sample). Hedonic indexes use matched and unmatched models and in doing so put an end to the matched models sample selection bias.[1] The need for hedonic indexes can be seen in the context of the need to reduce bias in the measurement of the U.S. Consumer Price Index (CPI), which has been the subject of three major reports: the Stigler (1961) Committee Report, the Boskin (1996) Commission Report, and the Schultze and Mackie (2002) Committee on National Statistics Panel Report. Each found the inability to properly remove the effect on price changes of changes in quality to be a major source of bias. Hedonic regressions were considered to be the most promising approach to control for such quality changes, though the Schultze panel cautioned for the need for further research on methodology:

> Hedonic techniques currently offer the most promising approach for explicitly adjusting observed prices to account for changing product quality. But our analysis suggests that there are still substantial unresolved econometric, data, and other measurement issues that need further attention. (Schultze and Mackie 2002, 6)

At first sight the two approaches to hedonic indexes appear quite similar. Both rely on hedonic regression equations to remove the effects on price of quality changes. They can also incorporate a range of weighting systems and can be formulated as a geometric, harmonic, or arithmetic aggregator function of quality-adjusted prices, and as chained or direct, fixed-base comparisons. Yet they can give quite different results, even when using comparable weights, functional forms, and the same method of making comparisons over periods. This is due to the fact that they work on different averaging principles. The dummy variable method constrains hedonic regression parameters to be the same over time. A hedonic imputation index conversely allows the quality adjustment parameters to change in each period and undertakes two sets of quality adjustments to prices for each comparison of prices between two periods and then averages over these two comparisons.

There has been some valuable research on the two approaches[2] though to

1. See for example, Cole et al. (1986), Silver and Heravi (2003, 2005), Pakes (2003), and Triplett (2004).

2. See Berndt, Griliches, and Rappaport (1995), Berndt and Rappaport (2001), Diewert (2003b), Silver and Heravi (2003), Pakes (2003), de Haan (2003, 2004), and Triplett (2004).

the authors' knowledge no formal analysis has been presented, with a few exceptions,[3] of the factors governing the differences between the approaches. Berndt and Rappaport (2001) and Pakes (2003) have highlighted the fact that the two approaches can give different results and both of these papers advise the use of hedonic imputation indexes when parameters are unstable, a proposal that will be considered in sections 4.5 and 4.7.

Section 4.2 looks at a simple unweighted two-period time dummy variable hedonic regression model. We focus on the estimation of the time dummy estimate of the change in log prices going from period 0 to 1 but we represent this measure of overall log price change as a difference in log price levels for the two periods. In section 4.3, we take the same unweighted model but run separate hedonic regressions for both periods and use these regression parameters to form two imputed measures of constant quality log price change. These two measures are then averaged to obtain an overall imputed measure of log price change.[4] An exact expression for the difference in constant quality log price change between the time dummy and imputation measures is also developed in section 4.3. It is found that in order for these two overall measures to differ, we require the following.

- Differences in the two variance covariance matrices pertaining to the model characteristics in each period
- Differences in average amounts of model characteristics present in each period[5]
- Differences in estimated hedonic coefficients for the two separate hedonic regressions

The analysis in sections 4.2 and 4.3 is repeated in the weighted context in sections 4.4 and 4.5. Section 4.6 provides an empirical study for desktop PCs and section 4.7 concludes by discussing the issue of choice between the approaches in light of the theoretical and empirical findings.

Appendix A considers two alternative methodologies for constructing measures of overall log price change using the hedonic imputation methodology where two separate hedonic regressions are estimated for the two periods under consideration. The first methodological approach is due to

3. The first exception is Silver and Heravi (2007a), who considered the case of one characteristic and used a rather different methodological approach based on the bias generated by omitted variables in regression models. The second exception is the comment by Jan de Haan, which follows this chapter, who developed an expression for the difference based on a framework outlined in Triplett and MacDonald (1977). The points made in Haan's commentary are developed more fully in de Haan (2007).

4. An alternative interpretation of this measure of price change is derived in appendix B.

5. If the models are exactly the same in the two periods being considered, then this set of differences will be zero and the characteristics variance covariance matrices will also be identical. Hence the hedonic time dummy and hedonic imputation estimates of price change will be identical under these conditions. Thus the two methods will give rise to substantial conflicting estimates only in markets where there are many new models being introduced into the marketplace or many disappearing models (or both).

Court (1939, 108) where individual prices in each period are quality adjusted using their characteristics vectors and the characteristics prices obtained from one of the two hedonic regressions and then the resulting quality-adjusted prices are compared across the two periods. Finally, the resulting two measures of quality-adjusted overall log price change are averaged. In the second methodological approach to hedonic imputation indexes, due originally to Griliches (1967), the mean vector of characteristics that pertains to the models observed in period 0 is calculated and then the distance between the two hedonic regressions at this mean characteristics point is calculated, which generates a first measure of overall price change (the Laspeyres measure of log price change). The Paasche measure of overall log price change is calculated using the mean vector of characteristics that pertains to the models observed in period 1 and then the distance between the two hedonic regressions at this mean characteristics point is calculated. Finally the two estimates of overall log price change are averaged. Appendix A shows that these two methodological approaches to hedonic imputation indexes lead to exactly the same numerical estimates of overall price change.

It is often thought that a major advantage of the time dummy variable method for obtaining measures of overall log price change is that a standard error for the log price change is obtained. In appendix B, a method for obtaining approximate standard errors for the Laspeyres and Paasche hedonic imputation measures of log price change is derived.

## 4.2 Unweighted Time Dummy Hedonic Regressions

We begin by considering a simple unweighted two-period time dummy variable hedonic regression model. We assume that there are $N(t)$ observations on the prices, $p_n^t$, of various models $n$ in period $t$ for $t = 0,1$. Observation $n$ in period $t$ has a vector of $K$ characteristics associated with it, say, $[z_{n1}^t, z_{n2}^t, \ldots, z_{nK}^t]$ for $t = 0,1$ and $n = 1, 2, \ldots, N(t)$. The time dummy regression model has the following form:

$$(1) \quad \ln p_n^t \equiv y_n^t = \alpha_t + \sum_{k=1}^{K} \mathbf{z}_{nk}^t \gamma_k + \varepsilon_n^t; \qquad t = 0, 1; n = 1, 2, \ldots, N(t)$$

where the $\varepsilon_n^t$ are independently distributed normal variables with mean 0 and constant variance and $\alpha_0, \alpha_1, \gamma_1, \ldots, \gamma_K$ are parameters to be estimated. The parameters $\alpha_0$ and $\alpha_1$ are measures of the *average level of constant quality prices* of the items in period 0 and 1, respectively, and the $\gamma_1, \ldots, \gamma_K$ are *quality adjustment factors* for the $K$ characteristics; that is, $\gamma_k$ is the contribution to the log price of the product of adding an extra unit of characteristic $k$. Note that we have parameterized the time dummy hedonic regression model in a slightly different way to the way it is usually done since we do not have an overall constant term in the regression plus a time dummy variable in period 1; instead we have separate constant terms for each period. The overall measure of *logarithmic price change* going from period 0 to period 1 is $\alpha_1 - \alpha_0$.[6] Let $1_t$ and $0_t$ be vectors of ones and zeros of dimension $N(t)$, let $\mathbf{y}^0$ and $\mathbf{y}^1$ be the $N(0)$ and $N(1)$ dimensional vectors of period 0 and 1 logarithms of product prices, let $\boldsymbol{\varepsilon}^0$ and $\boldsymbol{\varepsilon}^1$ be the $N(0)$ and $N(1)$ dimensional vectors of period 0 and 1 stochastic disturbances and let $\mathbf{Z}^0$ and $\mathbf{Z}^1$ be matrices of the product characteristics in periods 0 and 1, respectively. Then the model defined by equation (1) can be written in matrix notation as follows:

(2) $$\mathbf{y}^0 = 1_0\alpha_0 + 0_0\alpha_1 + \mathbf{Z}^0\gamma + \boldsymbol{\varepsilon}^0;$$

(3) $$\mathbf{y}^1 = 0_1\alpha_0 + 1_1\alpha_1 + \mathbf{Z}^1\gamma + \boldsymbol{\varepsilon}^1.$$

Let $\alpha_0^*, \alpha_1^*, \gamma_1^*, \ldots, \gamma_K^*$ be the maximum likelihood or least squares estimators for the parameters that appear in equations (2) and (3). Then letting $\mathbf{e}^0$ and $\mathbf{e}^1$ be the vectors of least squares residuals for equations (2) and (3), respectively, the following equations will be satisfied by the parameter estimates and the data:

(4) $$\mathbf{y}^0 = 1_0\alpha_0^* + 0_0\alpha_1^* + \mathbf{Z}^0\gamma^* + \mathbf{e}^0;$$

(5) $$\mathbf{y}^1 = 0_1\alpha_0^* + 1_1\alpha_1^* + \mathbf{Z}^1\gamma^* + \mathbf{e}^1.$$

Let $\mathbf{y} \equiv [\mathbf{y}^{0T}, \mathbf{y}^{1T}]^T$ and $\mathbf{e} \equiv [\mathbf{e}^{0T}, \mathbf{e}^{1T}]^T$ and define $\phi^* \equiv [\alpha_0^*, \alpha_1^*, \gamma_1^*, \ldots, \gamma_K^*]^T$. Now rewrite equations (4) and (5) as

(6) $$\mathbf{y} = X\phi^* + \mathbf{e}.$$

It is well known that the columns of the **X** matrix are orthogonal to the vector **e** of least squares residuals; that is, we have

(7) $$\mathbf{X}^T\mathbf{e} = \mathbf{X}^T[\mathbf{y} - \mathbf{X}\phi^*] = 0_{2+K}.$$

The first two equations in (7) are equivalent to the following two equations:[7]

(8) $$1_0^T\mathbf{y}^0 = N(0)\alpha_0^* + 1_0^T\mathbf{Z}^0\gamma^*;$$

(9) $$1_1^T\mathbf{y}^1 = N(1)\alpha_1^* + 1_1^T\mathbf{Z}^1\gamma^*.$$

Equations (8) and (9) can be used to solve for the following period 0 and 1 *constant quality log price levels:*

6. Our method of parameterization is equivalent to the standard method for parameterizing a time dummy hedonic regression model, which is to have a common constant term for the two periods and a time dummy variable for the second period regression.

7. Diewert (2003a, 335; 2003b, 39; 2006) and Silver and Heravi (2005) used this orthogonality method of proof to provide an interpretation of the hedonic time dummy in terms of quality-adjusted prices.

(10) $$\alpha_0^* = \frac{1_0^T \mathbf{y}^0}{N(0)} - \frac{1_0^T \mathbf{Z}^0 \boldsymbol{\gamma}^*}{N(0)} = \frac{1_0^T(\mathbf{y}^0 - \mathbf{Z}^0\boldsymbol{\gamma}^*)}{N(0)};$$

(11) $$\alpha_1^* = \frac{1_1^T \mathbf{y}^1}{N(1)} - \frac{1_1^T \mathbf{Z}^1 \boldsymbol{\gamma}^*}{N(1)} = \frac{1_1^T(\mathbf{y}^1 - \mathbf{Z}^1\boldsymbol{\gamma}^*)}{N(1)}.$$

Note that $1_t^T \mathbf{y}^t/N(t)$ is the arithmetic average of the log prices in period $t$ for $t = 0,1$. Furthermore, note that $1_0^T \mathbf{Z}^0/N(0)$ is the arithmetic average of the amounts of each characteristic that are present in the period 0 models and $1_1^T \mathbf{Z}^1/N(1)$ is the corresponding arithmetic average amount of each characteristic that is present in the period 1 models. Thus, each $\alpha_t^*$ is equal to the average of the log prices for the models present in period $t$ less a quality adjustment consisting of the inner product of the characteristic prices $\boldsymbol{\gamma}^*$ with the average amount of each characteristic across the models that are present in period $t$. Alternatively, the second set of equalities in equations (10) and (11) shows that each $\alpha_t^*$ is equal to the arithmetic average of the quality adjusted log prices, $\mathbf{y}^t - \mathbf{Z}^t\boldsymbol{\gamma}^*$, for the models present in that period. In any case, the (unweighted) *hedonic time dummy estimate of the change in log prices* going from period 0 to 1, $LP_{HD}$, is the following difference in the log price levels:[8]

(12) $$LP_{HD} \equiv \alpha_1^* - \alpha_0^*.$$

For later reference, we work out an expression for the estimated characteristic prices, $\gamma^*$. Recall equation (6), $\mathbf{y} = \mathbf{X}\phi^* + \mathbf{e}$, which defined the $N(0) + N(1)$ by $2 + K$ matrix $\mathbf{X}$. We rewrite $\mathbf{X}$ as follows:

(13) $$\mathbf{X} = [\mathbf{V}, \mathbf{Z}],$$

where $\mathbf{Z}^T \equiv [\mathbf{Z}^{0T}, \mathbf{Z}^{1T}]$ and $\mathbf{V}$ is an $N(0) + N(1)$ by 2 matrix that has the first column equal to $[1_0^T, 0_1^T]^T$ and second column equal to $[0_0^T, 1_1^T]^T$. Now solve the least squares minimization problem that corresponds to equation (6) in two stages. In the first stage, we condition on $\gamma$ and minimize with respect to the components of $\alpha \equiv [\alpha_0, \alpha_1]^T$. The resulting conditional least squares estimator for $\alpha$ is:

(14) $$\alpha(\gamma) \equiv (\mathbf{V}^T\mathbf{V})^{-1}\mathbf{V}^T(y - Z\gamma).$$

The second stage minimization problem is the problem of minimizing $f(\gamma)$ with respect to the components of $\gamma$ where $f$ is defined as follows:

8. This methodology can be traced back to Court (1939, 109–111) as his hedonic suggestion number two. Note also that if the models are the same in the two periods being considered, then $N(0)$ equals $N(1)$ (equals $N$, say) and $\mathbf{Z}^0$ equals $\mathbf{Z}^1$, so that the two characteristics matrices are identical and thus $\alpha_1^* - \alpha_0^* = 1_1^T[\mathbf{y}^1 - \mathbf{Z}^1\boldsymbol{\gamma}^*]/N(1) - 1_0^T[\mathbf{y}^0 - \mathbf{Z}^0\boldsymbol{\gamma}^*]/N(0) = 1_1^T\mathbf{y}^1/N - 1^T\mathbf{y}^0/N$, which is the arithmetic mean of the period 1 log prices less the arithmetic mean of the period 0 log prices. Thus under these conditions, there is no need to run a hedonic regression; the usual matched-model methodology can be used.

$$(15)\quad \begin{aligned} f(\gamma) &\equiv [\mathbf{y} - \mathbf{Z}\gamma - \mathbf{V}\alpha(\gamma)]^T[\mathbf{y} - \mathbf{Z}\gamma - \mathbf{V}\alpha(\gamma)] \\ &= [\mathbf{y} - \mathbf{Z}\gamma - \mathbf{V}(\mathbf{V}^T\mathbf{V})^{-1}\mathbf{V}^T(\mathbf{y} - \mathbf{Z}\gamma)]^T \\ &\quad [\mathbf{y} - \mathbf{Z}\gamma - \mathbf{V}(\mathbf{V}^T\mathbf{V})^{-1}\mathbf{V}^T(\mathbf{y} - \mathbf{Z}\gamma)] \qquad \text{using (14)} \\ &= (\mathbf{My} - \mathbf{MZ}\gamma)^T(\mathbf{My} - \mathbf{MZ}\gamma) \\ &= (\mathbf{y} - \mathbf{Z}\gamma)^T\mathbf{M}^T\mathbf{M}(\mathbf{y} - \mathbf{Z}\gamma) \\ &= (\mathbf{y} - \mathbf{Z}\gamma)^T\mathbf{M}(\mathbf{y} - \mathbf{Z}\gamma) \qquad \text{since } \mathbf{M} = \mathbf{M}^T \text{ and } \mathbf{M}^2 = \mathbf{M} \end{aligned}$$

where the projection matrix **M** is defined as follows:

$$(16)\qquad \mathbf{M} \equiv I - \mathbf{V}(\mathbf{V}^T\mathbf{V})^{-1}\mathbf{V}^T.$$

A simple way to solve the problem of minimizing $f(\boldsymbol{\gamma})$ with respect to $\boldsymbol{\gamma}$ is to make use of the third equality in equation (15); that is, define the projections of **y** and **Z** onto **M** as follows:

$$(17)\qquad \mathbf{y}^* \equiv \mathbf{M}y;\ \mathbf{Z}^* \equiv \mathbf{M}Z.$$

Using definitions (17), it can be seen that

$$(18)\qquad f(\gamma) = (\mathbf{y}^* - \mathbf{Z}^*\boldsymbol{\gamma})^T(\mathbf{y}^* - \mathbf{Z}^*\boldsymbol{\gamma}).$$

Thus, the solution to the second stage least squares minimization problem is:

$$(19)\qquad \boldsymbol{\gamma}^* \equiv (\mathbf{Z}^{*T}\mathbf{Z}^*)^{-1}\mathbf{Z}^{*T}\mathbf{y}^*.$$

Once $\boldsymbol{\gamma}^*$ has been determined by equation (19), then we can use equations (14) or (8) and (9) to determine the least squares estimators for $\alpha_0^*$ and $\alpha_1^*$.

Using the definition of **V**, it can be shown that the projection matrix **M** defined by (16) is block diagonal, with the two main diagonal blocks $\mathbf{M}^0$ and $\mathbf{M}^1$ defined as follows:

$$(20)\qquad \mathbf{M}^0 \equiv \mathbf{I}_0 - \frac{1_0 1_0^T}{N(0)};\quad \mathbf{M}^1 \equiv \mathbf{I}_1 - \frac{1_1 1_1^T}{N(1)},$$

where $\mathbf{I}_0$ and $\mathbf{I}_1$ are identity matrices of dimension $N(0)$ and $N(1)$, respectively. Using (20), we can determine more precisely what the vector $\mathbf{y}^*$ equal to $\mathbf{My}$ and the matrix $\mathbf{Z}^*$ equal to $\mathbf{MZ}$ look like. Let $\mathbf{y}^{*T} = [\mathbf{y}^{0*T}, \mathbf{y}^{1*T}]$ and $\mathbf{Z}^{*T} = [\mathbf{Z}^{0*T}, \mathbf{Z}^{1*T}]$. Then using (20), we have:

$$(21)\qquad \mathbf{y}^{t*} = \mathbf{y}^t - \frac{1_t 1_t^T \mathbf{y}^t}{N(t)};\qquad t = 0, 1;$$

$$(22)\qquad \mathbf{Z}^{t*} = \mathbf{Z}^t - \frac{1_t 1_t^T \mathbf{Z}^t}{N(t)};\qquad t = 0, 1.$$

Thus, each projected vector $\mathbf{y}^{t*}$ is equal to the corresponding period $t$ log price vector $\mathbf{y}^t$ less a vector of ones times the average of the log prices for period $t$, $\Sigma_{n=1}^{N(t)} y_n^t / N(t)$, and each projected matrix $\mathbf{Z}^{t*}$ is equal to the corresponding period $t$ characteristics matrix $\mathbf{Z}^t$ less a column vector of ones times a row vector equal to the average of the characteristics in each model for period $t$, $[\Sigma_{n=1}^{N(t)} \mathbf{z}_{n1}^t / N(t), \Sigma_{n=1}^{N(t)} \mathbf{z}_{n2}^t / N(t), \ldots, \Sigma_{n=1}^{N(t)} \mathbf{z}_{nK}^t / N(t)]$. Thus, $\mathbf{y}^{t*}$ and $\mathbf{Z}^{t*}$ are simply the corresponding $\mathbf{y}^t$ and $\mathbf{Z}^t$ with the period means subtracted from each component.

Using the block diagonal structure of $\mathbf{M}$, it can be verified that we have the following alternative representation for the least squares characteristics prices $\boldsymbol{\gamma}^*$ defined by (19):

$$\boldsymbol{\gamma}^* \equiv (\mathbf{Z}^{0*T}\mathbf{Z}^{0*} + \mathbf{Z}^{1*T}\mathbf{Z}^{1*})^{-1}(\mathbf{Z}^{0*T}\mathbf{y}^{0*} + \mathbf{Z}^{1*T}\mathbf{y}^{1*}). \tag{23}$$

We now turn our attention to hedonic imputation indexes.

### 4.3 Unweighted Hedonic Imputation Indexes

Instead of running one hedonic regression where the same characteristics prices are used to quality adjust prices in each period, we can run two entirely separate hedonic regressions with separate characteristics prices, $\boldsymbol{\gamma}^0$ in period 0 and $\boldsymbol{\gamma}^1$ in period 1. Thus using the same notation as in section 4.2, our models now are:

$$\mathbf{y}^0 = 1_0\beta_0 + \mathbf{Z}^0\boldsymbol{\gamma}^0 + \eta^0; \tag{24}$$

$$\mathbf{y}^1 = 1_1\beta_1 + \mathbf{Z}^1\boldsymbol{\gamma}^1 + \eta^1, \tag{25}$$

where $\eta^0$ and $\eta^1$ are independently distributed normal random variables with means zero and constant variance within each period. Let $\beta_0^*, \gamma_1^{0*}, \ldots, \gamma_K^{0*}$ be the maximum likelihood or least squares estimators for the parameters that appear in equation (24) and let $\beta_1^*, \gamma_1^{1*}, \ldots, \gamma_K^{1*}$ be the maximum likelihood or least squares estimators for the parameters that appear in equation (25). Then letting $\mathbf{u}^0$ and $\mathbf{u}^1$ be the vectors of least squares residuals for equations (24) and (25), respectively, the following equations will be satisfied by the parameter estimates and the data:

$$\mathbf{y}^0 = 1_0\beta_0^* + \mathbf{Z}^0\boldsymbol{\gamma}^{0*} + \mathbf{u}^0; \tag{26}$$

$$\mathbf{y}^1 = 1_1\beta_1{}^* + \mathbf{Z}^1\boldsymbol{\gamma}^{1*} + \mathbf{u}^1. \tag{27}$$

The counterparts to equations (8) and (9) in the present context are:

$$1_0^T\mathbf{y}^0 = N(0)\beta_0^* + 1_0^T\mathbf{Z}^0\boldsymbol{\gamma}^{0*}; \tag{28}$$

$$1_1^T\mathbf{y}^1 = N(1)\beta_1^* + 1_1^T\mathbf{Z}^1\boldsymbol{\gamma}^{1*}. \tag{29}$$

Equations (28) and (29) lead to the following counterparts to equations (8) and (9):

$$\beta_0^* = \frac{1_0^T\mathbf{y}^0}{N(0)} - \frac{1_0^T\mathbf{Z}^0\boldsymbol{\gamma}^{0*}}{N(0)} = \frac{1_0^T(\mathbf{y}^0 - \mathbf{Z}^0\boldsymbol{\gamma}^{0*})}{N(0)}; \tag{30}$$

$$(31)\qquad \beta_1{}^* = \frac{1_1^T \mathbf{y}^1}{N(1)} - \frac{1_1^T \mathbf{Z}^1 \boldsymbol{\gamma}^{1*}}{N(1)} = \frac{1_1^T(\mathbf{y}^1 - \mathbf{Z}^1 \boldsymbol{\gamma}^{1*})}{N(1)}.$$

Recall that the hedonic time dummy estimate of the change in log prices going from period 0 to 1, $LP_{HD}$, was defined by (12) as the difference in the log price levels, $\alpha_1^* - \alpha_0^*$. In the present context, we cannot simply take the difference between $\beta_1^*$ and $\beta_0^*$ as a measure of constant quality log price change between periods 0 and 1, because the quality adjustment parameters, $\boldsymbol{\gamma}^{0*}$ and $\boldsymbol{\gamma}^{1*}$, are *different* between the two periods. However, we can use the period 0 parameters, $\gamma^{0*}$, to form estimates of quality-adjusted log prices for the models present in period 1 and then take the average of the resulting quality-adjusted log prices, which we denote by $\delta_1^*$:

$$(32)\qquad \delta_1^* \equiv \frac{1_1^T \mathbf{y}^1}{N(1)} - \frac{1_1^T \mathbf{Z}^1 \boldsymbol{\gamma}^{0*}}{N(1)} = \frac{1_1^T(\mathbf{y}^1 - \mathbf{Z}^1 \boldsymbol{\gamma}^{0*})}{N(1)}.$$

Note that the previous estimate of a period 1 log price level is analogous to $\beta_1^*$, defined by equation (31) except that the period 0 hedonic quality adjustment factors, $\boldsymbol{\gamma}^{0*}$, are used in equation (32) whereas the period 1 hedonic quality adjustment factors, $\boldsymbol{\gamma}^{1*}$, were used in equation (31). Since the period 0 and 1 estimated price levels, $\beta_0^*$ and $\delta_1^*$, use the same quality adjustment factors $\boldsymbol{\gamma}^{0*}$ in order to form constant quality log prices in each period, we can take the difference $\delta_1^*$ less $\beta_0^*$ as a measure of quality-adjusted log price change between periods 0 and 1.[9] We call this hedonic imputation measure of log price change a *Laspeyres type measure* of price change and denote it by $\phi_L^* \equiv \delta_1^* - \beta_0^*$. This measure of overall log price change depends asymmetrically on the characteristics price vector $\boldsymbol{\gamma}^{0*}$ that was obtained from the period 0 hedonic regression. It can be seen that we can obtain an alternative measure of log price change between the periods using the period 1 hedonic regression characteristics price vector $\boldsymbol{\gamma}^{1*}$. Thus, use the period 1 characteristics price vector, $\boldsymbol{\gamma}^{1*}$, to form estimates of quality-adjusted log prices for the models present in period 0 and then take the average of the resulting quality-adjusted log prices, which we denote by $\delta_0^*$:

$$(33)\qquad \delta_0^* \equiv \frac{1_0^T \mathbf{y}^0}{N(0)} - \frac{1_0^T \mathbf{Z}^0 \boldsymbol{\gamma}^{1*}}{N(0)} = \frac{1_0^T(\mathbf{y}^0 - \mathbf{Z}^0 \boldsymbol{\gamma}^{1*})}{N(0)}.$$

Note that the previous estimate of a period 0 log price level is analogous to $\beta_0^*$ defined by equation (30) except that the period 1 hedonic quality adjustment factors, $\boldsymbol{\gamma}^{1*}$, are used in equation (33), whereas the period 0 hedonic quality adjustment factors, $\boldsymbol{\gamma}^{0*}$, were used in equation (30). Since the period 0 and 1 estimated price levels, $\delta_0^*$ and $\beta_1^*$, use the same quality adjustment factors $\boldsymbol{\gamma}^{1*}$ in order to form constant quality log prices in each

9. This basic idea can be traced back to Court (1939, 108) as his hedonic suggestion number one. His suggestion was followed up by Griliches (1971a, 59–60; 1971b, 6) and Triplett and McDonald (1977, 144).

period, we can take the difference $\beta_1^*$ less $\delta_0^*$ as a second measure of log price change between periods 0 and 1. We call this hedonic imputation measure of log price change a *Paasche type measure* of price change and denote it by $\phi_P^* \equiv \beta_1^* - \delta_0^*$.[10]

Following Griliches (1971b, 7) and Diewert (2003b, 12), it seems preferable to take a symmetric average of the above two estimates of log price change over the two periods. We choose the arithmetic mean[11] as our symmetric average and define the (unweighted) *hedonic imputation estimate of the change in log prices* going from period 0 to 1, $LP_{HI}$, as follows:[12]

$$
\begin{aligned}
(34)\quad LP_{HI} &\equiv \frac{1}{2}\phi_L^* + \frac{1}{2}\phi_P^* \\
&= \frac{1}{2}(\delta_1^* - \beta_0^*) + \frac{1}{2}(\beta_1^* - \delta_0^*) \\
&= \frac{1}{2}\left[\frac{1_1^T(\mathbf{y}^1 - \mathbf{Z}^1\boldsymbol{\gamma}^{0*})}{N(1)} - \frac{1_0^T(\mathbf{y}^0 - \mathbf{Z}^0\boldsymbol{\gamma}^{0*})}{N(0)} \right. \\
&\quad \left. + \frac{1_1^T(\mathbf{y}^1 - \mathbf{Z}^1\boldsymbol{\gamma}^{1*})}{N(1)} - \frac{1_0^T(\mathbf{y}^0 - \mathbf{Z}^0\boldsymbol{\gamma}^{1*})}{N(0)}\right] \qquad \text{using (30)–(33)} \\
&= 1_1^T\left\{\frac{\mathbf{y}^1 - \mathbf{Z}^1[(1/2)\boldsymbol{\gamma}^{0*} + (1/2)\boldsymbol{\gamma}^{1*}]}{N(1)}\right\} \\
&\quad - 1_0^T\left\{\frac{\mathbf{y}^0 - \mathbf{Z}^0[(1/2)\boldsymbol{\gamma}^{0*} + (1/2)\boldsymbol{\gamma}^{1*}]}{N(0)}\right\}.
\end{aligned}
$$

Recall that in the hedonic time dummy method for quality adjusting log prices $\mathbf{y}^t$ for each period $t$, we used the characteristics quality adjustments defined by $\mathbf{Z}^t\boldsymbol{\gamma}^*$, where $\boldsymbol{\gamma}^*$ was a constant across periods vector of quality adjustment factors. Looking at the right-hand side of (34), it can be seen that the hedonic imputation method for quality adjusting log prices in each period is similar but now the period $t$ vector of quality adjustments is $\mathbf{Z}^t[(1/2)\boldsymbol{\gamma}^{0*} + (1/2)\boldsymbol{\gamma}^{1*}]$ instead of $\mathbf{Z}^t\boldsymbol{\gamma}^*$. Thus for the hedonic imputation method of quality adjusting prices, the average of the two separate hedonic

10. In appendix B we develop a simple method for obtaining approximate standard errors for the hedonic imputation Laspeyres and Paasche measures of log price change between the two periods.

11. If we chose to measure price change instead of log price change, then the arithmetic mean estimator of log price change converts into a geometric mean of the two measures of level price change, $\exp[\delta_1^* - \beta_0^*]$ and $\exp[\beta_1^* - \delta_0^*]$.

12. In appendix A we show that the measure of quality-adjusted change in log prices defined by equation (34), which followed the methodology due originally to Court (1939, 108), can also be interpreted as a measure of the distance between the two hedonic regressions. The principles of such measures were discussed in Griliches (1967) and Dhrymes (1971, 111–12) and further developed by Feenstra (1995) and Diewert (2003a, 341–44). Empirical studies using this approach include Berndt, Griliches, and Rappaport (1995), Ioannidis and Silver (1999), Berndt and Rappaport (2001, 270), Koskimäki and Vartia (2001) and Silver and Heravi (2003, 2007b).

regression estimated quality adjustment factors, $(1/2)\boldsymbol{\gamma}^{0*} + (1/2)\boldsymbol{\gamma}^{1*}$, replaces the single regression estimated quality adjustment factor vector $\boldsymbol{\gamma}^*$ that was used in the hedonic time dummy method for quality adjustment.

Note also that if the models are the same in the two periods being considered, then $N(0)$ equals $N(1)$ (equals $N$, say) and $\mathbf{Z}^0$ equals $\mathbf{Z}^1$, so that the two characteristics matrices are identical, then $LP_{HI}$ defined by (34) collapses to $1_1^T\mathbf{y}^1/N - 1^T\mathbf{y}^0/N$, which is the arithmetic mean of the period 1 log prices less the arithmetic mean of the period 0 log prices. Thus under these conditions, there is no need to run hedonic regressions; the usual matched-model methodology can be used.

Using (12) and (34), we can form the following expression for the difference in the overall log price change using the two methods for quality adjustment:

$$(35)\quad LP_{HD} - LP_{HI} = -\frac{1_1^T\mathbf{Z}^1\boldsymbol{\gamma}^*}{N(1)} + \frac{1_0^T\mathbf{Z}^0\boldsymbol{\gamma}^*}{N(0)} + \frac{1_1^T\mathbf{Z}^1[(1/2)\boldsymbol{\gamma}^{0*} + (1/2)\boldsymbol{\gamma}^{1*}]}{N(1)} - \frac{1_0^T\mathbf{Z}^0[(1/2)\boldsymbol{\gamma}^{0*} + (1/2)\boldsymbol{\gamma}^{1*}]}{N(0)}$$

$$= \frac{1_1^T\mathbf{Z}^1[(1/2)\boldsymbol{\gamma}^{0*} + (1/2)\boldsymbol{\gamma}^{1*} - \boldsymbol{\gamma}^*]}{N(1)} - \frac{1_0^T\mathbf{Z}^0[(1/2)\boldsymbol{\gamma}^{0*} + (1/2)\boldsymbol{\gamma}^{1*} - \boldsymbol{\gamma}^*]}{N(0)}$$

$$= \left[\frac{1_1^T\mathbf{Z}^1}{N(1)} - \frac{1_0^T\mathbf{Z}^0}{N(0)}\right]\left(\frac{1}{2}\boldsymbol{\gamma}^{0*} + \frac{1}{2}\boldsymbol{\gamma}^{1*} - \boldsymbol{\gamma}^*\right).$$

Thus, the hedonic time dummy and hedonic imputation measures of log price change will be identical if *either* of the following two conditions are satisfied:

$$(36)\quad \frac{1_1^T\mathbf{Z}^1}{N(1)} = \frac{1_0^T\mathbf{Z}^0}{N(0)};$$

$$(37)\quad \boldsymbol{\gamma}^* = \frac{1}{2}\boldsymbol{\gamma}^{0*} + \frac{1}{2}\boldsymbol{\gamma}^{1*}.$$

Condition (36) says that the average amount of each characteristic for the models present in period 1 equals the corresponding average amount of each characteristic for the models present in period 0. Condition (37) says that the time dummy vector of quality adjustment factors, $\boldsymbol{\gamma}^*$, is equal to the arithmetic average of the two separate hedonic regression estimates for the quality adjustment factors, $(1/2)\boldsymbol{\gamma}^{0*} + (1/2)\boldsymbol{\gamma}^{1*}$.

Condition (36) is somewhat unanticipated. It tells us that if the average amount of characteristics present in the models in each period does not change much, then the hedonic time dummy and hedonic imputation estimates of quality-adjusted price change will be much the same, even if characteristic valuations change over the two periods.

Condition (37) can be refined. Recall (23) in the previous section, which provided a formula for the hedonic time dummy vector of quality adjustment factors, $\boldsymbol{\gamma}^*$. The techniques that were used to establish (23) can be used in order to establish the following expressions for the period 0 and 1 least squares estimates $\boldsymbol{\gamma}^{0*}$ and $\boldsymbol{\gamma}^{1*}$ that appear in (26) and (27):

$$(38) \qquad \boldsymbol{\gamma}^{0*} = (\mathbf{Z}^{0*T}\mathbf{Z}^{0*})^{-1}\mathbf{Z}^{0*T}\mathbf{y}^{0*};\ \boldsymbol{\gamma}^{1*} = (\mathbf{Z}^{1*T}\mathbf{Z}^{1})^{-1}\mathbf{Z}^{1*T}\mathbf{y}^{1*},$$

where the $\mathbf{y}^{t*}$ and $\mathbf{Z}^{t*}$ are the demeaned $\mathbf{y}^t$ and $\mathbf{Z}^t$ as in the previous section.[13] Now premultiply both sides of (23) by the matrix $\mathbf{Z}^{0*T}\mathbf{Z}^{0*} + \mathbf{Z}^{1*T}\mathbf{Z}^{1*}$ and we obtain the following equation:[14]

$$\begin{aligned}(39)\ (\mathbf{Z}^{0*T}\mathbf{Z}^{0*} + \mathbf{Z}^{1*T}\mathbf{Z}^{1*})\boldsymbol{\gamma}^* &= \mathbf{Z}^{0*T}\mathbf{y}^{0*} + \mathbf{Z}^{1*T}\mathbf{y}^{1*} \\ &= \mathbf{Z}^{0*T}\mathbf{Z}^{0*}(\mathbf{Z}^{0*T}\mathbf{Z}^{0*})^{-1}\mathbf{Z}^{0*T}\mathbf{y}^{0*} \\ &\quad + \mathbf{Z}^{1*T}\mathbf{Z}^{1*}(\mathbf{Z}^{1*T}\mathbf{Z}^{1*})^{-1}\mathbf{Z}^{1*T}\mathbf{y}^{1*} \\ &= \mathbf{Z}^{0*T}\mathbf{Z}^{0*}\boldsymbol{\gamma}^{0*} + \mathbf{Z}^{1*T}\mathbf{Z}^{1*}\boldsymbol{\gamma}^{1*} \qquad \text{using (38).}\end{aligned}$$

Equation (39) tells us that if $\boldsymbol{\gamma}^{0*}$ equals $\boldsymbol{\gamma}^{1*}$, then $\boldsymbol{\gamma}^*$ is necessarily equal to this common vector. We now use equation (39) in order to evaluate the following expression:

$$\begin{aligned}(40)\ 2(\mathbf{Z}^{0*T}\mathbf{Z}^{0*} + \mathbf{Z}^{1*T}\mathbf{Z}^{1*})&\left[\frac{1}{2}\boldsymbol{\gamma}^{0*} + \frac{1}{2}\boldsymbol{\gamma}^{1*} - \boldsymbol{\gamma}^*\right] \\ &= (\mathbf{Z}^{0*T}\mathbf{Z}^{0*} + \mathbf{Z}^{1*T}\mathbf{Z}^{1*})(\boldsymbol{\gamma}^{0*} + \boldsymbol{\gamma}^{1*}) \\ &\quad - 2(\mathbf{Z}^{0*T}\mathbf{Z}^{0*}\boldsymbol{\gamma}^{0*} + \mathbf{Z}^{1*T}\mathbf{Z}^{1*}\boldsymbol{\gamma}^{1*}) \qquad \text{using (39).} \\ &= (\mathbf{Z}^{0*T}\mathbf{Z}^{0*})(\boldsymbol{\gamma}^{1*} - \boldsymbol{\gamma}^{0*}) - (\mathbf{Z}^{1*T}\mathbf{Z}^{1*})(\boldsymbol{\gamma}^{1*} - \boldsymbol{\gamma}^{0*}) \\ &= -(\mathbf{Z}^{1*T}\mathbf{Z}^{1*} - \mathbf{Z}^{0*T}\mathbf{Z}^{0*})(\boldsymbol{\gamma}^{1*} - \boldsymbol{\gamma}^{0*})\end{aligned}$$

Now premultiply both sides of (40) by $(1/2)(\mathbf{Z}^{0*T}\mathbf{Z}^{0*} + \mathbf{Z}^{1*T}\mathbf{Z}^{1*})^{-1}$ and substitute the resulting expression for $(1/2)\boldsymbol{\gamma}^{0*} + (1/2)\boldsymbol{\gamma}^{1*} - \boldsymbol{\gamma}^*$ into equation (35) in order to obtain the following expression for the difference between the hedonic dummy estimate of constant quality price change and the corresponding symmetric hedonic imputation estimate:

$$\begin{aligned}(41)\quad \mathrm{LP_{HD}} - \mathrm{LP_{HI}} = &-\frac{1}{2}\left[\frac{\mathbf{1}_1^T\mathbf{Z}^1}{N(1)} - \frac{\mathbf{1}_0^T\mathbf{Z}^0}{N(0)}\right] \\ &(\mathbf{Z}^{0*T}\mathbf{Z}^{0*} + \mathbf{Z}^{1*T}\mathbf{Z}^{1*})^{-1}(\mathbf{Z}^{1*T}\mathbf{Z}^{1*} - \mathbf{Z}^{0*T}\mathbf{Z}^{0*}) \\ &(\boldsymbol{\gamma}^{1*} - \boldsymbol{\gamma}^{0*}).\end{aligned}$$

13. Note that $\mathbf{Z}^{t*T}\mathbf{y}^{t*}/N(t)$ can be interpreted as a vector of sample covariances between the log prices in period $t$ and the amounts of the characteristics present in the period $t$ models while $\mathbf{Z}^{t*T}\mathbf{Z}^{t*}/N(t)$ can be interpreted as a sample variance covariance matrix for the model characteristics in period $t$. In the main text, we refer to $\mathbf{Z}^{t*T}\mathbf{Z}^{t*}$ as a characteristics "total" variance covariance matrix.

14. In the single characteristic case, equation (40) tells us that $\gamma_1^*$ is a weighted average of $\gamma_1^{0*}$ and $\gamma_1^{1*}$.

Using equation (41), it can be seen that the hedonic time dummy and hedonic imputation measures of log price change will be identical if *any* of the following three conditions are satisfied:

- $1_1^T\mathbf{Z}^1/N(1)$ equals $1_0^T\mathbf{Z}^0/N(0)$ so that the average amount of each characteristic across models in each period stays the same
- $\mathbf{Z}^{1*T}\mathbf{Z}^{1*}$ equals $\mathbf{Z}^{0*T}\mathbf{Z}^{0*}$ so that the model characteristics total variance covariance matrix is the same across periods[15]
- $\gamma^{1*}$ equals $\gamma^{0*}$ so that separate (unweighted) hedonic regressions in each period give rise to the same characteristics quality adjustment factors.[16]

In the following sections, we will adapt the previous material to cover the case of weighted hedonic regressions.

## 4.4 Weighted Time Dummy Hedonic Regressions

We now consider a weighted two-period time dummy variable hedonic regression model. We again assume that there are $N(t)$ observations on the prices, $p_n^t$, of various models $n$ in period $t$ for $t = 0, 1$, but we now assume that the quantities purchased for each model $n$ in period $t$, $q_n^t$, are also observable. Model $n$ in period $t$ again has the vector of $K$ characteristics associated with it, $[z_{n1}^t, z_{n2}^t, \ldots, z_{nK}^t]$ for $t = 0, 1$ and $n = 1, 2, \ldots, N(t)$. The *expenditure share* of model $n$ in period $t$ is

$$(42)\qquad \mathbf{s}_n^t \equiv \frac{p_n^t q_n^t}{\sum_{i=1}^{N(t)} p_i^t q_i^t}; \qquad t = 0, 1; n = 1, 2, \ldots, N(t).$$

Let $\mathbf{s}^t \equiv [s_1^t, \ldots, s_{N(t)}^t]^T$ denote the period $t$ expenditure share vector for $t = 0, 1$ and let $\mathbf{S}^t$ denote the *diagonal period t share matrix* that has the elements of the period $t$ expenditure share vector $\mathbf{s}^t$ running down the main diagonal for $t = 0,1$. The matrix $(\mathbf{S}^t)^{1/2}$ is the *square root matrix* of $\mathbf{S}^t$; that is, the positive square roots of the elements of the period $t$ expenditure vector $\mathbf{s}^t$ are the diagonal elements of this diagonal matrix for $t = 0, 1$. As in the previous sections, $\mathbf{y}^t$ is the vector of period $t$ log price changes and $\mathbf{Z}^t$ is the period $t$ model characteristics matrix for $t = 0,1$.

With the previous notational preliminaries out of the way, the *weighted time dummy regression model* that is the counterpart to the unweighted model defined earlier by (2) and (3) is defined as follows:[17]

15. This condition for equality is also somewhat unanticipated.

16. Using equation (38), we can obtain a more "fundamental" condition in terms of variance covariance matrices for the equality of $\gamma^{0*}$ to $\gamma^{1*}$; namely the equality of $(\mathbf{Z}^{0*T}\mathbf{Z}^{0*})^{-1}\mathbf{Z}^{0*T}\mathbf{y}^{0*}$ to $(\mathbf{Z}^{1*T}\mathbf{Z}^{1*})^{-1}\mathbf{Z}^{1*T}\mathbf{y}^{1*}$.

17. Diewert (2003b, 26) explained the logic behind the weighting scheme in the regression model defined by equations (43) and (44). For additional material on weighting in hedonic regressions, see Diewert (2005, 563; 2006, 13). Basically, the form of weighting that is used in equations (43) and (44) leads to measures of price change that are comparable (in the case where

(43) $$(\mathbf{S}^0)^{1/2}\mathbf{y}^0 = (\mathbf{S}^0)^{1/2}(\mathbf{1}_0\alpha_0 + \mathbf{0}_0\alpha_1 + \mathbf{Z}^0\boldsymbol{\gamma}) + \boldsymbol{\varepsilon}^0;$$

(44) $$(\mathbf{S}^1)^{1/2}\mathbf{y}^1 = (\mathbf{S}^1)^{1/2}(\mathbf{0}_1\alpha_0 + \mathbf{1}_1\alpha_1 + \mathbf{Z}^1\boldsymbol{\gamma}) + \boldsymbol{\varepsilon}^1,$$

where the $\boldsymbol{\varepsilon}^t$ vectors have elements $\varepsilon_n^t$ that are independently distributed normal variables with zero means and constant variances.

Let $\alpha_0^*, \alpha_1^*, \gamma_1^*, \ldots, \gamma_K^*$ be the maximum likelihood or least squares estimators for the parameters that appear in (43) and (44). Then letting $\mathbf{e}^0$ and $\mathbf{e}^1$ be the vectors of least squares residuals for equations (43) and (44) respectively, the following equations will be satisfied by the parameter estimates and the data:

(45) $$(\mathbf{S}^0)^{1/2}\mathbf{y}^0 = (\mathbf{S}^0)^{1/2}(\mathbf{1}_0\alpha_0^* + \mathbf{0}_0\alpha_1^* + \mathbf{Z}^0\boldsymbol{\gamma}^*) + \mathbf{e}^0;$$

(46) $$(\mathbf{S}^1)^{1/2}\mathbf{y}^1 = (\mathbf{S}^1)^{1/2}(\mathbf{0}_1\alpha_0^* + \mathbf{1}_1\alpha_1^* + \mathbf{Z}^1\boldsymbol{\gamma}^*) + \mathbf{e}^1.$$

The counterparts to equations (10) and (11) are now:

(47) $$\alpha_0^* = \mathbf{s}^{0T}\mathbf{y}^0 - \mathbf{s}^{0T}\mathbf{Z}^0\boldsymbol{\gamma}^* = \mathbf{s}^{0T}(\mathbf{y}^0 - \mathbf{Z}^0\boldsymbol{\gamma}^*);$$

(48) $$\alpha_1^* = \mathbf{s}^{1T}\mathbf{y}^1 - \mathbf{s}^{1T}\mathbf{Z}^1\boldsymbol{\gamma}^* = \mathbf{s}^{1T}(\mathbf{y}^1 - \mathbf{Z}^1\boldsymbol{\gamma}^*).$$

Note that $\mathbf{s}^{tT}\mathbf{y}^t = \Sigma_{n=1}^{N(t)} s_n^t \ln p_n^t$ is the period $t$ expenditure share weighted average of the log prices in period $t$ for $t = 0,1$. Furthermore, note that $\mathbf{s}^{tT}\mathbf{Z}^t$ is a 1 by $K$ vector whose $k$th element is equal to the period $t$ expenditure share weighted average $\Sigma_{n=1}^{N(t)}\mathbf{s}_n^t\mathbf{z}_{nk}^t$ of the amounts of characteristic $k$ that are present in the period $t$ models for $t = 0, 1$ and $k = 1, \ldots, K$. Thus, each $\alpha_t^*$ is equal to the expenditure share weighted average of the log prices for the models present in period $t$ less a quality adjustment consisting of the inner product of the characteristic prices $\boldsymbol{\gamma}^*$ with an expenditure share weighted average amount of each characteristic across the models that are present in period $t$. Alternatively, the second set of equalities in equations (47) and (48) shows that each $\alpha_t^*$ is equal to the period $t$ expenditure share weighted average of the quality-adjusted log prices, $\mathbf{y}^t - \mathbf{Z}^t\boldsymbol{\gamma}^*$, for the models present in that period. Now use equations (47) and (48) in order to define the following *weighted hedonic time dummy estimate of the change in log prices* going from period 0 to 1: $LP_{WHD}$, is the following difference in the log price levels:

(49) $$LP_{WHD} \equiv \alpha_1^* - \alpha_0^* = \mathbf{s}^{1T}(\mathbf{y}^1 - \mathbf{Z}^1\boldsymbol{\gamma}^*) - \mathbf{s}^{0T}(\mathbf{y}^0 - \mathbf{Z}^0\boldsymbol{\gamma}^*).$$

Thus, the weighted hedonic time dummy estimate of the change in log prices is equal to a period 1 expenditure share weighted average of the quality-adjusted log prices, $\mathbf{y}^1 - \mathbf{Z}^1\boldsymbol{\gamma}^*$, less a period 0 expenditure share weighted average of the quality-adjusted log prices, $\mathbf{y}^0 - \mathbf{Z}^0\boldsymbol{\gamma}^*$.

the characteristics of the models can be defined by dummy variables) to the "best" measures of price change in bilateral index number theory. It should be noted that the present weighted model will be equivalent to the previous unweighted model (4) and (5) only if the number of observations in each period are equal, so that $N(0)$ equals $N(1)$, and each share component $s_n^t$ is equal to a common value.

For later reference, we can adapt the methodology presented at the end of section 4.2 in order to work out an explicit expression for the estimated characteristic prices, $\gamma^*$. Recall the definitions of the diagonal matrices $\mathbf{S}^0$ and $\mathbf{S}^1$. Define $\mathbf{S}$ as a block diagonal matrix that has the blocks $\mathbf{S}^0$ and $\mathbf{S}^1$ on the main diagonals and let $\mathbf{S}^{1/2}$ be the corresponding square root matrix; that is, this matrix has the elements of the period 0 expenditure share $\mathbf{s}^0$ and the period 1 expenditure share vector $\mathbf{s}^1$ running down the main diagonal. Adapting the analysis in section 4.1, we need to replace the $\mathbf{y}$ vector in that section by $\mathbf{S}^{1/2}\mathbf{y}$ and the $\mathbf{Z}$ matrix in that section by $\mathbf{S}^{1/2}\mathbf{Z}$, the $\mathbf{V}$ matrix by $\mathbf{S}^{1/2}\mathbf{V}$, and define the counterpart $\mathbf{M}°$ to the projection matrix $\mathbf{M}$ defined by equation (16) as follows:

(50)
$$\begin{aligned}\mathbf{M}° &\equiv \mathbf{I} - \mathbf{S}^{1/2}\mathbf{V}(\mathbf{V}^T\mathbf{S}\mathbf{V})^{-1}\mathbf{V}^T\mathbf{S}^{1/2} \\ &= \mathbf{I} - \mathbf{S}^{1/2}\mathbf{V}\mathbf{V}^T\mathbf{S}^{1/2},\end{aligned}$$

where the second equality in equation (50) follows from the fact that $\mathbf{V}^T\mathbf{S}\mathbf{V}$ equals $\mathbf{I}_2$, a two-by-two identity matrix. Now define $\mathbf{y}°$ and $\mathbf{Z}°$ in terms of $\mathbf{M}°$ and the original $\mathbf{y}$ vector and $\mathbf{Z}$ matrix as follows:

(51)
$$\begin{aligned}\mathbf{y}° &\equiv \mathbf{M}°\mathbf{S}^{1/2}\mathbf{y} \\ &= (\mathbf{I} - \mathbf{S}^{1/2}VV^T\mathbf{S}^{1/2})\mathbf{S}^{1/2}\mathbf{y} \qquad \text{using (50);} \\ &= \mathbf{S}^{1/2}(\mathbf{I} - \mathbf{V}\mathbf{V}^T\mathbf{S})\mathbf{y};\end{aligned}$$

(52)
$$\begin{aligned}\mathbf{Z}° &\equiv \mathbf{M}°\mathbf{S}^{1/2}\mathbf{Z} \\ &= (\mathbf{I} - \mathbf{S}^{1/2}\mathbf{V}\mathbf{V}^T\mathbf{S}^{1/2})\mathbf{S}^{1/2}\mathbf{Z} \qquad \text{using (50).} \\ &= \mathbf{s}^{1/2}(\mathbf{I} - \mathbf{V}\mathbf{V}^T\mathbf{S})\mathbf{Z}\end{aligned}$$

The new vector of time dummy quality adjustment factors $\gamma^*$ can now be defined as the following counterpart to equation (19):

(53)
$$\gamma^* \equiv (\mathbf{Z}^{°T}\mathbf{Z}°)^{-1}\mathbf{Z}^{°T}\mathbf{y}°.$$

Once $\gamma^*$ has been determined by equation (53), then we can use equations (47) and (48) to determine the weighted least squares estimators for $\alpha_0^*$ and $\alpha_1^*$.

It is possible to express the $\gamma^*$ defined by (53) in a more transparent way using our definitions of the matrices $\mathbf{Z}$, $\mathbf{V}$, and $\mathbf{S}$. Recall that in section 4.2, the demeaned log price change vectors $\mathbf{y}^{t*}$ defined by (20) and the demeaned characteristics matrices $\mathbf{Z}^{t*}$ defined by (21) proved to be useful. In those definitions, we used simple unweighted means. In the present context, we use *expenditure share weighted average means* as follows:

(54)
$$\mathbf{y}^{t*} \equiv \mathbf{y}^t - 1_t\mathbf{s}^{tT}\mathbf{y}^t; \qquad t = 0, 1;$$

(55)
$$\mathbf{Z}^{t*} \equiv \mathbf{Z}^t - 1_t\mathbf{s}^{tT}\mathbf{Z}^t; \qquad t = 0, 1.$$

Let the $n$th component of the vector $\mathbf{y}^{t*}$ be $\mathbf{y}_n^{t*}$ and let the $n$th row of the $N(t)$ by $K$ dimensional matrix $\mathbf{Z}^{t*}$ be $z_n^{t*}$ for $t = 0, 1$ and $n = 1, 2, \ldots, N(t)$. Then it can be shown that the vector of characteristics prices $\gamma^*$ defined by (53) can be written in terms of the components of the demeaned log price change vectors $\mathbf{y}^{t*}$, the components of the expenditure share vectors $\mathbf{s}^t$, and the rows of the demeaned characteristics matrices $\mathbf{Z}^{t*}$ as follows:

$$(56) \qquad \gamma^* = \left[\sum_{n=1}^{N(0)} s_n^0 z_n^{0*T} z_n^{0*} + \sum_{n=1}^{N(1)} s_n^1 z_n^{1*T} z_n^{1*}\right]^{-1} \left[\sum_{n=1}^{N(0)} s_n^0 z_n^{0*T} y_n^{0*} + \sum_{n=1}^{N(1)} s_n^1 z_n^{1*T} y_n^{1*}\right].$$

Note that $\Sigma_{n=1}^{N(t)} s_n^t z_n^{t*T} z_n^{t*}$ can be interpreted as a period $t$ expenditure share weighted sample variance covariance matrix[18] for the model characteristics present in period $t$ and $\Sigma_{n=1}^{N(t)} s_n^t z_n^{t*T} y_n^{t*}$ can be interpreted as a period $t$ expenditure share weighted sample covariance matrix between the period $t$ log prices and the characteristics of the models present in period $t$.

We now generalize the analysis on unweighted hedonic imputation indexes presented in section 4.3 to the weighted case.

### 4.5 Weighted Hedonic Imputation Indexes

Using the notation explained in the previous section, the two separate weighted hedonic regressions that are counterparts to the separate unweighted regressions (24) and (25) are now equations (57) and (58):

$$(57) \qquad (\mathbf{S}^0)^{1/2}\mathbf{y}^0 = (\mathbf{S}^0)^{1/2}(1_0\beta_0 + \mathbf{Z}^0\boldsymbol{\gamma}^0) + \eta^0;$$

$$(58) \qquad (\mathbf{S}^1)^{1/2}\mathbf{y}^1 = (\mathbf{S}^1)^{1/2}(1_1\beta_1 + \mathbf{Z}^1\boldsymbol{\gamma}^1) + \eta^1,$$

where $\eta^0$ and $\eta^1$ are independently distributed normal random variables with means zero and constant variance within each period. Let $\beta_0^*, \gamma_1^{0*}, \ldots, \gamma_K^{0*}$ be the maximum likelihood or least squares estimators for the parameters that appear in equation (57) and let $\beta_1^*, \gamma_1^{1*}, \ldots, \gamma_K^{1*}$ be the maximum likelihood or least squares estimators for the parameters that appear in equation (58). Then letting $\mathbf{u}^0$ and $\mathbf{u}^1$ be the vectors of least squares residuals for equations (57) and (58), respectively, the following equations will be satisfied by the parameter estimates and the data:

$$(59) \qquad (\mathbf{S}^0)^{1/2}\mathbf{y}^0 = (\mathbf{S}^0)^{1/2}(1_0\beta_0^* + \mathbf{Z}^0\boldsymbol{\gamma}^{0*}) + \mathbf{u}^0;$$

$$(60) \qquad (\mathbf{S}^1)^{1/2}\mathbf{y}^1 = (\mathbf{S}^1)^{1/2}(1_1\beta_1^* + \mathbf{Z}^1\boldsymbol{\gamma}^{1*}) + \mathbf{u}^1.$$

The weighted counterparts to equations (30) and (31) are:

$$(61) \qquad \beta_0^* = \mathbf{s}^{0T}\mathbf{y}^0 - \mathbf{s}^{0T}\mathbf{Z}^0\boldsymbol{\gamma}^{0*} = \mathbf{s}^{0T}(\mathbf{y}^0 - \mathbf{Z}^0\boldsymbol{\gamma}^{0*});$$

$$(62) \qquad \beta_1^* = \mathbf{s}^{1T}\mathbf{y}^1 - \mathbf{s}^{1T}\mathbf{Z}^1\boldsymbol{\gamma}^{1*} = \mathbf{s}^{1T}(\mathbf{y}^0 - \mathbf{Z}^1\boldsymbol{\gamma}^{1*}).$$

18. Note that for the present weighted model, $\Sigma_{n=1}^{N(t)} s_n^t z_n^{t*T} z_n^{t*}$ is a true period $t$ expenditure share weighted sample variance covariance matrix, whereas for the earlier unweighted model, the counterpart to this sample variance covariance matrix was $\mathbf{Z}^{t*T}\mathbf{Z}^{t*}$, which was the period $t$ total variance covariance matrix, equal to $N(t)$ times the sample variance covariance matrix for the characteristics present in period $t$ models.

As in section 4.3, we cannot simply take the difference between $\beta_1^*$ and $\beta_0^*$ as a measure of constant quality log price change between periods 0 and 1, because the quality adjustment parameters, $\boldsymbol{\gamma}^{0*}$ and $\boldsymbol{\gamma}^{1*}$, are again *different* between the two periods. As in section 4.3, we can use the period 0 parameters, $\boldsymbol{\gamma}^{0*}$, to form estimates of quality-adjusted log prices for the models present in period 1 and then take the period 1 weighted average of the resulting quality-adjusted log prices, which we denote by $\delta_1^*$:

$$(63) \qquad \delta_1^* \equiv \mathbf{s}^{1T}\mathbf{y}^1 - \mathbf{s}^{1T}\mathbf{Z}^1\boldsymbol{\gamma}^{0*} = \mathbf{s}^{1T}(\mathbf{y}^1 - \mathbf{Z}^1\boldsymbol{\gamma}^{0*}).$$

Note that the previous estimate of a period 1 log price level is analogous to $\beta_1^*$ defined by equation (62) except that the period 0 hedonic quality adjustment factors, $\boldsymbol{\gamma}^{0*}$, are used in equation (63), whereas the period 1 hedonic quality adjustment factors, $\boldsymbol{\gamma}^{1*}$, were used in equation (62). Since the period 0 and 1 estimated price levels, $\beta_0^*$ and $\delta_1^*$, use the same quality adjustment factors $\boldsymbol{\gamma}^{0*}$ in order to form constant quality log prices in each period, we can again take the difference $\delta_1^*$ less $\beta_0^*$ as a measure of quality-adjusted log price change between periods 0 and 1.[19] This measure of overall log price change depends asymmetrically on the characteristics price vector $\boldsymbol{\gamma}^{0*}$ that was obtained from the period 0 hedonic regression. It can be seen that we can obtain an alternative measure of log price change between the periods using the period 1 hedonic regression characteristics price vector $\boldsymbol{\gamma}^{1*}$. Thus, use the period 1 characteristics price vector, $\boldsymbol{\gamma}^{1*}$, to form estimates of quality-adjusted log prices for the models present in period 0 and then take the period 0 weighted average of the resulting quality-adjusted log prices, which we denote by $\delta_0^*$:

$$(64) \qquad \delta_0^* \equiv \mathbf{s}^{0T}\mathbf{y}^0 - \mathbf{s}^{0T}\mathbf{Z}^0\boldsymbol{\gamma}^{1*} = \mathbf{s}^{0T}(\mathbf{y}^0 - \mathbf{Z}^0\boldsymbol{\gamma}^{1*}).$$

Note that the previous estimate of a period 0 log price level is analogous to $\beta_0^*$ defined by equation (61) except that the period 1 hedonic quality adjustment factors, $\boldsymbol{\gamma}^{1*}$, are used in (64) whereas the period 0 hedonic quality adjustment factors, $\boldsymbol{\gamma}^{0*}$, were used in equation (61). Since the period 0 and 1 estimated price levels, $\delta_0^*$ and $\beta_1^*$, use the same quality adjustment factors $\boldsymbol{\gamma}^{1*}$ in order to form constant quality log prices in each period, we can take the difference $\beta_1^*$ less $\delta_0^*$ as a second measure of log price change between periods 0 and 1.[20]

Again following Diewert (2003b, 20) and de Haan (2003, 14; 2004), it seems preferable to take a symmetric average of the two previous estimates of log price change over the two periods. We again choose the arithmetic mean

19. Haan (2003, 12) defined the exponential of this measure of log price change as the geometric Laspeyres hedonic imputation index of price change, except that for the matched models in both periods, he used actual prices rather than predicted prices.

20. Haan (2003, 13) defined the exponential of this measure of log price change as the geometric Paasche hedonic imputation index of price change, except that for the matched models in both periods, he used actual prices rather than predicted prices. Diewert (2003b, 13–14) considered similar hedonic imputation indexes except that he worked with ordinary Paasche and Laspeyres type indexes rather than geometric Paasche and Laspeyres type indexes.

as our symmetric average and define the *weighted hedonic imputation estimate of the change in log prices* going from period 0 to 1, $LP_{WHI}$, as follows:[21]

$$\text{(65)} \quad LP_{WHI} \equiv \frac{1}{2}[\delta_1^* - \beta_0^*] + \frac{1}{2}[\beta_1^* - \delta_0^*].$$
$$= \frac{1}{2}[\mathbf{s}^{1T}(\mathbf{y}^1 - \mathbf{Z}^1\boldsymbol{\gamma}^{0*}) - \mathbf{s}^{0T}(\mathbf{y}^0 - \mathbf{Z}^0\boldsymbol{\gamma}^{0*}) + \mathbf{s}^{1T}(\mathbf{y}^1 - \mathbf{Z}^1\boldsymbol{\gamma}^{1*}) - \mathbf{s}^{0T}(\mathbf{y}^0 - \mathbf{Z}^0\boldsymbol{\gamma}^{1*})]$$
$$= \mathbf{s}^{1T}\left[\mathbf{y}^1 - \mathbf{Z}^1\left(\frac{1}{2}\boldsymbol{\gamma}^{0*} + \frac{1}{2}\boldsymbol{\gamma}^{1*}\right)\right] - \mathbf{s}^{0T}\left[\mathbf{y}^0 - \mathbf{Z}^0\left(\frac{1}{2}\boldsymbol{\gamma}^{0*} + \frac{1}{2}\boldsymbol{\gamma}^{1*}\right)\right].$$

Recall that in the weighted hedonic time dummy method for quality adjusting log prices $\mathbf{y}^t$ for each period $t$, we used the characteristics quality adjustments defined by $\mathbf{Z}^t\boldsymbol{\gamma}^*$, where $\boldsymbol{\gamma}^*$ was a constant across periods vector of quality adjustment factors. Looking at the right-hand side of equation (65), it can be seen that the weighted hedonic imputation method for quality adjusting log prices in each period is similar but now the period $t$ vector of quality adjustments is $\mathbf{Z}^t[(1/2)\boldsymbol{\gamma}^{0*} + (1/2)\boldsymbol{\gamma}^{1*}]$ instead of $\mathbf{Z}^t\boldsymbol{\gamma}^*$.

Using equations (49) and (65), we can form the following expression for the difference in the overall log price change using the two weighted methods for quality adjustment:

$$\text{(66)} \quad LP_{WHD} - LP_{WHI} = \mathbf{s}^{1T}[\mathbf{y}^1 - \mathbf{Z}^1\boldsymbol{\gamma}^*] - \mathbf{s}^{0T}[\mathbf{y}^0 - \mathbf{Z}^0\boldsymbol{\gamma}^*]$$
$$- \left\{\mathbf{s}^{1T}\left[\mathbf{y}^1 - \mathbf{Z}^1\left(\frac{1}{2}\boldsymbol{\gamma}^{0*} + \frac{1}{2}\boldsymbol{\gamma}^{1*}\right)\right] - \mathbf{s}^{0T}\left[\mathbf{y}^0 - \mathbf{Z}^0\left(\frac{1}{2}\boldsymbol{\gamma}^{0*} + \frac{1}{2}\boldsymbol{\gamma}^{1*}\right)\right]\right\}$$
$$= (\mathbf{s}^{1T}\mathbf{Z}^1 - \mathbf{s}^{0T}\mathbf{Z}^0)\left(\frac{1}{2}\boldsymbol{\gamma}^{0*} + \frac{1}{2}\boldsymbol{\gamma}^{1*} - \boldsymbol{\gamma}^*\right).$$

Thus, the hedonic time dummy and hedonic imputation measures of log price change will be identical if *either* of the following two conditions are satisfied:

$$\text{(67)} \quad \mathbf{s}^{1T}\mathbf{Z}^1 = \mathbf{s}^{0T}\mathbf{Z}^0;$$

$$\text{(68)} \quad \boldsymbol{\gamma}^* = \frac{1}{2}\boldsymbol{\gamma}^{0*} + \frac{1}{2}\boldsymbol{\gamma}^{1*}.$$

21. The exponential of this measure of price change is approximately equal to Haan's (2003, 14) geometric mean of his geometric Paasche and Laspeyres hedonic imputation indexes, which he regarded as an approximation to Törnqvist hedonic imputation index.

Condition (67) says that the expenditure share weighted average amount of each characteristic for the models present in period 1 equals the corresponding expenditure share weighted average amount of each characteristic for the models present in period 0. Condition (68) says that the time dummy vector of quality adjustment factors, $\boldsymbol{\gamma}^*$, is equal to the arithmetic average of the two separate weighted hedonic regression estimates for the quality adjustment factors, $(1/2)\boldsymbol{\gamma}^{0*} + (1/2)\boldsymbol{\gamma}^{1*}$.

As in section 4.3, condition (68) can be strengthened. Recall equation (56) in the previous section, which provided a formula for the hedonic time dummy vector of quality adjustment factors, $\boldsymbol{\gamma}^*$. Using the same notation to that used in the previous section, we can establish the following expressions for the period 0 and 1 weighted least squares estimates $\boldsymbol{\gamma}^{0*}$ and $\boldsymbol{\gamma}^{1*}$ that appear in equations (59) and (60):

$$(69)\qquad \boldsymbol{\gamma}^{0*} = \left(\sum_{n=1}^{N(0)} s_n^0 z_n^{0*T} z_n^{0*}\right)^{-1} \left(\sum_{n=1}^{N(0)} s_n^0 z_n^{0*T} y_n^{0*}\right);$$

$$(70)\qquad \boldsymbol{\gamma}^{1*} = \left(\sum_{n=1}^{N(1)} s_n^1 z_n^{1*T} z_n^{1*}\right)^{-1} \left(\sum_{n=1}^{N(0)} s_n^1 z_n^{1*T} y_n^{1*}\right).$$

where the $\mathbf{y}^{t*}$ and $Z^{t*}$ are the demeaned $\mathbf{y}^t$ and $Z^t$ as in the previous section. Now premultiply both sides of equation (56) by the matrix $[\Sigma_{n=1}^{N(0)} s_n^0 z_n^{0*T} z_n^{0*} + \Sigma_{n=1}^{N(1)} s_n^1 z_n^{1*T} z_n^{1*}]$ and we obtain the following equation that is the weighted counterpart to equation (40):

$$(71)\qquad \left[\sum_{n=1}^{N(0)} s_n^0 z_n^{0*T} z_n^{0*} + \sum_{n=1}^{N(1)} s_n^1 z_n^{1*T} z_n^{1*}\right]\boldsymbol{\gamma}^*$$

$$= \sum_{n=1}^{N(0)} s_n^0 z_n^{0*T} y_n^{0*} + \sum_{n=1}^{N(1)} s_n^1 z_n^{1*T} y_n^{1*}$$

$$= \left[\sum_{n=1}^{N(0)} s_n^0 z_n^{0*T} z_n^{0*}\right]\left[\sum_{n=1}^{N(0)} s_n^0 z_n^{0*T} z_n^{0*}\right]^{-1}\left[\sum_{n=1}^{N(0)} s_n^0 z_n^{0*T} y_n^{0*}\right]$$

$$+ \left[\sum_{n=1}^{N(1)} s_n^1 z_n^{1*T} z_n^{1*}\right]\left[\sum_{n=1}^{N(1)} s_n^1 z_n^{1*T} z_n^{1*}\right]^{-1}\left[\sum_{n=1}^{N(1)} s_n^1 z_n^{1*T} y_n^{1*}\right]$$

$$= \left[\sum_{n=1}^{N(0)} s_n^0 z_n^{0*T} z_n^{0*}\right]\boldsymbol{\gamma}^{0*} + \left[\sum_{n=1}^{N(1)} s_n^1 z_n^{1*T} z_n^{1*}\right]\boldsymbol{\gamma}^{1*}$$

using (69) and (70).

Equation (71) tells us if $\boldsymbol{\gamma}^{0*}$ equals $\boldsymbol{\gamma}^{1*}$, then $\boldsymbol{\gamma}^*$ is necessarily equal to this common vector. We now use equation (71) in order to evaluate the following expression:

$$(72)\quad 2\left[\sum_{n=1}^{N(0)} s_n^0 z_n^{0*T} z_n^{0*} + \sum_{n=1}^{N(1)} s_n^1 z_n^{1*T} z_n^{1*}\right]\left[\frac{1}{2}\boldsymbol{\gamma}^{0*} + \frac{1}{2}\boldsymbol{\gamma}^{1*} - \boldsymbol{\gamma}^*\right]$$

$$= \left[\sum_{n=1}^{N(0)} s_n^0 z_n^{0*T} z_n^{0*} + \sum_{n=1}^{N(1)} s_n^1 z_n^{1*T} z_n^{1*}\right][\boldsymbol{\gamma}^{0*} + \boldsymbol{\gamma}^{1*}]$$

$$- 2\left\{\left[\sum_{n=1}^{N(0)} s_n^0 z_n^{0*T} z_n^{0*}\right]\boldsymbol{\gamma}^{0*} + \left[\sum_{n=1}^{N(1)} s_n^1 z_n^{1*T} z_n^{1*}\right]\boldsymbol{\gamma}^{1*}\right\} \quad \text{using (71).}$$

$$= \left[\sum_{n=1}^{N(0)} s_n^0 z_n^{0*T} z_n^{0*}\right][\boldsymbol{\gamma}^{1*} - \boldsymbol{\gamma}^{0*}] - \left[\sum_{n=1}^{N(1)} s_n^1 z_n^{1*T} z_n^{1*}\right][\boldsymbol{\gamma}^{1*} - \boldsymbol{\gamma}^{0*}]$$

$$= -\left[\sum_{n=1}^{N(1)} s_n^1 z_n^{1*T} z_n^{1*} - \sum_{n=1}^{N(0)} s_n^0 z_n^{0*T} z_n^{0*}\right][\boldsymbol{\gamma}^{1*} - \boldsymbol{\gamma}^{0*}]$$

Now premultiply both sides of equation (72) by $(1/2)[\Sigma_{n=1}^{N(0)} s_n^0 z_n^{0*T} z_n^{0*} + \Sigma_{n=1}^{N(1)} s_n^1 z_n^{1*T} z_n^{1*}]^{-1}$ and substitute the resulting expression for $(1/2)\boldsymbol{\gamma}^{0*} + (1/2)\boldsymbol{\gamma}^{1*} - \boldsymbol{\gamma}^*$ into equation (66) in order to obtain the following expression for the difference between the hedonic dummy estimate of constant quality price change and the corresponding symmetric hedonic imputation estimate using weighted hedonic regressions in both cases:

$$(73)\quad \mathrm{LP_{WHD}} - \mathrm{LP_{WHI}} = (\mathbf{s}^{1T}\mathbf{Z}^1 - \mathbf{s}^{0T}\mathbf{Z}^0)\left(\frac{1}{2}\boldsymbol{\gamma}^{0*} + \frac{1}{2}\boldsymbol{\gamma}^{1*} - \boldsymbol{\gamma}^*\right)$$

$$= -\frac{1}{2}[\mathbf{s}^{1T}\mathbf{Z}^1 - \mathbf{s}^{0T}\mathbf{Z}^0]\left[\sum_{n=1}^{N(0)} s_n^0 z_n^{0*T} z_n^{0*} + \sum_{n=1}^{N(1)} s_n^1 z_n^{1*T} z_n^{1*}\right]^{-1}$$

$$\left[\sum_{n=1}^{N(1)} s_n^1 z_n^{1*T} z_n^{1*} - \sum_{n=1}^{N(0)} s_n^0 z_n^{0*T} z_n^{0*}\right][\boldsymbol{\gamma}^{1*} - \boldsymbol{\gamma}^{0*}].$$

Using equation (73), it can be seen that the weighted hedonic time dummy and the weighted hedonic imputation measures of log price change will be identical if *any* of the following three conditions are satisfied:

- $\mathbf{s}^{1T}\mathbf{Z}^1$ equals $\mathbf{s}^{0T}\mathbf{Z}^0$ so that the period expenditure share weighted amount of each characteristic across models in each period stays the same
- $\Sigma_{n=1}^{N(1)} s_n^1 z_n^{1*T} z_n^{1*}$ equals $\Sigma_{n=1}^{N(0)} s_n^0 z_n^{0*T} z_n^{0*}$ so that the expenditure share weighted model characteristics variance covariance matrix is the same in the two periods
- $\boldsymbol{\gamma}^{1*}$ equals $\boldsymbol{\gamma}^{0*}$ so that separate (weighted) hedonic regressions in each period give rise to the same characteristics quality adjustment factors

Which weighted method of quality adjustment is "best"? If *either* the weighted average amounts of each characteristic are much the same in the two periods being considered so that $\mathbf{s}^{1T}\mathbf{Z}^1$ is close to $\mathbf{s}^{0T}\mathbf{Z}^0$, or if the expenditure share weighted model characteristics variance covariance matrices are similar across periods, or if the separate weighted hedonic regression quality adjustment factors do not change much across the two periods, then it will not matter much which method is used, which is the new result demonstrated in this chapter. If, however, $\mathbf{s}^{1T}\mathbf{Z}^1$ is not close to $\mathbf{s}^{0T}\mathbf{Z}^0$, the expenditure share weighted model characteristics variance covariance matrices are different across periods, and the two separate weighted hedonic regressions (57) and (58) generate very different estimates for the quality adjustment factors, $\boldsymbol{\gamma}^{0*}$ and $\boldsymbol{\gamma}^{1*}$, then the method of quality adjustment could matter. If equations (57) and (58) are run together as a pooled regression model and an F test rejects the equality of $\boldsymbol{\gamma}^0$ and $\boldsymbol{\gamma}^1$, then it seems sensible to use the weighted hedonic imputation method, which does not depend on having $\boldsymbol{\gamma}^0$ equal to $\boldsymbol{\gamma}^1$ as does the hedonic time dummy method. If the F test does not reject the equality of $\boldsymbol{\gamma}^0$ and $\boldsymbol{\gamma}^1$ and there are a large number of characteristics in the model, then valuable degrees of freedom will be saved if the weighted time dummy hedonic regression model is used. However, in this case, since $\boldsymbol{\gamma}^0$ and $\boldsymbol{\gamma}^1$ are necessarily close, it should not matter much which method is used. Thus, it seems that the hedonic imputation methods probably give rise to "better" quality adjustments than dummy variable methods. We will revisit this discussion in section 4.7.

## 4.6 Empirical Illustration: Desktop Personal Computers (PCs)

The empirical study is of the measurement of changes in the quality-adjusted monthly prices of British desktop PCs in 1998. The data are monthly scanner data from the bar code readers of PC retailers. The data amounted to 7,387 observations (a particular make and model of a PC sold in a given month in an either specialized or nonspecialized PC store-type) representing a sales volume of 1.5 million models worth £1.57 billion. Table 4.1 shows that for the January to February price comparison there were 584 matched models available in both months for the price comparison. However, for the January to December price comparison only 161 matched models were available, with 509 unmatched "old" models (available in January, but unmatched in December) and 436 unmatched "new" models (available in December but unavailable in January for matching).[22] For product markets where there are a high proportion of unmatched models, Silver and Heravi (2005) demonstrated why matched-model indexes suffer from sample selectivity bias and why hedonic indexes should be used instead.

The calculation of hedonic indexes requires the estimation of hedonic regression equations. To simplify the illustration we first include only a single explanatory variable in the hedonic (price) regressions, the speed in MHz. The regressions were run separately for each month for the hedonic imputation indexes, and over January and the current month, including a dummy variable for the latter, for the hedonic dummy indexes. The estimated

22. Bear in mind that some of the indexes estimated in this chapter are also weighted by shares of sales values and that the fall off in the coverage of the matched sample by sales is even more dramatic: for the January to December comparison matched models made up only 71 percent of the January sales value and a mere 12 percent of the December sales value.

**Table 4.1** **Number of matched and unmatched observations**

| | Number of matched-models | Number of unmatched old models in January of the comparison | Number of unmatched new models in the current month of the comparison |
|---|---|---|---|
| February | 584 | 86 | 104 |
| March | 577 | 93 | 181 |
| April | 346 | 324 | 191 |
| May | 315 | 355 | 227 |
| June | 297 | 373 | 265 |
| July | 282 | 388 | 301 |
| August | 276 | 394 | 351 |
| September | 247 | 423 | 382 |
| October | 193 | 477 | 402 |
| November | 164 | 506 | 435 |
| December | 161 | 509 | 436 |

*Note:* Figures are for comparisons between January and each current month.

coefficients for speed in the hedonic regressions were statistically significant coefficients with the expected positive signs.[23]

Table 4.2 columns (1) and (2) show falls in the *unweighted* hedonic dummy and hedonic imputation indexes of 73.2 and 76.4 percent, respectively, a difference of 3.2 percentage points. Columns (4) through (6) show the constituent elements of equation (41) that make up this difference: column (4) is the change in mean characteristics, $[1_1^T\mathbf{Z}^1/N(1)] - [1_0^T\mathbf{Z}^0/N(0)]$, average speed increased by 127 MHz. over the year. Column (5) is the change in the (total) variance-covariance characteristics matrices relative to their sum in the two periods, $[\mathbf{Z}^{0*T}\mathbf{Z}^{0*} + \mathbf{Z}^{1*T}\mathbf{Z}^{1*}]^{-1}[\mathbf{Z}^{1*T}\mathbf{Z}^{1*} - \mathbf{Z}^{0*T}\mathbf{Z}^{0*}]$, with one characteristic in this illustration it is the relative change in the variance of speed, falling in some early months but increasing thereafter. Column (6) is the change in the characteristic parameter estimates, $[\gamma^{1*} - \gamma^{0*}]$, the estimated parameters decreased over time. The decomposition of the difference between the hedonic dummy and imputation indexes given in column (3) is exactly as demonstrated in column (7)—the difference is equal to one-half of the product of columns (4), (5), and (6), following equation (41). We stress that the decomposition is based on the *product* of these constituent parts. If either of these changes is zero, then there will be no difference between the indexes. While it is clear that there were large increases in the mean speed of PCs over the year (column [4]) they did not materialize in substantial difference

23. The F-statistics for the null hypothesis of coefficients being equal to zero averaged 34.2 for hedonic imputation indexes and 53.4 for hedonic dummy indexes, consistently rejecting the null at a 0.01 percent level and lower. The explanatory power of the estimated equations were naturally low for this specification with a single explanatory variable, especially since they did not include dummy variables on brand. Details of estimates from a fully specified model are available from the authors.

**Table 4.2** **Decomposition of differences between unweighted hedonic time dummy and imputation indexes for desktop PCs, 1998**

| | $LP_{HD}$ (1) | $LP_{HI}$ (2) | $LP_{HD}$–$LP_{HD}$ (3) | Change in mean characteristics (4) | Relative change in var-cov matrices (5) | Change in parameters (6) | (4) × (5) × (6) / 2 (7) |
|---|---|---|---|---|---|---|---|
| | | | *Change relative to fixed base, January 1998* | | | | |
| February | –0.0837 | –0.0837 | 0.0000 | –0.02 | 0.0564 | –0.00042 | 0.0000 |
| March | –0.1609 | –0.1611 | 0.0003 | 7.69 | 0.1485 | –0.00045 | 0.0003 |
| April | –0.2717 | –0.2713 | –0.0004 | 47.16 | –0.1895 | –0.00010 | –0.0004 |
| May | –0.4334 | –0.4348 | 0.0014 | 50.93 | –0.1444 | 0.00039 | 0.0014 |
| June | –0.4359 | –0.4347 | –0.0012 | 60.64 | –0.0390 | –0.00099 | –0.0012 |
| July | –0.4535 | –0.4540 | 0.0004 | 68.99 | 0.0119 | –0.00103 | 0.0004 |
| August | –0.4560 | –0.4672 | 0.0112 | 76.71 | 0.1484 | –0.00196 | 0.0112 |
| September | –0.4272 | –0.4467 | 0.0195 | 84.15 | 0.1787 | –0.00259 | 0.0195 |
| October | –0.5727 | –0.5945 | 0.0218 | 103.89 | 0.1906 | –0.00220 | 0.0218 |
| November | –0.6705 | –0.7046 | 0.0341 | 118.27 | 0.2317 | –0.00249 | 0.0341 |
| December | –0.7320 | –0.7643 | 0.0323 | 127.47 | 0.2050 | –0.00247 | 0.0323 |

between the formulas, being tempered by the smaller changes in columns (5) and (6). The formulation also provides insights into the factors behind any difference in the results from these methods. For example, in September and December the changes in the estimated parameters were about the same, yet the difference between the hedonic dummy and imputation indexes in column (3) was higher in December than in September, driven by the larger change in mean characteristics in December.

The indexes considered in table 4.2 were unweighted and thus unrepresentative if models differ in their popularity. Conventional index number theory requires that price changes should be weighted by relative expenditures shares and the same requirement should apply to hedonic indexes. In sections 4.4 and 4.5 *weighted* hedonic dummy and hedonic imputation indexes were formulated and equation (73) provided a decomposition of the difference between them. The results for PCs for weighted hedonic indexes, their difference, and the constituent elements underlying the difference are given in table 4.3. Again the difference depends on the product of three terms: the change in the expenditure share weighted mean of each characteristics, $[\mathbf{s}^{1T}\mathbf{Z}^1 - \mathbf{s}^{0T}\mathbf{Z}^0]$; the change in the expenditure share weighted characteristics variance-covariance matrix, $[\Sigma_{n=1}^{N(0)} s_n^0 z_n^{0*T} z_n^{0*} + \Sigma_{n=1}^{N(1)} s_n^1 z_n^{1*T} z_n^{1*}]^{-1} \times [\Sigma_{n=1}^{N(1)} s_n^1 z_n^{1*T} z_n^{1*} - \Sigma_{n=1}^{N(0)} s_n^0 z_n^{0*T} z_n^{0*}]$; and the change in the parameters estimates, $[\boldsymbol{\gamma}^{1*} - \boldsymbol{\gamma}^{0*}]$ from the separate (weighted) hedonic regressions in each period. Table 4.3 shows respective falls for the weighted hedonic dummy and weighted hedonic imputation indexes of 43.1 and 50.6 percent (imputation) over the year, compared with falls in the corresponding unweighted indexes of 73.2 and 76.4 percent in table 4.2, thus weighting matters. The decomposition in table 4.3 follows equation (73) and is exact with (one-half of) the product of columns (4) to (6) (in column [7]) equaling the difference between the formulas in column (3). The differences are at their highest in September and December at over 7 percentage points, in part due to the relatively high parameter changes. Again comparing September with December, the parameter changes in column (6) are similarly high at –0.0039. But again the change in the mean speed in column (4) at 139.6 MHz in December is much higher than its September figure of 94.45 MHz.[24] This should translate into a very much lower difference between the formulas in September compared with December, but for the weighted results it does not. This is because the much higher December change in characteristics, column (4), is largely offset by the much lower change in the relative variance in column (5).

The previous empirical example was limited to a single price-determining quality characteristic variable for illustrative purposes. The decomposition for more than one characteristic is similar in principle to the case of a single

24. The multiplication is of the change in average speed by the parameter estimate for speed. The result is invariant to the units of measurement used for speed since an accordingly lower coefficient would result if the units of measurement for speed were, say, doubled.

**Table 4.3** **Decomposition of differences between weighted hedonic time dummy and imputation indexes for desktop PCs, 1998**

| | $LP_{HD}$ (1) | $LP_{HI}$ (2) | $LP_{HD}$–$LP_{HD}$ (3) | Change in mean characteristics (4) | Relative change in var-cov matrices (5) | Change in parameters (6) | (4) × (5) × (6) / 2 (7) |
|---|---|---|---|---|---|---|---|
| | | | *Change relative to fixed base, January 1998* | | | | |
| February | –0.0622 | –0.0624 | 0.0002 | 8.84 | 0.0454 | –0.00076 | 0.0002 |
| March | –0.0920 | –0.0921 | 0.0001 | 14.81 | 0.0122 | –0.00092 | 0.0001 |
| April | –0.1750 | –0.1746 | –0.0004 | 31.44 | –0.0331 | –0.00074 | –0.0004 |
| May | –0.2306 | –0.2318 | 0.0012 | 42.74 | 0.0458 | –0.00122 | 0.0012 |
| June | –0.1873 | –0.2002 | 0.0129 | 54.79 | 0.1464 | –0.00321 | 0.0129 |
| July | –0.2782 | –0.2914 | 0.0131 | 65.76 | 0.1180 | –0.00338 | 0.0131 |
| August | –0.2974 | –0.3271 | 0.0297 | 81.67 | 0.2299 | –0.00316 | 0.0297 |
| September | –0.2336 | –0.3040 | 0.0704 | 94.45 | 0.3829 | –0.00390 | 0.0704 |
| October | –0.3891 | –0.4476 | 0.0586 | 118.52 | 0.2979 | –0.00332 | 0.0586 |
| November | –0.5080 | –0.5566 | 0.0486 | 131.90 | 0.2131 | –0.00346 | 0.0486 |
| December | –0.4311 | –0.5057 | 0.0745 | 139.59 | 0.2766 | –0.00386 | 0.0745 |

explanatory variable, but the constituent items of equation (73) are matrices and it is the product of these matrices that is required to account for the difference between the formulas. The regression estimates are now based on three quality characteristics, speed in MHz, the hard disk capacity (CAP), and random access memory (RAM), both in MB. The estimated coefficients for the three variables in the hedonic regressions were statistically significant with the expected positive signs.[25] The result of the decomposition of the difference between weighted hedonic dummy and weighted hedonic imputation indexes based on multiple characteristics for the January with December comparison only (for ease of exposition) is presented in the matrix format of equation (73) and as table 4.4.

The weighted hedonic dummy index in December compared with January, based on the extended specification, fell by 51.5 percent, compared with the fall in the weighted hedonic imputation index of 63.3, a sizable difference of 11.8 percentage points. From tables 4.2 and 4.3 we saw that weighting matters. Here we identify the importance of a fuller specification of the hedonic regression used and its effect on the magnitude of the index change and the spread between the two estimates. The fuller specification has led to an increase in the spread between the two indexes from 7.5 to 11.8 percentage points. Prices are estimated to have fallen further using the extended variable set: a fall for the weighted hedonic dummy hedonic of 51.5 compared with 43.1 and for the hedonic imputation index of 63.3 compared with 50.6 percent. Additional explanatory variables in a quality-adjusted hedonic regression based index are probably preferable.[26] Yet in spite of this illustration, a fuller specification of the hedonic regression need not necessarily lead to an increase in the difference between the formulas. If any component of an additional variable—its change in relative dispersion, covariance, parameter, or mean value—is negligible, then it will have little effect on the difference. Indeed, the overall impact of additional variables in the product of matrices in equation (73) may take a different sign and reduce the discrepancy. However, in general, product development in high technology products such as PCs takes the form of increased product differentiation (dispersion of characteristics values), improvements in many product dimensions at the same time (which will generally change means and covariances), and decreasing characteristic production costs and marginal utilities, as consumers realign their preferences to the new standards (which will generally lead to changes in parameter estimates). Thus, our expectation is that the HI and HD approaches to measuring price change may frequently give different estimates of overall price change in dynamic markets.

25. The adjusted-$R^2$ were 0.40 and 0.31 for the hedonic regression equations in January and November, respectively. The specification could be extended to include many more variables including dummy variables for brands. The exposition here was simplified to illustrate the decomposition for more than one explanatory variable.

26. There are statistical caveats to this statement; that is, it may not be useful to include additional explanatory variables if there are insufficient degrees of freedom or if multicollinearity between included and omitted variables is strong.

**Table 4.4** **Factors contributing to difference between weighted HD and weighted HI estimates for PCs for three variables: January to December comparison**

| | | |
|---|---|---|
| $LP_{HI}$ | –0.4311 | 0.0001 |
| $LP_{HI}$ | –0.5057 | –0.0004 |
| $LP_{HD}$–$LP_{HD}$ | 0.0745 | 0.0012 |

Factors contributing to change

| Change in mean characteristics | | Change in variances | |
|---|---|---|---|
| Speed | 139.593 | Speed | 1,728.1 |
| CAP | 180.140 | CAP | –3,672.3 |
| RAM | 14.405 | RAM | 167.3 |
| **Inverse of total variances** | | **Change covariances** | |
| Speed | 6,245.2 | Speed:CAP | 5,168.0 |
| CAP | 55,658.7 | Speed:RAM | 460.2 |
| RAM | 1,131.1 | CAP:RAM | –1,93.9 |
| **Inverse of total covariances** | | **Change in parameter estimates** | |
| Speed:CAP | 5,422.8 | Speed | –0.00743 |
| Speed:RAM | 637.2 | CAP | 0.00127 |
| CAP:RAM | 3,626.1 | RAM | –0.00612 |

The four terms in equation (73) are reproduced following as matrices, and as table 4.4, for the December with January comparison, the product of which is equal to the difference between the formulas, that is

$$-\frac{1}{2}[\mathbf{s}^{1T}\mathbf{Z}^1 - \mathbf{s}^{0T}\mathbf{Z}^0]\left[\sum_{n=1}^{N(0)} \mathbf{s}_n^0 z_n^{0*T} z_n^{0*} + \sum_{n=1}^{N(1)} \mathbf{s}_n^1 z_n^{1*T} z_n^{1*}\right]^{-1}$$

$$\left[\sum_{n=1}^{N(1)} \mathbf{s}_n^1 z_n^{1*T} z_n^{1*} - \sum_{n=1}^{N(0)} \mathbf{s}_n^0 z_n^{0*T} z_n^{0*}\right][\boldsymbol{\gamma}^{1*} - \boldsymbol{\gamma}^{0*}]$$

$$= -\frac{1}{2}[139.593,\ 180.140,\ 14.405] \times$$

$$\begin{bmatrix} 6{,}245.2 & 5{,}422.8 & 637.2 \\ 5{,}422.8 & 55{,}658.7 & 3{,}626.1 \\ 637.2 & 3{,}626.1 & 1{,}131.0 \end{bmatrix}^{-1} \times$$

$$\begin{bmatrix} 1{,}728.1 & 5{,}168.0 & 460.2 \\ 5{,}168.0 & -3{,}672.3 & -193.9 \\ 460.2 & -193.9 & 167.3 \end{bmatrix} \begin{bmatrix} -0.00743 \\ 0.00127 \\ -0.00612 \end{bmatrix}$$

$$= 0.1182.$$

The values of the elements in the first row or column of the matrices are for the characteristic variable speed, the second, the CAP, and third, RAM. The vectors and matrices in turn are the change in the mean value of the characteristics, which were all positive; the sum of the inverted variance-covariance characteristics matrix over the two months (the second matrix in equation [73] has been inverted); the change in the variance-covariance characteristics matrix over the two months; and the change in the estimated parameters. Thus in the third matrix, for example, the diagonal values of 1,728.1, –3,672.3, and 167.3 are the change in the variances of the characteristics speed, CAP, and RAM, respectively. Note that in the last matrix, the parameter estimates for speed and RAM fall over the period by a similar amount, but the increase in the average value of speed (in the first matrix) is much more than that of the mean RAM size, and thus is a more significant driver of the difference between the formulas. There is also a marked increase in the average CAP, yet its parameter difference estimate at 0.00127 is positive, so that a higher marginal value is attached to it in December as compared with January, yet the absolute value of this change, and thus its impact on the difference, is lower than the corresponding change for speed.

## 4.7 Concluding Remarks on the Choice between Hedonic Imputation Indexes and Hedonic Dummy Indexes

Having identified the factors behind the difference between the hedonic dummy and imputation indexes, we turn to consider which, if any, formula is more appropriate. Given that both approaches make symmetric use of information in the two periods and can be formulated to have the same functional form and weighting system, a plausible stance, when they produce different results, is to take a (geometric) mean of the two. Yet there may be reasons to prefer one against the other.

The main concern with the use of the hedonic time dummy index approach, as given by the respective unweighted and weighted equations (12) and (49), is that by construction, it constrains the parameters on the characteristic variables to be the same. Berndt and Rappaport (2001) found, for example, from 1987 to 1999 for desktop PCs, the null hypothesis of adjacent-year equality of the characteristics parameters to be rejected in all but one case. For mobile PCs the null hypothesis of parameter stability was rejected in eight of the twelve adjacent-year comparisons. Berndt and Rappaport (2001) preferred the use of hedonic imputation indexes if there was evidence of parameter instability. Pakes (2003), using quarterly data for hedonic regressions for desktop PCs over the period 1995 to 1999, rejected just about any hypothesis on the constancy of the coefficients. He also advocated hedonic imputation indexes on the grounds that ". . . since hedonic coefficients vary across periods it [the hedonic dummy approach] has no theoretical justification." Pakes (2003, 1593). The hedonic imputation method is inherently more *flexible* (in that it can deal with changes in purchasers' valuations of characteristics over the periods being compared) than the hedonic dummy method and this is a big advantage for the HI method.

Note also that the difference between the two approaches has been found to depend on three change factors: the change in the mean characteristics, relative variance-covariance characteristics matrix, and parameter estimates. More specifically, it was found that the difference depends on the *product* of such changes. As such, parameter instability by itself need not by itself be a cause for concern. Even if parameters were unstable, the difference between the indexes may be compounded or mitigated by a small change in any of the other components.

Nevertheless, the essence of the HD method is that only one regression is run, with the data in both periods appearing as dependent variables and with the restriction that the characteristics are valued at common "prices" for the two periods. In this interpretation, HD is not as flexible because of these restrictions. Why are these restrictions imposed? Perhaps for three reasons:

- To conserve degrees of freedom.
- To give an unambiguous estimate of the amount of price change going from period 0 to 1. Because the regression surfaces are parallel, we can measure the distance between the two surfaces at any characteristics point $z$ and get the same estimate of log price change, which is not the case in the HI methods.
- To minimize the influence of outliers, particularly in situations where degrees of freedom are small.

In view of the previous considerations, the advantages and disadvantages of the two methods can be seen: HI is "better" because it allows for changing characteristics prices over time; that is, it is more "flexible" but at the cost of:

- Using up more degrees of freedom.
- Leading to a less reproducible estimate of overall price change between the two periods, since we have to condition on one or more "reasonable" $z$ points to measure the distance between the two surfaces.

In practice, the last objection is not very serious; the Laspeyres and Paasche type estimates of price change are well established in index number theory, as is the idea that these equally valid estimates of price change should be averaged in order to come up with a single measure of price change.

Thus all things considered, we favor HI methods unless degrees of freedom are very limited.

Triplett (2004) recognized that extensive product differentiation with a high model turnover is an increasing feature of product markets. The motivation for the use of hedonic regression techniques lies in the failure of the matched-models method to adequately deal with price measurement in this context. Schultze and Mackie (2002) argued that hedonic indexes were the most promising approach to measuring price changes for such product markets, but advised that further research into such methods was needed: in particular, under what conditions will HD and HI measures of price change be different? This chapter has provided answers to this question.

## Appendix A

*An Alternative Interpretation of the Hedonic Imputation Estimate of Log Price Change*

In section 4.3, we derived an estimator for the logarithm of overall price change between the two periods, $LP_{HI}$ defined by equation (34), which we called the hedonic imputation estimate of the change in log prices going from period 0 to 1. We derived this estimator of price change following the methodology pioneered by Court (1939, 108); that is, individual prices in each period were quality adjusted using their characteristics vectors and the characteristics prices obtained from one of the two hedonic regressions pertaining to the two periods under consideration, and then the resulting quality-adjusted prices were compared across the two periods. However, there is an alternative method for estimating price change across two periods when separate hedonic regressions are run for each period. In this second method, we calculate the mean vector of characteristics that pertains to the models observed in period 0, say, and then calculate the distance between the two hedonic regressions at this mean characteristics point. This is called a Laspeyres-type measure of price change. Then we calculate the mean vector of characteristics that pertains to the models observed in period 1 and calculate the distance between the two hedonic regressions at this second mean characteristics point, leading to a Paasche-type measure of price change. Finally these two distances between the hedonic regression surfaces are averaged in order to obtain a final measure of price change between the two periods. This is the methodology originally proposed by Griliches (1967) and Dhrymes (1971, 111–12). In this appendix, we show that the first and second hedonic imputation methods lead to the same overall estimate of price change.

We first consider the unweighted hedonic imputation model that was described in section 4.3. Recall the notation used in section 4.3 where $\mathbf{y}^0$ was the $N(0)$ dimensional vector of log model prices in period 0, $\mathbf{y}^1$ was the $N(1)$ dimensional vector of log model prices in period 1 and $\mathbf{Z}^t$ was the $N(t)$ by $K$ matrix of characteristics by model in period $t$ for $t = 0,1$. Define the sample average of the log prices in period $t$, $\mathbf{y}^{t*}$, and the sample average vectors of model characteristics, $\mathbf{z}^{t*}$, as follows:

(A1) $$\mathbf{y}^{0*} \equiv \frac{1_0^T \mathbf{y}^0}{N(0)};\ \mathbf{y}^{1*} \equiv \frac{1_1^T \mathbf{y}^1}{N(1)};\ \mathbf{z}^{0*} \equiv \frac{1_0^T \mathbf{Z}^0}{N(0)};\ \mathbf{z}^{1*} \equiv \frac{1_1^T \mathbf{Z}^1}{N(1)}.$$

Using definitions (A1), equations (28) and (29) in section 4.3 can be rewritten as follows:

(A2) $$\mathbf{y}^{0*} = \beta_0^* + \mathbf{z}^{0*T}\boldsymbol{\gamma}^{0*};$$

(A3) $$\mathbf{y}^{1*} = \beta_1^* + \mathbf{z}^{1*T}\boldsymbol{\gamma}^{1*}.$$

For later reference, it can be seen that equations (A2) and (A3) imply the following expression for the difference in intercepts in the two hedonic regressions:

(A4) $$\beta_1^* - \beta_0^* = \mathbf{y}^{1*} - \mathbf{y}^{0*} - \mathbf{z}^{1*T}\boldsymbol{\gamma}^{1*} + \mathbf{z}^{0*T}\boldsymbol{\gamma}^{0*}.$$

Now we are ready to define some estimators of the distance between the two hedonic regression surfaces. We define the *Laspeyres-type measure of log price change* between periods 0 and 1, $LP_L$, and the *Paasche-type measure of log price change,* $LP_P$, as follows:

(A5) $$LP_L \equiv \beta_1^* + \mathbf{z}^{0*T}\boldsymbol{\gamma}^{1*} - (\beta_0^* + \mathbf{z}^{0*T}\boldsymbol{\gamma}^{0*});$$

(A6) $$LP_P \equiv \beta_1^* + \mathbf{z}^{1*T}\boldsymbol{\gamma}^{1*} - (\beta_0^* + \mathbf{z}^{1*T}\boldsymbol{\gamma}^{0*}).$$

It can be seen that equations (A5) and (A6) are both measures of the distance between the two hedonic regression surfaces: the Laspeyres-type measure holds the characteristics vector constant at the average of the period 0 levels, $\mathbf{z}^{0*}$, while the Paasche-type measure holds the characteristics vector constant at the average of the period 1 levels, $\mathbf{z}^{1*}$. Our final measure of log price change is the arithmetic average of the Laspeyres- and Paasche-type measures, which we call the Fisher type measure of log price change, $LP_F$:

(A7) $$\begin{aligned} LP_F &\equiv \frac{1}{2}(LP_L + LP_P) \\ &= \frac{1}{2}[\beta_1^* + \mathbf{z}^{0*T}\boldsymbol{\gamma}^{1*} - (\beta_0^* + \mathbf{z}^{0*T}\boldsymbol{\gamma}^{0*}) + \beta_1^* + \mathbf{z}^{1*T}\boldsymbol{\gamma}^{1*} \\ &\quad - (\beta_0^* + \mathbf{z}^{1*T}\boldsymbol{\gamma}^{0*})] \qquad \text{using (A6) and (A7)} \\ &= \beta_1^* - \beta_0^* + \frac{1}{2}(\mathbf{z}^{0*T} + \mathbf{z}^{1*T})(\boldsymbol{\gamma}^{1*} - \boldsymbol{\gamma}^{0*}) \\ &= \mathbf{y}^{1*} - \mathbf{y}^{0*} - \mathbf{z}^{1*T}\boldsymbol{\gamma}^{1*} + \mathbf{z}^{0*T}\boldsymbol{\gamma}^{0*} \\ &\quad + \frac{1}{2}(\mathbf{z}^{0*T}\boldsymbol{\gamma}^{1*} - \mathbf{z}^{0*T}\boldsymbol{\gamma}^{0*} + \mathbf{z}^{1*T}\boldsymbol{\gamma}^{1*} - \mathbf{z}^{1*T}\boldsymbol{\gamma}^{0*}) \qquad \text{using (A4)} \\ &= \mathbf{y}^{1*} - \mathbf{y}^{0*} + \frac{1}{2}(\mathbf{z}^{0*T}\boldsymbol{\gamma}^{1*} + \mathbf{z}^{0*T}\boldsymbol{\gamma}^{0*} - \mathbf{z}^{1*T}\boldsymbol{\gamma}^{1*} - \mathbf{z}^{1*T}\boldsymbol{\gamma}^{0*}) \\ &= \mathbf{y}^{1*} - \mathbf{y}^{0*} - \frac{1}{2}(\boldsymbol{\gamma}^{1*} - \boldsymbol{\gamma}^{0*})^T(\mathbf{z}^{1*} - \mathbf{z}^{0*}) \\ &= LP_{HI}, \end{aligned}$$

where $LP_{HI}$ was the hedonic imputation index defined by equation (34) in section 4.2. Thus, the two hedonic imputation methods for defining an estimate of price change coincide in the unweighted case.[27]

Now consider the weighted hedonic imputation model that was described in section 4.5. The equally weighted sample averages of the log prices ($\mathbf{y}^{0*}$ and $\mathbf{y}^{1*}$) and of the model characteristics (the vectors $\mathbf{z}^{0*}$ and $\mathbf{z}^{1*}$) defined in equation (A1) are now replaced by the following *expenditure share weighted averages:*

$$\text{(A8)} \qquad \mathbf{y}^{0*} \equiv \mathbf{s}^{0T}\mathbf{y}^{0}; \mathbf{y}^{1*} \equiv \mathbf{s}^{1T}\mathbf{y}^{1}; \mathbf{z}^{0*} \equiv \mathbf{s}^{0T}\mathbf{Z}^{0}; \mathbf{z}^{1*} \equiv \mathbf{s}^{1T}\mathbf{Z}^{1}.$$

Using the new definitions in equation (A8), it can be seen that equations (61) and (62) in section 4.5 imply that equations (A2) and (A3) continue to hold so that (A4) also holds, using these new definitions. We can again define the Laspeyres and Paasche type measures of log price change by equations (A5) and (A4) where we use the new hedonic regression estimates for the period 0 weighted regression, $\beta_0^*$and $\boldsymbol{\gamma}^{0*}$, and for the period 1 weighted regression, $\beta_1^*$ and $\boldsymbol{\gamma}^{1*}$, and the period 0 weighted average characteristics vector $\mathbf{z}^{0*}$ for the Laspeyres measure $LP_L$ and the period 1 weighted average characteristics vector $\mathbf{z}^{1*}$ for the Paasche measure $LP_P$. Now use $LP_L$ and $LP_P$ to define the Fisher measure $LP_F$ by the first line in equation (A7) and again we can show that this Fisher measure is equal to the weighted hedonic imputation index $LP_{WHI}$ defined by equation (65).

Thus we have shown that two rather different looking approaches to hedonic imputation indexes are equivalent.

## Appendix B

*A Method for Obtaining Approximate Standard Errors for the Hedonic Imputation Laspeyres and Paasche Measures of Log Price Change*

We consider the unweighted case first. Recall that the Laspeyres type hedonic imputation measure of log price change was defined as

$$\text{(A9)} \qquad \phi_L^* \equiv \delta_1^* - \beta_0^*,$$

where $\delta_1^*$ and $\beta_0^*$ are defined by equations (32) and (30), respectively. These last two equations can be rewritten as follows:

$$\text{(A10)} \qquad N(1)\delta_1^* = 1_1^T\mathbf{y}^1 - 1_1^T\mathbf{Z}^1\boldsymbol{\gamma}^{0*};$$

$$\text{(A11)} \qquad N(0)\beta_0^* = 1_0^T\mathbf{y}^0 - 1_0^T\mathbf{Z}^0\boldsymbol{\gamma}^{0*}.$$

27. It can also be verified that $LP_L$ is equal to $\beta_1^* - \delta_0^*$ where $\delta_0^*$ was defined by equation (33) and $LP_P$ is equal to $\delta_1^* - \beta_0^*$ where $\delta_1^*$ was defined by equation (32).

Recall also that the period 0 hedonic regression was written as equation (26) where $\beta_0^*$ was the period 0 estimated log price level and $\boldsymbol{\gamma}^{0*}$ was the period 0 vector of least squares estimates for the characteristics prices. Now use these estimated period 0 regression coefficients to quality adjust the period 1 log prices in the vector $\mathbf{y}^1$. After subtracting these quality adjustments from the vector of period 1 log prices $\mathbf{y}^1$, we are left with the period 1 vector $\mathbf{v}^1$ of quality-adjusted prices, less the period 0 log price level defined as follows:

$$\text{(A12)} \qquad \mathbf{v}^1 \equiv \mathbf{y}^1 - (1_1\beta_0^* + \mathbf{Z}^1\boldsymbol{\gamma}^{0*}) = (\mathbf{y}^1 - \mathbf{Z}^1\boldsymbol{\gamma}^{0*}) - 1_1\beta_0^*.$$

Now run a least squares regression of the period 1 residual vector $\mathbf{v}^1$ on a constant term with coefficient $\phi_0$. The resulting least squares estimator for $\phi_0$ is:

$$\text{(A13)} \qquad \begin{aligned} \phi_0^* &\equiv \frac{1_1^T\mathbf{v}^1}{N(1)} \\ &= \frac{1_1^T(\mathbf{y}^1 - \mathbf{Z}^1\boldsymbol{\gamma}^{0*})}{N(1)} - \frac{N(1)\beta_0^*}{N(1)} && \text{using (A12)} \\ &= \delta_1^* - \beta_0^* && \text{using (A10)} \\ &= \phi_L^* && \text{using (A9).} \end{aligned}$$

Thus, the Laspeyres type hedonic imputation measure of log price change $\phi_L^*$ defined by equation (A9) is numerically equal to the least squares estimator $\phi_0^*$ of the constant term in a regression of period 1 quality-adjusted log prices $\mathbf{v}^1$ defined by equation (A12) on a constant and the standard error on this auxiliary regression coefficient can serve as an approximate standard error for the Laspeyres hedonic imputation measure of constant quality log price change over the two periods under consideration.[28]

The previous algebra can be repeated for the Paasche type hedonic imputation measure of log price change, which was defined as

$$\text{(A14)} \qquad \phi_P^* \equiv \beta_1^* - \delta_0^*,$$

28. This is only an approximate standard error because it is conditional on period 0 estimated parameters, $\beta_0^*$ and $\boldsymbol{\gamma}_0^*$, which are subject to some sampling uncertainty. If we wanted to use the same methodology to obtain standard errors for the constant quality period 0 log price level, $\beta_0$, and the constant quality period 1 log price level, $\delta_1$, then we would use the period 0 estimated characteristics prices $\boldsymbol{\gamma}^{0*}$ in order to form period 0 and 1 quality-adjusted log price vectors $\mathbf{w}^0$ and $\mathbf{w}^1$, defined as $\mathbf{w}^t \equiv \mathbf{y}^t - \mathbf{Z}^t\boldsymbol{\gamma}^{0*}$ for $t = 0,1$. Now form two auxiliary regressions where $\mathbf{w}^0$ is regressed on a constant with coefficient $\beta_0$ and $\mathbf{w}^1$ is regressed on a constant with coefficient $\delta_1$. The least squares estimators for $\beta_0$ and $\delta_1$ turn out to be the $\beta_0^*$ and $\delta_1^*$, defined by equations (A10) and (A11). The standard errors for these coefficients in the auxiliary regression can be used as approximate standard errors for the log price levels in the two periods. These standard errors are conditional on the estimated period 0 characteristics prices, $\boldsymbol{\gamma}^{0*}$. Of course, the original period 0 hedonic regression can be used in order to obtain an unconditional standard error for the period 0 log price level $\beta_0$.

where $\beta_1^*$ and $\delta_0^*$ are defined by equations (31) and (33), respectively. These last two equations can be rewritten as follows:

(A15) $$N(1)\beta_1^* = 1_1^T\mathbf{y}^1 - 1_1^T\mathbf{Z}^1\boldsymbol{\gamma}^{1*}.$$

(A16) $$N(0)\delta_0^* = 1_0^T\mathbf{y}^0 - 1_0^T\mathbf{Z}^0\boldsymbol{\gamma}^{1*}.$$

Recall also that the period 0 hedonic regression was written as equation (27), where $\beta_1^*$ was the period 1 estimated log price level and $\boldsymbol{\gamma}^{1*}$ was the period 1 vector of least squares estimates for the characteristics prices. Now use these estimated period 1 regression coefficients to quality adjust the period 0 log prices in the vector $\mathbf{y}^0$. After subtracting these quality adjustments from the vector of period 0 log prices $\mathbf{y}^0$, we are left with the period 0 vector $\mathbf{v}^0$ of quality-adjusted prices, less the period 1 log price level defined as follows:

(A17) $$\mathbf{v}^0 \equiv \mathbf{y}^0 - [1_0\beta_1^* + \mathbf{Z}^0\boldsymbol{\gamma}^{1*}] = [\mathbf{y}^0 - \mathbf{Z}^0\boldsymbol{\gamma}^{1*}] - 1_0\beta_1^*.$$

Now run a least squares regression of the period 0 residual vector $\mathbf{v}^0$ on a constant term with coefficient $\phi_1$. The resulting least squares estimator for $\phi_1$ is:

(A18) $$\begin{aligned} \phi_1^* &\equiv \frac{1_0^T\mathbf{v}^0}{N(0)} \\ &= \frac{1_0^T(\mathbf{y}^0 - Z^0\boldsymbol{\gamma}^{1*})}{N(0)} - \frac{N(0)\beta_1^*}{N(0)} && \text{using (A17)} \\ &= \delta_0^* - \beta_1^* && \text{using (A16)} \\ &= -\phi_L^* && \text{using (A14).} \end{aligned}$$

Thus, the Paasche type hedonic imputation measure of log price change $\phi_P^*$ defined by equation (A14) is numerically equal to minus the least squares estimator $\phi_1^*$ of the constant term in a regression of period 0 quality-adjusted log prices $\mathbf{v}^0$ defined by equation (A17) on a constant and the standard error on this auxiliary regression coefficient can serve as an approximate standard error for the Paasche hedonic imputation measure of constant quality log price change over the two periods under consideration.

We leave the reader with the task of deriving the counterparts of these results to the case where we have weighted hedonic regressions.

## References

Berndt, E. R., Z. Griliches, and N. J. Rappaport. 1995. Econometric estimates of price indexes for personal computers in the 1990s. *Journal of Econometrics* 68: 243–68.

Berndt, E. R., and N. J. Rappaport. 2001. Price and quality of desktop and mobile personal computers: A quarter-century historical overview. *American Economic Review* 91 (2): 268–73.
Boskin, M. S. (Chair), Advisory Commission to Study the Consumer Price Index. 1996. Towards a more accurate measure of the cost of living. Interim report to the senate finance committee, Washington DC
Cole, R., Y. C. Chen, J. A. Barquin-Stolleman, E. Dullberger, N. Helvacian, and J. H. Hodge. 1986. Quality-adjusted price indexes for computer processors and selected peripheral equipment. *Survey of Current Business* 66 (1): 41–50.
Court, A. T. 1939. Hedonic price indexes with automotive examples. In *The dynamics of automobile demand,* 98–117. New York: General Motors Corporation.
de Haan, J. 2003. Time dummy approaches to hedonic price measurement. Paper presented at the Seventh Meeting of the International Working Group on Price Indices, (Ottawa Group), 27–29 May, National Institute for Statistics and Economic Studies (INSEE), Paris. Available at: http://www.insee.fr/en/nom_def_met/colloques/ottawa/ottawa_papers.htm.
———. 2004. Hedonic regressions: The time dummy index as a special case of the Törnqvist Index, time dummy approaches to hedonic price measurement. Paper presented at the Eighth Meeting of the International Working Group on Price Indices. 23–25 August, Helsinki: Statistics Finland.
———. 2007. Hedonic price indexes: A comparison of imputation, time dummy and other approaches. Room document at the Tenth Ottawa Group Meeting. 9–12 October, Ottawa. Available at: http://www.ottawagroup2007.ca/r004/pdf/ogo04_033_e.pdf.
Diewert, W. E. 2003a. Hedonic regressions: A consumer theory approach. In *Scanner data and price indexes,* studies in income and wealth, vol. 64, ed. R. C. Feenstra and M. D. Shapiro, 317–48. Chicago: University of Chicago Press.
———. 2003b. Hedonic regressions: A review of some unresolved issues. Paper presented at the Seventh Meeting of the Ottawa Group. 27–29 May, Paris.
———. 2005. Weighted country product dummy variable regressions and index number formulae. *The Review of Income and Wealth* 51 (4): 561–71.
———. 2006. Adjacent period dummy variable hedonic regressions and bilateral index number theory. *Annales d'économie et de statistique* 79/80: 1–28. Available at: http://www.econ.ubc.ca/discpapers/dp0511.pdf.
Dhrymes, P. J. 1971. Price and quality changes in consumer capital goods: An empirical study. In *Price indexes and quality change,* ed. Z. Griliches, 88–149. Cambridge, MA: Harvard University Press.
Feenstra, R. C. 1995. Exact hedonic price indexes. *Review of Economics and Statistics* 77 (4): 634–54.
Griliches, Z. 1967. Hedonic price indexes revisited: A note on the state of the art. *Proceedings of the Business and Economics Section of the American Statistical Association:* 332–34.
———. 1971a. Hedonic price indexes for automobiles: An econometric analysis of quality change. In *Price indexes and quality change,* ed. Z. Griliches, 55–87. Cambridge, MA: Harvard University Press.
———. 1971b. Introduction: Hedonic price indexes revisited. In *Price indexes and quality change,* ed. Z. Griliches, 3–15. Cambridge, MA: Harvard University Press.
Ioannidis, C., and M. Silver. 1999. Estimating exact hedonic indexes: An application to U.K. television sets. *Journal of Economics* 69 (1): 71–94.
Koskimäki, T., and Y. Vartia. 2001. Beyond matched pairs and Griliches-type hedonic methods for controlling quality changes in CPI sub-indices. In *International working group on price indices: Papers and proceedings of the sixth meeting* (the

Ottawa Group) held at Canberra, Australia, April 2–6, ed. K. Woolford, 12–40. Canberra: Australian Bureau of Statistics.
Pakes, A. 2003. A reconsideration of hedonic price indexes with an application to PCs. *The American Economic Review* 93 (5): 1576–93.
Schultze, C. L., and C. Mackie, eds. 2002. *At what price? Conceptualizing and measuring cost-of-living indexes,* Washington DC: National Academy Press.
Silver, M., and S. Heravi. 2003. The measurement of quality-adjusted price changes. In *Scanner data and price indexes,* ed. M. Shapiro and R. Feenstra, 277–317. Chicago: University of Chicago Press.
———. 2005. A failure in the measurement of inflation: Results from a hedonic and matched experiment using scanner data. *Journal of Business and Economic Statistics* 23 (5): 269–81.
———. 2007a. Hedonic imputation indexes and time dummy hedonic indexes. *Journal of Business and Economic Statistics* 25 (2): 239–46.
———. 2007b. Different approaches to estimating hedonic indexes. In *Hard-to-measure goods and services: Essays in honour of Zvi Griliches,* ed. E. R. Berndt and C. Hulten, 235–68. Chicago: University of Chicago Press.
Stigler, G., ed. 1961. *The price statistics of the federal government,* National Bureau of Economic Research. Chicago: University of Chicago Press.
Triplett, J. 2004. *Handbook on hedonic indexes and quality adjustments in price indexes: Special application to information technology products.* Directorate for Science, Technology and Industry Working Paper 2004/9, Paris: Organization for Economic Cooperation and Development (OECD).
Triplett, J. E., and R. J. McDonald. 1977. Assessing the quality error in output measures: The case of refrigerators. *The Review of Income and Wealth* 23 (2): 137–56.

## Comment Jan de Haan

Hedonic regression has now become one of the standard tools for statistical agencies to adjust their CPIs for quality changes in markets with a high turnover of differentiated models such as PCs. The authors address an important question, namely the difference between "hedonic imputation indexes" and time dummy hedonic indexes, which are the two main approaches to estimating hedonic price indexes (in the academic literature). They provide a novel exposition of the factors underlying the difference between these approaches, both for the unweighted and the preferred expenditure-share weighted case. In particular, the authors derive three conditions under which the two approaches lead to identical results: constancy (over time) of the average characteristics, constancy of the estimated characteristics parameters (used in the imputation approach), and constancy of the characteristics variance-covariance matrix. As the authors rightly claim, the third condition is somewhat unanticipated. Apart from being a valuable contribution to the literature, the chapter seems highly relevant for the work of statistical agencies. However, the use of matrix algebra makes the exposition very

Jan de Haan is a senior researcher at Statistics Netherlands.

technical, and the implications may not be readily understood by a typical price statistician (though the empirical illustration is certainly helpful). Following I present some of the authors' findings in a simplified way by avoiding matrix notation, comment on them, and take the opportunity to make a few additional observations. I focus on the unweighted case, just for the sake of simplicity, but spend a few words on weighting also.

A couple of choices have implicitly been made in the chapter right from the start. For example, it is assumed that the hedonic regressions are run on the price data that are collected for the CPI. There may be statistical offices that perform hedonic regressions on a different data set and then use the estimated coefficients to adjust the raw CPI data for quality changes (which, I agree, is a problematic approach). More importantly, the chapter discusses a specific type of hedonic imputation. Let $S^0$ and $S^1$ be the samples of items in periods 0 and 1; $S_M = S^0 \cap S^1$ is the matched sample with size $n_M$, $S_D^0$ the subsample of disappearing items, and $S_N^1$ the subsample of new items. For simplicity I assume a fixed sample size $n$; thus $n - n_M$ is the number of disappearing and new items. I distinguish three types of unweighted symmetric imputation indexes—single imputation (SI), double imputation (DI), and full imputation (FI) indexes, as follows:

(1) $$\hat{P}_{SI} = \prod_{i \in S_M} \left(\frac{p_i^1}{p_i^0}\right)^{1/n} \prod_{i \in S_D^0} \left(\frac{\hat{p}_i^1}{p_i^0}\right)^{1/2n} \prod_{i \in S_N^1} \left(\frac{p_i^1}{\hat{p}_i^0}\right)^{1/2n};$$

(2) $$\hat{P}_{DI} = \prod_{i \in S_M} \left(\frac{p_i^1}{p_i^0}\right)^{1/n} \prod_{i \in S_D^0} \left(\frac{\hat{p}_i^1}{\hat{p}_i^0}\right)^{1/2n} \prod_{i \in S_N^1} \left(\frac{\hat{p}_i^1}{\hat{p}_i^0}\right)^{1/2n};$$

(3) $$\hat{P}_{FI} = \prod_{i \in S_M} \left(\frac{\hat{p}_i^1}{\hat{p}_i^0}\right)^{1/n} \prod_{i \in S_D^0} \left(\frac{\hat{p}_i^1}{\hat{p}_i^0}\right)^{1/2n} \prod_{i \in S_N^1} \left(\frac{\hat{p}_i^1}{\hat{p}_i^0}\right)^{1/2n},$$

where $p_i^t$ denotes the price of item $i$ in period $t$ ($t = 0,1$) and $\hat{p}_i^t$ an imputed (predicted) price. If I am correct, the authors seem to consider (at least implicitly) a fourth type of imputation index, namely

(4) $$\hat{P}_{HI} = \left[\prod_{i \in S^0} \left(\frac{\hat{p}_i^1}{p_i^0}\right)^{1/n} \prod_{i \in S^1} \left(\frac{p_i^1}{\hat{p}_i^0}\right)^{1/n}\right]^{1/2},$$

(in case of a fixed sample size). They use a log-linear hedonic model that explains the logarithm of price $p_i^t$ from a set of $K$ characteristics $z_{ik}$ and an intercept term $\alpha^t$:

(5) $$\ln(p_i^t) = \alpha^t + \sum_{k=1}^{K} \beta_k^t z_{ik} + \varepsilon_i^t,$$

where $\beta_k^t$ is the parameter for $z_{ik}$. By assumption the random errors $\varepsilon_i^t$ have expected values of zero and constant (identical) variances.[1] Equation (9) is

1. Characteristics have no superscript for time $t$ as an individual item is supposed to be of constant quality so that its characteristics are fixed over time.

estimated separately in periods 0 and 1, that is on the data of the samples $S^0$ and $S^1$. Ordinary least squares (OLS) regression of equation (5) yields parameter estimates $\hat{\alpha}^t$ and $\hat{\beta}_k^t$ and predicted prices $\hat{p}_i^t = \exp[\hat{\alpha}^t + \Sigma_{k=1}^K \hat{\beta}_k^t z_{ik}]$. However, because the OLS regression residuals $e_i^t = \ln(p_i^t) - \ln(\hat{p}_i^t) = \ln(p_i^t/\hat{p}_i^t)$ sum to zero in each period (i.e., $\Sigma_{i\in S^t} e_i^t = 0$), the index given by equation (4) coincides with the full imputation index (3). In appendix A the authors show that this approach is equivalent to what is often called the characteristics prices approach. The full imputation index (3), and thus equation (4), can be related to the single imputation index (1) in the following way:

$$\hat{P}_{FI} = \hat{P}_{SI}\left[\frac{\exp(\bar{e}_N^1)}{\exp(\bar{e}_D^0)}\right]^{(1-f_M)/2}, \tag{6}$$

where $f_M = n_M/n$ denotes the fraction of matched items and $1 - f_M = (n - n_M)/n$ the fraction of unmatched items; $\bar{e}_D^0 = \Sigma_{i\in S_D^0} e_i^0/(n - n_M)$ and $\bar{e}_N^1 = \Sigma_{i\in S_N^1} e_i^1/(n - n_M)$ are the average residuals for the disappearing and new items. Dividing equation (2) by equation (1) yields

$$\hat{P}_{DI} = \hat{P}_{SI}\left[\frac{\exp(\bar{e}_D^0)}{\exp(\bar{e}_N^1)}\right]^{(1-f_M)/2}, \tag{7}$$

which relates the double imputation index (2) to the single imputation index. Equations (6) and (7) show that the choice of imputation method matters if the average residuals of the disappearing and new items differ, especially if they have different signs (and $f_M$ is relatively small). For example, $\hat{P}_{DI} < \hat{P}_{SI} < \hat{P}_{FI}$ if $\bar{e}_D^0 < 0$ and $\bar{e}_N^1 > 0$. This happens if disappearing items are sold at prices that are unusually low given their characteristics, perhaps due to "dumping," and new items are introduced at unusually high prices.

At first sight it is not obvious why we would prefer the full imputation index (3), and thus equation (4), to the other imputation methods. A drawback seems to be that the observed prices are replaced by model-based estimates: in general this increases the variance of the hedonic index as it adds model variance to the matched-item part and may give rise to unnecessary bias if the hedonic model would be misspecified (which almost certainly happens to some extent in practice). But this view might be too simplistic. It can easily be shown that the following expression applies to the full imputation index:

$$\hat{P}_{FI} = \frac{\prod_{i\in S^1}(p_i^1)^{1/n}}{\prod_{i\in S^0}(p_i^0)^{1/n}} \exp\left[\sum_{k=1}^{K} \hat{\beta}_k^{01}(\bar{z}_k^0 - \bar{z}_k^1)\right], \tag{8}$$

with $\hat{\beta}_k^{01} = (\hat{\beta}_k^0 + \hat{\beta}_k^1)/2$ and where $\bar{z}_k^t = \Sigma_{i\in S^t} z_{ik}/n$ is the average sample value of the $k$-th characteristic in period $t$ ($t = 0,1$). By taking logs of equation (8) the authors' equation (34) is obtained (for a fixed sample size). Since the average characteristics of matched items are the same across periods, by denoting the average characteristics of the disappearing and new items by

$\bar{z}^{0}_{Dk} = \Sigma_{i\in S^0_D} z_{ik}/(n - n_M)$ and $\bar{z}^{1}_{Nk} = \Sigma_{i\in S^1_N} z_{ik}/(n - n_M)$, respectively, expression (8) can be rewritten as

$$(9)\ \hat{P}_{FI} = \left[\prod_{i\in S_M}\left(\frac{p^1_i}{p^0_i}\right)^{1/n_M}\right]^{f_M}\left\{\frac{\prod_{i\in S^1_N}(p^1_i)^{1/(n-n_M)}}{\prod_{i\in S^0_D}(p^0_i)^{1/(n-n_M)}}\exp\left[\sum_{k=1}^{K}\hat{\beta}^{01}_k(\bar{z}^0_{Dk} - \bar{z}^1_{Nk})\right]\right\}^{1-f_M}.$$

Equation (9) shows that this hedonic index is a weighted average of the matched-item index $\Pi_{i\in S_M}(p^1_i/p^0_i)^{1/n_M}$ and a (quality-adjusted) index for the unmatched items. The latter index adjusts the ratio of geometric mean prices of new and disappearing items for differences in the average characteristics of those items. Equation (9) further shows that the matched items' price relatives are implicitly left unchanged. Thus, matching where possible remains the basic principle even if a hedonic index would be estimated that, at first glance, does not seem to rely on matching.[2]

Another advantage of the full imputation approach is its comparability with the time dummy approach. In its standard form the time dummy hedonic model reads

$$(10)\qquad \ln(p^t_i) = \alpha + \delta D^t_i + \sum_{k=1}^{K}\beta_k z_{ik} + \varepsilon^t_i,$$

where $D^t_i$ is a dummy variable that takes on the value of 1 if $i$ is sold period $t$ (i.e., for $i \in S^1$) and 0 otherwise (for $i \in S^0$). A pooled OLS regression yields predicted prices $\hat{p}^0_i = \exp[\hat{\alpha} + \Sigma^K_{k=1}\hat{\beta}_k z_{ik}]$ and $\hat{p}^1_i = \exp[\hat{\alpha} + \hat{\delta} + \Sigma^K_{k=1}\hat{\beta}_k z_{ik}]$. It follows that

$$(11)\qquad \hat{P}_{TD} = \exp(\hat{\delta}) = \frac{\hat{p}^1_i}{\hat{p}^0_i} = \frac{\prod_{i\in S^1}(p^1_i)^{1/n}}{\prod_{i\in S^0}(p^0_i)^{1/n}}\exp\left[\sum_{k=1}^{K}\hat{\beta}_k(\bar{z}^0_k - \bar{z}^1_k)\right],$$

using the fact that, since an intercept term is included in equation (10), the residuals again sum to zero in both periods. Expression (11) is well known (see, e.g., Triplett 2004) and is quite similar to equation (8). This means that the time dummy index can also be written in the form of equation (9) when we replace $\hat{\beta}^{01}_k$ by $\hat{\beta}_k$. Using this result we obtain

$$(12)\qquad \hat{P}_{TD} = \exp[(1 - f_M)\sum_{k=1}^{K}(\hat{\beta}_k - \hat{\beta}^{01}_k)(\bar{z}^0_{Dk} - \bar{z}^1_{Nk})]\hat{P}_{FI},$$

which makes clear that the difference between the time dummy index and the hedonic imputation will particularly be small if the set of matched items is large, the (average) regression coefficients from both approaches are close

2. This is of course not to say that statistical agencies should try to match as much as possible. Samples preferably reflect the population of items at any point in time, possibly by using (or trying to mimic) PPS sampling. The fact that the current period sample may differ substantially from the base period sample is what makes the use of hedonics so important.

to each other, and the differences in the average characteristics of the new and disappearing items are small.

Finally I turn to weighted hedonic price indexes. The authors choose expenditure shares pertaining to the single period as regression weights. The advantage is obvious: it is a straightforward generalization of the unweighted approach, yielding an estimator of the (full) imputation Törnqvist price index. The same set of regression weights is used for the weighted time dummy approach, so that both weighted approaches can easily be compared. The disadvantage, on the other hand, is that WLS regression might increase the variance of the estimated parameters compared to OLS (especially if, as the authors assume, the errors have identical variances). The use of the single imputation Törnqvist index

$$(13) \qquad \hat{P}_{T,SI} = \prod_{i \in S_M} \left( \frac{p_i^1}{p_i^0} \right)^{(s_i^0 + s_i^1)/2} \prod_{i \in S_D^0} \left( \frac{\hat{p}_i^1}{p_i^0} \right)^{s_i^0/2} \prod_{i \in S_N^1} \left( \frac{p_i^1}{\hat{p}_i^0} \right)^{s_i^1/2},$$

or its double imputation counterpart is, however, more flexible: explicit weighting makes it possible to apply all kinds of regression weights when estimating model (5), including equal weights. Moreover, the authors' weighted time dummy index violates the (weak) identity test in a matched-item context (without new or disappearing items), a property that was mentioned already by Diewert (2003).[3] My conclusion would be that the issue of weighting in hedonic regressions is still unresolved.

## References

de Haan, J. 2004. Hedonic regression: The time dummy index as a special case of the imputation Törnqvist index. Paper presented at the Eighth Meeting of the Ottawa Group. 23–25 August, Helsinki.

Diewert, W. E. 2003. Hedonic regressions: A review of some resolved issues. Paper presented at the Seventh Meeting of the Ottawa Group. 27–29 May, Paris.

Triplett, J. E. 2004. *Handbook on hedonic indexes and quality adjustments in price indexes: Special application to information technology products.* Directorate for Science, Technology and Industry Working Paper 2004/9. Paris: Organization for Economic Cooperation and Development (OECD).

3. De Haan (2004), following up on Diewert (2003), proposed using regression weights for the WLS time dummy approach that are identical to the weights of the price relatives in equation (14). In that case the time dummy index can be interpreted as a single imputation Törnqvist index, and of course, in a matched-item situation the matched-item Törnqvist will be obtained.

## Response

W. Erwin Diewert, Saeed Heravi, and Mick Silver

We are very grateful for the comments made by Jan de Haan on our chapter. In particular, his equations (1) through (4) make clear the various alternatives that could be used by statistical agencies in constructing elementary price indexes using hedonic regressions to quality adjust new and disappearing items or models for a narrowly specified commodity. The commentary by Haan provides statistical agencies with a very useful overview of the issues associated with quality adjustment of prices in a replacement sampling context. Moreover, the notation used in our chapter will not be familiar to most practitioners and so Jan has done us all a favor in translating our rather formal matrix algebra results into an easier to interpret framework.

In order to help the reader make the connection between our notation and the notation used by Haan, we will specialize our unweighted models discussed in sections 4.2 and 4.3 of our chapter to the case where the number of new items that enter the sample in period 1 is equal to the number of items that have disappeared from the sample in period 0 so that the total number of items in the sample in period 0, $N(0)$, is equal to the total number of items or models in period 1, $N(1)$, and we will follow Haan and set $n$ equal to this common number of models. With this replacement sampling simplification of our model, the exponential of $\text{LP}_{\text{HI}}$ defined by our equation (34), where $\text{LP}_{\text{HI}}$ is our hedonic imputation estimate of the change in log prices going from period 0 to 1, is indeed equal to Haan's hedonic imputation index, $\hat{P}_{HI}$, defined by his equation (4)—and as Haan notes, the exponential of our $\text{LP}_{\text{HI}}$ is also equal to Haan's full imputation index, $\hat{P}_{FI}$, defined by his equation (3). Furthermore, using our expressions (32) and (33) and the simplification that $N(0)$ equals $N(1)$, it is easy to show that the exponential of $\text{LP}_{\text{HI}}$ defined by our equation (34) is also equal to Haan's double imputation price index, $\hat{P}_{DI}$, defined by his equation (2). Note that Haan's double imputation price index uses the actual prices for the matched models and hence, using the aforementioned equalities, so does our hedonic imputation index, $\text{LP}_{\text{HI}}$. Thus, the main point to debate in this context is whether to use Haan's single imputation index $\hat{P}_{SI}$, defined by his equation (1), or the double imputation index that was defined (in logarithms) in our chapter by equation (34) and which is equal to Haan's expressions (2) and (3). For a discussion of the merits of the two methods, the reader is referred to Haan's commentary.

Haan also briefly discusses our weighted hedonic imputation indexes in his commentary and he provides a much more extensive discussion of the issues associated with weighting in hedonic regressions in Haan (2007). We recommend this paper to interested readers. The specific point that Haan makes in his commentary about our weighted hedonic imputation index (whose logarithm $\text{LP}_{\text{WHI}}$ is defined by equation [65] in our chapter) is that this index does not satisfy the strong identity test; that is, if the models are exactly the same in the two periods under consideration and the prices for each model remain unchanged, then the strong identity test asks that the index be equal to unity, no matter what the quantities are. Haan is correct in his assertion; the exponential of our $LP_{WHI}$ defined by equation (65) does not satisfy the strong identity test, whereas his preferred Törnqvist imputation index defined by his equation (13) does satisfy this test. Haan ends his commentary by noting that the issue of weighting in hedonic regressions seems to be unresolved; that is, is our form of weighting to be preferred over his or not? This issue requires more research but at this point in time, we do find Haan's suggested weighting scheme rather attractive!

## Reference

de Haan, J. 2007. Hedonic price indexes: A comparison of imputation, time dummy and other approaches. Room document at the Tenth Ottawa Group Meeting. 9–12 October, Ottawa. Available at: http://www.ottawagroup2007.ca/r004/pdf/ogo04_033_e.pdf.

# 5

# CPI Bias from Supercenters
## Does the BLS Know That Wal-Mart Exists?

Jerry Hausman and Ephraim Leibtag

## 5.1 Introduction

Hausman (2003) discusses four sources of bias in the present calculation of the Consumer Price Index (CPI). The most often discussed substitution bias is a second-order bias while the other three sources of bias are all first-order in their effects: "new good bias," "quality bias," and "outlet substitution bias." A "pure price" index based approach of surveying prices to estimate a Cost-of-Living Index (COLI) cannot succeed in solving the three problems of first-order bias. Neither the Bureau of Labor Statistics (BLS) nor the recent report *At What Price?* henceforth, AWP, by Schultze and Mackie (2002) recognizes that to solve these problems, which have been long known, both quantity and price data are necessary. We discuss economic and econometric approaches to measuring the first-order bias effects from outlet substitution bias. We demonstrate the use of scanner data that permits implementation of techniques that allow the problem to be solved.

Over the past decade, "nontraditional" shopping formats have captured significant share from "traditional grocery." Little (2004) describes the two categories of alternative retail outlets as "high-spend" outlets, which are low price, one-stop shopping destinations, and "low and medium-spend" stores,

Jerry Hausman is the John and Jennie S. MacDonald Professor of Economics at the Massachusetts Institute of Technology and a research associate of the National Bureau of Economic Research. Ephraim Leibtag is an economist with the Economic Research Service of the U.S. Department of Agriculture (USDA).

Earlier draft presented at Index Number conference in Vancouver, June 2004. We thank Jie Yang and Ketan Patel for outstanding research assistance. John Greenlees and Marshall Reinsdorf provided helpful comments. Author contact: jhausman@mit.edu. The views expressed in this study are those of the authors, and do not necessarily reflect those of the U.S. Department of Agriculture.

which are mostly convenience stores that serve a "fill-in" role in between trips to the "high-spend" outlets. He includes supercenters (Wal-Mart, Kmart, Meijer, etc.), warehouse clubs (Sam's Club, Costco, and BJ's), and mass merchants (Wal-Mart, Kmart, Target, etc.) as the primary outlets for these "high-spend" expenditures.[1] Using 2003 data, he estimates that these outlets have 24.8 percent of food expenditures, with supercenters having 45.6 percent of the category. Over the past few years Wal-Mart has become the largest supermarket chain in the United States. Wal-Mart—excluding its Sam's Club—now has supermarket-related revenues approximately 51 percent larger than the runner-up Kroger, and larger than Albertsons and Safeway (the third and fourth largest supermarket chains) combined. Nationwide Wal-Mart has a 14 percent market share (in 2003), despite not being in a number of regional markets, and an 18 percent share when Sam's Clubs are included. Within the "medium-low spend" category, Little estimates convenience stores that also sell gasoline as the fastest growing store type, with 85.5 percent of the 12.4 percent total share for the category. Little calculates that total traditional grocery outlets, including conventional supermarkets and superstores (a larger version of the conventional supermarket), have decreased to a 56.3 percent dollar share in 2003. He also forecasts that in five years, the "high-spend category" will grow from 24.8 percent to 31 percent, with supercenters comprising 54.8 percent of the total while traditional grocery outlets decrease from 56.3 percent to 48.3 percent. Thus, he expects Wal-Mart to become increasingly important over the next few years, continuing the trend of change over the past decade.

Wal-Mart began selling food in 1988 and in 2002 became the largest U.S. grocery chain. Significant consolidation has occurred in the supermarket industry, but Wal-Mart continues to grow at a significantly faster rate than other supermarket chains. The majority of Wal-Mart's grocery sales arise from its over 1,400 (as of April 2004) supercenters, which are 180,000-square-foot stores that are both discount stores and grocery stores, although it also has "Neighborhood Market" stores that are about the size (40,000 square feet) of an average supermarket.[2] While most of the stores are in the South and Southwest, Wal-Mart is increasingly moving into urban centers with openings expected in Los Angeles and Chicago, along with other urban centers.[3]

1. Sam's Club is owned by Wal-Mart.

2. Wal-Mart management has given guidance that it expects to open between 230 and 240 new supercenters in 2005 for an increase of about 16 percent. See Dow Jones, "Factiva," April 19, 2004. Morgan Stanley reports that Wal-Mart is seeking 16 to 17 percent growth in supermarket sales compared with 3 percent industry growth. See M. Wiltamuth and R. Fariborz, "Food Retail," June 2004. Wal-Mart has grown at a 16 percent rate over the past three years.

3. Wal-Mart has sometimes had difficulty in receiving planning approval for its stores. Currently, Wal-Mart has either no presence or an extremely limited presence in New England, the New York metro area, California, and the Pacific Northwest. However, its expansion into new areas has proceeded over the past few years.

Over the ten-year period from 1991 to 2001 margins increased in supermarkets as the price of food sold at supermarkets grew at approximately twice the rate of the Producer Price Index (PPI) for food. Over this period the PPI for finished food increased by 13.9 percent while the CPI for food at home increased by 27.7 percent. Profit margins for supermarkets also increased over the same time period, with Kroger's operating profit margin growing from 3.3 percent to 4.7 percent and Safeway's operating profit margin growing from 3.5 percent to 7.9 percent.[4] Various studies have demonstrated that food items at Wal-Mart are 8 to 27 percent lower priced than at the large supermarket chains, even after discounts for loyalty card and other special promotions are taken into account.[5] After entry by Wal-Mart, conventional supermarkets typically decrease their prices (or do not increase them as much as in non-Wal-Mart markets) because of the increased competition.

Remarkably, the large expansion and continuing expansion of Wal-Mart and other supercenter food outlets has almost no effect on the BLS calculation of the CPI for food.[6] The BLS employs a "linking procedure" that assumes "quality-adjusted" prices at Wal-Mart are exactly equal to prices at conventional supermarkets. Thus, when a Wal-Mart store replaces, say, a Kroger in the BLS sample of stores from which it collects prices, it links the lower Wal-Mart price to the higher Kroger price to remove any difference. Even though packaged food items are physically identical at the two stores, the BLS procedure does not recognize any price difference between the stores. This procedure is not based on any empirical study. Rather, it is based on mere assumption. The assumption is completely inconsistent with actual real world market outcomes where Wal-Mart has expanded very quickly in markets that it entered. Thus, the market impacts of Wal-Mart and other supercenters are nowhere in the food CPI so that we find that the BLS does not know that Wal-Mart "exists" in terms of the estimation of a CPI. We also believe that observed consumer behavior cannot be explained by the BLS assumption of a compensating "quality differential." We specify a theoretical model of consumer behavior that demonstrates this point following.

4. Calculations based on companies' SEC 10-K filings. Callahan and Zimmerman (2003) also report increased profit margins for supermarkets over this period.

5. A recent December 2003 study by UBS Investment Research found a price gap of 17.3 percent to 26.2 percent ("Price Gap Tightens, Competition Looks Hot Hot Hot"). The previous year UBS found a price gap of 20.8 percent to 39.1 percent. For example, for a specified identical market basket UBS finds Wal-Mart supercenters to have an average price that is 19.1 percent less expensive in Tampa and 22.8 percent less expensive in Las Vegas. In 2002, Salomon Smith Barney estimated the price gap to be between 5 percent and 25 percent. See L. Cartwright, "Empty Baskets," September 12, 2002.

6. When customers shift from conventional supermarkets to Wal-Mart no change occurs in the food CPI. To the extent that prices at Wal-Mart decrease (or increase) at a different rate than conventional stores, the food CPI will take account of this change with a lagged effect over time.

## 5.2 Current BLS Procedure

The BLS methodology updates its samples of stores from which it collects prices periodically. It makes two adjustments. First, the BLS updates the stores at which these purchases are made. Next, the BLS updates the products in the market basket that consumers purchase.[7] Cage (1996) describes the current BLS sampling procedure, in which the "Telephone Point-of-Purchase Survey" (TPOPS) is used to provide a sampling frame of outlets visited by urban consumers. Approximately 25 percent of all sampling units participate in a given year. While the products can change, note that the expenditure shares across categories did not change with this procedure. The expenditure shares are only updated on a considerably less frequent basis since the TPOPS does not collect expenditure data or quantity data at the product level (item category level), although overall expenditure at the outlet level is collected. Thus, the BLS probability sampling procedure works against solving the outlet bias problem discussed in this chapter.[8]

When the BLS collects data, it collects the name and address of the retail establishment reported by respondents and estimates of the total daily expenditure by TPOPS category. The expenditure weights are not used to update the expenditure weights used in the weighted average of prices, rather they are used in the selection of outlets so that those outlets with larger expenditure weights receive a greater probability of selection.

The TPOPS outlet rotation allows a closer approach to actual consumer shopping patterns as they change. As more households shop at Wal-Mart, the probability of a Wal-Mart being included in a given market increases. Item rotation also occurs as previously discussed. However, when an identical item is sampled at the new outlet, even if the product is physically identical to the item sampled in the old outlet, the BLS does not take account of the lower price. Thus, if a twelve ounce box of Kellogg's Rice Krispies is purchased at a Wal-Mart that is newly included to replace a Kroger that has been dropped, the BLS links the new lower price to the old higher price so no price change occurs. This linking procedure creates outlet substitution bias in the estimation of the CPI. In the AWP (Schultze and Mackie 2002, 169) discussion of BLS procedures, it is claimed that consumer shopping comprises a package and that nonmonetary benefits exactly balance out the effects of the lower price. This finding was based on absolutely no empirical evidence whatsoever. The finding is also completely inconsistent with the real world *market facts* that expenditures at supercenters grow quickly when

7. The BLS sometimes takes a very long time to incorporate new products in the market basket as in the case of cellular telephones, which were not included for fifteen years after their introduction. Hausman (1999) demonstrates the significant bias from the delay in the introduction of cellular telephone.

8. We thank John Greenlees and Marshall Reinsdorf for pointing out the problem arising from using the probability sampling procedure in terms of outlet bias.

they become available. Indeed, Wal-Mart is now the largest supermarket chain in the United States.

This "compensating service effect" explanation is also inconsistent with the "indirect price effect" that we estimate subsequently, where we find that as expenditure at superstores increases in a given market, the prices at traditional supermarkets decrease.[9] For example, after two Wal-Mart supercenters opened in Houston, a nearby Kroger's sales dropped 10 percent, the Kroger store reduced worker hours by 30 to 40 percent, and it decreased its prices.[10] Presumably this price decrease is caused by greater competition. Thus, consumers demonstrate with their expenditure choice that they prefer lower priced outlets, and the higher priced supermarket must respond in a competitive manner. The AWP description of the BLS assumption that markets are in equilibrium is inconsistent with the real world market data, which find that prices from traditional stores decrease from the increased competition.

Thus, when a new set of stores are included in the BLS sample, the linking procedure eliminates all of the price differences. Even though the box of Kellogg's Rice Krispies is identical in all respects, the BLS assumes that differences in outlet and product characteristics completely explains the difference in price. Thus, lower prices from increased expenditure at superstores have no effect on the CPI. In this sense, the BLS assumes that Wal-Mart does not exist in constructing the CPI.

Reinsdorf (1993) found that food and motor-fuel prices during a two-year overlap period led to new samples prices being lower by about 1.25 percent compared to the outgoing samples. Since sample rotation occurred every five years, this finding would create a 0.25 percent bias per year.[11] However, Reinsdorf's quantitative findings have not been totally accepted because of concerns about product quality as well as differences in coverage. The AWP (Schultze and Mackie 2002, 176) recommended that the BLS continue its current practice and disregard the effect of Wal-Mart and other supercenters on prices and price indices.

## 5.3 A Utility-Consistent Economic Model of Shopping Destination

The BLS assumes that an exact compensating "quality differential" exists between shopping at a supercenter store with its lower prices and a conventional supermarket. Service quality and other factors supposedly allow the BLS to assume that quality-adjusted prices are exactly the same when the BLS links the prices. However, this assumption is inconsistent with real world market behavior that finds when Wal-Mart opens a store in a new

9. Shapiro and Wilcox (1996) also noted this indirect effect.

10. Callahan and Zimmerman (2003) report on these effects. The regional head of Kroger's stated, "Wal-Mart made us look at ourselves and reinvent ourselves."

11. The BLS recently decreased the rotation cycle to every four years.

geographic market, it rapidly gains share while conventional supermarkets lose share.[12] We believe that a better model than the implicit BLS model is to consider Wal-Mart supercenters as a new choice to consumers. Some consumers find the choice to be superior while others continue to shop at conventional supermarkets.[13] Thus, the arrival of Wal-Mart in a given geographic market is similar to the introduction of a new good into the geographic market. Hausman (1997, 2003) discusses how new products should be included in a correct Cost-of-Living Index (COLI). Here, rather than a completely new product (e.g., cellular telephones), an existing product is expanded into a new geographic market. However, the effect on consumers is similar since they now have increased choice in their shopping trips.

For our economic model we consider the conditional choice of consumers to shop at either a conventional supermarket or at a lower price, and perhaps lower service quality, supercenter. For ease of exposition, we use a two-stage choice model in which at the lower stage the consumer considers his or her shopping behavior conditional on type of store. The consumer calculates a price index for shopping at either type of store, takes account of service and other quality differences, and then at the upper stage decides at which type of store to shop.[14] We use the two-stage approach of Hausman (1985) and Hausman, Leonard, and McFadden (1995), although neither of the models was designed precisely for the situation of shopping destination choice.

We allow for consumers' choice of shopping at either a conventional supermarket, $j = 1$, or at a supercenter, $j = 2$. Conditional on choosing to shop at one of these two types of stores the consumer has a *conditional expenditure function*

$$(1) \qquad y = e(\mathbf{p}_0, p_1^j, p_2^j, \ldots, p_n^j; \bar{u}) = e(p, \bar{u})$$
$$\text{solves min } ip_ix_i \text{ such that } u(x) = \bar{u},$$

where $\mathbf{p}_0$ is a vector of prices of all nonfood items assumed the same for destination choice, $p^j = \{p_1^j, p_2^j, \ldots p_n^j\}$ are the prices of the $n$ goods in the two types of outlets denoted by the superscript $j$, and $\bar{u}$ is the utility level of the consumer.[15] The conditional demand for each type of product, depending on the type of outlet $j$ chosen is:

12. Supermarket chains sometimes exit a geographic market after Wal-Mart enters. Albertsons exited the Houston market after Wal-Mart entry. However, in our model we assume that consumers continue to have access to traditional supermarkets, even if a given chain exits the market.

13. As we discussed previously, these conventional supermarkets typically decrease price because of the increased competition from Wal-Mart. If the BLS consistently applied its "quality adjustment" procedure it would ignore these price decreases at conventional supermarkets because presumably they arise from reduced service quality. However, the BLS fully incorporates these price decreases, demonstrating that its approach is based on no correct economic assumptions.

14. We assume that consumers do not divide their shopping trips between different types of stores, although this behavior could be incorporated into the model.

15. As written, equation (1) assumes that both types of stores carry all goods. To the extent that supermarkets carry a wider variety of products than supercenters, the prices for super-

$$(2) \qquad x_i^j = \frac{\partial e(\mathbf{p}_0, p^j, \bar{u})}{\partial p_i^j} = \frac{-\partial v(\mathbf{p}_0, p^j, y)/\partial p_i^j}{\partial v(\mathbf{p}_0, p^j, y)/\partial y}\ i = 1, \ldots, n,$$

where the indirect utility function $v(p,y)$ is derived from the duality relationship with the expenditure function. Using duality corresponding to any level of utility in equation (1) and any vector of prices, a price index exists that corresponds to the minimum expenditure required to achieve a given level of utility $\bar{u}$. Indeed, the utility consistent price index is the level of expenditure needed to achieve the utility level:

$$(3) \qquad \Pi(p^j, \bar{u}) = e(p^j, \bar{u}) = y^j(p^j, \bar{u}) = y^j = \sum_i p_i^j x_i^j.$$

An "average price" $\bar{p}^j$ can then be calculated by dividing $y^j$ by a quantity index $\bar{x}^j$ so that $y^j = \bar{p}^j \bar{x}^j$.[16]

We now move to the top level where the consumer decides whether to shop at the conventional supermarket or at the supercenter outlet. We expect $y^1 > y^2$ because most prices in supermarkets exceed the prices in supercenters. Consider the use of the binomial logit model for choice between traditional supermarkets and supercenters.[17] The probability of choosing the traditional supermarket is:

$$(4) \qquad pr(j = 1) = \frac{1}{1 + \exp[\beta_0 + \beta_1(\bar{p}^1 - \bar{p}^2)]},$$

where a log price index or other type of price index (e.g., a Stone price index) can also be used depending on the precise form of the underlying expenditure (utility) and demand functions in equations (1) and (2).[18]

If we can assume that the overall units of a good are the same—for example, Kellogg's Rice Krispies—we can simplify so that the overall demand for good $i$ becomes:

$$(5) \qquad \hat{x}_i(\mathbf{p}_0, p^1, p^2, y) = pr(j=1)x_i(\mathbf{p}_0, p^1, y) + pr(j = 2)x_i(\mathbf{p}_0, p^2, y),$$

where the right-hand side demands are the conditional demands from equation (2) and have common units. Similarly, to calculate the unconditional price for the representative consumer we take overall expenditure on good $i$ and divide by the quantity of equation (5):

$$(6) \qquad \hat{p}_i(\mathbf{p}_0, p^1, p^2, y) = \frac{\Xi_i(\mathbf{p}_0, p^1, p^2, y)}{\hat{x}_i(\mathbf{p}_0, p^1, p^2, y)},$$

centers can be entered as virtual prices that set demand to zero. See Hausman (1997) for an explanation of virtual prices.

16. Instead of the average price we can also divide expenditure by utility to get a "cost of utils" index.

17. Because of only two choices, the independence of irrelevant alternative assumption does not create a problem here. With more than two choices a nested logit or multinomial probit model could be used. See Hausman, Leonard, and McFadden (1995) for a derivation with the nested logit model.

18. An exact aggregation approach when using a Gorman generalized polar form appears in Hausman, Leonard, and McFadden (1995).

where $\Xi_i$ is expenditure on good $i$. If choice $j = 2$ does not exist in a given geographic market, then the price index of equation (6) is just the traditional supermarket price so that $\hat{p}_i(p^1, p^{2*}, y) = p^1$, where $p^{2*}$ are the virtual prices, which cause demand at supercenters to be zero.[19] But when supercenters become available, consumers who choose to shop at supercenters do so to maximize their utility and the correct price index is an expenditure weighted average of the two prices of the supermarket and supercenter. This expenditure weighted approach to price averages is the procedure we use in the empirical work that follows.

Thus, the exact Cost-of-Living Index becomes

$$(7) \qquad P(p_0, p^2, p^1, \bar{u}) = \frac{y^2(p_0, p^1, p^2, \bar{u})}{y^1(p_0, p^1, p^{2*}, \bar{u})} = \frac{e(p_0, p^1, p^2, \bar{u})}{e(p_0, p^1, p^{2*}, \bar{u})},$$

which gives the ratio of the required amount of income when supercenters are present in the market compared to the situation where supercenters are not present and prices are at the virtual level $p^{2*}$, which causes demand to be zero. Equation (7) demonstrates how the new good approach applies to supercenters when the correct unit of observation is a geographic market, rather than a new product. Taking the appropriate weighted averages of equation (7) leads to an expenditure share weighted approach.

Thus, we do not find support for the BLS assumption of an exact compensating quality differential when consumers can choose which type of outlet at which to shop. Some consumers continue to shop at traditional supermarkets when supercenters become available, while other consumers shift to shopping at supercenters. In terms of the representative consumer we calculate the probability weights for each type of choice multiplied by the demand at each type of outlet and divide this weighted demand into expenditure to derive the price index. As more supercenters become available in a given geographic market, more consumers choose to shop at supercenters and its expenditure weight increases. We continuously update the expenditure weights to allow for this observed market determined change in shopping destination choices. Consumers in their revealed preference choices determine the appropriate weights to be used in the price index.

In this section we have specified a model of consumer outlet choice and demonstrate how to calculate an exact COLI in equation (7). In Hausman-Leibtag (2007) we estimate this model and estimate the compensating variation that arises from the spread of supercenters. We reject the BLS hypoth-

19. To the extent that traditional supermarkets close because of increased supercenter competition, consumers have decreased choice, which could affect price index calculations. However, in the model we assume that consumers still have the choice to shop at one or more traditional supermarkets (i.e., that not all supermarkets in a given geographic market close). In this situation, which is consistent with actual market outcomes, the effect on a theoretical price index would be extremely small. Indeed, supermarkets that close typically have the smallest customer base, which further decreases the effect of store closings on a price index.

esis of a complete offsetting compensating "quality differential." Instead, we find that consumers gain significant amounts of consumers surplus (compensating variation) when a new supercenter opens that permits them to choose to purchase at lower prices. The compensating variation is the difference of the numeration and denominator of equation (7), while the exact Cost-of-Living Index is the ratio. As discussed in Hausman (2003), for example, the BLS has recognized (Abraham, Greenlees, and Moulton 1998) that a COLI provides the correct approach. The BLS approach attempts to approximate a true COLI with the CPI so that our theoretical derivation demonstrates that the current BLS CPI approach can potentially cause significant bias. We now apply a BLS-type procedure to the data and find that the CPI bias can be significant.

We find that Wal-Mart should exist in the estimation of a price index, contrary to the current BLS procedure. However, note that as Hausman (2003) emphasized, to implement this approach both *prices and quantities* need to be available, which necessitates the use of scanner data. The BLS approach, which only collects price data, cannot implement the correct price index approach. Without quantity data, the BLS will always be required to make one or another arbitrary assumption regarding "service adjusted" quality levels. Observation of actual consumer choice in terms of quantities purchased allows us to resolve the problem.

## 5.4 Data Description

This study uses a customized subset of the Nielsen Homescan scanner panel data for the four years 1998 to 2001. The Nielsen Homescan data is a consumer panel consisting of approximately 61,500 randomly selected households across the United States and includes purchase as well as demographic information for all households in the sample. Homescan households are randomly recruited to join the panel using sampling techniques to ensure household representation for demographic variables such as household income, family composition, education, and household location. Each household is equipped with an electronic home-scanning unit, and household members record every UPC-coded food purchase they make by scanning in the UPC of the food products that they buy from all retail outlets that sell food for home consumption.

The panel is recruited on a permanent basis, subject to turnover from normal attrition or adjustments to demographic targets necessitated by Census revisions.[20] The Homescan panel is considered by many in the food industry as the most reliable household-based panel data due to its long-standing

20. Households lost through attrition are replaced with others having similar key characteristics.

reputation in the marketplace and its utilization of handheld technology that minimizes the recording burden for participants.

The panel includes consumer shopping and purchase data from all outlet channels, including grocery, drug, mass and convenience stores. The panel is geographically dispersed and is demographically balanced so the sample profile matches the U.S. population as closely as possible. The panel data are also projected to census estimates that are updated regularly to reflect population changes.

Household panel data allow for observation of the ongoing purchase habits and practices of household and demographic groups. Tracking and analyzing this information over time can reveal the dynamics of consumer behavior such as who is buying what products, what different products are purchased during a given shopping trip, and how often a product is purchased. Panel data quantify the composition of category or brand volume, which can be used to measure the impact of store choice on the purchase level of product quantities and prices. Data are collected after each panelist shopping trip. Members of the panel record their purchases, capturing not only what is purchased, but also where the purchase was made, and whether the purchase was a promotional, sale, or coupon item.

These data are useful in price analysis since we are able to observe actual purchase choices by consumers. However, in terms of food purchase behavior, the key missing information is consumer purchases of food away from home (primarily restaurant meals) so one needs to assume that the unknown levels of food away from home purchases do not somehow bias the average prices paid by an individual household for their food at home purchases. Once this assumption is made these data are useful for analysis of the impact of store choice on average prices paid for food at home items. Consumer panel information can be used to measure the average prices paid by a representative group of households over time. This measurement of average price paid can be aggregated across households and/or across time to measure price change for different categories of products.

Along with the description of each product, the price and quantity that was purchased is recorded on a daily basis. National and regional level aggregates can be calculated using transaction data from households located in fifty local U.S. markets as well as households in nonmetro/rural areas that are included in this data set. For twenty-one of these fifty markets, a large enough number of panelists are included to enable comparisons across markets for all UPC-coded products.[21]

21. The fifty markets are Albany, Atlanta, Baltimore, Birmingham, Boston, Buffalo-Rochester, Charlotte, Chicago, Cincinnati, Cleveland, Columbus, Dallas, Denver, Des Moines, Detroit, Grand Rapids, Hartford-New Haven, Houston, Indianapolis, Jacksonville, Kansas City, Little Rock, Los Angeles, Louisville, Memphis, Miami, Milwaukee, Minneapolis, Nashville, New Orleans-Mobile, New York, Oklahoma City-Tulsa, Omaha, Orlando, Philadelphia, Phoenix, Pittsburgh, Portland, Raleigh-Durham, Richmond, Sacramento, Salt Lake City, San Antonio, San Diego, San Francisco, Seattle, St. Louis, Syracuse, Tampa, and Washington, DC.

The Economic Research Service (ERS) of the USDA purchased a subsample of transaction level data from the Fresh Foods Homescan Panel[22] comprised of households that not only recorded their UPC-coded transactions, but also recorded their random-weight (non-UPC coded) food purchases over the year(s) that they participated in the panel. This subsample was used for this study in order to be able to measure the entire market basket of household purchases of food for at-home consumption.[23] Of this group of 15,000 households per year, the sample was restricted to households that participated in the panel for at least ten out of twelve months per year.[24]

Standard demographic information is collected on an annual basis from each household and each household's home market/city and census region is identified for stratification purposes (see the following). Each household is then assigned a projection factor (weight) based on its demographics in order to aggregate the data to be representative at the market, regional, and national level.[25]

These data were constructed based on a stratified random sample with households as the primary sampling unit. A stratified random sample is used to ensure that the sample of households matches Census-based demographic and geographic targets. One function of the design is to allow description of eight major markets for cross-market comparisons.[26]

The strata for 1998 and 1999 are based on six cities (Nielsen major markets): Atlanta, Baltimore/Washington, Chicago, Los Angeles, New York, and San Antonio. All other households fall into one of four census regions: East, Central, South, and West. (See table 5.1.) There was no known or intentional clustering in the sample construction. The projection factor (weight) reflects the sample design and demographic distribution within the strata.

The information that is captured on a transaction level basis includes:

22. The Fresh Foods Homescan Panel contained 12,000 households in 1998 and 1999 and was expanded to 15,000 households in 2000 and 2001.

23. If only UPC-coded products were used to measure food-at-home expenditures, many fruit, vegetable, meat, and poultry purchases would not be recorded in the data and food-at-home expenditure shares by store type would not accurately measure true household and market expenditure shares. This is especially true in this situation, when alternative channel stores sell fewer random weight items than conventional retailers. Leaving out random weight items would then tend to overstate the shares of food expenditures of alternative retail outlets.

24. In total, there were 9,501 unique households in the data with some subset participating each year, creating a total of 28,996 household by year observations. In 1998 there were 7,624 households, 7,124 households in 1999, 7,523 households in 2000, and 8,216 households in 2001. Some households participated in the panel for more than one year. Of the 9,501 households in the data, 5,247 households participated for all four years, 1,877 households participated for three years, and 2,377 households were one year participants.

25. Age, gender, education, occupation, of head(s) of household, number of household members, household income, household composition, race, and ethnicity.

26. Atlanta, Baltimore/Washington, Chicago, Los Angeles, New York, Philadelphia, San Antonio, San Francisco.

**Table 5.1 List of market and regional stratum for Nielsen Fresh Foods Homescan, 1998–2001**

| Stratum | Description |
|---|---|
| | *1998–1999* |
| 1 | Atlanta |
| 2 | Baltimore-Washington |
| 3 | Chicago |
| 4 | Los Angeles |
| 5 | New York |
| 6 | San Antonio |
| *For all other households: Census Regions are used as strata* | |
| 7 | East |
| 8 | Central |
| 9 | South |
| 10 | West |
| | *2000–2001*[a] |
| 1 | Atlanta |
| 2 | Baltimore-Washington |
| 3 | Chicago |
| 4 | Los Angeles |
| 5 | New York City |
| 6 | Philadelphia |
| 7 | San Antonio |
| 8 | San Francisco |
| *For all other households: Census Regions are used as strata* | |
| 9 | East |
| 10 | Central |
| 11 | South |
| 12 | West |

[a]Nielsen augmented their stratification scheme in 2000, selecting two additional major markets.

date of purchase, store name and channel type identifier,[27] store department identifier,[28] item description, brand name, number of units purchased, price paid, and promotions/sales/coupons used (if any). For retail stores that Nielsen tracks with their store-level scanner data,[29] prices are verified through store-level price and promotion checks.

Warehouse shipment data are used to supplement scanner-generated data

27. Grocery, Drug, Mass Merchandiser, Supercenter, Club, Convenience, Other (including dollar stores, bakeries, military stores, online purchases, health food stores, and vending machines)

28. Dry Grocery, Dairy, Frozen-Produce-Meat, Random Weight.

29. The Nielsen store-level sample is updated through both replacement of canceled or closed stores and *Continuous Sample Improvement Program*—when the sample is changed intentionally to ensure that changes in the universe are reflected in the sample.

collected from households or provided to Nielsen through their store-level scanner data. Warehouse shipment data are used to estimate the balance of sales moving through other food retailers. This information is Census data (i.e., nonprojected, actual shipment data) supplied to Nielsen by wholesale cooperators.

Some question the quality of household panel data when they try to reconcile it with store-level scanner data. There is the perception that the volumetric data from each source should be the same. However, panel data and store data are not always equal because measurement methodologies differ. Store-level data record millions of shopping transactions while panel data record a specific group of shoppers. In addition, panel data only represent household-based purchases, so there are no small businesses or other institutional purchases included in the panel.

Both types of information have their uses, and by combining the two, one can quantify the composition of volume, understand the reasons behind consumer behavior changes, and measure the impact of store choice on average prices. Store-level scanning data may show that sales were down in a particular store for some group of products in a given time period. Panel data provide insight into whether the lost volume is due to fewer buyers or if the existing buyers purchased less at the given store or chain of stores. Panel data also provide information on which competitors gained the lost expenditures of the store in question.

## 5.5 Effects on Prices

In producing the CPI, BLS makes the implausible assumption that all differences in price between supercenters and other stores are due to quality differences. The empirical analysis in this section proceeds from the opposite assumption that the price differences in food items represents a gain to shoppers at supercenters. While this assumption may not be entirely accurate, we believe it is much closer to the actual economic outcome than the BLS assumption. In Hausman-Leibtag (2007) we estimate an econometric model that allows us to relax this assumption. However, the results presented following illustrate the size of the CPI bias that could arise from recognition of the consumer benefits arising from supercenters. Further, since the BLS has refused to use econometric estimates of demand parameters in calculating the CPI, the approach we use here is considerably more accurate than the current BLS approach as the Hausman-Leibtag (2007) results demonstrate.

Our empirical approach first investigates the effect of supercenters, mass merchandisers, and club stores, (hereafter SMC) on prices paid by households. Two effects are present. The "total" effect is that as more of these superstores operate in a given geographic market, the average prices paid by households will decrease. Prices for food categories in superstores are typically 5 to 48 percent less than prices for the same product in supermarkets and other conventional retail outlets. Thus, as a high proportion of households buy their food at nontraditional retail outlets, the average price paid in a market will decrease.

### 5.5.1 Price Difference between Supermarkets and Superstores

In table 5.2 we calculate the ratios of average prices across different types of outlets for twenty food categories. Column (2) compares the prices for the food categories in traditional supermarkets compared to prices for these same categories in SMCs (nontraditional stores).

The largest difference in average price was for lettuce, where SMC prices were about 50 percent lower than traditional supermarkets over the forty-eight month period. Bottled water was the lowest price difference, with SMC prices about 5 percent less expensive. Soda was the only item with a lower price in traditional supermarkets than in SMCs. When we take an average across all of the food categories we find that SMCs have prices that are twenty-seven percent lower than traditional supermarkets. We find this difference to be quite large.[30]

In considering the results of table 5.2 a concern can arise that superstores and supermarkets are selling a different mix of produce (e.g., types of apples could differ across the outlets). However, we estimate approximately the same price ratio for apples and apple juice across the two types of outlets. Thus, while different product mixes remain a topic for future research, the price differences we estimate across different outlet types are unlikely to arise primarily from different product mixes. Further, price comparisons of identical products that we discuss in the introduction have found price ratios of approximately the same size that we estimate in table 5.2.

In column (3) of table 5.2 we compare the price in all non-SMC outlets, including traditional supermarkets, to the price of these food categories in superstores. We find the results to be quite similar with the main differences occurring in soda and bottled water. We find the same overall results—that SMC stores offer significantly lower prices than other retail outlets.

### 5.5.2 Total and Indirect Effects on Prices from Superstores

Another important effect exists from the expansion of SMC stores. Their increasing presence also increases competition among traditional food retailers. These supermarkets must decrease prices to remain competitive. The well-publicized strike in the Los Angeles area in late 2003 through early 2004 when traditional supermarkets wanted to decrease health benefits for their employees demonstrates the effect that potential entry of supercenters can have on competition. We call this SMC effect on traditional supermarkets

30. The estimated difference is in line with stock analyst reports who have previously sampled the difference in prices over a very few markets.

**Table 5.2 Ratio of supermarket and other outlet prices to superstore prices for 37 cities, 1998–2001**

| Product | Supermarkets/SMC | All other/SMC |
|---|---|---|
| Apples | 1.546 | 1.531 |
| Apple juice | 1.585 | 1.596 |
| Bananas | 1.384 | 1.368 |
| Bread | 1.108 | 1.098 |
| Butter/margarine | 1.096 | 1.096 |
| Cereal | 1.172 | 1.166 |
| Chicken breast | 1.408 | 1.411 |
| Coffee | 1.373 | 1.383 |
| Cookies | 1.223 | 1.214 |
| Eggs | 1.312 | 1.305 |
| Ground beef | 1.372 | 1.367 |
| Ham | 1.967 | 1.984 |
| Ice cream | 1.320 | 1.331 |
| Lettuce | 2.117 | 2.107 |
| Milk | 1.207 | 1.199 |
| Potatoes | 1.412 | 1.402 |
| Soda | 0.891 | 0.974 |
| Tomatoes | 1.358 | 1.321 |
| Bottled water | 1.058 | 1.165 |
| Yogurt | 1.413 | 1.411 |
| Average | 1.300 | 1.306 |

the indirect price effect. Both the total and indirect price effects we estimate lead to lower average prices for households.

To investigate both the total and indirect effects on average prices, we do an econometric analysis using the Nielsen Homescan data. These data are particularly useful since they provide household data and allow for a stratified random sample of all households. Importantly, they provide both price and quantity data across all stores. Since Wal-Mart and some other large superstores no longer participate in the Information Resources, Inc. (IRI) or Nielsen store level data collection, household data collection provide a source of price and quantity data that are not available elsewhere.

We analyze data at the market level using a fixed effects specification with forty-eight monthly observations for each market during the period 1998 to 2001:

$$(8) \qquad p_{it} = \alpha_i + \delta_t + \beta e_{it} + \varepsilon_{it} \qquad i = 1, 34 \qquad t = 1, 48,$$

where $p_{it}$ is the average log price paid for a given product, $\alpha_i$ is a fixed effect for a market, $\delta_t$ is a monthly fixed effect, $e_{it}$ is percentage expenditure for a given product in superstores, and $\beta$ is the elasticity coefficient that we estimate. We use market fixed effects rather than random effects because expenditure in SMC stores is unlikely to be uncorrelated with the stochastic disturbance (e.g., Hausman 1978). In this situation a fixed effects estimator yields the efficient estimator. However, we make two further econometric adjustments. First, expenditure in superstores on a given product may well not be econometrically predetermined. Thus, we use instrumental variable estimation (2SLS) where as the instrument we use the overall proportion of food expenditure in SMC stores in a given market as the instrumental variable. Also, we use an autoregressive model for the stochastic disturbance (AR1) to capture the time series aspect of the data and to achieve more efficient estimates. However, least squares with robust standard errors leads to quite similar results.

For our econometric investigation of twenty food products we use thirty-four markets, each with over 12,000 food transactions per year. The thirty-four markets are listed in table 5.3.

For each of these markets we standardized purchases on a physical unit measure and estimated the effect of increasing purchases in SMC stores. Since we have fixed effects for each market, persistent cost and price differences should be taken into account as well as seasonal effects given the presence of monthly fixed effects. We give the econometric estimates for these twenty food categories across the thirty-four markets in table 5.4. All of the estimated elasticity coefficients are negative as expected. Thus as households spend increasing amounts of expenditure at SMCs, the average prices paid for food items decrease. While the effects are estimated with varying amount of precision, overall the results are highly significantly different from zero. No obvious pattern of coefficient size seems to exist: we find the largest effects for ham, lettuce, butter/margarine, tomatoes, potatoes, and coffee, which are a mix of branded and unbranded products. Yet we find relatively small effects for ground beef, apples, and bananas, which are typically unbranded products, but we also find relatively small effects for cereal and yogurt, which typically are branded products. Overall, we find a statistically

**Table 5.3** **Markets used in econometric analysis**

| | | |
|---|---|---|
| Boston | Denver | Hartford-New Haven |
| Chicago | Detroit | Phoenix |
| Houston | Miami | Salt Lake City |
| Indianapolis | Milwaukee | Columbus |
| Kansas City | Minneapolis | Charlotte |
| Los Angeles | Philadelphia | Des Moines |
| New York | Pittsburgh | Grand Rapids |
| San Francisco | Portland, OR | Omaha |
| Seattle | St. Louis | San Antonio |
| Atlanta | Tampa | Syracuse |
| Cincinnati | Baltimore | |
| Cleveland | Buffalo-Rochester | |

**Table 5.4** **Average price for food products across 34 markets: 1998–2001**

National results
AR(1) IV results
(Asymptotic standard errors)

| Product | All stores |
|---|---|
| Apples | –0.1036 |
| | (0.2298) |
| Apple juice | –0.2769 |
| | (0.3799) |
| Bananas | –0.01545 |
| | (0.1747) |
| Bread | –0.0642 |
| | (0.0898) |
| Butter/margarine | –0.8192 |
| | (0.2445) |
| Cereal | –0.1079 |
| | (0.1275) |
| Chicken breast | –0.5597 |
| | (0.4402) |
| Coffee | –0.6548 |
| | (0.4774) |
| Cookies | –0.4850 |
| | (0.1294) |
| Eggs | –0.4324 |
| | (0.0995) |
| Ground beef | –0.0679 |
| | (0.1637) |
| Ham | –1.3032 |
| | (0.7580) |
| Ice cream | –0.3516 |
| | (0.3053) |
| Lettuce | –1.6194 |
| | (1.0106) |
| Milk | –0.2411 |
| | (0.0748) |
| Potatoes | –0.6406 |
| | (0.2346) |
| Soda | –0.3756 |
| | (0.1489) |
| Tomatoes | –0.8157 |
| | (0.4942) |
| Bottled water | –0.7231 |
| | (0.9446) |
| Yogurt | –0.1832 |
| | (0.1635) |

Number of observations 1,632

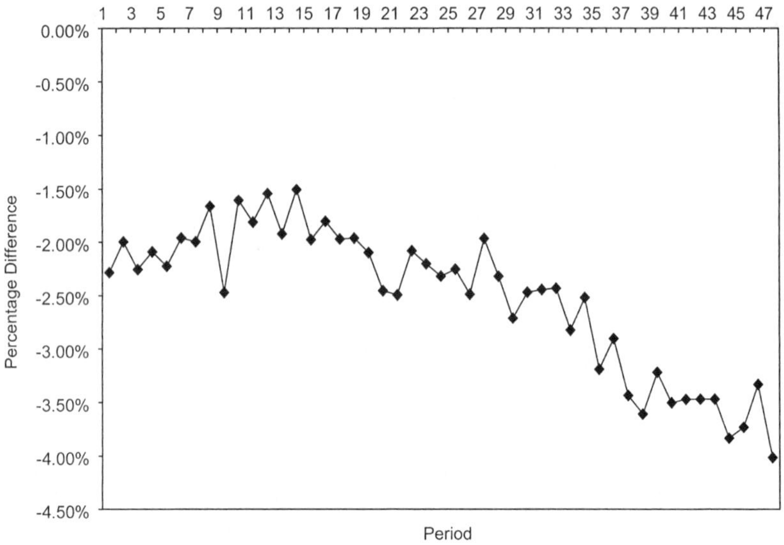


**Fig. 5.1 National difference in prices due to SMC stores**

negative effect on average prices as shopping in superstores increases. Thus, we find the "total effect" operates as households shift their expenditure from traditional supermarkets to lower priced superstore outlets.

In figure 5.1 we depict the difference in average prices paid by households due to the spread of SMC stores over the period. During the sample period from January 1998 to December 2001 the expenditure share of SMC stores increased from 10.9 to 16.9 percent, a 55.3 percent increase over the forty-eight months, or 11.6 percent per year. We take the econometric estimates from table 5.3 and use them to estimate the decrease in average price for each food category. We then average across food categories and plot the results in figure 5.1, which demonstrates the increasing effect on average food prices as SMCs become more available and households increase their expenditures at these retail outlets. We find that food prices are 3.0 percent lower than otherwise, or an effect of about 0.75 percent year.

We now consider two of the individual food products. In figure 5.2 we plot the effect of increased expenditure in superstores on the average price of butter/margarine.

The estimated coefficient for butter/margarine in table 5.3 is quite large at –0.8192. The estimated effect of the spread of superstores on the price of butter/margarine is –5.63 percent over the forty-eight month period. The effect on the price of yogurt is presented in figure 5.3. The estimated coefficient for the price of yogurt is considerably smaller at –0.1832. Thus, in figure 5.2 the effect on the average price of yogurt over the 48 month period is –1.1 percent. From figures 5.2 and 5.3 we see that significantly different

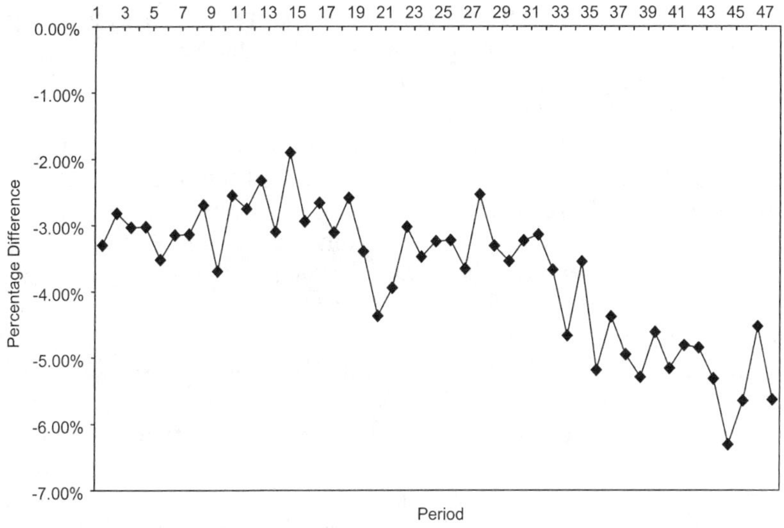


**Fig. 5.2 Butter/margarine difference**

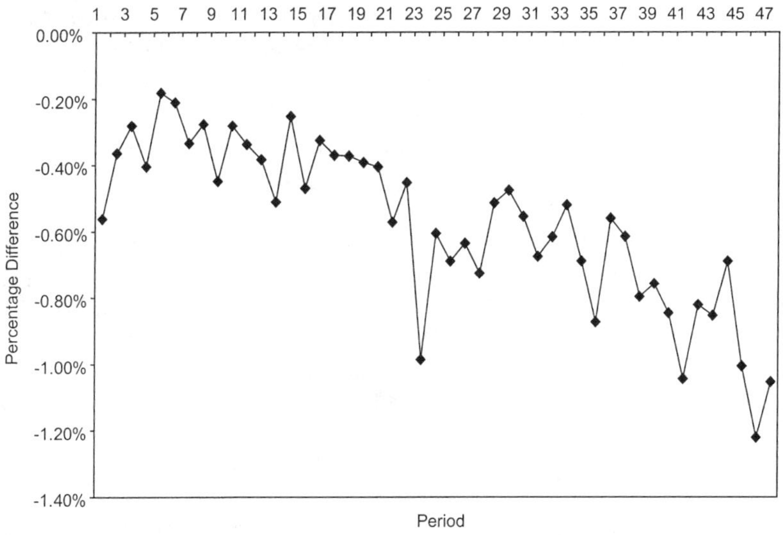


**Fig. 5.3 Yogurt price difference**

price effects exist for different food products due to the spread of SMCs and increased expenditure at those SMCs by households.

We now repeat the econometrics to test for the "indirect effect" of lower conventional supermarket prices because of increased competition from superstores. In equation (8) we replace the left-hand variable $p_{it}$, which is the average log price paid for a given product, with $\tilde{p}_{it}$, which is the average price paid in supermarkets. We give the results in table 5.5.

We estimate eighteen of the twenty coefficients to be negative, with the only exceptions being bread and cereal, neither of which is statistically significant.[31] As would be expected from economic theory, the effects of increased SMC expenditures are smaller for most of the products. Thus, the estimated "total effects" on average prices paid by households arising from substitution to lower priced SMCs typically exceeds the "indirect effects" of decreased prices in supermarkets. Nevertheless, we do find some quite large indirect effects as in lettuce, butter/margarine, coffee, ice cream, potatoes, tomatoes, and bottled water. The spread of supercenters leads to lower prices both for households that shift their food shopping from supermarket to SMC stores but also for households who continue to shop at supermarkets because of lower prices caused by the increased competition from expanding food offerings at SMCs.

In principle we could decompose the total effect into an "indirect effect" and a "direct effect" by using a share weighed average of prices into supercenters and traditional supermarkets. However, the econometrics of this approach are difficult because prices and shares for a given product are not econometrically predetermined. Further, expenditures in superstores for a given product are also unlikely to be predetermined as we explained previously. Thus, to estimate the decomposition we would need additional instrument variables, which we have been unable to determine.[32]

In terms of one of the questions we posed at the beginning of the chapter, the spread of supercenters does significantly affect prices paid by households. However, to correctly estimate the effect both *quantities and prices* must be utilized. Holding prices fixed as households shift their expenditures to nontraditional retail outlets, we find the average prices they pay decrease. However, prices also change because as households shift their purchasing behavior, the increased competition forces supermarkets to lower their prices. Both of these effects, the direct effect and indirect effect, lead to lower average prices paid by households for food items.

## 5.6 Effect on Price Indices

Since our scanner-based data set includes observation on both quantity and price, we are able to construct a price index that takes account of both

31. We find very similar results if we group the remaining Nielsen categories with supermarket: drug stores, convenience, and "other." These other outlet categories have relatively low expenditure levels compared to traditional supermarkets.

32. The approach I used earlier (e.g., Hausman and Leonard 2002; Hausman, Leonard, and Zona 1994) of using supermarket prices in one city as instruments for prices in another city does not work here since Wal-Mart has a common presence across all of the markets that we use in our econometric data set.

**Table 5.5 Average price for food products in supermarkets across 34 markets: 1998–2001**

National results for supermarkets
AR(1) IV results
(Asymptotic standard errors)

| Product | Supermarkets |
|---|---|
| Apples | –0.2307 |
| | (0.2233) |
| Apple juice | –0.5385 |
| | (0.5104) |
| Bananas | –0.0437 |
| | (0.1447) |
| Bread | 0.0066 |
| | (0.0890) |
| Butter/margarine | –0.6853 |
| | (0.2089) |
| Cereal | 0.0832 |
| | (0.1538) |
| Chicken breast | –0.5812 |
| | (0.5352) |
| Coffee | –0.4763 |
| | (0.6005) |
| Cookies | –0.4366 |
| | (0.1966) |
| Eggs | –0.1915 |
| | (0.0922) |
| Ground beef | –0.0303 |
| | (0.1538) |
| Ham | –2.1172 |
| | (1.2448) |
| Ice cream | –0.3985 |
| | (0.2895) |
| Lettuce | –2.4217 |
| | (1.5517) |
| Milk | –0.1247 |
| | (0.0887) |
| Potatoes | –0.5092 |
| | (0.2244) |
| Soda | –0.2728 |
| | (0.1513) |
| Tomatoes | –0.6956 |
| | (0.4791) |
| Bottled water | –0.5950 |
| | (0.8155) |
| Yogurt | –0.0759 |
| | (0.1833) |
| Number of observations 1,632 | |

increased expenditure at SMC stores as well as the effects of substitution when consumers face lower prices. Thus, we are to consider a source of first-order bias in the CPI, outlet substitution bias, as well as the source of second-order bias, substitution bias that occurs with the lower prices at the SMC outlets.

Food expenditures at SMC outlets have increased over the years in question. In January 1998, in our sample of thirty-four markets, we find an expenditure share of 0.1090. At the end of the sample, forty-eight months later, in December 2001 we find an expenditure share of 0.1693. Thus, the expenditure increased by .0603 or by 55.3 percent over the forty-eight months or 11.6 percent per year. The share has continued to increase as new SMC food outlets have continued to open and as consumers have increasingly shopped at these outlets.

We estimate the effect of this increased expenditure in lower priced SMC outlets on the twenty food categories we considered previously and an overall food price index. We consider four indexes in table 5.6. First is the continuous update: a continuously updated value index where aggregates food expenditure shares across outlets from the current month are used to construct a share weighted average price for each food category. Note that since we have scanner data we can update both the food expenditure shares

**Table 5.6** **Price index calculations for food expenditure: 1998–2001**

| Product | Continuous update | Constant weights | Yearly update | Biennial update |
|---|---|---|---|---|
| Apples | 1.016 | 1.028 | 1.032 | 1.032 |
| Apple juice | 0.939 | 0.961 | 0.955 | 0.960 |
| Bananas | 0.710 | 0.720 | 0.717 | 0.725 |
| Bread | 1.104 | 1.106 | 1.104 | 1.111 |
| Butter/margarine | 1.162 | 1.168 | 1.172 | 1.169 |
| Cereal | 1.043 | 1.054 | 1.051 | 1.056 |
| Chicken breast | 1.731 | 1.765 | 1.768 | 1.762 |
| Coffee | 0.897 | 0.909 | 0.915 | 0.926 |
| Cookies | 1.148 | 1.156 | 1.157 | 1.157 |
| Eggs | 0.893 | 0.905 | 0.903 | 0.909 |
| Ground beef | 1.368 | 1.392 | 1.392 | 1.388 |
| Ham | 0.755 | 0.774 | 0.791 | 0.799 |
| Ice cream | 1.092 | 1.112 | 1.110 | 1.108 |
| Lettuce | 1.016 | 1.059 | 1.056 | 1.045 |
| Milk | 1.083 | 1.091 | 1.091 | 1.095 |
| Potatoes | 1.355 | 1.373 | 1.381 | 1.378 |
| Soda | 1.084 | 1.074 | 1.081 | 1.077 |
| Tomatoes | 1.569 | 1.581 | 1.582 | 1.599 |
| Bottled water | 1.160 | 1.162 | 1.174 | 1.182 |
| Yogurt | 1.102 | 1.120 | 1.115 | 1.119 |
| Average difference/year | | 0.0032 | 0.0036 | 0.0042 |

(quantity data) and the price data each month. This continuous updating allows us to control for both outlet substitution bias, a first-order bias in the CPI, and substitution bias, a second-order bias in the CPI. Second are BLS Constant Weights: we keep the expenditure shares constant over the forty-eight months. We use current prices each month, but we take a weighted average using the expenditure weights as of January 1998. Thus, both outlet substitution bias and price substitution bias are present in the calculated index. This index is probably closest to the current BLS approach, although the BLS uses geometric means while we use arithmetic means. Third is the BLS with updated yearly expenditure weights: in January of each year we rotate stores and link the prices to the preceding December. We are assuming here that the BLS TPOPS procedure leads to a correctly reweighted sample each year, but that price linking removes the lower price effect of the shift by consumers to increasing expenditures at SMCs. Fourth is the Biennial Update: we now update the expenditure weights across stores based on the previous December. We continue to use the BLS linking procedure. Thus, we continue to have outlet substitution bias but we have reduced price substitution bias because of the yearly updates.

In table 5.6 we see that Method (1), the Continuous Update procedure, almost always leads to lower price increases or greater price decreases for all food products over the forty-eight month period. For example, apples have a price increase estimated at 1.6 percent. Method (2) calculates an increase of 2.8 percent. Thus, Method (2) overstates price change by 1.2 percentage points over four years, or by 75 percent of the true inflation rate. Method (3), which allows for yearly updated expenditure weights, calculates an increase of 3.2 percent per year, 1.6 percentage points or 100 percent more than Method (1). Lastly, Method (4), which uses biennial updates to the weights, again calculates an increase of 3.2 percent per year, or a difference of 100 percent. To our initial surprise, while Method (1) finds the lowest price increase as expected, Method (2) often estimates a lower price increase than Method (3) or Method (4). However, we now recognize this outcome as the result of the BLS linking procedure that eliminates the effect of the lower prices when customers switch outlets. Method (2) captures the "indirect effect" of lower prices when the presence of supercenters increases, but Methods (3) and (4) eliminate part of this indirect effect because they update the expenditure weights. Thus, the outcome of a more continual updating of expenditure weights leads to a perverse result because of the "linking out" of lower prices in SMCs.

When we take average yearly changes across all food categories we find the estimated difference between Method (1) and Method (2) to be 0.32 percent a year. This estimate is the same order of magnitude, but somewhat higher than Reinsdorf's (1993) estimate. In terms of the BLS CPI-U for food at home (which averaged 2.29 percent over this period) the 0.32 percent per year difference is 14.0 percent. Thus, we estimate that the Method (2) has an upward bias of approximately 14.0 percent because of its linking procedure, which eliminates the effect of households shifting their expenditure to lower price supercenter outlets such as Wal-Mart.

We next compare Method (1) to Method (3), which allows for updated expenditure weights each year. Here we find an estimated difference between Method (1) and Method (3) of increase of about 0.36 percent per year. We find the Method (3) measure of food at home to be upward biased by 15.7 percent. If we compare Method (4), the biennial update method, we find the estimated average difference to be 0.42 percent per year. In terms of Method (4) the 0.42 percent per year difference is 18.3 percent. The years 1998 to 2001 were generally a period of low inflation, but we still find significant difference in estimates of the food price indexes due to a shift toward lower price outlets. We find an upward bias in the range of 14.0 to 18.3 percent in the estimate of the CPI for food at home because of the use of the BLS linking procedure. Thus, updating the expenditure weights significantly reduces the bias in the estimated price index.

In figure 5.4 we plot the Method (1) price index where January 1998 is set equal to 1.0. Over the entire period we estimate a price increase of 12.1 percent or 3.0 percent per year.

While this estimate is for just the twenty food products we have investigated to date, we note that the BLS CPI-U food at home index increased by 9.48 percent over the same period, or 2.29 percent per year. The estimates are quite comparable, but the CPI-U index is over a much wider range of food products than the index we have computed.

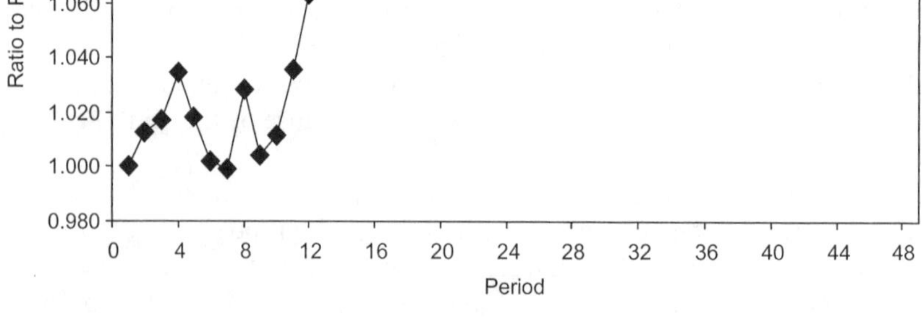

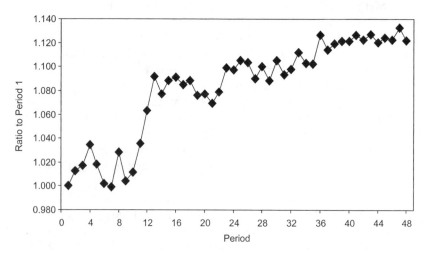


**Fig. 5.4 National price index, 20 food categories**

## 5.7 Conclusion

Over the past fifteen years the largest development in food retailing has been the start of Wal-Mart supercenters, which compete most closely with traditional supermarkets. Wal-Mart has expanded greatly, mostly in the South and Southwest, and become the largest supermarket chain in the United States. Wal-Mart is now expanding into additional geographic markets in California and the upper Midwest, so its effects will become even more important. Wal-Mart offers identical food items at an average price about 15 to 25 percent lower than traditional supermarkets. Wal-Mart's entry into a new geographic market creates a direct price effect by offering a lower price option to consumers and an indirect price effect by causing traditional supermarkets to lower their prices because of the increased competition.

The BLS procedure currently does not take account of the lower price option that Wal-Mart offers when it enters and expands in a given geographic market. The BLS only captures the indirect price effect. Instead, the BLS "links out" Wal-Mart's lower prices by assuming that an exact "compensating service quality differential" exists that exactly counteracts Wal-Mart's lower prices. If this assumption were correct, we would not see the rapid gain in market share by Wal-Mart after its entry into a market.

We find that a more appropriate approach to the analysis is to let the choice to shop at Wal-Mart be considered as a "new good" to consumers when Wal-Mart enters a geographic market. Some consumers continue to shop at traditional supermarkets while other consumers choose to shop at Wal-Mart. For the representative consumer we take a utility-consistent probability weighted average of the choice of shopping destination.[33] This approach leads to a continuously updated expenditure weighted average price calculation, which we apply to food data in thirty-four markets over a forty-eight month period. Of course, the BLS would need to implement our proposal using economic judgment because if the new market entrant were Starbucks instead of Wal-Mart, the assumption that the higher price of coffee in Starbucks did not represent a quality differential would be difficult to justify. The difference arises because much of the food products sold by Wal-Mart are the same as the products sold by supermarkets, while in the case of Starbucks a quality adjustment is necessary, as Hausman (2003) discusses.[34] The approach we recommend in this chapter requires quantity data as well as price data, so the BLS would need to begin to use scanner

33. The BLS approach assumes that consumers are not made better off by an expanded choice set, contrary to almost all economic theory.

34. However, if the higher quality aspect of Starbucks were correctly taken into account as Hausman (2003) discusses, the price index would typically decrease, even though Starbuck coffee prices are higher than the previous coffee shop charged.

data to implement our approach. Currently the BLS collects only price data, but does not collect quantity (or expenditure) data that it incorporates into the CPI except at lengthy intervals.

We find a significant difference between our approach and the BLS approach, even for the relatively low food inflation period of 1998 to 2001 that we study in this chapter. Our estimates are that the BLS CPI-U food at home inflation is too high by about 0.32 to 0.42 percentage points, which leads to an upward bias in the estimated inflation rate of about 15 percent per year. We intend to expand our approach to more food categories in further research, but we find that the BLS should take account of Wal-Mart and other nontraditional retail outlets, rather than making believe that Wal-Mart does not exist.

## Appendix

*Reply to Professor Silver*

Professor Silver correctly draws attention to the questions of sample selection and composition for the Nielsen Homescan panel data that we use. The use of panel data seems especially attractive since households remain the same when the presence of supercenter outlets increases in a given market. Indeed, in a related paper (see Hausman and Leibtag [2007]), we use econometric methods to estimate fixed effects for households, which is only possible with panel data. Hausman (1978) demonstrated that unobserved household effects that are correlated with observed variables can create significant bias in econometric and statistical analysis. Professor Silver raises the problem that sample selection of more price sensitive households can lead to an estimate upward bias in effects. As we describe in the current chapter, Nielsen chooses household using random sampling techniques. Professor Silver speculates that households that agree to join the Homescan panel "are likely [to] have lower search costs, be better informed about prices and be more price sensitive." He gives no reasons for this conclusion. However, we understand that Nielsen, and its competitor IRI, both use household panels to supplement their point of sale (POS) scanner data, which Professor Silver views as nearly problem-free. Thus, neither the companies nor their customers find the panel data to suffer from unacceptable bias.[35]

Professor Silver also discusses attrition and sample replacement and the

35. Hausman has used POS scanner data in many previous papers. However, since Wal-Mart no longer sells its scanner data to either Nielsen or IRI, we used panel data in this chapter to do the estimation. If the BLS were to use scanner data to estimate its CPI correctly as we suggest, hopefully it could buy the necessary scanner data from Wal-Mart.

possible problems that may arise with nonrandom attrition. Again, he speculates that only the more "price sensitive" households remain in the sample. He correctly states that nonrandom attrition "can potentially create estimation problems for researchers." Hausman and Wise (1979) were among the first authors to demonstrate the problems that can arise from nonrandom attrition in panel data. Professor Silver is also correct that "biased sample selection comes around in biased results." He states that whether the problem exists is "difficult to test."

To investigate the possible effect of nonrandom attrition we calculated the proportion of shopping trips to supercenters by three groups. Group 1 is households who exit in the sample in year 1; Group 2 exit in year 2; Group 3 exit in year 3; and Group 4 remain in the sample for the entire sample period. If nonrandom attrition created a problem, we would expect to see the proportion of trips to supercenters be greater the higher the group number since household exit the sample earlier may not be as "price sensitive" as other groups. The proportions and standard errors (S.E.) are given in table 5A.1. Table 5A.1 calculates the proportion of supercenter shopping trips across all market at three-month intervals. We do not find evidence that households that exit the sample earlier are more likely to shop at supercenters. For example, in month 3 of the sample Group 1 shops more at supercenters than Groups 2 through 4. In period 12 Group 3 shops more at supercenters than Group 2 but also more than Group 4, households who never exit the sample. If nonrandom attrition were a problem we would expect to see the proportions increase from left to right in each period. We do not observe this pattern. Further, the estimated standard errors are sufficiently small that we would very likely have found the pattern if it existed in the population.

While the question of a nonrandom sample cannot be answered definitively since it depends on unobserved household characteristics, these estimate and tests demonstrates that it is unlikely to be particularly large. Further, the main recommendation of our chapter, that the BLS not ignore the price differences of Wal-Mart and other supercenters compared to traditional outlets when they enter the BLS sample, remains unchanged.

**Table 5A.1 Supercenter shopping proportions**

| | Group 1 | | Group 2 | | Group 3 | | Group 4 | |
|---|---|---|---|---|---|---|---|---|
| Period | Proportion | Standard error | Proportion | Standard error | Proportion | Standard error | Proportion | Standard error |
| 3 | 0.151 | 0.009 | 0.143 | 0.012 | 0.139 | 0.013 | 0.136 | 0.008 |
| 12 | 0.184 | 0.010 | 0.149 | 0.013 | 0.154 | 0.014 | 0.147 | 0.008 |
| 24 | | | 0.160 | 0.011 | 0.173 | 0.013 | 0.166 | 0.008 |
| 36 | | | | | 0.173 | 0.010 | 0.173 | 0.009 |
| 48 | | | | | | | 0.191 | 0.009 |

## References

Abraham, K., J. Greenlees, and B. Moulton. 1998. Working to improve the Consumer Price Index. *Journal of Economic Perspectives* 12 (1): 27–36.
Cage, R. 1996. New methodology for selecting CPI outlet samples. *Monthly Labor Review* 119 (December): 49.
Callahan, P., and A. Zimmerman. 2003. Grocery chains fighting Wal-Mart for market share. *Wall Street Journal* May 31.
Hausman, J. 1978. Specification tests in econometrics. *Econometrica* 46 (6): 1251–71.
———. 1985. The econometrics of nonlinear budget sets. *Econometrica* 53 (6): 1255–82.
———. 1997. Valuation of new goods under perfect and imperfect competition. In *The economics of new goods,* ed. T. Bresnahan and R. Gordon, 209–248. Chicago: University of Chicago Press.
———. 1999. Cellular telephone, new products, and the CPI. *Journal of Business and Economics Statistics* 17 (2): 188–94.
———. 2003. Sources of bias and solutions to bias in the CPI. *Journal of Economic Perspectives* 17 (1): 23–44.
Hausman, J., and E. Leibtag. 2007. Consumer benefits from increased competition in shopping outlets: Measuring the effect of Wal-Mart. *Journal of Applied Econometrics* 22 (7): 1157–77.
Hausman, J., and G. Leonard. 2002. The competitive effects of a new product introduction: A case study. *Journal of Industrial Economics* 50 (3): 237–63.
Hausman, J., G. Leonard, and D. McFadden. 1995. A utility-consistent combined discrete choice and count data model: Assessing recreational use losses due to natural resource damage. *Journal of Public Economics* 56 (1): 1–30.
Hausman, J., G. Leonard, and D. Zona. 1994. Competitive analysis with differentiated products. *Annales, D'Economie et de Statistique* 34: 159–80.
Hausman, J., and D. Wise. 1979. Attrition bias in experimental and panel data: The Gary income maintenance experiment. *Econometrica* 47 (2): 455–73.
Little, P. 2004. Channel blurring redefines the grocery market. *Competitive Edge* June: 34.
Reinsdorf, M. 1993. The effect of outlet price differentials in the U.S. Consumer Price Index. In *Price measurements and their use,* ed. M. Foss, M. Manser, and A. Young, 227–54. Chicago: University of Chicago Press.
Schultze, C., and C. Mackie, eds. 2002. *At what price?* Washington, DC: National Academy of Sciences Press.
Shapiro, M., and D. Wilcox. 1996. Mismeasurement of the Consumer Price Index: An evaluation. *NBER Macroeconomics Annual* 11: 93–142.

## Comment Marshall Reinsdorf

### Overview of the Chapter's Results

This chapter uses transactions data collected from the households in the ACNielsen Fresh Foods Homescan Panel to obtain very interesting new

Marshall Reinsdorf is a senior research economist at the U.S. Department of Commerce, Bureau of Economic Analysis.

estimates of outlet substitution bias for twenty food items. These data permit direct estimation of the average price paid for an item by the households in a market area, such as Atlanta or Baltimore-Washington. The data include "random weight" items, which, despite their importance, are often omitted from scanner data sets because they lack bar codes.

The authors estimate the effect of the market share of supercenters, mass merchandisers, and club stores (SMC) on the average price paid by the households in an area. They include dummy variables to control for area-specific or time-specific fixed effects, and they use two-stage least squares to avoid any bias from a possible covariance between the regression error term and the SMC market share. The coefficient on SMC share is negative in every case, though only seven of the twenty items have statistically significant coefficients. The authors also estimate the effect of the SMC share on the average price paid in supermarkets, because evidence suggests that incumbent supermarkets tend to reduce their prices when SMCs enter or gain market share. For most items the regression coefficient is again negative, but smaller in magnitude than in the first set of regressions. Thus, the total negative effect of SMCs on overall average price paid seems to have a direct component reflecting outlet substitution and an indirect component reflecting price responses of supermarkets to competition from SMCs. The BLS indexes presumably capture the indirect effect, but miss the direct effect.

Next, the authors calculate four kinds of price index for each food product. The first uses contemporaneous weights and tracks the average price paid, which is equivalent to a unit value price. The second holds expenditure weights for outlets constant at their initial values. The third links in new outlet weights annually, and the fourth links in new outlet weights biannually.

Over the four years in the sample, the constant weight index rises an average of 0.32 percent per year faster than the preferred average-price-paid index. However, the description of the index construction procedure suggests that the authors have confused expenditure weights with quantity weights; if so, outlets with high prices received too much weight.[1] Presuming—as is commonly the case—that initially low prices tended to rise more than average, the effect of the confusion would have been to depress the constant-weight index, possibly causing an understatement of the difference between a constant basket index and an average-price-paid index.

Surprisingly, the authors also find that linking in updated outlet weights annually or biannually tends to make the indexes rise faster than they do with constant weights. They do not offer a detailed explanation of this finding, but I can suggest a plausible explanation. The theoretical result that chaining reduces a constant-weight index's upward substitution bias depends on an assumption that markets adjust immediately to their complete information

1. When averaging prices arithmetically, the weights should be proportional to quantities; weights proportional to current-period expenditures or to adjusted base-period expenditures can be used in a *harmonic* average of prices to obtain a unit-value, or its constant-basket average price.

equilibrium. The markets investigated in this chapter are, however, likely to be characterized by delayed responses. Supermarkets' losses of market share following the entry of SMCs occur gradually as information diffuses and consumers adjust their shopping patterns, and the supermarkets may make defensive price cuts in response to the losses of market share with an additional lag. If supermarket prices start to rise more slowly than SMC prices after the supermarkets have lost market share, linking in updated outlet weights will reduce the growth rate of the index.

### Some Caveats

Two effects that could make the chapter's estimates of outlet substitution bias too high have been hypothesized. A comment by Mick Silver suggests that the Homescan sample contains unusually price-sensitive consumers, and that the respondents who stay in the sample for all four years are more price-sensitive than average. In response, the authors show that the proportion of respondents who shop at SMCs is not lower in portions of the sample that are lost to early attrition. This suggests that nonrandom attrition does not cause an overstatement of the propensity to substitute lower SMC prices, contrary to Silver's hypothesis. On the other hand, no direct evidence is available on whether the process of initial selection into the Homescan sample favors those who are most price-sensitive. However, the continued purchases of Homescan data by commercial customers who can check them against store sales data shows that any such sample selection bias is not so severe as to undermine their usefulness. Moreover, store-level confirm the general finding that SMCs have made significant gains at the expense of supermarkets.

Second, consumers who shop at SMCs may be giving up some valuable elements of quality in exchange for lower prices. The SMC stores often offer less convenient locations than traditional supermarkets and a more limited selection of varieties and goods, and SMCs do not have the kind of upscale ambience that some supermarkets achieve by offering attractive displays of fresh produce and seafood and elaborate deli counters. Finally, the need to pay a membership fee to shop at a club store offsets some fraction of the savings from these stores' low prices. The importance of the services offered by retailers is analyzed in Betancourt and Gautschi (1992, 1993).

The authors are dismissive of the argument that consumers' price savings are offset by differences in outlet quality. The consumers who buy from the SMCs probably place a small enough value on the outlet quality differences to make the average-price-paid index, which makes no adjustment for outlet quality differentials, an acceptable measure for practical purposes. I therefore agree that their average-price-paid index is a reasonable benchmark for approximating outlet substitution bias. Nevertheless, in a perfect index, the adjustment for outlet quality would probably not be zero. A framework for analyzing the effect of quality variation when a lower-cost, lower-quality alternative is introduced was developed for treatment of the entry of generic pharmaceuticals by Griliches and Cockburn (1994) and Fisher and Griliches (1995). They estimate the average willingness-to-pay for brandedness of the buyers of generics by the midpoint of its theoretical bounds of zero and the total price savings offered by the generic, though I would argue that attributing half the price savings to quality overdoes the quality adjustment because the distribution of the willingness-to-pay for brandedness in the subpopulation that chooses generics is probably concentrated near zero.[2] A highly elastic response to a narrowing of the price gap between the two alternatives—implying that the value of the foregone quality approaches the price savings for many consumers—is more plausible in the SMC substitution case than in the generics substitution case. The likely existence of small net gains for some SMC shoppers is, however, offset in the aggregate by the likely existence of large gains for other SMC shoppers: the distribution of willingness-to-pay for the extra services offered by supermarkets probably has a lower bound of *below* zero because some consumers strictly prefer SMCs for reasons such as their broader assortments of nonfood products.

Although sample selection and outlet quality differentials are unlikely to have substantially affected the chapter's estimates of the bias inherent in the methods used in the CPI, a third potential source of error in the chapter's estimates should also be recognized. With the exception of bananas, the items in this study are aggregates of a range of varieties of varying qualities. Variation in the average price paid for an item caused by variation in the average quality of the varieties purchased is undoubtedly one of the reasons for the relatively high standard errors of the regression coefficients. However, in addition to high variances, differences in the quality of varieties are a likely source of bias. The varieties sold in supermarkets are likely to include more representatives of the high end of the quality range than the varieties sold in SMCs; for example, organic meat and produce is likely to be more widely available in supermarkets. If so, the varieties in sample of purchases from supermarkets will tend to represent higher average levels of quality.

These three possible problems of sample selection effects, outlet quality differentials, and variety noncomparability mean that the estimates in the chapter are subject to some uncertainty beyond the variance from sampling error that is inherent in all sample-based statistics. Nevertheless, even in combination, the effects of these problems seem unlikely to be large enough to explain away all of the upward bias that the authors find for the constant basket index, and for the annually and biannually linked indexes. The esti-

2. The midpoint of this distribution overestimates its expected value because many of the consumers who choose generics perceive the quality differences as inconsequential, and few would substitute back to the branded drug if the price differential narrowed slightly. Otherwise, manufacturers of the branded products are giving up significant profits by not making small price cuts that would allow them to regain most of their customers. A symmetric argument that the existence of large consumer surplus implies that the generics manufacturers would profit by raising their prices cannot be made, because competition with each other prevents them from raising prices.

mates remain valuable documentation of the existence and likely range of outlet bias in the CPI for the products covered by this study.

## Conclusion

Showing that a problem exists in the CPI is usually much easier than developing a workable and accurate solution for it. (That is, of course, the way things should be—we would expect all the easy problems to have been solved by now!) Alternatives to the assumption that the differences in price for items sold side-by-side in the same market are a measure of the value of their differences in quality are not easy to implement. In the case of outlet substitution bias, estimating quality adjustments for outlets from CPI samples is especially difficult because prices from different stores often represent varieties of differing quality levels. The diversity of varieties in the CPI follows from the need to obtain representative samples of the varieties purchased by consumers.

In the mid-1960s BLS asked Edward Denison to provide expert advice on improving the CPI. One of his remarks was that ideally prices should be collected from households rather than from stores, so the prices that are actually paid could be reflected in the index. Of course, he added, this would never be practical. Now the authors of the current chapter have used a unique data set to do just that. In doing so, they have provided important new evidence on the possible magnitude of outlet substitution bias in one component of the CPI.

## References

Betancourt, R. R., and D. Gautschi. 1992. The demand for retail products and the household production model: New views on complementarity and substitutability. *Journal of Economic Behavior and Organization* 17 (2): 257–75.

———. 1993. Two essential characteristics of retail markets and their economic consequences. *Journal of Economic Behavior and Organization* 21 (3): 277–94.

Griliches, Z., and I. Cockburn. 1994. Generics and new goods in pharmaceutical price indexes. *The American Economic Review* 84 (5): 1213–32.

Fisher, F., and Z. Griliches. 1995. Aggregate price indexes, new goods, and generics. *Quarterly Journal of Economics* 110 (1): 229–44.

# Comment Mick Silver

This excellent chapter addresses the important issue of outlet substitution bias. There is much in the methodology that is to be commended. The con-

Mick Silver is a senior economist in the Statistics Department of the International Monetary Fund. The views expressed herein are those of the author and should not be attributed to the IMF, its Executive Board, or its management.

cern of this comment lies with the empirical finding that the BLS CPI-U food at home inflation is too high by about 0.32 to 0.42 percentage points. The problem this comment draws attention to is the reliability of the finding given the data source employed, as opposed to econometric issues. It is first worth distinguishing between two types of scanner data: the consumer panel data used in this study that use handheld bar code scanners, as opposed to diaries to record purchases and retail bar code electronic point-of-sale (EPOS) scanner data.

### Scanner Data

The study used ACNeilsen Homescan data. Such data arise from a consumer panel regularly scanning the bar codes on their shopping basket purchases. The data benefit from the attachment of the demographic characteristics of the household to the purchases and a history of purchase behavior so that, for example, repeat purchases can be identified as well as switching patterns. The coverage and representativity of the panel, and its consistency over time is restricted to, and relies upon, the efficacy of the selection of panel members, their attrition, and replacement. If it is true that the sample members are selected in a manner that they are more price sensitive than other members of the population, then the estimates of outlet substitution effects will be overstated.

A second type of scanner data is bar code point-of sale (POS) scanner data. Such data are compiled from the scanned transactions at the point of sale and have an impressive coverage of transactions. In a period of, say, a month, the quantity of sales can be aggregated of a particular variety of a product, and its transaction price summed and a unit value calculated. The summation can be over outlet-types and the product variety codes can be linked to files that contain detailed product characteristics for each variety. Such data can cover the vast majority of transactions and are unlikely to be subject to selectivity bias. However, such data cannot identify the demographics of each purchaser nor their purchase history as they substitute between outlets. Therein lays the advantage of the consumer panel data.

The chapter[1] describes the data panel used in the study as consisting of a subsample of transaction level data from the Fresh Foods Homescan Panel, ". . . approximately 61,500 randomly selected households across the US [. . .] randomly recruited to join the panel using sampling techniques to ensure household representation for demographic variables such as household income, family composition, education, and household location." The chapter notes that the panel is ". . . subject to turnover from normal attrition or adjustments to demographic targets necessitated by Census revisions." Also, that "Households lost through attrition are replaced with others having

1. I use the NBER working paper version of the chapter as the most recent available: http://www.nber.org/papers/w10712.

similar key characteristics". Emphasis is given to the fact that the sample is geographically dispersed and demographically balanced so that the sample matches the U.S. population as closely as possible.

There are two issues of concern. The first is the representativity of the sample of households due to nonresponse (self-selectivity) bias and the second, the attrition rate and replacement policy.

**Nonresponse Selectivity Bias**

The authors have noted that the sample selected is a random one, that each household, within the practicalities of such things, will have an equal chance of selection. There is not, to the knowledge of author of this comment, nor referenced in the chapter, any information on sample design, but we take this on trust. The method used to recruit and maintain panel members is again, not to our knowledge, documented. Our understanding is that Homescan recruit their members by first mailing the sampled householders and asking if they are willing to take part in a (regular) survey of spending in return for coupons and product information. Those who respond form the potential sample. All (or a sample) of those who complete the forms regularly and well (to some standard) are then selected for membership of the panel. We know little of the reward structure for being a panel member. Such members are likely have lower search costs, be better informed about prices, and be more price sensitive. We have no information on the nonresponse rate—the number of recruits to a panel over the number of mailings sent out to households. There are not unreasonable grounds to believe that this may be very high. The sample was post-stratified according to a number of Census-based demographic and geographic targets. However, such post-stratification is of course not in itself sufficient to remove selectivity bias. The sample comprises those households in each stratum who are more price conscious in the sense that they respond to calls for filling out forms and recording their purchases for coupons and rewards and stay with it. Findings of high price sensitivity and substitution behavior remain open to the charge that they are artifacts of the selected data.

Of course the loose description of these methods may be false and the nonresponse rate may be very low. But when similar comments were made by the author to a group of researchers who use the data there was no disagreement with the essentials of the point previously made.[2]

2. http://www.farmfoundation.org/projects/documents/ScannerDataWorkshopSummaries2_000.pdf. A Workshop on the Use of Scanner Data in Policy Analysis, Economic Research Service, USDA and the Farm Foundation, Washington DC, June 2003. The website includes summaries of the papers where shortcomings of Homescan data, as well as its very real benefits, are highlighted. In particular, see Helen Jensen, "Demand for Enhanced Foods and the Value of Nutritional Enhancements of Food" and J. Michael Harris, "Properties of Scanner Data."

**Attrition and Replacement**

The study uses a subset of the data to represent household purchases of food for at-home consumption. The study was over the period 1998 to 2001 and the Homescan sample used included 12,000 households in 1998 and 1999, increasing to 15,000 in 2000 and 2001, but was restricted to households that participated in the panel for at least ten out of the twelve months per year. This reduced the sample size in 1998, 1999, 2000, and 2001 to 7,624, 7,124, 7,523, and 8,216 households, respectively; by about one-third in 1998 and 1999 and one-half in 2000 and 2001. This reinforces the predisposition of the sample to the price conscious shoppers. Of the price sensitive households recruited only the more committed ones remained in the sample.[3]

Yet the sample may be further biased since there were in fact only 9,501 unique households over the four years, of which only ". . . 5,247 households participated for all four years, 1,877 households participated for three years, and 2,377 households were one year participants." Thus, of those households with over ten to twelve months of membership who constituted this self-selected sample, whose purpose is to reflect the purchase patterns of a representative consumer, over a half (5,247/9,501) were price-conscious households who had chosen to monitor, in return for the incentives, their shopping behavior *for at least four years.*

There should always be in economic analysis an awareness that what goes around in biased sample selection comes around in biased results. But all of the above remains a suspicion about possible bias and, by the nature of the data, one difficult to test. Some such testing can be carried out. For example, data are available by duration of panel membership and the estimation of substitution effects by duration of panel membership will give some insights into possible bias, though there would remain the problem of determining the selectivity bias from the initial self-selectivity decision. The purpose of the comment is of course only to draw attention to such possible selectivity bias and is not to negate the usefulness of the chapter's contribution in drawing further attention to outlet-substitution bias and providing a methodological basis for analyzing its effects.

3. J. Michael Harris makes a similar point: "In the HomeScan data set only 12,000 households reported both UPC and random weight purchases. However, if you restrict the sample to households present in the data for 10 of 12 months in 1999, only purchases for 7,195 households are available. Indeed, it is clear that all households are not present in the purchase data for every month. This situation can potentially create estimation problems for researchers and can magnify the censoring problem, especially when individual products are examined." (p. 25 of website, see footnote 2.).

6

# Incorporating Financial Services in a Consumer Price Index

Dennis Fixler

## 6.1 Introduction

In recent years, the use of financial services by consumers has grown, with technological advances in both computers and telecommunications as well as with product innovation by financial firms. The national accounts measures of consumption include many financial services and as part of the comprehensive revision to the national accounts released in December 2003, the Bureau of Economic Analysis (BEA) improved its measure of the consumption of bank implicit financial services. However, the inclusion of financial services in a consumer price index has occurred to only a limited extent. Two complications are often cited that stand in the way of expanding the coverage of financial services. First, financial services involve activities that could be viewed as income generating and thus they are generally deemed outside the domain of such indexes. Second, financial service prices contain both explicit charges and implicit charges—the latter creates the problem of what value to place in the price index and this problem was the focus of the improvement by the BEA in its measure of financial services consumption.

Setting the domain of a consumer price index (CPI) involves a determination of the underlying purpose of the index. Most statistical agencies base their consumer price indexes on the cost of living (COL) conceptual

Dennis Fixler is chief statistician of the Bureau of Economic Analysis, U.S. Department of Commerce.

I am greatly indebted to George Smith and Gabriel Medeiros for their extensive work on compiling the indexes presented in the chapter. I also thank Susanto Basu, John Greenlees, Brent Moulton, Jeremy Nalewaik, and Marshall Reinsdorf for their comments. The analysis and comments solely reflect the view of the author and not necessarily those of the U.S. Bureau of Economic Analysis or the U.S. Department of Commerce.

framework.[1] That framework is not usually constructed with money or other financial assets in the utility function. The placement of money in a utility function has a long history in the literature and its justification rests on the fact that money facilitates transactions and provides a way of intertemporal transfers.[2] However, Alchian and Klein (1973) argued that assets in general should be placed in the utility function in order that a CPI should provide a better measure of inflation under the COL framework. More specifically they argued that assets must be included to obtain a meaningful answer to the question, "Does the individual need more or less money to remain at the same level of satisfaction?" (186).

Another way to place financial assets in the domain would be to view them as though they were durable goods that provide implicit services that attend their holding. This is the view of the user cost of money approach, developed by Donovan (1978), Diewert (1974), and Barnett (1978).[3] The precedent for putting such a framework in a CPI has already been set by the common treatment of housing in CPIs, which imputes a rental value of the services received from owner-occupied housing.

Both of these perspectives of financial services relate to a multiperiod analysis rather than the single period analysis in the standard cost of living framework. Pollak (1975) pointed out that there are several difficulties in constructing a multiperiod Cost-of-Living Index: futures markets are not always available, expectations about the future do not hold with certainty, and capital markets are not perfect. One way to handle the multiperiod problem in the context of the Cost-of-Living Index is to treat a single time period as a subindex of the multiperiod problem and apply the single period analysis. Similarly, Barnett (1980) constructs a multiperiod optimization problem for a consumer on the basis of separability of financial assets from other goods and services and shows that the optimization problem regarding financial assets can be reduced to a one period problem. Accordingly, this chapter also focuses on the one period problem; the attention is on the consumption of financial services within the period being considered.

Consumers purchase many types of financial services that are concomitant with financial assets and liabilities. The inclusion of such services in a CPI rests on their not being tied to a future receipt of money. For example, the purchase of automobile insurance is commonly included in CPIs, as are other forms of property and casualty insurance. Yet the purchase of life insurance is not included because it is viewed as both an intertemporal transaction, in the sense that the contract concerns the future transfer of a sum of money to others and as a tantamount purchase of an annuity, especially in the case of whole life insurance. Similarly, professional fees that are

1. See National Research Council (2002).
2. See, for example, Patinkin (1965).
3. As in the case of capital equipment, the idea is there is a flow of services that is received from a stock and the value of the services is given by the user cost of capital.

associated with financial management, such as accounting, are included in CPIs, while fees for services such as financial advice, or portfolio management are generally excluded.[4] However, this notion is inconsistent with the fact that the purchase of financial services by a consumer is consumption in the current period even though the purpose of the services is to increase income in subsequent periods. Therefore, these services should be included in the domain of a CPI. In principle, all financial services should be candidates for inclusion in a CPI.

As previously mentioned, setting the boundary of a CPI domain is only part of the complication of including financial services; the valuation of these services is sometimes not straightforward. This is especially true in the case of bank-provided financial services, for which there is no observable charge. Thus, a method of imputing the price of these services must be chosen.

Section 6.2 sets out more of the theory of incorporating financial services into a consumer price index. To give an idea of what a financial service component of a CPI might look like, section 6.3 presents three financial service price indexes that are constructed from data in the Personal Consumption Expenditures (PCE) component of the national accounts. Though the PCE price index is not based on a conceptual model of consumer behavior as is the CPI (as is typically compiled by statistical agencies), it is hoped that the illustration may serve as a useful guide to those considering the incorporation of financial services in a CPI. Section 6.4 provides a summary and conclusions.

## 6.2 Theory

Consumers are viewed as having a utility function that contains goods and services, inclusive of financial services. Woolford (2001) uses the following definition of financial services in discussing their incorporation into the Australian CPI: financial services are the services associated with the use, acquisition, or sale of financial and real assets.[5] This definition clearly captures expenditures on fees for portfolio management and investment advice.[6]

4. Further discussion on the inclusion of financial services in the domain of a CPI can be found in Woolford (2001), Triplett (2000), and chapter 10 in International Labour Organization (2004)—a new version of their CPI manual.

5. This definition is also used in the discussion of financial services in International Labour Organization (2004).

6. The definition, however, does not distinguish between intermediate and final demand and such a distinction is important when considering the acquisition of a home and the related expenses. More specifically, some of the financial services involved in the purchase of housing are not classified as consumption in the U.S. national accounts and in the accounts of most other countries. In the United States, a notional business is set up for households that produce housing services from the investment in a house and these services are resold to the homeowner.

Though the purchase of financial services is tied to the acquisition or holding of a financial asset or liability, either of which can be cast as a financial product, the multiperiod dimension of the demand for these is not considered here; the focus is on the per period consumption of the attending financial services.[7] One can think of the consumer as having both long-term and short-term optimization problems that are linked. In the long-term problem, the consumer plans consumption over time—the intertemporal optimization problem. This dynamic problem considers both consumption and the expected changes in income available for consumption. The short-run problem concerns the purchase of goods, services and assets/liabilities in a particular period, given the income and stock of financial assets available in the period.[8] The short-run problem therefore concerns the period purchase of any financial services that attend financial assets. For example, a depositor purchases the record keeping and safe keeping services implicit in the holding of deposits in the period that the deposit is held. Similarly, a portfolio manager is paid for his services (carrying out transactions and providing advice) in the period that they are provided. The fact that there are intertemporal considerations underlying the holding of deposits or a portfolio does not preclude the consideration of the purchases of the attending financial services in any period. The purchase of any asset, however, would not be included in the period measure of consumption.[9]

Banks provide numerous services; some have explicit charges and some have implicit charges. The valuation of the prices for implicit services is the major difficulty in forming a comprehensive set of bank services prices because many important financial services are provided implicitly. For example, the services of record-keeping and safekeeping are implicitly provided to depositors and there are no explicit charges for these services.

The user cost of money approach developed by Diewert (1974), Donovan (1978), and Barnett (1978) is one way to impute the price of the implicit

---

It follows that in the United States, the fees paid to real estate agents are not consumption, part is allocated for the purchase of land and is considered an intermediate purchase, and part is allocated for the purchase of the structure and is classified as residential fixed investment; Woolford (2001), in contrast, lists real estate broker services as part of the Australian CPI.

7. Some might be concerned that the definition of financial services transforms the CPI from an expenditure basis to a use basis, which affects the price recorded for goods and services that span more than one time period. For example, under the current expenditure approach the price of a purchased auto would be recorded in the CPI while under a use approach some estimate of the per-period value of the service flowing from the auto would be incorporated in the index. But this is not the intent. The focus is on the financial services inextricably attached to the asset/liability. One cannot purchase a deposit product without purchasing record-keeping and safekeeping services.

8. In the standard one period model underlying the cost of living framework, the dual optimization problem is employed: consumers minimize expenditures to achieve a given level of utility in the period in which the consumption is to take place.

9. Schreft (2006) describes how even the choice of a payment instrument can be the object of an intertemporal consumer optimization problem.

financial services.[10] This approach is taken below and it is identical with the one that underlies the user cost approach for implicit banking services that BEA implemented in the comprehensive revision released on December 10, 2003.[11]

The key to incorporating financial services is characterizing their prices so that they include both the implicit and explicit charges, which are viewed as given to consumers. The user cost of money approach focuses on the cash flow resulting from the purchase of the financial product. For deposit products, the cash flow consists of an initial deduction from cash holdings and a return of the cash plus an interest component at the end of the time period. Let $D$ denote the deposit amount, $r_D$ the interest rate paid on deposits and $\rho$ the risk-free interest rate that serves as an opportunity cost of money. The cash flow without any explicit service fee is given by:

$$-D + \frac{(1 + r_D)D}{1 + \rho} = \left[\frac{(r_D - \rho)}{1 + \rho}\right]D;$$

this assumes no withdrawals during the period.[12] The bracketed term on the right-hand side of the equality is the user cost of deposits from the consumer perspective. This expression says the difference between the reference rate and the deposit interest rate represents the implicit price paid by the depositor for the uncharged-for financial services. The explicit fee component can be considered in one of two ways. One could include a service fee in the previous expression, but it would have to be defined on a per dollar basis, which may be counter to the way that the actual charge is assessed. For example, the charge for certifying a check is usually a flat fee that is independent of the amount of the check. Alternatively, explicit service fees can be treated separately and that is the approach used in the example presented in section 6.3.

The deposit user cost price above is the negative of the user cost price of deposits from a bank's point of view; the one used in the 2003 comprehensive revision to the national accounts (see Fixler, Reinsdorf, and Smith [2003]).[13] The sign difference results entirely from the fact that the asset and liability

10. See Fixler and Zieschang (2001) for a discussion of the application of the user cost approach to CPIs.

11. See Moulton and Seskin (2003) and Fixler, Reinsdorf, and Smith (2003) for a discussion of the changes in the measure of implicit banking services in the national accounts that were implemented in the comprehensive revision.

12. Barnett (1978) uses a dynamic optimization model to derive the user cost of money prices.

13. In the computation of the user cost prices from bank data it is quite frequently found that for deposit products, $(\rho - r_D) > 0$, implying that the bank treats the deposit product as an output. In the consumer problem this means that the parenthetical term above is negative. The negativity is consistent with the notion of a payment for financial services by consumers and the positive sign for the bank is indicative of a receipt.

designations for the consumer are the reverse of that for the financial intermediary; a deposit product is an asset to the consumer but a liability to the supplying bank. In keeping with the assumption that consumers are price takers, the form of the user cost price for deposits will be that charged by a bank and the discount factor is suppressed:

$$p_D = \rho - r_D. \tag{1}$$

The previous characterization of the deposit price is consistent with Dick (2002), who found that the demand for deposit services is based on both the service fee and interest rates.[14]

A similar analysis applies in the case of loans. From a consumer's perspective a loan is a liability that provides an amount $L$ at the beginning of the period and at the end of the period requires the payment of $L$ plus interest $r_L L$, where $r_L$ is the loan interest rate. From the financial intermediary's perspective, however, the cash flow is the exact opposite, as the loan is an asset that provides earnings. The user cost price of the loan from a bank's perspective is thus:

$$p_L = r_L - \rho.^{15} \tag{2}$$

The interest rate differential in the previous loan price captures the idea that consumers go to banks because it is relatively easier to convince a bank of one's creditworthiness than the market (or even one's relatives) and the consumer pays the bank a fee for its assumption of this credit risk. Equation (2) is the implicit price of loan services. The explicit price for loan services are separate, as in the case of deposit products.

In the previous characterizations of the prices of the loan and deposit implicit services, the idea is that the transaction is in effect repeating itself in each period. In the case of loans, the implicit charge represented by the interest rate differential is a per period charge because if the loan continues, that is, if it is neither paid-off or canceled by the bank, then the borrower pays for the continued assumption of the credit risk by the bank for the outstanding balance. Similarly, if the depositor leaves money on deposit then deposit services are repurchased in the period.

The user cost price concept can be applied to numerous financial services. In countries where there is universal banking (one-stop financial service centers) the set of financial products is quite large and thereby creates more possibilities for implicit financial services. The extension of the user

14. Furthermore, it is not just the deposit rate that is important but also the loan rate—evidently consumers consider the potential costs of having to switch to another bank in order to obtain a loan.

15. Holding gains or losses can also be included here and in principle in the deposit user cost as well. In the national accounts the inclusion of such values as part of valuation of financial services is currently being studied.

cost approach to different kinds of financial services is in Schreyer and Stauffer (2002).

A key component of the user cost price is the reference rate or benchmark rate. In theory, this rate should represent an opportunity cost of funds that guides decision making with respect to either the demand or supply of financial products. As can be seen from the discussion of the mirror images between the consumer user cost price and the financial intermediary user cost price, it is assumed that both banks and consumers have the same reference rate.[16] It is also assumed that this single reference rate applies to all financial products. To illustrate, instead of depositing funds in a bank, consumers could purchase Treasury bonds. Though they would earn a higher interest rate by doing so they would forgo transaction services and some liquidity. From a bank's perspective, deposited funds can be invested in Treasury securities—they provide a credit-risk-free source of investment income and a source of liquidity. This role for Treasury securities implies that they serve as an alternative to making a particular loan. Thus, the difference between the loan rate and the reference rate reflects the credit risk associated with the borrower; if the borrower did not have any credit risk then in principle he should be able to borrow at the reference rate.[17]

There are several interest rates that have been mentioned as candidates for the reference rate and as the previous examples indicate, U.S. Treasury rates are good candidates because they are default risk-free and available to all. In the European Union, Eurostat requires an interbank rate. Though Fixler and Zieschang (1992) show that quantity indexes are robust with respect to the selection of the reference rate, the selection of the rate does affect the nominal level of financial services.

The inclusion of interest rates in the user cost prices raises the general question of whether to use book or market rates. Some considerations are: (a) individuals hold assets and liabilities over time so that the actual flow of interest expenses and receipts can be different from the one that is consistent with the market rate for any specific period; (b) the detail available on the financial products held by individuals may not permit an assignment of a correct market rate; and (c) there is a national accounting convention to use book rates instead of market rates. Accordingly, interest rates here are computed in a way that reflects book rather than market values. More specifically, all interest rates used in the following example are computed by dividing some interest flow (receipt or expense) by the stock of the cor-

16. Barnett (1995), for example, also assumes that one benchmark rate applies to all agents; in his model the benchmark asset provides no services other than its yield.

17. Some may argue that the reference rate should be adjusted for the default risk of the borrower to properly measure the credit service that is being provided. However, if a bank determines the loan rate on the basis of the borrower's default risk then such an adjustment may produce a downward bias in the valuation of the service being provided.

responding financial product at a point in time.[18] This method of computation implies that all of the interest rates used in the user cost prices take into account the different maturities of the underlying financial product. For example, the computed reference rate reflects all the maturities of U.S. Treasury securities held by banks and the computed loan rate reflects the maturities of outstanding loans.[19]

As is well known, the nominal interest rate in any period is directly related to the expected rate of inflation in that period, which implies that the interest rate-dependent financial service prices can be affected by inflation. As a result, the user cost prices are deflated by a general price index; the gross domestic purchases chain price index is used to deflate the user cost price relative between $t$ and $t-1$. The appendix illustrates how inflation rates are captured by the unit value interest rates.

In addition to the general price level changing over time, the characteristics of financial products change over time and thereby create a need for quality adjustment as well. For example, suppose that in period $t$ a deposit product has a minimum balance requirement and a service fee $s$ and in period $t+1$, this minimum balance requirement is dropped and the service fee increased. Because there is a change in the quality of the service—the customer has more of the amount of deposit available to him, one would want to adjust the change in $s$ for the change in the quality of the service.[20] Fixler and Zieschang (1999) demonstrate one way of adjusting the user cost prices for changes in the quality of financial services. The price indexes constructed in the next section are not adjusted for change in the quality of the financial services. This omission largely derives from the absence of a readily available set of data that contains the information needed. More specifically, information on transaction restrictions (such as minimum balance requirements or number of checks allowed per month) or the number of ATMs is neither collected by the regulatory authorities, the prime source of data, nor by the Bureau of the Census in the Economic Census for banks. However, inasmuch as the purpose of the example in the next section is to show how a financial services component of a consumer price index might be constructed and how the resulting indexes behave rather than provide augmentations to official estimates, the absence of quality adjustments does not detract from the analysis. Of course, any official implementation of a

18. As described in Fixler, Reinsdorf, and Smith (2003), the change in the valuation of implicit services in the national accounts also employed a unit value computation of interest rates.

19. In the July 2005 annual revision the computation of the reference rate was changed to eliminate mortgage-backed securities, which have recently become risky because of reporting irregularities from the issuing firms.

20. In some instances the characteristics of the financial product and the financial service coincide. If the characteristic set of a deposit product were amended to include Internet banking, then there would simultaneously be a new form of transaction service. However it is viewed, a quality adjustment would be necessary.

financial services component to a consumer price index must examine the issue of quality adjustment.

## 6.3 A PCE-based Financial Services Price Index

To illustrate what a financial service component of a CPI might look like, data from the BEA's Personal Consumption Expenditures (PCE) are used to construct such an index. Because the purpose of PCE is to record expenditures of consumers (and nonprofit institutions serving households) as part of the overall measure of economic activity, PCE is not based on a cost of living framework and includes many types of expenditures that are associated with income generation. Table 6.1 lists the financial services included in PCE and provides their average share of the total for these financial services in 2000. Most of the listed financial services are components of the personal

**Table 6.1 The set of financial services**

*Brokerage charges and investment counseling*

Equities commissions
1. Exchange listed equities (2.4 percent)
2. Market making in over-the-counter equity securities (1.3 percent)
3. Other equity securities, including specialists on registered exchanges and dealer trading (0.97 percent)
4. Listed options transactions (0.22 percent)
5. All other securities transactions (4.6 percent)
6. Broker charges on mutual fund sales (1.8 percent)
7. Trading profits on debt securities (0.22 percent)
8. Trust services of commercial banks (0.47 percent)
9. Investment advisory services of brokers (2.4 percent)
10. Commodities revenues (0.43 percent)
11. Investment counseling services (3.1 percent)

*Bank service charges, trust services, and safe deposit box rental*

12. Commercial bank service charges on deposit accounts (3.2 percent)
13. Commercial bank fees on fiduciary accounts (2.5 percent)
14. Commercial bank other fee income (3.3 percent)
15. Charges and fees of other depository institutions (2.6 percent)

*Services furnished without payment by financial intermediaries*

16. Commercial banks (11.5 percent)
17. Other financial institutions (18.4 percent)
18. Expenses of handling life insurance and pension plans (17.2 percent)
19. Household insurance (0.69 percent)
20. Auto insurance (7.7 percent)

*Health insurance*

21. Medical and hospital insurance (12.2 percent)
22. Income loss insurance (0.3 percent)
23. Workers' Compensation (2.5 percent)

*Note:* Number in parentheses is the average share of Financial Services in 2000.

business category within PCE while other financial services are classified in the category related to the service—for example, auto insurance is in the transportation category. These financial services totaled 559 billion dollars in 2000. There is some overlap with the services included in the U.S. CPI. In fact, the BEA uses the information regarding the explicit fees included in the CPI when computing real explicit bank services in PCE.

Most of the data that are used to compile the PCE components for bank-provided financial services come from the Reports of Condition and Income (the Call Reports) that banks have to file quarterly with the Federal Deposit Insurance Corporation. Because these data are bank reported, there is no identification of the buyer of the financial services and so allocations are made using the Federal Reserve's Flow of Funds Accounts data. For example, the household portion of bank implicit financial services is determined by looking at the household share of deposits and loans in the Flow of Funds data.[21] In some cases it is straightforward to identify the purchaser—for example, personal loans can be confidently assigned to the household sector. These allocations change annually. The time period of consideration is 1987Q1 to 2002Q4. This period was selected because it is one in which the bank reporting requirements are relatively unchanged.

Though the December 2003 comprehensive revision to the national accounts, as described in Moulton and Seskin (2003) and Fixler, Reinsdorf, and Smith (2003), implemented a user cost of money approach to compute the nominal value of the implicit bank services, there was no change in the computation of real values or constant dollar measure of implicit bank services. The constant-dollar measure of banks' implicit output equals (a) the constant-dollar value of banks' total output, estimated by extrapolating the base-year (2000) current-dollar estimate of banks' total (both explicitly and implicitly priced) output by the BLS estimate of the growth in banks' total output less[22] (b) the constant dollar real value of banks' explicitly priced output, estimated by deflating banks' service charges on deposit accounts and other noninterest income with the Bureau of Labor Statistics (BLS) CPI for checking account and other bank services and then adding an estimate of banks' real fiduciary activities based on the growth of the number of trust department discretionary accounts. This real implicit service output measure is then used to obtain an implicit price index (current dollar divided by constant dollar) for the implicit bank services. Observe that this price index does not directly relate to the user cost prices presented previously.

Similarly, Moulton and Seskin (2003) and Chen and Fixler (2003) describe

21. In the 2005 annual revision some adjustments were made to the set of deposit products that were considered to be consumer oriented. In particular, some large deposit products that arguably could be viewed as being more associated with businesses than with households were removed.

22. The BLS methodology for measuring bank output is explained in Kunze, Jablonski, and Sieling (1998).

the changes in the nominal measure of property and casualty insurance output that were implemented in the comprehensive revision. These changes were the addition of premium supplements and the use of a measure of normal claims instead of actual claims; the nominal value of property and casualty insurance became premium plus premium supplement less normal claims.[23] Again, the computation of real values was not altered. The computation of the real values generally involves the use of various components of the BLS' CPI and PPI programs to deflate premiums (and premium supplements) and (normal) claims components, the methods of deflation are not the same across the various lines of insurance.[24] These price indexes are used to compute real values in terms of the base year and then these real values are used to compute an implicit price deflator, which is the price index published by BEA.[25] Some might argue that a premium less claims-based measure of price is inappropriate for a CPI. It is beyond the scope of this chapter to discuss the merits of different approaches to measuring insurance services in a consumer price index. The purpose here is to present an example of such an index in the context of Personal Consumption Expenditures, which uses the premiums less claims-based measure of price.

Three financial service price indexes reflecting three different methods for estimating bank real implicit services are computed below: one is based on the current BEA procedure that uses an implicit price deflator, a second is an offshoot of the current method that separates depositor and borrower services and the third is a user cost based price index. In the first, the published BEA price indexes for all of the services listed in table 6.1 are used to form a financial services price index component for PCE. Many of the service prices included in these indexes are explicit charges. For the implicit services provided by banks as well as for auto insurance, the BEA published price indexes are actually implicit price deflators that reflect the changes in the computation of nominal values that were implemented in the 2003 comprehensive revision.

Because the financial services shown in table 6.1 are found in different categories of PCE, the corresponding implicit price deflators must be aggregated in some way. In keeping with the fixed-base nature of the indexes,

23. Premiums supplements are the income earned by the insurer from investing unearned premiums and unpaid claims and this income is attributed to policyholders. Normal claims are computed as a moving average of actual claims—the idea is that insurers base their pricing on expected rather than actual claims.

24. In the case of homeowner's insurance double deflation is used because of the availability of a BLS CPI on household insurance premiums for renters. However, automobile insurance is singly deflated by the CPI for motor vehicle insurance premiums. In the case of expenses for handling life insurance, the BEA uses a composite index of BLS measures of earnings—that is, the deflation is based on input prices.

25. The BEA recognizes that this method of deflation is limited and has on its research agenda improving the method of deflation. One aspect of that research will be the possible use of the PPI for property and casualty insurance, which already incorporates investment income in its price index.

the aggregation is performed by using a Laspeyres-type aggregation—each implicit price deflator is weighted by its share of financial service expenditures in the base period. More specifically, let $IPD_i^{fs}$ $(t,2000)$ be the implicit price deflator for the $i$th financial services listed in table 6.1. The aggregate fixed weight price index for financial services is then:

$$P_{FW}^{FinServ} = \sum_i IPD_i^{fs}(t,2000)s_{i,2000}^{fs}, \tag{3}$$

where $s_{i,2000}^{fs}$ is the share of the $i$th financial service in the base year, 2000.

Figure 6.1 shows the fixed weighted financial services price index in equation (3). It is compared to an aggregate PCE price index that is computed by weighting the PCE component prices by their shares in 2000, as done in equation (3). Clearly the financial services index is more volatile, but that volatility does not appear to affect the overall PCE because the 2000 share of the financial services subset in table 6.1 is approximately 8 percent. Interestingly, the share remains approximately constant throughout the period examined.

Under the current method for determining the real value of implicit banking services a total is computed and then allocated to deposit and loan services. This allocation is made according to the nominal shares of implicit deposit and borrower services. A subsequent allocation of implicit deposit and borrower services is made to households and businesses according to their respective shares of deposits and loan balances. Thus, the sector allo-

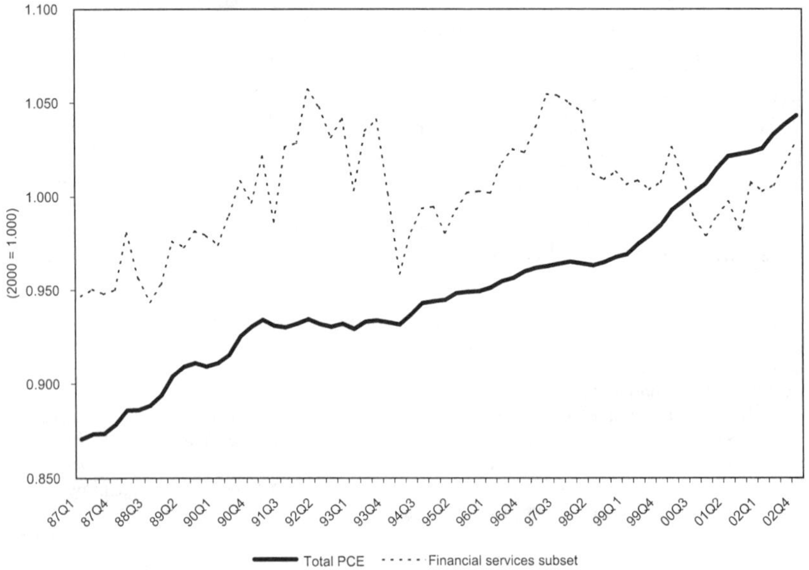


**Fig. 6.1 Fixed-weight price indexes (IPD), PCE, financial services subset**

cation of nominal implicit services reflects both changes in user costs for depositor and borrower services and changes in sector shares of nominal deposit and loan balances. Because about 60 percent of the deposits at commercial banks are owned by persons and given that this percentage has not changed much over time, an implication of the current procedure is that a change in the user cost price of deposits will affect the share of real implicit deposits services allocated to households. To illustrate, suppose that the user cost price of deposits increases, ceteris paribus, and results in an increase in the share of nominal implicit deposits services from 65 to 70 percent. Using the 60 percent value for household deposits, the share of real implicit deposits allocated to households will increase from 39 percent to 42 percent. Thus, the real implicit deposit services consumed by households will increase because of the increase in the user cost price of deposits.

One way to remove the influence of changing user costs on the real consumption of implicit services would be to perform the quantity extrapolation by type of service—depositor and borrower services.[26] This second method is possible because the BLS measure distinguishes between these two types of services. More specifically, estimates of the overall real implicit depositor services are determined by extrapolating the base-year estimate of total (implicit and explicitly-priced) depositor services with the deposit component of the BLS quantity index and then subtracting a deflated measure of explicitly-priced depositor services. The amount of the personal consumption of real implicit depositor services is determined by the share of nominal deposit balances owned by persons. Therefore, changes in real personal consumption of implicit depositor services reflect changes in the BLS quantity index, changes in deflated measures of explicitly-priced depositor services, and changes in the personal sector's share of nominal deposits, but not changes in the user cost of deposits. The same approach is applied to borrower services.

Figure 6.2 illustrates the price indexes (implicit price deflators) that result from these more detailed and published methods of quantity extrapolation. The extrapolation by type has a large influence on total PCE after about 2000Q3 that reflects its greater influence on financial services at about that time. Note that the pattern of the financial services index does not change with the quantity extrapolation by type.

Figure 6.3 shows the effect of the change in the method of quantity extrapolation on the banks' implicit services component. Observe that the implicit depositor services price index for banks, when the quantity extrapolation is by type, has a substantial positive impact on total implicit services by type after 2000Q3. It should be noted that approximately 80 percent of the implicit services consumed by persons are deposit services. Accordingly, when treated separately the influence of implicit depositor services will be

26. This procedure was suggested by George Smith.

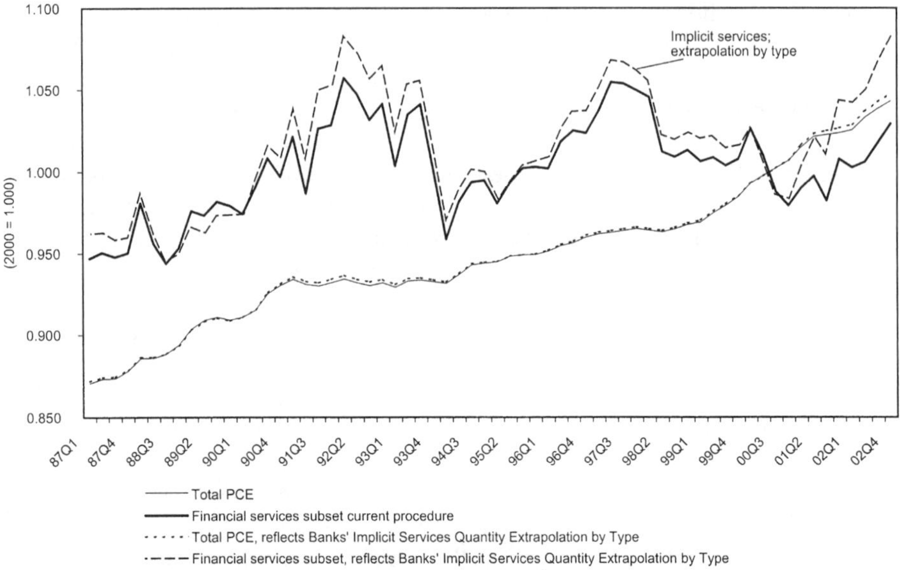


**Fig. 6.2 Comparison of fixed-weight price indexes for financial services and total PCE**

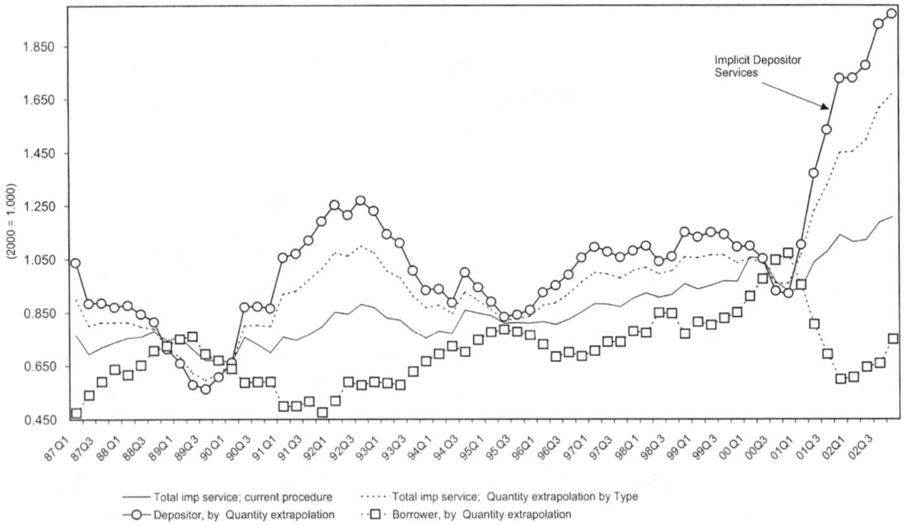


**Fig. 6.3 Price indexes (implicit price deflators) for total implicit services: Two methods of quantity extrapolation**

more pronounced; the joint treatment of depositor and borrower services obscures the relative weight difference.

A third method of computing bank real implicit service output uses the user cost prices in equations (1) and (2) to construct a Törnqvist financial service price index. The Törnqvist formula is used for mathematical simplicity; it easily allows for the isolation of subindexes and allows for an easy rescaling of expenditure shares. Furthermore, because the Törnqvist formula and Fisher index formula used by the BEA are both superlative, there will be no loss in the ability to compare the movements of this index with PCE chain Fisher price index published by the BEA.[27] The general form of a Törnqvist price index is given by

$$P_{Tornq}(t, t-1) = \prod_i \left( \frac{p_i^t}{p_i^{t-1}} \right)^{0.5(s_i^t + s_i^{t-1})},$$

where $p_i$ is the price of the $i$th good or service and $s_i$ is the expenditure share of the $i$th good.

The financial services Törnqvist price index contains two subindexes: one containing the explicit financial service prices (some bank services, brokerage services, and insurance) and one containing the implicit financial service prices for implicit services (particularly some deposit and loan services provided by banks). For the first component, the Törnqvist index formula is used; the prices are derived from actual charges and the shares are the expenditure on these services as a fraction of the expenditures on all of the financial services listed in table 6.1. This index is denoted by $P_{Tornq}^{explicit}(t, t-1)$.

For the implicitly priced services, the following Törnqvist formula is used

$$\text{(4)} \quad P_{Tornq}^{implicit}(t,t-1) = \prod_i \left[ \frac{p_{Li}^t / p_{Li}^{t-1}}{\delta(t,t-1)} \right]^{0.5(s_{Li}^t + s_{Li}^{t-1})} \prod_j \left[ \frac{p_{Dj}^t / p_{Dj}^{t-1}}{\delta(t,t-1)} \right]^{0.5(s_{Dj}^t + s_{Dj}^{t-1})},$$

where $p_L$ identifies loan prices, as in equation (2), and $s_L$ shares (implicit loan services as a fraction of total financial services) and $p_D$ identifies the deposit prices, as in equation (1), and $s_D$ shares (implicit deposit services as a fraction of total financial services). There are 4 loan products and 11 deposit products. The term $\delta$ is given by

$$\delta(t, t-1) = \frac{\text{Gross Domestic Purchases Price Index } (t, 2000)}{\text{Gross Domestic Purchases Price Index } (t-1, 2000)},$$

27. See Diewert (1976) for the concept of a superlative index. Diewert (1978) showed that the numerical difference among commonly used superlative index number formulas is very small, on the order of .001 index points.

and is intended to adjust the user cost prices for general inflation. In the following example, $\delta(t, t-1)$ is based on a four quarter moving average of the published Gross Domestic Purchases Price Index.[28]

The complete financial services price index is thus given by

$$(5) \qquad P_{Tornq}^{FinServ}(t,t-1) = P_{Tornq}^{explicit}(t,t-1) \cdot P_{Tornq}^{implicit}(t,t-1) \ .$$

This bilateral index is a component of the chain Törnqvist price index that is used to compute the financial service price index for more than two periods.

Figure 6.4 shows the relationship among the book value based interest rates used to construct the user cost prices. Note that there are downward trends in all of the interest rates during the 1990 to 1991 and 2001 recessions, despite these rates not being market rates.

Figure 6.5 shows a comparison between the chain Törnqvist financial services price index and the published chain Fisher PCE price index. Though the financial services price index is more volatile, the volatility of those prices does not appear to present itself in the overall PCE price index because, as noted earlier, the financial services subset of PCE amounts to approximately 8 percent of PCE for the period under consideration.

Figure 6.6 presents a closer examination of the movements of the components of the Törnqvist financial services price index. The overall steady increase in the total financial services price index is driven by the steady increase in the insurance subset that contains the insurance services listed in table 6.1. The insurance subset amounts to approximately 40 percent of financial services in 2000, with the share not varying much over the considered time period. Observe that there is a decrease in price in 2001Q3 owing to the terrorist attacks on September 11, 2001.[29] The explicit fees component share in 2000 was approximately 18 percent and remained fairly constant. Bank implicit services had a share of about 12 percent, with 9 percent deriving from depositor services and 3 percent from borrower services. Observe that some of the movement in the implicit financial services index influences the movement of the overall financial services index.

Figure 6.7 presents a closer look at the movement of banks' implicit financial services by presenting the depositor and borrower price indexes

28. Gross Domestic Purchases is defined as the market value of goods and services purchased by U.S. residents, regardless of where those goods and services were produced. It is measured as Gross Personal Consumption Expenditures plus Gross Private Domestic Investment plus Government Consumption Expenditures and Gross Investment. Because this price index contains financial services it may appear that its use as a deflator for the user cost price relative is problematic. Based on an examination using fixed weight implicit price deflators, the inclusion of financial services has a very small impact on the deflated value of the user cost price relative. This small influence derives from the fact that the financial services in table 6.1, on average, amount to about 5 percent of nominal Gross Domestic Purchases.

29. This reduction would have been larger without the change in the measure of insurance implemented in the December 2003 comprehensive revision; see Chen and Fixler (2003) for a detailed description of that change.

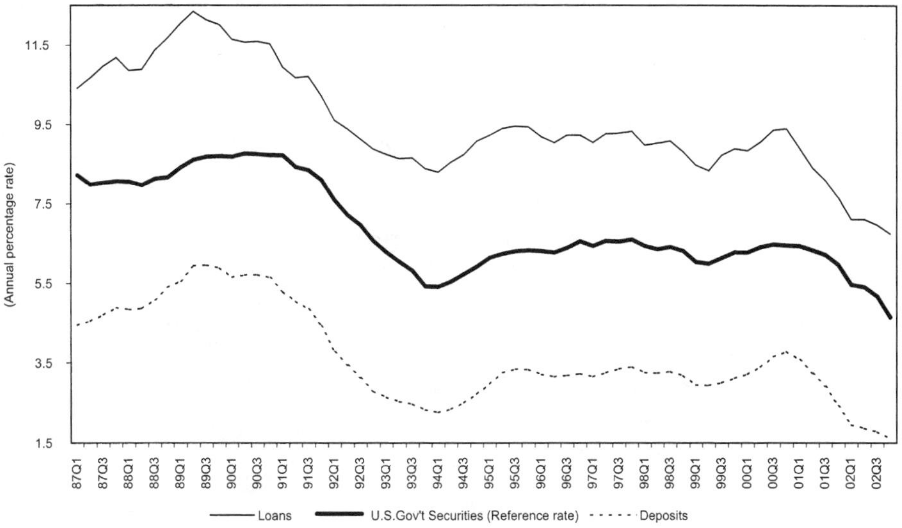


**Fig. 6.4 Average interest received and paid by banks, book values**

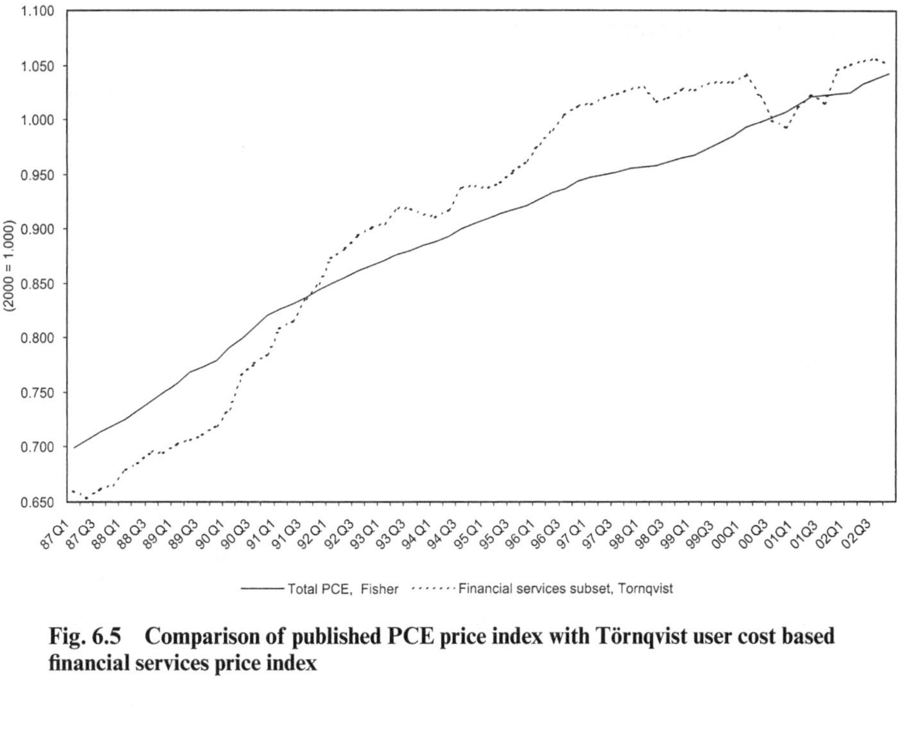


**Fig. 6.5 Comparison of published PCE price index with Törnqvist user cost based financial services price index**

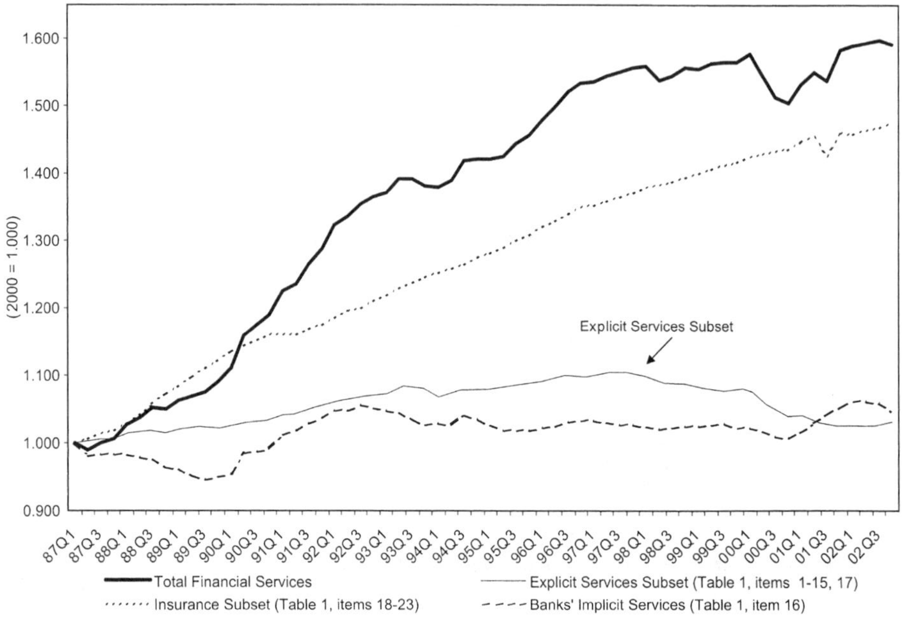


**Fig. 6.6 Törnqvist chained price indexes for financial services**

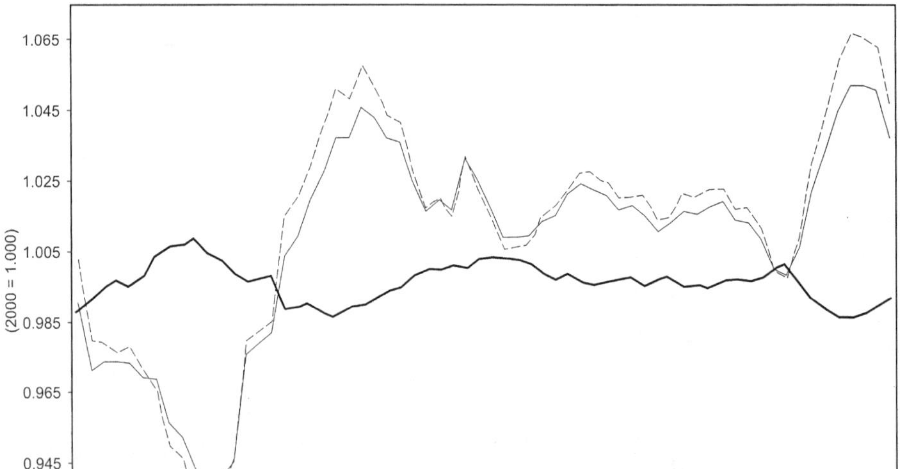

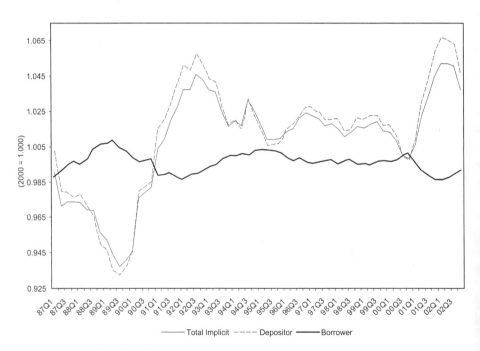

**Fig. 6.7 Törnqvist price indexes: Total implicit, depositor and borrower services**

separately. Clearly the implicit services subindex follows the movement in the depositor series and this is due to the fact that depositor services range from 60 to 90 percent of implicit services while borrower services range from 10 to 40 percent. In 2000Q4 depositor services start to rise toward their peak of 90 percent while borrower services move toward their low of 10 percent. Looking at figure 6.4 one can see that during this time all of the interest rates are falling but that rate of decline in deposit rates is relatively great, which serves to increase the user cost price of deposits. Note that the decrease in deposit rates in the early 1990s also contributed to the large increase in the deposit user cost price index.

Figures 6.8 and 6.9 compare the movement of the user cost prices of deposit and borrower implicit services with the respective implicit price deflator. Figure 6.8 shows the user cost price of deposits with and without its deflation by a four quarter moving average of the Gross Domestic Purchases price index.[30] The implicit price deflator for depositor services is computed by dividing the nominal value of implicit depositor services by a corresponding real value that reflects quantity extrapolation with the BLS deposit output index. Though the levels are different the movement in all three series is very similar. This result derives from the fact that both the amount of deposits, which together with the user costs yields the nominal measure, and the quantity extrapolator do not change much over the period. In other words, the variation in all three series is due to the variation in the user cost price.[31] The borrower counterparts for these series are presented in figure 6.9 and the same analysis applies.[32] Though the patterns in the depositor and borrower services prices are nearly the same among the different measures of depositor and borrower service prices, the difference in levels affect the attending quantities of depositor and borrower services.

Figures 6.10 through 6.14 present the quantity indexes that correspond to the price indexes discussed previously. The quantity indexes are computed by taking the quantity in year *t* and dividing by the quantity in 2000. Figure 6.10 shows that the quantity index for total PCE is not changed when the quantity extrapolation is done separately by type of service instead of by a single combined service—the two quantity index series effectively lie on top of each other. This result seems to be due to the small weight of financial services subset in total PCE. Observe that the two financial services indexes differentiated by the method of quantity extrapolation show different levels, though the paths are very similar. Figure 6.11 focuses on the fixed weight

30. In any period the user cost deposit price is computed as a deposit share weighted sum of the individual deposit user cost prices. The value without deflation is the user cost price indexes with 2000Q3 = 1.

31. The movement in the moving average of the Gross Domestic Purchases price index is fairly stable.

32. As in the case of deposits, the borrower user cost price is a loan share weighted sum of the individual loan user cost prices.

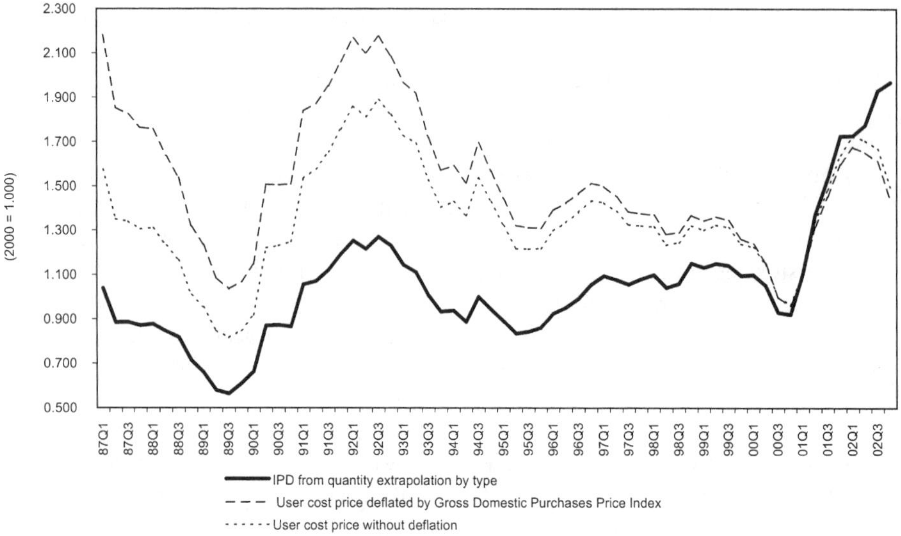


**Fig. 6.8 Comparison of depositor service prices: Implicit price deflator versus user cost**

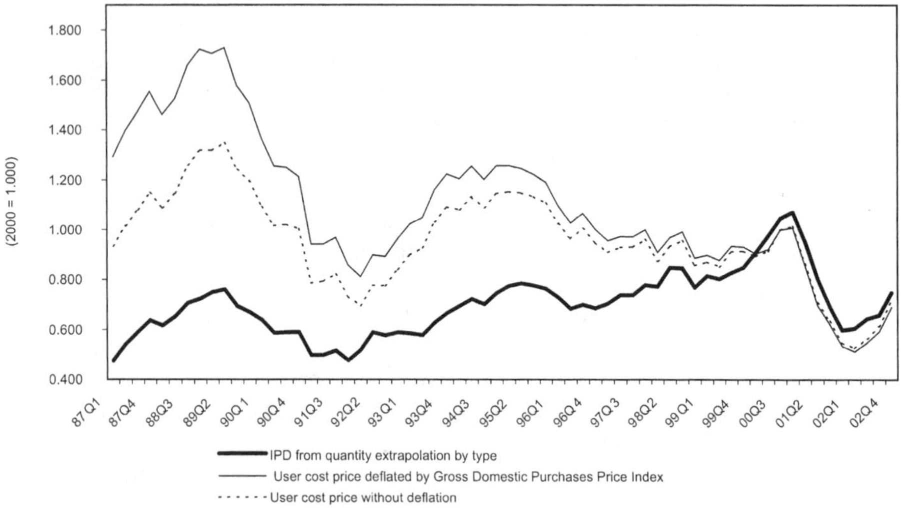


**Fig. 6.9 Comparison of borrower service prices: Implicit price deflator versus user cost price**

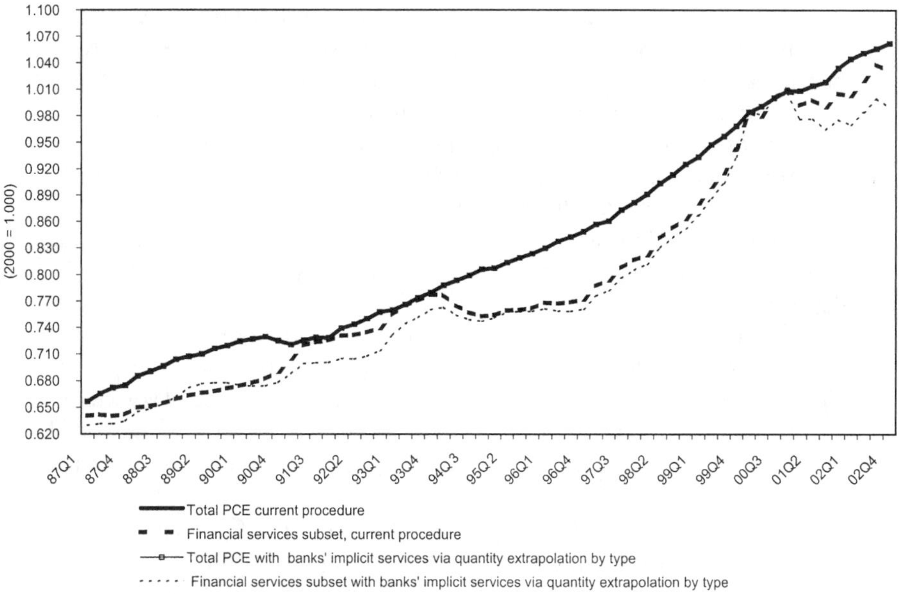


**Fig. 6.10 Comparison of fixed-weighted quantity indexes**

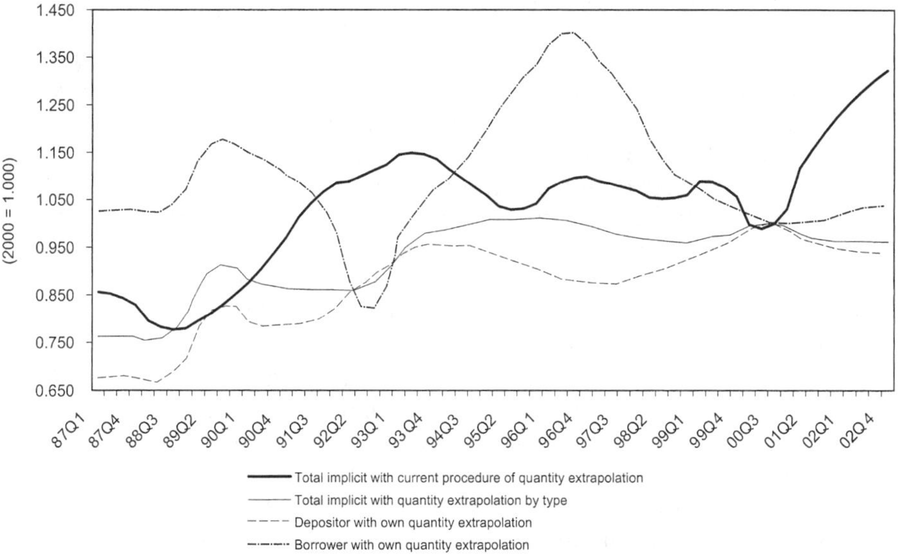


**Fig. 6.11 Fixed-weighted quantity indexes banks' implicit services**

quantity indexes for bank implicit services and shows that there is considerably more volatility in the quantity index for borrower services. The total implicit services have similar patterns but note that the large discrepancy that began in 2000Q4 is akin to the difference presented in early 1990s. In the earlier period depositor services increase slightly, and given their higher share of implicit services it makes sense that the implicit services index would increase. The index with the combined quantity extrapolation, the current procedure, gives depositor services a relatively higher weight because, as explained earlier, the deposit share is influenced by the rising user cost of deposits for the period that is illustrated in figure 6.8. The influence of the user cost prices on the shares also explains the divergence in the two total implicit services index in the later period. Starting in 2000Q4, borrower services rise relative to depositor services and this difference in trend is accentuated by the fact that the user cost of borrower services is rising, as illustrated in figure 6.9, while the user cost of depositor services is falling, as illustrated in figure 6.8.

Figure 6.12 compares the published chained Fisher PCE quantity index with the Törnqvist quantity index—computed implicitly using the Törnqvist price index.[33] The amount of real implicit depositor services allocated to personal consumption is determined by the proportion of nominal deposit balances owned by persons—the real implicit borrower services allocated to personal consumption is analogously determined. This method of sector allocation is similar to that with the quantity extrapolation by type. Observe that the Törnqvist financial services quantity index does not rise as steadily as the PCE quantity index. The indexes approach each other in 2000 because that is their common base period. Again, the movements in the financial services index do not have much influence on the movement in the overall PCE index because of its relatively small weight.

Figure 6.13 presents the quantity index for bank implicit services and its component depositor and borrower services quantity indexes. Observe that the large differences between the borrower and depositor indexes occurs in the period 1990Q2 to 1992Q1, which includes the 1990 to 1991 recession, and in the period 2000Q4 to 2001Q4, which includes the last recession. In both cases, the beginning is characterized by a falling quantity of implicit borrower services and a rising quantity of implicit depositor services. Figure 6.9 shows that both the implicit price deflator and the user cost price of borrower services are declining in these periods. The implication is that the volume of borrower services did not increase with the fall in borrower services prices. In fact, the growth rate of total consumer credit, as measured by the Flow of Funds, fell continuously in the period 1990 to 1992 and in the

33. For period *t*, the nominal value was deflated by the Törnqvist price index for *t*. This value was then divided by the quantity index for 2000 to obtain a quantity index between periods *t* and 2000.

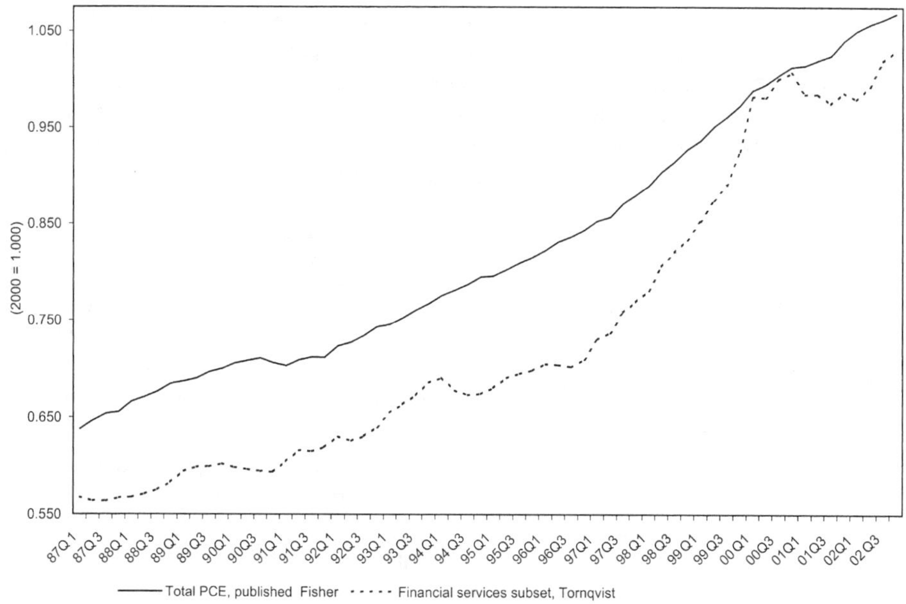


**Fig. 6.12 Chain-weighted quantity indexes, PCE and financial services**

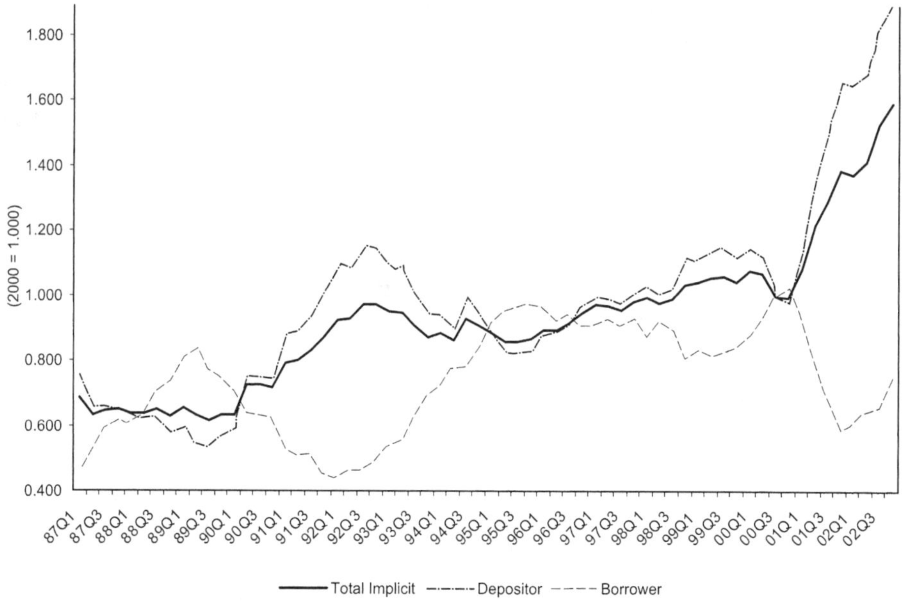


**Fig. 6.13 Implicit quantity indexes from Törnqvist price indexes: Total implicit, depositor, and borrower services**

period 2000 to 2002. Regarding the quantity of implicit depositor services, it increases during both of these periods. Figure 6.8 shows that large increases in the user cost price of implicit deposit services occurs in the period 1990Q2 to 1992Q1 and the period 2000Q4 to 2001Q4. The implication is that the volume of deposits did not fall during these periods. Yet, as measured by the Flow of Funds, checkable deposits at commercial banks fell in 1990, increased in 1991 and 1992, fell in 2000 and 2001, and increased in 2002. Thus, the increase in the user cost price of implicit deposit services offset the decrease in checkable deposits when they occurred.

Figure 6.14 compares the different quantity indexes for implicit services from the different implicit service price indexes. In the most recent periods the current procedure leads to an understatement of the quantity of implicit financial services relative to the user cost price index. Observe that the understatement is even greater with the quantity extrapolation by type of service. The difference in the two fixed weighted quantity indexes is due to the influence that changes in user cost prices have on the sector allocations under the current procedure. For example, the large quantity increases under the current procedure immediately after 1988Q3 and 2000Q3 primarily reflect large increases in depositor user costs that flow through to the quantity measures. This movement is not observed with the quantity index that is based

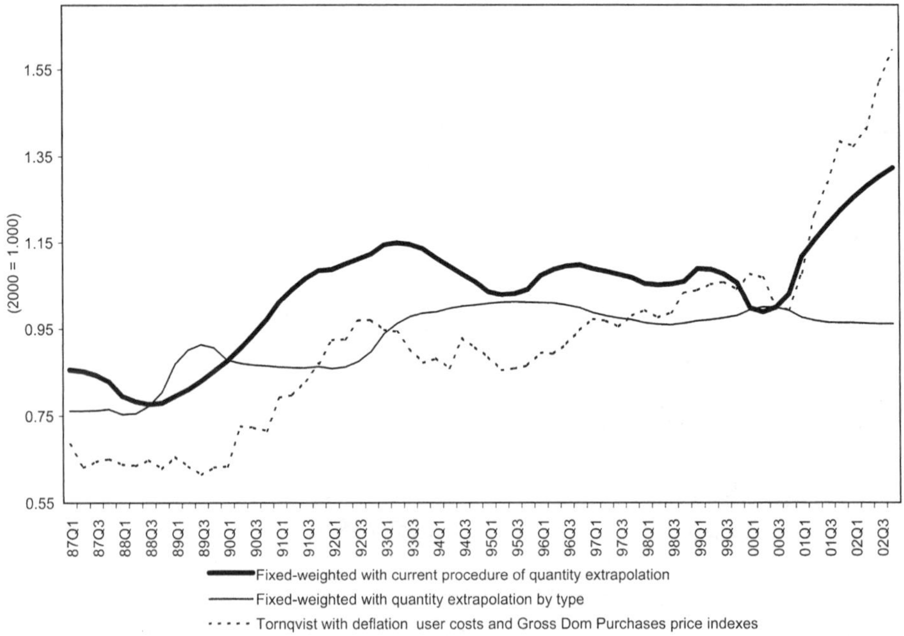


**Fig. 6.14 Comparison of quantity indexes for PCE banks' implicit services**

on the extrapolation by type of service because, as discussed earlier, changes in user cost prices do not flow through to the quantity measures.

Given the differences between the quantity indexes derived implicitly via deflation by the Törnqvist price index and directly computed via extrapolation, it is natural to look at differences in the underlying measurement concept. Deflation is used to measure the quantities of services in most cases because services are generally difficult to count. Measuring services by quantity extrapolation focuses on the observable aspect of the transaction and thus may miss unobservable aspects of the service that is being purchased. For example, an individual is purchasing more deposit services with a deposit of ten thousand dollars than with a deposit of one hundred dollars—more safekeeping and record-keeping are being purchased. In the transaction approach, one would only count the deposit and there would be no recording of the amount deposited. Thus, the growth in deposit services illustrated in figure 6.11 (especially in the late 1990s) does not capture any changes in the amount deposited, which is reflected in the depositor services index in figure 6.13.

## 6.4 Summary and Conclusions

The importance of financial services to personal (household) consumption has grown over time. However, the domain of consumer price indexes generally excludes such services if they involve the future generation of income. This chapter maintains that expenditures on such services ought to be included in current consumption because they are outlays for services that are consumed in the period. For example, brokerage fees are payments for services provided at a point in time and similarly a depositor pays for the implicit services attending a deposit in each period that the deposit is maintained. The difficult operational question is how to measure the current period price of the implicit financial services.

The user cost of money approach has been used in several studies of bank output and price measurement and, most recently, by the BEA in the nominal valuation of bank implicit services. In this chapter the user cost based prices of implicit financial services are used to form a price index for bank implicit services, which can then be included in a financial services price index. To illustrate, a financial services price index is constructed from a set of financial services covered in Personal Consumption Expenditures. It is shown that the quantity of implicit financial services using a user cost price measure can be substantially different from the quantity measured using the current BEA procedures for producing quantity indexes for implicit bank services. Given the differences among the quantity indexes, which one is likely to be the most accurate measure? The user cost price based index has two key advantages over the index under the current procedure. First, it directly relates to the user cost prices of the implicit services and thereby has a direct link to the nominal value of the implicit services. Second, the data are available quarterly—the quantity extrapolations used in the current method and in the alternative type of service method are based on an annual index provided by the BLS. Currently the Bureau of Labor Statistics is developing a user cost based price measure for banking services that will be part of the Producer Price Index. The BEA is also investigating possible improvements in its price index for implicit bank services.

## Appendix

### *Using Unit Value Interest Rates*

Unit values rates are used to compute the interest rate components of the user cost price expressions. Because interest rates reflect rates of inflation, it is useful to show how unit value rates can properly account for inflation.

Consider loans $L$ made by a bank in two periods, 0 and 1. In period 0 let the $r_0L_0$ denote the interest income and let $r_0 = \rho_0$ (that is, the nominal rate in period 0 is equal to the real rate). In period 1 let the interest income be given by $r_1L_1$ with $r_1 = \rho + \pi_1$, where $\pi_1$ denotes the inflationary expectations in period 1.

At the end of period 1, assuming that both loans are still on the books, the balance sheet entry for the amount of loans is $L_0 + L_1$ and the interest income is given by $r_0L_0 + r_1L_1$. Dividing the latter by the former gives the estimate of the interest rate for period 1:

$$\hat{r}_1 = \frac{r_0L_0 + r_1L_1}{L_0 + L_1}$$
$$= r_0\left(\frac{L_0}{L_0 + L_1}\right) + r_1\left(\frac{L_1}{L_0 + L_1}\right).$$

Writing the nominal interest rate in terms of the real rates yields,

$$\hat{r}_1 = \rho\left(\frac{L_0}{L_0 + L_1}\right) + (\rho + \pi_1)\left(\frac{L_1}{L_0 + L_1}\right)$$
$$= \rho + \pi_1\left(\frac{L_1}{L_0 + L_1}\right).$$

The second equality shows that the estimated interest rate is the real rate plus an adjustment for inflationary expectations that is weighted by the share of loans in the first period. Observe that the weights are nominal, which makes sense given that the estimation is of a nominal rate. Also observe that if there were no inflationary expectations in period 1 then the estimated interest rate is the real rate. Generally in the $n$th period,

$$\hat{r}_n = \rho + \sum_{j=1}^{n} \pi_j \left( \frac{L_j}{\sum_{j=0}^{n} L_j} \right).$$

Thus the nominal interest estimate in a period is the real rate and assumed to be constant, plus the weighted average of inflationary expectations in each period.

An analogous computation would hold for the liability interest rates and for the reference rate.

The previous interest rate computation, by definition, provides consistency between income and balance sheet data. Furthermore, the nominal interest rate measure provides a consistent measure of the nominal value of implicit services.

The computation of a price index, however, would require the that loan values shown previously be deflated; the idea follows from the use of the loans as an indicator of the volume of activity.

## References


Alchian, A., and B. Klein. 1973. On a correct measure of inflation. *Journal of Money Credit and Banking* 5 (1): 173–91.

Barnett, W. 1978. The user cost of money. *Economics Letters* 1 (2): 145–49.

———. 1980. Economic monetary aggregates: An application of index number and aggregation theory. *Journal of Econometrics* 14 (1): 11–48.

———. 1995. Exact aggregation under risk. In *Social choice, welfare, and ethics: Proceedings of the eighth International Symposium in Economic Theory and Econometrics,* ed. W. A. Barnett, H. Moulin, M. Salles, and N. J. Schofield, 353–74. Cambridge: Cambridge University Press.

Chen, B., and D. Fixler. 2003. Measuring the services of property-casualty insurance in the NIPAs: Changes in concepts and methods. *Survey of Current Business* 83 (October): 10–26.

Diewert, W. E. 1974. Intertemporal consumer theory and the demand for durables. *Econometrica* 42 (3): 497–516.

———. 1976. Exact and superlative index numbers. *Journal of Econometrics* 4 (2): 115–45.

———. 1978. Superlative index numbers and consistency in aggregation. *Econometrica* 46 (4): 883–900.

Dick, A. 2002. Demand estimation and consumer welfare in the banking industry. Finance and Economic Discussion Series, Federal Reserve Board Discussion Paper no. 2002–58.

Donovan, D. 1978. Modeling the demand for liquid assets: An application to Canada. *IMF Staff Papers* 25 (December): 676–704.

Fixler, D., M. Reinsdorf, and G. Smith. 2003. Measuring the services of commercial

banks in the NIPAs: Changes in concepts and methods. *Survey of Current Business* 83 (9): 33–43.
Fixler, D., and K. D. Zieschang. 1992. User costs, shadow prices, and the real output of banks. In *Output measurement in the service sectors,* ed. Z. Griliches, 219–43. Chicago: University of Chicago Press.
———. 1999. The productivity of the banking sector: Integrating financial and production approaches to measuring financial service output. *The Canadian Journal of Economics* 32 (2): 547–69.
———. 2001. Price indices for financial services. Paper presented at the April 2001 Ottawa Group meeting. 2–6 April, Canberra, Australia.
International Labour Organization. 2004. *Consumer Price Index manual: Theory and practice.* (Draft, chapter 10). Available at: http://www.ilo.org/public/english/bureau/stat/guides/cpi/index.htm.
Kunze, K., M. Jablonski, and M. Sieling. 1998. Measuring output and labor productivity of commercial banks (SIC 602): A transactions-based approach. Paper presented at the Brookings Institution Workshop on Banking Output. 20 November, Washington, DC.
Moulton, B., and E. Seskin. 2003. Preview of the 2003 comprehensive revision of the National Income and Product Accounts: Changes in definitions and classifications. *Survey of Current Business* 83 (June): 17–34.
National Research Council. 2002. *At what price? Conceptualizing and measuring cost of living and price indexes.* Panel on Conceptual, Measurement and Other Statistical Issues in Developing Cost of Living Indexes, ed. C. I. Schultz and C. Mackie. Washington, DC: National Academy Press.
Patinkin, D. 1965. *Money, interest and prices,* 2nd Edition. New York: Harper and Row.
Pollak, R. 1975. The intertemporal cost-of-living index. *Annals of Economic and Social Measurement* 4 (Winter): 179–85.
Schreyer, P., and P. Stauffer. 2002. Financial services in national accounts: Measurement issues and progress. Organization for Economic Cooperation and Development (OECD) Task Force on Financial Services in the National Accounts.
Schreft, S. 2006. How and why do consumers choose their payment method. Working Paper RWP-06-04, Federal Reserve Bank of Kansas City.
Triplett, J. 2000. Hedonic valuation of "Unpriced" banking services: Application to national accounts and Consumer Price Indexes. Unpublished Manuscript, July. Paper presented at NBER Summer Institute. 10 July, Cambridge, MA.
Woolford, K. 2001. Financial services in the Consumer Price Index. Paper presented at the April 2001 Ottawa Group meeting. 2–6 April, Canberra, Australia.

## Comment Susanto Basu

In this chapter, Fixler takes on a very important and very challenging task—thinking hard about the measure of nominal financial sector output, and decomposing that output into a price index and a volume index. This is a long-standing problem in the economics of measurement, made more urgent

Susanto Basu is a professor of economics at Boston College, and a research associate of the National Bureau of Economic Research.

by the growing share of the service sector in most industrialized countries and the importance of the financial sector specifically in the total factor productivity (TFP) acceleration in the United States since 1995.

No method of measuring financial sector prices (and hence real output) has yet commanded a consensus.[1] In fact, there is even disagreement about how to measure *nominal* output in one of the most important financial sectors, namely banking![2] Thus, it is not surprising that I shall propose different answers than Fixler to the questions that he raises. But more important than the specifics of any particular issue is a general contention: in economics, when a conceptual disagreement has lasted a long time with no resolution in sight, it is usually a sign that economic theory has not been applied sufficiently rigorously. The only way to make progress in this area is to start from detailed models of what financial institutions actually do, and the market environment in which they operate. Once that is done, the measurement implications are usually obvious in principle, although the implied measures may be exceedingly difficult to implement in practice.

Although I shall move to theory of this sort, I begin from the simple example of constructing a price index for bank deposit services to fix some ideas. Bank deposits are a good case because it is one where Fixler and I agree on the measure of nominal output. That is, we agree that consumers buy implicitly-priced services from banks in the amount of

$$\frac{\rho - r^D}{1 + \rho} D \equiv p^D D. \tag{1}$$

The notation in equation (1) follows that in the chapter. (Here I follow the chapter and ignore explicit fees; it reintroduces them in section 6.3.) Now if equation (1) defines nominal output, then the temptation is obviously to define $p^D$ as the price and $D$ as the real volume of output. But of course this leads to the uncomfortable realization that the "real" $D$ is in fact nominal. The usual solution is to divide $D$ by some general price index (and multiply $p^D$ by the same price index). But what is the right price index? One might divide by the GDP deflator, on the grounds that it is the most comprehensive, or by the CPI, on the grounds that consumers use bank deposits to buy consumption goods. When issues of this importance are left ambiguous, it is usually a sign that more detailed theorizing is necessary.

Regardless of the deflator used, the upshot is that in the approach that Fixler advocates, real depositor output is taken to be linearly proportional to the stock of deflated balances that people hold in their bank accounts. Given an observed measure of nominal output, this is the only way to justify a $p^D$ of the sort used to construct the price index in the chapter. That is, the

1. See, for example, the exchange between Bosworth, Triplett, and Fixler in Triplett and Bosworth (2004, chapters 5 and 6 and subsequent comment by Fixler).

2. See the contribution by Wang, Basu, and Fernald (chapter 7, this volume).

basic price measurement framework advocated in this chapter rests on the assumption that the *flow* of real financial services, which we can denote $S_t$, is linearly proportional to some measure of the *stock* of real deposit balances:

(2) $$s_t = kD_t,$$

where $k$ is a constant. Thus, even though the focus of Fixler's chapter is on measuring prices, my focus will be on the implied measure of real output. But given an agreed-upon measure of nominal output—mostly true, with a caveat that I discuss at the end of my comments—the two issues are isomorphic.

How realistic is the assumption in equation (2) that is central for the chapter? Before turning to theory, consider an example to build intuition.

Suppose two people keep the same amount of money in their banks. But Bank 1 pays a lower interest rate on deposits, because it offers access to a larger ATM network than does Bank 2. (For simplicity, let us suppose that ATM transactions are the only implicitly-priced depositor services that are provided.) The procedure advocated by Fixler would say unequivocally that Bank 1 charges a higher price than Bank 2. In fact, we see that the issue is one of quality difference in the services provided to depositors, so that the correct, quality-adjusted price charged by Bank 1 may be higher or lower than the price charged by Bank 2.

This sort of issue is clear to advocates of the method that Fixler proposes in this chapter. For example, Fixler and Zieschang (1999) propose ways "quality adjust" the outputs (or equivalently, the prices) of financial firms generally and banks particularly. That is, they propose a modification of the assumption maintained in the present chapter, and allow for a time-varying relationship between services and deposit stocks of the form

(3) $$s_t = k(\mathbf{x}_t)D_t,$$

where $k$ is no longer a constant but a function of a vector of characteristics $\mathbf{x}$. Note that adjustments of this sort, which are necessary to make measurement conform more closely to intuition, are rather ad hoc in terms of the formal theory underlying the measurement of depositor prices as $p^D$, which is Sidrauski's (1967) model of money in the utility function.

If one comes so far, then why not take one extra step, and dispense with the proportionality to $D$ completely? That is, why not say that depositors at both banks are buying access to ATM networks, the flow of service output is the number of ATM transactions, but the quality of the service provided is different across the two banks, which complicates the proper computation of an average price? Conceptually, this would make banking and financial services the same as other personal and professional services, such as hair cuts and legal representation, with the same issues of quality adjustment. The only extra complication would be that consumers are paying implicitly for the services by accepting deposit rates lower than ρ rather than paying explicit fees. But one can figure out the amount of the payment from equation (1)—which continues to hold in the framework I have sketched—and figure out an implicit price deflator by knowing the quantities of nominal and real output. The real output would need to be adjusted for quality, just as haircuts and legal services need to be adjusted for quality, which may be difficult in practice, but is not problematic in principle. (This approach is developed further in Wang and Basu, 2009.)

Why then has the literature on financial output measurement foregone this straightforward approach, which treats financial services as a garden-variety service industry like many others, and hewed to the notion that real output must be proportional to real balances in some manner? The assumption that real financial services are linearly proportional to real financial balances is strong and not very realistic. With the assumption of a fixed $k$ as in equation (2)—the approach adopted in Fixler's current chapter—it can lead to undesirable results where price changes are confounded with quality changes. The answer is that the literature has sought microeconomic foundations for its approach by putting its faith in money-in-the-utility-function models and has assumed that this formulation, which originated as a shortcut, is in fact a structural economic relationship.

The idea of using real balances as a quantity measure and foregone interest as price goes back at least to the classic paper of Sidrauski (1967). He proposed a shortcut to modeling financial services—putting real balances in the utility function:

$$U = U(C_t, M_t), \tag{4}$$

where $C$ is real consumption and $M$ represents real money balances. Normalizing the price of consumption goods to 1, the first-order conditions for optimization are:

$$U_c(C_t, M_t) = \lambda_t,$$

and

$$U_M(C_t, M_t) = \lambda_t(\rho_t - r_t^m).$$

Here $\lambda$ is the marginal utility of wealth, $\rho$ as before is the real interest rate, and $r^m$ is the real return to holding "money"—equal to the negative of the inflation rate in the case of cash, and equal to $r^D$ in the case of bank deposits. Thus, by analogy to consumption, it appears from this formulation that *if* the stock of real balances is the correct measure of real financial service consumption *then* the interest spread is its price. But of course Sidrauski did not prove the "if" part of the proposition—he simply (and rather apologetically) took it for granted.

It was left to Feenstra (1986) to provide a beautiful analysis of the microfoundations of Sidrauski's approach. Feenstra showed that the "money in the utility function" formulation can be justified as an *indirect* utility function if holding "money" helps to economize on the real transactions cost of purchasing consumption goods. He then demonstrated that a number of classic models of the transactions demand for money, including the Baumol-Tobin model, have such a property.

While Feenstra provided a classic analysis of the microfoundations of Sidrauski's approach, he did so in a setting where all transactions technologies are static. But this assumption, while a sensible shortcut for his purposes, does not accord with the evident reality of massive innovation in all aspects of finance. Basu and Wang (2006) investigate this issue. They analyze a growth model where bank deposits (the only form of "money") are used to make transactions. Consumers need to pay a fixed cost intermittently to cash part of their holdings of capital (which they hold in mutual funds) and transfer them to banks as deposits. Banks charge for the costs they incur in clearing transactions by paying a lower-than-market interest rate on bank deposits, exactly as assumed by Fixler. Mutual funds charge explicit fees for each transaction.

In this framework, Basu and Wang show, first, that if the technologies used by *both* banks and mutual funds are constant over time, then the quantity of real bank service output *is* proportional to the stock of real deposits (deflated by the CPI). Thus, there is indeed a set of conditions that validates Fixler's approach in the current chapter. Unfortunately, the necessary conditions are very restrictive. If there is technological progress *either* in banking *or* in the mutual fund industry, the result is broken—there is no longer a fixed proportionality between actual bank services (the number of transactions cleared) and the real deposit balances that consumers hold. This result implies, for example, that the real output measure for financial industries that is implicit in Fixler's approach cannot be used to estimate TFP in finance, since the measure is valid only if such TFP growth is zero. On the other hand, Basu and Wang show that the value of nominal bank services to depositors is still correctly measured as $p^D D$, even when the real output is not proportional to $D$ deflated by some general price index.

Since deposit balances are not, in general, a valid index of real service output, Basu and Wang (2006) propose a method of constructing real output (and thus, given the observed $p^D D$, an implicit price deflator) that is robust to technological change. Conceptually it is very simple—just count the services provided by banks as one would count any traditional good or service output. In the context of their model, this just amounts to counting the number of transactions that banks clear. Inklaar and Wang (2007) show that there are practical difficulties when one tries to implement this approach in real data, but that these difficulties can be overcome. Basu, Inklaar, and Wang (2006) do the same for the measurement of nominal financial output.

As noted earlier, all of these issues of the appropriate measure of real quantities have direct implications for the measurement of prices, which is the subject of Fixler's current chapter.

Finally, this discussion so far has been couched in a nonstochastic framework, where there is no issue of risk. This is appropriate for analyzing bank deposits in the United States, where there is deposit insurance.[3] Wang (2003) and Wang, Basu, and Fernald (chapter 7, this volume) show that when risk is present—for example, in the case of bank loans—the "reference rate" used to construct $p^D$ (the analogue of $r^D$) must be adjusted for risk. Together, these papers—all following from the original work of Wang (2003)—present an alternative to the approach that Fixler exposits in his current chapter. The alternative has firmer roots in theory, and can be implemented in practice. However, it is true that the Wang approach significantly complicates the measurement of nominal financial output, real output, and a financial services price deflator. Thus, I must confess that there are days when I yearn for the simplicity of measurement promised by the approach that Fixler advocates in his current chapter. But unfortunately there is no guarantee that better measures of prices and output in hard-to-measure service industries will also be easier to construct than the current measures.

## References

Basu, S., R. Inklaar, and J. C. Wang. 2006. The value of risk: Measuring the services of U.S. commercial banks. Working Paper, Federal Reserve Bank of Boston.

Basu, S., and J. C. Wang. 2006. Technological progress, "Money" in the utility function, and the "user cost of money." Working Paper, Federal Reserve Bank of Boston.

Feenstra, R. C. 1986. Functional equivalence between liquidity costs and the utility of money. *Journal of Monetary Economics* 17 (2): 271–91.

Fixler, D., and K. D. Zieschang. 1999. The productivity of the banking sector: Integrating financial and production approaches to measuring financial service output. *The Canadian Journal of Economics* 32 (2): 547–69.

Inklaar, R., and J. C. Wang. 2007. Measuring real output in banking. Working Paper, Federal Reserve Bank of Boston.

Sidrauski, M. 1967. Rational choices and patterns of growth in a monetary economy. *American Economic Review* 57: 534–44.

Triplett, J. E., and B. P. Bosworth. 2004. *Productivity in the U.S. services sector: New sources of economic growth.* Washington, DC: Brookings Institution Press.

Wang, J. C. 2003. Loanable funds, risk, and bank service output. Federal Reserve Bank of Boston, Working Paper Series, no. 03-4. Available at: http://www.bos.frb.org/economic/wp/wp2003/wp034.htm.

Wang, J. C., and S. Basu. 2009. Risk bearing, implicit financial services, and specialization in the financial industry. *Price and productivity measurement* (3). Ed. W. E. Diewert, B. M. Balk, D. Fixler, K. J. Fox, and A. O. Nakamura.

3. However, these issues arise even for bank deposits in countries without deposit insurance—for example, Switzerland. And even in the United States, deposits over $100,000 are not insured.

7

# A General Equilibrium Asset-Pricing Approach to the Measurement of Nominal and Real Bank Output

J. Christina Wang, Susanto Basu, and John G. Fernald

In many service industries, measuring real output is a challenge, because it is difficult to measure quality-adjusted prices. In financial services, however, there is not even an agreed upon conceptual basis for measuring *nominal,* let alone *real,* output.[1] This chapter presents a dynamic, stochastic, general equilibrium (DSGE) model in which nominal and real values of bank output—and hence the price deflator—are clearly defined. We use the model to assess the inadequacy of existing national accounting measures, and we derive a theoretically preferred alternative. Our model is a general equilibrium (GE) extension of Wang's (2003a) partial equilibrium framework, and it validates Wang's proposed bank service flow measure.

The biggest challenge for measurement is that banks and other financial service providers often do not charge explicit fees for services. Instead, they charge indirectly by the spread between the interest rates they charge and pay. The *System of National Accounts, 1993* (United Nations et al. 1993; hereafter SNA93) thus recommends measuring these "financial intermediation services indirectly measured" (FISIM) using net interest, defined as "the total property income receivable by financial intermediaries minus

J. Christina Wang is a senior economist at the Federal Reserve Bank of Boston. Susanto Basu is a professor of economics at Boston College and a research associate of the National Bureau of Economic Research. John G. Fernald is vice president of macroeconomic research at the Federal Reserve Bank of San Francisco.

We thank Erwin Diewert, Dennis Fixler, Charles Hulten, Alice Nakamura, Emi Nakamura, Marshall Reinsdorf, Paul Schreyer, Jack Triplett, and Kim Zieschang for helpful discussions, and we thank Felix Momsen for data assistance. The views in this chapter are those of the authors and should not be construed as necessarily reflecting the views of the Board of Governors or anyone else affiliated with the Federal Reserve System.

1. For a recent sample, see chapter 7 in Triplett and Bosworth (2004a), the comment on that chapter by Fixler (2004), and the authors' rejoinder.

their total interest payable, excluding the value of any property income receivable from the investment of their own funds."[2] The so-called user cost approach to banking is taken to be the theoretical basis for measuring nominal output via interest rate margins and for interpreting interest rate spreads as implicit prices for financial services.[3] As a practical matter, the SNA93 approach more or less equates nominal output from FISIM with the net interest income that flows through banks.

Net interest income from lending is the conceptual difference between interest income received and the opportunity cost of funds lent. As currently implemented (e.g., in SNA93), net interest is imputed using the difference between actual lending rates and a riskless interest rate, such as a short-term Treasury rate, which is meant to capture the opportunity cost of funds. However, Wang (2003a) shows that net interest contains not only nominal compensation for bank services but also the return due to the systematic risk of bank loans. This return is part of the opportunity cost of funds, and according to the essence of the user cost framework, it should be excluded from bank output. In modern finance theories of asset pricing, the required rate of return depends on risk. Hence, the user cost of money needs to be adjusted for risk. Wang's (2003a) key contribution is the extension of the user cost approach to a world with risk. This contrasts with the unrealistic riskless framework in the existing literature. Thus, the net interest portion of Wang's service flow measure of nominal bank output can also be characterized as total net income of the opportunity cost of funds, provided this opportunity cost is correctly adjusted for risk. (All agree that explicit fee income received is also part of nominal bank output.)

The GE model here verifies the partial equilibrium conclusion reached by Wang (2003a). As in Wang (2003a), we use a user cost framework in which banks' optimal choice of interest rates must cover the (risk-adjusted) opportunity cost of funds, as well as the cost of implicitly provided services. The primary contribution of our GE model is to endogenize the cost of funds, which Wang (2003a) takes as exogenously given by financial markets.

Like SNA93, the 2003 U.S. National Income and Product Accounts (NIPAs) benchmark revisions allocate the FISIM between borrowers and depositors using a reference rate. The NIPAs impute the nominal value of services to borrowers as the volume of interest-earning assets multiplied by the difference between the (average) lending rate and that reference rate—the user cost of funds. Likewise, it imputes nominal output of services to depositors as the volume of deposits multiplied by the difference between that reference rate and the (average) deposit rate (Fixler, Reinsdorf, and Smith 2003).

2. SNA 1993, paragraph 6.125.

3. See, for example, Fixler and Zeischang (1992). Important contributors to the user cost approach also include Diewert (1974), Barnett (1978), and Hancock (1985).

The challenge is to determine the appropriate reference rate or rates. The NIPAs use a basically risk-free rate for both borrower and depositor services. As in Wang (2003a), however, we show that the risk-free rate is not appropriate for borrowers. Because the cost of funds is risk dependent, the reference rate must incorporate the systematic risk of a bank's loan portfolio. Hence, the imputed value of banks' implicit borrower services *excludes* the risk premium. The premium represents capital income to bank shareholders and uninsured debt holders for bearing the systematic risk on funds used in production *outside* the bank.

A simple example shows the intuition for excluding the risk premium from bank output and illustrates the shortcomings of the NIPAs approach. Consider two otherwise identical borrowers who seek to obtain additional financing in a world with no transactions costs or informational asymmetries; one borrows in the bond market, the other borrows from a bank. The bond-financed firm's expected return equals the risk-free rate plus a risk premium. It is clear that the entire return represents the value added of the borrower.

Now consider the bank-financed firm. To keep things simple, suppose that banks hire *no* labor or capital and produce no services whatsoever. Banks are merely an accounting device that records loans (perhaps funded by bank shareholder equity) to borrowers. They are a perfect substitute for the bond market, so they charge the risk-free interest rate plus the same risk premium paid by the bond-financed firm: by construction, the risk is the same, and in equilibrium, there is no arbitrage. (Note that in equilibrium, bank shareholders are indifferent between buying the bonds or holding shares in the bank.) But NIPAs would attribute positive value added to a bank equal to the risk premium multiplied by the face value of the loan—even though, by assumption, the bank does nothing!

Conceptually, the two firms should be treated symmetrically: they are identical, apart from an arbitrary and (to the firm) irrelevant financing choice. But under NIPAs conventions, they appear to have different value added, inputs of financial services, and productivities. In contrast, the approach we recommend would treat the two firms symmetrically by excluding the risk premium from the bank's nominal financial output—a premium the borrowing firm must pay, regardless of whether it is financed by bonds or bank loans.

Thus, the national accounting measure leads to inconsistency, even in the very simplest of possible models, where banks produce no services that use real resources. Our model, as well as Wang's (2003a), shows that the conceptual inconsistency extends to realistic cases, where banks provide actual services. The NIPAs measure corresponds to the empirically irrelevant special case, when either investors are risk neutral or bank loans have no systematic risk.

Quantitatively, the potential mismeasurement under the current system is large. In 2001, commercial banks in the United States had nominal output of $187 billion,[4] of which half was final consumption and half was intermediate services to businesses. Our theoretical results imply that the measured figures overstate true output; Wang (2003b) suggests that NIPAs banking output measures are about 20 percent too high. This figure reflects both an overestimate of lending services provided to consumers (hence an overstatement of gross domestic product [GDP]) and an overestimate of intermediate services provided to firms (which does not overstate GDP but distorts measures of industry output and productivity).

Similar considerations apply to measuring the output of financial services more generally, so the total NIPAs mismeasurement can be substantial. Furthermore, the distortions affect relative GDP measures across countries. For example, banking services account for 37 percent of Luxembourg's exports, which in turn are 150 percent of GDP. Thus, our work suggests that Luxembourg's GDP could be overstated by about 11 percent—substantial by any measure.

In addition, time variation in risk premia distorts growth rates (Wang 2003b). The distortion is particularly large during transitions such as those taking place now. For example, as banks securitize a growing fraction of their loans, they move the risk premium off their books, even if they continue to provide substantially the same real services (e.g., screening and servicing loans). Several studies find that financial services contributed importantly to the post-1995 U.S. productivity growth revival, so it is important to measure the growth as well as the level of these sectors' outputs correctly.

The model provides additional insights. First, to measure real output (and hence the banking price deflator), one wants to count just the productive activities of banks (such as those related to screening loans), not the (real) amounts of associated financial assets (i.e., the loans). Importantly, the two are not generally in fixed proportion to one another, so one cannot use the volume of loans as a proxy or indicator for the value of services. The model provides conceptual guidance on how to weight different real services in the absence of clearly attributable nominal shares in cost or revenue. Second, being dynamic, our model highlights the potential timing mismatch between when a service is performed (e.g., screening when a loan is originated) and when that service is compensated (with higher interest income over the life of the loan). Third, being stochastic, the model points out that the *expected* nominal output of monitoring (services that are performed during the lifetime of a loan, after it is originated) can be measured from ex ante interest rate spreads, but the *actual* monitoring services produced are difficult to measure from ex post revenue flows. Finally, our service-flow perspective suggests major shortcomings of the book-value output mea-

4. Figures are from Fixler, Reinsdorf, and Smith (2003) and reflect the December 2003 comprehensive revisions.

sures that are universally used in the empirical microeconomic literature on bank efficiencies.

Our use of a DSGE model offers several advantages for studying measurement issues. First, national income accounting imposes a set of adding-up constraints that must hold in the aggregate; GE models impose the same restrictions. By applying actual national income accounting procedures to the variables generated by the model, we can ask whether and under what conditions the objects measured in the national accounts correspond to the economic concepts we want to measure.

Second, and more specific to our current project, the study of banking intrinsically concerns both goods- and asset-market interactions among different agents, which endogenously determine goods prices, quantities, and interest rates. This nexus of economic connections is naturally studied in a GE setting, which ensures the comprehensive consideration of all the key elements of an economy. For example, one needs to specify an environment in which intermediation is necessary: in the model, households cannot or will not lend directly to firms for well-specified informational reasons. We also need to specify how banks then produce real intermediation services and what determines required rates of return on bank assets.

The DSGE model endogenizes the risk premium on loans that fund business capital, as well as the required rate of return on banks' equity. Our model follows Bernanke and Gertler (1989) and Bernanke, Gertler, and Gilchrist (1999), among others, but it explicitly models the screening and monitoring technology of financial intermediaries, which these authors use to resolve asymmetric information problems in investment. The model highlights the proper measurement of bank service output in both nominal and real terms.

We abstract from some activities banks undertake (mainly transactions services to depositors), as well as from realistic complications (e.g., deposit insurance and taxes). These abstractions, which could be incorporated, are unlikely to interact in important ways with the issues we address here. For example, our approach extends naturally to valuing activities by banks other than making loans and taking deposits, such as underwriting derivatives contracts and other exotic financial instruments; we present one such example. Thus, we begin the process of bringing measurement into line with the new roles that banks play in modern economies, as discussed, for example, by Allen and Santomero (1998, 1999).

One might worry that results from our bare-bones model do not apply to the far more complex real world. But our model provides a controlled setting, where we know exactly what interactions take place and what outcomes result. Even in this relatively simple setting, current methods of measuring nominal and real bank output generate inconsistent results that can be economically substantial. It is implausible that these methods will magically succeed in the far more complex world.

The chapter has four main sections. Sections 7.1 and 7.2 present the basic setup of the model with minimal technicality to build intuition for the economic reasoning behind our conclusions. (The rigorous solution of the model is included in the appendix.) Section 7.1 solves the model with symmetric information between borrowers and lenders and uses this simple setup to show by example the flaws in existing proposals for measuring bank output. Section 7.2 introduces asymmetric information and assumes that banks and rating agencies have a technological advantage in resolving such asymmetries. We derive the correct, model-based measure of bank output in this setting, where financial institutions provide real services. Section 7.3 discusses implications of the model for measuring nominal and real financial sector output. Section 7.4 discusses extensions, and section 7.5 concludes and suggests priorities for future research and data collection.

## 7.1 The Model with Symmetric Information

### 7.1.1 Overview

Our model has three groups of agents: households, who supply labor and who ultimately own the economy's capital; entrepreneurs, who hire workers and buy capital to operate projects; and competitive financial institutions (banks and rating agencies), which resolve information problems between the owners and the final users of capital. It also has a bond market in which entrepreneurs can issue corporate debt.

First, households are the only savers in this economy and thus are the ultimate owners of all capital. Their preferences determine the risk premium on all financial assets in the economy, and their accumulated saving determines the amount of capital available for entrepreneurs to rent in a given period.

Second, entrepreneurs operate projects that produce the economy's final output. There is only one homogeneous final good, sold in a competitive market, that can be consumed or invested. Entrepreneurs' projects differ from one another because the entrepreneurs differ in their ability levels (or equivalently, in the intrinsic productivity of their projects). The technology for producing final goods in any project has constant returns to scale. Thus, without asymmetric information, the social optimum would be to give all the capital to the most efficient project. But we assume that due to asymmetric information problems, entrepreneurs face a supply curve for funds that is convex in the amount borrowed.[5] We also assume that entrepreneurs are born without wealth—they are the proverbial impoverished geniuses,

5. Given that all entrepreneurs are borrowing without collateral, this seems quite realistic. Our specific modeling assumption is that the cost of screening is convex in the size of the project, but other assumptions—such as leveraging each entrepreneur's net worth with debt—would also lead to this result. See Bernanke, Gertler, and Gilchrist (1999).

whose heads are full of ideas but whose purses hold only air—so that one way or another, they will need to obtain funds from households.

The focus of this chapter is on how the entrepreneurs obtain the funds for investment from households and on the role of financial intermediaries in the process. A large literature on financial intermediation explains (in partial equilibrium) financial institutions' role as being to resolve informational asymmetries between the ultimate suppliers of funds (i.e., the households in our model) and the users of funds (i.e., the entrepreneurs who borrow to buy capital and produce). We incorporate this result into our general equilibrium model.[6]

We consider both types of information asymmetry—hidden information and hidden actions. Households face adverse selection ex ante as they try to select projects to finance: they know less about the projects (e.g., default probabilities under various economic conditions) than the entrepreneurs, who have an incentive to understate the risk of their projects. Moral hazard arises ex post, as savers cannot perfectly observe borrowers' actions (e.g., diverting project revenue for their own consumption).

Thus, the third group of actors in our model are institutions such as banks that exist (in the model and largely in practice) to mitigate these informational problems.[7] We focus on two specific services they provide: (a) screening to lessen (in our model, to eliminate) entrepreneurs' private information about the viability of their projects and (b) monitoring project outcomes (e.g., auditing after a default) to discover entrepreneurs' hidden actions.[8] To conduct screening and monitoring, intermediaries engage in a production process that uses real resources of labor, capital, and an underlying technology. The production process is qualitatively similar to producing other information services, such as consulting and data processing.[9]

We call the financial intermediaries banks mainly for convenience, although the functions they perform have traditionally been central to the activities of commercial banks. But the analysis is general, as we will show

6. Most general equilibrium models of growth or business cycles abstract from this issue: implicitly, households own and operate the firms directly, so there are no principal-agent problems.

7. Financial institutions prevent market breakdown (such as in Akerlof [1970]) but cannot eliminate deadweight loss. Another major function of banks is to provide services to depositors, as discussed in the introduction. But we omit them from the formal model, because their measurement is less controversial and has no bearing on our conclusion about how to treat risk in measuring lending services. Yet, we note practical measurement issues about them in section 7.3.

8. Many studies, all partial equilibrium, analyze the nature and operation of financial intermediaries. See, for example, Leland and Pyle (1977), who model banks' role as resolving ex ante adverse selection in lending; Diamond (1984) studies delegated monitoring through banks; Ramakrishnan and Thakor (1984) look at nondepository institutions.

9. Only a handful of studies analyze the effects of financial intermediaries on real activities in a general equilibrium framework. None of them, however, consider explicitly the issue of financial intermediaries' output associated with the process of screening and monitoring, nor the properties of the screening and monitoring technology.

that loans subject to default are equivalent to a risk-free bond plus a put option. So, our analysis also applies to implicit bank services associated with other financial instruments, as well as to other types of intermediaries, such as rating agencies and finance companies. We assume that banks and other financial service providers are owned by households and are not subject to informational asymmetries with respect to households.[10]

As suppliers of funds, households demand an expected rate of return, commensurate with the systematic risk of their assets. This is of course true in any reasonable model with investor risk aversion, regardless of whether there are informational asymmetries. Banks must ensure that the interest rate charged compensates their owners, the households, with the risk-adjusted return in expectation. Banks must also ensure that they charge explicit or implicit fees to cover the costs incurred by screening and monitoring.

The primary focus of this chapter is on how to correctly measure the nominal and real service output provided by these banks, when the services are not charged explicitly, but rather are charged implicitly in the form of higher interest rates. Hence, we need to detail the nature of the contract between entrepreneurs and banks, because that determines the interest rates banks charge. Indeed, most of the complexity in the formal model in the appendix comes from the difficulty of solving for the interest rate charged under the optimal debt contract and from decomposing total interest income into a compensation for bank services—screening and monitoring—and a risk-adjusted return for the capital that households channel to firms through the bank. The payoff from this complexity is that the model provides definite insights on key measurement issues.

For the most part, we try to specify the incentives and preferences of the three groups of agents in a simple way in order to focus on the complex interactions among the agents. We now summarize the key elements of the incentives and preferences of each agent to give the reader a working knowledge of the economic environment. We then derive the key first-order conditions for the optimal pricing of risky assets, which must hold in any equilibrium, to draw implications from the model that are crucial for measurement purposes. At the end of this section, the reader may proceed to the detailed discussion of the model found in the appendix or may proceed to section 7.3 to study the implications for measurement.

### 7.1.2 Households

We assume households are infinitely lived and risk averse. For most of the chapter, we assume that households can invest their wealth only through a financial intermediary, because they lack the ability to resolve information asymmetries with entrepreneurs directly. In contrast, households own

10. We could extend our model to allow for this two-tier information asymmetry at the cost of considerable added complexity. We conjecture, however, that our qualitative results would be unaffected by this change.

and have no informational problems with respect to the intermediaries. All households are identical, and they maximize the expected present value of lifetime utility—expressed here in terms of a representative household:

(1) $$E_t\left[\sum_{s=0}^{\infty}\rho^s V(C^H_{t+s},1-N)\right],$$

subject to the budget constraint:

(2) $$C^H_t = W_t N_t + \prod_t + \tilde{R}^H_{t+1} X_t - X_{t+1}.$$

The variable $C^H_t$ is the household's consumption, $N_t$ is its labor supply, and $\rho$ is the discount factor. The variable $E_t(.)$ is the expectation, given the information set at time $t$. We assume that the utility function $V(.)$ is concave and that $V'(0) = \infty$. The variable $W_t$ is the wage rate, $X_t$ is the household's total assets (equal to the capital stock in equilibrium), and $\Pi_t$ is pure economic profit received from ownership of financial intermediaries (equal to zero in equilibrium because we assume that this sector is competitive). The variable $\tilde{R}^H_{t+1}$ is the ex post gross return on the household's asset portfolio (real capital, lent to various agents to enable production in the economy). Corresponding to the ex post return is an expected return—the required rate of return on risky assets, which we denote $R^H_{t+1}$. This is a key interest rate in the following sections, so we discuss it further.

We define the intertemporal pricing kernel (also called the stochastic discount factor), $m_{t+1}$, as

(3) $$m_{t+1} \equiv \frac{\rho V_c(C^H_{t+1}, 1 - N_{t+1})}{V_c(C^H_t, 1 - N_t)},$$

where $V_C$ is the partial derivative of utility with respect to consumption. In this notation, the Euler equation for consumption (which is also a basic asset-pricing equation in the consumption capital asset-pricing model [CCAPM]) is:

(4) $$E_t(m_{t+1}\tilde{R}^H_{t+1}) = 1.$$

Now suppose a one-period asset, whose return is risk free because it is known in advance. Clearly, for this asset, the rate of return $R^f_{t+1}$ satisfies $E_t(m_{t+1}R^f_{t+1}) = R^f_{t+1}E_t(m_{t+1}) = 1$. So,

(5) $$R^f_{t+1} = \frac{1}{E_t(m_{t+1})}.$$

As is standard in a CCAPM, the Euler equation (3) allows us to derive the risk-free rate, even if no such asset exists—which is the case in our economy, where the only asset is risky capital.[11]

11. For more discussion, see chapter 2 in Cochrane (2001).

From equations (4) and (5), the gross required (expected) rate of return on the risky asset, $R^H_{t+1}$, is:

(6) $$R^H_{t+1} \equiv E_t(\tilde{R}^H_{t+1}) = R^f_{t+1}[1 - \mathrm{cov}_t(m_{t+1}, \tilde{R}^H_{t+1})],$$

where $\mathrm{cov}_t$ is the covariance, conditional on the information set at time $t$. The risk premium then equals

$$R^H_{t+1} - R^f_{t+1} = -R^f_{t+1}\,\mathrm{cov}_t(m_{t+1}, \tilde{R}^H_{t+1}).$$

Note that when $R^H_{t+1}$ is the *required* rate of return on debt (e.g., loans) subject to the risk of borrower default, there is a subtle but important conceptual difference between $R^H_{t+1}$ and the interest rate (the so-called yield for corporate bonds) that is *charged* on loans—the rate that a borrower must pay if not in default. To illustrate in a simple example, suppose there is probability $p$ that a borrower will pay the interest rate charged (call it $R_{t+1}$) and probability $(1 - p)$ otherwise, in which case lenders get nothing. Then, $R_{t+1}$ must satisfy

$$p \cdot R_{t+1} + (1 - p) \cdot 0 = R^H_{t+1} \quad \Rightarrow \quad R_{t+1} = \frac{R^H_{t+1}}{p}.$$

So, $R_{t+1}$ exceeds the required return $R^H_{t+1}$; the margin $R_{t+1} - R^H_{t+1}$ is the so-called default premium. Thus, $R_{t+1}$ differs from the risk-free rate for two reasons. First, there is the default premium. The borrower repays less to nothing in bad states of the world, so he must pay more in good states to ensure an adequate average return. Second, there is a risk premium, as previously shown. The risk premium exists if the probability of default is correlated with consumption (or more precisely, with the marginal utility of consumption). If defaults occur when consumption is already low, then they are particularly costly in utility terms. Thus, the consumer requires an extra return, on average, to compensate for bearing this systematic, nondiversifiable risk.

In addition to the intertemporal Euler equation, consumer optimization requires a static trade-off between consumption and leisure within a period:

(7) $$W_t V_C(C^H_t, 1 - N_t) = -V_N(C^H_t, 1 - N_t).$$

In equilibrium, households' assets equal the total capital stock of the economy: $X_t = K_t$. The capital stock evolves in the usual way:

$$K_{t+1} = (1 - \delta)K_t + I_t.$$

Capital is used by intermediaries to produce real financial services or is rented by firms for production.[12]

12. Because we have assumed identical households, we abstract from lending among households (e.g., home mortgages).

### 7.1.3 Entrepreneurs

Each entrepreneur owns and manages a nonfinancial firm that invests in one project, producing the single homogeneous final good and selling it in a perfectly competitive market. So entrepreneur, firm, and project are all equivalent and interchangeable in this model. Entrepreneurs are a set of agents, distinct from households in that each lives for only two periods, which coincides with the duration of a project. Thus, there are two overlapping generations of entrepreneurs in each period. The number of entrepreneurs who are born and die each period is constant, so the fraction of entrepreneurs is constant in the total population of agents. The reason for having short-lived entrepreneurs in the economy is to create a need for external financing and thus the screening and monitoring by financial intermediaries. Long-lived entrepreneurs could accumulate enough assets to self-finance all investment, without borrowing from households. In addition, by having each borrower interact with lenders only once, we avoid complex supergame Nash equilibria, where entrepreneurs try to develop a reputation for being good risks in order to obtain better terms from lenders.

We assume that entrepreneurs, like households, are risk averse.[13] But we abstract from the issue of risk sharing and assume that the sole income an entrepreneur receives is the residual project return, if any, net of debt repayment.[14] That also means entrepreneurs have no initial endowment.[15] In choosing project size in the first period, entrepreneurs seek to maximize their expected utility from consumption in the second period, which is the only period in which they consume. Thus, the utility of entrepreneur $i$ born at time $t$ is

$$U(C_{t+1}^{E,i}), \tag{8}$$

where $U' > 0$, $U'' < 0$, and $U(0) = 0$. We denote entrepreneurs' aggregate consumption by $C_t^E$, which is the sum over $i$ of $C_t^{E,i}$.

Firms differ only in their exogenous technology parameters. We denote

13. If entrepreneurs were risk neutral, they would insure the households against all aggregate shocks, leading to a degenerate—and counterfactual—outcome, where lenders of funds would face no aggregate risk.

14. In fact, this model implicitly allows for the sharing of project-specific risk (i.e., $z^i$) across entrepreneurs (e.g., through a mutual insurance contract covering all entrepreneurs), as all the results would remain qualitatively the same. The model assumes that there is no risk sharing between entrepreneurs and households, because the only contract that lenders offer borrowers is a standard debt contract. Given our desire to study banks, this assumption is realistic.

15. The assumption of zero endowment is mainly to simplify the analysis. Introducing partial internal funds (e.g., with entrepreneurs' own labor income) affects none of the model's conclusions. One potential problem with zero internal funds is that it gives entrepreneurs incentive to take excessive risk (i.e., adopting projects with a high payoff when successful but possibly a negative net present value), but we rule out such cases by assumption. The usual principal-agent problem between shareholders and managers does not arise here because entrepreneurs are the owners-operators.

the parameter $A^i_{t+1}$ for a firm $i$ created in period $t$, because the owner produces in the second period—$t + 1$. We assume that $A^i_{t+1} = z^i A_{t+1}$, where $A_{t+1}$ is the stochastic aggregate technology level in period $t + 1$, and $z^i$ is the idiosyncratic productivity level of $i$, drawn at time $t$ when the owner is born. The variable $z^i$ is assumed to be independently and identically distributed across firms and time, with bounded support, and independent of $A_{t+1}$, with $E(z^i) = 1$. Conditional on $z^i$, the firm borrows to buy capital from the households at the end of period $t$. In keeping with our desire to study banking operation in detail, we assume that lenders offer borrowers a standard debt contract. (We discuss the borrowing process, first under symmetric information and then under asymmetric information, in the next several subsections.)

The aggregate technology level ($A_{t+1}$) is revealed at the start of period $t + 1$, and it determines $A^i_{t+1}(= z^i A_{t+1})$. But because $A_{t+1}$ is unknown when the capital purchase decision is made, there is a risk involved for both the borrower and the lender. Conditional on $A^i_{t+1}$ and the *precommitted* level of capital input, the firm hires the optimal amount of labor at the going wage of time ($t + 1$) and produces the final good. Entrepreneurs first pay their workers, then pay the agreed upon interest to households (as well as return the loan principal, the value of the stock of capital rented for production), and then consume all the output leftover.

If a bad realization of $A_{t+1}$ leaves an entrepreneur unable to cover the gross interest on his borrowed funds, he declares bankruptcy. The lenders (households) seize all of the assets and output of the firm leftover after paying the workers, which will be shown to be less than what the lenders are owed and expect to consume. Entrepreneurs are left with zero consumption—less than what they expected as well. The risk to both borrowers and lenders is driven by the aggregate uncertainty of the stochastic technology, $A$.

### 7.1.4 Equilibrium with Symmetric Information

In order to make an important point about the SNA93 method for measuring nominal bank output, we first consider a case where households can costlessly observe all firms' idiosyncratic productivity, $z^i$.

We assume that the production function of each potential project has constant returns to scale (CRS):

(9) $$Y^i_t = A_t z^i (K^i_t)^{\alpha} (N^i_t)^{1-\alpha}.$$

Given CRS production, households will want to lend all their capital only to the entrepreneur with the highest level of $z$—or to paraphrase in market terms, the entrepreneur with the highest productivity will be willing and able to outbid all the others and to hire all the capital in the economy. (We assume that he or she will act competitively, taking prices as given, rather than act as a monopolist or monopsonist.)

We define $\bar{z} = \max_i\{z_i\}$.[16] Then, the economy's aggregate production function will be (that of $\bar{z}$):

$$Y_t = A_t \bar{z} K_t^{\alpha} N_t^{1-\alpha}.$$

The entrepreneur with the $\bar{z}$ level of productivity will hire capital at time $t$ to maximize

$$(10) \qquad E_t U\{\max[A_{t+1}\bar{z}K_{t+1}^{\alpha}N_{t+1}^{1-\alpha} - (R_{t+1} - 1 + \delta)K_{t+1} - W_{t+1}N_{t+1}, 0]\}.$$

The expression in equation (10) indicates that the entrepreneur gets either the residual profits from his project if he is not bankrupt or gets nothing if he has to declare bankruptcy.

The labor choice will be based on the realization of $A_{t+1}$ and the market wage and will be

$$(11) \qquad N_{t+1} = \left[\frac{(1-\alpha)\bar{z}A_{t+1}}{W_{t+1}}\right]^{1/\alpha} K_{t+1}.$$

Production, capital and labor payments, and consumption will take place as outlined in the previous subsection. Note that producing at the highest available level of $z$ does not mean that bankruptcy will never take place or even that it will necessarily be less likely. Ceteris paribus, a higher expected productivity of capital raises the expected return $R_{t+1}^H$ but does not eliminate the possibility of bankruptcy conditional on that higher-required return.[17] Thus, debt will continue to carry a risk premium relative to the risk-free rate.

The national income accounts identity in this economy is

$$Y_t = C_t^H + C_t^E + I_t.$$

### 7.1.5 The Bank That Does Nothing

There is no bank in the economy summarized in the previous subsection, nor is there any need for one. Households lend directly to firms at a required rate of return $R_{t+1}^H$. Suppose, however, a bank is formed simply as an accounting device. Households transfer their capital stock to banks, and in return, they own bank equity. The bank rents the capital to the single most productive firm at the competitive market price.

Because households see through the veil of the bank to the underlying

16. The maximum is finite because we have assumed the $z$ has a bounded support.

17. Let us assume, as in section 7.2, that a continuum of entrepreneurs is born every period, so we are guaranteed that $\bar{z}$ is always the upper end of the support of $z_i$. Then, all that happens by choosing the most productive firm every period is that the mean level of technology is higher than if we chose any other firm (e.g., the average firm). But nothing in our derivations turns on the mean of $A$; it is simply a scaling factor for the overall size of the economy, which is irrelevant for considering the probability of bankruptcy.

assets the bank holds—risky debt issued by the entrepreneur—they will demand the same return (i.e., $R^H_{t+1}$) on bank equity as they did on the debt in the economy without a bank. Because the bank acts competitively (and thus makes zero profit), it will lend the funds at marginal cost (expected return of $R^H_{t+1}$, hence a contractual interest rate of $R_{t+1}$) to the firm, which will then face the same cost of capital as before.

However, applying the SNA93 calculation for FISIM to this model economy, the value added of bank, effected via book entries of the capital transfer (the only sign of the bank's existence here), would be

$$(R^H_t - R^f_t)K_t.$$

The variable $K_t$ is the value of bank assets, as well as the economy-wide capital stock. Thus, by using the risk-free rate as the opportunity cost of funds instead of the correct risk-adjusted interest rate, the current procedure attributes positive value added to the bank that in fact produces nothing.[18]

At the same time, from the expenditure side, the value of national income will be unchanged—still equal to $Y_t$—because the bank output (if any) is used as an intermediate input of service by firms producing the final good.[19] But industry values added are mismeasured: for a given aggregate output, the productive sector has to have lower value added in order to offset the value added incorrectly attributed to the banking industry. Clearly, the production sector's true value added is all of $Y_t$, but it will be measured, incorrectly, as:

$$Y_t - (R^H_t - R^f_t)K_t.$$

Thus, the general lesson from this example is that whenever banks make loans that incur aggregate risk (i.e., risk that cannot be diversified away), the current national accounting approach attributes too much of aggregate value added to the banking industry and too little to the firms that borrow from banks. This basic insight carries over to the more realistic cases next, where banks do in fact produce real services.

We shall also argue later that our simplifying assumption of a fully equity-funded bank is completely unessential to the result. The reason is that in our setting, the theorem of Modigliani and Miller (1958; hereafter MM) applies to banks. The MM theorem proves that a firm's cost of capital is independent of its capital structure. Thus, the bank that does nothing can finance itself by issuing debt (taking deposits) as well as equity, without

18. Financial intermediation services indirectly measured (FISIM) also impute a second piece of bank output—depositor services. But because bank deposits are zero in our model, FISIM would correctly calculate this component of output to be zero.

19. Mismeasuring banking output would distort GDP if banks' output is used as a final good (e.g., lending and depository services to consumers, or perhaps more importantly, net exports).

changing the previous result in the slightest, either qualitatively or quantitatively.[20]

Even in more realistic settings, the lesson in this subsection is directly relevant for one issue in the measurement of bank output. Banks buy and passively hold risky market assets, as in the example here. Even though banks typically hold assets with relatively low risk, such assets (e.g., high-grade corporate bonds) still offer rates of return that exceed the risk-free rate, sometimes by a nontrivial margin. Whenever a bank holds market securities that offer an average return higher than the current reference rate, it creates a cash flow—the difference between the securities' return and the safe return, multiplied by the market value of the securities held—that the current procedure improperly classifies as bank output.

## 7.2 Asymmetric Information and a Financial Sector That Produces Real Services

### 7.2.1 Resolving Asymmetric Information I: Nonbank Financial Institutions

Now we assume, more realistically, that information is in fact asymmetric. Entrepreneurs know their idiosyncratic productivity and actual output, but households cannot observe them directly. In this case, as we know from Akerlof (1970), the financial market will become less efficient and may break down altogether.

We introduce two new institutions into our model. The first is a rating agency, which screens potential borrowers and monitors those who default to alleviate the asymmetric information problems. The other is a bond market; that is, a portfolio of corporate debt. The two combined fulfill the function of channeling funds from households to entrepreneurs so that the latter can invest. Both institutions have real-world counterparts, which will be important when we turn to our model's implications for output measurement.

The purpose of introducing these two new institutions will become clear in the next subsection when we compare them with banks. There, we will show that a bank can be decomposed into a rating agency plus a portfolio of corporate debt, and the real output of banks—informational services—is equivalent to the output of the agency alone. Thus, it makes sense to understand the two pieces individually before studying the sum of the two. Understanding the determination of bond market interest rates is particularly

20. This is assuming there is no deposit insurance. See Wang (2003a) for a full treatment of banks' capital structure with risk and deposit insurance. Of course, in the real world, taxes and transactions costs break the pure irrelevance result of Modigliani-Miller. But the basic lesson—that the reference rate must take risk into account—is unaffected by these realistic but extraneous considerations.

important when we discuss measurement, because we shall argue that corporate debt with the same risk-return characteristics as bank loans provides the appropriate risk-adjusted reference rate for measuring bank output.

We discuss rating agencies first. These are institutions with specialized technology for assessing the quality (i.e., productivity) of prospective projects, and they are also able to assess the value of assets if a firm goes bankrupt. Thus, these institutions are similar to the rating agencies found in the real world, such as Moody's and Standard and Poor's, which not only rate new issues of corporate bonds but also monitor old issues.

The technology of each rating agency for screening ($S$) and monitoring ($M$) is as follows:

$$Y_t^{JA} = A_t^J (K_t^{JA})^{\beta^J} (N_t^{JA})^{1-\beta^J},\ J = M \text{ or } S. \tag{12}$$

We use the superscript $A$ to denote prices and output of the agency. The variables $K_t^{JA}$ and $N_t^{JA}$ are the capital and labor, respectively, used in the two activities. The variables $A_t^M$ and $A_t^S$ differ when the pace of technological progress differs between the two activities. Difference between output elasticities of capital $\beta^M$ and $\beta^S$ means that neither kind of task can be accomplished by simply scaling the production process of the other task.

We assume there are many agencies in a competitive market, so the price of their services equals the marginal cost of production. The representative rating agency solves the following value maximization problem:

$$E_0\left[\sum_{t=0}^{\infty}\left(\prod_{t=0}^{t} R_t^{SV}\right)^{-1}(f_s^{SA}Y_t^{SA} + f_t^{MA}Y_t^{MA} - W_t N_t^A - I_t^A)\right], \tag{13}$$

$$Y_t^{SA} = A_t^S (K_t^{SA})^{\beta^S} (N_t^{SA})^{1-\beta^S}, \tag{14}$$

$$Y_t^{MA} = A_t^M (K_t^{MA})^{\beta^M} (N_t^{MA})^{1-\beta^M},\ \text{and}\ Y_0^{MA} = 0, \tag{15}$$

$$N_t^A = N_t^{SA} + N_t^{MA},\ \text{and}\ K_t^A = K_t^{SA} + K_t^{MA}, \tag{16}$$

$$K_{t+1}^A = K_t^A (1 - \delta) + I_t^A. \tag{17}$$

In equation (13), $Y_t^{SA}$ and $Y_t^{MA}$ are the rating agency's respective output of screening and monitoring services. The variables $f_t^S$ and $f_t^M$ are the corresponding prices (mnemonic: *f*ees), and as assumed, are equal to the respective marginal cost. The variable $W_t$ is the real wage rate, and $N_t^A$ is the agency's total labor input. Equations (14) and (15) are the production functions for screening and monitoring, respectively, with the inputs defined as in equation (12). Total labor and capital inputs are given in equation (16), and equation (17) describes the law of motion for the agency's total capital.

The agency is fully equity funded. Thus, the discount rate for the agency's value maximization problem (i.e., $R_t^{SV}$ [$SV$ standing for services]) is exactly its shareholders' required rate of return on equity. The variable $R_t^{SV}$, analogous to $R_{t+1}^H$ in equation (6), thus is determined by the systematic risk of the agency's entire cash flow. According to the pricing equation (6), and equivalently equation (4), $R_t^{SV}$ equals

$$(18)\quad R_{t+1}^{SV} = R_{t+1}^{f}\left\{1 - \text{cov}_t\left[m_{t+1}, \frac{f_{t+1}^{SA}Y_{t+1}^{SA} + f_{t+1}^{MA}Y_{t+1}^{MA} - W_{t+1}N_{t+1}^{A} + (1-\delta)K_{t+1}^{A}}{K_{t+1}^{A}}\right]\right\}.$$

The denominator ($K_{t+1}^A$) in the covariance is the agency's capital used in production at time $t + 1$, funded by its shareholders at time $t$. The numerator is the ex post return on that capital, consisting of its operating profits (revenue minus labor costs), plus the return of the depreciated capital lent by the stockholders at time $t$.[21]

Even though the agency is paid contemporaneously for its services, the fact that it must choose its capital stock a period in advance creates uncertainty about the cash flow accruing to the owners of its capital. This uncertainty arises fundamentally because the demand for screening and monitoring is random, driven by the stochastic process for aggregate technology, $A_{t+1}$. Thus, the implicit rental rate of physical capital in period $t$ for this agency is ($R_t^{SV} - 1 + \delta$),[22] where $R_t^{SV}$ will generally differ from the risk-free rate.

Because a rating agency is of little use unless one can borrow on the basis of a favorable rating, we assume that a firm can issue bonds of the appropriate interest rate in the bond market once it is rated. That is, once an agency finishes screening a firm's project, it issues a certificate that reveals the project's type (i.e., $z^i$). Armed with this certificate, firms sell bonds to households in the market, offering contractual rates of interest $R_{t+1}^i$ that vary according to each firm's risk rating. The variable $R_{t+1}^i$ depends on households' required rate of return on risky debt, but $R_{t+1}^i$ is not the required return per se. The two differ by the default premium, as discussed in subsection 7.1.2. (Determining the appropriate interest rate to charge an entrepreneur of type $i$ is a complex calculation, in part because the probability of default is endogenous to the interest rate charged. We thus defer this derivation to the appendix.)

There is an additional complication: because entrepreneurs are born without wealth, they are unable to pay their screening fees up front. Instead, they must borrow the fee from the bond market, in addition to the capital they plan to use for production next period, and must dash back to the rating agency within the period to pay the fee they owe. In the second period, they must pay the bondholders a gross return on the borrowed productive capital, plus a same return on the fee that was borrowed to pay the agency.

21. The payoff to the shareholder depends, of course, on the marginal product of capital. The assumption of constant-returns, Cobb-Douglas production functions allows us to express the result in terms of the more intuitive average return to capital. Note that the capital return in equation (18) is actually an average of the marginal revenue products of capital in screening and monitoring, with the weights being the share of capital devoted to each activity.

22. Recall that all $R$ variables are gross interest rates, so the net interest rate $r = R - 1$.

In the second period of his or her life, after his or her productivity is determined by the realization of $A_{t+1}$, an entrepreneur may approach his or her bondholders and inform them that his or her project was unproductive and that he or she is unable to repay his or her debt with interest. The households cannot assess the validity of this claim directly. Instead, they must engage the services of the rating agency to value the firm (its output plus residual capital). The agency charges a fee equal to its marginal cost, as determined by the maximization problem in equations (13) through (17). We assume that the agency can assess the value of the firm perfectly. Whenever a rating agency's services are engaged, the bondholders get to keep the entire value of the project after paying the agency its monitoring fee.[23] The entrepreneur gets nothing. Under these circumstances, the entrepreneur always tells the truth and only claims to be bankrupt when that is in fact the case.

Note that in this asymmetric information environment, entrepreneurs require additional inputs of real financial services from the agencies to obtain capital. The production function for gross output for a firm of type $i$ is still given by equation (9). But now, entrepreneurs have two additional costs. In the first period, when they borrow capital, they must buy certain units of certification services. The amount of screening varies with the size of the project (see the appendix for a detailed discussion of the size dependence of these information processing costs). A project of size $K^i_{t+1}$ needs $\upsilon^S_t(K^i_{t+1})$ units of screening services. Then, in the second period, a firm is required to pay for $Z^M_{t+1}\upsilon^M_t(K^i_{t+1})$ units of monitoring services, where $Z^M$ equals one if the firm defaults and equals zero otherwise. Functions $\upsilon^S(.)$ and $\upsilon^M(.)$ determine how many units of screening, and possibly monitoring, are needed for a project of size $K^i$. Either $\upsilon^S(.)$ or $\upsilon^M(.)$ is strictly convex, and this effectively leads firms to have diminishing returns to scale.[24] Thus, it is no longer optimal to put all the capital at the most productive firm, and the equilibrium involves production by a strictly positive measure of firms.

Given these two additional costs, firm $i$ producing in period $t + 1$ maximizes

$$E_t U\{\max[A_{t+1}z^i(K^i_{t+1})^{\alpha}(N^i_{t+1})^{1-\alpha} - (R^i_{t+1} + \delta)K^i_{t+1} - W_{t+1}N^i_{t+1} \\ - \upsilon^S_t(K^i_{t+1}) - Z^M_{t+1}\upsilon^M_t(K^i_{t+1}), 0]\}.$$

The variable $R^i_{t+1}$ is the contractual interest rate appropriate for a project of type $i$—the analogue to the full information contractual rate for the highest productivity project in equation (10). As in the situation with perfect information, either the entrepreneur gets positive residual profits, or he or she declares bankruptcy and gets nothing.

23. We assume that a project always has a *gross* return large enough to pay the fee. This assumption seems reasonable—even Enron's bankruptcy value was high enough to pay similar costs (amounting to over one billion dollars).

24. A convex cost of capital is needed to obtain finite optimal project scale; we discuss this issue further in the appendix.

We define $\tilde{R}^{Ki}_{t+1}$ as the ex post gross return on capital for the project. It is the project's total output net of labor cost and depreciation, $(\tilde{R}^{Ki}_{t+1} - 1)K^i_{t+1} = Y^i_{t+1} - W_{t+1}N^{i*}_{t+1} - \delta K^i_{t+1}$, where $N^{i*}_{t+1}$ is the optimal quantity of labor. Thus, the ex ante required rate of return on the bonds issued by firm $i$, $R^{Li}_{t+1}$, is the required return implied by the asset-pricing equation

(19)

$$E_t\left\{m_{t+1}\cdot\frac{R^i_{t+1}[K^i_{t+1}+f^S_t\upsilon^S(K^i_{t+1})](1-Z^{Mi}_{t+1})+[\tilde{R}^{Ki}_{t+1}K^i_{t+1}-f^M_{t+1}\upsilon^M(K^i_{t+1})]Z^{Mi}_{t+1}}{[K^i_{t+1}+f^S_t\upsilon^S(K^i_{t+1})]}\right\}=1.$$

So, as usual, $R^{Li}_{t+1}$ depends on the conditional covariance between the cash flow and the stochastic discount factor. The expression in the numerator of the fraction is the state-contingent payoff to bondholders. If the realization of technology $(A_{t+1})$ is sufficiently favorable, then the project will not default (i.e., $Z^M = 0$), and the bondholders will receive the contractual interest promised by the bond—$R^i_{t+1}[K^i_{t+1} + f^S_t\upsilon^S(K^i_{t+1})]$. Otherwise, if the realization of technology is bad enough, the firm will have to declare bankruptcy, and bondholders will receive the full value of the firm, net of the monitoring cost—$[\tilde{R}^{Ki}_{t+1}K^i_{t+1} - f^M_{t+1}\upsilon^M(K^i_{t+1})]$. The contracted interest rate on the bond issued by a project $(R^i_{t+1})$ depends on its ex ante required rate of return $R^{Li}_{t+1}$, which in turn depends on the risk characteristics of that project. For details, see the appendix.

The denominator of equation (19) is the total amount of resources the firm borrows from households. The variable $K^i_{t+1}$ is the capital used for production, while $f^S_t\upsilon^S(K^i_{t+1})$ is the screening fee. As discussed previously, entrepreneurs need to borrow to pay the screening fees, because they have no endowments in the first period of their lives.

In general, households will hold a portfolio of bonds, not just one. For comparison in the next subsection with the case of a bank, it will be useful to derive the required return on this portfolio. Because each bond return must satisfy equation (19), we can write the return to the portfolio as a weighted average of the individual returns. Then, for a large portfolio of infinitesimal projects, the required rate of return is set by the equation

(20)

$$E_t\left(m_{t+1}\cdot\frac{\int_{i:K^i_{t+1}>0}\{R^i_{t+1}[K^i_{t+1}+f^s_t\upsilon^s(K^i_{t+1})](1-Z^{Mi}_{t+1})+[\tilde{R}^{Ki}_{t+1}K^i_{t+1}-f^M_{t+1}\upsilon(K^i_{t+1})]Z^{Mi}_{t+1}\}}{\int_{i:K^i_{t+1}>0}[K^i_{t+1}+f^S_t\upsilon^S(K^i_{t+1})]}\right)=1.$$

where the integral is taken over all firms whose bonds are in the investor's portfolio.[25]

25. To illustrate the derivation, consider an example of discreet projects. Suppose a lender holds bonds from $N$ firms. Equation (19) holds for every firm $i$ and can be rearranged by pulling the denominator $K^i_{t+1} + f^S_t\upsilon^S(K^i_{t+1})$ outside the expectations sign, because it is known at time $t$. Then, multiply each firm's equation (19) by the firm's share in the aggregate resources borrowed (i.e., $[K^i_{t+1} + f^S_t\upsilon^S(K^i_{t+1})]/\Sigma^N_{i=1}[K^i_{t+1} + f^S_t\upsilon(K^i_{t+1})]$), and add up the $N$ resulting equations.

### 7.2.2 Resolving Asymmetric Information II: Banks That Produce Real Services

We are finally ready to discuss bank operations. Now the banking sector performs real services, unlike the accounting device in subsection 7.1.5. We assume that banks assess the credit risk of prospective borrowers and lend them capital, and if a borrower claims to be unable to repay, banks investigate, liquidate the assets, and keep the proceeds. That is, in our model—and in the world—banks perform the functions of rating agencies and the bond market under one roof. As important, especially for measurement purpose, note that banks, rating agencies, and the bond market all coexist, both in the model and in reality. Our banks are completely equity funded.[26] They issue stocks in exchange for households' capital. Part of the capital is used to generate screening and monitoring services, with exactly the same technology as in equation (12). The rest of the capital is lent to qualified entrepreneurs. At time $t$, a bank must make an ex ante decision to split its total available capital into in-house capital (used by the bank for producing services in period $t + 1$, denoted $K^B_{t+1}$) and loanable capital (lent to entrepreneurs, used to produce the final good in period $t + 1$). Because the banking sector is competitive, banks price their package of services at marginal cost.

The exact statement of the bank's value maximization problem is tedious and yields little additional insight, so it, too, is deferred to the appendix. In summary, entrepreneurs are shown to be indifferent between approaching the bank for funds or going to a rating agency and then to the bond market,[27] given that banks have the same screening and monitoring technology as the agency (production functions in equations [14] and [15]).

Instead, in the rest of this section, we illustrate the intuition of the model's conclusion—a bank's cash flow equivalent to that of a rating agency plus a bond portfolio—and its implication for bank output measure.

First, we describe a bank's total cash flow. At any time $t$, banks cannot charge explicit fees for the service of screening young entrepreneurs' applications for funds, because the applicants have no initial wealth. Instead, banks have to allow the fees to be paid in the next period and must obtain additional equity in the current period to finance the production costs of

The right-hand side clearly sums up to one, while $\sum_{i=1}^{N}[K^i_{t+1} + f^S_t \upsilon(K^i_{t+1})]$ becomes the common denominator for the left-hand side. Consequently, we find that $E_t(m_{t+1} \cdot \sum_{i=1}^{N}\{R^i_{t+1}[K^i_{t+1} + f^S_t \upsilon^S(K^i_{t+1})](1 - Z^{Mi}_{t+1}) + [\tilde{R}^{Ki}_{t+1}K^i_{t+1} - f^M_{t+1}\upsilon^M(K^i_{t+1})]Z^{Mi}_{t+1}\}/\sum_{i=1}^{N}[K^i_{t+1} + f^S_t \upsilon(K^i_{t+1})]) = 1$. That is, the weighted average of the $N$ firms' conditions equals the sum of the numerators over the sum of the denominators.

26. Again, our assumption that the bank does not issue debt is irrelevant for our results. See the discussion of the Modigliani-Miller (1958) theorem at the end of section 7.1.5.

27. We assume that in equilibrium, both the banking sector and agencies/the bond market get the same quality of applicants on average. In equilibrium, entrepreneurs will be indifferent about which route they should take to obtain their capital, so assigning them randomly is an innocuous assumption.

screening. Upon concluding the screening process, banks will lend the appropriate amount of capital to each firm. The firm must either repay the service fees and the productive capital with interest in period $t + 1$ or declare bankruptcy. In case of a default, the bank monitors the project and takes all that is left after deducting fees, exactly as if the firm had defaulted on a bond. At the same time, the bank also gets the fees, so unlike a bondholder, a bank truly gets the full residual value of the project!

Next, it is illuminating to partition the bank's cash flow as if it were produced by two divisions. The first, which we term the service division, does the actual production of screening and monitoring services, using capital chosen in the previous period ($K^B_{t+1}$) and labor hired in the current period. Monitoring services are paid by firms that have declared bankruptcy. But because the entrepreneurs have no resources in the first period of life, the fees for the screening services are paid by the other part of the bank, which we call the loan division. (Ultimately, of course, the bank will have to obtain these resources from its shareholders, as we will show next.) Once the screening is done, the loan division lends to entrepreneurs the funds it received as equity capital. The cash inflow of the loan division comes solely from returns on loans—either their contractual interest or the bankruptcy value of the firm, net of monitoring costs—exactly as in the case of bondholders. See figure 7.1 for a diagram showing the cash flows through a bank in any pair of periods.

The key to understanding our decomposition of a bank's cash flow is to realize that each period, the bank's shareholders must be paid the full returns

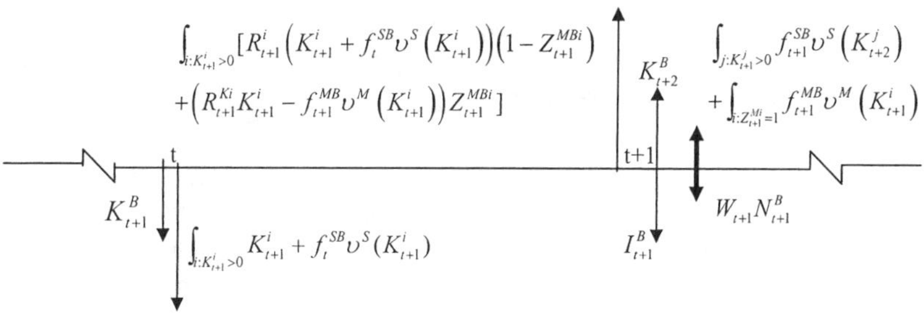


**Fig. 7.1 Cash flows for a bank's shareholders who invest in $K^A_{t+1}$ and generation-*t* firms' capital**

*Notes:* The bank's shareholders invest in both the bank's productive capital $K^B_{t+1}$ and generation-$t$ firms' productive capital $\int_{i:K^i_{t+1}>0}K^i_{t+1}$, as well as the associated screening fee $\int_{i:K^i_{t+1}>0}f^{SB}_t\upsilon^S(K^i_{t+1})$ at the end of period $t$. The variable $K^B_{t+1}$ is used in the bank's production in period $t + 1$, while $\int_{i:K^i_{t+1}>0}K^i_{t+1}$ is used in firms' production. From the bank's operation (i.e., screening generation-$t + 1$ and monitoring generation-$t$ projects), the shareholders receive a variable profit of $\int_{j:K^j_{t+1}>0}f^{SB}_{t+1}\upsilon^S(K^j_{t+2}) + \int_{i:Z^{Mi}_{t+1}=1}f^{MB}_{t+1}\upsilon^M(K^i_{t+1}) - W_{t+1}N^B_{t+1}$. The variable $I^B_{t+1}$ is investment, and $K^B_{t+2} - I^B_{t+1} = (1 - \delta)K^B_{t+1}$; that is, part of the shareholders' gross return is the initial bank capital, net of depreciation. At the end of period $t + 1$, the shareholders either receive the contracted interest rate $R^i_{t+1}$ from a firm or pay the necessary monitoring fee $f^{MB}_{t+1}\upsilon^M(K^i_{t+1})$ and receive all the residual payoff.

on their investment in the previous period. The intuition is the no-arbitrage condition as follows: suppose an investor chooses to hold the bank's stock for only one period; then he must be fully compensated for his entire initial investment when he sells the stock at the end of the period.[28] Because investors always have the option of selling out after one period, this condition must hold, even when investors keep the stock for multiple periods; otherwise, arbitrage would be possible.

This principle of shareholders receiving the full return on their investment every period is most important for understanding the cash flow associated with screening. At time $t$, a group of investors invest in a bank's equity, conditional on the expected return at time $t + 1$. It is these time-$t$ shareholders who implicitly pay the fees for the bank's screening of new projects at time $t$, because screening enables them to invest in worthy projects and thus earn the returns at time $t + 1$.

We now demonstrate the equivalence between a bank and a rating agency plus a bond portfolio. We use a superscript $B$ to denote bank decision variables. We denote by $R^H$ the rate of return that the households require in order to hold a bank's equity. Then, $R^H$ will be determined by the following asset-pricing equation:

$$(21)\quad E_t[m_{t+1}(\{\mathbf{[}f^{SB}_{t+1}Y^{SB}_{t+1} + f^{MB}_{t+1}Y^{MB}_{t+1} - W_{t+1}N^B_{t+1} + (1-\delta)K^B_{t+1}\mathbf{]} + \\ \mathbf{(}\textstyle\int_{i:K^i_{t+1}>0}\{R^{Bi}_{t+1}[K^i_{t+1} + f^{SB}_t \upsilon^S(K^i_{t+1})](1 - Z^{Mi}_{t+1}) + [\tilde{R}^{Ki}_{t+1}K^i_{t+1} - f^{MB}_{t+1}\upsilon^M(K^i_{t+1})]Z^{Mi}_{t+1}\}\mathbf{)}\} \\ \div \{K^B_{t+1} + \textstyle\int_{i:K^i_{t+1}>0}[K^i_{t+1} + f^{SB}_t \upsilon^S(K^i_{t+1})]\})] = 1.$$

The numerator equals the bank's total cash flow in period $t + 1$. It is organized into two parts (in bold brackets and parentheses) to correspond to the cash flows of the two hypothetical divisions in order to facilitate the comparison of a bank with a rating agency plus a bond portfolio. The first part is the cash flow of the service division, which does all the screening and monitoring; every term there is defined similarly to its counterpart in the numerator of equation (18)—the cash flow for the rating agency. The second part is the cash flow of the loan division, equal to the interest income, summed over all the entrepreneurs to whom the bank has made loans, net of the monitoring costs. Every term is defined similarly to its counterpart in equation (20), which is the return on a diversified portfolio of many bonds, each of which has a payoff similar to the numerator of equation (19).

The denominator of equation (21) is the sum of bank capital, which

28. Alternatively, one can think of the bank paying off the full value of its equity each period—returning the capital that was lent the previous period, together with the appropriate dividends—and then issuing new equity to finance its operations for the current period. Of course in practice, most of the bank's shareholders at time $t + 1$ are the same as the shareholders at time $t$, but the principle remains the same.

comprises the amount the bank uses for screening and monitoring ($K^B$), the amount it lends to entrepreneurs, and the screening fees put up by this period's shareholders—which is best conceptualized as a form of intangible capital.[29]

Note that in order to derive the respective cash flows of the two divisions in the numerator, we deliberately add monitoring income $f^{MB}Y^{MB}$ to the first term and subtract monitoring costs $\int f^{MB}\upsilon^M Z^{Mi}$ from the second. But this manipulation on net leaves the bank's overall cash flow unchanged, because

$$Y^{MB}_{t+1} = \int_{i:K^i_{t+1}>0} [\upsilon^M(K^i_{t+1})Z^{Mi}_{t+1}]. \tag{22}$$

The reason is that the monitoring services produced generate income for the service division, and those are exactly the services the loan division must buy in order to collect from defaulting borrowers.

We have so far accounted for all of the cash inflow and outflow of the loan division and for the cash inflow corresponding to the provision of monitoring services for the service division. The next component is the cash inflow from providing screening services by the service division. According to the logic of fully compensating shareholders every period (discussed earlier), these screening services are implicitly paid for by time-$t + 1$ shareholders, and the fees constitute part of time-$t$ shareholders' return. They are the analogue of the screening fees in the denominator, which amount to $f^{SB}_t Y^{SB}_t$ (for a reason similar to equation [22]), and were paid by time-$t$ shareholders to compensate time-($t - 1$) shareholders. The final component of the capital return for the service division is the return of the depreciated capital to shareholders. (Depreciated capital is in the capital return of the loan division implicitly, because we use gross rates of return in that part of the numerator.)

### 7.2.3 Equilibrium with Asymmetric Information

We do not solve for the full set of equilibrium outcomes for all the variables, because we need only a subset of the equilibrium conditions to make the important points regarding bank output measurement. A major use of general equilibrium in our model is that it allows us to derive asset prices (and risk premia) endogenously in terms of the real variables (in particular, the marginal utility of consumption). Thus, in the context of this model, it is clear where everything comes from in the environment facing banks.

The first step toward proving the nature of the equilibrium is to note that the cash flow of any bank can be thought of as coming from two assets that households can choose to hold separately, each corresponding to equity

29. That is, even though not recorded on balance sheets, the screening fees are nonetheless part of the overall investment funded by the investors today, and they expect to benefit from the payoff of that investment in the subsequent period.

claims on just one division of the bank. For the purpose of valuing an asset, it is immaterial whether the asset actually exists. Thus, it is immaterial whether the bank actually sells separate claims on the different streams of cash flows coming from its different operations; no bank does. But investors will still value the overall bank as the sum of two separate cash flows, each discounted by its own risk-based required rate of return. To take an analogy, Ford Motor Company shareholders in the United States certainly make different forecasts for the earnings of its Jaguar, Volvo, and domestic divisions, and they know that exchange rate risk applies to earnings from the first two but not to the third. Shareholders then add these individual discounted components to arrive at their valuation of the entire company.

It is important to note that no asset-pricing theory implies a unique way to split up a bank's—or indeed any firm's—cash flow generated by its various operations. Investors can choose to think of a bank as comprising the sum of any combination of its operations that adds up to the entire bank's cash flow. The crucial point is that the asset-pricing equation (4) must apply to *any* and *all* subsets of a bank's overall cash flow. But the service versus loan division is the most meaningful way of partitioning a bank's operations for the purpose of understanding real bank output, because it separates the bank's production of real output from its holding of assets on behalf of its investors. Moreover, this division generates two entities that both have real-world counterparts (i.e., rating agencies and bond markets). Therefore, this division is most useful, both for understanding and for measuring bank output (see our discussion of measurement next). This argument is made formally in the working paper version of this chapter (Wang, Basu, and Fernald 2004).

In conclusion, in any equilibrium, the service division of the bank must have a required rate of return on capital of $R^{SV}$, and each loan that the bank makes must have the same required return, $R^{Li}$, as it would have were it made in the bond market.[30]

### 7.2.4 The Model Applied to Measurement

We have presented the essential features of a simple DSGE model with financial intermediation. The model shows that because banks perform several functions under one roof, investors view a bank as a collection of assets—a combination of a bond mutual fund (of various loans) and a stock mutual fund (one that holds the equities of rating agencies). Investors value the bank by discounting the cash flow from each asset using the relevant risk-adjusted required rate of return for that asset. But in general, all of the

30. We have shown that in any equilibrium that exists, households demand the same rate of return on each division of the bank as the rate on the rating agency and the bond portfolio, respectively. We have not claimed that an equilibrium must exist in this model or that the equilibrium previously described is unique—there may be multiple equilibria, with different asset prices associated with each one.

cash flows will have some systematic risk, and thus none of the required rates will be the risk-free interest rate.

In the context of the model, it is clear that proper measurement of nominal and real bank output requires that we identify the actual services banks provide (and are implicitly compensated for) and recognize that these services are qualitatively equivalent to the (explicitly priced) services provided by rating agencies. So, it is logical to treat bank output the same as the explicit output of those alternative institutions.

Another benefit of our approach—and a different intuition for its validity—is that the measure of bank output it implies is invariant to alternative modes of operation in banks. The prime example is the securitization of loans, which has become increasingly popular in recent years, where banks originate loans (mostly residential mortgages) and then sell pools of such loans to outside investors, who hold them as they would bonds. In this case, a bank turns itself into a rating agency, receiving explicit fees for screening (and servicing over the lifetime of the loan pool). Securitization should not change a reasonable measure of bank output, because banks perform similar services, regardless of whether a loan is securitized. Our model, which counts service provision as the only real bank output, indeed will generate the same measure of bank output, regardless of whether loans are securitized. But if one follows SNA93, then a bank that securitizes loans will appear to have lower output on average, because it will not be credited with the output, which is actually the transfer of the risk premium to debt holders. Thus, under SNA93, an economy with increasing securitization will appear to have declining bank output, even if all allocations and economic decisions are unchanged.

### 7.2.5 Different Capital Structures for Banks

The previous subsections of section 7.2 have all assumed that banks are 100 percent equity financed. This is unusual, in that we are used to thinking of banks as being financed by debt (largely deposits). But we will show next that the MM (1958) theorem holds in our model, so all of our previous conclusions are completely unaffected by introducing debt (deposit) financing. Of course, there is a large literature in corporate finance discussing how differential tax treatment of debt and equity and information asymmetry (between banks and households, that is) cause the MM theorem to break down. But we have deliberately avoided such complications in order to exposit the basic intuition of our approach. Once that intuition is clear, it will be simple to extend the model to encompass such real-world complications.

We have an environment where information is symmetric between banks and households, so there is no need for screening and monitoring when raise funds from (i.e., sell equity shares to) households. Thus, we reasonably assume that there are no transaction costs of any kind between banks and households. We also assume that interest payments and dividends receive the same tax treatment. In this setting, banks' capital structure is irrelevant, in that the required rate of return on banks' total assets is the same, with or without debt. When banks are leveraged, the required rates of return on the bank's debt and equity are determined by the risk of the part of the cash flow promised to the debt and the equity holders, respectively. Because debt holders have senior claim on the bank's cash flow, the ex ante rate of return they require is almost always lower than the rate required by shareholders. But the rate of return on the bank's total assets is the weighted average of the return on debt and equity, and it equals the return on the assets of an unlevered (i.e., all-equity) bank. This result is a simple application of the MM (1958) theorem.

The implication of this result is that all the preceding analysis of the imputation of implicit bank service output remains valid, even when banks are funded partly by deposits. We discuss the extension to deposit insurance in section 7.3.2; Wang (2003a) analyzes it fully.

The preceding overview of the model and the intuition for the key results should equip the reader for analytical details of the model in the appendix.[31] Alternatively, a reader more interested in the measurement implications now has the theoretical background for the measurement discussion that follows in section 7.3.

## 7.3 Implications for Measuring Bank Output and Prices

This model yields one overarching principle for measurement: focus on the flow of actual services provided by banks. This principle applies equally to measuring both nominal and real banking output, and thus the implied (implicit) price deflator. Following theories of financial intermediation, we model banks as providing screening and monitoring services that mitigate asymmetric information problems between borrowers and investors. Because screening and monitoring represent essential aspects of financial services in general, we would want any measure of bank output to be consistent with the model's implications. But the SNA93 recommendations for measuring implicit financial services—and the NIPAs implementation—are not. They generally do not accurately capture actual service flows.

The model highlights three conceptual shortcomings of the SNA93/NIPAs framework. First, the model shows that the appropriate reference rate for measuring nominal bank lending services must incorporate the borrower's risk premium, which is not part of bank output. Intuitively, the

31. The appendix focuses on solving analytically the joint determination of the optimal contractual interest rate and each entrepreneur's choice of capital and labor in production. In particular, it spells out (a) the exact terms of the debt contract for entrepreneur's projects (including the interest rate charged) that is consistent with bank profit maximization and (b) each entrepreneur's utility-maximizing choice of capital and labor, given the debt contract.

borrowing firm must pay that premium, determined by the intrinsic risk profile of its cash flow, regardless of whether it obtains the funds through a bank or through the bond market (after getting certified by a credit rating agency). The return on the risky assets—loans or bonds—is part of the cost of capital to the borrowing firm and is income to households.

Second, the model shows that the timing of bank cash flows often does not match the timing of actual bank service output. As a prime example, screening is typically done before the loan generates income. This problem does not necessarily disappear, even when the origination fees are explicitly paid up front (ruled out in the model), because generally accepted accounting principles (GAAP) often require banks to artificially smooth these revenues over the lifetime of the loan, thus inadvertently reinstating the problem.

Third, the *measured* value of implicit output of services such as monitoring, whose *expected* value is incorporated in advance into the interest rate charged, most likely deviates from the *actual* output. This is because the realization of such services is contingent on loans' ex post realized return, which almost surely deviates from the ex ante expected return. Our model suggests that when the observed bank interest income is the realized return, the most suitable reference rate is actually the matched holding-period rate of return, not the ex ante expected rate, on a portfolio of debt with comparable risk and no financial services.

We now discuss further implications of these issues in the context of nominal and then real output.

### 7.3.1 Nominal Bank Output

Nominal bank services should correspond to the value of *service flows* provided by banks. It should exclude the value of any revenue that might flow through a bank that does not, in fact, correspond to actual financial services provided by the bank. This principle is embedded in the key first-order condition for a bank's optimal choice of contractual loan interest rate, $R^{Bi}_{t+1}$ (i.e., equation [A11] in the appendix):[32]

$$(23)\quad [(1-p^i_t)R^{Bi}_{t+1}K^i_{t+1} + p^i_t E_t(Int^i_{t+1} \mid Default^i_{t+1})] - R^{Li}_{t+1}K^i_{t+1}$$
$$= R^{Li}_{t+1} f^S_t \upsilon^S_t(K^i_{t+1}) + p^i_t E_t[f^M_{t+1}\upsilon^M_{t+1}(K^i_{t+1})].$$

The variable $p^i_t$ is the probability that the borrower defaults, $(1-p^i_t)$ otherwise. The expected interest payment by the borrower in case of default is denoted as $E_t(Int^i_{t+1} \mid Default^i_{t+1})$. Thus, the terms in square brackets on the left-hand side is the expected interest from lending $K^i_{t+1}$ to a borrower of risk type $i$; that is, the default probability-weighted average interest income the bank expects to receive. The variable $R^{Li}_{t+1}$ is the required rate of return that the bond market would charge borrower $i$ for a debt of the same size (and

32. Note the distinction between the contractual rate and the required rate of return for a defaultable loan (section 7.1.1).

by our reasoning in the preceding sections, it is also the return that bank shareholders demand for financing such a bank loan). The variable $\upsilon_t^S(K_{t+1}^i)$ is the amount of screening services, the price per unit of which is $f_t^S$, and the variables $\upsilon_{t+1}^M(K_{t+1}^i)$ and $f_{t+1}^M$ are the counterparts for monitoring services.

Thus, the left-hand side is the difference between the expected bank income from loans of risk type $i$ and the (hypothetical) income on a bond of the same size with the same risk characteristics. The right-hand side is the nominal value of the bank's *expected* services of screening and monitoring that loan.[33]

Equation (23) incorporates our three main points regarding measurement. First, consider reference rates. We define $F(R_{t+1}^{Bi}) \equiv [p^i R_{t+1}^{Bi} K_{t+1}^i + (1 - p^i)E_t(Int_{t+1}^i \mid Default_{t+1}^i)]/K_{t+1}^i$ as the interest rate the bank expects to receive, net of defaults, on loans to borrowers of type $i$. Then, the left-hand side of equation (23), an interest margin, can be expressed as an interest spread multiplied by the loan size, $K_{t+1}^i$:

$$(24) \qquad [F(R_{t+1}^{Bi}) - R_{t+1}^{Li}]K_{t+1}^i.$$

As Fixler, Reinsdorf, and Smith (2003; hereafter FRS) suggest, one can use "interest margins as values of implicit services of banks" (34). The key issue is deciding what reference rate(s) to use. Equation (24) makes clear that $R_{t+1}^{Li}$ is the appropriate reference rate for imputing the implicit value of bank output.

Importantly, this reference rate must be *risk adjusted* (i.e., contain a risk premium reflecting the systematic risk associated with the loans). In sharp contrast, U.S. and other national accounts stipulate a reference rate that explicitly *excludes* borrower risk. The 2003 benchmark revisions of the U.S. NIPAs define the reference rate as the average rate earned by banks on U.S. Treasury and U.S. agency securities.[34] As FRS argue, "If a highly liquid security with no credit risk is available to banks, the banks forego the opportunity to earn this security's rate of return . . . when they invest in loans instead" (34). That's true; but it's also true that banks forego the opportunity to invest in high-risk/high-yielding junk bonds!

Our model clarifies the apparent ambiguity inherent in the opportunity cost argument by incorporating modern asset-pricing theories (the CCAPM, specifically). Indeed, by combining theories of asset pricing and financial intermediation, our model (and Wang's [2003a]) extends and generalizes the user cost framework to take account of uncertainty and asymmetric information.

33. The potential monitoring cost is not known in advance but must be expected, because it depends on wages and productivity that will be realized in period $t + 1$. The variable $E_t$ is the expectations operator, conditional on time-$t$ information.

34. This average rate is not, in fact, a risk-free rate, even in nominal terms. In particular, U.S. agency securities have a positive and time-varying interest spread, reflecting credit risk, over Treasuries of matching maturities.

Asset-pricing theories imply that an asset's required rate of return depends (positively) on its systematic risk. In two special cases, the required return equals the risk-free rate: if there is no systematic risk (i.e., only idiosyncratic risk, which creditors can diversify away) or if investors are risk neutral. In such a world, there would be no risk premia. Otherwise, the correct reference rate (i.e., opportunity cost of funds) for imputing bank lending services must be adjusted for systematic risk. Thus, our model makes clear that the current NIPAs implementation of the user cost approach—with a *risk-free* reference rate for lending services—is not appropriate in the realistic world with uncertainty.

What is the intuition for risk-adjusted reference rates? When a bank keeps loans on its balance sheet and charges implicitly for services, it sets each loan rate to cover both the services provided *and* the riskiness of the loan. In equilibrium, the loan interest rate, net of implicit service charges, must compensate the ultimate suppliers of funds (i.e., households in this model) for the disutility arising from the risk. Conversely, the borrower could (at least conceptually) go to a rating agency, get certified, and then issue bonds at the risk-adjusted rate. Adjusting reference rates for risk thus preserves neutrality with respect to economically identical institutional arrangements for obtaining external funds.

Comparison with securitization further illustrates the rationale for risk-adjusted reference rates.[35] When banks securitize loans, they receive explicit payments for services; household optimization implies that the securitized asset yields a service-free interest rate that reflects each loan's risk properties. However, banks perform the same kinds of screening and monitoring services and arrive at much the same optimization rule, which governs the service-free interest rates (along with other choice variables), whether loans are held on the balance sheet or securitized. The principle of neutrality across economically identical lending arrangements implies that bank output measurement should be invariant. Otherwise, measured bank output fluctuates with the share of securitized loans, even if actual bank services are constant over time.

Securitization thus provides a useful conceptual benchmark against which to judge the validity of any measure of implicitly priced bank services. Our model, in effect, imputes implicit bank output to be invariant, regardless of whether loans are securitized. That is, the nominal value of bank services equals total bank interest income minus the amount of service-free pure interest—corresponding to the rate that would be charged on a securitized loan pool with matching risk (i.e., if the loans were securitized).

Furthermore, the model implies that the NIPAs mismeasure the oppor-

35. By the end of 2003, over 80 percent of residential mortgage loans and 30 percent of consumer credit were securitized (Federal Reserve Board 2009) and are an increasing share of loans to businesses.

tunity cost of banks' own funds (i.e., financial assets minus liabilities). The SNA93 recommends that the opportunity cost of a bank's own funds be netted out of its imputed service output; the version implemented in the 2003 NIPAs revision uses the risk-free rate as the user cost of banks' own funds (see FRS 2003, 36). Our model can be construed as implying a similar netting-out principle, because any reference rate can be expressed as a weighted average of the respective user cost of banks' debt and own funds. However, the model makes clear that both rates ought to be risk adjusted, according to the different risk on banks' debt and own funds, respectively.

More importantly, our model-implied measure of implicit bank service output does not depend on the bank's capital structure, which is but a coincidental state variable. That is, the opportunity cost of funds for a loan needs to be risk adjusted according to the same asset-pricing theories, regardless of whether the lending is financed by intermediation (i.e., deposit taking) or by banks' own funds.

Counting the risk premium as part of bank output also overstates GDP. In the model, GDP is not mismeasured, because financial services are an intermediate input into nonfinancial firms' production. An SNA93-based measure misallocates some value added to banks. But the logic of the model applies to consumer loans (e.g., mortgages and credit cards), which also involve risk and risk-assessment services. So, final services to consumers and GDP would be overstated if we include the risk premium in bank output.

The second general issue that equation (23) highlights is the timing mismatch between the provision of screening services and the resulting cash flow. Banks screen borrowers in period $t$, but these services are not compensated until period $t + 1$. The borrower's (future) payment of $R^{Li}_{t+1} f^S_t \upsilon^S_t(K^i_{t+1})$ for screening services thus exceeds the contemporaneous nominal value of the services, $f^S_t \upsilon^S_t(K^i_{t+1})$. Ideally, one would attribute those services to period $t$, when the bank screens and originates the loans, rather than to $t + 1$.

In principle, if banks charge explicit origination fees upfront—rather than rolling these fees into the interest rate—then the timing mismatch becomes less important. In practice, firms often do pay explicit origination fees. But GAAP require that banks amortize the origination fee over the life of a loan. So, the reported income stream is artificially smoothed relative to the timing of service provision. If true screening services vary over time, then accounting data might not properly reflect this variation. In this case, direct quantity data (such as counting the number of loans originated) can help ensure correct timing.

The third general point from equation (23) is that *actual* monitoring output differs from *expected* (i.e., $p^i_t E_t[f^M_{t+1} \upsilon^M_{t+1}(K^i_{t+1})]$ on the right-hand side of equation [23]), the value of which is included in the expected interest margin (i.e., the left-hand side of equation [23]). That is, the contractual rate covers expected monitoring services based on ex ante probability of default, but monitoring takes place only when a borrower actually defaults ex post. In fact, *neither* ex ante *nor* ex post interest margins match the actual value of monitoring, while the two margins almost surely do not equal each other. We suspect that in good times, banks do less monitoring than expected, while enjoying higher-than-expected interest margins; in bad times, they do more monitoring than expected, while suffering lower-than-expected interest margins. Thus, in a boom, ex post interest margins exceed ex ante margins, and in turn exceed the value of banks' actual service flows. In a recession, ex post interest margins fall short of ex ante margins, and in turn fall short of the actual value of service flows.[36]

In general, adjusting the ex post interest margin for the actual rate of default yields more accurate measurement of nominal bank service output. Such adjustments can be implemented; for example, Wang (2003b) uses bank holding company data to adjust the ex post interest income for the default realizations.[37]

This problem of mismeasuring monitoring services is unlikely to disappear, even when one averages over a large number of loans, unless there was no aggregate risk. This nondiversifiable deviation of actual from expected cash flow is precisely the *reason* why there is a risk premium. That is, in good times, when output and consumption are high (so marginal utilities are low), banks generate more residual cash flow for shareholders; in bad times, when output and consumption are low, banks generate less residual cash flow.

We conclude this section by discussing how to extend the model to include bank depositor services (e.g., direct transaction and payment services, safe deposit boxes, etc.). Conceptually, they raise fewer complications than lending services, especially regarding the treatment of risk. Without the service component, deposits are simply fixed-income securities. A straightforward extension of the model implies that nominal depositor services equal the margin between interest paid and interest imputed, using reference rates based on market debt securities with comparable risk. For balances covered by deposit insurance, the correct reference rate is the risk-free rate, as used in the NIPAs. For balances not covered or without deposit insurance, however, depositors would demand a higher expected return that depends on the default risk of a bank's asset portfolio and its capital structure. So, the NIPAs measure is appropriate only for insured balances and is unlikely to remain correct for countries without deposit insurance, such as New Zealand.

36. See appendix 2 in Wang, Basu, and Fernald (2004; hereafter WBF) for technical derivations of these results and for how to adjust for actual default.

37. Going forward, more relevant data is likely to be generated in the coming implementation of the Basel II accord for capital requirement, which encourages banks to develop internal risk management systems.

### 7.3.2 Is Risk Assumption a Service?[38]

One interpretation of the NIPAs choice of the reference rate is that they construe risk bearing as an additional service provided by banks.[39] Our model, on the contrary, considers only screening and monitoring services to be bank output, produced using capital and labor. Presumably, one could write down alternative internally consistent *accounting* systems that are consistent with any given *economic* model. So, one could probably write down another accounting system, also internally consistent, where bearing risk is treated as service output in all transactions.[40]

Nevertheless, at least two intuitive criteria help in choosing between different, internally consistent accounting frameworks. First, one wants to choose an accounting framework where the quantities measured have natural economic interpretation. Second, the framework should treat identical market transactions identically. The system we propose meets these two criteria. The current system, in contrast, does not.

We have already discussed several examples that illustrate these criteria. For example, if firms are indifferent between borrowing from banks or from the bond market, then we would want to treat them identically with respect to their marginal decisions. The current national accounts do not do so.

More generally, the current system does not treat risk bearing consistently across alternative market arrangements. Indeed, the current accounting system leads to very peculiar outcomes when applied to outside banks narrowly defined. Consider mutual funds. The account holders of mutual funds are owners of the assets—shareholders. Because the current system credits bank shareholders with the risk premium for assuming risk, mutual fund shareholders should be treated in the same way. Thus, the NIPAs framework would seem to imply that the mutual fund management industry should be credited with producing services equal to actual asset returns in excess of the risk-free return (multiplied by the market value of the assets).

We do not think it appropriate to credit the mutual fund industry with producing trillions of dollars of value added, corresponding to the difference between average stock returns and risk-free interest. Our framework would say that we should credit mutual funds only with providing the services that people think they are buying from mutual funds—transactions, bookkeeping services, and sometimes financial advice. We think this corresponds much more closely to the economic reality.

38. We thank Paul Schreyer, whose comment on this chapter stimulated us to add this section.

39. For example, FRS (2003) say, "The spread between the reference rate of return and the lending rate is the implicit price that the bank receives for providing financial services to borrowers, which include the cost of bearing risk."

40. We are not aware of any fully worked out models that explore the full implications of treating risk assumption as a service output.

Finally, counting risk assumption as a bank service causes conceptual difficulties when the resulting measure of output is used in productivity studies. Suppose one bank turns down very risky loans, whereas another seeks out high-risk projects and lends to them at high interest rates. Suppose also that both banks use the same amount of capital and labor to provide exactly the same processing services, such as screening and monitoring. They have the same output and productivity by our definition. It is undesirable to claim instead that the bank making more risky loans—which the other bank could have made but declined—is the more productive bank, *solely* because of the riskiness of its loan portfolio.

### 7.3.3 Real Bank Output

It is clear that one wants to measure real output as the actual service flow provided by banks. The model aims to focus on the issue of risk and bank output measurement; hence, it considers only bank lending activities, which essentially involve processing information—specifically, financial and credit data. These services are qualitatively similar to other information services, such as accounting and consulting.

Banks provide many distinct types of services. The model captures this by the different production functions for screening and monitoring. Screening depends on the number of *new* loans issued, whereas monitoring depends on the number of *outstanding* loans (in the model, inherited from last period). There is also heterogeneity within either activity. The amount of screening and monitoring, respectively, that is needed for a loan depends on many factors that differ across loans.[41] The model captures this in the form of size differences across loans. The multiproduct nature of bank services implies that aggregate bank output should be defined as a Törnqvist or Fisher index of the quantity (index) of each distinct service type.

Measuring the real value of monitoring services presents the same difficulty that affects nominal value measurement: measured output based on deflated nominal value (assuming both the risk premium and the cost of screening are properly accounted for) generally differs from *both* the actual and the expected output of monitoring. Thus, in a downturn, productivity analysts would see a banking sector experience lower imputed output, despite absorbing as much (if not more) primary or intermediate inputs. Then, measured banking total factor productivity (TFP) would fall sharply in a downturn, even if actual TFP did not change.

The way around this difficulty is to measure real monitoring services using

41. For example, a loan's denomination, the borrower's industry and geographic location, and his or her previous interaction with the bank are all relevant factors. In practice, the amount of screening and monitoring needed differ more across commercial and industrial loans than across (conforming) residential mortgage and consumer loans. See WBF (2004) for a more detailed discussion of the heterogeneity in information services across different categories of loans.

direct quantity indicators. For instance, one can make use of the number of loans overdue or delinquent in each period to gauge the actual amount of monitoring performed; one may be able to collect data also on the associated costs of restructuring and foreclosure to estimate the quality-adjusted output of monitoring different loans.

How do these conceptual issues relate to what the national accounts actually measure (or attempt to measure)? The national accounts base their estimates of real output on a real index of banking services calculated by the Bureau of Labor Statistics (BLS). In terms of lending activities, the BLS (1998) tries to count activities such as the number of loans of various types (commercial, residential, credit card, etc.). Within each category, different loans are weighted by interest rates, the presumption being that loans that bear a higher interest rate involve more real services. Across categories of services, output is then aggregated using employment weights.

As the BLS technical note makes clear, limitations on the availability of appropriate data force many of their choices. Conceptually, at least, we highlight a few of the issues suggested by the model.

First, one should try to distinguish new loans from the stock of old loans, because they involve different services (that is, screening and monitoring, respectively). In particular, the timing of when each type of service is undertaken differs. Second, interest rates are probably not the right weights to use within loan category. Relative interest rates contain the compensation for (a) systematic risk, (b) screening services, and (c) expected monitoring services (tied to expected default probability). Thus, the relative interest rate weights are probably correlated with the proper weights–but imperfectly and certainly not linearly. Third, nominal output, instead of employment requirement, should be used as the weight for aggregating output across categories of services. Last, as noted earlier, one should try to measure real monitoring output more directly. Even using the number of outstanding loans—as the BLS does, on the grounds that existing and new loans require some services—will not capture the likely countercyclical pattern of actual monitoring services. (In fact, the number of outstanding loans is more likely to be procyclical.)

### 7.3.4 Price Deflators for Bank Output

Conceptually, what do we mean by the price of financial services? We use what seems like a natural definition of the price deflator: the nominal value of services divided by the real quantity index. So, the deflator is directly implied by the preceding discussions of both nominal and real output measures.

Our definition, although natural and intuitive, differs entirely from the common meaning of prices for financial instruments. The latter often refer to interest rates themselves, as in "the interest rate is the price of money," or as in "pricing a loan," which refers to setting the proper interest rate.

Similarly, the user cost approach refers to the interest rate *spread* (between the loan rate and a reference rate, scaled by a general deflator such as the Consumer Price Index [CPI]) as the user cost price of a loan.

This sometimes loose reference to financial prices can be appropriate in the context of discussing rates of return on financial *instruments.* But the model makes clear that neither the interest rate nor the interest rate spread is the price for financial *services,* even though banks often charge for these services indirectly via an interest rate spread. Similarly, the book value of loans is not the right quantity measure of lending services. (Bank efficiency studies often inappropriately treat loans' book value—deflated with a general price deflator, such as the CPI—as the quantity of bank output and treat interest rate as the price.)

As an explicit example, consider depositor services. Depositors implicitly pay for the services they receive by accepting a lower interest rate. Suppose a depositor decides to purchase *fewer* financial services by putting the *same* deposits in an Internet bank that offers a higher interest rate. The natural interpretation is that the nominal quantity of services falls (as measured by a lower interest margin) because the real quantity of services falls. It would clearly be mistaken to claim that nominal output falls because the price (i.e., the interest rate spread) falls, while the quantity (measured by the dollar value of deposits) is fixed.

In summary, the model implies the proper price of financial services by providing theoretical guidance for measuring the nominal and real values of such services. As important, we now discuss how to meet the practical challenges of implementing the model's implied nominal and real output measures.

### 7.3.5 Implementing the Model's Recommendations in Practice

To properly measure the value of nominal bank services, we must first estimate and remove the risk premium on bank loans. The risk premium on comparable market securities (i.e., commercial papers, mortgage-backed securities, etc., that are subject to the same systematic risk) serves as a good proxy. Such proxies are readily available. Wang (2003b) suggests some securities one may use and provides a preliminary estimate of bank service output, free of the risk premium. (Her estimate suggests that on average, the risk premium may amount to 20 to 25 percent of imputed bank service output.)

Arguably, a better alternative is a rate that is adjusted for the risk, as assessed according to each bank's internal risk-rating system. Indeed, Basel II requires that banks assess their risks even more carefully than they already do—offering an opportunity for improving the accuracy of the estimate of risk premia. This should then lead to a more accurate estimate of (a Törnqvist or Fisher index of) aggregate real bank output, where the nominal output share of each distinct type of bank service serves as the aggregation weight.

Second, we need the timing of measured output—screening, in particular—to match when services are rendered rather than when services generate revenue. If explicit origination fees are available for a type of loan, national accountants can collect cash-based accounting data on total origination income for that type of loan and estimate the true screening output by deflating the income with the explicit fee. The fee can also serve as a proxy for the price of similar charges that are implicit. Or, one can derive quantity indexes from direct counts of distinct activities (e.g., the number of new credit card loans made), and the weighted sum of the growth rates of these indexes gives the growth of aggregate service output.

Third, to address the issue that actual monitoring services (both nominal and real) are likely to differ from both the expected and the measured value, one can make use of bank data on actual loan default rates, as noted previously. In addition, because the correct reference rate equals the rate of return on market securities with comparable risk-return characteristics as bank loans, one can use ex post returns on such matched fixed-income market securities to more accurately infer bank service flows.

Finally, consider depositor services. It seems easier to define a product for depositor services than for lending services, because depositor services are more homogeneous across banks and in terms of product characteristics.[42] Conceptually, each distinct type of transaction should be viewed as one depositor service output. Thus, each ATM or teller-assisted transaction is presumably a composite good of several distinct activities. But for practical reasons, we can define each visit to an ATM or a teller as one unit of a service product. Similarly, without data on the number of each distinct type of transaction, we can treat maintaining each account of a given type as one product and use the number of deposit accounts of different types to measure output. This amounts to assuming that each account of a given type requires the same amount of bookkeeping, payment processing, and so forth, every period.

## 7.4 Further Implications for Measurement

The model's framework helps clarify several other issues in the literature. These include the use of assets/liabilities themselves as a measure of bank output, the question of whether to include capital gains as part of bank output, and how to measure other financial services/instruments provided by banks.

First, the model provides no theoretical support for the widespread practice of using the dollar value of interest-bearing assets (loans plus market

42. For instance, safe deposit box rentals are a relatively homogeneous activity, as are wire transfers, money orders, and cash withdrawals. To a lesser degree, so are cashing checks and opening accounts of a specific type.

securities) on bank balance sheets deflated by, for example, the GDP deflator, as real bank output.[43] This practice is standard in the empirical microeconomic literature on bank cost and profit efficiency.[44] Our model suggests a simple counterexample, in the spirit of the bank that does nothing. Suppose a bank has accumulated a loan portfolio by doing prior screening and monitoring but originates no new loans and does not need to monitor any old ones at a particular point in time. Then, our model makes it clear that the bank has zero service output in that period. But the microliterature would conclude that the bank's output is arbitrarily large, depending on the size of its existing loan portfolio.

Second, although the model does not explicitly consider capital gains, it provides a guiding principle for answering the question of whether capital gains should be counted in banking or financial output. Capital gains and interest income are two often interchangeable ways of receiving asset returns, with the former related more often to unexpected returns and the latter related more to expected returns. If interest income is often employed as implicit compensation for financial services provided without explicit charge, then in principle, capital gains can be used in place of interest for the same purpose. By design, such capital gains will be *expected* gains, because the service provider expects to be compensated. These gains should be recognized as implicit compensation for real financial services. Otherwise, capital gains should not be recognized.

To illustrate this principle, we use the same example of screening services in lending. Suppose that instead of holding loans on its balance sheet, a bank sells them after its shareholders have put up the initial funding, consisting of both the productive capital lent to the firms and the screening fees. Also assume that the bank only records the value of the capital lent, but not the screening fees, as assets on its balance sheet.[45] Accordingly, the loans' contractual interest rates are quoted with respect to just the capital lent, although the expected value of the interest will cover the screening fees as well. Then, when the bank sells these loans (i.e., debt claims on the firms' cash flows), it will enjoy a capital gain equal to the value of the screening fees, because the present value of those claims exceeds the book value by exactly the amount of the fees. Clearly, the capital gain in this case is qualitatively the same as the extra interest income the bank would receive in compensation for its services if it kept the loans. So, this capital gain should be counted as bank output.

43. Some existing studies also use deposit balance to measure depositor services, implicitly assuming that the service flow is in fixed proportion to the account balance. But Wang (2003a) shows, in realistic settings, that the relationship between the quantity of services and the account balance is likely to be highly nonlinear and time varying.

44. See, for example, Berger and Mester (1997) and Berger and Humphrey (1997) for surveys of the literature.

45. This is a quite likely scenario, because the fees are like intangible assets, which are often poorly or simply not accounted for on balance sheets.

On the other hand, following the same principle, capital gains or losses purely due to the random and unexpected realization of asset returns should not be counted as financial output. This can be seen in the model from the fact that the ideal reference rate is an ex post rate. The economic intuition is fairly clear, although it is best illustrated with multiperiod debts. Suppose we modify the model so that entrepreneurs and their projects last three periods. Then firms would borrow two-period debt, which would be screened and monitored in the usual way. Suppose also that aggregate technology is serially correlated. Then, a favorable realization of technology would lead to a capital gain on all bonds and bank loans that have yet to mature, because a good technology shock today raises the probability of good technology in the next period, which reduces the probability of bankruptcy in that period. But these capital gains do not reflect any provision of bank services—in fact, loans one period from maturity would be past the screening phase and would not yet require monitoring—and thus, the capital gains should not be counted as part of output. Intuitively, the only exception to this rule would arise if the capital gains on the loans are due to the provision of some banking service. For example, if banks provide specialized services to firms that make them more productive, which leads to an appreciation in the value of their assets, one would want to count some of that gain. This seems unlikely in the context of banks but may be realistic for venture capital firms.

Third, our model can be readily applied to value implicit services generated by banks when they create financial instruments other than loan contracts, and it can also be applied to measure implicit services generated by other financial institutions that create a wide variety of complex financial instruments.

The general applicability of our method stems from the fact that a loan (i.e., bond) subject to default risk is equivalent to a default-free loan combined with a short position in a put option[46] (i.e., giving the borrower the option of selling the project to the lender at a prespecified price). We denote the contractual interest rate as $R^i$ and a project's actual rate of payoff as $R^A$. Then, the payoff on a defaultable loan equals min $(R^i, R^A)$; a lender receives either the promised interest or the project's actual payoff, whichever is less. We can rewrite the risky loan's payoff as:

$$\min(R^i, R^A) = R^i - \max(0, R^i - R^A). \tag{25}$$

The first term describes the payoff from a riskless loan guaranteed to pay $R^i$; the second term, max(.), is the payoff to a put option on the project with a strike price of $R^i$. When the project pays less than $R^i$, the option holder would exercise the option (selling the project and receiving $R^i$) and earn a net

46. Put options, in general, offer the holder the option to sell an asset (real or financial) at a prespecified price to the party that offered (i.e., shorted) the option contract.

return of $R^i - R^A$.[47] When the project pays more than $R^i$, the option holder would not exercise the option and thus earn zero return. The negative sign in front of the second term means the lender of the defaultable loan is shorting (i.e., selling to the borrower) the put option. More generally, equation (25) describes the fact, well known in corporate finance, that a firm's bondholders essentially write a put option to the firm's shareholders.

In banks' cases, this means that issuing a loan is qualitatively the same as writing (i.e., holding a short position in) a put option to the borrower. The processing costs incurred should be the same as well, because all the risk in a defaultable loan lies in the embedded put option. So, screening and monitoring is only needed for that risky component, whereas the other component—the riskless loan—should involve little information processing. Therefore, the implicit services that banks produce in the process of underwriting a loan can be viewed as equivalent to services generated in the process of creating a financial derivatives contract.

This means the measure of implicit bank services implied by our model can be applied equally well to similar services that financial institutions generate in creating other types of financial instruments. The general principle is the same: apply asset-pricing theories to price the financial instrument by itself; the difference between that value and the contract's actual value yields the nominal value of the implicit services. Measurement issues similar to those related to lending, as previously discussed at length, will no doubt arise; our recommendations for implementing the output measure in practice apply then as well.

## 7.5 Conclusions

We develop a dynamic stochastic GE model to address thorny issues in measuring financial service output. Financial institutions perform screening and monitoring services to resolve asymmetric information. Measuring real output involves measuring the flow of actual financial services produced; measuring nominal output requires measuring the income that correspond to these services. Equilibrium asset-pricing conditions help resolve some of the perplexing conceptual issues in the literature.

A key result, as in Wang (2003a), is that the risk premium on loans is not part of banks' nominal output, because it does not correspond to the screening and monitoring services provided by banks. The risk premium is part of the capital income transfer from the final users to the ultimate suppliers of loanable funds (i.e., from the borrowing firms to households). The

47. This is, in effect, one way to describe default: a defaulted borrower's zero total payoff can be decomposed into two pieces—a negative net worth of $R^A - R^i$ exactly offset by a positive payoff of $R^i - R^A$ from holding the option.

rationale is intuitive enough: one wants to measure the output of economically similar institutions the same way. In the model and in the world, bank services to borrowers essentially combine the services of a rating agency with funding through the bond market. But the bond market is clearly just a conduit for transferring funds from households to firms; equally clear, the return on those funds, including any risk premium, is not the output of the rating agency!

Conversely, our implied output measure also satisfies the intuitive principle that a firm's output is invariant to the specific institutional source of external funding, as long as its liabilities have the same risk-return profile and incur the same informational services. The firm pays the same risk premium and the same service charges (implicit or explicit), regardless of whether the funds flow through a bank or through the bond market.

The model highlights the conceptual shortcomings in the existing national accounting measure of bank output. By counting the risk premium as part of nominal bank output, the current SNA93 and NIPAs measures treat economically identical alternative funding institutions differently and alter the output of the borrowing firm, depending on its source of funding. At the same time, the model makes clear that the book value of financial instruments on the balance sheet of banks, commonly used as the measure of bank output in the large body of bank efficiency studies, generally does not correspond to the true bank output, nominal or real.

In addition, we highlight two practical problems. First, the timing of cash flows often does not match the timing of actual bank services, because the bank screens in advance and then generates income over time. Second, expected bank net interest income incorporates the ex ante expected value of providing monitoring services; but ex post the quantity and nominal value of these services do not match the realized net interest income of the bank. We have discussed ways to resolve these problems.

More generally, we advocate a model-based approach to measurement for conceptually challenging areas of financial services and insurance.[48] We suggest that researchers write down an explicit optimizing model of what each firm/industry does. A model clarifies what we *want* to measure and thus what the ideal data set is. Only after we know how to do measurement in principle can we begin to compromise in practice. And if the shadow costs of the data availability constraints are too high, the measurement community can call for additional data collection projects.

Our approach suggests several priorities for extending theory and collecting data. Our method applies directly to bank services produced in the process of generating financial instruments other than loans (e.g., lines

48. For recent studies, see, for example, Schreyer and Stauffer (2003), who consider an extensive set of services provided by financial firms; chapter 6 in Triplett and Bosworth (2004b) discusses the measurement of insurance output.

of credit, derivatives). Likewise, our model applies to the production of financial services by nonbank intermediaries. Thus, our work serves as a template for measuring financial service output of the financial sector more generally. Also, our method connects financial measurement to the vast body of research on asset pricing and corporate finance. Thus, conclusions from these literatures on some real-world complexities (e.g., realistic tax treatment of interest and capital gains) can be readily incorporated. Wang (2003a) discusses some of these issues in depth, such as the effects of deposit insurance.

On data collection, Basel II reporting requirements can generate data on the risk profiles of banks' assets. Also, constructing an index of real bank output requires improved surveys; for example, direct quantity counts for a wider variety of bank activities would be useful, and data on how marginal costs of originating and monitoring loans vary with size and other attributes would help with quality adjustment.

We conclude by summarizing the answers to the four questions posed in the abstract. First, the correct reference rates on loans must incorporate risk. Second, one does not want to use an ex ante measure of the risk premium on bank funds in each reference rate—using an ex post holding return on bonds of comparable riskiness comes closer to measuring the actual production of bank services. But the timing mismatch and other problems mean that in general, no single reference rate provides a perfect measurement of the nominal value of implicit service output. Third, the price deflator for financial services generally is not the overall price level. Financial services are an information product, qualitatively similar to other information processing services (e.g., consulting); in general, the price of financial services relative to final output will not be constant. Fourth, we should count capital gains as part of financial service output only if the gains are expected as implicit compensation for actual services provided.

## Appendix

### *Financial Intermediation under Asymmetric Information and Bank Output*

This appendix solves a bank's and its borrower's joint optimization problem to derive analytically why and how implicit bank output can be measured by decomposing a bank's overall cash flow.[49] The key equation underlying the decomposition is the one that sets the optimal interest rate on a bank loan.

49. This is a summary of appendix 1 in WBF (2004), which the reader is urged to consult for more detailed derivations.

### Screening and Monitoring

In the model, each project (operated by a firm that is owned by an entrepreneur) spans two periods. Banks' first function is to screen each project in the first period to uncover its credit risk, which determines the loan's interest rate. We assume that banks' screening technology can fully discern a project's type, denoted $\theta^i$, to avoid unnecessary complications. Because entrepreneurs have no initial wealth, banks price the implicit fee into the interest charged, to be paid next period. Firms then use the loans to purchase capital.

In the second period, each firm uses the capital to produce the single homogeneous final good of the economy and is liquidated at period end. The lending bank takes no further action unless a firm defaults, in which case the bank incurs a cost to monitor the firm and extracts all the residual payoff.[50]

In summary, banking service output consists of screening the *new* projects born in each period and monitoring the *old* projects that fail. Screening and monitoring have different production functions. They parsimoniously represent the myriad of tasks performed by banks in their general role as information processors in the credit market. So, the analysis here can be readily adapted to study (implicit) bank output in creating other financial instruments, such as derivatives contracts.

### Bank Cost Functions for Screening and Monitoring

A loan's interest rate depends in part on the bank's cost of screening and monitoring. So, we first detail properties of these two cost functions. Banks have the same CRS technology as the rating agency for screening and monitoring, respectively (see equation [12]).[51] The cost of screening or monitoring varies with each loan's attributes, most likely in a nonlinear fashion. The model represents loan attributes with a single dimension of size. Then, the cost of screening ($S$) or monitoring ($M$) a *single* loan of size $L^i$ in time $t$ can be written as

$$\text{(A1)} \qquad c_t^J = \upsilon^J(L_t^i)f^J(W_t, R_t^{SV} - 1 + \delta)$$
$$= \frac{\upsilon^J(L_t^i)}{A^J}\left(\frac{W_t}{1-\beta^J}\right)^{1-\beta^J}\left(\frac{R_t^{SV} - 1 + \delta}{\beta^J}\right)^{\beta^J}, \qquad J = S, M.$$

The term $f_t^J(.)$ is the cost of processing a numeraire loan (whose size is normalized to one). So, it only depends on factors common to all ($S$ and

50. That is, we adopt the standard costly state verification setup from Townsend (1979). See WBF (2004) for a discussion of its distinction from the monitoring function in Diamond (1991).

51. That is, referring to the constant marginal cost of processing each *additional loan* of given attributes. The CRS assumption is made for simplicity, given that the degree of returns to scale does not matter for deriving the right measure of bank output.

$M$)s output: input prices (the wage rate $W_t$ and the shadow rental price of bank capital $R_t^{SV} - 1 + \delta$; see section 7.1), output elasticities ($\beta^J$), and the technology parameter ($A^J$). The other term $\upsilon^J(L^i)$, which depends solely on size, then scales the numeraire cost across loans of different sizes. Given perfect competition for both screening and monitoring, $f_t^J$ will also be the price (relative to the price of the final good) of the respective numeraire service, and $\upsilon^J(L^i)$ will be the weight for aggregating services.

We assume, intuitively, that the cost of monitoring a loan grows more slowly than linearly in loan size; that is, $\upsilon^{M\prime} > 0$, and $\upsilon^{M\prime\prime} < 0$. Aggregate monitoring output then depends on not only the sum but also the distribution of loan sizes. On the other hand, $\upsilon^S(.)$ is assumed to be convex for technical reasons (explained next).

**Terms of the Loan Contract for Entrepreneurs' Projects**

We now describe terms of the loan contract, which will enter a bank's optimization problem in the next section. For a penniless entrepreneur $i$ born in period $t$ (called generation-$t$) to purchase capital $K_{t+1}^i$ for his or her project, he or she must borrow $K_{t+1}^i$ (the subscript denoting the period in which the capital is used in production), plus the screening fee $f_t^S\upsilon^S(K_{t+1}^i)$, and must pay off everything at the end of period two from the project's payoff.

Project $i$, arriving in period $t$, pays $\theta^i R_{t+1}^K$ for every unit of investment, where $R_{t+1}^K$ is the average ex post gross return (to be realized in period $t + 1$) across all potential projects, while $\theta^i$ is the project-specific risk parameter of $i$ (i.e., type) uncovered by the bank screening process. The variable $\theta^i$ depends on the random draw of $i$ from the distribution of project productivities, $z^i$.[52] So, $\theta^i$ is independently and identically distributed across time and projects. We denote its cumulative distribution function as $G(\theta)$, with $E(\theta) = 1$. The variable $R_{t+1}^K$ represents the aggregate risk and thus depends on the realization of the aggregate productivity shock in period $t + 1$ (i.e., $A_{t+1}$).[53] We denote the conditional cumulative distribution function as simply $F(R_{t+1}^K)$, which is assumed to be differentiable over a nonnegative support. The variable $\theta^i$ is uncorrelated with $R_{t+1}^K$, because $z^i$ and $A_{t+1}$ are uncorrelated.

Because project payoff is borrowers' sole source of income for repayment, it is intuitive to map the contractual rate for loan $i$ (call it $R_{t+1}^i$) into a (unique) threshold value of the aggregate return $R_{t+1}^K$ (call it $R_{t+1}^{Ki}$), such that $R_{t+1}^i[K_{t+1}^i + f_t^S\upsilon^S(K_{t+1}^i)] = \theta^i R_{t+1}^{Ki} K_{t+1}^i$. So, $F(R_{t+1}^{Ki})$ is the endogenous default probability of $i$. The lender's expected gross return is $F(R_{t+1}^{Ki})\theta^i K_{t+1}^i$, where $\Phi(R_{t+1}^{Ki}) \equiv [1 - F(R_{t+1}^{Ki})]R_{t+1}^{Ki} + \int_0^{R_{t+1}^{Ki}} R_{t+1}^K dF(R_{t+1}^K)$—the two terms being the expected rate of return, conditional on no default and default, respectively.

52. Section 1.G of appendix 1 in WBF (2004) derives the exact mapping between $\theta^i$ and $z^i$ for given $A_{t+1}$: $\theta^i = [\Upsilon(z^i)^{1/\alpha} + (1 - \delta)]/[\Upsilon\kappa + (1 - \delta)]$, where $\kappa \equiv \int_{z_{\min}}^{\infty} z^{1/\alpha} K_{t+1}^i d\vartheta(z)/K_{t+1}^{NF}$ and $\Upsilon \equiv (A_{t+1})^{1/\alpha}\, \alpha[(1 - \alpha)/W_{t+1}]^{(1/\alpha - 1)}$. It is omitted here due to space constraint.

53. Wang, Basu, and Fernald (2004) explain in detail why omitting project-specific noises in each project's realized return does not alter the model's implications for output measurement.

### Financial Intermediaries' Optimization Problem

This subsection solves banks' optimal production plan and loan interest rate. The representative bank maximizes the present value of cash flows by choosing $R^{Ki}_{t+1}$ (conditional on $K^i_{t+1}$), $N^S_t$, $N^M_t$, and $I^B_t$:

$$\text{(A2)} \quad V^B_0 = E_0\left[\sum_{t=1}^{\infty}\left(\prod_{\tau=1}^{t} R^H_\tau\right)^{-1}\left\{\int_0^{\hat\theta}[\theta K^i_{t+1}R^K_{t+1} - f^M_{t+1}\upsilon^M(K^i_{t+1})]dG(\theta)\right.\right.$$
$$+ \int_{\hat\theta}^{\infty}\theta K^i_{t+1}R^{Ki}_{t+1}dG(\theta) - \int_0^{\infty}K^i_{t+2}dG(\theta) + \int_0^{\infty}f^S_{t+1}\upsilon^S(K^i_{t+2})dG(\theta)$$
$$\left.\left. + \int_0^{\hat\theta}f^M_{t+1}\upsilon^M(K^i_{t+1})dG(\theta) - W_{t+1}N^B_{t+1} - I^B_{t+1}\right\}\right],$$

subject to the constraints:

$$\text{(A3)} \quad R^{Ki}_{t+1}(\hat\theta) = R^K_{t+1},$$

$$\text{(A4)} \quad \int_0^{\infty}\upsilon^S(K^i_{t+1})dG(\theta) = A^S_t(K^S_t)^{\beta^S}(N^S_t)^{1-\beta^S},$$

$$\text{(A5)} \quad \int_0^{\hat\theta}\upsilon^M(K^i_{t+1})dG(\theta) = A^M_{t+1}(K^M_{t+1})^{\beta M}(N^M_{t+1})^{1-\beta M},$$

$$\text{(A6)} \quad N^B_t = N^S_t + N^M_t, \text{ and } N^M_0 = 0,$$

$$\text{(A7)} \quad K^B_{t+1} = K^B_t(1-\delta) + I^B_t, \text{ where } K^B_t = K^S_t + K^M_t; \text{ Given } K^B_0 = K^S_0,$$

$$\text{(A8)} \quad K^{NF}_{t+1} = K^{NF}_t(1-\delta) + I^{NF}_t, \text{ where } K^{NF}_t = \int_0^{\infty}K^i_t dG(\theta); \text{ Given } K^{NF}_0,$$

$$\text{(A9)} \quad K^S_{t+1} + K^M_{t+1} + \int_0^{\infty}[K^i_{t+1} + f^S_t\upsilon^S(K^i_{t+1})]dG(\theta) = V^B_t.$$

Expectations in equation (A2) are taken over the distribution of $R^K_{t+1}$. The first two integrals are the overall interest (net of monitoring fees $f^M_{t+1}\upsilon^M[K^i_{t+1}]$) the bank will receive in period $t + 1$. The third integral is the productive capital the bank passes on to generation-$t + 1$ entrepreneurs after screening them. So, the sum of the three terms constitutes the cash flow of the loan division. The remaining terms form the cash flow of the bank's services division, whose implicit outputs of screening ($Y^S_{t+1}$) and monitoring ($Y^M_{t+1}$) are $\int_0^{\infty}\upsilon^S(K^i_{t+2})dG(\theta)$ and $\int_0^{\hat\theta}\upsilon^M(K^i_{t+1})dG(\theta)$, respectively. The variables $f^S_{t+1}$ and $f^M_{t+1}$ are the respective shadow prices, and $W_{t+l}$ is the wage rate in period $t + 1$; $N^B_{t+1}$ is the bank's total labor input, and $I^B_{t+1}$ is its total investment. Bank shareholders both pay (as debtholders of nonfinancial firms) and receive (as owners of the bank) the monitoring fees, so the two flows exactly offset each other in the bank's overall cash flow.

In equation (A3), $\hat\theta$ identifies the type of borrowers who are just able to pay their loan interest, given the realized $R^K_{t+1}$. Equations (A4) and (A5) are the production functions for screening in period $t$ and monitoring in period

$t + 1$, respectively. Total labor input is given in equation (A6), and $N_0^M = 0$ (and $K_0^M = 0$), given no monitoring at $t = 0$. Equations (A7) and (A8) describe the motion of the bank's and nonfinancial firms' capital, respectively.

Equation (A9) is the bank's balance sheet: the value of equity ($V_t^B$) equals the value of assets, consisted of productive capital to be used in screening ($K_{t+1}^S$) and monitoring ($K_{t+1}^M$) next period, funds $[\int_0^\infty K_{t+1}^i dG(\theta)]$ transferred to borrowing firms, and this period's screening fees, which can be thought of as an intangible asset that will generate income in the next period, because it will be repaid by borrowing firms, on average.

The variable $R^H$ in equation (A2) needs elaboration. It is bank shareholders' required rate of return, equivalent to the return on total assets for a fully equity-funded bank. Thus, $R^H$ is determined by the risk profile of *total* bank cash flow, according to households' Euler equation (6). Section 7.1 has shown that $R^H$ is the weighted average of (implicit) required rates on the two partial cash flows generated by the loan division and the services division—$R^L$ and $R^{SV}$, respectively. Correspondingly, equation (A2) can be decomposed into two terms, as follows:[54]

$$\text{(A10)}\quad E_0\left[\left(1-\frac{K_1^B}{V_0^B}\right)\sum_{t=1}^{\infty}\left(\prod_{\tau=1}^{t}R_\tau^L\right)^{-1}\left\{\int_0^{\hat\theta}[\theta K_{t+1}^i R_{t+1}^K - f_{t+1}^M \upsilon^M(K_{t+1}^i)]dG(\theta) + \int_{\hat\theta}^{\infty}\theta K_{t+1}^i R_{t+1}^i dG(\theta) - K_{t+2}^{NF}\right\}\right.$$
$$\left. + \left(\frac{K_1^B}{V_0^B}\right)\sum_{t=1}^{\infty}\left(\prod_{\tau=1}^{t}R_\tau^{SV}\right)^{-1}\left\{\int_0^{\infty} f_{t+1}^S \upsilon^S(K_{t+2}^i)dG(\theta) + \int_0^{\hat\theta} f_{t+1}^M \upsilon^M(K_{t+1}^i)dG(\theta) - W_{t+1}N_{t+1}^B - I_{t+1}^B\right\}\right].$$

This partition maps into a bank's cash flow under securitization: banks receive origination fees up front and servicing fees over the lifetime of the loan pool. (See section 7.3 for more discussions.) Investors then receive the residual interest payments. This also maps into a rating agency plus a bond issue (section 7.1).

## The Determination of the Contractual Interest Rate

The loan division's optimal decision (the first component in equation [A10]) sets the contractual interest rate. It contains all the relevant cash flows—including the processing cost—for the debtholders. It expresses the condition that the interest rate charged must generate an expected return (net of the monitoring cost) equal to the ex ante rate of return required by households on their investment. This condition must hold for every loan

54. This is under the implicit assumption that bank services are paid first, before shareholders receive the residual interest.

to avoid arbitrage. So, the optimal rate ($R^{Ki}_{t+1}$) on a loan to a generation-$t$ entrepreneur ($i$) must satisfy:[55]

$$\text{(A11)}\quad [1 - F(R^{Ki}_{t+1})]\theta^i R^i_{t+1} K^i_{t+1} + \int_0^{R^{Ki}_{t+1}} \theta^i R^K_{t+1} K^i_{t+1} dF(R^K_{t+1}) - E_t[f^M_{t+1}]\upsilon^M(K^i_{t+1})F(R^{Ki}_{t+1}) - R^{Li}_{t+1} f^S_t \upsilon^S(K^i_{t+1}) = R^{Li}_{t+1} K^i_{t+1}.$$

This is the key first-order condition from the bank's maximization problem set up in equations (A2) through (A9). Note that the relevant discount rate for the risky debt return is $R^{Li}$ but not $R^{Hi}$. As intuition suggests, equation (A11) implies that the higher the screening or monitoring costs, the worse the project types, and lower means of $R^K_{t+1}$ all lead to higher $R^{Ki}_{t+1}$.[56] To ensure a finite scale of operation at each firm, we assume that $R^{Ki}_{t+1}$ falls with loan size ($K^i_{t+1}$).

## Optimal Choice of Capital by Nonfinancial Firms

Entrepreneur $i$ chooses $K^i_{t+1}$ to maximize the expected utility of his residual return:[57]

$$\text{(A12)}\qquad \max E_t(U^i_{t+1}) = \max \int_{R^{Ki}_{t+1}}^{\infty} U[(R^K_{t+1} - R^{Ki}_{t+1})\theta^i K^i_{t+1}] dF(R^K_{t+1}),$$

subject to the constraint in equation (A11). The variable $U(.)$ is the usual concave utility function, as defined in equation (8). The first-order condition for $K^i_{t+1}$ is:

$$\text{(A13)}\quad \int_{R^i_{t+1}}^{\infty} U'(.)\left[(R^K_{t+1} - R^{Ki}_{t+1}) - \left(\frac{\partial R^{Ki}_{t+1}}{\partial K^i_{t+1}}\right) K^i_{t+1}\right]\theta^i dF(R^K_{t+1}) = 0.$$

The implicit relationship between $R^{Ki}_{t+1}$ and $K^i_{t+1}$ is represented by $\partial R^{Ki}_{t+1}/\partial K^i_{t+1}$, embedded in equation (A11). Clearly, $R^{Ki}_{t+1}$ and $K^i_{t+1}$ are jointly determined by the bank and the firm's optimization problems.

Equation (A13) makes it clear that for given $F(R^K_{t+1})$, the contractual loan rate needs to rise in the size of the loan (i.e., $\partial R^{Ki}_{t+1}/\partial K^i_{t+1} > 0$) to obtain a finite optimal $K^i_{t+1}$.[58] For individual $K^i_{t+1}$ to be determinate, an upward-sloping supply curve for funds is also necessary (i.e., the optimal solution of $K^i_{t+1}$ rises in the mean of $R^K_{t+1}$), given that firms' technology is CRS. In fact, this means that production will not happen just at the most efficient firm

55. Note that $f^M_{t+1}$ is not known when $R^{Ki}_{t+1}$ is chosen in period $t$, and hence the expectations operator.

56. See WBF (2004) for derivations of these and all the other comparative statics, and if relevant, the conditions under which they are obtained. None of the conditions affect the model's conclusion regarding bank output measurement.

57. This formulation is consistent with equation (10) in the text, except that here, the entrepreneur's payoff is expressed all in terms of his or her residual return on capital, which has already accounted for the cost of labor and bank information services implicitly. Section G of appendix 1 in WBF (2004) shows the exact mapping between the two formulations.

58. Wang, Basu, and Fernald (2004) discuss in detail the conditions under which this result arises. In general, it seems to call for more than simple processing costs. But the exact mechanism matters not for our purpose—deriving the proper output measure.

(i.e., with the highest $\theta^i$, corresponding to $\bar{z}$ in section 7.1). Instead, banks lend to a group of firms with a descending order of $\theta^i$ until aggregate capital stock is all utilized; the more efficient a firm, the larger its capital size. All else equal, the more capital available, the larger the set of firms that invest. On the other hand, given the aggregate capital stock, higher screening or monitoring cost means a larger set of firms will invest, and the efficiency level of the marginal firm will be lower.

## References

Akerlof, G. 1970. The market for "lemons": Quality uncertainty and the market mechanism. *Quarterly Journal of Economics* 84 (3): 488–500.

Allen, F., and A. M. Santomero. 1998. The theory of financial intermediation. *Journal of Banking and Finance* 21 (11/12): 1461–85.

———. 1999. What do financial intermediaries do? FIC Working Paper no. 99-30-B. University of Pennsylvania, Wharton Financial Institutions Center.

Barnett, W. A. 1978. The user cost of money. *Economic Letters* 1 (2): 145–9.

Berger, A. N., and D. B. Humphrey. 1997. Efficiency of financial institutions: International survey and directions for future research. *European Journal of Operational Research* 98 (2): 175–212.

Berger, A. N., and L. J. Mester. 1997. Inside the black box: What explains differences in the efficiencies of financial institutions? *Journal of Banking and Finance* 21 (7): 895–947.

Bernanke, B. S., and M. Gertler. 1989. Agency costs, net worth, and business fluctuations. *American Economic Review* 79 (1): 14–31.

Bernanke, B. S., M. Gertler, and S. Gilchrist. 1999. The financial accelerator in a quantitative business cycle framework. In *Handbook of macroeconomics,* vol. 1C, *Handbooks in economics,* vol. 15, ed. B. S. Bernanke, M. Gertler, and S. Gilchrist, 1341–93. New York: Elsevier Science.

Cochrane, J. H. 2001. *Asset pricing.* Princeton, NJ: Princeton University Press.

Diamond, D. W. 1984. Financial intermediation and delegated monitoring. *Review of Economic Studies* 51 (3): 393–414.

———. 1991. Monitoring and reputation: The choice between bank loans and directly placed debt. *Journal of Political Economy* 99 (4): 688–721.

Diewert, W. E. 1974. Intertemporal consumer theory and the demand for durables. *Econometrica* 42 (3): 497–516.

Fixler, D. J. 2004. Discussion of output measurement in the insurance and the banking and finance industries. In *Productivity in the U.S. services sector: New sources of economic growth,* ed. J. E. Triplett and B. P. Bosworth, 217–30. Washington, DC: Brookings Institution.

Fixler, D. J., M. B. Reinsdorf, and G. M. Smith. 2003. Measuring the services of commercial banks in the NIPAs: Changes in concepts and methods. *Survey of Current Business* 83 (9): 33–44.

Fixler, D. J., and K. D. Zieschang. 1992. User costs, shadow prices, and the real output of banks. In *Studies in income and wealth,* vol. 56, *Output measurement in the service sector,* ed. Z. Griliches, 219–45. Cambridge, MA: National Bureau of Economic Research.

Hancock, D. 1985. The financial firm: Production with monetary and nonmonetary goods. *Journal of Political Economy* 93 (5): 859–80.

Leland, H. E., and D. H. Pyle. 1977. Informational asymmetries, financial structure, and financial intermediation. *Journal of Finance* 32 (2): 371–87.
Modigliani, F. F., and M. H. Miller. 1958. The cost of capital, corporation finance, and the theory of investment. *American Economic Review* 48 (3): 261–97.
Ramakrishnan, R., and A. V. Thakor. 1984. Information reliability and a theory of financial intermediation. *Review of Economic Studies* 51 (3): 415–32.
Schreyer, P., and P. Stauffer. 2003. Financial services in national accounts: Measurement issues and progress. Paper presented at the meeting of the Organization for Economic Cooperation and Development (OECD) Task Force on Financial Services in the National Accounts, October.
Townsend, R. M. 1979. Optimal contracts and competitive markets with costly state verification. *Journal of Economic Theory* 21 (1): 265–93.
Triplett, J. E., and B. P. Bosworth. 2004a. Measuring banking and finance: Conceptual issues. In *Productivity in the U.S. services sector: New sources of economic growth,* ed. J. E. Triplett and B. P. Bosworth, 177–211. Washington, DC: Brookings Institution.
———. 2004b. Price, output, and productivity of insurance: Conceptual issues. In *Productivity in the U.S. services sector: New sources of economic growth,* ed. J. E. Triplett and B. P. Bosworth, 123–77. Washington, DC: Brookings Institution.
United Nations, Eurostat, International Monetary Fund, Organization for Economic Cooperation and Development, and World Bank. 1993. *System of National Accounts, 1993.* New York: United Nations.
U.S. Department of Labor, Bureau of Labor Statistics. 1998. Technical note on commercial banks, SIC 602: Output components and weights. Manuscript, December. Washington, DC: GPO.
U.S. Federal Reserve Board. 2009. Z.1: Flow of funds accounts of the United States. Available at http://www.federalreserve.gov/releases/z1/current/data.htm.
Wang, J. C. 2003a. Loanable funds, risk, and bank service output. Federal Reserve Bank of Boston, Working Paper no. 03-4, July. Available at http://www.bos.frb.org/economic/wp/wp2003/wp034.htm.
———. 2003b. Service output of bank holding companies in the 1990s, and the role of risk. Federal Reserve Bank of Boston, Working Paper no. 03-6, September. Available at http://www.bos.frb.org/economic/wp/wp2003/wp036.htm.
Wang, J. C., S. Basu, and J. F. Fernald. 2004. A general-equilibrium asset-pricing approach to the measurement of nominal and real bank output. Federal Reserve Bank of Boston, Working Paper no. 04-7, October. Available at http://www.bos.frb.org/economic/wp/wp2004/wp047.htm.

## Comment Paul Schreyer

### Introduction

The topic of banking output has long been a thorny issue for national accountants and analysts of banking performance and productivity. Christina Wang, Susantu Basu, and John Fernald (see chapter 7 of this volume;

Paul Schreyer is head of the National Accounts Division of the Organisation for Economic Cooperation and Development.

WBF in what follows) provide us with an explicit model of the behavior of households, financial firms, and nonfinancial firms, with a view to drawing conclusions for the measurement of implicitly priced output of banks. Such a model is useful, because it spells out the assumptions underlying the statements about measurement, making them transparent and focusing the discussion. The WBF contribution is also timely, because the topic of banking output has attracted renewed attention at the national and international level in the past two or three years: in Europe, member countries of the European Union agreed on a common method and timeline for the treatment of financial intermediation services indirectly measured (FISIM) in their respective national accounts (Commission of the European Communities 2002); the United States recently introduced a revised treatment of FISIM into their National Income and Product Accounts (Fixler, Reinsdorf, and Smith 2003; NIPAs); and the Organization for Economic Cooperation and Development (OECD) discussed the topic in the context of a Task Force on the Measurement of the Production of Financial Institutions (Schreyer and Stauffer 2003). This was complemented by other contributions, such as those of Triplett and Bosworth (2004), who also discuss the measurement of banking output and make several proposals to advance the matter. It is against this background—new developments in the international debate and existing prescriptions in the System of National Accounts (SNA)—that I will discuss WBF's contribution.

## A Point to Reemphasize: Financial Institutions Provide Financial Services

An important feature of WBF's model and its conclusions for measurement is the focus on the actual flow of *financial* services provided by banks. More specifically, in WBF's model, banks provide financial services in the form of screening and monitoring to mitigate asymmetric information problems between potential investors and those seeking funds. This differs from a strand of research (e.g., Ruggles 1983) that sees banks as providers of *finance*[1] (to borrowers) and consequently recommends that the output of banks be measured by the flow of revenues from providing *financing* services—note the subtle but important difference between *financing* and *financial* services.

The emphasis of WBF on financial services as the output of financial institutions is a point worth reiterating. According to WBF, banks exist and create value essentially because there are information asymmetries that make it costly for households and investors with surpluses of funds to lend directly to nonfinancial firms with requirements for funds. There is in fact a significant body of literature that has considered information asymmetries as an explanation for the existence and activity of banks, as documented,

1. See Triplett and Bosworth (2004) for a fuller discussion.

for example, in a survey by Gorton and Winton (2002). However, the step from acknowledging this reason for the existence of financial institutions to bringing out the implications for the measurement of output is much scarcer, and this effort is an important merit of WBF's chapter. A similar conclusion—to put forward financial services as the output of financial institutions—has been reached by the OECD Task Force on Financial Services Measurement (Schreyer and Stauffer 2003), albeit in the context of a much simpler accounting model.

Wang, Basu, and Fernald limit their focus to screening and monitoring services. Other services could easily be put forward—in particular, convenience services (say, for depositors—for example, safeguarding, automatic payments, and provision of checks). This makes little difference to their qualitative conclusions, however. And WBF's limitation to screening and monitoring services reflects the trade-off between providing an explicit modeling approach for important services and keeping the model tractable.

## Should the Reference Rate Reflect Risk?

One of the central conclusions put forward by WBF is that the reference rate for measuring nominal bank lending services "must be *risk adjusted* (i.e., contain a risk premium reflecting the systematic risk associated with the loans)" (see chapter 7 of this volume). This is in contrast to current practice in the U.S. NIPAs, where the reference rate is an (implicitly) maturity-weighted rate of government bonds and thus a default-free rate. Similarly, the directives for the implementation of the new FISIM measures in the European Union require that countries use an interbank rate; that is, an interest rate that is short-term but also essentially risk free. The choice of the right reference rate is important, because it influences the measured level of banking output and potentially influences gross domestic product, as well as its growth rates. Some more discussion is required to shed light on this point.

### The Question behind the Reference Rate: Who Bears Risk?

The first point to make is that it is not the reference rate as such that is at stake; it is the more general question about whether banks assume risk. Consider an investment decision by a bank, say, in a loan. In an efficient market, the value of this financial asset to the bank at the beginning of a year ($P^L$) will equal the discounted value of expected interest payments at the end of the year ($R^L$) and the discounted market value of the loan at the end of the year ($P_1^L$), minus the value of financial services ($S^L$) that the bank provides to the borrower, where these services are implicitly priced[2] and assumed to be provided at the beginning of the year.

2. We ignore explicitly priced services, because they add nothing to the present debate and can easily be integrated.

The appropriate rate for discounting should be the required return that an investment of equal risk and maturity is expected to yield on the financial market. This is also the definition of a risk-adjusted opportunity cost for the bank's investment. Call this required rate of return $r^H$, following WBF's notation. We can further decompose this required rate into a risk-free rate and a risk premium: $(1 + r^H) = (1 + r^F)(1 + rp)$, where $r^F$ is a risk-free rate and $rp$ is the risk premium. An asset market equilibrium should then be characterized by the following condition:

$$\text{(C1)} \qquad P^L = \frac{1}{1 + r^F} - S^L.$$

After inserting $(1 + r^H) = (1 + r^F)(1 + rp)$ and after a few transformations, equation (C1) becomes:

$$\text{(C2)} \qquad (1 + rp)(1 + s^L) = \frac{1}{1 + r^F}\left(r^L + \frac{P_1^L}{P^L}\right),$$

where $s^L \equiv S^L/P^L$ is the value of financial services implicitly provided per dollar of the value of the asset, and $r^L \equiv R^L/P^L$ is the rate of return that reflects the regular (interest) payments on the asset (loan).

The left-hand side of equation (C2) is the discount factor that combines the risk premium and the rate of implicitly priced services. Let us call this combined rate $\tilde{s}^L$, where $(1 + \tilde{s}^L) \equiv (1 + rp)(1 + s^L)$. If one inserts this relation into equation (C2), one gets

$$\text{(C3)} \qquad \tilde{s}^L = \frac{1}{1 + r^F}\left(r^L + \frac{P_1^L}{P^L}\right) - 1 = \frac{1}{1 + r^F}(r^L + \pi - r^F),$$

where the rate of price change $P_1^L/P^L - 1$ has been labeled $\pi$. For simplicity, we shall assume that the loan is not traded and the price change is zero. Thus,

$$\text{(C4)} \qquad \tilde{s}^L = \frac{1}{1 + r^F}(r^L - r^F).$$

Equation (C4) corresponds to the simplest form of the user cost price that features in the NIPAs calculation of FISIM.[3] What then does one make of all this in relation to the WBF critique of the reference rate?

User cost prices of loans, as in equation (C4), reflect implicitly priced services to borrowers and risk premia. By construction, the reference rate $r^F$ is a risk-free rate; otherwise, the user cost price would not comprise a risk premium. But there is no claim that the risk-free rate constitutes the risk-adjusted required return on investments for financial firms—the latter was assumed to be $r^H$, and this rate correctly entered as the discount factor in

3. The national accounts measure does not comprise the factor $1/(1 + r^F)$, but this is of secondary importance and depends only on the assumptions about the timing of interest payments during the accounting period.

the equilibrium condition in equation (C1). In equation (C4), the reference rate serves simply as a device to capture the risk premium with a view to reflecting risk-assumption services provided by the bank to the borrower. Thus, it is not the required return to the financial firm that is at issue in the discussion about the reference rate. By challenging the risk-free reference rate, WBF challenge the existence of this service: it is not the bank but is its shareholders who ultimately bear systematic risk, and consequently, measured bank output is overstated. The real question therefore, is, whether there is a risk-assumption service by the financial institution.

Scope of Assets and Liabilities

The discussion so far has been in terms of a loan in isolation, and statements about the right measure of banking output have to consider both the asset and liability side of the bank's balance sheet. And while the source of a bank's funds (equity, deposits, bonds issued, etc.) is without importance in WBF's model, it is not without importance in a national accounts context. In essence, WBF state that the systematic risk of loans is borne by the bank's shareholders and not by the bank itself—hence, the risk-assumption service should not be identified as part of bank output. Indeed, if one brings in shareholder considerations and computes the user cost price of the bank's shares from the perspective of shareholders, a computation parallel to the preceding one can be applied to yield

$$\tilde{s}^{SI} = \frac{1}{1 + r^F}(d^{SI} + \pi^{SI} - r^F). \tag{C5}$$

In equation (C5), $\tilde{s}^{SI}$ is the user cost price for the bank's shareholders, $d^{SI}$ are dividends paid by the bank, $\pi^{SI}$ are expected holding gains, and $r^F$, as before, is a risk-free rate. As in WBF, take the simple case, where a bank is only funded by equity and only invests in loans, and where the value of equity equals the value of loans, which we shall call $y^L$. Then, correcting the user cost price on loans in equation (C4) by the user cost price of shareholders' investment in equation (C5), we get

$$(\tilde{s}^L - \tilde{s}^{SI})y^L = [r^L - (d^{SI} + \pi^{SI})]y^L. \tag{C6}$$

In equation (C6), the rate of return on loans $r^L$ is compared with the expected rate of return on the bank's equity $(d^{SI} + \pi^{SI})$, which in equilibrium would equal the bank's opportunity cost $r^H$. But if $(d^{SI} + \pi^{SI}) = r^H$, one ends up with a value for bank output that corresponds to WBF's formula with a risk-adjusted reference rate $r^H$, rather than the risk-free rate $r^F$.

Thus, the two approaches would yield the same result if the national accounts corrected for shareholders' user costs, as specified in equation (C5). However, the national accounts do not perform this correction, as by convention, no user costs are computed on equity. There is thus an underlying issue of scope—which financial instruments are carriers of financial services—that needs addressing in the national accounts. In its narrowest form, implemented, for example, in the European Union, the national accounts measure of financial services is solely based on deposits and loans. The U.S. NIPAs takes a wider perspective and considers all assets and liabilities that earn interest or imputed interest. Obviously, the broader the scope of assets and liabilities that the national accounts take into account, the smaller the difference to the WBF results, even if the national accounts employ a risk-free reference rate.

A different way of interpreting WBF's results vis-à-vis the national accounts is to say that the national accounts implicitly take a perspective where a financial firm and its owners constitute one economic entity. Wang, Basu, and Fernald's model sees banks separately from their shareholders, and by implication, any risk premia charged by banks are passed on to shareholders, who bear the systematic risk of investment. The authors conclude that banking output as presently measured is overstated by the risk premium, because financial firms should be considered different entities from their shareholders.

### A Practical Point: Choosing the Required Rate of Return for Shareholders

If one accepts WBF's suggestion to use a risk-adjusted reference rate and/or to correct the national accounts computation for user costs to shareholders, the practical question arises: how do we choose the appropriate risk-adjusted rate that reflects the required return to shareholders? As shown in WBF's model, the theoretically correct rate is determined by the representative consumers' expected consumption path, or more specifically, the required rate equals the risk-free rate, plus a risk premium that depends on the covariance between the consumer's intertemporal pricing kernel and the assets in which the bank invests.

The empirical implementation of this risk-adjusted rate is a difficult issue. Typically, the covariance between asset returns and consumption is weak—a finding that is well established in the literature on the equity premium puzzle (see Kocherlakota [1996] for an overview). A weak covariance implies a small adjustment to the risk-free rate, however, and would diminish the empirical impact of the choice. For example, using the components of the Federal Reserve System monetary aggregates, Barnett, Liu, and Jensen (1997) found that risk adjustments were small. Of course, such empirical considerations have no bearing on the theoretical points made by WBF, but they are of interest to statistical agencies that have to implement measures.

### Is the Test of "The Bank That Does Nothing" a Valid One?

One test proposed by WBF to substantiate the plausibility of their model is to ask what their measure of production would be for a bank that "does nothing" (see chapter 7 of this volume). More specifically, a hypothetical situation is invoked, where banks are simple accounting devices, only there to receive households' capital (they buy the bank's shares) and to lend out these funds to entrepreneurs, but not to provide screening or monitoring services—shareholders themselves see right through the bank and are able to screen borrowers and to monitor them. Then, WBF argue, the measure of this bank's output should be zero. The national accounts measure, under the same circumstances, produces a positive value of output, because in the previous notation, it would correspond to the user costs of the loans, $(r^L - r^F)y^L$, and they are positive if there is systematic risk.

This raises again the question about the source of financing. In WBF's model, the Modigliani-Miller theorem applies to banks as well as to nonfinancial firms; therefore, banks' financing structures are of no consequence for the required rate of return. Consequently, allowing for debt financing of banks makes no difference to WBF's argument that national accounts overstate banking output by the risk premium on loans and other assets. This is correct if one accepts the assumptions underlying the Modigliani-Miller theorem (perfect capital markets, equal access, homogenous expectations, etc.), which we shall do for the present argument. Thus, the structure of bank financing has no influence on the bank's required rates of return. However, the structure of financing *does* make a difference when applying the test of the bank that does nothing, because different sources of financing are not treated symmetrically in the national accounts. Take a bank that does nothing—a pure accounting device in WBF's terms—but assume that it is deposit financed, not equity financed. Applying national accounts methodology to this case yields a zero measure of production.

This is easily demonstrated by considering the national accounts' FISIM calculation, where $y^D$ and $r^D$ are the value of deposits and the interest rate paid on them, respectively:

$$\text{National accounts' banking output} = y^L(r^L - r^F) - y^D(r^D - r^F).$$

In WBF's case of a bank that does nothing, there are no implicitly priced depositor services, and the rate that is paid on deposits must equal the loan rate, itself equal to the return required by the financing units, the depositors: $r^L = r^D$. In the absence of equity financing and in the equilibrium situation postulated by WBF, $y^L = y^D$ and the banking output measured by the national accounts equals zero. This makes the relevance of the test of the bank that does nothing dependent on an empirical issue: national accounts fail to register zero output, to the extent that bank loans are equity financed—in the more realistic case of deposit-financed banks, the argument applies to a much smaller extent.

### Timing of Provision and Measurement of Financial Services

Wang, Basu, and Fernald's model assumes that screening services are provided at the beginning of a contractual relationship between banks and borrowers, and the authors rightly point out that there is an issue of timing when the flow of services is measured via flows of interest that are observed during the life of the loan. This is not a contentious issue, and the accrual principle, one of the cornerstones of the SNA, suggests that efforts be made to enter payments for a service at a time as close as possible to the provision of the service. The tricky empirical issue of implementing this principle in the context of a flow of service payments that cannot be directly observed remains!

### Another Point Worth Emphasizing: Holding Gains

The authors rightly observe, "If interest income is often employed as implicit compensation for financial services provided without explicit charge, then in principle, capital gains can be used in place of interest for the same purpose" (see chapter 7 of this volume). To illustrate, WBF use the example of a loan that is sold off and argue that only expected capital gains should enter the computation of financial services output, whereas capital gains or losses purely due to the random realization of asset returns should not be counted as financial output.

This is an important observation that lines up with a suggestion made by Fixler and Moulton (2001) and the discussion in Schreyer and Stauffer (2003). At the same time, any consideration of holding gains or losses in measures of production turns out to be highly controversial in the context of national accounts, because the SNA does not consider holding gains to be production. But the basic issue remains: there are many items on a bank's balance sheets with remunerations other than interest payments, and if an argument can be made that financial services are somehow associated with these assets and liabilities, expected holding gains cannot be ignored. Thus, WBF have raised another important and valid point here.

### Conclusions

There are many advantages to having an explicit model when devising proposals for measurement, and WFB should be commended for that. Explicit statements of assumptions and behavior of economic agents and the use of a model to bring things together are most valuable to make informed choices about measurement.

A core issue that arises from the discussion and that probably deserves further research is the role of risk and the question of whether, from an accounting perspective, banks or their shareholders bear the risk involved in lending.

Generally, WBF's model is relevant, raises the right issues, and treats them in a rigorous way: (a) we should view banks as institutions that provide financial services and then should be clear about what these services are and how they should be measured; (b) the choice of the reference rate is important, and its theoretical foundations need to be clearly put down; (c) measuring service flows at the time when they are produced and consumed can be difficult; (d) expected holding gains are an integral part of the return of certain financial instruments and should not be ignored in measuring financial services; and (e) interest rates are not normally the appropriate measures of financial service prices.

## References

Barnett, W., Y. Liu, and M. Jensen. 1997. CAPM risk adjustment for exact aggregation over financial assets. *Macroeconomic Dynamics* 1 (2): 485–512.

Commission of the European Communities. 2002. Report from the Commission to the Council and the European Parliament concerning the allocation of financial intermediation services indirectly measured (FISIM). Unpublished manuscript, June.

Fixler, D. J., and B. Moulton. 2001. Comments on the treatment of holding gains and losses in the national accounts. Paper presented at the Organization for Economic Cooperation and Development (OECD) Meeting of National Accounts Experts, October.

Fixler, D. J., M. B. Reinsdorf, and G. M. Smith. 2003. Measuring the services of commercial banks in the NIPAs: Changes in concepts and methods. *Survey of Current Business* 83 (9): 33–44.

Gorton, G., and A. Winton. 2002. Financial intermediation. NBER Working Paper no. 8928. Cambridge, MA: National Bureau of Economic Research, May.

Kocherlakota, N. R. 1996. The equity premium: It's still a puzzle. *Journal of Economic Literature* 34 (1): 42–71.

Ruggles, R. 1983. The United States national income accounts, 1947–77: Their conceptual basis and evolution. In *Studies in income and wealth,* vol. 47, *The United States national income accounts: Selected topics,* ed. M. F. Foss, 15–107. Chicago: University of Chicago Press.

Schreyer, P., and P. Stauffer. 2003. Measuring the production of financial corporations. Background report on the OECD Task Force on Financial Services in National Accounts, presented at the workshop on Rethinking Total Factor Productivity, October, Ottawa.

Triplett, J. E., and B. Bosworth. 2004. *Productivity in the U.S. services sector: New sources of economic growth.* Washington, DC: Brookings Institution.

8

# Can A Disease-Based Price Index Improve the Estimation of the Medical Consumer Price Index?

Xue Song, William D. Marder, Robert Houchens, Jonathan E. Conklin, and Ralph Bradley

## 8.1. Introduction

This chapter examines the effects of two separate factors that make it particularly challenging to construct health care price indexes in the United States. The first challenge is to obtain real prices for representative medical treatments. The widespread use of third-party reimbursement for services covered by health insurance plans puts the consumer of health care, the patient, in the unusual position of having another institution pay for the bulk of services consumed. Third-party reimbursement is characterized by complicated price negotiations that are not visible to the consumer at the time of purchase. It is also not visible to the Bureau of Labor Statistics (BLS) data collection efforts that depend on point-of-purchase surveys and follow-up monthly price checks. Thus, questions can be raised about the accuracy of the Medical Care component of the Consumer Price Index (MCPI), which relies on the general approach of the BLS to price the same bundle of goods and services that would be purchased by consumers. Which health plan reimbursement negotiations would be relevant or accessible to the data collector? In the absence of special efforts, the data collector is most likely to capture a (possibly discounted) list price, rather than an appropriately sampled real transaction price.

The second challenge is to keep pace with treatment innovations. Like

Xue Song is research leader at Thomson Reuters. William D. Marder is senior vice president and general manager of Thomson Reuters. Robert Houchens is senior director of Thomson Reuters. Jonathan E. Conklin is vice president of Thomson Reuters. Ralph Bradley is a research economist at the U.S. Department of Labor, Bureau of Labor Statistics.

Support for this work was provided to Thomson Reuters under contract to the Bureau of Labor Statistics. Opinions expressed are those of the authors and do not represent the official position of the Bureau of Labor Statistics.

many parts of the economy, the health care sector in recent years has experienced rapid technological change. New drugs have been introduced that can radically alter the style of treatment available for many common and rare conditions. New surgical and medical techniques have been developed and put into widespread use. Consequently, the treatment of many conditions has moved away from inpatient settings to outpatient settings or prescription drugs.

The nature of demand for health care services provides opportunities for measurement that are not applicable in most other sectors. Following Grossman (1972), physician visits, prescription drugs, and overnight stays in hospitals are not viewed as direct arguments in a consumer's utility function. The demand for health care services is a derived demand generated from an underlying demand for health, not health care. Health can be produced through preventive services in advance of illness or with curative services in the event of illness. By examining episodes of care for carefully selected illnesses, a number of authors (e.g., Berndt et al. 2002; Cutler, McClellan, and Newhouse 1998, 1999) have successfully examined the changing price of treatment for specific illnesses, such as depression and acute myocardial infarction. These studies look at the types of treatments patients receive to help them recover from illness. The ultimate demand is for recovery. As the technology available to health care providers improves, the inputs used in an episode of care will change. By measuring the total cost of the restructured episode, these authors were able to track the price of care.

Based largely on this evidence, a Committee on National Statistics (CNSTAT) panel recommended that the BLS develop an experimental version of the MCPI that derives prices for the total treatment costs of randomly sampled diagnoses.[1] Additionally, CNSTAT suggested that instead of collecting price quotes directly from providers, the MCPI could use the reimbursement information on retrospective claims databases. Pricing based on diseases and treatment episodes allows for medical care substitution across medical inputs in the treatment of patients. Because it does not rely on subjective response, claims-based pricing also eliminates respondent burden and may have the advantages of larger sample size and greater data validity.

This study uses medical insurance claims data to investigate both issues: (a) obtaining real prices for representative medical treatments to examine the impact of third-party reimbursement on measured trends in health care inputs of prescription drugs, physician services, and hospital services; and (b) capturing the substitution effects of health care inputs on the trend in medical care prices captured by episodes of care for some randomly selected conditions.

In section 8.2, we describe the data that are employed. Section 8.3 focuses on the replication analysis of the current BLS methodology. Section 8.4 provides the analysis of episodes of care, and the results are summarized

1. See Schultze and Mackie (2002).

in section 8.5. Section 8.6 discusses potential improvements that could be applied to studies in this area and the limitations of relying solely on claims data to produce medical CPI.

## 8.2 Data

Data for this study come from the MarketScan® Research Databases from Thomson Reuters. These databases are a convenience sample reflecting the combined health care service use of individuals covered by Thomson Reuters employer clients nationwide. Personally identifiable health information is sent to Thomson Reuters to help its clients manage the cost and quality of health care they purchase on behalf of their employees. MarketScan is the pooled and deidentified data from these client databases. Two MarketScan databases are used in this MCPI study: the Commercial Claims and Encounters (Commercial) Database and the Medicare Supplemental and Coordination of Benefits (COB; Medicare) Database.

The Commercial Claims and Encounters Database contains the health care experience of approximately four million employees and their dependents in 2002. These individuals' health care is provided under a variety of fee-for-service, fully capitated, and partially capitated health plans, including preferred provider organizations, point-of-service plans, indemnity plans, and health maintenance organizations. The database consists of inpatient admissions, inpatient services, outpatient services (including physician, laboratory, and all other covered services delivered to patients outside of hospitals and other settings where the patient would spend the night), and outpatient pharmaceutical claims.

The 2002 Medicare Supplemental and COB Database contains the health care experience of almost nine hundred thousand individuals with Medicare supplemental insurance paid for by employers. Both the Medicare-covered portion of payment (represented as the COB amount) and the employer-paid portion are included in this database. The database also consists of inpatient admissions, inpatient services, outpatient services, and outpatient pharmaceutical claims.

Our analysis is limited to three metropolitan areas that serve as primary sampling units (PSUs) for the BLS MCPI and that have significant numbers of covered lives captured in MarketScan databases. These metropolitan areas are New York City (CPI area A109), Philadelphia (A102), and Boston (A103). While the number of covered lives in each of the cities varies by year, MarketScan has many more respondents in Boston (146,000 in 1998) than in Philadelphia (104,901) or New York (43,520).

## 8.3 Replication of the Medical CPI

The BLS CPI is constructed using a two-stage process. In the first stage, price indexes are generated for 211 different item categories for each of thirty-eight urban areas. The indexes in the first stage are then used to generate an all-items-all-cities index. The overall medical CPI is an expenditure weighted average of such item indexes. Although the medical CPI includes eight of the 211 item categories—including, for example, dental services, nonprescription drugs, and medical supplies—this study only constructed price indexes for prescription drugs, physician services, and hospital services.

The initial BLS sample at the item-area level is implemented with two surveys. The first is a telephone point-of-purchase survey (TPOPS), where randomly selected households are asked where they purchase their medical goods and services and how much they spend at each outlet. In the second survey, the results of TPOPS are used to select outlets where the probability of selection for a particular outlet is proportional to its expenditure share in TPOPS.

Once an outlet is drawn, the BLS field representative goes to the outlet to select either a good or a service that falls within a certain item category. There is a detailed checklist of important characteristics of the item. The field representative determines the expenditure share for each characteristic, and the probability that an item is drawn is proportional to the expenditure share of its characteristics within the outlet. For pharmaceuticals, a key characteristic is the National Drug Code (NDC); for physicians, it is the Current Procedure Terminology (CPT) code; and for hospitals, it is based on the Diagnosis Related Group (DRG).

Once the outlets and items are selected, they stay in the BLS sample for four years.[2] The implicit assumption of this fixed sample is that the inputs used to treat each specific disease are constant. As Cutler, McClellan, and Newhouse (1998, 1999) and Shapiro and Wilcox (1996) argued, if less expensive inputs are substituted for more expensive ones, this will not be reflected as a decrease in the BLS price index.

On a monthly or bimonthly basis, the BLS reprices the items in its sample.[3] For all medical items except pharmaceuticals, the BLS generates an arithmetic mean (Laspeyres-type) price index in each area. For pharmaceuticals, a geometric mean index is computed. The Laspeyres formula is then used to aggregate the area indexes to the national level.

No claims database contains the information needed to precisely mimic these procedures. Appendix A provides the eleven detailed steps we took to create analytic files that would provide as much of the information just described as possible. All outlets and items were selected using probability in proportion to size with replacement, the same method that the BLS uses to collect its samples.

2. Beginning in 2001, the BLS began reselecting prescription drugs within its outlet sample at two-year intervals—that is, midway between outlet resamplings.

3. Most areas have on-cycle and off-cycle months. For some areas, the on-cycle months are the even ones, and for others, they are the odd ones. Repricing is only done in the on-cycle months, and the price index represents the price change over a two-month period.

We developed two sets of input-based indexes. One is based on the same sample sizes as those of the BLS MCPI,[4] and the other is based on much larger sample sizes (ten times as large as the BLS sample sizes wherever possible). We used the small-sample index to investigate if the price distribution was statistically different between the claims database and the BLS sample. The large-sample index was intended to examine whether the sample sizes had a significant impact on indexes.[5]

## 8.4 Episode-Based Price Indexes

A number of studies previously cited have studied the changing cost of treating specific illnesses by examining episodes of care for those illnesses and how the cost of a treatment episode changed over time. Based on that literature, the CNSTAT recommended a study of a generalization of this approach (Schultze and Mackie 2002, 6–9):

> BLS should select between 15–40 diagnoses from the ICD (International Classification of Diseases), chosen randomly in proportion to their direct medical treatment expenditures and use information from retrospective claims databases to identify and quantify the inputs used in their treatment and to estimate their cost. On a monthly basis, the BLS could re-price the current set of specific items (e.g., anesthesia, surgery, and medications), keeping quantity weights temporarily fixed. Then, at appropriate intervals, perhaps every year or two, the BLS should reconstruct the medical price index by pricing the treatment episodes of the 15 to 40 diagnoses—including the effects of changed inputs on the overall cost of those treatments. The frequency with which these diagnosis adjustments should be made will depend in part on the cost to BLS of doing so. The resulting MCPI price indexes should initially be published on an experimental basis. The panel also recommends that the BLS appoint a study group to consider, among other things, the possibility that the index will "jump" at the linkage points and whether a prospective smoothing technique should be used.

### 8.4.1 Description of Medstat Episode Grouper

In order to implement the committee's recommendation with the data available for this study, we used the Medstat Episode Grouper (MEG) to transform a stream of claims data into episodes of care for the full range

4. The BLS sample sizes are:

| City | Drug | Physician | Hospital |
|---|---|---|---|
| Philadelphia | 34 | 32 | 31 |
| Boston | 42 | 27 | 46 |
| New York City | 41 | 35 | 59 |

5. McClelland and Reinsdorf (1999) found that the small sample bias of the geometric means index was larger than that of the seasoned index.

of conditions covered by the ICD system. The MEG is predicated on the Disease Staging patient classification system, developed initially for the Healthcare Cost and Utilization Project. The MEG uses sophisticated logic to create clinically relevant, severity-rated, and disease-specific groupings of claims. There are 593 episode groups. Episodes can be of several types:

- *Acute Condition* type includes episodes of care of acute conditions, which are generally reversible, such as an episode of sinusitis or otitis media.
- *Chronic Maintenance* episodes refer to episodes of routine care and management for a chronic, typically nonreversible condition or lifelong illness, such as diabetes mellitus episodes. All cancers are considered chronic.
- *Acute Flare-Up* type includes episodes of acute, generally reversible, and ideally preventable exacerbations of chronic conditions—such as an episode of diabetes with gangrene.
- *Well Care* type includes administrative and preventative care provided to a patient for ongoing health maintenance and wellness.

For the acute conditions and flare-ups identified in the claims, we define clean periods that mark the beginning or end of an episode of care. For chronic maintenance episodes, the first occurrence of the diagnosis can open an episode, and the calendar year is used to define endpoints.

Figure 8.1 illustrates how a stream of claims can be transformed into three episodes of care for a fifty-five-year-old male patient. In this example, episodes of care occur for two conditions: acute prostatitis and a herniated disc.

An episode for the care of the herniated disc (Episode 1) begins with an office visit on January 10. It includes all services related to an identified health problem of low back pain, including diagnostic imaging and a hospitalization. The episode ends with a follow-up physician office visit on May 8.

The treatment of acute prostatitis is divided into two episodes (Episodes 2 and 3). First, the patient is seen in his physician's office for acute prostatitis on February 4. The length of time between the February 4 visit and the May 18 visit is sufficiently long enough to begin a new episode, rather than continue the first episode. Consequently, a second episode (Episode 3) is initiated with the office visit for acute prostatitis on May 18. A complication of prostatitis, pyelonephritis, occurs within a short time, so the June 1 visit is a continuation of the second prostatitis episode.

This example also illustrates the difference between complications and comorbidities. A disease complication arises from the progression of an underlying disease. For example, pyelonephritis is a complication of acute prostatitis and is therefore a part of the episode for acute prostatitis. Disease comorbidities are diseases that are concurrent but not related to one another.

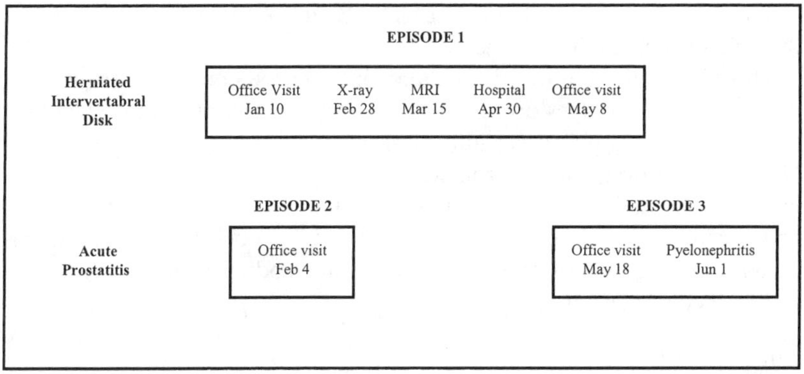


**Fig. 8.1 Three episodes of care**

For instance, the acute prostatitis and the herniated disc are comorbidities unrelated to one another. Therefore, separate disease episodes are created for the two comorbidities.

An episode of care is initiated with a contact with the health delivery system. In a claims-based methodology, the beginning of an episode is the first claim received for an episode grouping. The MEG methodology allows physician office visits and hospitalizations to open or extend patient episodes. As the coding of claims for laboratory tests and x-rays are not always reliable, these services can join existing episodes but cannot open an episode. Frequently in the practice of medicine, a physician will order a test prior to seeing a patient. To recognize this, a look-back mechanism has been incorporated in MEG. When a lab or x-ray service is encountered that occurred prior to the date of the claim that established an episode, MEG checks to see if an episode with the same episode group number has been opened within fifteen days following the test. If so, the lab or x-ray will be added to the episode.

An episode ends when the course of treatment is completed. Because the end of an episode is not designated on a claim, the clean period decision rule has been employed to establish the end date. Clean periods represent the period of time for a patient to recover from a disease or condition. If a subsequent visit for a disease occurs within the clean period, then it is assumed to be a part of the episode containing previous visits for that disease. If a visit for a disease occurs later than the clean period, then it defines the beginning of a new episode. The duration of clean periods was empirically and clinically reviewed and varies by disease.

Nonspecific initial diagnoses are relatively common in the billing of treatments of patients. For instance, an initial visit may be coded as abdominal pain but later be classified as appendicitis. The MEG incorporates logic to link nonspecific diagnoses and costs to specific episodes. The linkage occurs when a nonspecific claim has a date close in time to the specific episode and the linkage makes clinical sense.

The MEG incorporates drug claims into episode groups, even though drug claims themselves do not contain diagnostic information. The process of integrating pharmacy information into MEG begins with obtaining NDC information from Micromedex, a Thomson Reuters affiliate. Micromedex staff, made up of recognized pharmacological experts, map NDC codes from product package inserts to ICD-9-CM codes. This information is then reviewed by Thomson Reuters clinical and coding experts and mapped to MEG episode groups.

### 8.4.2 Construction of Episode-Based Disease Indexes

To construct episode-based disease indexes, we identified all claims for patients residing in the three metropolitan areas. We processed this group of claims with the episode software and created a file containing all of the episodes of care. Less than ten episode groups computed by MEG were excluded because they represent a collection of disparate conditions. This group contains only a small dollar amount.

Because diseases with low incidence (for example, cancer and kidney failure) usually command a much higher expenditure share than population share, it is possible that expenditure-based indexes and population-based indexes are very different. The cost-of-living theory is based on the cost functions of the individual consumer, but disease incidence and medical care spending are very skewed, both across individuals and over time for any given individual. Disease selection based on expenditure share increases the chances that less common but more severe diseases are selected; thus, the sample of selected diseases will not be representative of a typical consumer's experience in a given year. For example, in 2002, 5.7 percent of the national medical expenditure went to the treatment of acute myocardial infarction, while only 0.2 percent of the national population had this disease. Therefore, it is interesting to contrast indexes based on expenditure weighting with those based on population weighting.

To investigate the differences between the expenditure-based price index and the population-based price index, we randomly selected forty episodes with probability in proportion to their direct medical expenditures and another forty episodes with probability in proportion to the frequency of their occurrence in the population. Both sets of episodes were selected with replacement. All sample selection was carried out independently in each metropolitan area using MarketScan 1998 data. Because there could be more than one episode of a specific type chosen in this random selection, for the conditions represented in the selected episodes, all episodes of the same type in the city were selected, and the inputs used in these episode types were identified. For each selected episode, the volumes of inputs were updated at yearly intervals, and prices were estimated monthly from January 1999 to December 2002.

Appendixes B and C present the characteristics of the specific episode types that comprise the expenditure-based samples and the population-based samples in each city. For the expenditure-based samples, acute myocardial infarction, angina pectoris chronic maintenance, type 2 diabetes, and osteoarthritis were selected in all three cities. Neoplasm (with different types) also showed up in all cities. Only three diseases were commonly selected into the population-based samples in all three cities: aneurysm, thoracic; asthma, chronic maintenance; and tibial, iliac, femoral, or popliteal artery disease. Again, different types of neoplasm were sampled in all cities.

Standard grouping methods were utilized to compute the inputs into each episode type. For inpatient stays, we examined DRGs. For physician services and hospital outpatient services, we used the Berenson-Eggers Type of Service codes (BETOS, a transformation of the CPT-4 codes) developed by the Center for Medicare and Medicaid Services. For prescription drugs, we used Red Book therapeutic classes. The motivating factor in the decision to use grouped data was the desire to examine the full range of services that might appear in the episode and the concern with the magnitude of the detail that would need to be captured. The more detailed data we use, the bigger the concern with adequate cell size for monthly reporting. That is, grouping helps avoid months with no observations on price for detailed inputs that are rarely used. As we use grouped data, however, we introduce the potential for month-to-month changes within the group service mix.

For each year $t$, we identified all the inpatient discharges (DRGs), physician services (BETOS), and prescription drugs (therapeutic classes) used to treat episodes of care of each type in each city. This captures local variation in practice patterns that have been the subject of much discussion. Given the mix of inputs in year $t-1$, we captured monthly prices for each input in each city in year $t$ and computed a Laspeyres index. We allowed the mix of inputs to vary from year to year to capture the substitution effect. Because the total number of episodes of a specific type could also differ from one year to another, we used the average volume of inputs for each episode type, which was the total volume of each DRG, BETOS, or therapeutic class, divided by the total number of episodes in that group.

The hospital prices driving the hospital index in each city were city-specific average prices in MarketScan. We were concerned that there would be a large number of months with no observation of a discharge in specific DRGs that occasionally appeared in the treatment episode. Our general strategy for months with no relevant observation on price was to assume that the price was the same as the last month with a valid observation.

We first constructed component indexes for prescriptions, outpatient, and inpatient, and then we calculated their relative expenditure share within each episode as weight. The overall disease index was constructed as a weighted sum of these component indexes.

The expenditure shares that we calculated for experimental price indexes were different from those of BLS MCPI; in particular, the weight for prescription drugs was much smaller for the experimental price indexes than for the BLS index. The difference in the expenditure shares was much larger in New York City than in Philadelphia and Boston. For example, in 1999, the expenditure shares for inpatient and physician office visits were 71 percent and 28 percent in New York City for the experimental price index, while the corresponding shares were 40 percent and 44 percent for the BLS MCPI; the expenditure share of prescription drugs was around 16 percent for the BLS index but less than 1 percent for the experimental price index. The low share for prescription drugs could be explained by the following: (a) In the MarketScan database, drugs administered in hospitalizations are not recorded separately from other inpatient costs, which would lower the expenditure share for drugs and raise the expenditure share for hospitalizations. (b) The MEG grouper did not assign all prescription claims with an episode number. (c) The BLS drug weight comes from the Consumer Expenditure Survey (CEX), which includes individuals who are not insured and who are publicly insured; because the uninsured have a low inpatient utilization rate, their inpatient expenditure share might be extremely low and their drug share relatively high. (d) The CEX includes all prescription purchases, regardless of whether they are reimbursed, but the claims database only includes prescription purchases made by privately insured individuals that are reimbursed by health plans.

### 8.4.3 Bootstrapping Method

To decompose the differences between the episode-based price index and the BLS MCPI and to test their statistical significance, we need to estimate the mean and standard errors from the original sample first, and then use a parametric model (random walk with normal errors) to generate bootstrap samples. The standard error from the original sample was estimated using bootstrapping. In each month, we bootstrapped the ratio of the prices in that month and prices in the month prior to obtain the standard errors for prescription, outpatient, and inpatient separately. The monthly price change and standard error in Month 1 were set to one and zero, respectively. This section describes how bootstrapping was carried out for the cumulative indexes (across forty-eight months in 1999 to 2002) in this study.

Let $I_{i,a,t}$ be the month-to-month percentage change for index $i$, city $a$, and month $t$. The forty-eight-month cumulative index is

$$I_{i,a} = \prod_{t=1}^{48} I_{i,a,t}.$$

The individual $I_{i,a,t}$ is a mean with the variance of $\sigma^2_{i,a,t}$, which is the square of the standard error of the original sample. We assume a random walk with a drift, and the random variable is $I_{i,a,t} + \varepsilon_{i,a,t}$, where $\varepsilon_{i,a,t}$ is drawn from $N(0, \sigma^2_{i,a,t})$.[6] To bootstrap, we took 999 samples. For each sample $b = 1$ to 999, we drew $\varepsilon_{i,a,t}$ from $N(0, \sigma^2_{i,a,t})$ and added it to $I_{i,a,t}$ to get $\hat{I}_{i,a,t}$ for $t = 1$ to 48, which represents the forty-eight months from 1999 to 2002. This was done for prescription, outpatient, and inpatient services separately. The overall index was a weighted mean of these component indexes using their relative expenditure as weights $R_{i,a}$. So, the overall index for each of the 999 samples became

$$I_{b,t} = \Pi_{i,a} \hat{I}_{i,a,t,b} R_{i,a}.$$

We replicated each index one thousand times to obtain an estimate of variances for all MarketScan indexes. The BLS variances are the square of the BLS standard errors provided by the BLS. With the variances, we could calculate the difference between the claims-based index and the BLS index and its 95 percent confidence intervals. If zero falls between the confidence intervals, then the difference is not statistically significant.

## 8.5 Results

### 8.5.1 Price Trends

The small-sample and large-sample indexes reported in figure 8.2 suggest a slower price increase than that suggested by the BLS city-specific medical care indexes over the period 1999 to 2002 (January 1999 = 100). The BLS indexes presented in figure 8.2 include only drugs, physicians, and hospital services to be comparable with the experimental price indexes that we have calculated. Except in New York City, the BLS indexes are bimonthly, with the Boston index repriced in odd months and the Philadelphia index repriced in even months.

In Philadelphia, the trends of large-sample and small-sample prices are very similar, and both are below the BLS trend most of the time; in Boston, the small-sample index presents a much larger price variation in 2001 and early 2002 than the large-sample index, and in most of the months, the small-sample index is above the BLS index, while the large-sample index is below the BLS index. In New York City, the trends of large-sample and small-sample prices are very similar, and both are below or above the BLS trend in about the same months: from the end of 1999 to mid-2001, both large-sample and small-sample indexes show a price decrease and are well

6. This assumption is similar to those often used in modeling of financial asset prices.

A

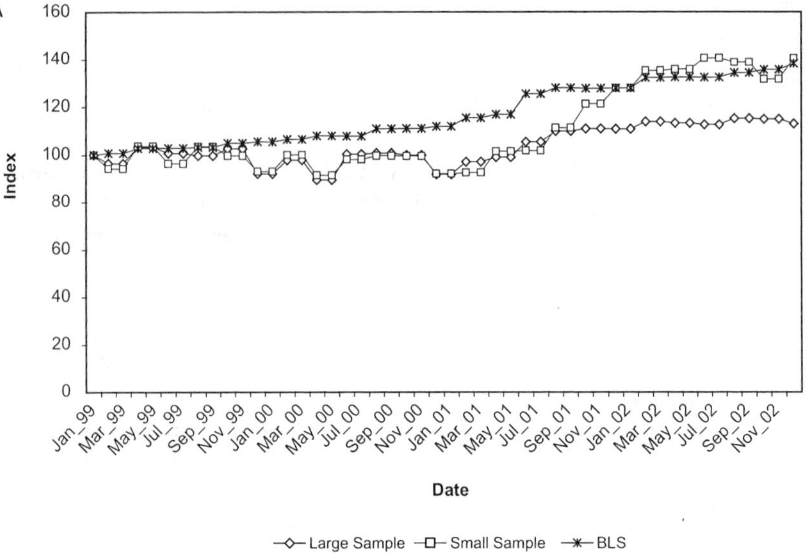


B

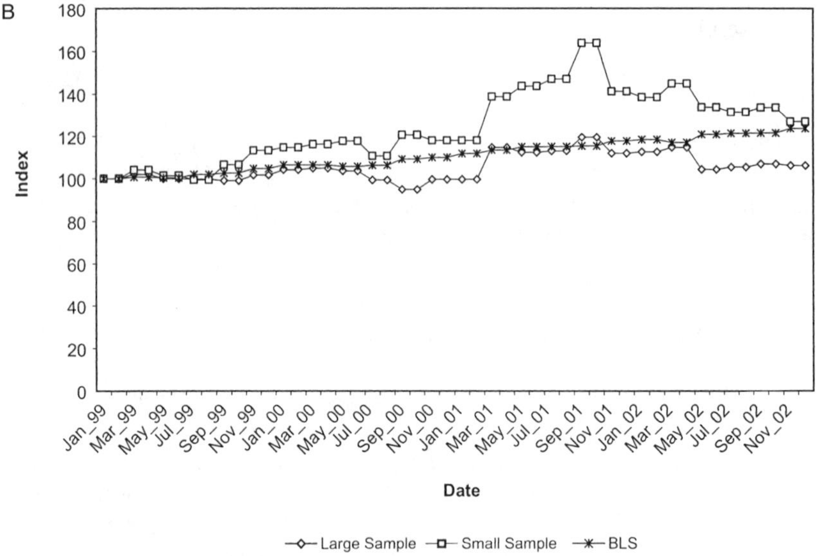


**Fig. 8.2 Large-sample index vs. small-sample index vs. BLS index: *A*, Philadelphia; *B*, Boston; *C*, New York City**

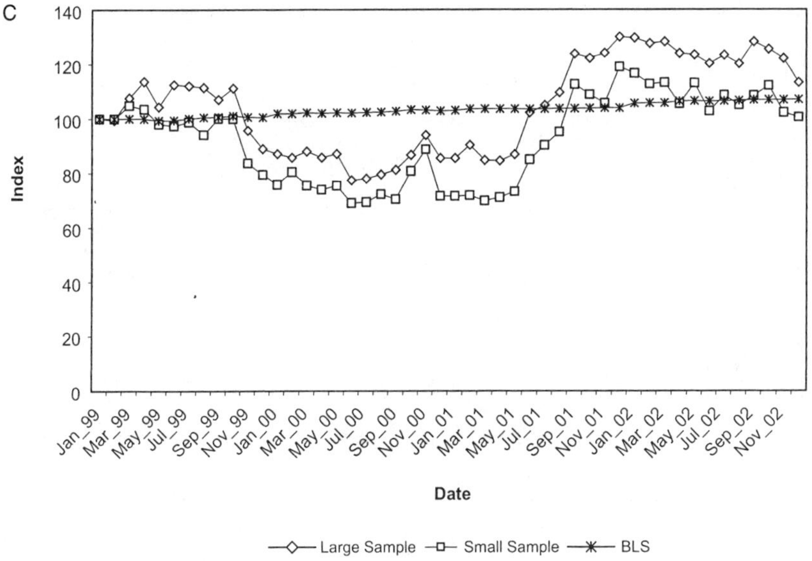


**Fig. 8.2 (cont.)**

below the BLS trend. As the sample sizes for the small sample are quite limited, the price variation we have found might just be random.

The episode-based indexes reported in figure 8.3 demonstrate that between January 1999 and December 2002, the cost of treatment has declined in all three cities for all indexes, except the population-based index in Philadelphia, which has risen, but much less than the corresponding BLS index. In fact, the correlation between the BLS index levels and the expenditure-based episode index levels is –0.68 in Boston, –0.57 in New York City, and –0.03 in Philadelphia, and the correlation between the BLS index levels and the population-based episode index levels is –0.06, –0.19, and 0.11, respectively.

As expected, the expenditure-based and population-based indexes present a different, although not statistically significant, price trend. In general, the expenditure-based index is lower than the population-based index in Philadelphia and Boston but is higher in New York City. In spite of these differences, these two indexes do give the three cities the same rank when considering the relative magnitude of the cumulative price changes from 1999 to 2002: New York City experiences the largest price decline, and Philadelphia sees the smallest price decline (expenditure-based index) or even a price increase (population-based index).

Overall, episode-based indexes fluctuate much more than the BLS MCPI, and one of the reasons is that we allowed the mix of inputs of treatment to

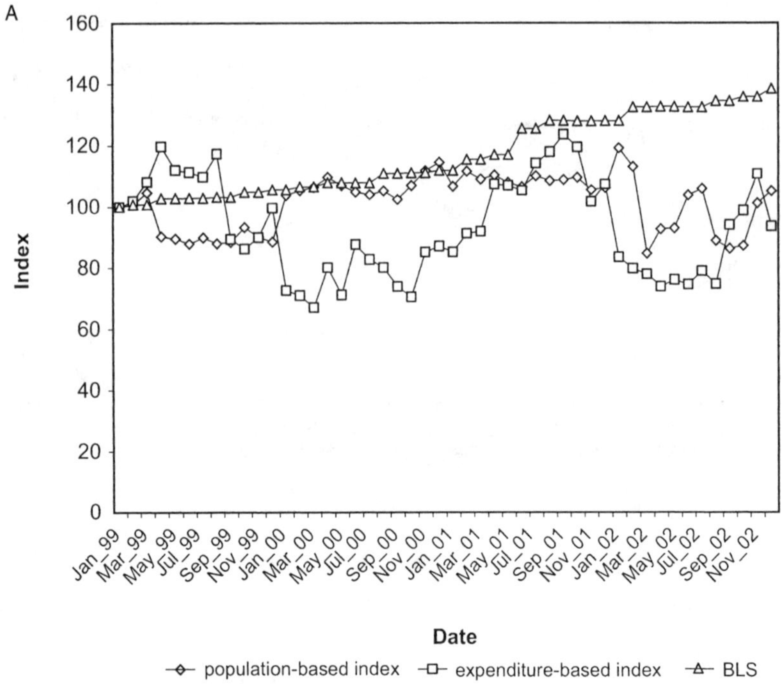


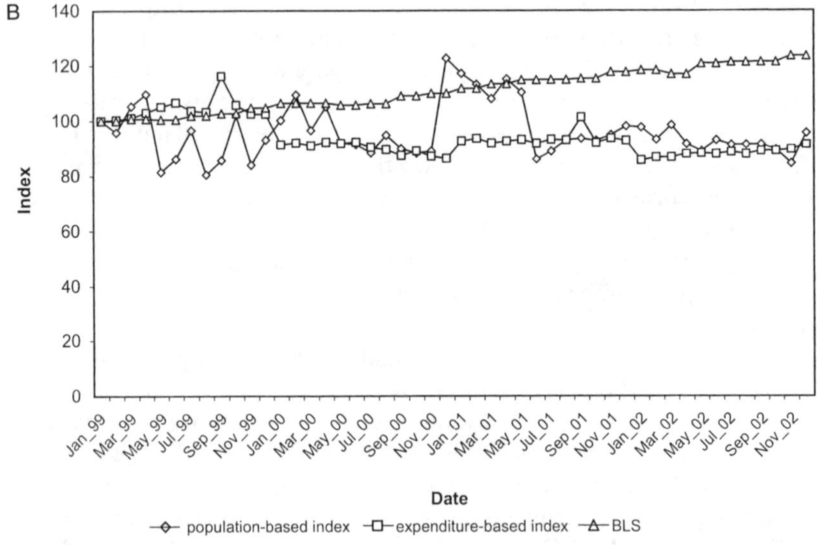


**Fig. 8.3 Population-based disease index vs. expenditure-based disease index vs. BLS index: *A*, Philadelphia; *B*, Boston; *C*, New York City**

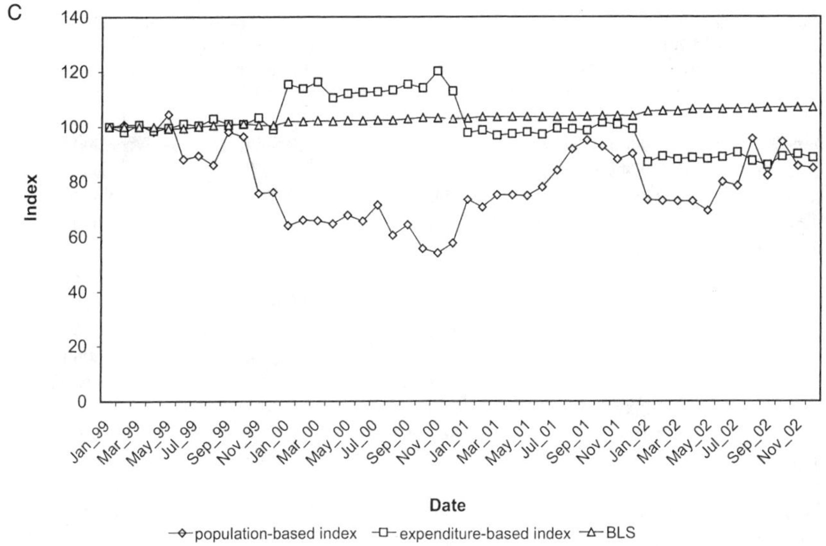


**Fig. 8.3 (cont.)**

change from year to year. Because the volume of inputs was updated in January of each year, the largest price jump usually occurs between December and January. Song et al. (2004) provide a close look at the mix of inputs of treating two specific episodes of angina pectoris with chronic maintenance and malignant neoplasm of female breast. We find that it is the change in volumes, not in prices, that produces such a dramatic jump.

To examine the statistical significance of the differences between the BLS index and the experimental price indexes, we bootstrapped their forty-eight-month cumulative changes and standard errors, as discussed in section 8.4.3. Tables 8.1 and 8.2 present the month-to-month percentage changes and estimated standard errors of the large-sample index, small-sample index, BLS MCPI, expenditure-based disease index, and population-based disease index in each city. Based on these statistics, we derived the forty-eight-month cumulative change for each index, their differences, and the lower and upper bound of the 95 percent confidence intervals of these differences.

The comparison of disease indexes for expenditure-based episodes and population-based episodes is reported in table 8.3.[7] From January 1999 to December 2002, we found a consistent decrease in the overall episode-based index in Boston and New York City: –8 percent in Boston and –10 percent in New York City for expenditure-based episodes, and –9 percent and

7. The cumulative index levels in tables 8.3 and 8.4 differ slightly from those shown in figures 8.2 and 8.3 as a result of the bootstrapping process.

Table 8.1 **Comparison of MarketScan large-sample index and small-sample index**

| Months | Large-sample index | | Small-sample index | |
|---|---|---|---|---|
| | Month-to-month percentage change | Standard errors | Month-to-month percentage change | Standard errors |
| | | *Philadelphia* | | |
| Jan_99 | 0.0000 | 0.0000 | 0.0000 | 0.0000 |
| Feb_99 | –0.0344 | 0.0113 | –0.0573 | 0.0332 |
| Mar_99 | 0.0000 | 0.0000 | 0.0000 | 0.0000 |
| Apr_99 | 0.0702 | 0.0218 | 0.1001 | 0.0505 |
| May_99 | 0.0000 | 0.0000 | 0.0000 | 0.0000 |
| Jun_99 | –0.0260 | 0.0148 | –0.0706 | 0.0389 |
| Jul_99 | 0.0000 | 0.0000 | 0.0000 | 0.0000 |
| Aug_99 | –0.0094 | 0.0192 | 0.0751 | 0.0756 |
| Sep_99 | 0.0000 | 0.0000 | 0.0000 | 0.0000 |
| Oct_99 | 0.0289 | 0.0168 | –0.0375 | 0.0541 |
| Nov_99 | 0.0000 | 0.0000 | 0.0000 | 0.0000 |
| Dec_99 | –0.1021 | 0.0342 | –0.0662 | 0.0694 |
| Jan_00 | 0.0000 | 0.0000 | 0.0000 | 0.0000 |
| Feb_00 | 0.0623 | 0.0170 | 0.0744 | 0.0584 |
| Mar_00 | 0.0000 | 0.0000 | 0.0000 | 0.0000 |
| Apr_00 | –0.0845 | 0.0305 | –0.0857 | 0.0341 |
| May_00 | 0.0000 | 0.0000 | 0.0000 | 0.0000 |
| Jun_00 | 0.1194 | 0.0327 | 0.0727 | 0.0411 |
| Jul_00 | 0.0000 | 0.0000 | 0.0000 | 0.0000 |
| Aug_00 | 0.0049 | 0.0210 | 0.0160 | 0.0509 |
| Sep_00 | 0.0000 | 0.0000 | 0.0000 | 0.0000 |
| Oct_00 | –0.0082 | 0.0164 | –0.0012 | 0.0629 |
| Nov_00 | 0.0000 | 0.0000 | 0.0000 | 0.0000 |
| Dec_00 | –0.0815 | 0.0284 | –0.0753 | 0.0466 |
| Jan_01 | 0.0000 | 0.0000 | 0.0000 | 0.0000 |
| Feb_01 | 0.0585 | 0.0133 | 0.0053 | 0.0484 |
| Mar_01 | 0.0000 | 0.0000 | 0.0000 | 0.0000 |
| Apr_01 | 0.0198 | 0.0255 | 0.0972 | 0.0619 |
| May_01 | 0.0000 | 0.0000 | 0.0000 | 0.0000 |
| Jun_01 | 0.0640 | 0.0212 | 0.0016 | 0.0395 |
| Jul_01 | 0.0000 | 0.0000 | 0.0000 | 0.0000 |
| Aug_01 | 0.0432 | 0.0270 | 0.0940 | 0.0702 |
| Sep_01 | 0.0000 | 0.0000 | 0.0000 | 0.0000 |
| Oct_01 | 0.0082 | 0.0182 | 0.0902 | 0.0629 |
| Nov_01 | 0.0000 | 0.0000 | 0.0000 | 0.0000 |
| Dec_01 | –0.0006 | 0.0196 | 0.0546 | 0.0782 |
| Jan_02 | 0.0000 | 0.0000 | 0.0000 | 0.0000 |
| Feb_02 | 0.0273 | 0.0141 | 0.0573 | 0.0301 |
| Mar_02 | 0.0000 | 0.0000 | 0.0000 | 0.0000 |
| Apr_02 | –0.0054 | 0.0152 | 0.0049 | 0.0381 |
| May_02 | 0.0000 | 0.0000 | 0.0000 | 0.0000 |
| Jun_02 | –0.0050 | 0.0312 | 0.0336 | 0.0633 |
| Jul_02 | 0.0000 | 0.0000 | 0.0000 | 0.0000 |
| Aug_02 | 0.0225 | 0.0234 | –0.0120 | 0.0447 |
| Sep_02 | 0.0000 | 0.0000 | 0.0000 | 0.0000 |
| Oct_02 | –0.0014 | 0.0289 | –0.0513 | 0.0367 |
| Nov_02 | 0.0000 | 0.0000 | 0.0000 | 0.0000 |
| Dec_02 | –0.0172 | 0.0192 | 0.0664 | 0.0282 |

Table 8.1 (continued)

| Months | Large-sample index: Month-to-month percentage change | Large-sample index: Standard errors | Small-sample index: Month-to-month percentage change | Small-sample index: Standard errors |
|---|---|---|---|---|
| | | *Boston* | | |
| Jan_99 | 0.0317 | 0.0125 | 0.0016 | 0.0405 |
| Feb_99 | 0.0000 | 0.0000 | 0.0000 | 0.0000 |
| Mar_99 | 0.0200 | 0.0119 | 0.0397 | 0.0353 |
| Apr_99 | 0.0000 | 0.0000 | 0.0000 | 0.0000 |
| May_99 | –0.0186 | 0.0113 | –0.0243 | 0.0303 |
| Jun_99 | 0.0000 | 0.0000 | 0.0000 | 0.0000 |
| Jul_99 | –0.0031 | 0.0134 | –0.0190 | 0.0380 |
| Aug_99 | 0.0000 | 0.0000 | 0.0000 | 0.0000 |
| Sep_99 | –0.0075 | 0.0225 | 0.0709 | 0.0473 |
| Oct_99 | 0.0000 | 0.0000 | 0.0000 | 0.0000 |
| Nov_99 | 0.0264 | 0.0205 | 0.0630 | 0.0513 |
| Dec_99 | 0.0000 | 0.0000 | 0.0000 | 0.0000 |
| Jan_00 | 0.0252 | 0.0116 | 0.0112 | 0.0254 |
| Feb_00 | 0.0000 | 0.0000 | 0.0000 | 0.0000 |
| Mar_00 | 0.0060 | 0.0100 | 0.0139 | 0.0318 |
| Apr_00 | 0.0000 | 0.0000 | 0.0000 | 0.0000 |
| May_00 | –0.0116 | 0.0133 | 0.0132 | 0.0347 |
| Jun_00 | 0.0000 | 0.0000 | 0.0000 | 0.0000 |
| Jul_00 | –0.0409 | 0.0187 | –0.0601 | 0.0438 |
| Aug_00 | 0.0000 | 0.0000 | 0.0000 | 0.0000 |
| Sep_00 | –0.0447 | 0.0418 | 0.0897 | 0.0651 |
| Oct_00 | 0.0000 | 0.0000 | 0.0000 | 0.0000 |
| Nov_00 | 0.0495 | 0.0246 | –0.0220 | 0.0497 |
| Dec_00 | 0.0000 | 0.0000 | 0.0000 | 0.0000 |
| Jan_01 | 0.0000 | 0.0000 | 0.0000 | 0.0000 |
| Feb_01 | 0.0000 | 0.0000 | 0.0000 | 0.0000 |
| Mar_01 | 0.1509 | 0.0456 | 0.1767 | 0.0938 |
| Apr_01 | 0.0000 | 0.0000 | 0.0000 | 0.0000 |
| May_01 | –0.0211 | 0.0204 | 0.0357 | 0.0296 |
| Jun_01 | 0.0000 | 0.0000 | 0.0000 | 0.0000 |
| Jul_01 | 0.0063 | 0.0175 | 0.0233 | 0.0290 |
| Aug_01 | 0.0000 | 0.0000 | 0.0000 | 0.0000 |
| Sep_01 | 0.0570 | 0.0540 | 0.1145 | 0.1122 |
| Oct_01 | 0.0000 | 0.0000 | 0.0000 | 0.0000 |
| Nov_01 | –0.0629 | 0.0414 | –0.1383 | 0.0575 |
| Dec_01 | 0.0000 | 0.0000 | 0.0000 | 0.0000 |
| Jan_02 | 0.0065 | 0.0104 | –0.0197 | 0.0280 |
| Feb_02 | 0.0000 | 0.0000 | 0.0000 | 0.0000 |
| Mar_02 | 0.0172 | 0.0119 | 0.0470 | 0.0371 |
| Apr_02 | 0.0000 | 0.0000 | 0.0000 | 0.0000 |
| May_02 | –0.0890 | 0.0199 | –0.0769 | 0.0364 |
| Jun_02 | 0.0000 | 0.0000 | 0.0000 | 0.0000 |
| Jul_02 | 0.0105 | 0.0178 | –0.0180 | 0.0396 |
| Aug_02 | 0.0000 | 0.0000 | 0.0000 | 0.0000 |
| Sep_02 | 0.0141 | 0.0169 | 0.0167 | 0.0502 |
| Oct_02 | 0.0000 | 0.0000 | 0.0000 | 0.0000 |
| Nov_02 | –0.0072 | 0.0167 | –0.0498 | 0.0323 |
| Dec_02 | 0.0000 | 0.0000 | 0.0000 | 0.0000 |

(*continued*)

**Table 8.1** (continued)

| Months | Large-sample index | | Small-sample index | |
|---|---|---|---|---|
| | Month-to-month percentage change | Standard errors | Month-to-month percentage change | Standard errors |
| | | *New York City* | | |
| Jan_99 | 0.0483 | 0.0167 | 0.0039 | 0.0340 |
| Feb_99 | –0.0061 | 0.0149 | –0.0001 | 0.0403 |
| Mar_99 | 0.0838 | 0.0253 | 0.0488 | 0.0446 |
| Apr_99 | 0.0556 | 0.0199 | –0.0127 | 0.0236 |
| May_99 | –0.0820 | 0.0133 | –0.0532 | 0.0274 |
| Jun_99 | 0.0779 | 0.0159 | –0.0069 | 0.0138 |
| Jul_99 | –0.0036 | 0.0101 | 0.0143 | 0.0239 |
| Aug_99 | –0.0067 | 0.0141 | –0.0468 | 0.0309 |
| Sep_99 | –0.0389 | 0.0111 | 0.0636 | 0.0436 |
| Oct_99 | 0.0386 | 0.0220 | –0.0010 | 0.0411 |
| Nov_99 | –0.1393 | 0.0282 | –0.1629 | 0.0472 |
| Dec_99 | –0.0702 | 0.0286 | –0.0518 | 0.0358 |
| Jan_00 | –0.0209 | 0.0087 | –0.0451 | 0.0291 |
| Feb_00 | –0.0152 | 0.0100 | 0.0613 | 0.0357 |
| Mar_00 | 0.0259 | 0.0124 | –0.0614 | 0.0256 |
| Apr_00 | –0.0252 | 0.0105 | –0.0209 | 0.0400 |
| May_00 | 0.0154 | 0.0104 | 0.0206 | 0.0417 |
| Jun_00 | –0.1114 | 0.0322 | –0.0847 | 0.0509 |
| Jul_00 | 0.0087 | 0.0128 | 0.0048 | 0.0393 |
| Aug_00 | 0.0189 | 0.0185 | 0.0413 | 0.0274 |
| Sep_00 | 0.0208 | 0.0229 | –0.0246 | 0.0433 |
| Oct_00 | 0.0676 | 0.0520 | 0.1473 | 0.0794 |
| Nov_00 | 0.0845 | 0.0491 | 0.0968 | 0.0597 |
| Dec_00 | –0.0907 | 0.0340 | –0.1926 | 0.0393 |
| Jan_01 | 0.0000 | 0.0000 | 0.0000 | 0.0000 |
| Feb_01 | 0.0570 | 0.0145 | 0.0036 | 0.0401 |
| Mar_01 | –0.0622 | 0.0099 | –0.0272 | 0.0284 |
| Apr_01 | –0.0019 | 0.0119 | 0.0160 | 0.0591 |
| May_01 | 0.0278 | 0.0236 | 0.0319 | 0.0513 |
| Jun_01 | 0.1761 | 0.0668 | 0.1594 | 0.0778 |
| Jul_01 | 0.0259 | 0.0169 | 0.0615 | 0.0399 |
| Aug_01 | 0.0451 | 0.0185 | 0.0553 | 0.0348 |
| Sep_01 | 0.1301 | 0.0454 | 0.1828 | 0.0538 |
| Oct_01 | –0.0130 | 0.0128 | –0.0329 | 0.0437 |
| Nov_01 | 0.0155 | 0.0192 | –0.0301 | 0.0365 |
| Dec_01 | 0.0475 | 0.0181 | 0.1273 | 0.0494 |
| Jan_02 | –0.0030 | 0.0112 | –0.0197 | 0.0307 |
| Feb_02 | –0.0153 | 0.0135 | –0.0342 | 0.0264 |
| Mar_02 | 0.0053 | 0.0117 | 0.0049 | 0.0372 |
| Apr_02 | –0.0338 | 0.0102 | –0.0689 | 0.0259 |
| May_02 | –0.0046 | 0.0126 | 0.0714 | 0.0415 |
| Jun_02 | –0.0258 | 0.0199 | –0.0908 | 0.0304 |
| Jul_02 | 0.0254 | 0.0146 | 0.0568 | 0.0569 |
| Aug_02 | –0.0255 | 0.0171 | –0.0327 | 0.0423 |
| Sep_02 | 0.0673 | 0.0306 | 0.0328 | 0.0484 |
| Oct_02 | –0.0212 | 0.0189 | 0.0341 | 0.0396 |
| Nov_02 | –0.0265 | 0.0166 | –0.0885 | 0.0423 |
| Dec_02 | –0.0741 | 0.0231 | –0.0173 | 0.0425 |

**Table 8.2** **Comparison of BLS MCPI and episode-based index**

| | BLS | | Expenditure-based disease index | | Population-based disease index | |
|---|---|---|---|---|---|---|
| Months | Month-to-month percentage change | Standard errors | Month-to-month percentage change | Standard errors | Month-to-month percentage change | Standard errors |
| | | | *Philadelphia* | | | |
| Jan_99 | 0.0000 | 0.0000 | –0.1005 | 0.0241 | 0.1145 | 0.1018 |
| Feb_99 | 0.0085 | 0.0033 | 0.0189 | 0.0210 | 0.0070 | 0.0218 |
| Mar_99 | 0.0000 | 0.0000 | 0.0613 | 0.0638 | 0.0398 | 0.1560 |
| Apr_99 | 0.0203 | 0.0125 | 0.1067 | 0.0591 | –0.1379 | 0.1073 |
| May_99 | 0.0000 | 0.0000 | –0.0638 | 0.0552 | –0.0089 | 0.0081 |
| Jun_99 | 0.0001 | 0.0013 | –0.0065 | 0.0232 | –0.0188 | 0.0133 |
| Jul_99 | 0.0000 | 0.0000 | –0.0141 | 0.0484 | 0.0235 | 0.0298 |
| Aug_99 | 0.0028 | 0.0039 | 0.0689 | 0.0412 | –0.0219 | 0.0192 |
| Sep_99 | 0.0000 | 0.0000 | –0.2385 | 0.0495 | 0.0062 | 0.0525 |
| Oct_99 | 0.0168 | 0.0114 | –0.0348 | 0.0342 | 0.0540 | 0.0561 |
| Nov_99 | 0.0000 | 0.0000 | 0.0434 | 0.0483 | –0.0337 | 0.0522 |
| Dec_99 | 0.0065 | 0.0062 | 0.1069 | 0.0891 | –0.0177 | 0.0480 |
| Jan_00 | 0.0000 | 0.0000 | –0.2710 | 0.0863 | 0.1733 | 0.3120 |
| Feb_00 | 0.0094 | 0.0065 | –0.0230 | 0.0742 | 0.0147 | 0.0310 |
| Mar_00 | 0.0000 | 0.0000 | –0.0552 | 0.0469 | 0.0107 | 0.0828 |
| Apr_00 | 0.0127 | 0.0035 | 0.1950 | 0.1284 | 0.0302 | 0.0288 |
| May_00 | 0.0000 | 0.0000 | –0.1112 | 0.1018 | –0.0246 | 0.0185 |
| Jun_00 | –0.0007 | 0.0049 | 0.2315 | 0.1104 | –0.0199 | 0.0164 |
| Jul_00 | 0.0000 | 0.0000 | –0.0568 | 0.0844 | –0.0082 | 0.0412 |
| Aug_00 | 0.0286 | 0.0079 | –0.0306 | 0.0425 | 0.0119 | 0.0131 |
| Sep_00 | 0.0000 | 0.0000 | –0.0787 | 0.0882 | –0.0269 | 0.0229 |
| Oct_00 | 0.0012 | 0.0060 | –0.0457 | 0.0411 | 0.0445 | 0.0449 |
| Nov_00 | 0.0000 | 0.0000 | 0.2080 | 0.0980 | 0.0456 | 0.0664 |
| Dec_00 | 0.0073 | 0.0077 | 0.0228 | 0.0253 | 0.0237 | 0.0300 |
| Jan_01 | 0.0000 | 0.0000 | –0.0219 | 0.1094 | –0.0679 | 0.1421 |
| Feb_01 | 0.0321 | 0.0234 | 0.0713 | 0.0469 | 0.0460 | 0.0553 |
| Mar_01 | 0.0000 | 0.0000 | 0.0066 | 0.0466 | –0.0234 | 0.0859 |
| Apr_01 | 0.0128 | 0.0068 | 0.1695 | 0.1074 | 0.0125 | 0.0757 |
| May_01 | 0.0000 | 0.0000 | –0.0038 | 0.0236 | –0.0220 | 0.0325 |
| Jun_01 | 0.0725 | 0.0603 | –0.0162 | 0.0640 | –0.0136 | 0.0427 |
| Jul_01 | 0.0000 | 0.0000 | 0.0851 | 0.0555 | 0.0341 | 0.0406 |
| Aug_01 | 0.0211 | 0.0029 | 0.0321 | 0.0623 | –0.0138 | 0.0236 |
| Sep_01 | 0.0000 | 0.0000 | 0.0487 | 0.0220 | 0.0026 | 0.0085 |
| Oct_01 | –0.0019 | 0.0024 | –0.0339 | 0.0223 | 0.0064 | 0.0138 |
| Nov_01 | 0.0000 | 0.0000 | –0.1494 | 0.0533 | –0.0379 | 0.0318 |
| Dec_01 | 0.0010 | 0.0045 | 0.0563 | 0.0327 | 0.0069 | 0.0135 |
| Jan_02 | 0.0000 | 0.0000 | –0.2223 | 0.1054 | 0.1224 | 0.5559 |
| Feb_02 | 0.0346 | 0.0268 | –0.0442 | 0.0363 | –0.0512 | 0.0504 |
| Mar_02 | 0.0000 | 0.0000 | –0.0232 | 0.0666 | –0.2509 | 0.1659 |
| Apr_02 | 0.0015 | 0.0023 | –0.0516 | 0.0743 | 0.0943 | 0.1308 |
| May_02 | 0.0000 | 0.0000 | 0.0297 | 0.0456 | 0.0025 | 0.0124 |
| Jun_02 | –0.0011 | 0.0023 | –0.0208 | 0.0659 | 0.1161 | 0.0789 |
| Jul_02 | 0.0000 | 0.0000 | 0.0603 | 0.0358 | 0.0208 | 0.0181 |
| Aug_02 | 0.0151 | 0.0005 | –0.0539 | 0.0290 | –0.1600 | 0.0743 |

(*continued*)

**Table 8.2** (continued)

| Months | BLS | | Expenditure-based disease index | | Population-based disease index | |
|---|---|---|---|---|---|---|
| | Month-to-month percentage change | Standard errors | Month-to-month percentage change | Standard errors | Month-to-month percentage change | Standard errors |
| Sep_02 | 0.0000 | 0.0000 | 0.2575 | 0.2232 | –0.0300 | 0.0175 |
| Oct_02 | 0.0097 | 0.0064 | 0.0508 | 0.0575 | 0.0114 | 0.0419 |
| Nov_02 | 0.0000 | 0.0000 | 0.1213 | 0.2059 | 0.1594 | 0.1535 |
| Dec_02 | 0.0194 | 0.0154 | –0.1552 | 0.0930 | 0.0386 | 0.0795 |
| | | | *Boston* | | | |
| Jan_99 | 0.0190 | 0.0073 | 0.0042 | 0.0033 | 0.1136 | 0.0511 |
| Feb_99 | 0.0000 | 0.0000 | 0.0033 | 0.0013 | –0.0424 | 0.0493 |
| Mar_99 | 0.0100 | 0.0081 | 0.0079 | 0.0049 | 0.0998 | 0.1241 |
| Apr_99 | 0.0000 | 0.0000 | 0.0188 | 0.0110 | 0.0413 | 0.0777 |
| May_99 | –0.0023 | 0.0015 | 0.0208 | 0.0093 | –0.2572 | 0.0987 |
| Jun_99 | 0.0000 | 0.0000 | 0.0142 | 0.0088 | 0.0577 | 0.0396 |
| Jul_99 | 0.0122 | 0.0140 | –0.0279 | 0.0137 | 0.1206 | 0.0763 |
| Aug_99 | 0.0000 | 0.0000 | –0.0051 | 0.0051 | –0.1662 | 0.0652 |
| Sep_99 | 0.0069 | 0.0043 | 0.1267 | 0.0547 | 0.0650 | 0.1775 |
| Oct_99 | 0.0000 | 0.0000 | –0.0902 | 0.0262 | 0.1898 | 0.0774 |
| Nov_99 | 0.0198 | 0.0080 | –0.0299 | 0.0178 | –0.1762 | 0.1515 |
| Dec_99 | 0.0000 | 0.0000 | –0.0014 | 0.0065 | 0.1076 | 0.0828 |
| Jan_00 | 0.0155 | 0.0076 | –0.1081 | 0.0344 | 0.0771 | 0.1130 |
| Feb_00 | 0.0000 | 0.0000 | 0.0065 | 0.0026 | 0.0912 | 0.1344 |
| Mar_00 | 0.0013 | 0.0089 | –0.0105 | 0.0027 | –0.1173 | 0.1451 |
| Apr_00 | 0.0000 | 0.0000 | 0.0128 | 0.0066 | 0.0888 | 0.0946 |
| May_00 | –0.0070 | 0.0101 | –0.0036 | 0.0043 | –0.1256 | 0.0553 |
| Jun_00 | 0.0000 | 0.0000 | 0.0053 | 0.0057 | –0.0054 | 0.0341 |
| Jul_00 | 0.0053 | 0.0031 | –0.0205 | 0.0057 | –0.0328 | 0.0249 |
| Aug_00 | 0.0000 | 0.0000 | –0.0091 | 0.0024 | 0.0716 | 0.0488 |
| Sep_00 | 0.0233 | 0.0135 | –0.0227 | 0.0094 | –0.0508 | 0.0562 |
| Oct_00 | 0.0000 | 0.0000 | 0.0181 | 0.0071 | –0.0178 | 0.0362 |
| Nov_00 | 0.0080 | 0.0112 | –0.0219 | 0.0136 | 0.0075 | 0.0463 |
| Dec_00 | 0.0000 | 0.0000 | –0.0095 | 0.0027 | 0.3784 | 0.3084 |
| Jan_01 | 0.0157 | 0.0043 | 0.0724 | 0.0337 | –0.0446 | 0.1016 |
| Feb_01 | 0.0000 | 0.0000 | 0.0094 | 0.0094 | –0.0347 | 0.0408 |
| Mar_01 | 0.0147 | 0.0073 | –0.0181 | 0.0092 | –0.0454 | 0.0649 |
| Apr_01 | 0.0000 | 0.0000 | 0.0079 | 0.0015 | 0.0660 | 0.0632 |
| May_01 | 0.0117 | 0.0043 | 0.0058 | 0.0045 | –0.0421 | 0.1024 |
| Jun_01 | 0.0000 | 0.0000 | –0.0143 | 0.0026 | –0.2203 | 0.1693 |
| Jul_01 | 0.0005 | 0.0030 | 0.0155 | 0.0041 | 0.0346 | 0.0454 |
| Aug_01 | 0.0000 | 0.0000 | –0.0017 | 0.0036 | 0.0452 | 0.0446 |
| Sep_01 | 0.0027 | 0.0034 | 0.0893 | 0.0526 | 0.0056 | 0.0389 |
| Oct_01 | 0.0000 | 0.0000 | –0.0921 | 0.0377 | –0.0078 | 0.0514 |
| Nov_01 | 0.0198 | 0.0056 | 0.0180 | 0.0022 | 0.0223 | 0.0610 |
| Dec_01 | 0.0000 | 0.0000 | –0.0092 | 0.0041 | 0.0340 | 0.0844 |
| Jan_02 | 0.0059 | 0.0079 | –0.0777 | 0.0314 | –0.0050 | 0.1089 |
| Feb_02 | 0.0000 | 0.0000 | 0.0123 | 0.0040 | –0.0458 | 0.0751 |

**Table 8.2** (continued)

| Months | BLS: Month-to-month percentage change | BLS: Standard errors | Expenditure-based disease index: Month-to-month percentage change | Expenditure-based disease index: Standard errors | Population-based disease index: Month-to-month percentage change | Population-based disease index: Standard errors |
|---|---|---|---|---|---|---|
| Mar_02 | –0.0124 | 0.0100 | –0.0001 | 0.0024 | 0.0570 | 0.0595 |
| Apr_02 | 0.0000 | 0.0000 | 0.0153 | 0.0018 | –0.0697 | 0.0394 |
| May_02 | 0.0317 | 0.0372 | 0.0028 | 0.0038 | –0.0279 | 0.0319 |
| Jun_02 | 0.0000 | 0.0000 | –0.0034 | 0.0035 | 0.0447 | 0.0614 |
| Jul_02 | 0.0042 | 0.0027 | 0.0081 | 0.0076 | –0.0185 | 0.0436 |
| Aug_02 | 0.0000 | 0.0000 | –0.0077 | 0.0018 | 0.0011 | 0.0218 |
| Sep_02 | 0.0006 | 0.0010 | 0.0131 | 0.0021 | 0.0011 | 0.0346 |
| Oct_02 | 0.0000 | 0.0000 | 0.0012 | 0.0023 | –0.0203 | 0.0451 |
| Nov_02 | 0.0175 | 0.0031 | 0.0046 | 0.0022 | –0.0571 | 0.0393 |
| Dec_02 | 0.0000 | 0.0000 | 0.0200 | 0.0021 | 0.1322 | 0.0593 |
| | | | *New York City* | | | |
| Jan_99 | 0.0092 | 0.0038 | 0.0485 | 0.0074 | –0.0066 | 0.0376 |
| Feb_99 | 0.0000 | 0.0000 | –0.0206 | 0.0076 | 0.0078 | 0.0253 |
| Mar_99 | 0.0007 | 0.0007 | 0.0287 | 0.0076 | –0.0014 | 0.0065 |
| Apr_99 | –0.0010 | 0.0007 | –0.0220 | 0.0039 | –0.0247 | 0.0230 |
| May_99 | –0.0056 | 0.0031 | 0.0108 | 0.0047 | 0.0643 | 0.0797 |
| Jun_99 | 0.0005 | 0.0003 | 0.0155 | 0.0065 | –0.1563 | 0.0941 |
| Jul_99 | 0.0062 | 0.0137 | –0.0071 | 0.0067 | 0.0141 | 0.0209 |
| Aug_99 | 0.0039 | 0.0053 | 0.0250 | 0.0058 | –0.0370 | 0.0408 |
| Sep_99 | 0.0013 | 0.0015 | –0.0186 | 0.0042 | 0.1401 | 0.1567 |
| Oct_99 | 0.0047 | 0.0062 | –0.0009 | 0.0048 | –0.0175 | 0.0131 |
| Nov_99 | –0.0042 | 0.0020 | 0.0227 | 0.0040 | –0.2146 | 0.1699 |
| Dec_99 | –0.0009 | 0.0010 | –0.0415 | 0.0047 | 0.0058 | 0.0084 |
| Jan_00 | 0.0127 | 0.0053 | 0.1671 | 0.1223 | –0.1595 | 0.1465 |
| Feb_00 | 0.0000 | 0.0000 | –0.0142 | 0.0080 | 0.0305 | 0.0289 |
| Mar_00 | 0.0033 | 0.0063 | 0.0211 | 0.0059 | –0.0030 | 0.0237 |
| Apr_00 | –0.0020 | 0.0045 | –0.0494 | 0.0092 | –0.0174 | 0.0090 |
| May_00 | 0.0036 | 0.0015 | 0.0138 | 0.0058 | 0.0493 | 0.0275 |
| Jun_00 | –0.0022 | 0.0032 | 0.0043 | 0.0092 | –0.0329 | 0.0226 |
| Jul_00 | 0.0032 | 0.0023 | 0.0011 | 0.0083 | 0.0891 | 0.1732 |
| Aug_00 | 0.0005 | 0.0005 | 0.0055 | 0.0039 | –0.1540 | 0.0647 |
| Sep_00 | 0.0037 | 0.0019 | 0.0189 | 0.0070 | 0.0644 | 0.0481 |
| Oct_00 | 0.0045 | 0.0028 | –0.0111 | 0.0066 | –0.1355 | 0.1113 |
| Nov_00 | –0.0009 | 0.0009 | 0.0530 | 0.0073 | –0.0281 | 0.0205 |
| Dec_00 | –0.0031 | 0.0017 | –0.0599 | 0.0038 | 0.0653 | 0.1122 |
| Jan_01 | 0.0023 | 0.0021 | –0.1336 | 0.1111 | 0.2766 | 0.2492 |
| Feb_01 | 0.0053 | 0.0025 | 0.0091 | 0.0059 | –0.0394 | 0.0202 |
| Mar_01 | –0.0008 | 0.0115 | –0.0190 | 0.0043 | 0.0646 | 0.0592 |
| Apr_01 | 0.0004 | 0.0013 | 0.0048 | 0.0041 | 0.0001 | 0.0022 |
| May_01 | 0.0000 | 0.0000 | 0.0064 | 0.0045 | –0.0032 | 0.0045 |
| Jun_01 | –0.0012 | 0.0007 | –0.0079 | 0.0038 | 0.0420 | 0.0363 |
| Jul_01 | 0.0013 | 0.0031 | 0.0223 | 0.0065 | 0.0772 | 0.0733 |

(*continued*)

**Table 8.2** (continued)

| | BLS | | Expenditure-based disease index | | Population-based disease index | |
|---|---|---|---|---|---|---|
| Months | Month-to-month percentage change | Standard errors | Month-to-month percentage change | Standard errors | Month-to-month percentage change | Standard errors |
| Aug_01 | 0.0009 | 0.0034 | –0.0023 | 0.0069 | 0.0922 | 0.1489 |
| Sep_01 | 0.0000 | 0.0000 | –0.0051 | 0.0049 | 0.0350 | 0.0423 |
| Oct_01 | 0.0011 | 0.0041 | 0.0293 | 0.0058 | –0.0236 | 0.0343 |
| Nov_01 | 0.0012 | 0.0028 | –0.0075 | 0.0050 | –0.0514 | 0.0516 |
| Dec_01 | –0.0010 | 0.0017 | –0.0148 | 0.0037 | 0.0232 | 0.0172 |
| Jan_02 | 0.0173 | 0.0062 | –0.1228 | 0.0731 | –0.1851 | 0.1781 |
| Feb_02 | 0.0020 | 0.0057 | 0.0248 | 0.0087 | –0.0042 | 0.0216 |
| Mar_02 | –0.0005 | 0.0103 | –0.0128 | 0.0070 | –0.0021 | 0.0235 |
| Apr_02 | 0.0071 | 0.0044 | 0.0064 | 0.0064 | 0.0006 | 0.0006 |
| May_02 | 0.0007 | 0.0016 | –0.0041 | 0.0051 | –0.0478 | 0.0222 |
| Jun_02 | –0.0006 | 0.0011 | 0.0078 | 0.0037 | 0.1506 | 0.1338 |
| Jul_02 | 0.0009 | 0.0005 | 0.0182 | 0.0043 | –0.0187 | 0.0558 |
| Aug_02 | 0.0007 | 0.0007 | –0.0337 | 0.0074 | 0.2182 | 0.1595 |
| Sep_02 | 0.0030 | 0.0026 | –0.0173 | 0.0031 | –0.1405 | 0.0676 |
| Oct_02 | 0.0004 | 0.0010 | 0.0363 | 0.0055 | 0.1505 | 0.1514 |
| Nov_02 | 0.0005 | 0.0004 | 0.0091 | 0.0099 | –0.0944 | 0.0581 |
| Dec_02 | 0.0002 | 0.0001 | –0.0134 | 0.0027 | –0.0091 | 0.0502 |

–16 percent for population-based episodes. In both cases, New York City experiences a much larger price decline than Boston. The expenditure-based index and population-based index display an opposite trend in Philadelphia: the former has dropped by 4 percent, while the latter has gone up by 8 percent.

The component indexes are not consistent across cities, either. In fact, the expenditure-based and population-based indexes often show an opposite trend. Both the expenditure-based index and the population-based index have moved in the same direction for prescription drug prices: they have gone up in Philadelphia and Boston but have gone down in New York City. In fact, the prescription price index has gone up by 97 percent in Philadelphia and 10 percent in Boston, but it has dropped by 39 percent in New York City for the expenditure-based episodes. The outpatient prices have increased in Boston and decreased in New York City for both expenditure-based and population-based episodes; in Philadelphia, it has gone up for the expenditure-based episodes but dropped for the population-based episodes. The inpatient index has dropped in all cases, except for population-based episodes in Philadelphia. It is difficult to know what factors might explain the differences between the cities. Part of the story could relate to the size of the claims database in each city; for example, Boston constitutes the largest

**Table 8.3** **Decomposition of the difference between expenditure-based disease index and population-based disease index using raw payments: 48-month cumulative effect**

| | Expenditure-based disease index | | Population-based disease index | | | 95% CI for total difference | |
|---|---|---|---|---|---|---|---|
| | Percentage change | SE | Percentage change | SE | Difference | Lower bound | Upper bound |
| Philadelphia | | | | | | | |
| RX | 0.9742 | 0.4864 | 1.3281 | 0.4190 | –0.3539 | –1.6122 | 0.9043 |
| OP | 0.8074 | 0.7541 | –0.0639 | 0.0455 | 0.8713 | –0.6093 | 2.3519 |
| IP | –0.2571 | 0.6124 | 0.0147 | 0.9816 | –0.2718 | –2.5394 | 1.9958 |
| All-item | –0.0422 | 0.5435 | 0.0815 | 0.8260 | –0.1237 | –2.0616 | 1.8142 |
| Boston | | | | | | | |
| RX | 0.1021 | 0.0995 | 0.2341 | 0.0822 | –0.1320 | –0.3850 | 0.1210 |
| OP | 0.3791 | 0.4697 | 0.0107 | 0.0493 | 0.3684 | –0.5573 | 1.2940 |
| IP | –0.2308 | 0.0654 | –0.1526 | 0.8023 | –0.0782 | –1.6558 | 1.4995 |
| All-item | –0.0803 | 0.1055 | –0.0861 | 0.6123 | 0.0058 | –1.2120 | 1.2236 |
| New York City | | | | | | | |
| RX | –0.3941 | 0.2070 | –0.2827 | 0.2232 | –0.1114 | –0.7080 | 0.4851 |
| OP | –0.1001 | 0.2087 | –0.2354 | 0.0841 | 0.1353 | –0.3057 | 0.5763 |
| IP | –0.1313 | 0.2062 | –0.1263 | 0.7582 | –0.0051 | –1.5451 | 1.5350 |
| All-item | –0.1005 | 0.1710 | –0.1592 | 0.5382 | 0.0586 | –1.0482 | 1.1654 |

*Note:* “SE” = standard errors; “RX” = prescriptions; “OP” = outpatient treatment; “IP” = inpatient treatment; “CI” = confidence interval.

of the three city samples in MarketScan but is the smallest of the three BLS PSUs. Discrepancy in the health delivery systems in the three cities could be another potential explanation.

Despite the different trends that expenditure-based and population-based indexes demonstrated in some cases, we found that there is no significant difference between these two disease indexes. For all three cities, zero falls inside the 95 percent confidence intervals of the differences for the overall index, as well as all component indexes.

### 8.5.2 Decomposition Analysis

An initial look at the monthly index difference showed no statistical significance at the monthly level, so we examined the cumulative forty-eight-month indexes from 1999 to 2002. Three potential sources could contribute to the difference between the forty-eight-month cumulative BLS index and disease index: different index construction methods, different sample sizes, and different price distributions. To identify the importance of these sources, we decomposed the difference according to the following formula:

$$\begin{aligned} \text{DPIMDT}_{m,y} - \text{MPIBLS}_{m,y} = {} & (\text{DPIMDT}_{m,y} - \text{MPIMDTL}_{m,y}) \\ & + (\text{MPIMDTL}_{m,y} - \text{MPIMDTS}_{m,y}) \\ & + (\text{MPIMDTS}_{m,y} - \text{MPIBLS}_{m,y}). \end{aligned}$$

That is, TotalDifference = Method + SampleSize + DifferentPriceDistributions, where $m,y$ = index month and year, DPIMDT = the disease index generated with claims data, MPIBLS = the BLS Medical CPI index with BLS data, MPIMDTL = the large-sample BLS CPI index with claims data, and MPIMDTS = the BLS CPI index with claims data using BLS sample sizes.

Table 8.4 reports the differences in the forty-eight-month cumulative changes between the expenditure-based disease index, the BLS index, the large-sample index, and the small-sample index. From January 1999 to December 2002, the BLS index shows a 38 percent increase in Philadelphia, a 23 percent increase in Boston, and a 7 percent increase in New York City, while our expenditure-based disease index presents a consistent decline in Philadelphia (–4 percent), Boston (–8 percent), and New York City (–10 percent).

The differences between the overall expenditure-based disease index and the BLS MCPI are –42 percent, –31 percent, and –17 percent in Philadelphia, Boston, and New York City, respectively, but only the –31 percent is statistically different from zero. Most episode-based component indexes are not significantly different from the BLS medical component indexes, either. In fact, the only significant difference is the difference in the inpatient index in Boston and the difference in the prescription index in New York City.

In sum, the decomposition results suggest that differences between the

**Table 8.4** **Decomposition of differences between BLS index, expenditure-based disease index, large-sample index, and small-sample index using raw payments: 48-month cumulative effect**

| | Expenditure-based disease index | | BLS MCPI | | 95% CI for total difference | | |
|---|---|---|---|---|---|---|---|
| | Percentage change | SE | Percentage change | SE | Total difference | Lower bound | Upper bound |
| Philadelphia | | | | | | | |
| RX | 0.9742 | 0.4864 | 0.1650 | 0.0525 | 0.8092 | –0.1496 | 1.7681 |
| OP | 0.8074 | 0.7541 | 0.2959 | 0.2003 | 0.5116 | –1.0176 | 2.0408 |
| IP | –0.2571 | 0.6124 | 0.6486 | 0.1600 | –0.9057 | –2.1462 | 0.3349 |
| All-item | –0.0422 | 0.5435 | 0.3803 | 0.1002 | –0.4224 | –1.5055 | 0.6607 |
| Boston | | | | | | | |
| RX | 0.1021 | 0.0995 | 0.1893 | 0.0700 | –0.0872 | –0.3257 | 0.1513 |
| OP | 0.3791 | 0.4697 | 0.0400 | 0.0470 | 0.3391 | –0.5861 | 1.2643 |
| IP | –0.2308 | 0.0654 | 0.5055 | 0.1832 | –0.7362 | **–1.1175** | **–0.3549** |
| All-item | –0.0803 | 0.1055 | 0.2291 | 0.0627 | –0.3093 | **–0.5499** | **–0.0687** |
| New York City | | | | | | | |
| RX | –0.3941 | 0.2070 | 0.1294 | 0.0457 | –0.5235 | **–0.9389** | **–0.1081** |
| OP | –0.1001 | 0.2087 | 0.0178 | 0.0407 | –0.1179 | –0.5346 | 0.2988 |
| IP | –0.1313 | 0.2062 | 0.1012 | 0.0666 | –0.2326 | –0.6573 | 0.1922 |
| All-item | –0.1005 | 0.1710 | 0.0701 | 0.0320 | –0.1706 | –0.5116 | 0.1703 |

| | Large sample size: Replication | | | 95% CI for method difference | |
|---|---|---|---|---|---|
| | Percentage change | SE | Method difference | Lower bound | Upper bound |
| Philadelphia | | | | | |
| RX | 0.3129 | 0.0071 | 0.6613 | –0.2921 | 1.6147 |
| OP | –0.0697 | 0.1589 | 0.8771 | –0.6333 | 2.3875 |
| IP | 0.1502 | 0.3161 | –0.4073 | –1.7581 | 0.9434 |
| All-item | 0.1328 | 0.1268 | –0.1749 | –1.2687 | 0.9188 |
| Boston | | | | | |
| RX | 0.1191 | 0.1731 | –0.0170 | –0.4084 | 0.3745 |
| OP | 0.1051 | 0.1286 | 0.2740 | –0.6805 | 1.2285 |
| IP | –0.1833 | 0.1962 | –0.0475 | –0.4529 | 0.3579 |
| All-item | 0.0571 | 0.1279 | –0.1373 | –0.4623 | 0.1876 |
| New York City | | | | | |
| RX | 0.1830 | 0.0142 | –0.5771 | **–0.9837** | **–0.1705** |
| OP | –0.1640 | 0.1562 | 0.0639 | –0.4470 | 0.5748 |
| IP | –0.0189 | 0.3537 | –0.1124 | –0.9148 | 0.6899 |
| All-item | 0.1220 | 0.1786 | –0.2225 | –0.7072 | 0.2622 |

(*continued*)

**Table 8.4** (continued)

| | Small sample size: Replication | | | 95% CI for sample size difference | |
|---|---|---|---|---|---|
| | Percentage change | SE | Sample size difference | Lower bound | Upper bound |
| Philadelphia | | | | | |
| RX | 0.3283 | 0.0203 | –0.0153 | –0.0575 | 0.0268 |
| OP | 0.2860 | 0.7094 | –0.3557 | –1.7806 | 1.0692 |
| IP | 0.2654 | 0.5761 | –0.1152 | –1.4031 | 1.1728 |
| All-item | 0.4037 | 0.3528 | –0.2710 | –1.0058 | 0.4638 |
| Boston | | | | | |
| RX | 0.1144 | 0.0234 | 0.0046 | –0.3378 | 0.3470 |
| OP | –0.0115 | 0.3576 | 0.1166 | –0.6283 | 0.8614 |
| IP | 0.3405 | 0.5411 | –0.5238 | –1.6520 | 0.6044 |
| All-item | 0.2535 | 0.2959 | –0.1964 | –0.8283 | 0.4354 |
| New York City | | | | | |
| RX | 0.1719 | 0.1076 | 0.0110 | –0.2017 | 0.2238 |
| OP | –0.3538 | 0.3809 | 0.1898 | –0.6170 | 0.9966 |
| IP | –0.0512 | 0.3734 | 0.0323 | –0.9757 | 1.0403 |
| All-item | 0.0022 | 0.2901 | 0.1198 | –0.5480 | 0.7875 |

| | BLS MCPI | | | 95% CI for sample size difference | |
|---|---|---|---|---|---|
| | Percentage change | SE | Price difference | Lower bound | Upper bound |
| Philadelphia | | | | | |
| RX | 0.1650 | 0.0525 | 0.1633 | **0.0531** | **0.2736** |
| OP | 0.2959 | 0.2003 | –0.0098 | –1.4547 | 1.4350 |
| IP | 0.6486 | 0.1600 | –0.3832 | –1.5550 | 0.7887 |
| All-item | 0.3803 | 0.1002 | 0.0235 | –0.6954 | 0.7423 |
| Boston | | | | | |
| RX | 0.1893 | 0.0700 | –0.0749 | –0.2195 | 0.0698 |
| OP | 0.0400 | 0.0470 | –0.0515 | –0.7584 | 0.6554 |
| IP | 0.5055 | 0.1832 | –0.1650 | –1.2847 | 0.9548 |
| All-item | 0.2291 | 0.0627 | 0.0244 | –0.5685 | 0.6173 |
| New York City | | | | | |
| RX | 0.1294 | 0.0457 | 0.0426 | –0.1865 | 0.2717 |
| OP | 0.0178 | 0.0407 | –0.3716 | –1.1223 | 0.3791 |
| IP | 0.1012 | 0.0666 | –0.1524 | –0.8959 | 0.5910 |
| All-item | 0.0701 | 0.0320 | –0.0679 | –0.6400 | 0.5041 |

*Note:* Numbers in bold are significantly different from 0. "SE" = standard errors; "RX" = prescriptions; "OP" = outpatient treatment; "IP" = inpatient treatment; "CI" = confidence interval.

large- and small-sample indexes are never significant, which is not a surprise, as the large sample and the small sample were both drawn from the same MarketScan population data file. The majority of differences due to methods and the majority of differences due to price distributions are not significant, either. However, it is important to keep in mind that because the city-specific indexes are measured with only limited precision, the differences between the methods may reflect random differences.

In addition to differences in sample sizes, methods, and price distributions, another reason for the difference in the all-item indexes is the different relative weighting of prescription drugs, as we have discussed.

## 8.6 Summary and Discussion

The findings reported here suggest that using medical claims data to measure price changes in health care based on episodes of care is feasible, although claims data alone are not sufficient to replace the current medical CPI.

To summarize the finding from this study, the analysis of trends in treatment costs for a randomly selected set of diseases yields a different picture than the BLS overall medical care price index. Where the current methods indicate consistent price increases over time, the disease-based indexes suggest that treatment prices (i.e., cost for an episode of care) have dropped in Philadelphia, Boston, and New York City during 1999 to 2002. These results on the trends in treatment costs are similar to a generalized version of the findings in cataract surgery, depression, and acute myocardial infarction as reported by Berndt, Cockburn, and Griliches (1996), Berndt et al. (2002), Busch, Berndt, and Frank (2001), Cutler, McClellan, and Newhouse (1998, 1999), and Shapiro, Shapiro, and Wilcox (2001). In addition, in this case, the finding of a substantially different trend in price change is for forty diagnoses randomly selected from a sampling frame that contains virtually all potential diagnoses. However, despite the different trends, the forty-eight-month cumulative changes of the expenditure-based disease index and the BLS index are not significantly different from each other in Philadelphia or New York City.

The results we have obtained suggest that the disease-based index may measure the real price changes better than the current MCPI, because the disease index allows for the substitution effect among treatment inputs. The percentages of the total expenditures on prescriptions, outpatient, and inpatient treatment of the forty randomly selected expenditure-based episodes have changed considerably in all three cities during 1999 to 2002. In Philadelphia, the share of prescription expenditure went up from 2.1 percent in January 1999 to 4.6 percent in December 2002, the share of outpatient expenditure increased from 16.9 percent to 34.1 percent, and the inpatient expenditure share dropped from 81.0 percent to 61.4 percent. In Boston, these expenditure shares were 3.6 percent, 22.7 percent, and 73.7 percent in January 1999 and became 4.4 percent, 34.6 percent, and 61.0 percent in December 2002. In New York City, the outpatient expenditure share rose from 28.4 percent to 34.4 percent, the hospitalization share dropped from 71.0 percent to 65.2 percent, and the prescription share decreased slightly from 0.6 percent to 0.4 percent. A similar pattern was also observed for population-based episodes over the same time period. Overall, the treatment pattern of disease episodes seems to move away from inpatient hospitalizations to outpatient settings.

It is important to note that all results presented in this chapter are based on raw payments in the claims database, which could help explain the large variance we observed in claims data indexes. To avoid the small-sample issues with hospital stays and procedures, one could use the nationwide database and a two-level random-effect model to produce a Bayes estimate of the monthly payment for each DRG and BETOS at the city level. Song et al. (2004) report disease indexes that are constructed using Bayes-estimated prices for BETOS and DRGs for the same two sets of forty episodes. The overall trend of payments is determined from the overall MarketScan trend, and an adjustment is made to the intercept of each city. Indexes based on Bayes-estimated prices present a more consistent trend and reveal less fluctuation than indexes based on raw payments. However, depending on how big a value should be placed on consistency, it is not clear whether the addition of analytic complexity is worth the computational burden for the BLS.

The sampling method taken in this chapter selected drugs, physician office visits, hospitals, and disease episodes using probability in proportion to size with replacement, as the BLS does for the MCPI. However, sampling without replacement is more efficient than sampling with replacement (Foreman 1991). A further advantage to sampling without replacement is that the episode groupers can be randomly ordered within a body system, and then the body systems can be randomly ordered in the MEG list. This would cause the sample of episodes to be implicitly stratified by body systems, ensuring that the sample of episodes tended to be representative of the various body systems, so there is no chance of selecting only metabolic diseases, for example. We could select diseases from each body system in proportion to the expenditures or frequency of occurrence for treatment of that body system.

Disease-based price indexes rely heavily on MEG in this study. In addition to MEG, there exist several other proprietary episode grouper software products. Rosen and Mayer-Oakes (1999) compared four such episode groupers based on characteristics such as purpose, case-mix adjustment, comprehensiveness, and clinical flexibility. Although it would be interesting to see whether different episode groupers would generate different trends in treatment costs, we believe that correcting the information technology failure in the medical market is more important in the calculation of the cost of episode care using claims databases than trying to choose the best episode grouper. The current medical record-keeping system does not adequately keep track of all the inputs that are used to treat a patient disease or patient episode. The lack of sufficient record-keeping and the existence of incomplete claims are two examples of the information technology failure. For instance, in the Medical Expenditure Panel Survey 2003 data, about 8 percent of medical expenditures were due to orphan records (i.e., records with a dollar amount for the use of a service but no diagnoses). In each year of 1998 to 2003, orphan records had the highest expenditure share. No episode grouper can correctly bundle orphan records into a particular disease. We do not think we can generate any type of accurate price index from claims data until this information technology failure is corrected. To achieve this, all physicians, public insurers, and private insurers must be responsible for maintaining an audited record-keeping system that is consistently updated for the inputs used to treat diseases, for corrections or changes in diagnosis, and for an established beginning and end date established by the physician for every acute disease.

In addition to the information technology failure, there are four limitations in using claims data to generate a medical CPI. One limitation of the price index developed in this study is that it does not include health insurance premiums. A true CPI needs to account for the role of health insurance, because it represents a major medical purchase for most consumers. Unfortunately, information on health insurance premiums and characteristics is not available in a medical claims database. Secondly, it is important to point out that all indexes constructed in this study are indexes only for those covered by health plans in the United States. We did not estimate price indexes for the uninsured population, who may face different incidence of diseases, and who, for a particular disease, may consume different inputs. A third limitation of using the claims data set is that treating a disease may require more types of inputs than those reimbursed by an insurer. For example, over-the-counter medicines may play an important role, and products such as sunscreen, gym memberships, and dental floss are often used to prevent disease and should be considered as part of the mix of goods used to stay healthy. Finally, whether the insured people in a claims database are representative of the whole privately insured population in the United States remains to be seen. Thus, a medical CPI cannot be generated solely on claims databases.

# Appendix A

## *Analytic File Construction for BLS MCPI Replication Analysis*

The analytic file was built from the MarketScan databases, following the steps summarized below.

1. Using the first three digits of providers' ZIP codes, we selected all inpatient admissions, inpatient services, outpatient services, and pharmacy claims for the following metropolitan areas from the Commercial and Medicare Databases between January 1, 1998, and December 31, 2002: New York City (A109), Philadelphia (A102), and Boston (A103).
2. We combined the resulting data sets from the Commercial and Medicare Databases.
3. To sample pharmacies, we randomly selected a given number of pharmacy IDs in proportion to their expenditure share within a city. Because MarketScan databases do not record the annual expenditure of any pharmacy, we summed up all payment to a given pharmacy in a year recorded in MarketScan to calculate the probability of selecting that pharmacy. The computed total payment to a pharmacy could differ from its actual annual revenue, as some large pharmacies may have a small number of patients in MarketScan databases.
4. For each selected pharmacy ID, we randomly selected one NDC in proportion to its expenditure share within that pharmacy at yearly intervals. All drugs and medical supplies dispensed by prescription, including prescription-dispensed over-the-counter drugs, were included in this random selection. Inpatient hospital prescriptions and prescriptions paid by Medicaid or worker's compensation were ineligible for the medical price index. For each NDC selected, both the insurance reimbursement and the patient co-pay, if any, were included to arrive at the total reimbursement for that prescription.
5. Hospitals that are owned and operated by health maintenance organizations (HMOs) should be excluded, because they are not eligible for CPI pricing; but because hospital ownership is not included in the MarketScan databases, these hospitals cannot be identified directly. Instead, we excluded all services that are paid by the capitation method, and by default, these hospitals were excluded from our sample.
6. We relied on the provider type variable (STDPROV) to exclude ophthalmologists, dentists, podiatrists, and other medical practitioners who are not medical doctors or osteopaths from our sample, because they are not eligible for medical price indexes. We also excluded services reimbursed by capitation.
7. To calculate physician indexes, we first randomly selected a given number of physicians in proportion to their expenditure share within a city,

and then we randomly selected one CPT in proportion to its expenditure share for that physician. As MarketScan databases do not record the annual revenue of any physician, we summed up all payment to a given physician in a year recorded in MarketScan to calculate the probability of selecting that physician. It is important to note that the computed total payment to a physician could differ from his or her actual annual revenue.

8. MarketScan outpatient services database does not contain the same hospital ID that is contained in the inpatient admissions and inpatient services databases; therefore, we could not link inpatient stays and outpatient visits that occur within the same hospital. We used hospital IDs (UNIHOSP) in the inpatient data sets to identify hospitals, and we used provider IDs (PROVID) in the outpatient data set to identify hospitals.

9. To sample a given number of hospitals for the hospital indexes, we randomly selected the same number of hospitals in proportion to their expenditure share within a city. As MarketScan databases do not record the annual revenue of any hospital, we summed up all payment to a given hospital in a year recorded in MarketScan to calculate the probability of choosing that hospital. It is important to note that the computed total payment to a hospital could differ from its actual annual revenue, as some large hospitals may have a small number of patients in MarketScan database.

10. For each selected hospital ID, we randomly chose one hospital stay in proportion to its expenditure share within all inpatient hospital stays; for each selected provider ID, we randomly selected one outpatient visit in proportion to its expenditure share within all outpatient services in that hospital. Thus, for each hospital ID, we selected one inpatient stay; for each provider ID, we selected one outpatient visit. All random selection occurred at yearly intervals. Hospital outpatient services were identified using the place of service variable (STDPLAC).

11. We calculated the final reimbursements for each selected NDC, CPT, and hospital stay/visit in each month. The PAY variable in MarketScan measures total payment reimbursed from all sources.

# Appendix B

**Table 8B.1** **Expenditure-based sampling characteristics: Conditions sampled with probability proportional to expenditure with replacement**

| Episode group number | Episode label | Total payments ($) | Number of times drawn | Expected number of times drawn |
|---|---|---|---|---|
| | *Philadelphia* | | | |
| 10 | Angina pectoris, chronic maintenance | 16,594,049 | 6 | 2.965 |
| 187 | Renal failure | 9,538,311 | 2 | 1.704 |
| 11 | Acute myocardial infarction | 8,740,579 | 2 | 1.562 |
| 374 | Osteoarthritis | 8,349,565 | 1 | 1.492 |
| 397 | Cerebrovascular disease with stroke | 6,531,667 | 2 | 1.167 |
| 426 | Complications of surgical and medical care | 5,092,074 | 1 | 0.910 |
| 212 | Neoplasm, malignant: Breast, female | 4,802,802 | 1 | 0.858 |
| 336 | Neoplasm, malignant: Prostate | 3,671,757 | 2 | 0.656 |
| 274 | Cholecystitis and cholelithiasis | 2,868,658 | 1 | 0.513 |
| 51 | Diabetes mellitus with complications | 2,393,106 | 1 | 0.428 |
| 189 | Urinary tract infections | 2,231,736 | 2 | 0.399 |
| 405 | Injury: Spine and spinal cord | 1,955,954 | 1 | 0.349 |
| 50 | Diabetes mellitus type 2 and hyperglycemic states, maintenance | 1,779,928 | 1 | 0.318 |
| 535 | Infections of skin and subcutaneous tissue | 1,359,153 | 1 | 0.243 |
| 1 | Aneurysm, abdominal | 1,103,927 | 1 | 0.197 |
| 411 | Neoplasm: Central nervous system | 967,351 | 1 | 0.173 |
| 357 | Fracture or sprain: Ankle | 899,572 | 1 | 0.161 |
| 285 | Pancreatitis | 812,379 | 1 | 0.145 |
| 149 | Functional digestive disorders | 805,771 | 1 | 0.144 |
| 556 | Injury: Other | 690,768 | 1 | 0.123 |
| 138 | Appendicitis | 591,180 | 1 | 0.106 |

| | | | | |
|---|---|---|---|---|
| 204 | Dysfunctional uterine bleeding | 387,773 | 1 | 0.069 |
| 366 | Infectious arthritis | 372,816 | 1 | 0.067 |
| 386 | Anomaly: Musculoskeletal system | 336,946 | 2 | 0.060 |
| 206 | Endometriosis | 288,676 | 1 | 0.052 |
| 220 | Pelvic inflammatory disease | 125,016 | 1 | 0.022 |
| 547 | Adverse drug reactions | 119,754 | 1 | 0.021 |
| 304 | Herpes simplex infections | 77,815 | 1 | 0.014 |
| 58 | Neoplasm, benign: Adenoma, parathyroid, or hyperparathyroidism | 63,178 | 1 | 0.011 |
| | *Boston* | | | |
| 10 | Angina pectoris, chronic maintenance | 27,424,386 | 4 | 2.690 |
| 374 | Osteoarthritis | 16,971,880 | 3 | 1.665 |
| 11 | Acute myocardial infarction | 16,192,922 | 1 | 1.588 |
| 13 | Essential hypertension, chronic maintenance | 13,013,202 | 2 | 1.277 |
| 397 | Cerebrovascular disease with stroke | 11,187,732 | 2 | 1.097 |
| 187 | Renal failure | 10,737,384 | 2 | 1.053 |
| 92 | Cataract | 8,905,881 | 1 | 0.874 |
| 500 | Chronic obstructive pulmonary disease | 8,752,026 | 1 | 0.859 |
| 6 | Arrhythmias | 8,653,448 | 1 | 0.849 |
| 212 | Neoplasm, malignant: Breast, female | 8,542,333 | 1 | 0.838 |
| 348 | Fracture: Femur, head, or neck | 7,267,359 | 2 | 0.713 |
| 426 | Complications of surgical and medical care | 6,681,475 | 1 | 0.655 |
| 50 | Diabetes mellitus type 2 and hyperglycemic states, maintenance | 5,312,060 | 1 | 0.521 |
| 24 | Tibial, iliac, femoral, or popliteal artery disease | 5,176,366 | 1 | 0.508 |
| 203 | Delivery, vaginal | 4,850,220 | 1 | 0.476 |
| 398 | Dementia: Primary degenerative (Alzheimer's or Pick's disease) | 2,540,752 | 1 | 0.249 |
| 536 | Neoplasm, malignant: Carcinoma, basal cell | 2,236,696 | 1 | 0.219 |
| 209 | Neoplasm, benign: Breast | 1,994,974 | 1 | 0.196 |

(*continued*)

**Table 8B.1** (continued)

| Episode group number | Episode label | Total payments ($) | Number of times drawn | Expected number of times drawn |
|---|---|---|---|---|
| 361 | Fracture, dislocation, or sprain: Humerus (head) or shoulder | 1,968,915 | 2 | 0.193 |
| 164 | Peptic ulcer disease | 1,916,376 | 1 | 0.188 |
| 88 | Sinusitis | 1,915,297 | 1 | 0.188 |
| 23 | Thrombophlebitis | 1,848,311 | 2 | 0.181 |
| 357 | Fracture or sprain: Ankle | 1,589,749 | 1 | 0.156 |
| 149 | Functional digestive disorders | 1,564,679 | 1 | 0.153 |
| 491 | Schizophrenia | 1,021,690 | 1 | 0.100 |
| 2 | Aneurysm, thoracic | 888,311 | 1 | 0.087 |
| 355 | Fracture: Tibia | 624,201 | 1 | 0.061 |
| 516 | Pulmonary embolism | 515,951 | 1 | 0.051 |
| 387 | Injury: Other and ill-defined musculoskeletal sites | 427,259 | 1 | 0.042 |
| | *New York City* | | | |
| 203 | Delivery, vaginal | 3,580,789 | 5 | 1.816 |
| 10 | Angina pectoris, chronic maintenance | 2,737,849 | 3 | 1.388 |
| 374 | Osteoarthritis | 2,379,435 | 1 | 1.207 |
| 212 | Neoplasm, malignant: Breast, female | 1,868,716 | 2 | 0.948 |
| 11 | Acute myocardial infarction | 1,407,383 | 1 | 0.714 |
| 411 | Neoplasm: Central nervous system | 1,173,222 | 2 | 0.595 |
| 508 | Neoplasm, malignant: Lungs, bronchi, or mediastinum | 1,150,206 | 1 | 0.583 |
| 6 | Arrhythmias | 989,755 | 1 | 0.502 |
| 209 | Neoplasm, benign: Breast | 926,921 | 1 | 0.470 |
| 341 | Bursitis | 880,225 | 1 | 0.446 |
| 510 | Pneumonia: Bacterial | 632,472 | 1 | 0.321 |

| | | | | |
|---|---|---|---|---|
| 211 | Neoplasm, benign: Uterus (leiomyomas) | 574,949 | 1 | 0.292 |
| 152 | Hernia, external | 552,161 | 1 | 0.280 |
| 427 | Encounter for chemotherapy | 533,949 | 1 | 0.271 |
| 158 | Neoplasm, benign: Adenomatous polyps, colon | 530,215 | 1 | 0.269 |
| 274 | Cholecystitis and cholelithiasis | 528,935 | 1 | 0.268 |
| 85 | Otitis media | 433,414 | 1 | 0.220 |
| 50 | Diabetes mellitus type 2 and hyperglycemic states, maintenance | 425,695 | 1 | 0.216 |
| 317 | Rheumatic fever | 357,445 | 1 | 0.181 |
| 173 | Gastroenteritis | 330,471 | 1 | 0.168 |
| 213 | Neoplasm, malignant: Cervix uteri | 307,638 | 1 | 0.156 |
| 370 | Injury, open wound, or blunt trauma: Lower extremity | 209,390 | 1 | 0.106 |
| 163 | Neoplasm, malignant: Stomach | 177,219 | 1 | 0.090 |
| 289 | Neoplasm, malignant: Other hepatobiliary tract | 166,445 | 1 | 0.084 |
| 398 | Dementia: Primary degenerative (Alzheimer's or Pick's disease) | 152,349 | 1 | 0.077 |
| 114 | Macular degeneration | 136,377 | 1 | 0.069 |
| 434 | Neoplasm, benign: Other sites | 122,331 | 1 | 0.062 |
| 487 | Eating disorders: Anorexia nervosa | 85,993 | 1 | 0.044 |
| 443 | Anomaly: Defects of kidney | 67,282 | 1 | 0.034 |
| 190 | Neoplasm, benign: Urinary tract | 40,339 | 1 | 0.020 |
| 307 | Infectious mononucleosis | 22,333 | 1 | 0.011 |
| 343 | Dislocation: Knee | 14,330 | 1 | 0.007 |

# Appendix C

**Table 8C.1 Population-based sampling characteristics: Episodes sampled with probability proportional to population with replacement**

| Episode group number | Episode label | Number of patients | Number of times drawn | Expected number of times drawn |
|---|---|---|---|---|
| | *Philadelphia* | | | |
| 425 | Abnormal lab, x-ray, and clinical findings | 2,438 | 2 | 1.0079 |
| 331 | Benign prostatic hypertrophy | 2,275 | 2 | 0.9405 |
| 371 | Injury, open wound, or blunt trauma: Upper extremity | 2,206 | 1 | 0.9120 |
| 402 | Headache | 2,125 | 1 | 0.8785 |
| 496 | Asthma, chronic maintenance | 2,116 | 1 | 0.8748 |
| 535 | Infections of skin and subcutaneous tissue | 2,069 | 1 | 0.8554 |
| 158 | Neoplasm, benign: Adenomatous polyps, colon | 1,427 | 1 | 0.5899 |
| 24 | Tibial, iliac, femoral, or popliteal artery disease | 1,385 | 3 | 0.5726 |
| 536 | Neoplasm, malignant: Carcinoma, basal cell | 1,368 | 1 | 0.5656 |
| 173 | Gastroenteritis | 1,327 | 2 | 0.5486 |
| 49 | Diabetes mellitus type 1 maintenance | 1,036 | 1 | 0.4283 |
| 489 | Generalized anxiety disorder | 1,016 | 4 | 0.4200 |
| 150 | Gastritis | 972 | 1 | 0.4018 |
| 51 | Diabetes mellitus with complications | 945 | 1 | 0.3907 |
| 267 | Anemia: Other | 906 | 1 | 0.3746 |
| 361 | Fracture, dislocation, or sprain: Humerus (head) or shoulder | 888 | 1 | 0.3671 |
| 199 | Ante- and postpartum complications | 770 | 1 | 0.3183 |
| 368 | Injury, knee, ligamentous | 741 | 1 | 0.3063 |
| 156 | Irritable bowel syndrome | 725 | 1 | 0.2997 |
| 98 | Detachment of the retina | 683 | 1 | 0.2824 |
| 152 | Hernia, external | 622 | 1 | 0.2571 |
| 541 | Psoriasis vulgaris | 398 | 1 | 0.1645 |
| 363 | Gout | 388 | 1 | 0.1604 |

| | | | | |
|---|---|---|---|---|
| 354 | Fracture: Radius, lower end | 380 | 1 | 0.1571 |
| 339 | Neoplasm, benign: Male reproductive system | 285 | 1 | 0.1178 |
| 79 | Neoplasm, benign: Sinuses | 240 | 1 | 0.0992 |
| 497 | Asthma with complications | 228 | 1 | 0.0943 |
| 213 | Neoplasm, malignant: Cervix uteri | 211 | 1 | 0.0872 |
| 304 | Herpes simplex infections | 159 | 1 | 0.0657 |
| 172 | Complications of gastrointestinal treatment | 94 | 1 | 0.0389 |
| 2 | Aneurysm, thoracic | 69 | 1 | 0.0285 |
| 552 | Laceration: Esophagus | 37 | 1 | 0.0153 |
| | *Boston* | | | |
| 496 | Asthma, chronic maintenance | 5,174 | 1 | 1.0959 |
| 189 | Urinary tract infections | 4,746 | 1 | 1.0053 |
| 539 | Neoplasm: Atypical nevus | 4,511 | 1 | 0.9555 |
| 425 | Abnormal lab, x-ray, and clinical findings | 4,364 | 1 | 0.9244 |
| 24 | Tibial, iliac, femoral, or popliteal artery disease | 3,731 | 3 | 0.7903 |
| 370 | Injury, open wound, or blunt trauma: Lower extremity | 3,585 | 1 | 0.7594 |
| 536 | Neoplasm, malignant: Carcinoma, basal cell | 3,402 | 1 | 0.7206 |
| 153 | Hernia, hiatal, or reflux esophagitis | 3,385 | 3 | 0.7170 |
| 51 | Diabetes mellitus with complications | 3,036 | 1 | 0.6431 |
| 158 | Neoplasm, benign: Adenomatous polyps, colon | 2,718 | 1 | 0.5757 |
| 149 | Functional digestive disorders | 2,550 | 1 | 0.5401 |
| 543 | Neoplasm, benign: Skin or subcutaneous tissue | 2,162 | 1 | 0.4579 |
| 93 | Conjunctivitis: Bacterial | 2,033 | 1 | 0.4306 |
| 378 | Osteoporosis | 1,985 | 1 | 0.4205 |
| 204 | Dysfunctional uterine bleeding | 1,842 | 1 | 0.3902 |
| 49 | Diabetes mellitus type 1 maintenance | 1,781 | 1 | 0.3772 |
| 226 | Vulvovaginitis | 1,726 | 1 | 0.3656 |
| 362 | Fracture, dislocation, or sprain: Wrist, hand, or fingers | 1,551 | 1 | 0.3285 |
| 365 | Herniated intervertebral disc | 1,302 | 1 | 0.2758 |
| 151 | Hemorrhoids | 1,288 | 1 | 0.2728 |

(*continued*)

**Table 8C.1** (continued)

| Episode group number | Episode label | Number of patients | Number of times drawn | Expected number of times drawn |
|---|---|---|---|---|
| 305 | Herpes zoster | 723 | 1 | 0.1531 |
| 421 | Obesity | 661 | 1 | 0.1400 |
| 477 | Bipolar disorder: Manic episode | 654 | 3 | 0.1385 |
| 404 | Injury: Craniocerebral | 628 | 1 | 0.1330 |
| 253 | Neoplasm, malignant: Lymphoma, diffuse large cell | 384 | 1 | 0.0813 |
| 75 | Labyrinthitis | 371 | 1 | 0.0786 |
| 476 | Bipolar disorder: Major depressive episode | 359 | 1 | 0.0760 |
| 283 | Hepatitis, chemical | 292 | 1 | 0.0619 |
| 275 | Cirrhosis of the liver | 246 | 1 | 0.0521 |
| 490 | Obsessive-compulsive neurosis | 216 | 1 | 0.0458 |
| 356 | Fracture or dislocation: Patella | 180 | 1 | 0.0381 |
| 522 | Tuberculosis | 137 | 1 | 0.0290 |
| 138 | Appendicitis | 132 | 1 | 0.0280 |
| 2 | Aneurysm, thoracic | 101 | 1 | 0.0214 |
| | *New York City* | | | |
| 209 | Neoplasm, benign: Breast | 1,029 | 1 | 1.135 |
| 539 | Neoplasm: Atypical nevus | 989 | 1 | 1.09 |
| 204 | Dysfunctional uterine bleeding | 923 | 1 | 1.018 |
| 496 | Asthma, chronic maintenance | 821 | 1 | 0.905 |
| 173 | Gastroenteritis | 768 | 1 | 0.847 |
| 50 | Diabetes mellitus type 2 and hyperglycemic states, maintenance | 765 | 2 | 0.843 |
| 405 | Injury: Spine and spinal cord | 576 | 2 | 0.635 |
| 543 | Neoplasm, benign: Skin or subcutaneous tissue | 576 | 1 | 0.635 |
| 150 | Gastritis | 514 | 2 | 0.567 |
| 93 | Conjunctivitis: Bacterial | 491 | 1 | 0.541 |

| | | | | |
|---|---|---|---|---|
| 331 | Benign prostatic hypertrophy | 437 | 1 | 0.482 |
| 153 | Hernia, hiatal, or reflux esophagitis | 409 | 1 | 0.451 |
| 151 | Hemorrhoids | 407 | 2 | 0.449 |
| 211 | Neoplasm, benign: Uterus (leiomyomas) | 378 | 1 | 0.417 |
| 519 | Rhino, adeno, and corona virus infections | 349 | 1 | 0.385 |
| 368 | Injury, knee, ligamentous | 311 | 1 | 0.343 |
| 125 | Strabismus | 246 | 1 | 0.271 |
| 436 | Neoplasm, malignant: Unspecified primary site | 240 | 3 | 0.265 |
| 361 | Fracture, dislocation, or sprain: Humerus (head) or shoulder | 228 | 1 | 0.251 |
| 506 | Influenza | 226 | 1 | 0.249 |
| 24 | Tibial, iliac, femoral, or popliteal artery disease | 217 | 2 | 0.239 |
| 23 | Thrombophlebitis | 147 | 1 | 0.162 |
| 5 | Aortic stenosis | 134 | 1 | 0.148 |
| 2 | Aneurysm, thoracic | 101 | 1 | 0.0214 |
| 210 | Neoplasm, benign: Ovary | 100 | 1 | 0.11 |
| 477 | Bipolar disorder: Manic episode | 84 | 1 | 0.093 |
| 137 | Anorectal suppuration | 72 | 1 | 0.079 |
| 339 | Neoplasm, benign: Male reproductive system | 54 | 1 | 0.06 |
| 395 | Cerebrovascular disease, chronic maintenance | 47 | 1 | 0.052 |
| 71 | Foreign body: Nasopharynx, throat, or bronchus | 42 | 1 | 0.046 |
| 435 | Neoplasm, malignant: Nonspecific sites | 37 | 1 | 0.041 |
| 214 | Neoplasm, malignant: Endometrium | 31 | 1 | 0.034 |
| 284 | Neoplasm, malignant: Pancreas | 29 | 1 | 0.032 |

## References

Berndt, E. R., A. Bir, S. Busch, R. Frank, and S. Normand. 2002. The treatment of medical depression, 1991–1996: Productive inefficiency, expected outcome variations, and price indexes. *Journal of Health Economics* 21 (3): 373–96.

Berndt, E. R., I. Cockburn, and Z. Griliches. 1996. Pharmaceutical innovations and market dynamics: Tracking effects on price indexes on anti-depressant drugs. *Brookings Papers on Economic Activity, MicroEconomics:* 133–88.

Busch, S. H., E. R. Berndt, and R. G. Frank. 2001. Creating price indexes for measuring productivity in mental health care. In *Frontiers in health policy research,* vol. 4, ed. A. Garber, 115–47. Cambridge, MA: MIT Press.

Cutler, D., M. McClellan, and J. Newhouse. 1998. Are medical prices declining? Evidence from heart attack treatments. *Quarterly Journal of Economics* 113 (4): 991–1024.

———. 1999. The costs and benefits of intensive treatment for cardiovascular disease. In *Measuring the prices of medical treatments,* ed. J. Triplett, 34–72. Washington, DC: Brookings Institution.

Foreman, E. K. 1991. *Survey sampling principles.* New York: Marcel Dekker.

Grossman, M. 1972. On the concept of health capital and the demand for health. *Journal of Political Economy* 80 (2): 223–55.

McClelland, R., and M. Reinsdorf. 1999. Small sample bias in geometric mean and seasoned CPI component indexes. BLS Working Paper no. 324. U.S. Department of Labor, Bureau of Labor Statistics.

Rosen, A. K., and A. Mayer-Oakes. 1999. Episodes of care: Theoretical framework versus current operational realities. *Joint Commission Journal on Quality and Patient Safety* 25 (3): 111–28.

Schultze, C., and C. Mackie, eds. 2002. *At what price? Conceptualizing and measuring cost-of-living and price indexes.* Washington, DC: National Academies Press.

Shapiro, I., M. Shapiro, and D. Wilcox. 2001. Measuring the value of cataract surgery. In *Studies in income and wealth,* vol. 62, *Medical care output and productivity,* ed. D. M. Cutler and E. R. Berndt, 411–39. Chicago: University of Chicago Press.

Shapiro, M., and D. Wilcox. 1996. Mismeasurement in the Consumer Price Index: An evaluation. In *NBER macroeconomics annual 1996,* ed. B. S. Bernanke and J. J. Rotemberg, 93–142. Cambridge, MA: MIT Press.

Song, X., D. W. Marder, O. Baser, R. Houchens, E. J. Conklin, and R. Bradley. 2004. Can health care claims data improve the estimation of the medical CPI? Available at: http://www.ipeer.ca/papers/Song,Marder,Baser,%20Houchens,Conklin, Brakley,%20Oct.2004CRIW%20Paper_Oct1404.doc.

## Comment Ernst R. Berndt

Chapter 8 in this volume addresses a very important set of issues regarding implications of using retrospective medical claim transactions data to construct price indexes for the treatment of episodes of various randomly chosen medical conditions and diseases. Price index data initially collected by the Bureau of Labor Statistics (BLS) in Boston, New York City, and Philadelphia for use in its medical Consumer Price Index (CPI) are compared with medical claims data in the Thomson Reuters MarketScan Research Databases, the latter based on transactions with providers/retailers in the same three cities, all over the January 1999 to December 2002 time period. That the BLS commission this type of experimental study was recommended by the panel convened by the Committee on National Statistics.[1] This chapter represents the first empirical evidence on the feasibility of constructing disease treatment-based price indexes that allow for substitutability among medical inputs and on comparisons of their price trends with those published by the BLS in its medical CPI.[2]

The authors construct a number of alternative price indexes, based on forty conditions randomly selected using expenditure versus population weights (the latter a simple count of the number of episodes treated), small samples (the same size as those used by the BLS in collecting data for the CPI), and large samples (about ten times the BLS sample size). Using medical CPI standard error data provided by the BLS and standard error estimates for the episode-based price indexes obtained by implementing bootstrapping procedures, the authors then test whether any of the cumulative forty-eight-month price trends are statistically significantly different.

The central finding reported is that for the most part, while there appear to be very different trends among cities and methods over shorter time periods, after forty-eight months, the cumulative estimated price changes for the various methods are typically not statistically significantly different. In

Ernst R. Berndt is the Louis E. Seley Professor in Applied Economics at the Alfred P. Sloan School of Management, Massachusetts Institute of Technology, and director of the Program on Technological Progress and Productivity Measurement at the National Bureau of Economic Research.

I thank Ralph Bradley and especially John Greenlees for clarifications and constructive suggestions on an earlier version of these comments.

1. Schultze, C., and C. Mackie, eds. 2002. *At what price? Conceptualizing and measuring cost-of-living and price indexes.* Washington, DC: National Academies Press.

2. I note in passing that the version of the paper given at the Vancouver conference had a slightly different title and contained considerably different material than was in the initial revised version from late 2006. The version I comment on here is dated July 1, 2007, and it already incorporates responses to some of my comments made in 2006. The Vancouver version was a draft by Xue Song, William D. Marder, Onur Baser, Robert Houchens, Jonathan E. Conclin, and Ralph Bradley, entitled "Can Health Care Claims Data Improve the Estimation of the Medical CPI?" dated June 17, 2004.

general and with several exceptions, while point estimates of the disease-based price indexes tend to suggest smaller price index growth after forty-eight months than does the medical CPI for each of the three cities, the boostrap-based estimated standard errors are very large, resulting in the inability to reject the null hypothesis of no difference between them at usual *p*-values. Specifically, as reported in table 8.4, while the BLS all-medical-item CPIs have cumulative increases of 38 percent in Philadelphia, 23 percent in Boston, and 7 percent in New York City, the expenditure-based disease indexes all have negative cumulative price changes: –4 percent in Philadelphia, –8 percent in Boston, and –10 percent in New York City. Although the differences between the two are extremely large, being –42 percent for Philadelphia, –31 percent for Boston, and –17 percent for New York City, only that for Boston (which has the largest claims sample size) is statistically significantly different from zero.

What is one to make of this initial evidence? I am reminded of my first statistics course professor, who exhorted us students never to forget that absence of evidence is not the same as evidence of absence. I say this for several reasons.

First, relatively little information is given on how the bootstrap method was implemented and on the validity of the assumptions on which it is based. Specifically, it appears that the authors' computation of bootstrap standard errors is based on the assumption of a random walk specification, which is well-known to generate nonstationarity. It would have been useful for the authors to test for nonstationarity using available unit root tests and to assess the robustness of their estimated bootstrap standard errors under alternative specifications, such as stationary ones around a trend. If the random walk hypothesis is empirically invalid, it likely results in exaggerated standard error estimates. Whether alternative specifications of the underlying stochastic processes would have resulted in sufficiently smaller standard errors to change qualitatively the general findings of no difference in cumulative price growth over time is of course unknown. Admittedly, the random walk hypothesis is commonly used in financial analyses of stock market movements, but its applicability to health care price changes is unclear. Careful and detailed discussion of this bootstrap specification and computational procedure would have been useful. While analysts of claims expenditure (not price) data have long noted that large outlier observations are a trademark in health care, the standard errors of price ratios reported here are cause for concern.

Second, the research initiative reported by the authors seems remarkably preliminary and incomplete. Why, for instance, is the statistical comparison undertaken only after forty-eight months, and not, for example, at yearly intervals? How would results have looked if the sample set of diseases were fixed for the four years, rather than being updated annually, or after every two years? How important is the abrupt change of weights from December of one year to January of the next year, when the basket of treatment inputs is updated for each disease? What would have been the consequences of smoothing the weights over that year end to the beginning of the next year time interval or of using some other overlapping methods? Why do the expenditure weights for inpatient, outpatient, and prescription drugs differ so much in both the CPI and claims data across cities and between the CPI and claims data for the same cities? How important are the various implementation methods that increase churning in contributing to the relatively large standard errors? If one formed a three-city aggregate of both the CPI and the various disease-based measures, would the price trends have become statistically significantly different, due to smaller standard errors? Although regional variations are of interest, in typical policy discussions, we are most concerned about measuring medical inflation at an aggregate rather than city-specific level of aggregation. Unfortunately, these types of rather obvious questions are not addressed in detail by the authors, and thus the reader is left rather puzzled, with the study raising enormous issues about both the CPI and Thomson Reuters underlying databases. Admittedly, the authors suggest that in future research, it might be useful to implement a two-stage disease selection method, first by major body organ system and then within that (an eminently reasonable suggestion that should not have been that difficult to carry out). In general, the analysis undertaken and reported in the chapter is spartan and truly preliminary.

A number of other issues deserve attention. First, while economic theory provides a strong rationale for using expenditure weights, what is the rationale for sampling based on population weights? The BLS and Bureau of Economic Analysis do not generally publish democratic weights (expenditure weights underlie plutocratic weighting schemes), so why even consider them here? Given the skewness of health care spending, one should expect substantial differences between expenditure- and population-weighted price indexes, and that is exactly what is reported. Why not instead devote more resources to a deeper analysis of the expenditure-weighted indexes? In any case, the expenditure-based and population-based indexes often display opposite trends for which no explanation is given.

Second, the careful reader will note from tables 8.1 and 8.2 that for the BLS medical CPI, in both Philadelphia (even-numbered months) and Boston (odd-numbered months), but not in New York City, the BLS only samples bimonthly. This creates a number of statistical complications when comparing their cumulative growth to all monthly disease-based measures and raises the issue of why the periodicity for the disease-based measures for Philadelphia and Boston differ from those of the BLS for those cities. A related puzzling result in table 8.3 is, why is it that the expenditure-based price index for prescription drugs goes up by 97 percent in Philadelphia and by 10 percent in Boston but drops by 39 percent in New York City? This regional variation in price changes is most puzzling.

Third, because the transaction claims data represent the total payment to the provider (consumers' out-of-pocket payments, plus third-party payer's payments to the provider), in some sense, the price index computed here better resembles a producer price index by medical care providers than a CPI, particularly because the medical care CPI relies so very heavily on a reallocation of insurance premiums into insurance payouts and gross margins.[3] While the Producer Price Index scope is generally confined to domestically produced goods and services, whereas the CPI tracks price changes of goods and services, regardless of where they are produced, my understanding is that for health care goods and services, relatively few are produced abroad, and thus the claims-based price index is more like a producer rather than consumer price index. A more complete discussion of these various issues would have been most useful.

Finally, a critical component of the analysis reported here involves the use of the Medstat Episode Grouper, which groups distinct medical claims over time into an episode of care, which in turn provides the basis for pricing inputs. The construction of such data into episode groupers involves combining medical knowledge with insights from claims processors and statisticians and reflects a great deal of art. It is my understanding that there are a number of alternative episode groupers available commercially (and some in the public domain), and thus it would have been useful for the authors to devote some attention in the chapter to the existing literature that examines and compares the various episode groupers on criteria such as their internal and external validity.[4]

In summary, the topic addressed by this chapter is extremely important. That so little in-depth analysis was undertaken, however, is disappointing. While the desirability of further research is typically mentioned in the concluding section of empirical chapters, in this case, that need is truly great.

3. For further discussion, see Schultze and Mackie, 2002, *At What Price?*

4. A study by Ana Aizcorbe, Nicole Nestoriak, and others that compares price indexes from alternative episode groupers (including the Symmetry Episode Treatment Group product commercially available from Ingenix, a subsidiary of United Health Care; available at http://www.ingenix.com/content/File/EvolutionofSymmetry.pdf) is currently underway. Initial findings have been reported by Ana Aizcorbe and Nicole Nestoriak in a Powerpoint presentation at the Bureau of Economic Analysis Advisory Committee Meeting, entitled "Episode-Based Price Indexes: Plans and Progress," on May 4, 2007. Available at www.bea.gov.

9

# Price and Real Output Measures for the Education Function of Government

## Exploratory Estimates for Primary and Secondary Education

Barbara M. Fraumeni, Marshall Reinsdorf,
Brooks B. Robinson, and Matthew P. Williams

### 9.1 Introduction

This chapter presents new measures of real output for government-provided education in the United States. The research refines the measures in our previous experimental work (see Fraumeni et al. 2004) and also takes important steps forward by calculating chain-type Fisher quantity indexes and implicit price deflators.

Measuring the education output of the government is difficult, even though education is a near-market activity. For services, defining nominal output measures can be problematic, and measuring real output is challenging (Griliches 1994). Education is a service with significant nonmarket inputs, notably student and parent time, and the outcome of education depends upon factors outside the control of providers of educational services, such as student ability, family, peer group, and neighborhood factors (Rivkin 2000). Accordingly, isolating the contribution of providers of educational

Barbara M. Fraumeni is associate dean of research, chair of the PhD in Public Policy program, and professor of public policy at the Muskie School of Public Service, University of Southern Maine. She was chief economist of the Bureau of Economic Analysis when this chapter was drafted. Marshall Reinsdorf is a senior research economist at the Bureau of Economic Analysis, U.S. Department of Commerce. Brooks B. Robinson, a supervisory economist, most recently served as chief of the Government Division, Bureau of Economic Analysis, U.S. Department of Commerce. He currently works for the U.S. Department of the Navy. Matthew P. Williams served as economist at the Office of the Chief Economist, Bureau of Economic Analysis, U.S. Department of Commerce when this chapter was drafted.

This paper represents views of the authors and is not an official position of the Bureau of Economic Analysis or the Department of Commerce. All of the authors were employees of the Bureau of Economic Analysis when this chapter was drafted. Marshall B. Reinsdorf is the only author currently at the Bureau of Economic Analysis. We thank Michael Christian and Barbara Silk, both former employees of the Bureau of Economic Analysis, for their assistance on this project.

services is not easy. In addition, not all benefits of education are measurable, because education has broader effects on the welfare of individuals and of society than just raising earnings, for example. As this research continues, the exploratory measures presented may be substantially altered and refined and will be expanded to include other levels and types of education.

The objective of the government is to educate all individuals of school age, including those least and most able. The cost of educating students will vary substantially across students, with the cost particularly high for special education students and those requiring supplemental help beyond that available in a typical classroom. A recent National Education Association (NEA) report indicates that the average U.S. cost per special education student is more than twice the average cost across all students. As well, the report notes that the number of special education students has risen 30 percent over the last ten years.[1] Educating these students is clearly more expensive than educating other types of students. Bringing about marginal improvements in their educational attainment is probably also more expensive than for more able students. Our current experimental output measures do not adjust for student composition, except to reflect the number of students in high school versus lower grades. Accordingly, given the growth in special education students and the associated higher costs, it is not surprising that the price measures presented in this chapter grow at a faster rate than the gross domestic product (GDP) or gross domestic purchases price indexes. In addition, to the extent that our measures do not capture all quality improvements occurring over time, quantity changes may be underestimated and price changes may be overestimated.

In 2001, the education function of government accounted for approximately 5 percent of nominal GDP, as measured by final expenditures, ranking it with health and income security as among the three largest government function categories.[2] The Bureau of Economic Analysis (BEA) began publishing functional tables with quantity and/or price indexes for government in 2004. However, these output quantity and price indexes are estimated with a cost-of-inputs-based approach, as is currently performed for total government: federal, state, and local.[3] Such input-based approaches do not recognize changes in output resulting from intangible inputs or from varying relationships between inputs and outputs, such as those arising from qualitative changes, and they do not allow for a meaningful estimate of productivity change.

1. National Education Association (2004).

2. See tables 1.1.5, 3.15.5, and 3.16 of the Bureau of Economic Analysis (BEA) National Income and Product Accounts (NIPAs). As government-by-function tables (3.15 and 3.16) appear later than other NIPAs tables (last published in the October 2002 *Survey of Current Business* [BEA 2002a, 12–13]), the data cited in this chapter do not reflect results of the NIPAs comprehensive revision published in December 2003. See BEA (2002a, 2002b, 2003).

3. The 2003 comprehensive revision new NIPAs table family 3.10 presents an alternative breakout of consumption expenditures.

Output-based measures of government output are preferred to input-based measures of output but are difficult to develop and implement. In recent years, national income accountants in other countries have looked to volume indicators using an output approach to improve measures of government education output (Powell and Pritchard 2002; Konijn and Kleima 2000a, Australian Bureau of Statistics 2000b).[4] The emphasis in all cases has been on real output—or volume—measures, rather than on price measures. These volume indicators, such as those based on number of pupils or hours spent in school, may or may not be quality adjusted. Others have suggested an outcome-based approach directly to adjust for quality change, such as those based on test scores or incremental earnings (O'Mahony and Stevens 2003, 2004; Jorgenson and Fraumeni 1992).[5] A third approach is a housing value approach, such as those that look at differential prices paid for houses near borders of school districts with differential performance ratings (Black 1998).

Volume indicators using an output approach are commonly not really independent of input measures. For example, teacher experience and pupil-teacher quality adjustments both depend upon an input measure. Although measures are becoming less reliant on input measures, as real output is not set equal to real input, education output measures still frequently rely on input measures.

This exploratory chapter begins by presenting a simple education production function and by discussing the issue of outputs versus outcomes. It next summarizes and analyzes the progress made by other countries to measure the education output of government to set the stage for a description of the U.S. initial efforts.[6] It then focuses on a few possible quality-adjusted volume indicators for the United States for primary and secondary public education.[7] Subsequent research at the BEA will continue this line of investigation and will look at quality-adjusted volume indicators for public higher education, libraries, and other education, and at the other output-based approaches for all subcategories of the education function of government. The sample of possible quality-adjusted volume indicator alternatives to the BEA's current methodology is presented within the context of the literature, and empirical estimates are developed.

4. Following the international *System of National Accounts* (Commission of the European Communities et al. 1993), most countries use the term volume to refer to what U.S. economists typically call quantity. In this chapter, the terms are used interchangeably.

5. Currie and Thomas (1999) show the relationship between test scores and future educational attainment and labor market outcomes.

6. Recent attempts to measure the education output of government in the national accounts from the output side (as opposed to the input side) began outside the United States.

7. In this chapter, primary education refers to kindergarten through eighth-grade education, and secondary education refers to ninth- through twelfth-grade education.

## 9.2 Prior Research on Output-Based Measures of Education Services of Government

As part of a general movement in the international statistical community toward using an output-based approach to measuring government output in their national accounts, a number of countries have implemented or experimented with the output-based measures of real government educational services.[8] The Office of National Statistics (ONS) in the United Kingdom has gone the furthest with this approach, with nearly 70 percent of government expenditure being measured using direct volume measures.[9] New Zealand measures over 60 percent of government expenditure in a similar fashion. Australia, the Netherlands, and Italy have also followed suit, each measuring up to 50 percent of government expenditures using direct volume measures. Other countries, such as Canada, Italy, Germany, Norway, Finland, Sweden, and Israel, have also developed real output measures, either recently implementing them for a small portion of government expenditures or currently considering doing so in the near future. Education and health are the two functions of government most commonly measured with an output-based approach.

A topic of debate in these efforts is the extent to which output measures can be based on outcomes. Sherwood (1994) gives the example of a teacher who faces a class of poor students. If the students learn nothing, is the output of the school for that class zero? Sherwood suggests that whether a service output, such as education, should be quality adjusted with an outcome measure, as opposed to being derived from a pure transactions count approach, depends upon the particular service. He points out that the price that individuals pay for a market service, such as a football game, in part depends upon the expected outcome of the game.

A few countries have experimented with output measures that use data on outcomes to quality adjust a quantity index of student years of education. Test scores are one such measure, and the Atkinson Report suggests using real earnings growth in an experimental measure of education output.[10]

8. See in particular Jenkinson (2003) and Pritchard (2002b). See also other documents, such as those authored by the Australian Bureau of Statistics (ABS; 1998, 1999, 2000a, 2000b, 2001b, 2002a, and 2003), by the Office for National Statistics (ONS; 1997, 2000, and 2005)—including others by A. Pritchard of the ONS (Pritchard and Powell 2001; Powell and Pritchard 2002; Pritchard 2002a, 2003) and by Caplan, formerly of the ONS (Caplan 1998; Neuburger and Caplan 1998)—and by Algera (1998) of Statistics Netherlands (CBS), by Konijn, formerly of the CBS, and by Kleima of the CBS (Konijn and Kleima 2000a, 2000b).

9. This is according to an e-mail on November 25, 2003, from A. Pritchard of the ONS, unconfirmed by the ABS, who states that implementing current ABS research on direct volume measures for justice (police, courts, and prisons), taxation, and social security would bring coverage of government output (using real measures) to 90 percent, making the ABS the world leader.

10. See Atkinson Commission (2005) and ONS (2005). Note that this approach requires either a strong assumption that the change in the price of education in the labor market can

Refinements to the use outcomes data that remove the influence of non-school factors from the output measure have not yet been developed. Next, we review prior results on measuring the output for the education function of government employed by statistical agencies of the United Kingdom, Australia, the Netherlands, and other countries.

### 9.2.1 United Kingdom

In the United Kingdom, the ONS produces both an official and an experimental quality-adjusted volume measure of the education function of government. Both use full-time equivalent number of pupils as the volume indicator, under the assumption that hours in school per pupil are constant across time, although it is recognized that pupil hours would be preferred. Both exclude higher education.

The official volume indicator is quality adjusted for all education categories. A 0.25 percent quality-adjustment factor per year is utilized, because "there is significant evidence that educational standards have been rising over a number of years," and "there is evidence that the quality of teaching is rising."[11] This is justified by General Certificate of Secondary Education (GCSE) examination results, which show a pattern of increases in the average point scores of pupils over a period of eleven years. An index of the number of pupils enrolled in nursery schools, primary schools, secondary schools, further education, and special education is constructed, with weights proportional to the expenditure on education in the base period to form the official volume indicator.

Pritchard (2002a) introduced the idea of using a lesson quality adjustment. In the United Kingdom, government inspectors make assessments regarding the quality of lessons. Powell and Pritchard note that weights could be assigned to the three ratings categories for lessons: good/very good lessons, satisfactory lessons, and unsatisfactory/poor lessons. If these assessments were used to form a lesson quality adjustment, the rate of growth of the volume indicator would be raised over the period 1995 to 2000. However, Powell and Pritchard say that they would prefer a "more coherent basis for estimates,"[12] so this adjustment is not used as part of the official measure, although it is part of the unofficial measure.[13]

be measured by a general deflator or the availability of a customized deflator to separate out the price and volume components of the increment to earnings resulting from additional education.

11. Caplan (1998, 48). Caplan also indicates that there may be a declining proportion of students completing higher education courses; therefore, an upward quality adjustment for these students may not be justified. Ronald Ehrenberg of Cornell University indicated in a recent discussion that in his opinion, an upward quality adjustment may not be justified for U.S. higher education.

12. See Powell and Pritchard (2002, 8).

13. See Powell and Pritchard (2002) for a description of the official measure and Pritchard (2002a, 30), for the unofficial measure estimates.

The official and experimental ONS estimates show how sensitive results can be to methodology. From 1995 to 2000, the annual rate of growth of the volume indicator for the experimental estimates with the "quality of lessons received" adjustment is 1.74 percent.[14] The comparable figure for the official index with the 0.25 percent quality adjustment is 0.88 percent.[15]

From 1995 to 2000, the annual rate of growth of the implicit price deflator for the official estimate is 3.76 percent. This reflects a typical pattern seen for the few countries, including the United States (see table 9.3 and figure 9.2), for which a price can be calculated based upon published information. In all these countries, the rates of growth in the prices account for at least two-thirds of the rates of growth of nominal expenditures, with the United Kingdom being on the high side for that time period at approximately 80 percent.[16] In contrast, the rates of growth of the GDP price may account for less than half of the rates of growth of nominal GDP for the countries for which education prices can be calculated: Australia, the United Kingdom, the Netherlands, and the United States.[17] However, to the extent that quality improvements occurring over time are not captured in the quality adjustments made to the education volume indicators, the price growth rates are overestimated, and the volume indicator growth rates are underestimated. Measuring the output of services is difficult, and measuring quality changes in the output of services is even more difficult. Accordingly, it is reasonable to assume that quality is imperfectly estimated in the education volume indicators of all countries.

### 9.2.2 Australia

The Australian Bureau of Statistics (ABS) examined a variety of approaches when researching possible volume indicators for education.[18] These approaches included a volume indicator with and without quality adjustment and a modified incremental earnings approach. The quality adjustments considered include quality indicators such as class size, examination results, the quantity and quality of research publications, grants received, and the number of student research completions. In the official

14. See table 10 in A. Pritchard (2002a, 30).

15. See annex B in A. Pritchard (2002b, 11).

16. Rough estimates of a volume indicator for the United States covering higher education as well as primary and secondary education were calculated using quality-unadjusted enrollment for higher education to compare with the Australian, Netherlands, and U.K. estimates. From 1990 to 2001, the rate of growth of prices is about three-quarters the rate of growth of nominal expenditures.

17. The comparison is made here to GDP prices rather than to gross domestic purchases prices, as the former are available for all of the countries. Frequently, the term gross domestic final expenditures prices is used by other countries in place of the term gross domestic purchases prices used by the BEA.

18. The ABS does not distinguish between public and private education in its estimates; therefore, it is not possible to separate the government education function from the private education function.

index, class size was not adopted as a quality adjuster because of uncertainty about the relationship between class size and the quality of education received. Examination results are not adopted as a quality adjuster because of concern about the comparability of scores over time, particularly because of external factors, such as social capital, which can affect these scores.[19] The modified incremental earnings approach, if ever adopted in the national accounts, would indirectly infer the "direction and size of long-term quality change" from a human capital model similar to that developed by Jorgenson and Fraumeni (1992), a model that has been implemented in a satellite account for Australia by the ABS.[20]

The official volume indicator now used by the ABS does not quality adjust the output indicator. For primary and secondary education, the output index is an index of enrollment numbers converted to an equivalent full-time student unit (EFTSU) basis. For vocational education, module hours are used. For higher education, enrollments are converted to an EFTSU basis and weighted by the Higher Education Contribution Scheme (HECS) charges levied on students to form the final higher education index. A university research index depends upon the number of publications and student research completions. Other education services, such as preschool education, are still measured using input price indexes. All of the individual indexes are weighted together using cost shares.[21]

The new education output method results in growth rates that are higher and more stable than the previous input method. For years ending June 30, the average annual rate of growth of gross value added from 1993 to 1994 through 1999 to 2000 under the new method is 1.9 percent, compared to 1.5 percent under the previous method.[22]

For years ending June 30, the 1994 to 2003 annual rate of growth of the implicit price deflator is 3.3 percent. This accounts for two-thirds of the rate of growth of nominal expenditures.

### 9.2.3 The Netherlands

Statistics Netherlands (CBS)[23] experimented with five possible volume indicators to replace their current input-based output index (Statistics Netherlands National Accounts Branch 2003; Konijn and Kleima 2000a). Edu-

19. Examination results were considered according to ABS (1998, 4) but were not used according to ABS (2002b, 3).

20. ABS (1998, 4), ABS (2002b, 3), and ABS (2001a).

21. ABS (2001b, 4–5) and ABS (1999, 13), the latter for the definition of a equivalent full-time student unit.

22. ABS (2002b, 3–4). David Bain of ABS provided the authors on April 30, 2004, with a worksheet containing education nominal and chain volume measures through the year ending June 30, 2003. (All ABS annual economic statistics are calculated from July 1 through June 30.) Growth rates for the nominal and implicit price deflator were calculated by the authors.

23. Both Statistics Netherlands and the Central Bureau of Statistics of Israel are referred to as CBS.

cation is divided into ten levels, from primary through university, and each level's output is measured using an appropriate index. Two indexes depend only on number of pupils. One is an unweighted index; the other weights number of pupils by expenditures per type. Three combination indexes use number of pupils for primary education along with number of pupils, number of pupils moving up, and/or number of graduates for other levels or types of education. In some cases, a two-year moving average of number of graduates is used to smooth the series. For several categories of secondary education and above, part-time students are counted as 0.5 in the pupil count.

Other quality adjustments are considered. For primary education, these include the composition of the pupil stock, the percentage of pupils that move up each year, and the scores of the level test, which is the National Institute for Educational Measurement (CITO) test. A quality adjustment for the composition of the pupil stock incorporates information on the share of students who have a lower level of education for two subcategories: those whose parents are Dutch and those whose parents are foreigners. This quality adjustment was not included in an estimate because of the uncertainty in the resource cost factors to serve these different students. A quality adjustment for pupils moving up was not incorporated into the estimate, because these adjustments would be almost constant over the years. The CITO test results changed little during 1995 to 2000, so they are not employed as a quality adjustment, but new tests may be a fruitful source of quality adjustment in later versions of a volume indicator. Pupils moving up was not used as an indicator for any of the university education volume indicators, because the financial grant period was shortened during this time period; accordingly, the study duration decreased. Pupils moving up was not used as an indicator for vocational colleges, because data were not available on this for the whole period 1990 to 1998.

The conclusion of Konijn and Kleima is that the best volume indicators are those that go beyond just tracking the number of pupils. Of the three combination indexes, the index that uses: the number of pupils for primary, secondary, and vocational education; a two-period moving average of the number of graduates of vocational colleges and universities; and pupils moving up as the quality adjuster for all other categories of education is their first choice.[24] Cost shares are used as weights. A volume indicator very similar to this index is now used in their national accounts.[25]

Konijn and Kleima estimate volume indicators with the current input method and five alternative indexes; however, they indicate that current

24. Konijn and Kleima (2000a, 19, 25). The two-period moving average is used to mitigate the effect of a small absolute change looking large in relative terms, compared to a small population of graduates.

25. E-mail from Kleima on November 14, 2003.

input method estimates for 1996 to 1998 may not be reliable. In 1995, the volume of labor input to education was adjusted upward by 15 percent. Unrevised estimates for 1990 to 1995 show labor input to education almost constant.[26] The 1991 to 1995 annual growth rates of the volume indicators vary from 0.34 percent for the two pupil numbers indexes to 1.42 percent for the preferred combination index. The 1991 to 1995 annual growth rate of the current input method is 0.86 percent. The 1991 to 1998 annual growth rates of the volume indicators vary from 0.23 percent for the weighted pupil numbers index to 1.25 percent for the preferred combination index.[27] From 1991 to 1997, the annual rate of growth of the implicit price deflator is 2.41 percent, which is two-thirds the rate of growth of nominal expenditures.

Figure 9.1 shows the implicit price deflator for all levels of the government function of education for Australia, the Netherlands, and the United Kingdom. As the implicit price deflators for these countries are not available separately for the category primary and secondary education, the U.S. implicit price deflator is not shown. As there are at most only five overlap years, always including the base year 1996, it is difficult to make comparisons.[28]

### 9.2.4 Other Countries

While a half dozen or so other countries have developed real output measures for a portion of government expenditures, in many cases, it is difficult to get a clear indication of the approaches used, much less a full description of the methodologies. Much of the work is still in developmental stages, and published explanations are hard to come by. Nevertheless, other approaches to measuring the output of the education function of government by other nations contribute valuable insight.

A number of countries use the number of pupils as a volume indicator, with quality-adjustment factors under consideration or already adopted. Among the countries that have adopted this approach are: Statistics Canada, the Federal Statistical Office of Germany, the National Institute of Statistics of Italy, and the Central Bureau of Statistics of Israel (CBS). Canada and Germany use or plan to use the number of pupils without a quality adjustment.[29] Italy uses the number of pupils for education-based functions, with some qualitative adjustments related to class size as captured by a congestion measure. In some cases, weights used in output aggregation also adjust for the use of equipment and teaching aids. For service-based functions in education, Italy uses the number of employees, the number of

26. Konijn and Kleima (2000a, 23).
27. Calculations based on estimates in Konijn and Kleima (2000a, 22).
28. The base year is set to 1996 in this chapter, because the U.S. data used in this chapter is the pre-NIPAs comprehensive revision data that has 1996 as its base year.
29. Jenkinson (2003, 4).

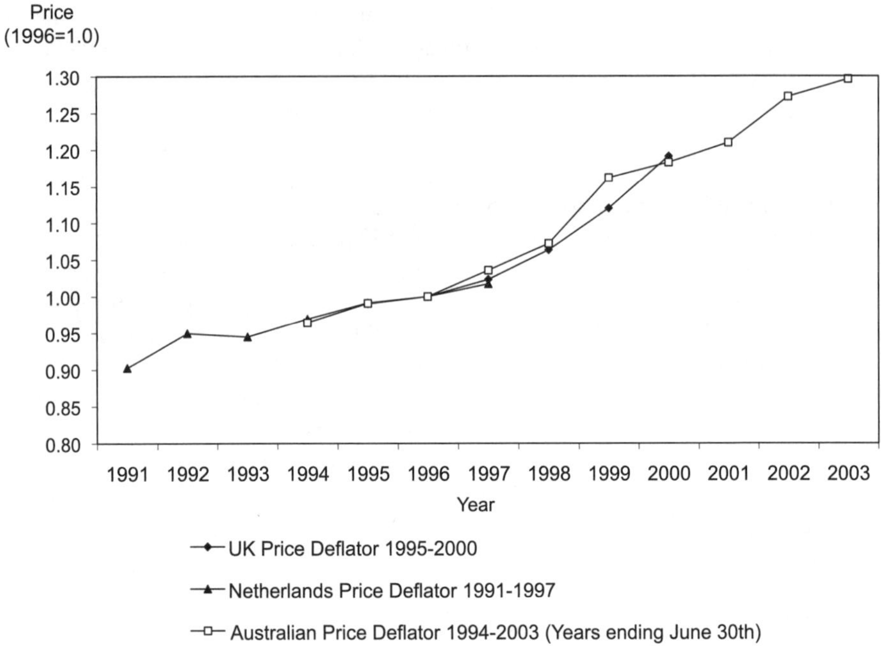


**Fig. 9.1 The United Kingdom, the Netherlands, and Australia: All levels of education price deflator**

users of the services, or the number of services provided.[30] Israel may be quality adjusting the number of pupils with a variety of indicators of quality change for higher education: the percentage of students succeeding in their studies each year; the number of students receiving diplomas or academic degrees; the percentage of students studying toward first, second, and third degrees; and the number of students in various study disciplines.[31]

Statistics Finland uses a variety of volume indicators. Teaching hours are the volume indicator for 99 percent of educational services produced by municipalities, which include services provided by vocational institutes and community colleges, as well as primary and secondary education institutions. The number of degrees completed, generally separated into graduate and postgraduate, measures university education output. Either the number of days of study or courses completed measures adult and continuing education, depending upon the university. The number of publications is used for the output of research, and the number of visitors is used for libraries.[32]

30. Malizia (1998, 18–24).
31. Hadar, Madler, and Barzel (1998, 9–13).
32. Niemi (1998).

## 9.3 Experimental Estimates for the United States

### 9.3.1 Introduction

In this section, quality-adjusted volume indicators are presented that might serve as a basis for measurement of output of government educational services. Each begins with the number of pupils enrolled as the base index, then considers possible quality adjustments to this base index. The list of possible quality adjusters is not exhaustive, and improvements to these experimental estimates are still underway. Accordingly, these estimates should not be taken as an indication of what measure (if any) may be adopted in the future by the BEA. Estimates are presented for 1980 to 2001 for primary and secondary education.[33] Quality adjustments presented include adjustments by teaching staff composition indexes, pupil-teacher ratios, and high school dropout rates.

### 9.3.2 Defining a Production Function for Education

A difficult question in the development of an output volume measure for the education function of government is whether outcome ought to be distinguished from output. Outcome generally refers to the level of knowledge or skills possessed by those who have received education. Outcome can be affected by a host of factors other than schools themselves (e.g., ability, parental support, the quality of home life, and social capital in general). On the other hand, output generally refers only to the impact of schools on the level of knowledge and skills of students. For example, test scores or graduation rates are frequently used to quality adjust volume indicators for education, yet these are often affected by factors other than schools. Cipollone and Rosolia (2007), for example, find that conscription prospects and peer group outcomes affect graduation rates. Students' ability and prior preparation also affect current educational outcomes. Finally, families provide inputs into the learning process; so for example, students from families that do not speak English will generally require more educational services to achieve the same outcome as measured by test scores than will native speakers of English.

Some of the services that schools provide are in areas other than education itself, such as athletics and socialization, but for the sake of convenience, we will refer to our quality-adjustment factor for outcomes as learning. Let $\theta_{it}$ denote the average learning outcome by a student at education level $i$ (primary, secondary, or higher education), and let $q_{it}$ denote the number of students completing a year of education at level $i$ in year $t$. Then, volume of learning in year $t$ is:

33. The estimates do not incorporate revised data from the December 2003 NIPAs comprehensive revision.

$$(1) \qquad Q_t = \Sigma_i \theta_{it} q_{it}.$$

Changes in $\theta_{it}$ result both from changes in the educational services produced by schools using inputs of teachers, other staff, supplies, and capital stock and from changes in nonschool factors. Let teacher inputs be represented by the vector of $\mathbf{T}_i$, where the elements of $\mathbf{T}_i$ are the numbers of teachers of each experience and education level teaching at school type *i*. Also, let $\mathbf{A}_i$ represent administrative and support staff, let $\mathbf{K}_i$ represent the capital stock, and let $\mathbf{M}_i$ represent intermediate inputs, such as supplies. Finally, let the factors that influence outcomes but not output be $e_i$, an index of factors other than teachers or schools that influence student effort levels, and $b_i$, an index of student background and ability levels. Then, the outcome function at educational level $i$ for learning per pupil is:

$$(2) \qquad \theta_i = f_i(\mathbf{T}_i, \mathbf{A}_i, \mathbf{K}_i, \mathbf{M}_i, e_i, b_i, q_i).$$

If $\theta_i$ is measured by average test scores, $f_i(\cdot)$ equals the maximum score achievable by the school with inputs $\mathbf{T}_i$, $\mathbf{A}_i$, $\mathbf{K}_i$, $\mathbf{M}_i$, given the external factors $e_i$ and $b_i$ and student body size of $q_i$.

Over the relevant range for the arguments of equation (2), the average amount of learning by a student at level $i$ is increasing in $\mathbf{T}_i$, $e_i$, and $b_i$. Also, $f_i(\cdot)$ is decreasing in $q_i$ in the region where we expect schools to operate, meaning that the marginal effect of a rise in the student-teacher ratio is to reduce learning per student. It is also increasing in $\mathbf{A}_i$, $\mathbf{K}_i$, and $\mathbf{M}_i$ in some local region (though in the case of $\mathbf{A}_i$, it is not always clear that schools are operating in that region). Finally, we assume that $f_i(0, 0, 0, 0, e_i, b_i, q_i) = 0$.

Because $f_i(\mathbf{T}_i, \mathbf{A}_i, \mathbf{K}_i, \mathbf{M}_i, e_i, b_i, q_i) > f_i(\mathbf{T}_i, \mathbf{A}_i, \mathbf{K}_i, \mathbf{M}_i, 0, 0, q_i)$ for $e_i > 0$ and $b_i > 0$, the average product of the inputs $\mathbf{T}_i$, $\mathbf{A}_i$, $\mathbf{K}_i$, $\mathbf{M}_i$ depends on the levels of $e_i$ and $b_i$. To measure the per-student educational output produced by the inputs into production, we must therefore condition on some set of reference values of $e_i$ and $b_i$. If $e_i$ and $b_i$ are constant over time, we can use their actual values as the reference values and treat the observed $\theta_i$ as a measure of the educational services produced by $\mathbf{T}_i$, $\mathbf{A}_i$, and $\mathbf{K}_i$. Otherwise, we must choose some level of reference values of $e_i$ and $b_i$, such as their initial level, their final level, or some average in between these. Letting $\hat{e}_i$ and $\hat{b}_i$ denote these reference values, the conditional education production function is defined as:

$$(3) \qquad \phi_i = (\mathbf{T}_{it}, \mathbf{A}_{it}, \mathbf{K}_{it}, \mathbf{M}_{it}, q_{it}, \hat{e}_i, \hat{b}_i) = q_{it} f_i(\mathbf{T}_{it}, \mathbf{A}_{it}, \mathbf{K}_{it}, \mathbf{M}_{it}, \hat{e}_i, \hat{b}_i, q_{it}).$$

Equation (3) can be used to measure the change in output of educational services from time $t$ to time $s$ as $\phi_i(\mathbf{T}_{is}, \mathbf{A}_{is}, \mathbf{K}_{is}, \mathbf{M}_{is}, q_{is}; \hat{e}_i, \hat{b}_i) - \phi_i(\mathbf{T}_{it}, \mathbf{A}_{it}, \mathbf{K}_{it}, \mathbf{M}_{it}, q_{it}; \hat{e}_i, \hat{b}_i)$. To estimate this change, the observed $\theta_{it}$ and $\theta_{is}$ must be adjusted for the effect of substituting $\hat{e}_i$ and $\hat{b}_i$ for the actual values $e_{it}$ and $b_{it}$ and of $e_{is}$ and $b_{is}$.

We make no such an adjustment in this chapter, however. As a result, the change in outcome probably understates the growth in output of educational services in the recent past. In particular, increasing numbers of special education students and students whose parents do not speak English have probably had adverse effects on student outcomes.

The basic measures developed here lay the foundation for future research on adjustment of outcomes to reflect changes in nonschool factors. Furthermore, outcome is the appropriate variable for some important questions. Perhaps for this reason, in other industries where external factors heavily influence outcomes, the convention is to ignore the external factors and to accept outcomes as measures of output. In agriculture, for example, weather is a crucial determinant of the size of the harvest, and the spread across borders of disease-causing organisms can affect deliveries of animal products to industry customers. No provision is made for these effects in the calculation of real agricultural output for national accounts purposes.

### 9.3.3 Use of Input Quantity and Quality to Infer Changes in Output

Empirical research has shown that some input quantity and quality measures are linked to improved educational outcomes, as measured by test scores. These include pupil-teacher ratios and teaching staff composition measures, such as years of education and experience. When direct measures of educational outcomes are unavailable, counting the expected change in educational outcomes that would arise from changes in input quantities or quality in the output measure is better than assuming that output per student educated is constant. A common practice, therefore, is to quality adjust volume indicators by factors that measure the amount or quality of inputs that have been shown to have an important effect on output. The difficult part is to estimate the precise value of the change in output resulting from a given change in inputs. For example, if class sizes drop by 10 percent, does $\theta_{it}$ increase by 10 percent? Furthermore, if the quantitative impact of inputs on output is estimated at some point in time, changes in other factors, such as the composition of the student body, might alter the relationship.

### 9.3.4 Enrollment Data

The U.S. Census Bureau (Census) Current Population Survey student enrollment statistics are used in preference to other sources, such as the U.S. National Center for Education Statistics (NCES). The NCES enrollment data were incomplete in some years. While considered superior, the Census enrollment figures used are also imperfect. Over the time period we consider (1980 to 2001),[34] three adjustments to the data had to be made, as can be found in table 9.1: the data for 1981 to 1992 are revised to be consistent with the 1990 Census estimates; interpolation is used for 1980 to deal with the lack of a public/private breakdown of students; and estimates of students aged

34. See appendix B-1 in Williams (2003) for a note on the time series.

**Table 9.1 Adjusted census enrollment figures (in thousands)**

| Year | Primary and secondary | Primary Grades K–8 | Secondary Grades 9–12 | College |
|---|---|---|---|---|
| 2001 | 47,775 | 32,945 | 14,830 | 12,421 |
| 2000 | 46,982 | 32,551 | 14,431 | 12,008 |
| 1999 | 47,069 | 32,431 | 14,638 | 11,659 |
| 1998 | 46,551 | 32,252 | 14,299 | 11,984 |
| 1997 | 47,213 | 32,579 | 14,634 | 12,091 |
| 1996 | 45,618 | 31,506 | 14,113 | 12,014 |
| 1995 | 45,308 | 31,558 | 13,750 | 11,372 |
| 1994 | 44,948 | 31,409 | 13,539 | 11,694 |
| 1993 | 44,852 | 31,867 | 12,985 | 11,594 |
| 1992 | 43,878 | 31,201 | 12,677 | 11,765 |
| 1991 | 43,182 | 30,738 | 12,444 | 11,436 |
| 1990 | 42,605 | 30,446 | 12,159 | 11,166 |
| 1989 | 41,947 | 29,661 | 12,287 | 10,644 |
| 1988 | 41,649 | 29,281 | 12,368 | 10,624 |
| 1987 | 41,365 | 28,549 | 12,816 | 10,368 |
| 1986 | 40,755 | 27,805 | 12,950 | 9,803 |
| 1985 | 40,220 | 27,286 | 12,934 | 9,916 |
| 1984 | 40,140 | 27,282 | 12,857 | 9,886 |
| 1983 | 39,960 | 27,066 | 12,894 | 9,466 |
| 1982 | 40,304 | 27,232 | 13,072 | 9,547 |
| 1981 | 40,983 | 27,426 | 13,557 | 9,254 |
| 1980 | 40,548 | 27,088 | 13,460 | 8,785 |

thirty-five years and over are added in for years before 1994, because these students are not included in the Census enrollment figures.[35]

### 9.3.5 Teaching Staff Composition

The U.S. Department of Education NCES "Monitoring School Quality: An Indicators Report" (2000) found that "students learn more from teachers with strong academic skills and classroom experience than they do from teachers with weak academic skills and less experience."[36] Rivkin, Hanushek, and Kain's (2001) analysis "identifies large differences in the quality of schools in a way that rules out the possibility that they are driven by non-school factors. . . . We conclude that the most significant [source of achievement variation] is . . . teacher quality."[37] Hanushek (1998) states that the "differences in student achievement with a good versus a bad teacher can be more than 11/2 grade levels of achievement within a single school year."[38] The NCES report identified thirteen indicators of school quality that recent research suggests are related to school learning; of these, four relate to the

35. See appendix B-2 in Williams (2003) for a full explanation of adjustments.
36. NCES (2000, i).
37. Rivkin, Hanushek, and Kain (2001, 32).
38. Hanushek (1998, 35).

quality of teachers: teacher academic skills, teacher assignment, teacher experience, and professional development.[39]

Data produced by the NEA "Status of the American Public School Teacher" provide information on teacher educational attainment. Although educational attainment does not perfectly predict how well a person will teach, there is "broad agreement that teachers' academic skills are linked to student learning."[40] Students appear to learn more from teachers with strong academic training. For example, Darling-Hammond (2000) concludes, "The most consistent highly significant predictor of student achievement in reading and mathematics in each year tested is the proportion of well-qualified teachers in a state."[41] Surveys by the NEA and NCES separate teachers with no degree, a bachelor's degree, a master's degree, a professional diploma, and a doctor's (PhD) degree. Indicating quality change, results show that from 1961 to 1996, the percentage of public elementary and secondary school teachers with a master's degree, specialist's degree, or doctor's degree almost doubled.[42]

Independent of educational attainment, teacher assignment can directly affect student learning and the quality of education. Many teachers are currently teaching courses in disciplines other than those in which they have been formally trained, and the student achievement has suffered.[43] The NCES report states, "Given the apparent benefits students receive from being taught by well-qualified teachers, it is worth assessing the extent to which students are taught by teachers who are teaching without proper qualifications."[44] While teacher assignment is an important indicator of school quality, defining a teacher as qualified versus unqualified is difficult, and meaningful data are not available.

Studies show that students also learn more when taught by more experienced teachers. Rivkin, Hanushek, and Kain (2002) show that fourth- and fifth-grade students in Texas whose teachers had more than two years of experience increased their math and reading test scores by between 0.12 and 0.19 standard deviations more over the course of a year than those whose teachers had fewer than two years of experience. The NEA and NCES surveys report detailed information regarding teacher experience.

Even though experts would likely agree that professional development should enhance student learning, there is no concrete statistical evidence of such an association.[45] Conceptually, professional development opportuni-

39. NCES (2000, 4).
40. NCES (2000, 5).
41. See Darling-Hammond (2000, 27).
42. NCES (2003, 82).
43. NCES (2000, 12).
44. NCES (2000, 11).
45. NCES (2000, 14).

ties seem important to help retain quality teachers, but research is needed to document such a relationship.

Of the four indicators of school quality associated with teachers, teacher academic skills (educational attainment) and teacher experience offer the best hope of empirically capturing quality change. Using NEA and NCES survey data that are available for selected school years, the Government Division of the BEA computes a quality-adjusted constant-dollar estimate of labor compensation for education. Educational attainment and experience are taken into account to adjust average real compensation estimates to represent changes in the teaching staff composition. Specifically, annual estimates of the number of teachers cross-classified by experience categories and highest degree obtained are multiplied by 1996 average wages for these same groups, then divided by the total number of teachers in each year to derive an estimate of an annual real average wage.[46] This series, normalized to 1.0 in 1996, is an index of teaching staff composition. It is used in this chapter as a quality adjuster, under the assumption that differences in average wages paid reflect teacher quality differences.[47] Table 9.2 shows that although this index of teaching staff composition increased for the period as a whole and for the first subperiod, 1980 to 1990, it decreased during the 1990 to 2001 subperiod. This is probably a reflection of the significant changes in teacher experience shown between the 1990/1991 and 1999/2000 NCES surveys of teachers. This indicator of teaching staff composition change is applied to both primary and secondary education, as there is no evidence of a differing impact upon different grades.

### 9.3.6 Class Size

Does size matter? Intuition says it must. If class size did not matter, it would be perfectly logical to increase a second-grade class from thirty to sixty students—or to 120, for that matter. Supplemental, out-of-class tutoring would be just as effective when done with groups of ten students as with one-on-one instruction. Although intuition necessitates this conclusion, the measurable impact of class-size variation is debatable and tough to measure.

Finn (1998b) summarizes the findings of some pivotal studies on class size.[48] Glass and Smith's (1978) statistical meta-analysis of the findings of

46. The NEA and NCES provided the BEA with their survey data, cross-classified by experience and highest degree obtained categories. Experience categories include less than five years of experience, five to ten years of experience, eleven to fifteen years of experience, sixteen to twenty years of experience, twenty-one to twenty-five years of experience, and over twenty-five years of experience. Highest degree obtained categories include no degree, two-year degree, bachelor's degree, master's degree, and doctor's degree.

47. Experience-based adjustments to labor input indexes implicitly assume that wage differentials reflect actual relative marginal productivity differences (perhaps as determined by a merit pay system) as opposed to wage differentials primarily arising from seniority-based wage systems.

48. Finn (1998b).

**Table 9.2** **Annual rates of growth in prospective quality-adjustment factors (percentages)**

| | 1980–2001 | 1980–1990 | 1990–2001 |
|---|---|---|---|
| Teaching staff composition | 0.13 | 0.49 | –0.20 |
| Pupil-teacher ratio | –0.77 | –0.83 | –0.71 |
| High school dropout rate | –1.31 | –1.52 | –1.11 |
| College enrollment rate | 1.07 | 2.00 | 0.24 |

over eighty empirical studies show that "reduced class size can be expected to produce increased academic achievement."[49] The Educational Research Service analyzed a much larger set of studies, finding mixed results.[50] One of Robinson's conclusions is that the class-size effects are more apparent with early primary education. Tennessee's Project STAR (Student-Teacher Achievement Ratio), a controlled scientific experiment that assigned over ten thousand students to small and large classes at random and then tracked their progress over four years, "provided educators with definitive answers about the impact of small classes in the primary grades." Project STAR found that statistically significant differences existed among the students in the different size classes on every achievement measure for every year of the study.[51] After returning to regular-size classes, the students of Project STAR were subsequently tracked by the Lasting Benefits Study. It found small but positive carryover effects through at least eighth grade.[52] Finn's study (1998b, 4) concludes that "small classes (17 pupils or below) are more effective academically than larger classes (22 and above) in the primary grades in all subject areas." Class sizes seem especially important, as "teachers spend more time in direct instruction and less time in classroom management when the number of students is small" (4).

Ivor Pritchard (1999) also synthesized previous studies, concluding "the pattern of research findings points more and more clearly toward the beneficial effects of reducing class size."[53] He noted Slavin's (1989) findings that "reduced class size had a small positive effect on students that did not persist after their reduced class experience."[54] Robinson and Wittebols (1986) found that the clearest evidence of the positive effects of smaller classes is in the primary grades. Ferguson (1991), using data on more than eight

49. Glass and Smith (1978, iv).
50. Robinson (1990).
51. Finn reaches this conclusion (1998b, 4). Mosteller (1995) and Krueger (1999) both support the conclusion that Project STAR results show that class size does matter, especially with younger and more economically disadvantaged children.
52. This is the conclusion of I. Pritchard (1999, 4), who cites Finn's (1998a) citation of Nye et. al. (1995).
53. I. Pritchard (1999, 1).
54. I. Pritchard (1999, 2) gives Slavin's conclusion, citing Finn (1998a) as the source. Finn's bibliography does not give a citation for Slavin (1989) as a sole author source. Finn's bibliography includes a 1989 article by Slavin and Madden and a 1989 book edited by Slavin.

hundred districts and 2.4 million students in Texas, found that in grades one through seven, "district student achievement fell as the student/teacher ratio increased for every student above an 18 to 1 ratio."[55] Krueger (1998), "in an external re-analysis of the Project STAR data, reconfirmed the original finding that 'students in small classes scored higher on standardized tests than students in regular classes' even when the data analysis took into account adjustments for school effects, attrition, rerandomization after kindergarten, nonrandom transitions, and variability in actual class size."[56] Ivor Pritchard makes the following conclusions to his synthesis:

- Existing research shows that smaller classes in the early grades lead to higher achievement.
- Reducing class size from over twenty students to under twenty students moves the average student from the fiftieth percentile to the sixtieth percentile in achievement measures.
- Students, teachers, and parents all agreed that smaller classes increase the quality of classroom activity.

On the other side of the debate, Hanushek (1998) claims that in 277 independent studies, only 15 percent found a statistically significant correlation.[57] "The evidence about improvements in student achievement that can be attributed to smaller classes turns out to be meager and unconvincing."[58] The results suggest that while some factors, such as teacher quality, do affect the output of education, class size does not. Using National Assessment of Educational Progress standardized tests data in conjunction with aggregate data on national pupil-teacher ratios over time, Hanushek concluded that smaller classes simply do not outperform larger classes on a consistent basis and that the data do not support the assertion that smaller classes ensure a higher level of output.

Hanushek (2002) suggests possible explanations for the lack of correlation between small classes and improved performance. One is that intraschool class sizes are not decided at random: schools put their lower-achieving students who need extra resources in smaller classes. Also, identification of exogenous determinants of class size is extremely difficult; accordingly, the generalizability of any findings may be jeopardized. As an example, he cites a study by Lazear (2001). Lazear looks at the probability that a student may impede his own learning or others' learning and suggests that higher-quality teachers may be more capable of keeping students on track. This study raises the question in Hanushek's mind of whether the probability of disruption should be considered an exogenous factor or dependent upon the teacher's

55. As cited and quoted in I. Pritchard (1999, 2).
56. I. Pritchard (1999, 5).
57. Krueger (2002) disputes Hanushek's conclusions after reviewing the same studies covered in Hanushek (1998).
58. Abstract in Hanushek (1998).

classroom management ability.[59] Except for a few scientifically controlled studies such as Project STAR, the bulk of the studies have no way to control for exogenous factors and simply compare achievement by class size. Other experiments (California, 1996; Indiana's Prime Time Project, 1994; Burke County, North Carolina, 1990; Wisconsin's Student Achievement Guarantee in Education Program, 1996) that systematically reduce class size across a school, district, or state may miss some of the benefits of having smaller classes, because they require hiring new, inexperienced teachers to accomplish the class-size reductions.[60]

Actual class sizes are unavailable, but pupil-teacher ratios, which are available, are a proxy for class size.[61] We therefore use pupil-teacher ratios for quality adjustment. Primary and secondary education pupil-teacher ratios have declined from 18.7 in 1980 to 15.9 in 2001.[62] Table 9.2 shows the rate of decline in this ratio for the whole period and two subperiods. Ceteris paribus, this trend improves the quality of education, resulting in an increase in the output. Because of the controversy regarding the link between pupil-teacher ratios and the quality of education, we dampen, the effect of pupil-teacher ratios by raising them to the 0.1 power, a conservative assumption.[63] Letting $\rho_{it}$ denote the student-teacher ratio in year $t$ and $w_{i0}$ denote a weight proportional to expenditures on educational level $i$ (where the levels are primary and secondary), we can define a Laspeyres index of the educational services volume measure in equation (1):

$$(4) \qquad Q^{\text{Laspeyres}} = \Sigma_i w_{i0} \left( \frac{q_{it}}{q_{i0}} \right) \left( \frac{\rho_{it}}{\rho_{i0}} \right)^{-0.1}.$$

With this quality adjustment, a 10 percent decrease in class size results in a 1 percent increase in the output measure. Pupil-teacher ratios are applied as a quality adjustment just for primary education (grades K–8), because an effect on primary education output has greater support in the literature than an effect on both primary and secondary education output.

### 9.3.7 High School Completion Factor

Two additional quality-adjustment factors that are worth considering are the percentage of the relevant population who complete high school and the percentage who go on to higher education. Two possible proxies for these

59. Hanushek (2002, 48–51).

60. I. Pritchard (1999, 9).

61. Pupil-teacher ratios are not the best measure of class size but are the best data available. See Hanushek (1998, 16) for reasons that the two measures differ, such as effect of special education teachers and aids on pupil-teacher ratios.

62. Eventually, it would be preferred to substitute pupil-teacher ratios for K–8, but these are not readily available, even through the NCES or other sources. The pupil-teacher ratios used come from table 65 in the NCES *Digest of Educational Statistics, 2002* (2003).

63. Krueger (1999) shows that a one-third reduction in class size over four years produced an average gain of 0.2 standard deviations in student achievement. See Hanushek (2002, 65).

factors were considered briefly: the high school dropout rate and college enrollment rates. Additional research is needed to identify and quantify these and other possible quality adjusters.

Research literature needs to be examined to answer two basic questions: To what extent are dropout rates determined by what schools do as opposed to other factors, such as social (including cultural) capital? And, are rising college enrollment rates primarily a sign of schools better preparing students for higher education (e.g., producing higher-quality students), or is this phenomenon mainly a function of changing labor market conditions? To give a sense of how important these potential quality adjustments might be, volume indicators are calculated with and without a dropout rate quality adjustment. The rates of growth of dropouts and college enrollments for recent high school graduates are shown in table 9.2.[64] The dropout rate quality adjustment is implemented at a 0.1 power, as dropout rates are taken to be an indicator of success for a portion of the high school population.[65] If the college enrollment quality adjustment is incorporated at a later date after further research, it also might be incorporated at a rate less than 1:1. Table 9.2 shows that the high school dropout rate reduction is larger in absolute value terms (if employed at a 1:1 rate instead of a 10:1 rate) than in any other possible quality-adjustment factor, where a decrease in the dropout rate would produce a higher adjustment than any other shown, with the exception of college enrollment rates for 1980 to 1990.[66] Over the 1980 to 2001 period, the increase in the college enrollment rate (again if employed at a 1:1 rate) would have the next-largest impact; however, in 1990 to 2001, this possible quality-adjustment factor would have a significantly smaller effect, as college enrollment rates peaked in 1997 at 67.0 percent before dropping to 61.7 percent in 2001.[67]

### 9.3.8 Prices and Volume Indicators

Table 9.3 presents annual growth rates of a number of alternative prices and volume indicators for selected periods. These fall into three categories: (a) unweighted quality-unadjusted total enrollment; (b) quality-unadjusted enrollment, where the volume indicators are chain-type Fisher quantity indexes; and (c) quality-adjusted enrollment, where the volume indicators are chain-type Fisher quantity indexes. In all cases, the prices are implicit

64. Tables 108 and 183 in the NCES *Digest of Educational Statistics, 2002* (2003). A caveat to the dropout rate table states, “Because of changes in data collection procedures, data may not be comparable with figures for earlier years.”

65. The high school dropout rate for persons aged sixteen to twenty-four years varies from a high of 14.1 percent in 1980 to a low of 10.7 percent in 2001. This rate is the average rate across public and private school students. See table 108 in NCES (2003).

66. As with the pupil-teacher ratio, the quality-adjustment factor for the dropout rate is the negative of the growth rates shown in table 9.2.

67. The economy may explain the drop in 2001 or even 2000, but the drop in 1998 and 1999 cannot be explained by an economic slowdown.

**Table 9.3** **Annual rates of growth in prices and quantities (volume indicators) for primary and secondary public education and gross domestic purchases (percentages)**

| | | 1980–2001 | | 1980–1990 | | 1990–2001 | |
|---|---|---|---|---|---|---|---|
| | | Price | Quantity | Price | Quantity | Price | Quantity |
| 1 | Quality-unadjusted enrollment, unweighted: Total | 6.02 | 0.78 | 7.29 | 0.50 | 4.88 | 1.05 |
| 2 | Primary growth rate | 6.17 | 0.94 | 7.33 | 1.18 | 5.12 | 0.72 |
| 3 | Secondary growth rate | 5.83 | 0.46 | 7.55 | –1.01 | 4.29 | 1.82 |
| | *Enrollment, chain-type Fisher quantity indexes, and implicit price deflators* | | | | | | |
| 4 | Quality-unadjusted enrollment: Total | 6.05 | 0.76 | 7.41 | 0.38 | 4.83 | 1.10 |
| 5 | Primary contribution | 4.19 | 0.65 | 4.88 | 0.80 | 3.57 | 0.51 |
| 6 | Secondary contribution | 1.90 | 0.14 | 2.52 | –0.33 | 1.34 | 0.56 |
| | *Quality-adjusted enrollment: Totals* | | | | | | |
| 7 | Adjusted by teaching staff composition index | 5.91 | 0.89 | 6.88 | 0.88 | 5.04 | 0.90 |
| 8 | Adjusted by 0.1 × pupil-teacher ratio | 6.00 | 0.81 | 7.35 | 0.44 | 4.78 | 1.15 |
| 9 | Adjusted by 0.1 × high school dropout rate | 5.99 | 0.81 | 7.34 | 0.45 | 4.79 | 1.14 |
| 10 | Adjusted by teaching staff composition index and 0.1 × pupil-teacher ratio | 5.86 | 0.94 | 6.82 | 0.93 | 4.99 | 0.95 |
| 11 | Adjusted by teaching staff composition index, 0.1 × pupil-teacher ratio, and 0.1 × high school dropout rate | 5.80 | 0.99 | 6.75 | 1.00 | 4.95 | 0.99 |
| 12 | Gross domestic purchases | 3.05 | 3.29 | 4.16 | 3.35 | 2.06 | 3.23 |

*Note:* The sum of rows 5 and 6 may not equal the total in row 4 because of rounding.

price deflators. The third category of volume indicators is being used or is under consideration in the most countries. The first two categories of volume indicators are presented in this chapter mainly for purposes of comparison.

Each one of the methods used in table 9.3 can be criticized. An unweighted quality-unadjusted enrollment volume indicator assumes that all pupils in primary and secondary education receive the same quantity of education (e.g., that the output of schools is the same, regardless of whether they are educating a kindergartner or a twelfth grader). Also, it assumes that the quantity of education represented by a pupil year does not change over time. Clearly, these are simplifying assumptions. The growth rates shown for primary education versus secondary education are the unweighted growth rates for these subcategories; accordingly, they do not add up to the growth rate for the total. The methodology underlying the second and third categories, quality-unadjusted and quality-adjusted enrollment, where the volume indicators are chain-type Fisher quantity indexes, is preferred to the methodology underlying the first category, because under certain assumptions, including the assumption that public schools allocate their budget between primary and secondary education to maximize the output produced, cost shares used in Fisher indexes reflect relative marginal products of resources devoted to primary versus secondary education. The growth rates shown for primary education versus secondary education are Fisher index decompositions for these subcategories; accordingly, they do add up to the growth rate for the total. As is true for the first category of indicators, using a quality-unadjusted volume indicator assumes that the quantity of educational output per pupil year within either primary education or secondary education has not changed over time. This seems unlikely, even during the twenty-one-year-period examined.

The preferred approach uses a chain-type Fisher quantity index and includes adjustments for quality changes. However, the question of which quality indicators to include in the measure of quality change and of how to specify the equations for their effect are difficult to answer. Table 9.3 shows the prices and volume indicators implied by three possible indicators and by two possible combinations of these indicators. At this time, because further research needs to be performed on the use of high school completion as a quality indicator, the enrollment volume indicator, quality adjusted by an index of teaching staff composition and pupil-teacher ratios, and the implicit price derived from the volume indicators are favored. However, all measures are exploratory.

The second and third category of alternative volume indicators can be written as follows: Let $z_{p,y}$ represent enrollment in primary school in year $y$, and let $z_{s,y}$ represent enrollment in secondary education in year $y$. The enrollment growth rates for primary and secondary education are calculated as $\mathrm{GR}(z_{p,1980,2001}) = (z_{p,2001}/z_{p,1980})^{1/21} - 1$ and $\mathrm{GR}(z_{s,1980,2001}) = (z_{s,2001}/z_{s,1980})^{1/21} - 1$, respectively.

Let $GR(TSCI_{1980,2001})$ denote the growth rate of the teacher composition index, and let $GR(z_{p,1980,2001})$ and $GR(z_{s,1980,2001})$ denote the growth rates of primary and secondary school enrollment. Then, the growth rate of the volume indicator with a teaching staff composition adjustment for primary education is:

$$(5) \quad GR(z_{p,1980,2001}, TSCI_{1980,2001}) = GR(z_{p,1980,2001}) + GR(TSCI_{1980,2001}),$$

and the growth rate of the volume indicator with a teaching staff composition adjustment for secondary education is:

$$(6) \quad GR(z_{s,1980,2001}, TSCI_{1980,2001}) = GR(z_{s,1980,2001}) + GR(TSCI_{1980,2001}).$$

The growth rate of the volume indicator with a pupil-teacher ratio (PTR) adjustment for primary education is:

$$(7) \quad GR(z_{p,1980,2001}, PTR_{1980,2001}) = GR(z_{p,1980,2001}) - 0.1\ GR(PTR_{1980,2001}),$$

and the growth rate for secondary education is $GR(z_{s,1980,2001})$ as calculated above, as the pupil-teacher adjustment is only applied to primary education. The growth rate of the pupil-teacher ratio is entered with a negative, as an increase in the ratio is associated with a decline in output quality, and a decrease is associated with a rise in output quality.

To adjust for changes in the dropout rate (DOR), the growth rate of the volume indicator adjusted for changes in school completion rates for secondary education as proxied by the changes in the dropout rate is:

$$(8) \quad GR(z_{s,1980,2001}, DOR_{1980,2001}) = GR(z_{s,1980,2001}) - 0.1\ GR(DOR_{1980,2001}).$$

The growth rate in the dropout rate is entered with a negative, as an increase in the rate is associated with a decline in output quality, and a decrease is associated with a rise in output quality. The growth rate for primary education is $GR(z_{p,1980,2001})$ as calculated above, as the dropout rate adjustment is only applied to secondary education.

The growth rate of the primary education volume indicator adjusted for changes in teaching staff composition and the pupil-teacher ratio is:

$$(9) \quad GR(z_{p,1980,2001}, TSCI_{1980,2001}, PTR_{1980,2001}) \\ = GR(z_{p,1980,2001}) + GR(TSCI_{1980,2001}) - 0.1\ GR(PTR_{1980,2001}).$$

The growth rate for secondary education is $GR(z_{s,1980,2001}, TSCI_{1980,2001})$ as calculated above, as the pupil-teacher adjustment is only applied to primary education.

The growth rate of the volume indicator adjusted for changes in teaching staff composition, the pupil-teacher ratio, and the high school dropout rate for secondary education is:

$$(10) \quad GR(z_{s,1980,2001}, TSCI_{1980,2001}, PTR_{1980,2001}, DOR_{1980,2001}) \\ = GR(z_{s,1980,2001}) + GR(TSCI_{1980,2001}) - 0.1\ GR(PTR_{1980,2001}) \\ - 0.1\ GR(DOR_{1980,2001}).$$

The growth rate for primary education is $\mathrm{GR}(Z_{p,1980,2001}, \mathrm{TSCI}_{1980,2001}, \mathrm{PTR}_{1980,2001})$ as calculated previously, as the high school dropout rate adjustment is only applied to secondary education.

Quality-adjusted volume indicators are then calculated for primary and secondary education by applying the quality-adjusted growth rates to a 1996 base set equal to enrollment in 1996. Implicit price indexes are estimated by dividing nominal expenditures by the volume indicators. The resulting implicit price index is normalized to 1.0 in 1996. The final step is to calculate a chain-type Fisher quantity index with quality-adjusted enrollment and implicit prices for primary and secondary education as the inputs and to calculate the implicit price index associated with the chain-type Fisher quantity index.[68]

Decomposing the Fisher chain-type indexes allow for estimation of the contribution of the subcomponents: primary and secondary education to growth in prices and quantities for the aggregate. The results of a decomposition for the quality-unadjusted estimates for the preferred indexes (that which uses teaching staff composition and the pupil-teacher ratio to adjust enrollment) is shown in the middle panel of table 9.3.

The growth rate of the decomposition of the chain-type Fisher quality-unadjusted volume index, $c_i$, is calculated as

$$\mathrm{GR}(c_{iy}) = \bar{s}_{iy}\left(\frac{q_{iy+1}}{q_{iy}} - 1\right), \tag{11}$$

for $i$ = primary education or secondary education, where

$$\bar{s}_{iy} = \frac{F^P p_{iy} q_{iy} + p_{iy+1} q_{iy}}{F^P(\Sigma_j p_{jy} q_{jy}) + \Sigma_j p_{jy+1} q_{jy}}. \tag{12}$$

The variable $F^P$ is a chain-type Fisher price index for year $y$; $p_{iy+1} q_{it}$ represents expenditures on education level $i$ in year $y$, adjusted for price change between year $y$ and year $y + 1$; and $\bar{s}_{iy}$ may be interpreted as a weighted average of the expenditure share for education level $i$ in year $y$ and its hypothetical share at year $y + 1$ if only prices had changed. The quality-unadjusted chain-type Fisher quantity indexes for primary and secondary education are then calculated from the growth rates in the same manner as previously described.

The decomposition of the chain-type Fisher quality-unadjusted price index is calculated using equations (10) and (11), with the price relative substituted for the quantity relative in equation (10) and with chain-type Fisher quantity indexes, $F^Q$, substituted in for the Fisher price indexes in equation (11). The quality-unadjusted chain-type Fisher price indexes and implicit price indexes for primary and secondary education are then calculated in

68. For an explanation of how chain-type Fisher indexes are constructed and a discussion of their properties, see Young (1992), Diewert (1993), and Triplett (1992). Because of the properties of Fisher indexes, the implicit price indexes are Fisher price indexes.

a manner parallel to the quality-unadjusted chain-type Fisher quantity indexes and implicit price indexes, with appropriate normalization.

Table 9.3 shows that price change is always greater than quantity change for the periods listed, with the price change typically being in the ballpark of twice the U.S. gross domestic purchases price change. When making comparisons, it should be remembered that the price changes in table 9.3 are probably overstated and the quantity changes understated. This is because of quality improvements occurring over time that have not yet been, or perhaps never will be (due to lack of data), captured in the estimates and because of other factors leading to higher expenditures per pupil, such as the increase in the number of special education students. For example, has the quality of education received in high school increased, as evidenced by an increase in Advanced Placement courses? The comparison is made to gross domestic purchases prices rather than to GDP prices to exclude exports, which are included in GDP and excluded in gross domestic purchases, and to include imports, which are excluded in GDP and included in gross domestic purchases. Figure 9.2 plots the preferred price deflator (derived from the volume indicator that uses the teaching staff composition index and the pupil-teacher ratio to adjust enrollment) against the gross domestic pur-

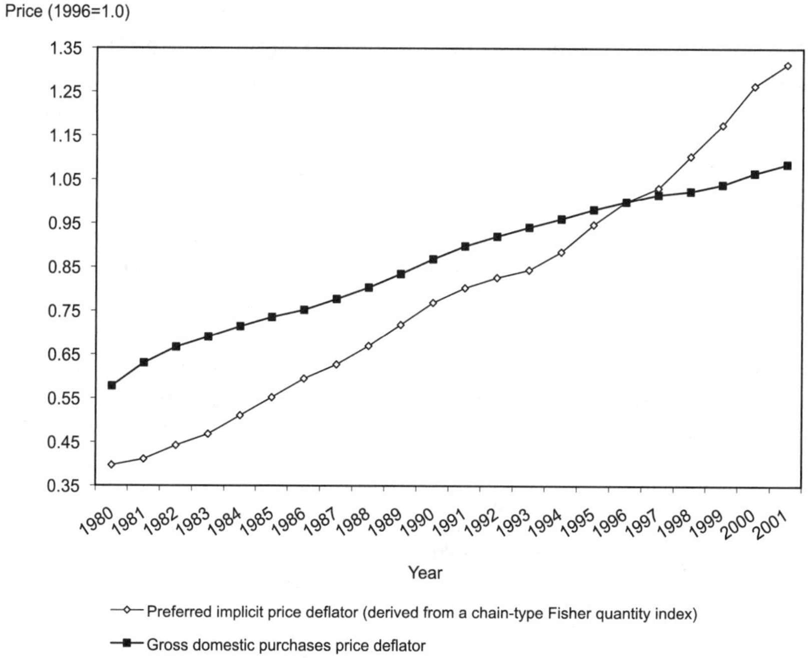


**Fig. 9.2 Preferred implicit price deflator versus the gross domestic purchases price deflator**

chases price deflator. Except for a brief period during the early nineties, the preferred price deflator rises at a rate faster than the gross domestic purchase price deflator. The decomposition of the price deflators derived from chain-type Fisher quality-unadjusted enrollment indexes in the middle panel of table 9.3 show that this is primarily because of the significantly higher contribution of primary education price change (4.19 percent versus 1.90 percent, 4.88 percent versus 2.52 percent, and 3.57 percent versus 1.34 percent). The rate of price change did moderate significantly in the last period, 1990 to 2001, compared to the first period, 1980 to 1990.

Enrollment data, which are the foundation for all volume indicators, show the influence of demographics. Noticeable is the decline in the population of high school students during 1980 to 1990, which ripples through all measures, but it is most apparent in the unweighted quality-unadjusted enrollment growth rates for secondary education in the top panel of table 9.3. Total enrollments nonetheless have increased during all three periods.

The difference between the top panel and the middle panel total growth rates reflect the fact that it is substantially more expensive to educate a secondary-school student than a primary-school student. The average expenditure per secondary student is estimated to be significantly higher than that per primary student.[69] On average, only either 30 percent or 31 percent of all primary and secondary students attend secondary school. Relative expenditures enter into the Fisher index calculation.

Looking at the middle panel of table 9.3, the total growth rates for the quality-unadjusted measures can be compared directly to the quality-adjusted enrollment volume indicators growth rates. Note that the change in the quantity index is offset by a change in the opposite direction in the price deflators.[70] This fact again highlights the sensitivity of the price results to quality adjustment of the quantity indexes. It is easiest to compare the quality-unadjusted estimates with those adjusted by the teaching staff composition index, as this difference, except for rounding, is exactly equal to the growth rate for the teaching staff composition index, shown in table 9.2. However, as the pupil-teacher ratio and high school dropout rate quality adjustments affect only one part of enrollments—not all enrollments, as with the teaching staff composition index—it is much more difficult to make a direct comparison. The impact of both are reduced, because the

69. It is difficult to estimate expenditure per student for primary versus secondary students, because expenditures may be reported on a school district basis, aggregated across primary and secondary schools, and because of different school formats (e.g., middle schools versus junior high schools). Our expenditure per-student estimates are based on *Digest of Educational Statistics* tables. See various issues of the NCES, *Digest of Educational Statistics.*

70. With Fisher indexes, the growth rates are related by the following equation:

$$(1 + n) = (1 + p) \cdot (1 + q),$$

where $n$ is the nominal growth rate, $p$ is the price growth rate, $q$ is the quantity growth rate, and the growth rates are in decimal format (e.g., a 6.00 percent growth rate appears as .0600).

weights are less than one and because minus the pupil-teacher ratio and the dropout rate, both are entered at a 0.1 power. Accordingly, even though the absolute value of the rates of growth of the pupil-teacher ratio and the dropout rate are greater than that for the teaching staff composition index (see table 9.2), the volume indicators with the pupil-teacher ratio and the dropout rate adjustments grow at a slower rate for 1980 to 2001 than that with the teaching staff composition adjustment.[71]

These estimates show that quality adjusting a volume indicator can have a significant effect on estimated output and prices. The difference between the growth rates for the quality-unadjusted measure and the preferred quality-adjusted measure (that using the teaching staff composition index and the pupil-teacher ratio) is 0.18 percent, 0.55 percent, and –0.15 percent for 1980 to 2001, 1980 to 1990, and 1990 to 2001, respectively.[72] The impact on output is greater than the impact on prices, as the rates of growth of quantities are much smaller than the rates of growth of prices. Chained BEA 2000 dollar estimates for primary and secondary education using an input cost-based output approach became available in October 2004. A comparison can be made between those estimates and the quality-adjusted output estimates presented here.[73]

## 9.4 Conclusion

Given its goal of continuously improving the U.S. national accounts, the BEA is examining a number of possible changes to the way it measures the output of the government sector. This exploratory chapter looks at one possible methodology that might be adopted if a change is made. Focusing on prices particularly highlights that much additional research needs to be undertaken, both for primary and secondary education and for other components of the government education function (e.g., for higher education and libraries). For primary and secondary education, beyond looking at high school completion factors, additional research is needed. This includes research on trends in numbers of teaching specialists; and research on the number and sizes of special education classes, English as a second language (ESL) classes, and other special classes to interpret or modify the pupil-teacher ratios; research on the impact and growth of school-sponsored activities; and research on the composition of the student body, as it affects

71. The fact that the growth rates for the volume indicator with a pupil-teacher quality adjustment and for the volume indicator with a high school dropout rate quality adjustment are almost identical is coincidental. The product of the (higher) expenditure weight for primary school with the absolute value of the (lower) rate of growth for the pupil-teacher growth rate is equal the product of the (lower) expenditure weight for secondary school with the absolute value of the (higher) rate of growth for the high school dropout rate.

72. Recall that changes in the experience distribution seem to be driving the decline in the teaching staff composition index over the 1990 to 2001 period. See table 9.2.

73. The relevant BEA category is titled "elementary and secondary education."

learning—these are just a few possible avenues of future work. As the title indicates, this chapter is exploratory.

## References


Algera, S. 1998. The measurement of price and volume changes of government output: The case of the Netherlands. Paper presented at the joint meeting of the Economic and Social Commission for Asia and the Pacific (ESCAP) and the Organization for Economic Cooperation and Development (OECD); System of National Accounts, 1993: Five Years on. 4–8 May, Bangkok.

Atkinson Commission. 2005. *Atkinson Review: Final report; measurement of government output and productivity for the national accounts.* Hampshire, England: Palgrave Macmillan.

Australian Bureau of Statistics (ABS). 1998. Measuring non-market sector output: Recent work by the Australian Bureau of Statistics. Paper presented at the OECD Meeting of National Accounts Experts, STD/NA(98)3. 22–25 September, Paris.

———. 1999. Non-market output: Recent work by the Australian Bureau of Statistics. Paper presented at the OECD Meeting of National Accounts Experts, STD/NA(99)41. 21–24 September, Paris.

———. 2000a. Australian national accounts: Concepts, sources and methods. ABS Publication no. 5216.0, December.

———. 2000b. Non-market output: Recent work by the Australian Bureau of Statistics. Paper presented at the OECD Meeting of National Accounts Experts, STD/NA/RD(2000)04. 26–29 September, Paris.

———. 2001a. Experimental estimates of human capital for Australia. Paper presented at the OECD Meeting of National Accounts Experts. 9–12 October, Paris.

———. 2001b. New chain volume estimates for the services sector. Australian national accounts: National income, expenditure and product. ABS Publication no. 5206, March.

———. 2002a. Australian national accounts: Non-profit institutions satellite account. ABS Publication no. 5256.0, November.

———. 2002b. New volume estimates for health and education services. *Year book Australia, 2002.* ABS Publication no. 1301.0, January.

———. 2003. Outputs and outcomes. *Measuring learning in Australia: A framework for education and training statistics, 2003,* chap. 9. ABS Publication no. 4213.0, January.

Black, S. 1998. Measuring the value of better schools. *FRBNY Economic Policy Review* 4 (1): 87–94.

Caplan, D. 1998. Measuring the output of non-market services. *Economic Trends* 539 (October): 45–49.

Cipollone, P., and A. Rosolia. 2007. Social interactions in high school: Lessons from an earthquake. *American Economic Review* 97 (3): 948–65.

Commission of the European Communities, International Monetary Fund, Organization for Economic Cooperation and Development, United Nations, and World Bank. 1993. *System of National Accounts, 1993.* New York: United Nations.

Currie, J., and D. Thomas. 1999. Early test scores, socioeconomic status and future outcomes. NBER Working Paper no. 6943. Cambridge, MA: National Bureau of Economic Research, February.

Darling-Hammond, L. 2000. Teacher quality and student achievement: A review of state policy evidence. *Education Policy Analysis Archives* 8 (1). Available at: http://epaa.asu.edu/epaa/v8n1/.

Diewert, W. E. 1993. Fisher ideal output, input and productivity indexes revisited. In *Essays in index number theory,* vol. 1, ed. W. E. Diewert and A. O. Nakamura, 317–54. Amsterdam: North-Holland.

Ferguson, R. F. 1991. Paying for public education: New evidence on how and why money matters. *Harvard Journal on Legislation* 28 (2): 465–98.

Finn, J. D. 1998a. *Class size and students at risk: What is known? What is next?* Washington, DC: U.S. Department of Education.

———. 1998b. Class size: What does research tell us? *Laboratory for student success: Spotlight on student success,* no. 207: 2–4.

Fraumeni, B. M., M. B. Reinsdorf, B. B. Robinson, and M. P. Williams. 2004. Real output measures for the education function of government: A first look at primary and secondary education. Paper presented at the National Institute of Economic and Social Research Public Services Performance workshop. 2 March, London.

Glass, G., and M. L. Smith. 1978. *Meta-analysis of the relationship of class size and student achievement.* San Francisco: Far West Laboratory for Educational Research.

Griliches, Z. 1994. Productivity, R&D, and the data constraint. *American Economic Review* 84 (1): 1–23.

Hadar, E., P. Mandler, and A. Barzel. 1998. Indicators for changes in output of non-market services. Paper presented at the OECD Meeting of National Accounts Experts. 22–25 September, Paris.

Hanushek, E. A. 1998. The evidence on class size. University of Rochester, W. Allen Institute of Political Economy. Occasional Paper no. 98-1, February.

———. 2002. Publicly provided education. NBER Working Paper no. 8799. Cambridge, MA: National Bureau of Economic Research, February.

Jenkinson, G. 2003. Measuring the volume of government outputs. Paper presented at the OECD Meeting of National Accounts Experts. 7–10 October, Paris.

Jorgenson, D. W., and B. M. Fraumeni. 1992. The output of the education sector. In *Studies in income and wealth,* vol. 56, *Output measurement in the service sectors,* ed. Z. Griliches, 303–43. Chicago: University of Chicago Press.

Konijn, P., and F. Kleima. 2000a. Volume measurement of education. Paper presented at the OECD Meeting of National Accounts Experts, STD/NA(2000)27. 26–29 September, Paris.

———. 2000b. Volume measurement of education. Statistics Netherlands. Occasional paper, November.

Krueger, A. B. 1998. Experimental estimates of educational production functions. NBER Working Paper no. 6051. Cambridge, MA: National Bureau of Economic Research, March.

———. 1999. Experimental estimates of educational production functions. *Quarterly Journal of Economics* 114 (2): 497–532.

———. 2002. Economic considerations and class size. NBER Working Paper no. 8875. Cambridge, MA: National Bureau of Economic Research, April.

Lazear, E. P. 2001. Educational production. *Quarterly Journal of Economics* 116 (3): 777–803.

Malizia, R. 1998. The estimation of general government services at constant prices: Methodology and application proposal for Italy. Paper presented at the joint meeting of ESCAP and OECD; System of National Accounts, 1993: Five Years on. 4–8 May, Bangkok.

Mosteller, F. 1995. The Tennessee study of class size in the early school grades. *The Future of Children: Critical Issues for Children and Youths* 5 (2): 113–27.

National Center for Education Statistics. 2000. Monitoring school quality: An indicators report. U.S. Department of Education, Office of Educational Research and Improvement. December.
———. 2003. *Digest of education statistics, 2002.* Available at: http://www.nces.ed.gov/programs/digest/.
National Education Association. 2004. Special education and the Individuals with Disabilities Act. Available at: http://www.nea.org/specialed/.
Neuburger, H., and D. Caplan. 1998. The measurement of real public sector output in the national accounts. *Economic Trends* 531 (February): 29–35.
Niemi, M. 1998. Measuring government sector output and productivity in Finland: Application of the Output Indicator Method. Paper presented at the OECD Meeting of National Accounts Experts. 22–25 September, Paris.
Nye, B., B. D. Fulton, J. Boyd-Zaharias, and V. A. Cain. 1995. *The last benefits study: Eighth grade technical report.* Nashville: Center of Excellence for Research in Basic Skills, Tennessee State University.
Office for National Statistics, United Kingdom. 1997. Use of productivity estimates in the United Kingdom output measure of gross domestic product. Paper presented at the joint meeting of ECE, OECD, and Eurostat on National Accounts, STD/NA(97)26. 3–6 June, Paris.
———. 2000. Development in the measurement of general government output. Paper presented at the OECD Meeting of National Accounts Experts. 26–29 September, Paris.
Office for National Statistics, U.K. Center for the Measurement of Government Productivity, United Kingdom. 2005. Public service productivity: Education. Available at: http://www.statistics.gov.uk/articles/nojournal/Education_productivity_2007_main.pdf.
O'Mahony, M., and P. Stevens. 2003. International comparisons of performance in the provision of public services: Outcome based measures for education. National Institute of Economic and Social Research (NIESR). November.
———. 2004. International comparisons of performance in the provision of public services: Outcome based measures for education. Paper presented at the National Institute of Economic and Social Research Public Services Performance workshop. 2 March, London.
Powell, M., and A. Pritchard. 2002. Measuring government output: Mystical or misunderstood? Paper presented at the twenty-seventh general conference of the International Association for Research in Income and Wealth. 18–24 August, Djurhamn, Sweden.
Pritchard, A. 2002a. Measuring productivity change in the provision of public services. *Economic Trends* 582 (May): 20–32.
———. 2002b. Measuring productivity change in the provision of public services. Paper presented at the NIESR conference on Productivity and Performance in the Provision of Public Services. 19 November, London.
———. 2003. Understanding government output and productivity. *Economic Trends* 596 (July): 27–40.
Pritchard, A., and M. Powell. 2001. Direct measures of government output: A few conceptual and practical issues. Paper presented at the OECD Meeting of National Accounts Experts. 9–12 October, Paris.
Pritchard, I. 1999. Reducing class size: What do we know? National Institute of Student Achievement, Curriculum and Assessment. Office of Educational Research and Improvement, U.S. Department of Education. Available at: http://www.ed.gov/pubs/ReducingClass/index.html.
Rivkin, S. G. 2000. The estimation of productivity change in education. Amherst College. April.

Rivkin, S. G., E. A. Hanushek, and J. F. Kain. 2001. Teachers, schools and academic achievement. Revised 1998 NBER Working Paper no. 6691. Cambridge, MA: National Bureau of Economic Research.

———. 2002. Teachers, schools and academic achievement. Revised 1998 NBER Working Paper no. 6691. Cambridge, MA: National Bureau of Economic Research, July.

Robinson, G. E. 1990. Synthesis of research on effects of class size. *Educational Leadership* 47 (7): 80–90.

Robinson, G. E., and J. H. Wittebols. 1986. Class size research: A related cluster analysis for decision-making. Arlington, VA: Education Research Service.

Sherwood, M. K. 1994. Difficulties in the measurement of service outputs. *Monthly Labor Review* 117 (3): 11–19.

Slavin, R. E., and N. A. Madden. 1989. What works for students at risk: A research synthesis. *Educational Leadership* 46 (5): 4–13.

Statistics Netherlands, National Accounts Branch. 2003. Inventory of sources and methods for price and volume measures in the Dutch national accounts. BPA no. 02254-02-MNR.

Triplett, J. E. 1992. Economic theory and BEA's alternative quantity and price indexes. *Survey of Current Business* (April): 49–52.

U.S. Department of Commerce, Bureau of Economic Analysis. 2002a. Annual NIPA revision: Newly available tables. *Survey of Current Business* (October): 12–19.

———. 2002b. Table 3.15.1: Percent change from preceding period in real government consumption expenditures and gross investment by function. Available at: http://www.bea.gov/national/nipaweb/TableView.asp?SelectedTable=307&Freq=Year&FirstYear=2006&LastYear=2007.

———. 2003. Table 1.1.5: Gross domestic product. Available at: http://www.bea.gov/national/nipaweb/TableView.asp?SelectedTable=58&Freq=Qtr&FirstYear=2006&LastYear=2008.

Williams, M. P. 2003. Real output measures for the education function of government: A more relevant approach. Draft, December.

Young, A. H. 1992. Alternative measures of change in real output and prices. *Survey of Current Business* (April): 32–48.

10

# Measuring the Output and Prices of the Lottery Sector
## An Application of Implicit Expected Utility Theory

Kam Yu

### 10.1 Introduction

This chapter studies the output and price measurement of the lottery sector using an economic approach. Perhaps as a result of the accumulating effects in jackpots when there are no major prize winners in previous weeks, lottery industries in Canada and elsewhere are growing steadily. In 1997, according to the Survey of Household Spending (SHS), 68.4 percent of all households in Canada bought government-run pool and lottery tickets, with the average expenditure per household equal to $238, which translates to 0.3 percent of total expenditures. Expenditure in gambling, however, has been found to be consistently underreported in the SHS. The actual amount of money spent on gambling, according to revenue reported by the government, is three times the amount reported by households (Marshall 1998, 31). Therefore, the lottery industry has become a significant part of the gross domestic product (GDP) and a more accurate method of measuring its output is needed. Moreover, prices in any game of chance are not currently included in the Consumer Price Index (CPI). If we are able to calculate the real output of a lottery, then an implicit price index can also be computed. This price index can be used both as a deflator in the national accounts and as a subindex in the CPI.

In the theory of consumption under uncertainty, the typical consumer

Kam Yu is an associate professor of economics at Lakehead University, e-mail: Kam.Yu@lakeheadu.ca.

The author wishes to thank Ernst Berndt, Alice Nakamura, Alan White, the editors of this volume, and two anonymous reviewers for valuable suggestions and comments and to thank Lottery Canada for providing the data on Lotto 6/49.

is traditionally assumed to follow an optimal decision rule with risk-averse preferences. This leads to the well-known expected utility hypothesis (EUH) in which the degree of risk averseness is often assumed to be decreasing in wealth. A wealthy person is more willing to invest in a risky but high-yielding portfolio than an average person. The EUH has been successfully applied to problems in insurance and financial investment. Its linear structure, however, also implies that a risk-averse expected utility maximizer will never buy lottery tickets, unless the payout prizes are exceedingly large. In reality, we observe that consumers who are fully insured in their houses and cars also engage in a variety of gambling activities. Therefore, we need a different approach other than the EUH. In the past two decades, new theories on economic uncertainty have been developed. For example, Diewert (1995) shows that the real output of a simple gambling sector can be measured using implicit expected utility theory. This theory successfully models consumers' risk averseness involving large portions of their wealth, and at the same time, it captures risk-seeking gambling activities involving small amounts of money. In this chapter, Diewert's model will be generalized from a simple two-outcome lottery to an $N$-outcome one (the 6/49 lotto has six outcomes with different payouts). The functional form of the estimating equation will be derived and estimated with Canadian data.

The portion of government output in the national accounts of industrialized countries has been increasing over the past several decades. There has been an ongoing debate on the concept and practice of measuring government output. Due to the absence of market prices in government services, statistical agencies traditionally use total factor costs as a proxy for the output. This practice has become less acceptable as the government sector has expanded. The Inter-Secretariat Working Group on National Accounts (1993)[1] recommends that government output should be measured directly whenever possible. In fact, statistical bureaus in Australia, the United Kingdom, and the Netherlands have switched to various forms of direct methods recently. In the case of government lotteries, the price of a lottery ticket is not an appropriate price to measure the output of the lottery. In the absence of a suitable output price, government statisticians usually take lottery total factor cost as a proxy for the value of output and use the CPI to deflate this value into a measure of real output. This chapter proposes a more satisfactory direct method of measuring government services in lotteries. Our results show that by using a direct utility approach, the measured output of Lotto 6/49 in Canada is three times higher than the official statistics. We also find that the estimated price elasticity of demand is found to be very similar to those of other countries.

This chapter also addresses a question raised by Hulten (2001), who contrasted the consumer's perspective in measuring output with the pro-

1. This manual is often referred to as SNA93.

ducer's perspective. From the producer's perspective, the lottery corporations simply provide a service to consumers to redistribute income after each draw.[2] Therefore, output can be interpreted as the fee charged by the lottery corporations to provide the services. In this chapter, we take the view that for any services involving risk, the ex ante welfare of the consumers is more relevant. It seems if we do not take this point of view, the insurance and gambling industries are simply wasteful.

The structure of the chapter is as follows. Section 10.2 examines the classical and new economic theories of uncertainty and some of their applications. In section 10.3, we briefly discuss the gambling sector in Canada and apply the new theory to the economics of a lottery. A money-metric measure of the real output of the sector will be derived. In practice, a two-parameter equation is estimated using a nonlinear regression. The next step is to use the Canadian Lotto 6/49 as an example to test the feasibility of the model. The results are presented in section 10.4. Finally, section 10.5 concludes.

## 10.2 The Economic Analysis of Risk: A Brief Review

### 10.2.1 The Expected Utility Hypothesis

The classical analysis of economic uncertainty begins with Friedman and Savage (1948) and Von Neumann and Morgenstern (1953). Their writings form the basis for what is generally known as the expected utility hypothesis. The EUH has been successfully applied to a number of economic problems, such as asset pricing and insurance. It has also been used as the premise in statistical decision theory.[3] In the basic model, the uncertainty is represented by a set of simple lotteries $\mathcal{L}$ over a set of outcomes $\mathcal{C}$. A simple lottery $L \in \mathcal{L}$ in the discrete case can be represented by a vector of outcomes and a vector of probabilities; that is, $L = (p_1, p_2, \ldots, p_N)$, where $\sum_{i=1}^{N} p_i = 1$. This notation means that outcome $C_i \in \mathcal{C}$ will occur with probability $p_i$, $i = 1, \ldots, N$. A consumer or a decision maker is assumed to have a complete and transitive preference structure $\succsim$ on $\mathcal{L}$. In addition, the preferences are supposed to be continuous and independent. The latter assumption means that for all $L, L', L'' \in \mathcal{L}$ and $0 < \alpha < 1$, we have

$$L \succsim L' \text{ if and only if } \alpha L + (1 - \alpha)L'' \succsim \alpha L' + (1 - \alpha)L''.$$

Therefore, the ranking on $L$ and $L'$ remains unchanged if we mix the lotteries with another one to form compound lotteries. Together, the continuity and independence assumptions imply the existence of an expected utility function $U : \mathcal{L} \rightarrow \mathbb{R}$, such that

2. This perspective follows the treatment of insurance services from the viewpoint of a producers' approach to output measurement in risky industries.

3. See, for example, Luce and Raiffa (1957) and Pratt, Raiffa, and Schaifer (1995).

$$U(L) = \sum_{i=1}^{N} u_i p_i, \tag{1}$$

where $u_i$, $i = 1, \ldots, N$ are utility numbers assigned to the outcomes $C_i \in \mathscr{C}$, respectively. Therefore,

$$L \succsim L' \text{ if and only if } U(L) \geq U(L').$$

The independence assumption, which gives rise to the linear structure of the expected utility function, has been controversial from the beginning. Samuelson (1952) defends the independence axiom by arguing that in a stochastic situation, the outcomes $C_i$ are mutually exclusive and therefore are statistically independent. Consequently, $U(L)$ must be additive in structure. Moreover, using a theorem by Gorman (1968), Blackorby, Davidson, and Donaldson (1977) show that continuity and independence imply that the utility structure under uncertainty is additively separable.

In spite of its solid theoretical foundation and normative implications, some applications of the EUH do not conform well with real behavior.[4] The most serious challenge is the Allais (1953) paradox, which can be illustrated by the following example. It involves decisions over two pairs of lotteries. The outcomes are cash prizes $(C_1, C_2, C_3)$ = ($2,500,000; $500,000; 0). In the first pair, the subjects are asked to choose between $L_1 = (0, 1, 0)$ and $L_1' = (0.10, 0.89, 0.01)$. That is, $L_1$ is getting $500,000 for sure, while $L_1'$ has a 10 percent chance of winning $2,500,000, an 89 percent chance of winning $500,000, and a 1 percent chance of winning nothing. The second part involves choosing between $L_2 = (0, 0.11, 0.89)$ and $L_2' = (0.10, 0, 0.90)$. Allais claims that most people choose $L_1$ and $L_2'$. This contradicts the EUH, because if we denote $u_{25}$, $u_{05}$, and $u_0$ to be the utility numbers that correspond to the three prizes, then $L_1 \succ L_2$ means that

$$u_{05} > 0.1u_{25} + 0.89u_{05} + 0.01u_0.$$

Adding $0.89u_0 - 0.89u_{05}$ to both sides of the above inequality gives

$$0.11u_{05} + 0.89u_0 > 0.1u_{25} + 0.9u_0.$$

This implies people should choose $L_1'$ instead of $L_2'$.

The linear structure of the EUH also implies that a risk-averse consumer will never gamble, even for a fair game, no matter what the degree of risk aversion the consumer has.[5] Friedman and Savage (1948) try to correct this problem by proposing a utility function $u$ with concavity varying with wealth level. This ad hoc fix does not solve the problem for small gambles, because both the normal wealth level and the payout prizes are far out in the concave

4. See, for example, Machina (1982), Rabin (2000), and Rabin and Thaler (2001).

5. See Diewert (1993, 425). Rabin and Thaler (2001) provide numerical illustrations on the absurdity of some implications of the EUH. Also see comments by Watt (2002) and the response from Rabin and Thaler.

section of $u$, given the insurance-buying behavior of the typical consumer. Cox and Sadiraj (2001) propose a new expected utility of income and initial wealth model, which assumes that the outcomes are ordered pairs of initial wealth and income (prize). Their model may have applications in other areas, but they concede that "the empirical failure of lottery payoffs is a failure of expected utility theory" (16). The EUH may be a good theory in prescribing how people should behave, but it fails as a model to describe how people actually behave. Therefore, in order to model a small gamble like the Lotto 6/49, we need a preferences structure that is more flexible than the EUH.

### 10.2.2 Nonexpected Utility Theories

Most of the theories developed to resolve the Allais paradox involve replacing or relaxing the independence axiom.[6] For example, by taking a general approach to the idea of a mean function, Chew (1983) replaces the independence axiom with the betweenness axiom. Instead of discrete probabilities on events in $\mathcal{C}$, let $\mathcal{L}$ now denote the set of probability distribution functions. The betweenness axiom assumes that for all $F$ and $G$ in $\mathcal{L}$, $F \sim G$ requires that

$$\alpha F + (1 - \alpha)G \sim F, \qquad 0 < \alpha < 1, \tag{2}$$

where $F \sim G$ means $F \succsim G$ and $G \succsim F$; that is, the consumer is indifferent between the lotteries $F$ and $G$. This means that if a consumer is indifferent between lotteries $F$ and $G$, then every convex combination of $F$ and $G$ is indifferent to them as well. As a consequence, the indifference curves are still straight lines. The independence axiom in EUH, on the other hand, can be characterized as

$$F \sim G \Rightarrow \alpha F + (1 - \alpha)H \sim \alpha G + (1 - \alpha)H, \qquad 0 < \alpha < 1, \tag{3}$$

for any $H \in \mathcal{L}$. We can see that equation (3) reduces to equation (2) if $H = F$. The involvement of a third lottery $H$ in equation (3) implies that the indifference curves are parallel straight lines. This additional restriction gives rise to the Allais paradox. The betweenness axiom together with other regularity conditions imply that preferences can be represented by a general mean function $M : \mathcal{L} \to \mathbb{R}$, such that[7]

$$M(F) = \phi^{-1}\left(\frac{\int \alpha \phi dF}{\int \alpha dF}\right), \tag{4}$$

where $\phi$ is a strictly monotonic and increasing function, and $\alpha$ is a continuous and nonvanishing function, both on the domain of $F$. In equation (4), $\phi$ is similar to the Von Neumann-Morgenstern utility function $u$ in equa-

6. For surveys of the nonexpected utility theories, see Epstein (1992), Machina (1997), and Starmer (2000).
7. For details, see Chew (1983), Dekel (1986), and Epstein (1992).

tion (1), while $\alpha$ is an additional weighting function. The mean function $M$ can be interpreted as the certainty equivalent of $F$.[8] This two-parameter generalization of the EUH is less restrictive and can be used to resolve the Allais paradox.

Other developments in nonexpected utility theory include, for example, Kahneman and Tversky's (1979) prospect theory, Gul's (1991) theory of disappointment aversion, and the rank-dependent utility theory.[9] In Gul's analysis, for example, a lottery is decomposed into an elation component and a disappointment component. A weak independence axiom is defined in terms of the elation/disappointment decompositions of lotteries. The combination of disappointment aversion and a convex Von Neumann-Morgenstein utility function may represent preferences that are risk averse to even chance gamblers and gamblers facing large losses with small probabilities, but also to risk-loving gamblers facing large prizes with small probabilities. Basically, this provides the fanning out effect to avoid the Allais paradox (Machina 1997).

Using the contingent commodity approach of Arrow (1964) and Debreu (1959), Diewert (1993) develops an implicit utility function as follows:

$$\sum_{i=1}^{N} p_i \phi_u(x_i) - \phi_u(u) = 0, \tag{5}$$

where $\phi : \mathbb{R}^2 \rightarrow \mathbb{R}$ is function of the utility $u$ and $x_i$. In this formulation, $x_i = f(y_i)$, where $y_i$ is a choice vector in the state of nature $i$, $i = 1, \ldots, N$, and $f$ is the consumer's certainty utility function.[10] The function $u = F(y_1, y_2, \ldots, y_N)$ is the consumer's overall state-contingent preference function. Notice that $u$ is implicitly a solution of equation (5). For aggregation purposes, if we assume that the consumers have homothetic preferences, equation (5) reduces to

$$\sum_{i=1}^{N} p_i \gamma\left(\frac{x_i}{u}\right) - \gamma(1) = 0, \tag{6}$$

where $\gamma$ is an increasing and continuous function of one variable.

A common property of nonexpected utility theories is that they can represent consumers with first-order risk aversion, which implies that the risk premium of a small gamble is proportional to the standard deviation of the gamble.[11] For a consumer with an expected utility function, on the other hand, second-order risk aversion is exhibited, where the risk premium is

8. In the context of equation (1), the certainty equivalent $\mu(L)$ of lottery $L$ is defined as $u[\mu(L)] = U(L)$. For a risk-averse decision maker, the risk premium of $L$ is the difference between the expected value of $L$ and $\mu(L)$.

9. See, for example, Yaari (1987), Chew and Epstein (1989a), Quiggin (1993), and Diecidue and Wakker (2001).

10. The function $f$ is the counterpart of the Von Neumann-Morgenstein utility function.

11. See Segal and Spivak (1990) and Epstein (1992).

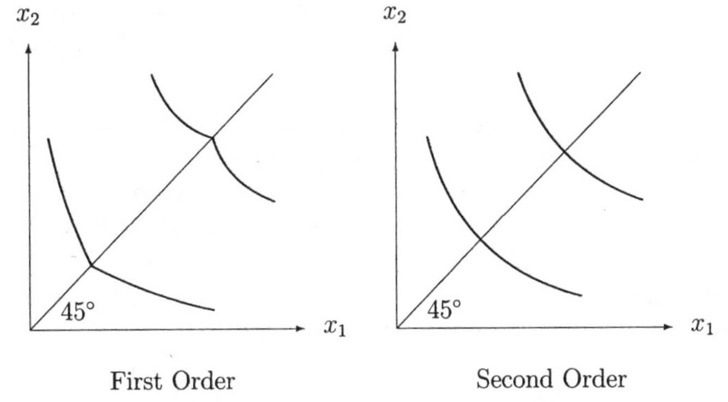


**Fig. 10.1 First- and second-order risk aversion**

proportional to the variance of the gamble. The difference can be illustrated graphically for the case $N = 2$. In figure 10.1, $x_1$ and $x_2$ represent the monetary outcome of states of nature 1 and nature 2, respectively. We assume that $p_1 = p_2 = 1/2$, so the indifference curves are symmetric about the forty-five degree certainty line. First-order risk aversion is represented on the left with a kink at the certainty line, whereas second-order aversion is represented by the smooth indifference curve on the right.[12] At the lower indifference curve, the kink implies a lot of risk aversion, and the consumer would not want to gamble for low levels of income (and will be willing to pay a premium for insurance). At the higher indifference curve, there is now a willingness to engage in small gambles (and the premium the consumer is willing to pay for insurance is now less). Extensive discussion on this point can be found in Diewert (1993).

Intuitively, both standard derivation and variance are statistical measures of spread of the distribution. In other words, they measure how far the random variable is away from the mean over the whole distribution. The standard derivation is conceptually equivalent to measuring the absolute distance between the variable and the mean, $|x - \mu|$, while the variance is equivalent to measuring the square of distance, $(x - \mu)^2$. This explains the kinks for the first-order risk aversion and the smoothness in the second-order risk aversion.

### 10.2.3 Applications of the New Theories

The EUH has been applied to many areas in economics involving uncertainty. Because observed behavior and experimental results sometimes contradict the theory, it is interesting to see whether the nonexpected utility theories can be successfully applied to those areas. In this section, we

12. Machina (2001) provides a detailed discussion of kinks on an indifference curve.

review some applications of the newly developed theory to intertemporal consumption analysis, asset pricing, and output analysis in insurance and gambling.

Chew and Epstein (1989b) first extend the implicit expected utility to an axiomatic analysis of a two-period intertemporal preferences. They find that in order for the new theory to be admissible, one of the two axioms (consistency and timing indifference, which imply the EUH) has to be relaxed. The application is later extended to the case of multiple-period consumption-saving decision with a recursive structure (Chew and Epstein 1990; Epstein 1992). In traditional consumption-saving analysis, the use of a one-parameter utility function cannot separate intertemporal substitution and the degree of risk aversion. For example, a typical intertemporal utility function is

$$U(c_0, p) = f(c_0) + \beta E \sum_{t=1}^{\infty} \beta^{t-1} f(c_t)$$

and

$$f(c) = \begin{cases} c^{1-\alpha}/(1-\alpha), & 0 < \alpha \neq 1 \\ \log c & \alpha = 1, \end{cases}$$

where $c_t$ is the consumption expenditure in period $t$, $t = 0, 1, \ldots, \infty$; $p$ is the probability measure of the future (uncertain) consumption vector $(c_1, c_2, \ldots)$; and $\beta \in (0, 1)$ is the discount factor. Here, $\alpha$ serves both as a relative risk-aversion parameter and the reciprocal of the elasticity of substitution. By modifying the recursivity axiom, Chew and Epstein (1990) show that the two concepts can be untangled by a class of utility functions that exhibits first-order risk aversion; for example, the one suggested by Yaari (1987, 113).[13] If the recursivity axiom is not assumed, however, then preferences may be inconsistent; that is, a consumption plan formulated at $t = 0$ may not be pursued in subsequent periods. The situation can be modeled as a noncooperative game between the decision maker at different times, and a perfect Nash equilibrium is taken to describe the behavior.

Using a similar approach, Epstein and Zin (1989) develop a generalized intertemporal capital asset-pricing model (CAPM). This model is used to study the equity premium puzzle in the United States, which has a historical average value of 6.2 percent. Using calibration of preferences by simulation technique, empirical results by Epstein and Zin (1990) show that the use of nonexpected utility function can explain at least a part (2 percent) of the equity premium. Epstein and Zin (1991) also apply the intertemporal CAPM to update the permanent income hypothesis of Hall (1978). In this study, the utility function takes the form

13. The recursivity axiom assumes that the recursive preference structure of a consumer is consistent over time and across states of the world. See Chew and Epstein (1990, 62–63) for details.

$$\tilde{U}_t = W[c_t, \mu(U_{t+1}|I_t)],$$

where $\mu$ is the certainty equivalent of the recursive utility $\tilde{U}_{t+1}$ at period $t + 1$, given the information $I_t$ in period $t$. The separation of intertemporal substitution and risk aversion makes the model more realistic. The resulting estimating equation is the weighted sum of two factors: a relation between consumption growth and asset return (intertemporal CAPM) and a relation between the risk of a particular asset and the return of the market portfolio (static CAPM). They conclude that the expected utility hypothesis is rejected, but the performance of the nonexpected utility model is sensitive to the choice of the consumption measure (nondurable goods, durable goods, services, etc.). Average elasticity of substitution is less than one, and average relative risk aversion is close to one.

Using the implicit utility function as described in equation (5), Diewert (1993, 1995) outlines simple models for measuring the real outputs of the insurance and gambling sectors. Here, we describe the model of a two-state lottery game. This simple model will be extended in the next section into a six-state lottery. The two-state lottery is $L = (p_1, p_2)$, with $p_2 = 1 - p_1$. The corresponding outcomes are

$$x_1 = y - w, \qquad x_2 = y + Rw, \tag{7}$$

where $y$ is the consumer's income, $w$ is the wager, and $R$ is the payout ratio. Assuming homothetic preferences, the implicit utility function $\phi_u$ can be written as $\gamma$ in equation (6):

$$\phi_u(z) = \gamma\left(\frac{z}{u}\right).$$

In order to provide a kink in the indifference curve, we employ the following functional form for $\gamma$:

$$\gamma(z) = \begin{cases} \alpha + (1 - \alpha)z^{\beta}, & z \geq 1 \\ 1 - \alpha + \alpha z^{\beta}, & z < 1, \end{cases} \tag{8}$$

where $0 < \alpha < 1/2$, $\beta < 1$, $\beta \neq 0$. The implicit expected utility in equation (5) for this game is

$$p_1\phi_u(x_1) + p_2\phi_u(x_2) - \phi_u(u) = 0. \tag{9}$$

Substituting $\gamma$ in equation (8) into equation (9) as $\phi_u$, we have for $x_1 < x_2$,

$$u = [\delta x_1^{\beta} + (1 - \delta)x_2^{\beta}]^{1/\beta}, \tag{10}$$

where $\delta \equiv p_1\alpha/[p_1 + (1 - p_1)(1 - \alpha)]$. Putting equation (7) into equation (10), the consumer's utility maximization problem is

$$\max_w [\delta(y - w)^{\beta} + (1 - \delta)(y + Rw)^{\beta}]^{1/\beta},$$

where $0 \leq w \leq y$. The first-order condition is

$$\frac{y + Rw^*}{y - w^*} = \left[\frac{1 - \delta}{\delta}R\right]^{1/(1-\beta)}$$

$$= \left[\frac{(1 - p_1)(1 - \alpha)R}{p_1\alpha}\right]^{1/(1-\beta)}$$

$$\equiv b.$$

Solving for the optimal $w^*$, we have

$$w^* = \frac{y(b - 1)}{b + R}.$$

Because $y$, $R$, and $w^*$ are observable, we can calculate $b$ in each period. Then, $\alpha$ and $\beta$ can be estimated with a regression model. Having estimated $\alpha$ and $\beta$, we can calculate the consumer's utility level without gambling:

$$u^0 = [\delta y^\beta + (1 - \delta)y^\beta]^{1/\beta} = y.$$

Similarly, the utility level with gambling is

$$u^* = [\delta(y - w)^\beta + (1 - \delta)(y + Rw)^\beta]^{1/\beta}.$$

The real output of the gambling service is then

$$Q = u^* - u^0.$$

## 10.3 Modeling the Gambling Sector

### 10.3.1 Gambling Sectors in Canada

The gambling industry in Canada has been growing in size and in revenue over the last decade. For example, revenue increased from \$2.7 billion in 1992 to \$7.4 billion in 1998, while employment grew from 11,900 in 1992 to 39,200 in 1999. In 1992, government lotteries were the major component in all games of chances, representing 90 percent of all gambling returns. They peaked at \$2.8 billion and have been declining at a moderate rate. On the other hand, video lottery terminals (VLTs) and casinos have grown rapidly. In 1998, revenue from the latter has overtaken government lotteries as the dominant player (Marshall 2000).

Government lotteries are administered by five regional crown corporations: namely, Atlantic Lottery Corporation, Loto-Québec, Ontario Lottery and Gaming Corporation, Western Canada Lottery Corporation, and British Columbia Lottery Corporation. Most of these corporations offer their own local lottery games. The national games, Lotto 6/49, Celebration (a special event lottery), and Super 7, however, are shared by all the corporations through the coordination of the Canadian Interprovincial Lottery Corporation, which was established in 1976 to operate joint lottery games

**Table 10.1** **Prizes of Canadian Lotto 6/49**

| Prize | Rule | Probability of winning, $\pi_i$ | Share of the pool fund |
|---|---|---|---|
| Jackpot | 6 numbers | 0.0000000715 | 50% |
| Second | 5 numbers + bonus | 0.000000429 | 15% |
| Third | 5 numbers | 0.00001802 | 12% |
| Fourth | 4 numbers | 0.0009686 | 23% |
| Fifth | 3 numbers | 0.01765 | $10 |

across Canada. Lotto 6/49 games are held twice a week on Wednesday and Saturday. Forty-five percent of the sales revenue goes to the prize fund. The fifth prize, which requires matching three numbers out of the six drawn, has a fixed prize of ten dollars. The prize fund, after subtracting the payout for all the fifth prizes, becomes the pool fund. This pool fund is divided among the other prizes by fixed shares, as shown in table 10.1. The prize money is shared equally among the winners of a particular prize category. If there is no winner for the jackpot, the prize money will be accumulated (rollover) to the prize fund of the next draw. About 13.3 percent of the sales revenue is used as the administration and retailing costs. This portion is used by Statistics Canada as the output of the Lotto 6/49 game in the GDP. As a consequence, the lottery corporation retains 41.7 percent (55 percent minus 13.3 percent) of the revenue as profit. This profit margin can be regarded as a tax on the output of the lottery sector. Thus from the final demand perspective, the value of lottery output should be listed as 55 percent of the sales volume, which is about four times the value from the industry accounts perspective (13.3 percent).

### 10.3.2 The Output of Government Lotteries

In this section, we extend Diewert's (1995) simple model to the measurement problem of a common lottery sector. A typical game of lottery—for example, Lotto 6/49 in Canada—involves choosing six numbers out of forty-nine. Five prizes are awarded, according to the rules listed in table 10.1.[14]

For example, the probability of winning the jackpot for one single ticket is $1/C^6_{49} = 1/13{,}983{,}816 = 0.0000000715$—a one in 14 million chance. The probability of the second prize is six times the probability of the jackpot; that is, $6/13{,}983{,}816 = 0.000000429$, and so on.[15] The following notation is used in the model: $w$ = wager; $p_i$ = probability of winning the $i$th prize, $i = 1, \ldots, 5$; $p_6$ = probability of not winning any prize; $x_i$ = state-contingent consumption, $i = 1, \ldots, 6$; $y$ = real disposable income; and $R_i$ = payout for the $i$th prize, $i = 1, \ldots, 6$.

Buying more than one ticket increases the chance of winning. Therefore,

14. See Ziemba (1986).
15. For details of computing all the probabilities, see Hoppe (1996).

(11) $$p_i = w\pi_i, \qquad i = 1, \ldots, 5,$$

where $\pi_i$ is the probability of winning the $i$th prize for one single ticket. Also, we have

(12) $$p_6 = 1 - \sum_{i=1}^{5} p_i = 1 - w\sum_{i=1}^{5}\pi_i$$

and

(13) $$x_i = y + R_i - w, \qquad i = 1, \ldots, 6.$$

We assume a representative consumer with homothetic preferences, so his or her state-contingent preference function $u = F(x_1, \ldots, x_6, p_1, \ldots, p_6)$ can be defined implicitly using equation (6). Using the kinked functional form in equation (8), equation (6) becomes

$$\sum_{i=1}^{5} p_i\left[\alpha + (1-\alpha)\left(\frac{x_i}{u}\right)^{\beta}\right] + p_6\left[1 - \alpha + \alpha\left(\frac{x_6}{u}\right)^{\beta}\right] - 1 = 0.$$

Solving for $u$ and using equations (11), (12), and (13), we have

(14) $$u(w) = \left[\frac{(1-\alpha)w\sum_{i=1}^{5}\pi_i(y + R_i - w)^{\beta} + \alpha(1 - w\sum_{i=1}^{5}\pi_i)(y - w)^{\beta}}{\alpha + (1-2\alpha)w\sum_{i=1}^{5}\pi_i}\right]^{1/\beta}.$$

The consumer's utility maximization problem is to maximize $u(w)$, subject to the constraint $0 \leq w \leq y$. For notational convenience, we define the following variables as

(15)
$$d = y - w,$$
$$p = \sum_{i=1}^{5}\pi_i,$$
$$q = \sum_{i=1}^{5}\pi_i(y + R_i - w)^{\beta-1}, \text{ and}$$
$$r = \sum_{i=1}^{5}\pi_i(y + R_i - w)^{\beta}.$$

The first-order condition for the utility maximization problem (assuming that a boundary solution does not occur) can be written as

$$\alpha(1-\alpha)r - \beta q(1-\alpha)[\alpha + (1-2\alpha)wp]w - \alpha\beta(1-wp)[\alpha + (1-2\alpha)wp]d^{\beta-1} - \alpha(1-\alpha)pd^{\beta} = 0.$$

Rearranging terms, we get a quadratic equation in $w$:

$$\{\beta p[\alpha(1-2\alpha)pd^{\beta-1} - (1-\alpha)(1-2\alpha)^2 q]\}w^2 + \{\alpha\beta[\alpha pd^{\beta-1} - (1-\alpha)q - (1-2\alpha)pd^{\beta-1}]\}w + \alpha[(1-\alpha)r - \alpha\beta d^{\beta-1} - (1-\alpha)pd^{\beta}] = 0.$$

Solving for this quadratic equation gives us the following equation involving the optimal level of the wager $w$:

$$(16) \qquad w^* = [-\alpha\beta[\alpha p d^{\beta-1} - (1-\alpha)q - (1-2\alpha)pd^{\beta-1}] \pm (\{\alpha\beta[\alpha p d^{\beta-1} - (1-\alpha)q - (1-2\alpha)pd^{\beta-1}]\}^2 - 4\alpha[(1-\alpha)r - \alpha\beta d^{\beta-1} - (1-\alpha)pd^{\beta}] \{\beta p[\alpha(1-2\alpha)pd^{\beta-1} - (1-\alpha)(1-2\alpha)q]\})^{1/2}] \div 2\{\beta p[\alpha(1-2\alpha)pd^{\beta-1} - (1-\alpha)(1-2\alpha)q]\}.$$

Equation (16) is the estimation equation for the parameters $\alpha$ and $\beta$, given the data for the other variables. Notice that $w$ appears in the right-hand side of equation (16) through the variables $d$, $q$, and $r$, which were defined in equation (15). But the effects of $w$ on $d$, $q$, and $r$ are negligible, because the disposable income $y$ and the sum of $y$ and the payout prizes $R_i$ are so much larger than $w$, and hence we can simply set $w$ equal to zero in those definitions. Another functional form, the kinked quadratic-generating function,

$$\gamma(z) = \begin{cases} z + \alpha(z-1) + \beta(z-1)^2, & z \geq 1 \\ z, & z < 1, \end{cases}$$

was attempted in addition to equation (8), but the analysis yielded no explicit solution for $w$.

The output of services provided by Lotto 6/49 is equal to the difference between utility level with the lotteries and utility without the lottery using equation (14); that is,

$$(17) \qquad Q^t = u(w^t) - u(0),$$

where $w^t$ is the observed wager in period $t$. An implicit price level can also be obtained as

$$(18) \qquad P^t = \frac{(1-\rho)w^t}{Q^t},$$

where $\rho$ is the proportion of the prize fund from the total revenue. In the case of Lotto 6/49, $\rho = 0.45$. The approach here follows the final demand perspective discussed in section 10.3.1. The resulting price index is an implicit cost-of-living index and can be included as a subindex in the CPI.

## 10.4 Estimating the Output of Government Lotteries

### 10.4.1 Data

Data on the winning numbers, payout prizes, and sales volume provided by Lottery Canada are available from November 11, 1997, to November 3, 2001, for Lotto 6/49, a total of 419 draws. Monthly data on the CPI and annual data on the number of households, personal disposable income, and participation rates in government lotteries are available from Statistics Canada. The sales volume of each draw is divided by the number of participating households, which gives the average wager per participating household, $w_t$.

The average personal disposable income per household, adjusted by the CPI, is used as a proxy for $y_t$.

Figure 10.2 depicts the number of ticket sales for the sample period. We see that there is a downward trend in sales, reflecting the switch from government lotteries to other games, such as VLTs and casinos. Table 10.2 summarizes the average sales, number of winners, and the payout prizes of the observed draws. The biggest jackpot during the sample period was $15 million, won by a single ticket on September 30, 2000. In table 10.2, we also calculate the expected average number of winners using the probabilities in table 10.1. We see that in each prize, the observed average number of winners is slightly smaller than the expected number. One possible explanation of the difference is that some players pay more than one dollar for the same numbers, which often happens in lottery pools. Of the 419 draws, 151 end up with a rollover, which is 36 percent. Given that the expected number of jackpot winners is 1.2 on average, this rollover percentage seems high. In fact, this agrees with previous observations in Canada (Ziemba 1986; Stern and Cover 1989), the United States (Chernoff 1981), and the United Kingdom

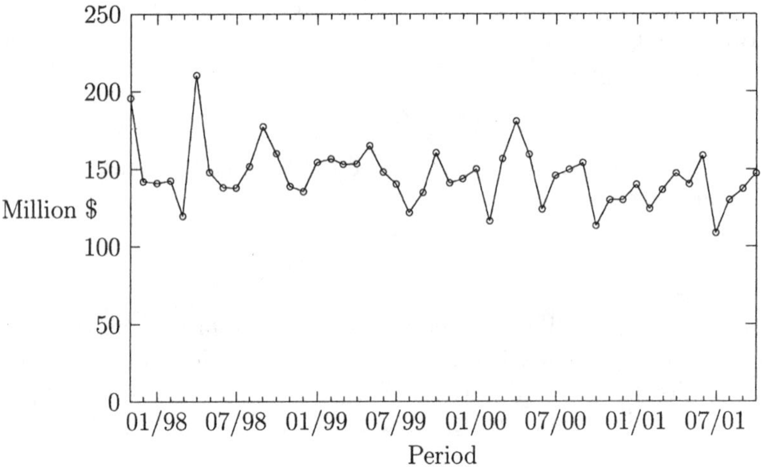


**Fig. 10.2 Monthly sales of Lotto 6/49: November 1997 to November 2001**

**Table 10.2 Descriptive statistics of Canadian Lotto 6/49: November 11, 1997, to March 11, 2001**

| | Sales | Jackpot | Second | Third | Fourth | Fifth |
|---|---|---|---|---|---|---|
| Average number of winners | 16,717,385 | 1.12 | 7.13 | 299 | 16,036 | 292,604 |
| Expected number of winners | | 1.20 | 7.17 | 308 | 16,199 | 293,287 |
| Prize ($) | | 3,249,108 | 133,903 | 1,976 | 68 | 10 |

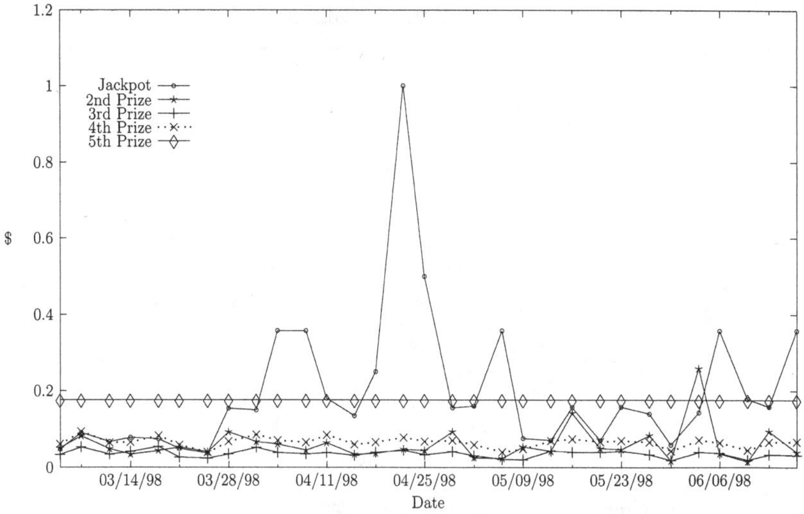


**Fig. 10.3 Expected values of the various prizes**

(Walker 1998; Simon 1999) that people have "conscious selection" (Cook and Clotfelter 1993); that is, some numbers on average are more popular than the others.[16] For example, the six most popular numbers of Lotto 6/49 in Canada were 3, 5, 6, 9, 12, and 13 in 1986. One possible reason is that a lot of people use their birthdays as their choices. Therefore, numbers starting from thirty-two onward are among the most unpopular numbers.

A lot of attention is concentrated on the jackpot prizes, particularly when there are rollovers and the pool fund becomes very big. Figure 10.3, however, shows that the average expected value is highest for the smallest prize. In the figure, EV1 to EV5 are the products of the payout prized and their respective probability of winning from March 4 to June 17, 1998. Because the payout is fixed at ten dollars, EV5 is constant. In only one draw is EV2 higher than EV5, and EV1 is higher than EV5 in several occasions. The fifth prize has a high expected value because of the relatively high probability of winning. The pleasure and thrill from buying a lottery ticket, nevertheless, comes from buying the big jackpot ticket, which has an extremely low probability of winning. This is why a nonlinear expected utility theory is needed to capture the risk-loving side of consumers.

### 10.4.2 Estimation and Results

The parameters $\alpha$ and $\beta$ in equation (16) are estimated by a nonlinear regression equation using the maximum likelihood method. Theoretically,

16. For a general discussion, see also Haigh (1997).

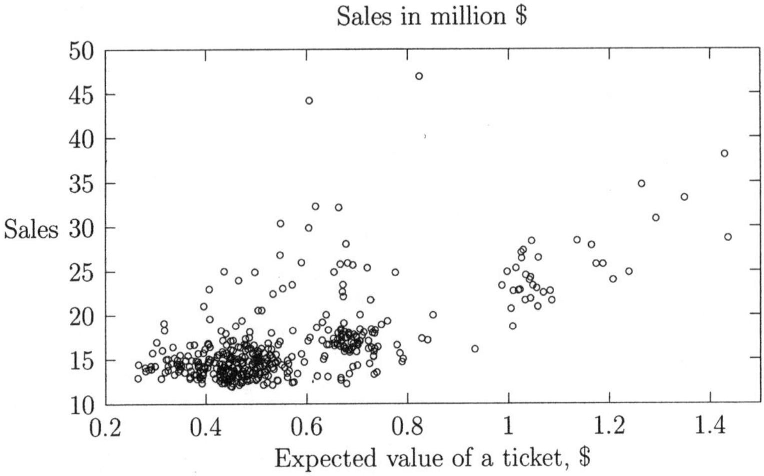


**Fig. 10.4 Sales and expected values of Lotto 6/49**

demand depends on the expected values of the payout prizes $R_1, \ldots, R_4$, which in turn depend on the sales volume. The actual payout prizes, however, are used in the estimation. Following Walker (1998, 371), we invoke the rational expectations assumption, which implies that consumers do not make systematic mistakes in forecasting the sales. Figure 10.4 is a scatter plot of the sales volume against the ex post expected value of a ticket. It clearly shows the positive relation between the two. The estimated values of $\alpha$ and $\beta$ are 0.10458 and –31.986, with standard errors equal to 0.003165 and 5.9527, respectively, which implies *t*-ratios of 33 and –5.4. The estimated values satisfy the constraints $0 < \alpha < 1/2$, $\beta < 1$, $\beta \neq 0$ in equation (8). These estimated values are then used to calculate the money-metric utility $u(w_t)$ and the output level $Q^t$ of the lottery using equations (14) and (17), respectively, for each draw. Outputs are aggregated into monthly results before the implicit price $P^t$ is calculated using equation (18). A fixed-base price index is then calculated using the price level of November 1997 as the base.

Figures 10.5 and 10.6 show the monthly price index and output of the Lotto 6/49 using this procedure. In figure 10.6, the factor cost (13.3 percent of sales revenue) is also included for comparison. Notice that the estimated output using the economic approach is much higher than the official GDP at factor cost, but the former has a steeper downward trend. The average monthly output using the economic approach is \$57.7 million, compared to the official total cost approach of \$19.4 million. We also observe in figure 10.6 that the utility-based output measure is more volatile than the factor cost measure. This is due to the rollover of the prize money when there is no jackpot winner for a particular draw. These rollovers create occasional

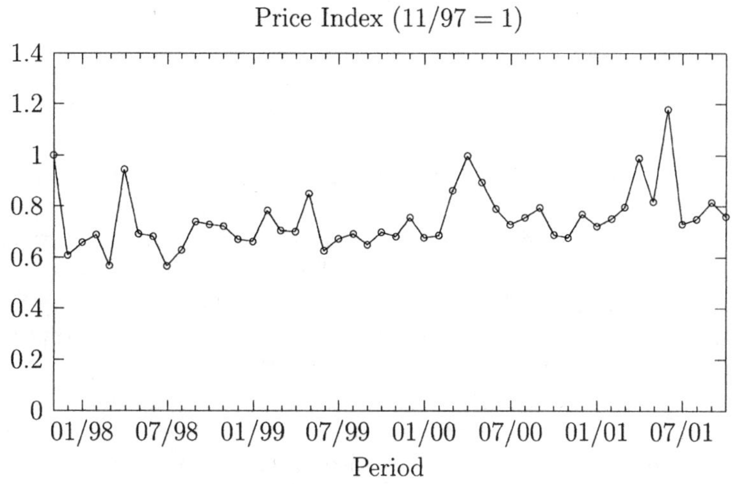


**Fig. 10.5 Price index of Lotto 6/49**

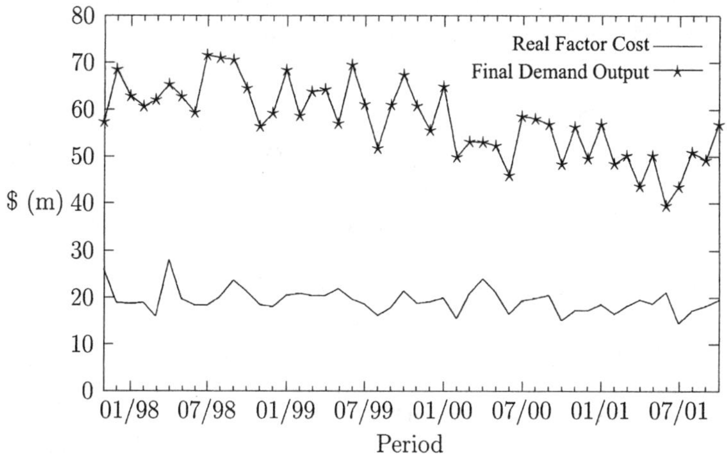


**Fig. 10.6 Output of Lotto 6/49**

excitement and effectively reduce the unfairness for the next draw. The effects are reflected in the utility measure of the game.[17]

17. This rollover effect creates substantial volatility in both the price and quantity of the final demand consumption of lottery output, and hence, statistical agencies may be reluctant to adopt this approach to measuring the price of lottery services in their CPIs. This problem could be solved by smoothing the raw data. This type of smoothing would automatically occur if statistical agencies adopted a rolling-year methodology for their CPIs; see Diewert (1998) for an explanation of this methodology.

We also estimate the elasticity of demand for the lottery using a simple log-linear model:

$$\log Q = \log P + \log y + T,$$

where $T$ is a trend variable, which is included to capture change in taste over time. The resulting price elasticity of demand is –0.672, with a standard error of 0.017. This result is comparable to the values of –0.66 estimated by Forrest, Gulley, and Simmons (2000), who use a two-stage ordinary least squares estimation, with the difference between the ticket price and the expected value as the effective price of lottery. Using a similar approach, Gulley and Scott (1993) estimated the price elasticities of four state-operated lottos in the United States, with results ranging from –0.40 to –2.5. Farrell and Walker (1999) used cross-sectional data to study the demand for lotteries in the United Kingdom using the Heckman selection model. Their estimated price elasticity was –0.763. Also, Beenstock and Haitovsky (2001) studied the demand for lotto in Israel using time-series data, with the estimated long-run price elasticity equal to –0.65. It is surprising that these results, although differing in methods, nature of data, and countries, show very close estimates of price elasticities of demand.

## 10.5 Conclusion

The classical expected utility hypothesis fails to capture a consumer's risk-averse behavior in facing big losses with small probabilities and the risk-loving behavior involving large gains with small probabilities. New nonexpected utility theories have been developed to overcome that difficulty. In this chapter, we have applied implicit expected utility theory to the problem of measuring outputs of lotteries. The results show that output levels of Lotto 6/49 in Canada is almost three times higher than the official statistics, which uses the total cost of providing the service approach as the output measurement principle. This kind of direct economic approach is recommended by the *System of National Accounts, 1993* (Inter-Secretariat Working Group on National Accounts 1993) for government and nonprofit organization output measurement. The approach taken here is the ex ante welfare measure of the consumers facing risk and uncertainty. The method developed can potentially be applied to other games of chance.[18] The estimated price elasticity of demand for lottery in Canada is close to that of the United Kingdom and Israel in previous studies.

18. See Dubins and Savage (1965) and R. Epstein (1977) for the mathematical analysis of a whole variety of games.

## References


Allais, M. 1953. Le comportement de l'homme rationnel devant le risque: Critique des postulats et axiomes de l'ecole Americaine. *Econometrica* 21 (4): 503–46.

Arrow, K. J. 1964. The role of securities in the optimal allocation of risk-bearing. *Review of Economic Studies* 31 (2): 91–96.

Beenstock, M., and Y. Haitovsky. 2001. Lottomania and other anomalies in the market for lotto. *Journal of Economic Psychology* 22 (6): 721–44.

Blackorby, C., R. Davidson, and D. Donaldson. 1977. A homiletic exposition of the expected utility hypothesis. *Economica* 44 (176): 351–8.

Chernoff, H. 1981. How to beat the Massachusetts numbers game. *Mathematical Intelligencer* 3 (4): 166–72.

Chew, S. H. 1983. A generalization of the quasilinear mean with applications to the measurement of income inequality and decision theory resolving the Allais paradox. *Econometrica* 51 (4): 1065–92.

Chew, S. H., and L. G. Epstein. 1989a. A unifying approach to axiomatic nonexpected utility theories. *Journal of Economic Theory* 49 (2): 207–40.

———. 1989b. The structure of preferences and attitudes towards the timing of the resolution of uncertainty. *International Economic Review* 30 (1): 103–17.

———. 1990. Nonexpected utility preferences in a temporal framework with an application to consumption-savings behaviour. *Journal of Economic Theory* 50 (1): 54–81.

Cook, P. J., and C. T. Clotfelter. 1993. The peculiar scale economies of lotto. *American Economic Review* 83 (3): 634–43.

Cox, J. C., and V. Sadiraj. 2001. Risk aversion and expected utility theory: Coherence for small- and large-stakes gambles. University of Arizona, Department of Economics. Working Paper no. 01-03, July.

Debreu, G. 1959. *Theory of value.* New Haven, CT: Yale University Press.

Dekel, E. 1986. An axiomatic characterization of preferences under uncertainty: Weakening the independence axiom. *Journal of Economic Theory* 40 (2): 304–18.

Diecidue, E., and P. P. Wakker. 2001. On the intuition of rank-dependent utility. *Journal of Risk and Uncertainty* 23 (3): 281–98.

Diewert, W. E. 1993. Symmetric means and choice under uncertainty. In *Essays in index number theory,* vol. 1, ed. W. E. Diewert and A. O. Nakamura, 335–433. Amsterdam: North-Holland.

———. 1995. Functional form problems in modeling insurance and gambling. *Geneva Papers on Risk and Insurance Theory* 20 (1): 135–50.

———. 1998. High inflation, seasonal commodities, and annual index numbers. *Macroeconomic Dynamics* 2 (4): 456–71.

Dubins, L. E., and L. J. Savage. 1965. *How to gamble if you must.* New York: McGraw-Hill.

Epstein, L. G. 1992. Behavior under risk: Recent developments in theory and applications. In *Advances in economic theory,* vol. 2, ed. J.-J. Laffont, 1–63. Cambridge: Cambridge University Press.

Epstein, L. G., and S. E. Zin. 1989. Substitution, risk aversion, and the temporal behavior of consumption and asset returns: A theoretical framework. *Econometrica* 57 (4): 937–69.

———. 1990. "First-order" risk aversion and the equity premium puzzle. *Journal of Monetary Economics* 26 (3): 387–407.

———. 1991. Substitution, risk aversion, and the temporal behavior of consumption and asset returns: An empirical analysis. *Journal of Political Economy* 99 (2): 263–86.

Epstein, R. A. 1977. *The theory of gambling and statistical logic.* New York: Academic Press.
Farrell, L., and I. Walker. 1999. The welfare effects of lotto: Evidence from the UK. *Journal of Public Economics* 72 (1): 99–120.
Forrest, D., O. D. Gulley, and R. Simmons. 2000. Elasticity of demand for UK National Lottery tickets. *National Tax Journal,* pt. 1 #53 (4): 853–63.
Friedman, M., and L. J. Savage. 1948. The utility analysis of choices involving risk. *Journal of Political Economy* 56 (4): 279–304.
Gorman, W. M. 1968. The structure of utility functions. *Review of Economic Studies* 35 (4): 367–90.
Gul, F. 1991. A theory of disappointment aversion. *Econometrica* 59 (3): 667–86.
Gulley, O. D., and F. A. Scott, Jr. 1993. The demand for wagering on state-operated lotto games. *National Tax Journal* 45 (1): 13–22.
Haigh, J. 1997. The statistics of the National Lottery. *Journal of the Royal Statistical Society* A 160 (2): 187–206.
Hall, R. E. 1978. Stochastic implications of the life cycle-permanent income hypothesis: Theory and evidence. *Journal of Political Economy* 86 (6): 971–87.
Hoppe, F. M. 1996. Mathematical appendix to the *Maclean's Magazine* article by John Schofield; November 4, 1996. McMaster University, Department of Mathematics. Available at http://icarus.mcmaster.ca/fred/Lotto/.
Hulten, C. R. 2001. Total factor productivity: A short biography. In *New developments in productivity analysis,* ed. C. R. Hulten, E. R. Dean, and M. J. Harper, 1–47. Chicago: University of Chicago Press.
Inter-Secretariat Working Group on National Accounts. 1993. *System of National Accounts, 1993.* Paris: Organization for Economic Cooperation and Development.
Kahneman, D., and A. Tversky. 1979. Prospect theory: An analysis of decisions under risk. *Econometrica* 47 (2): 263–91.
Luce, R. D., and H. Raiffa. 1957. *Games and decisions: introduction and critical survey.* New York: John Wiley and Sons. Repr., Mineola, NY: Dover Publications, 1989.
Machina, M. J. 1982. "Expected utility" analysis without the independence axiom. *Econometrica* 50 (2): 277–323.
———. 1997. Choice under uncertainty: Problems solved and unsolved. In *The environment and emerging development issues,* vol. 1, ed. P. Dasgupta and K.-G. Mäler, 201–55. Oxford: Clarendon Press.
———. 2001. Payoff kinks in preferences over lotteries. *Journal of Risk and Uncertainty* 23 (3): 207–60.
Marshall, K. 1998. The gambling industry: Raising the stakes. *Services Indicators* 5 (4): 29–38.
———. 2000. Update on gambling. *Perspectives on Labour and Income* 12 (1): 29–35.
Pratt, J. W., H. Raiffa, and R. Schlaifer. 1995. *Introduction to statistical decision theory.* Cambridge, MA: MIT Press.
Quiggin, J. 1993. *Generalized expected utility theory: The rank-dependent model.* Norwell, MA: Kluwer Academic.
Rabin, M. 2000. Risk aversion and expected-utility theory: A calibration theorem. *Econometrica* 68 (5): 1281–92.
Rabin, M., and R. H. Thaler. 2001. Risk aversion. *Journal of Economic Perspectives* 15 (1): 219–32.
Samuelson, P. A. 1952. Probability, utility, and the independence axiom. *Econometrica* 20 (4): 670–8.

Segal, U., and A. Spivak. 1990. First order versus second order risk aversion. *Journal of Economic Theory* 51 (1): 111–25.
Simon, J. 1999. An analysis of the distribution of combinations chosen by UK National Lottery players. *Journal of Risk and Uncertainty* 17 (3): 243–76.
Starmer, C. 2000. Developments in non-expected utility theory: The hunt for a descriptive theory of choice under risk. *Journal of Economic Literature* 38 (2): 332–82.
Stern, H., and T. M. Cover. 1989. Maximum entropy and the lottery. *Journal of the American Statistical Association* 84 (408): 980–5.
Von Neumann, J., and O. Morgenstern. 1953. *Theory of games and economic behavior.* Princeton, NJ: Princeton University Press.
Walker, I. 1998. The economic analysis of lotteries. *Economic Policy* 13 (27): 359–401.
Watt, R. 2002. Defending expected utility theory. *Journal of Economic Perspectives* 16 (2): 227–30.
Yaari, M. E. 1987. The dual theory of choice under risk. *Econometrica* 55 (1): 95–115.
Ziemba, W. T. 1986. *Dr Z's 6/49 lotto guidebook.* Vancouver: Dr. Z Investments.

## Comment Alan G. White

### Overview: Methods, Data, and Results

In chapter 10 of this volume, Kam Yu presents an economic approach to measuring the output and prices of a hard-to-measure sector—that of the lottery sector. Yu applies implicit expected utility theory by developing a money metric of utility of playing the Canadian Lotto 6/49 game.

Yu argues that the lottery is becoming an increasingly important component of gross domestic product (GDP) in Canada. He notes that according to the 1997 Survey of Household Spending (SHS), over two-thirds of families in Canada purchased lottery tickets, and average expenditure on lottery tickets was approximately $238. Given that expenditure on gambling is likely underreported in the SHS, the lottery industry may be a more important and significant component of GDP than currently measured, necessitating a more accurate method for measuring its output.

In the theory of consumption under uncertainty, a risk-averse consumer maximizes an expected utility function in which risk averseness is often assumed to be decreasing in wealth. Although this theory has been applied to problems in insurance and investment decisions, it predicts that a risk-averse expected utility maximizer would never purchase a lottery ticket unless the payout is extremely large. This, however, is not consistent with reality, where the purchase of lottery tickets and gambling among consum-

Alan G. White is a vice president at Analysis Group, Inc.

ers is commonplace. Yu notes that "in order to model a small gamble like the Lotto 6/49, we need a preference structure that is more flexible than the EUH [expected utility hypothesis]" (see chapter 10 of this volume).

Yu notes that under the nonexpected utility theory, first-order risk aversion implies that the risk premium of a small gamble is proportional to the standard deviation of the gamble, whereas under standard expected utility theory, the risk premium is proportional to the variance of the gamble. In the case of $N = 2$ (i.e., a world with two possible outcomes), the nonexpected utility theory allows for kinks around the forty-five-degree certainty line. I would like Yu to give a little more intuition to the reader (in section 10.2.2) on what nonexpected utility theory is and to give an explanation of the distinction between the risk premium being proportional to the standard deviation/variance of the gamble, so it is easier to better understand differences between expected and nonexpected utility theories. This might be aided by a clearer description of such things as the independence axiom and recursivity axiom that Yu refers to in the chapter but does not fully explain.

In the nonexpected utility theory, as applied in this chapter, the output of the lottery sector is defined as the difference in utility levels between a situation involving gambling and one not involving gambling, once the optimal wager has been solved for from the first-order conditions for the utility maximization problem. Yu extends the two-outcome model developed by Diewert (1993) to model a six-outcome result for the Lotto 6/49.

Yu uses data on winning numbers, payouts, and sales volume provided by Lottery Canada for November 1997 through November 2001, covering a total of 419 draws. Yu combines this with Statistics Canada data on the Consumer Price Index (CPI) and annual data on the number of households, personal disposable income, and participation rates in government lotteries. He uses these data to calculate the average wager per household and the average personal disposable income per household.

Yu notes that sales of Lotto 6/49 have declined over the period he examined, perhaps because of a shift to Video Lottery Terminals (VLTs) and casinos. Yu does not account for these in his chapter, and it would be interesting for Yu to speculate on the potential methods of measuring the output of these two other components and on how (if at all) Statistics Canada is currently measuring them. He notes that approximately 13.3 percent of the sales revenue for Lotto 6/49 is used for administrative and retailing costs, and it is this number that is used by Statistics Canada as the output of this lottery.

The first-order condition for the optimal wager is estimated using maximum likelihood methods. The final results show that the average monthly output using the economic approach is \$57.7 million, compared to the official total factor cost approach, which is \$19.4 million.

## Future Research and Specific Comments

1. Yu compares the lottery output under both the economic approach and the approach used by Statistics Canada. It is clear that the statistical agency method understates the true output of the lottery sector, as measured by the nonexpected utility approach. What is somewhat surprising is the differences in trends between the two different methods. Specifically, the economic approach yields a sharper downward trend than that of the method used by Statistics Canada. I would like to see some speculation or explanation for the possible divergence between the two trends. Was there a change in administrative costs of the lottery during this period that could have caused this?

2. Given that Statistics Canada uses the administrative costs for its estimate of output, is it appropriate to use some variation of sales to measure output? It might not be practical for Statistics Canada to estimate a function of the type proposed in the chapter, and I would like to see a discussion of alternative measures that might be more feasible and of how they might compare with the results presented in this chapter.

3. I would like to see a very brief discussion of how lotteries, gambling, and so forth are handled by other statistical agencies (if at all). For example, how does the approach adopted by Statistics Canada compare with that of the Bureau of Labor Statistics or Statistics Netherlands?

4. Yu has not addressed VLTs or casinos in this chapter—at least as they relate to the measurement of output. How does Statistics Canada handle these, and what does Yu think the likely implications are for measuring these particular items?

5. Although Yu computes an implicit price index for the Lotto 6/49, I would like to see some intuition for how to interpret it. Should it be properly viewed as a cost-of-living subindex for those families who play the Lottery 6/49, or is there some other interpretation? How does one interpret the price elasticity of demand? Does the price index or elasticity have any implications for the pricing of lottery tickets?

## Reference

Diewert, W. E. 1993. Symmetric means and choice under uncertainty. In *Essays in index number theory,* vol. 1, ed. W. E. Diewert and A. O. Nakamura, 355–433. Amsterdam: North-Holland.

11

# Consumption of Own Production and Cost-of-Living Indexes

T. Peter Hill

## 11.1 Introduction

The Cost-of-Living index, or COLI, defined as the ratio of the minimum expenditures needed to maintain a constant level of utility under two different price regimes, is underpinned by the economic theory of consumer behavior in which rational utility-maximizing individuals react to changes in relative prices by adjusting the relative quantities they consume.[1] A COLI is widely regarded as the appropriate target index for consumer price index (CPI). However, in general, not all the prices and quantities needed to calculate a COLI are available, for two reasons.

First, the quantities that enter into a COLI are hypothetical for at least one of the periods. They are the quantities that *would be* consumed *if* the prices were different from those actually prevailing in the period. This problem has always been recognized. It may be dealt with by calculating a superlative index as defined by Diewert (1976).[2] A superlative index is an index calculated from the actual prices and quantities in both periods that may be expected to provide a satisfactory approximation to a COLI under most conditions, provided the prices and quantities used are appropriate.

The second problem is less tractable and not widely appreciated. Consumption is an activity in which households use goods and services to satisfy

T. Peter Hill was head of the Economic Statistics and National Accounts division at the Organization for Economic Cooperation and Development (OECD), and before that he was professor of economics at the University of East Anglia, Norwich.

1. Originally proposed by Konüs (1924), the properties of the Cost-of-Living Index are explained in detail in chapter 17 of the international *Consumer Price Index Manual* (International Labor Office et al. 2004) entitled "The Economic Approach to Index Number Theory," written by E. Diewert.

2. See chapter 17 of the *CPI Manual* (International Labor Office et al. 2004).

their own personal needs and wants. The quantities of goods and services that enter into personal utility functions are those that are actually consumed by households. They are not necessarily the same goods and services that households purchase in retail outlets and that are classified as consumers' expenditure in national accounts and household expenditure surveys. They also are not necessarily the goods and services for which prices are collected for CPI purposes.

Recent research has shown that even in developed countries, the majority of the goods and services purchased by households for purposes of consumption are used to provide inputs into various kinds of household production processes. They are used to produce other goods or services from which households actually derive utility. Some of these production processes may be quite simple, but others are complex, involving not merely the consumption of purchased goods or services as intermediate inputs but also the inputs of own (and possibly hired) labor services and inputs of capital services provided by household-fixed assets in the form of dwellings and household durable equipment. For example, expenditure on fuels may be a major item of consumers' expenditures, but fuels are obviously not consumed directly and instead are used as intermediate inputs into household production processes.

Utility is derived from consuming the outputs from household production. The difficulty for CPIs is that there are no prices to be observed for the outputs because they are not traded in market transactions. The problem has long been recognized in one or two special cases, such as the consumption of housing services produced by owner occupiers or the consumption of own agricultural produce. However, recent research indicates that consumption of own production is much more extensive than seems to be generally realized. Moreover, as in other fields of production, the technologies used in many kinds of household production have improved dramatically over the longer term.[3]

In practice, statistical offices seem to tacitly ignore the problem and treat the inputs purchased by households as if they were consumption goods and services. However, given advancing technology, the prices of the outputs from household production from which utility is derived can be expected to rise less fast than those of the inputs. There is a prima facie case for arguing that CPIs are likely to be subject to an upward bias, at least if a COLI is being targeted.

If the target is a cost-of-goods index, or COGI, rather than a COLI, the situation is rather different. The use of actual prices, even input prices, might be justified by *defining* the CPI as an index that measures changes in the market prices of goods and services purchased by households *for purposes of*

3. Nordhaus (1997) has provided a dramatic illustration of the effects of technological advance in the production of light by households.

*consumption*. In this case, it would not matter whether the goods and services are consumed directly without further processing or are used as inputs into household production of goods and services for own consumption. Such a definition is suggested in paragraphs 3.77 and 3.78 of the *2004 CPI Manual* (International Labor Organization et al. 2004). In this case, it has to be made clear to users that many, indeed most, of the goods and services included in the index are not actually consumed directly.

There is a parallel with public consumption. In principle, a price index for public consumption should refer to the prices of the consumption goods and services produced, or purchased, by government and provided to individual households or collectively to the community. As the goods and services in question are typically not sold but are provided free, or at a nominal charge, to households, there are usually no prices to be observed or collected. As a result, it is common for the price index for the output from government production to be estimated from changes in the market prices of the inputs, including labor inputs.

However, calculating the price index for public consumption on the basis of the prices of the inputs into its production is generally not considered to be acceptable. Again, assuming that there are advances in technology, it is likely that the prices of the outputs from government production rise less rapidly than the prices of the inputs. In this case, a price index based on the inputs is likely not only to overestimate the rate of inflation for government output but also to lead to an underestimation of the corresponding rate of real growth. These are matters of serious concern to government. They have lead governments in a number of countries to promote research into the development of improved methods of estimating inflation and growth for government production and consumption.[4]

However, there seems to be not so much concern about the fact that the same problem occurs for CPIs. The purpose of this chapter is to draw attention to the nature and the scale of the problem. This has been made possible by the fact that for quite different reasons, a large amount of research into household production has been undertaken in recent years in a number of countries. Household production and consumption is no longer a black box.

## 11.2 Consumption and Consumption Expenditures

Consumption is a basic economic concept that is often not even defined, because its meaning is taken to be self-evident. However, it can mean different things in different contexts. In the present context, it is necessary to underline the fundamental distinction between consumption and consumption expenditures, even though the two terms are often casually used interchangeably.

4. For example, see Atkinson (2005) and Diewert (2008).

Consumption and production are opposite kinds of economic activities. Consumption, whether final or intermediate, is an activity in which goods and services are used up, whereas production is an activity in which goods and services are created.

Household final consumption is a particular type of economic activity in which members of households use goods or services to satisfy their personal needs, wants, or desires. By definition, a final consumption good or service provides utility to the person or household that consumes it. A final consumption good or service cannot be identified by its physical characteristics alone, however, as some goods or services may be used either for final consumption or as intermediate inputs into production.

Nondurable goods and services are single use, in the sense that they can be used once only. On the other hand, household durables are goods that may be used continuously or repeatedly over long periods of time to meet the needs and wants of households.[5] The consumption of durables therefore takes place gradually over time. It has become customary to describe the repeated use by saying that durables provide a flow of services.[6] Consumer durables are used directly for consumption, but durables such as boilers or cookers that provide a flow of capital services into household production in principle should be classified as fixed assets. In practice, only dwellings are classified as fixed assets in CPIs and national accounts. Dwellings provide flows of capital services into the production of housing services for household final consumption.

Household consumption expenditures may be defined as expenditures incurred by households to *acquire* goods and services that they intend to use for purposes of final consumption. They include expenditures on durables (but not, of course, purchases of dwellings). Most countries conduct periodic household budget surveys to collect information about household consumption expenditures, which are also used to derive expenditure weights for CPIs.

However, relatively few surveys have been undertaken on household consumption. One reason may be that production in national accounts has traditionally been confined mostly to market production. *By convention*, the production boundary in the international *System of National Accounts*, or SNA (Eurostat et al. 1993), and in the U.S. *National Income and Product Accounts*, or NIPAs, is drawn in such a way that with one important

5. Hicks introduced the terminology single-use goods and durable-use goods to emphasize that fixed assets and consumer durables are *in use*. He pointed out that some single-use goods, such as cans of food and drink, may be highly durable, in the sense that they do not deteriorate over time. He stated that the "common characteristic [of durable-use goods] is that they can go on being used for considerable periods of time" (1942, 27–30).

6. For example, Fisher described capital goods as providing a flow of services over time. He argued, "The services of an instrument of wealth are the desirable changes effected (or undesirable changes prevented) by means of that instrument. For instance, the services of a loom consist of changing yarn into cloth, . . ." (Fisher 1922, 19).

exception, the production of services within households is excluded.[7] The exception is the production of housing services by owner occupiers, which have always been included within the production boundary. Placing certain kinds of production outside the production boundary does not mean that the activities are regarded as nonproductive. It reflects the reluctance to include large nonmonetary flows in the accounts for which values have to be imputed.

Therefore, most of the value added created by household production does not enter into GDP. However, there is considerable interest among certain groups in knowing how much GDP would increase if the production boundary were to be extended to include all household production. As it is widely believed that the greater part of the unrecorded production may be carried out by women, the national accounts and GDP have often been criticized as understating the contribution of women to production and failing to reflect their role in the economy.

Many countries, including the United States, have therefore constructed satellite accounts[8] in order to be able to record household production for consumption. A recent study of household production and consumption in the United States by Landefeld and McCulla (2000, 300), using U.S. Bureau of Economic Analysis data, estimates that "the inclusion of household nonmarket services raises GDP by 43 percent in 1946 and by 24 percent in 1997." They also conclude that only "12 percent of the conventional estimate of final consumption expenditures [for 1992 in the national income and product account (NIPAs)], is actually final consumption," and adding household consumption of own production "to this remaining market consumption yields a new estimate of consumption, 91 percent of which is made up of own consumption" (304). The estimates made by Landefeld and McCulla are presented in more detail next.

Studies such as these show conclusively that consumption and consumers' expenditures are quite different flows. Prices can be collected for the goods and services purchased by households in market transactions but not for goods and services produced and consumed within the same household.

## 11.3 A Household Production Account

In order to get a better picture of household production, it is useful to set up an illustrative production account. Consider the production of a final

7. In principle, the production of goods for own use within households is included within the production boundary, but in practice, few countries attempt to measure it systematically in their main accounts.

8. Satellite accounts are intended to supplement or complement the main national accounts. They respect the accounting rules and conventions of the main national accounts as much as possible but deliberately deviate from them in certain respects in order to be able to record activities or flows that are omitted from the main system.

consumption good such as bread, cake, or a cooked meal. The account has the same format as a production account for an enterprise engaged in food manufacturing. If the inputs and outputs are independently priced, the total values of the inputs and outputs will not be identical. In this case, the account is balanced by defining the difference between total values of the outputs and the inputs as the net operating profit or loss. However, if the value of the output is estimated as the sum of the inputs, the two totals must be identical, and there is no need for a balancing item. These valuation issues are considered further in table 11.1.

The first group of intermediate inputs consists of foodstuffs such as flour, eggs, sugar, spices, and so forth. If they have been bought on the market, their purchase would have been recorded under household final consumption expenditures, even though they are meant for intermediate, not final, consumption. As several different kinds of productive activities may be carried on within the same household, even some of the intermediate inputs, such as the foodstuffs or fuel in the example, may themselves have been produced within the household. For example, the electricity could have been produced for own use by the household's own generator, or the oven could have been fired by wood collected by the household.

If the kitchen durables had been bought on the market, the purchases would have been recorded under household consumption expenditures. However, the relevant inputs consist of the capital services they provide. The expenditures would only approximate the value of the services if the durables have very short service lives and high rates of depreciation (or the accounting period is very long). In any case, total measured household purchases would still fall far short of the total value of the bread and cakes produced and consumed, as the labor services provided by members of the household are not purchased and would not be recorded under household consumption expenditures.

**Table 11.1** **Illustrative household production account**

| Inputs | | Outputs |
|---|---|---|
| Intermediate inputs | | Bread, cake, or other output |
| Foodstuffs used as ingredients | | |
| Electricity, gas, or other fuel; water | | |
| Other inputs | | |
| Inputs of labor and capital services | | |
| Labor inputs | | |
| Capital services from fixed assets | | |
| Kitchen equipment | | |
| The dwelling | | |
| Total | = | Total |

## 11.4 Some Estimates of the Magnitude of Consumption of Own Production

Interest in production for own consumption as a household activity stretches back many decades—at least to Margaret Reid's 1934 book, *Economics of Household Production.* On the economic theoretical side, it received a considerable boost from Gary Becker's influential paper "*A Theory of the Allocation of Time*" (1965).[9] It is now becoming feasible to make reasonably reliable estimates of household production by utilizing information derived from time-use surveys in which members of households are required to keep detailed diaries of the various ways in which they spend their time throughout all twenty-four hours of the day. Time-use surveys are being undertaken in an increasing number of countries.[10] While these surveys provide information about the quantities of labor inputs into household production, there still remains the major problem of how to value these inputs. One possibility is to value them at the wage rate payable for the same kind of work on the market (external opportunity costs). Alternatively, the inputs could be valued at the maximum wage rate that the household worker could have earned on the market for other kinds of work (internal opportunity costs). These alternatives are discussed in more detail later.

Estimates reported by Goldschmidt-Clermont and Pagnossin-Aligisakis (1999) in their report on time-use surveys undertaken in fourteen countries indicate that for thirteen out of the fourteen countries covered, the total amount of time spent by household members on unrecorded own account production is equal to or greater than the total amount of time spent working in SNA-type production that falls within the national accounts production boundary. Again, in thirteen out of fourteen countries, men tend to spend most of their time in SNA-type production, while women tend to spend most of their time on the unrecorded *non*-SNA-type activities.

A major new ongoing survey in the United States, the *American Time-Use Survey*, has recently been started by the U.S. Bureau of Labor Statistics. This survey is administered using computer-assisted telephone interviewing, rather than the paper diaries used in most other countries. A full description and some summary results for 2004 are published in the paper by Frazis and Stewart (2006).

These data are averages covering both the employed and the unemployed.

9. Diewert (2001, 231–38) develops the cost-of-living implications of Becker's theory, both under the assumption that time-use data are available and under the assumption that they are not available. In the latter case, Diewert (2001, 234) presents a justification of the traditional acquisitions approach to the CPI but notes that his justification suffers from the problem of technical progress in the household production functions, and hence his blended utility function will not remain constant over time.

10. See, for example, the collection of papers presented at the International Conference on Time Use in Luneberg, Germany in 1998 and published in *Time Use: Research, Data, and Policy,* edited by J. Merz and M. Ehling (1999).

**Table 11.2 Where does the time go? Hours spent in major activities (United States, 2004)**

| Activity | Men | Women |
|---|---|---|
| Personal care activities (including sleeping) | 9.13 | 9.54 |
| Working on SNA-type production | 4.57 | 2.87 |
| Household productive activities outside the SNA production boundary | 4.61 | 6.42 |
| Leisure, sports, religious activities | 5.70 | 5.18 |
| Total | 24.0 | 24.0 |

*Source:* This table condenses data from table 1 in Frazis and Stewart (2006).

Employed men spend an average of 6.26 hours per day at work. The results in table 11.2 are broadly consistent with the generalizations previously noted on the basis of the survey undertaken by Goldschmidt-Clermont and Pagnossin-Aligisakis (1999).

Time-use surveys provide data that may be used for the construction of household satellite accounts, although the surveys usually do not try to record actual quantities of goods and services produced. In general, the values of the outputs are estimated from the input side by summing the estimated costs of production, with the value of the labor inputs being one of the principal costs. Even valuing the outputs on the basis of the inputs presents serious difficulties, and these valuation problems are considered in more detail next, as they are relevant to the possible compilation of price indexes covering own-account consumption.

Goldschmidt-Clermont and Pagnossin-Aligisakis (1999) also report on the effects on GDP of including household production within the SNA production boundary. For the fourteen countries surveyed, the inclusion of household own-account production would increase GDP by amounts ranging from about 25 percent to 55 percent. As already noted, the estimates for the United States by Landefeld and McCulla (2000) increase GDP by 43 percent in 1946 and 24 percent in 1997. All the evidence indicates that household production makes a major contribution to the total production and consumption in both developing and developed countries.

One difficulty is that existing classifications of productive activities, such as standard industrial classifications, have been developed in relation to market production. However, some of the productive activities carried on within households may not have exact market equivalents or counterparts. Similarly, some of the outputs produced may not be exactly the same as commodities traded on markets. Good classifications are a prerequisite for useful analysis, and the lack of internationally agreed classifications in this area is an obstacle. Researchers into household production and consumption usually devise their own classifications of both the activities and their outputs.

The set of satellite household production accounts for the United States compiled by Landefeld and McCulla (2000) include an input-output table for household production. The data in this table make it possible to examine the interrelationship between household consumption and consumers' expenditures in some detail, even if the data cannot be expected to achieve the same standards and reliability as those in the regular national accounts. Thirteen household production activities and commodities are distinguished: food preparation, cleaning, laundry, household management, animals and plants, repair, yard work, child care, health care, shopping, services, travel, and other. The activities consume intermediate inputs purchased from outside the household, labor services provided by members of the household, and capital services provided by the fixed assets owned by the households. As proposed in this chapter, household durables used in production are treated as household-fixed assets. The outputs from the activities are entirely consumed within the household.

Landefeld and McCulla compare the values of the outputs of household production consumed by households with the values of household expenditures on the same kinds of goods or services purchased in shops or other outlets. They give the following examples. The value of household food preparation in 1992 was $717 billion,[11] compared with household food expenditures of $253 billion on prepared meals in the marketplace. Household laundry output was valued at $90 billion, whereas the value of expenditures on cleaning, storage, and the repair of clothing and shoes was only $11 billion.

The figures in table 11.3 are found in Landefeld and McCulla's paper (2000, 304).

Only 12 percent of the goods and services purchased on the market by U.S. households for purposes of consumption in 1992 were directly consumed by households without further processing. Of the remaining 88 percent, 62 percent were used as intermediate inputs into household production of other goods and services for own consumption, while the remaining 26 percent were reclassified either as capital formation or as household value added.

Using data from the input-output table in Landefeld and McCulla's paper (2000, 303), it is possible to construct the aggregate production account for all households shown in table 11.4.

It should be noted that the total value of household consumption is actually $5,713 billion, comprised of the $5,189 billion produced by households *plus* the expenditures of $524 billion shown in table 11.3 on goods and services that were consumed directly. Thus, only 9 percent of the final consumption of households consisted of goods and services purchased by households that were directly consumed without further processing.

11. Goldschmidt-Clermont and Pagnossin-Aligasakis (1999) report that in all of their countries except one, "food preparation requires the largest share of non-SNA time" (521).

**Table 11.3 Breakdown of household consumption expenditures by type or use (United States, 1992)**

| | $ (billions) | % |
|---|---|---|
| Personal (household) consumption expenditures (as recorded in the NIPAs), of which: | 4,209 | 100 |
| Goods and services subsequently used as intermediate inputs into household production | 2,596 | 62 |
| Purchases of durables (reclassified as gross capital formation) | 471 | 11 |
| Consumption of housing services produced by owner occupiers (reclassified as household value added) | 618 | 15 |
| Goods and services directly consumed by households without further processing | 524 | 12 |

**Table 11.4 Aggregate production account for household production for own consumption (United States, 1992)**

| Inputs | $ (billions) | Outputs | $ (billions) |
|---|---|---|---|
| Total value of households' personal expenditures on goods and services used as intermediate inputs | 2,596 | Total value of consumption goods and services produced and consumed by households | 5,189 |
| Gross value added produced within households, of which: | 2,593 | | |
| Labor services provided by household members | 1,449 | | |
| Capital services provided by household-fixed assets, including dwellings | 1,144 | | |
| Total | 5,189 | Total | 5,189 |

The $5,713 billion of total household consumption exceeds the $4,209 billion of total household consumption expenditures by $1,504 billion, which is largely explained by the additional value created by the labor services provided by household members. The difference is also affected by various reclassifications, however, as neither durables nor housing services are treated as being consumed directly, both being treated as providing flows of capital services into household production.

### 11.4.1 Valuing Household Consumption

As no monetary transactions occur for goods and services that are produced and consumed within the same household, no prices are generated. In this situation, there are two alternative ways of valuing the nonmarket output of household production. One is to try to find market prices that can be used to value the outputs, and the other is to value the outputs by their costs of production. As already noted, the same valuation problem occurs with the output of nonmarket services produced by government enterprises or nonprofit institutions.

If the same goods and services are sold on the market and market prices can be found for them, they can be used to value the goods and services produced by households for own use. Valuation at market prices is the procedure adopted in national accounting whenever possible. For example, market rents may be used to value the output of housing services produced by owner occupiers. However, the qualities of the goods and services produced within households tend to systematically differ from those of similar kinds of goods and services sold on the market, if any. In general, there seem to be very few cases where appropriate market prices can be found to value the output of household production, so other valuation methods have to be adopted.

The alternative is to value the outputs by their costs of production. This method is widely used in national accounts to value all kinds of nonmarket output. For example, in the production account in table 11.4, the figure of $5,713 billion for the output of household production is obtained as the sum of the intermediate and primary inputs on the left side of the account. There is assumed to be no net operating surplus or profit. This method shifts the problem of valuation from the outputs to the inputs.

There are three main inputs: intermediate inputs, capital services, and labor services. When purchased on the market, the value of the intermediate inputs is given straightforwardly by the expenditures incurred. The value of inputs of capital services is given by the user costs incurred—that is, by the sum of the depreciation and interest costs on the household-fixed assets. The main problem with the input approach is the valuation of the labor inputs. The labor inputs themselves are nonmarket, like the outputs they are being used to value. The valuation of labor inputs into household production is one of the more controversial topics in household production accounting.

The quantities of labor inputs can be estimated by using data on hours worked from time-use surveys, but they have to be valued. As already noted, the procedure adopted in national accounts is to value nonmarket flows of goods and services whenever possible at the prices at which the same goods and services are bought and sold on markets. To be consistent with this general principle, the labor inputs should be valued using the market wages payable to employees doing the same kind of work.

However, a case can also be made for valuing at internal opportunity costs—that is, what the person could have earned by taking paid employment. Valuing at internal opportunity costs is not generally favored in studies on household production, because it makes the value of the labor inputs depend on who does the work, rather than on the nature of the work done. In any case, most paid employees are not able to vary the amount of paid work they do to suit their own preferences. If they take on a second job instead of working in the home, they are likely to be paid less than in their main job.

A further complication is that people may engage in certain household productive activities, such as child care, because they enjoy it. Certain types of work may actually be undertaken as a form of leisure activity. For example, many people undertake do-it-yourself activities, ranging from cooking and gardening to constructing extensions to dwellings, because they derive satisfaction from the work itself, not merely from the output produced. The trade-off may not be between do-it-yourself activities and paid employment but between do-it-yourself activities and other forms of leisure activities, such as watching television or sports activities. The motivation behind some household activities may be quite complex. For example, the activity of gardening is recognized to be a good form of exercise, so it may be undertaken as a substitute for going to the gym (and savings on gym subscriptions). At the same time, it produces fruit and vegetables for eating and flowers and pleasant surroundings that enhance the value of the house. The concept of the opportunity cost in these kinds of circumstances is not altogether clear. On balance, it seems preferable to value work done in household production at the corresponding market wage rate for that type of work. This is a simple, objective, and rational method of valuation.

### 11.4.2 Price Indexes for Household Consumption

Notwithstanding the difficulties of valuing the labor inputs, estimating the value of the output of household production and consumption by summing the values of the inputs is likely to produce estimates of the right order of magnitude for a single period of time. From a CPI perspective, however, it is necessary to factor changes over time in the current values of household consumption into their price and quantity components. This is an altogether more difficult undertaking.

Although the total values of inputs and outputs may be identical for a single period of time, there is no corresponding identity between changes in the real values of inputs and outputs over time or between average changes in input and output prices. They diverge because of changes in productivity. Thus, even if satisfactory price indexes could be compiled for each of the inputs, a weighted average of the price indexes for the inputs into household production would not provide a satisfactory estimate of the price index for the outputs, except possibly in the very short term.[12]

As already noted, the problem is the same as that of measuring inflation and real growth for government nonmarket output. However, the problem

12. However, Diewert has shown that even in the longer term, an acceptable estimate of a COLI could be obtained if there were no technical progress and if household time were valued appropriately; see Diewert (2001, 233).

is even more acute for household production, because the values of the labor inputs have to be imputed, whereas the values of the labor inputs into government production can be measured by the compensation of employees actually paid.

It is only possible to make a satisfactory estimate of the rate of inflation or real growth of nonmarket output from input data if there is an independent estimate of the rate of growth of productivity. However, there is little to no hard evidence about changes in productivity for household production. It may be conjectured that household productivity has been rising over the long term, because as the general standard of living rises, households tend to equip themselves with more and better quality household-fixed assets, while the technology of household production is also likely to be improving over time. Estimating the rate of inflation or growth of the output from household production from the rates of inflation or growth of the inputs cannot be acceptable if no account is taken of household productivity growth.

It may be concluded that there is not much possibility of constructing a satisfactory price index for the consumption of own production within households, regardless of whether the price changes are estimated on the basis of movements in equivalent market prices or whether they are imputed from changes in input prices. Certainly, it is unlikely that such an index could be compiled on a regular monthly basis and used for policy purposes.

No price or volume indexes are provided in the satellite accounts for U.S. household production referred to previously. Landefeld and McCulla (2000) comment as follows: "Given the absence of output price data for household production, no real inflation adjusted estimates are presented here. The use of wage rates or other input costs to deflate household production would result in low or zero productivity in the household sector and bias real growth in household relative to market production" (300). Goldschmidt-Clermont and Pagnossin-Aligisakis (1999) conclude that "valuation will have to be output based, *i.e.*, it will have to start with the physical measurement of household output and value it at market prices. . . . Unfortunately, very little experience is available, as yet, with this approach at national levels" (528).

## 11.5 Summary and Conclusions

The chapter shows that there is a serious but neglected problem concerning the estimation of cost of living indexes. The problem is that most of the goods and services from which consumption households derive utility are produced by the households themselves. No prices are generated in the process. They are not the same goods and services that households purchase and for which statistical offices collect prices.

In the last two decades, satellite accounts for household production have been constructed for a number of countries, which make it possible to obtain a fairly clear picture of the scale and nature of household production for own use, both for own consumption and own gross fixed capital formation. The accounts have shown that a surprisingly large proportion of the goods and services purchased by households and classified as final consumption expenditures in national accounts, household budget surveys, and CPIs are not in fact consumed directly.

This research has been motivated largely by interest in the quantities produced and consumed, not by their prices. Living standards and welfare are determined by the quantities. Moreover, the status of the quantities and the prices that determine the imputed values of the relevant flows are quite different. In fact, only the prices are hypothetical and imputed. The quantities are real and therefore observable and measurable. Imputed values are therefore generally acceptable to analysts or policymakers primarily interested in volume changes, because they reflect changes in actual quantities. However, analysts interested in actual price movements are unlikely to regard price indexes based largely on movements in hypothetical imputed prices as acceptable.

Moreover, systematically imputing the prices in a price index is scarcely feasible. It may not be possible to find equivalent market prices for many goods and services produced on own account, because they are intrinsically different from those purchased on the market. For example, child care provided by the parents is a unique product that is not the same as nursery care. Meals prepared at home are not the same as restaurant meals. Driving one's own car is different from taking a taxi, and so on. There are substantial qualitative differences between own-produced products and superficially similar products sold on the market. It is likely to be impossible to adjust for such differences satisfactorily.

In any case, a price index that is calculated mainly from imputed prices would not be acceptable to most users. A CPI is a key statistic for policy purposes that can have important financial implications, as it is widely used for indexation purposes. It has to be objective, transparent, reliable, and credible.

In practice, CPIs measure changes in the market prices of the goods and services included in household final consumption expenditures as defined in national accounts and household expenditures surveys. Such an index can be interpreted as a consumer price index that measures changes in the prices of goods and services that households purchase with the intention of using them directly *or indirectly* for purposes of consumption—that is, to satisfy their personal needs or wants. Market prices are readily available for them and can be collected as frequently as desired.

The difficulty with a pragmatic approach of this kind is that such an index is likely to have an upward bias when compared with a COLI. The goods and services included in a COLI should be those from which consumption utility is derived, as distinct from the goods and services purchased in retail outlets. Goods or services that are used as inputs into household production should not simply be treated as if they were final consumption goods and services. Consumer price indexes that are meant to target COLIs but that in fact make extensive use of input prices are likely to have an upward bias, given that the technologies used in household production are continually improving.[13] As recent studies have shown that most of the goods and services purchased by households are used as inputs rather than consumed directly, this is not a trivial problem.

## References

Atkinson, T. 2005. *Atkinson Review: Final report; Measurement of government output and productivity for the national accounts.* New York: Palgrave Macmillan.

Becker, G. S. 1965. A theory of the allocation of time. *Economic Journal* 75 (299): 493–517.

Diewert, W. E. 1976. Exact and superlative index numbers. *Journal of Econometrics* 4 (2): 114–45.

———. 2001. The Consumer Price Index and index number purpose. *Journal of Economic and Social Measurement* 27 (3/4): 167–248.

———. 2008. The measurement of nonmarket sector outputs and inputs using cost weights. Discussion Paper no. 08-03. University of British Columbia, Department of Economics.

Eurostat, International Monetary Fund (IMF), Organization for Economic Cooperation and Development (OECD), United Nations (UN), and World Bank. 1993. *System of National Accounts, 1993.* New York: United Nations.

Fisher, I. 1922. *The nature of capital and income.* New York: August M. Kelly.

Frazis, H., and J. Stewart. 2006. Where does the time go? Concepts and measurement in the American Time Use Survey. In *Studies in income and wealth,* vol. 67, *Hard-to-measure goods and services: Essays in memory of Zvi Griliches,* ed. E. Berndt and C. Hulten, 73–97. Chicago: University of Chicago Press.

Goldschmidt-Clermont, L., and E. Pagnossin-Aligisakis. 1999. Households' non-SNA production: Labour time, value of labour and of product, and contribution to extended private consumption. *Review of Income and Wealth* 45 (4): 519–29.

Hicks, J. R. 1942. *The social framework.* Oxford: University Press.

International Labor Office, IMF, OECD, Eurostat, United Nations Economic Commission for Europe (UN ECE), and World Bank. 2004. *Consumer Price Index manual: Theory and practice.* New York: United Nations.

Konüs, A. A. 1924. The problem of the true index of the cost of living. *Economic Bulletin of the Institute of Economic Conjuncture,* no. 9/10: 64–71.

Landefeld, J. S., and S. H. McCulla. 2000. Accounting for nonmarket household

13. As already noted, Diewert (2001) has shown that input prices can be used in the estimation of a COLI in a model that integrates household production and consumption but only when there is no technical progress.

production within a national accounts framework. *Review of Income and Wealth* 46 (3): 289–307.
Merz, J., and M. Ehling, eds. 1999. *Time use: Research, data, and policy.* Baden-Baden, Germany: Nomos Verlagsgesellschaft.
Nordhaus, W. D. 1997. Do real-output and real-wage measures capture reality? The history of lighting suggests not. In *Studies in income and wealth,* vol. 58, *The economics of new goods,* ed. T. F. Bresnahan and R. J. Gordon, 29–71.
Reid, M. G. 1934. *Economics of household production.* New York: John Wiley and Sons.

12

# Durables and Owner-Occupied Housing in a Consumer Price Index

W. Erwin Diewert

## 12.1 Introduction

When a durable good (other than housing) is purchased by a consumer, national consumer price indexes typically attribute all of that expenditure to the period of purchase, even though the use of the good extends beyond the period of purchase.[1] This is known as the acquisitions approach to the treatment of consumer durables in the context of determining a pricing concept for the Consumer Price Index (CPI). However, if one takes the cost-of-living approach as the measurement objective for the CPI, then it is more appropriate to take the cost of *using the services* of the durable good during the period under consideration as the pricing concept. There are two broad approaches to estimating this imputed cost for using the services of a durable good during a period:

W. Erwin Diewert is a professor of economics at the University of British Columbia and a research associate of the National Bureau of Economic Research.

This research was supported by Statistics Sweden and a Social Sciences and Humanities Research Council of Canada grant. The author thanks Bert Balk, Kevin Fox, John Greenlees, Rosmundur Gudnason, Alan Heston, Peter Hill, Johannes Hoffman, Charles Hulten, Arnold Katz, Anders Klevmarken, Timo Koskimäki, Anne Laferrère, Alice Nakamura, Marshall Reinsdorf, and Carmit Schwartz for helpful comments on earlier versions of this chapter. The above people and institutions are not responsible for any errors or opinions expressed in this chapter. Some of the material in this chapter overlaps with chapter 23 in the *Consumer Price Index Manual: Theory and Practice* (International Labor Organization et al. 2004).

1. This treatment of the purchases of durable goods dates back at least to Alfred Marshall (1898, 594–95): "We have noticed also that though the benefits which a man derives from living in his own house are commonly reckoned as part of his real income, and estimated at the net rental value of his house; the same plan is not followed with regard to the benefits which he derives from the use of his furniture and clothes. It is best here to follow the common practice, and not count as part of the national income or dividend anything that is not commonly counted as part of the income of the individual."

- If rental or leasing markets for a comparable consumer durable exist, then this market rental price could be used as an estimate for the cost of using the durable during the period. This method is known as the *rental equivalence approach.*
- If used or second-hand markets for the durable exist, then the imputed cost of purchasing a durable good at the beginning of the period and selling it at the end could be computed, and this net cost could be used as an estimate for the cost of using the durable during the period. This method is known as the *user cost approach.*

The major *advantages* of the acquisitions approach to the treatment of consumer durables are as follows:

- It is conceptually simple and entirely similar to the treatment of non-durables and services.
- No complex imputations are required.

The major *disadvantage* of the acquisitions approach, compared to the other two approaches, is that the acquisitions approach is not likely to reflect accurately the consumption services of consumer durables in any period. Thus, suppose that real interest rates in a country become very high due to some sort of macroeconomic crisis. Under these conditions, typically purchases of automobiles, houses, and other long-lived consumer durables drop dramatically, perhaps to zero. However, the actual consumption of automobile and housing services of the country's population will not fall to zero under these circumstances: consumers will still be consuming the services of their existing stocks of automobiles and houses. Thus, for at least some purposes, rather than taking the cost of *purchasing* a consumer durable as the pricing concept, it will be more useful to take the cost of *using* the services of the durable good during the period under consideration as the pricing concept.

The previous paragraphs provide a brief overview of the three major approaches to the treatment of consumer durables. In the remainder of this introduction, we explore these approaches in a bit more detail and give the reader an outline of the detailed discussion that will follow in subsequent sections.

We first consider a formal definition of a consumer durable. By definition, a durable good delivers services longer than the period under consideration.[2] The *System of National Accounts, 1993* (SNA) defines a *durable good* as follows:

> In the case of goods, the distinction between acquisition and use is analytically important. It underlies the distinction between durable and non-durable goods extensively used in economic analysis. In fact, the distinc-

2. An alternative definition of a durable good is that the good delivers services to its purchaser for a period exceeding three years: "The Bureau of Economic Analysis defines consumer durables as those durables that have an average life of at least 3 years" (Katz 1983, 422).

tion between durable and non-durable goods is not based on physical durability as such. Instead, the distinction is based on whether the goods can be used once only for purposes of production or consumption or whether they can be used repeatedly, or continuously. For example, coal is a highly durable good in a physical sense, but it can be burnt only once. A durable good is therefore defined as one which may be used repeatedly or continuously over a period of more than a year, assuming a normal or average rate of physical usage. A consumer durable is a good that may be used for purposes of consumption repeatedly or continuously over a period of a year or more. (Eurostat et al. 1993, 208)

According to the SNA definition, durability is more than the fact that a good can physically persist for more than a year (this is true of most goods): a durable good is distinguished from a nondurable good due to its ability to deliver useful services to a consumer through repeated use over an extended period of time.

Because the benefits of using the consumer durable extend over more than one period, it does not seem appropriate to charge the entire purchase cost of the durable to the initial period of purchase. If this point of view is taken, then the initial purchase cost must be distributed somehow over the useful life of the asset. This is *a fundamental problem of accounting.*[3] Hulten (1990) explains the consequences for accountants of the durability of a purchase as follows:

Durability means that a capital good is productive for two or more time periods, and this, in turn, implies that a distinction must be made between the value of using or renting capital in any year and the value of owning the capital asset. This distinction would not necessarily lead to a measurement problem if the capital services used in any given year were paid for in that year; that is, if all capital were rented. In this case, transactions in the rental market would fix the price and quantity of capital in each time period, much as data on the price and quantity of labor services are derived from labor market transactions. But, unfortunately, much capital is utilized by its owner and the transfer of capital services between owner and user results in an implicit rent typically not observed by the statistician. Market data are thus inadequate for the task of directly estimating the price and quantity of capital services, and this has led to the development of indirect procedures for inferring the quantity of capital, like the perpetual inventory method, or to the acceptance of flawed measures, like book value. (120–1)

3. "The third convention is that of the annual accounting period. It is this convention which is responsible for most of the difficult accounting problems. Without this convention, accounting would be a simple matter of recording completed and fully realized transactions: an act of primitive simplicity" (Gilman 1939, 26). "*All* the problems of income measurement are the result of our desire to attribute income to arbitrarily determined short periods of time. Everything comes right in the end; but by then it is too late to matter" (Solomons 1961, 378). Note that these authors do not mention the additional complications that are due to the fact that future revenues and costs must be discounted to yield values that are equivalent to present dollars.

Thus, the treatment of durable goods is more complicated than the treatment of nondurable goods and services due to the simple fact that the period of time that a durable is used by the consumer extends beyond the period of purchase. For nondurables and services, the price statistician's measurement problems are conceptually simple: prices for the same commodity need only be collected in each period and compared. However, for a durable good, the periods of payment and use do not coincide, so complex imputation problems arise if the goal of the price statistician is to measure and compare the price of *using* the services of the durable in two time periods.

The three major approaches to the treatment of durables will be discussed more fully in sections 12.2, 12.3, and 12.4. However, there is a fourth approach to the treatment of consumer durables that has only been used in the context of pricing owner-occupied housing (OOH), and that is the *payments approach.*[4] This is a kind of a cash flow approach, which is not entirely satisfactory,[5] so it will not be discussed any further.

The preceding three approaches to the treatment of durable purchases can be applied to the purchase of any durable commodity. However, historically, it turns out that the rental equivalence and user cost approaches have *only* been applied to owner-occupied housing.[6] In other words, the acquisitions approach to the purchase of consumer durables has been universally used by statistical agencies, with the exception of owner-occupied housing. A possible reason for this is tradition; that is, Marshall set the standard, and statisticians have followed his example for the past century. However, another possible reason is that unless the durable good has a very long useful life, it usually will not make a great deal of difference in the long run, regardless of whether the acquisitions approach or one of the two alternative approaches is used.[7]

A major component of the user cost approach to valuing the services of owner-occupied housing is the depreciation component. General methods

4. This is the term used by Goodhart (2001, F350–F351).

5. This approach recognizes some costs of housing (such as nominal mortgage interest) but ignores other costs (such as the opportunity cost of equity funds tied up in the housing unit). It also ignores some benefits, such as anticipated appreciation of the equity part of the housing unit, and this factor is particularly important when there is high or moderate inflation. Thus, when there is very high inflation over the period and mortgage interest payments blow up, the payments approach will indicate a big increase in price of housing. However, the real cost to the homeowner will not be proportional to these monetary interest payments; there is an offsetting gain due to appreciation of the underlying housing asset. Put another way, an interest rate is a rather complex type of price. It is a payment for the use of funds over a specified time period. But the value of money is not the same at the beginning and end of the specified time period, and this fact should be taken into account if interest enters a CPI. This type of reasoning suggests that nominal interest rates should not be used in a CPI, but some form of real interest rate could be acceptable, as in the user cost approach (to be discussed later).

6. The Boskin Commission recommended that a flow of services approach be applied to all types of consumer durables, but this recommendation has not yet been implemented; see Boskin et al. (1996).

7. See Diewert (2002, 617–9).

for determining depreciation rates when information on used-asset prices is available[8] have been worked out by Hall (1971), Beidelman (1973, 1976), and Hulten and Wykoff (1981a, 1981b, 1996).[9] However, many durables (such as housing) are custom produced, and it turns out that the standard methods for determining depreciation rates are more difficult to implement. The special problems caused by these uniquely produced consumer durables are considered in section 12.5.

Sections 12.6 through 12.11 treat some of the special problems involved in implementing the user cost and rental equivalence methods for valuing the services provided by owner-occupied housing. Section 12.6 presents a derivation for the user cost of OOH and various approximations to it. Section 12.7 looks at some of the problems associated with obtaining constant-quality prices for housing. Section 12.8 considers some of the costs that are tied to home ownership, while section 12.9 considers how a landlord's costs might differ from a homeowner's costs. This material is relevant if the rental equivalence approach to valuing the services of OOH is used: care must be taken to remove some costs that are imbedded in market rents that homeowners do not face.

Section 12.10 tries to bring together all of the material on the problems associated with pricing owner-occupied housing and to outline possible CPI measurement strategies. Finally, section 12.11 concludes with another approach to the measurement of the services provided by OOH: the *opportunity cost approach,* which sets the price of OOH to the *maximum* of its user cost and its market rent. The very interesting critique of the user cost approach made by Verbrugge (2006) is also discussed in this final section.

## 12.2 The Acquisitions Approach

The *net acquisitions approach* to the treatment of owner-occupied housing is described by Goodhart as follows:

> The first is the net acquisition approach, which is the change in the price of newly purchased owner occupied dwellings, weighted by the net purchases of the reference population. This is an asset based measure, and therefore comes close to my preferred measure of inflation as a change in the value of money, though the change in the price of the stock of existing houses rather than just of net purchases would in some respects be even better. It is, moreover, consistent with the treatment of other durables. A few countries, e.g., Australia and New Zealand, have used it, and it is, I understand, the main contender for use in the Euro-area Harmonized

8. General models relating capital services, depreciation, and asset values in a set of vintage accounts have been worked out by Jorgenson (1973, 1989) and Hulten (1990, 127–9; 1996, 152–60).

9. See also Jorgenson (1996) for a review of the empirical literature on the estimation of depreciation rates.

> Index of Consumer Prices (HICP), which currently excludes any measure of the purchase price of (new) housing, though it does include minor repairs and maintenance by home owners, as well as all expenditures by tenants. (2001, F350)

Thus, the weights for the net acquisitions approach are the net purchases of the household sector of houses from other institutional sectors in the base period. Note that in principle, purchases of second-hand dwellings from other sectors are relevant here; for example, a local government may sell rental dwellings to owner occupiers. However, typically, newly built houses form a major part of these types of transactions. Thus, the long-term price relative for this category of expenditure will be primarily the price of (new) houses (quality adjusted) in the current period relative to the price of new houses in the base period.[10] If this approach is applied to other consumer durables, it is extremely easy to implement: the purchase of a durable is treated in the same way as a nondurable or service purchase is treated.

One additional implication of the net acquisitions approach is that major renovations and additions to owner-occupied dwelling units could also be considered in scope for this approach. In practice, these costs typically are not covered in a standard consumer price index. The treatment of renovations and additions will be considered in more detail in section 12.8.4.

Traditionally, the net acquisitions approach also includes transfer costs relating to the buying and selling of second-hand houses as expenditures that are in scope for an acquisitions-type consumer price index. These costs are mainly the costs of using a real estate agent's services and asset-transfer taxes. These transfer costs will be further discussed in sections 12.8.2 and 12.8.5.

The major advantage of the acquisitions approach is that it treats durable and nondurable purchases in a completely symmetric manner, and thus no special procedures have to be developed by a statistical agency to deal with durable goods. The major disadvantage of this approach is that the *expenditures* associated with this approach will tend to *understate* the corresponding expenditures on durables that are implied by the rental equivalence and user cost approaches.[11]

Some differences between the acquisitions approach and the other approaches are as follows:

- If rental or leasing markets for the durable exist and the durable has a long useful life, then the expenditure weights implied by the rental

10. This price index may or may not include the price of the land that the new dwelling unit sits on; for example, a new house price construction index would typically not include the land cost. The acquisitions approach concentrates on the purchases by households of goods and services that are provided by suppliers from outside the household sector. Thus, if the land on which a new house sits was previously owned by the household sector, then presumably, the cost of this land would be excluded from an acquisitions-type new house price index.

11. See Diewert (2002, 618–9) on this point.

equivalence or user cost approaches will typically be much larger than the corresponding expenditure weights implied by the acquisitions approach.

- If the base year corresponds to a boom year (or a slump year) for the durable, then the base-period expenditure weights may be too large or too small. Put another way, the aggregate expenditures that correspond to the acquisitions approach are likely to be more volatile than the expenditures for the aggregate that are implied by the rental equivalence or user cost approaches.
- In making comparisons of consumption across countries where the proportion of owning versus renting or leasing the durable varies greatly,[12] the use of the acquisitions approach may lead to misleading cross-country comparisons. The reason for this is that opportunity costs of capital are excluded in the net acquisitions approach, whereas they are explicitly or implicitly included in the other two approaches.

More fundamentally, whether the acquisitions approach is the right one depends on the overall purpose of the index number. If the purpose is to measure the price of current-period *consumption services,* then the acquisitions approach can only be regarded as an approximation to a more appropriate approach (which would be either the rental equivalence or user cost approach). If the purpose of the index is to measure *monetary* (or non-imputed) *expenditures* by households during the period, then the acquisitions approach is preferable, because the rental equivalence and user cost approaches necessarily involve imputations.

## 12.3 The Rental Equivalence Approach

The *rental equivalence approach* simply values the services yielded by the use of a consumer durable good for a period by the corresponding market rental value for the same durable for the same period of time (if such a rental value exists). This is the approach taken in the *System of National Accounts, 1993* for owner-occupied housing:

> As well-organized markets for rented housing exist in most countries, the output of own-account housing services can be valued using the prices of the same kinds of services sold on the market with the general valuation rules adopted for goods and services produced on own account. In other words, the output of housing services produced by owner-occupiers is valued at the estimated rental that a tenant would pay for the same accommodation, taking into account factors such as location, neighbour-

12. According to Hoffmann and Kurz (2002, 3–4), about 60 percent of German households lived in rented dwellings, whereas only about 11 percent of Spaniards rented their dwellings in 1999.

> hood amenities, etc. as well as the size and quality of the dwelling itself. (Eurostat et al. 1993, 134)

However, the SNA follows Marshall (1898, 595) and does *not* extend the rental equivalence approach to consumer durables other than housing. This seemingly inconsistent treatment of durables is explained in the SNA as follows:

> The production of housing services for their own final consumption by owner-occupiers has always been included within the production boundary in national accounts, although it constitutes an exception to the general exclusion of own-account service production. The ratio of owner-occupied to rented dwellings can vary significantly between countries and even over short periods of time within a single country, so that both international and intertemporal comparisons of the production and consumption of housing services could be distorted if no imputation were made for the value of own-account services. (Eurostat et al. 1993, 126)

Eurostat's (2001) *Handbook on Price and Volume Measures in National Accounts* also recommends the rental equivalence approach for the treatment of the dwelling services for owner-occupied housing:

> The output of dwelling services of owner occupiers at current prices is in many countries estimated by linking the actual rents paid by those renting similar properties in the rented sector to those of owner occupiers. This allows the imputation of a notional rent for the service owner occupiers receive from their property. (99)

The U.S. statistical agencies, the Bureau of Labor Statistics (BLS) and the Bureau of Economic Analysis (BEA), both use variants of the rental equivalence approach to value the services of owner-occupied housing. Katz describes the BEA procedures as follows:

> Basically, BEA measures the gross rent (space rent) of owner occupied housing from data on the rent paid for similar housing with the same market value. To get the service value that is added to GNP (gross housing product), the value of intermediate goods and services included in this figure (e.g., expenditures for repair and maintenance, insurance, condominium fees, and closing costs) are subtracted from the space rent. To obtain a net return (net rental income), depreciation, taxes, and net interest are subtracted from, and subsidies added to, the service value. (Katz 1983, 411)

Basically, the BEA applies estimated rent to asset-value ratios for rental units to asset values for owner-occupied dwellings of the same type in order to obtain estimated rents for these owner-occupied units.

Another method for determining rental price equivalents for owned consumer durables is to *ask* owners what they think their durables would rent for. This approach was used by the BLS in order to determine expenditure weights for owner-occupied housing prior to the 1998 CPI revision; that is, homeowners were asked to estimate what their house would rent for if it were rented to a third party (see BLS 1983). These estimated expenditures were then used as weights in a fixed-weight-type index, where the price relatives that were matched to these weights were market rent price relatives that corresponded to the type of owner-occupied unit. However, Lebow and Rudd (2003, 169) noted that these consumer expenditure survey-based estimates of imputed rents in the United States differed from the corresponding BEA estimates for imputed rents, which were based on applying a rent-to-value ratio for rented properties to the owner-occupied stock of housing. Lebow and Rudd (2003) noted that the expenditure survey estimates may be less reliable than the rent-to-value ratio method due to the relatively small size of the consumer expenditure survey, plus the difficulties households may have in recalling or estimating expenditures.[13] The current BLS procedures for estimating rents for owner-occupied dwellings are different from the pre-1998 procedures and are described in Ptacek and Baskin (1996).[14]

There are some problems with the preceding treatment of housing, and they will be discussed in later sections, after the user cost approach to durables has been discussed.

To summarize the previous material, it can be seen that the rental equivalence approach to the treatment of durables is conceptually simple: set the rental equivalence price equal to a current-period rental or leasing price for a comparable product. However, in implementing the approach, many practical difficulties arise. The most important difficulty is that comparable rental markets may not exist, particularly for a unique asset, such as a house. Even if some comparable rental markets exist, there may be difficulties in determining *exactly* how to choose the comparable rental price for the specific consumer durable at hand.

Note that the rental equivalence approach to pricing the services of a consumer durable is a type of *opportunity cost approach;* that is, the price for using the services of the durable over the reference period is taken to be the income that is foregone by not leasing or renting the durable.[15] In the following section, a different type of opportunity cost approach is taken—namely, the *user cost approach.* In this alternative approach, the opportunity

13. Garner et al. (2003) compared the BLS and BEA approaches to the measurement of housing services and found that in 1992, the estimate of dwelling services of renters and owners was about 9 percent higher in the BEA than the BLS. In addition, they found that the two series have consistently grown apart from 1992 to 2000. For additional material on the two approaches, see Heston and Nakamura (2009).

14. For information on current BLS procedure, see Ptacek and Baskin (1996, 34). In both the pre- and post-1998 BLS methodologies for OOH, once the OOH expenditure weights were determined, the weights were multiplied by rental unit price relatives.

15. As will be seen in section 12.9, when a market rental opportunity cost approach is taken to valuing the services of an owned durable, it may be necessary to adjust the comparable market rental price somewhat in order to convert it into a true opportunity cost to the owner.

cost is essentially taken to be *the loss of financial income* that the consumer forgoes in tying up his or her capital in the durable good.

## 12.4 The User Cost Approach

The user cost approach to the treatment of durable goods is in some ways very simple: it calculates the cost of purchasing the durable at the beginning of the period, using the services of the durable during the period, then netting off from these costs the benefit that could be obtained by selling the durable at the end of the period, taking into account the interest forgone in tying up one's capital in purchasing the durable. However, there are several details of this procedure that are somewhat controversial. These details involve the treatment of depreciation, interest, and capital gains or holding gains.

Another complication with the user cost approach is that it involves making distinctions between current-period (flow) purchases within the period under consideration and the holdings of physical stocks of the durable at the beginning and the end of the accounting period. Up to this point, all prices and quantity purchases were thought of as taking place at a single point in time, say the middle of the period under consideration, and consumption was thought of as taking place within the period as well. Thus, there was no need to consider the valuation of stocks of consumer durables that households may have at their disposal. The rather complex problems involved in accounting for stocks and flows are unfamiliar to most price statisticians.

To determine the net cost of using the durable good during, say, period 0, assume that one unit of the durable good is purchased at the beginning of period 0 at the price $P^0$. The used or second-hand durable good can be sold at the end of period 0 at the price $P_S^1$. It might seem that a reasonable net cost for the use of one unit of the consumer durable during period 0 is its initial purchase price $P^0$, less its end of period 0 scrap value $P_S^1$. However, *money received at the end of the period is not as valuable as money that is received at the beginning of the period.* Thus, in order to convert the end-of-period value into its beginning-of-period equivalent value, it is necessary to *discount* the term $P_S^1$ by the term $1 + r^0$, where $r^0$ is the beginning-of-period 0 nominal interest rate that the consumer faces. Hence, the *period 0 user cost* $u^0$ for the consumer durable[16] is defined as

$$u^0 \equiv P^0 - \frac{P_S^1}{1 + r^0}. \tag{1}$$

There is another way to view the user cost formula in equation (1): the consumer purchases the durable at the beginning of period 0 at the price

16. This approach to the derivation of a user cost formula was used by Diewert (1974), who in turn based it on an approach due to Hicks (1946, 326).

$P^0$ and charges himself or herself the rental price $u^0$. The remainder of the purchase price, $I^0$, defined as

(2) $$I^0 \equiv P^0 - u^0,$$

can be regarded as an *investment* that is to yield the appropriate opportunity cost of capital $r^0$ that the consumer faces. At the end of period 0, this rate of return could be realized, provided that $I^0$, $r^0$, and the selling price of the durable at the end of the period $P_S^1$ satisfy the following equation:

(3) $$I^0(1 + r^0) = P_S^1.$$

Given $P_S^1$ and $r^0$, equation (3) determines $I^0$, which in turn, given $P^0$, determines the user cost $u^0$ via equation (2).[17]

Note that user costs are not like the prices of nondurables or services, because the user cost concept involves pricing the durable at *two* points in time rather than at a single point in time.[18] Because the user cost concept involves prices at two points in time, money received or paid out at the first point in time is more valuable than money paid out or received at the second point in time, so *interest rates* creep into the user cost formula. Furthermore, because the user cost concept involves prices at two points in time, *expected prices* can be involved if the user cost is calculated at the beginning of the period under consideration instead of at the end. With all of these complications, it is no wonder many price statisticians would like to avoid using user costs as a pricing concept. However, even for price statisticians who would prefer to use the rental equivalence approach to the treatment of durables over the user cost approach, there is some justification for considering the user cost approach in some detail, because this approach gives insights into the economic determinants of the rental or leasing price of a durable. As will be seen in section 12.9, the user cost for a house can differ substantially for a landlord compared to an owner, and thus adjustments should be made to market rents for dwelling units if these observed rents are to be used as imputations for owner-occupied rents.

The user cost formula in equation (1) can be put into a more familiar form if the period 0 *economic depreciation rate* $\delta$ and the period 0 ex post *asset inflation rate* $i^0$ are defined. We define $\delta$ as

17. This derivation for the user cost of a consumer durable was also made by Diewert (1974, 504).

18. Woolford suggested that interest should be excluded from an ideal price index that measured inflation. In his view, interest is not a *contemporaneous price;* that is, an interest rate necessarily refers to *two* points in time: a beginning point, when the capital is loaned, and an ending point, when the capital loaned must be repaid. Thus, if one wanted to restrict attention to a domain of definition that consisted of only contemporaneous prices, interest rates would be excluded. Woolford (1999, 535) noted that his ideal inflation measure "would be contemporary in nature, capturing only the current trend in prices associated with transactions in goods and services. It would exclude interest rates on the ground that they are intertemporal prices, representing the relative price of consuming today rather than in the future."

$$(4) \qquad (1 - \delta) \equiv \frac{P_S^1}{P^1},$$

where $P_S^1$ is the price of a used asset at the end of period 0, and $P^1$ is the price of a new asset at the end of period 0. The *period 0 inflation rate* for the new asset, $i^0$, is defined as

$$(5) \qquad 1 + i^0 \equiv \frac{P^1}{P^0}.$$

Eliminating $P^1$ from equations (4) and (5) leads to the following formula for the end-of-period 0 used-asset price:

$$(6) \qquad P_S^1 = (1 - \delta)(1 + i^0)P^0.$$

Substitution of equation (6) into equation (1) yields the following expression for the *period 0 user cost* $u^0$:

$$(7) \qquad u^0 = \frac{[(1 + r^0) - (1 - \delta)(1 + i^0)]P^0}{1 + r^0}.$$

Note that $r^0 - i^0$ can be interpreted as a period 0 *real interest rate,* and $\delta(1 + i^0)$ can be interpreted as an *inflation-adjusted depreciation rate.*

The user cost $u^0$ is expressed in terms of prices that are discounted to the *beginning* of period 0. However, it is also possible to express the user cost in terms of prices that are discounted to the *end* of period 0.[19] Thus, we define the *end-of-period 0 user cost* $p^0$ as

$$(8) \qquad p^0 \equiv (1 + r^0)u^0 = [(1 + r^0) - (1 - \delta)(1 + i^0)]P^0,$$

where the last equation follows, using equation (7). If the real interest rate $r^{0*}$ is defined as the nominal interest rate $r^0$, less the asset inflation rate $i^0$, and the small term $\delta i^0$ is neglected, then the end-of-period user cost defined by equation (8) reduces to

$$(9) \qquad p^0 = (r^{0*} + \delta)P^0.$$

Abstracting from transactions costs and inflation, it can be seen that the end-of-period user cost defined by equation (9) is an *approximate rental cost;* that is, the rental cost for the use of a consumer (or producer) durable good should equal the (real) opportunity cost of the capital tied up, $r^{0*}P^0$,

19. Thus, the beginning-of-period user cost $u^0$ discounts all monetary costs and benefits into their dollar equivalent at the beginning of period 0, whereas $p^0$ accumulates or appreciates all monetary costs and benefits into their dollar equivalent at the end of period 0. This leaves open how flow transactions that take place within the period should be treated. Following the conventions used in financial accounting suggests that flow transactions taking place within the accounting period be regarded as taking place at the end of the accounting period; hence, following this convention, end-of-period user costs should probably be used by the price statistician. For additional material on beginning- and end-of-period user costs, see Diewert (2005a).

plus the decline in value of the asset over the period, $\delta P^0$. Equations (8) and (9) thus cast some light on the economic determinants of rental or leasing prices for consumer durables.

If the simplified user cost formula defined by equation (9) is used, then forming a price index for the user costs of a durable good is not very much more difficult than forming a price index for the purchase price of the durable good, $P^0$. The price statistician needs only to:

- Make a reasonable assumption as to what an appropriate monthly or quarterly real interest rate $r^{0*}$ should be.
- Make an assumption as to what a reasonable monthly or quarterly depreciation rate $\delta$ should be.[20]
- Collect purchase prices $P^0$ for the durable.
- Make an estimate of the total stock of the durable that was held by the reference population during the base period for quantities. In order to construct a superlative index, estimates of the stock held will have to be made for each period.

If it is thought necessary to implement the more complicated user cost formula in equation (8) in place of the simpler formula in equation (9), then the situation is more complicated. As it stands, the end-of-period user cost formula in equation (8) is an ex post (after the fact) *user cost:* the asset inflation rate $i^0$ cannot be calculated until the end of period 0 has been reached. Equation (8) can be converted into an ex ante (before the fact) *user cost* formula if $i^0$ is interpreted as an *anticipated asset inflation rate.* The resulting formula should approximate a market rental rate for the asset under inflationary conditions.[21] However, in section 12.11, it will be seen that this approximate equality is indeed only an approximate one.

Note that in the user cost approach to the treatment of consumer durables, the *entire* user cost formula in equation (8) or (9) is the period 0 price. Thus, in the time-series context, it is *not* necessary to deflate each component of the formula *separately;* the period 0 price, $p^0 \equiv [r^0 - i^0 + \delta(1 + i^0)]P^0$, is compared to the corresponding period 1 price, $p^1 \equiv [r^1 - i^1 + \delta(1 + i^1)]P^1$, and so on.

20. The geometric model for depreciation requires only a single monthly or quarterly depreciation rate. Other models of depreciation may require the estimation of a sequence of vintage depreciation rates. If the estimated annual geometric depreciation rate is $\delta_a$, then the corresponding monthly geometric depreciation rate $\delta$ can be obtained by solving the equation $(1 - \delta)^{12} = 1 - \delta_a$. Similarly, if the estimated annual real interest rate is $r_a^*$, then the corresponding monthly real interest rate $r^*$ can be obtained by solving the equation $(1 + r^*)^{12} = 1 + r_a^*$.

21. Because landlords must set their rent at the beginning of the period (and in fact, they usually set their rent for an extended period of time), if the user cost approach is used to model the economic determinants of market rental rates, then the asset inflation rate $i^0$ should be interpreted as an expected inflation rate rather than an after-the-fact actual inflation rate. This use of ex ante prices in this price measurement context should be contrasted with the preference of national accountants to use actual or ex post prices in the SNA.

Here is a list of some of the problems and difficulties that might arise in implementing a user cost approach to purchases of a consumer durable:[22]

- It is difficult to determine what the relevant nominal interest rate $r^0$ is for each household. If a consumer has to borrow to finance the cost of a durable good purchase, then this interest rate will typically be much higher than the safe rate of return that would be the appropriate opportunity cost rate of return for a consumer who had no need to borrow funds to finance the purchase.[23] It may be necessary to simply use a benchmark interest rate that would be determined by either the government, a national statistical agency, or an accounting standards board.
- It will generally be difficult to determine what the relevant depreciation rate is for the consumer durable.[24]
- *Ex post user costs* based on the formula in equation (8) will be too volatile to be acceptable to users[25] (due to the volatility of the asset inflation rate $i^0$), and hence an *ex ante user cost* concept will have to be used. This creates difficulties, in that different national statistical agencies will generally make different assumptions and use different methods in order to construct forecasted structures and land inflation rates; hence, the resulting ex ante user costs of the durable may not be comparable across countries.[26]
- The user cost formula in equation (8) should be generalized to accom-

22. For additional material on difficulties with the user cost approach, see Diewert (1980, 475–9; 2005a) and Katz (1983, 415–22).

23. Katz (1983, 415–6) comments on the difficulties involved in determining the appropriate rate of interest to use: "There are numerous alternatives: a rate on financial borrowings, on savings, and a weighted average of the two; a rate on nonfinancial investments. e.g., residential housing, perhaps adjusted for capital gains; and the consumer's subjective rate of time preference. Furthermore, there is some controversy about whether it should be the maximum observed rate, the average observed rate, or the rate of return earned on investments that have the same degree of risk and liquidity as the durables whose services are being valued."

24. It is not necessary to assume declining-balance depreciation in the user cost approach: any pattern of depreciation can be accommodated, including one-hoss shay depreciation, where the durable yields a constant stream of services over time until it is scrapped. See Diewert and Lawrence (2000) for some empirical examples of Canada using different assumptions about the form of depreciation. For references to the depreciation literature and for empirical methods for estimating depreciation rates, see Hulten and Wykoff (1981a, 1981b, 1996) and Jorgenson (1996).

25. Goodhart (2001, F351) comments on the practical difficulties of using ex post user costs for housing as follows: "An even more theoretical user cost approach is to measure the cost foregone by living in an owner occupied property as compared with selling it at the beginning of the period and repurchasing it at the end. . . . But this gives the absurd result that as house prices rise, so the opportunity cost falls; indeed the more virulent the inflation of housing asset prices, the more negative would this measure become. Although it has some academic aficionados, this flies in the face of common sense; I am glad to say that no country has adopted this method." As will be seen later, Iceland has in fact adopted a simplified user cost framework.

26. For additional material on the difficulties involved in constructing ex ante user costs, see Diewert (1980, 475–86) and Katz (1983, 419–20). For empirical comparisons of different user cost formulae, see Harper, Berndt, and Wood (1989) and Diewert and Lawrence (2000).

modate various taxes that may be associated with the purchase of a durable or with the continuing use of the durable.[27]

## 12.5 Unique Durable Goods and the User Cost Approach

In the previous section, it was assumed that a newly produced unit of the durable good remained the same from period to period. This means that the various vintages of the durable good repeat themselves from period to period, and hence a particular vintage of the good in the current period can be compared with the same vintage in the next period. In particular, consider the period 0 user cost of a new unit of a durable good $p_0^0$, defined earlier by equation (8). Recall that $P^0$ is the beginning of period 0 purchase price for the durable, $r^0$ is the nominal opportunity cost of capital that the household faces in period 0, $i^0$ is the anticipated period 0 inflation rate for the durable good, and $\delta_0$ is the one-period depreciation rate for a new unit of the durable good. In previous sections, it was assumed that the period 0 user cost $p_0^0$ for a new unit of the durable could be compared with the corresponding period 1 user cost $p_0^1$ for a new unit of the durable purchased in period 1. This period 1 user cost can be defined as follows:

$$(10) \quad p_0^1 = [(1 + r^1) - (1 - \delta_0)(1 + i^1)]P^1 = [r^1 - i^1 + \delta_0(1 + i^1)]P^1.$$

However, many durable goods are produced as *one-of-a-kind* models. For example, a new house may have many features that are specific to that particular house. An exact duplicate of it is unlikely to be built in the following period. Thus, if the user cost for the house is constructed for period 0 using the formula in equation (8), where the new house price $P^0$ plays a key role, then because there will not necessarily be a comparable new house price for the same type of unit in period 1, it will not be possible to construct the period 1 user cost for a house of the same type, $p_0^1$, defined by equation (10), because the comparable new house price $P^1$ will not be available.

Let $P_v^t$ be the second-hand market price at the beginning of period $t$ of a unit of a durable good that is $v$ periods old. Define $\delta_v$ to be the depreciation rate for a unit of the durable good that is $v$ periods old at the beginning of the period under consideration. Using this notation, the user cost of the house (which is now one period old) for period 1, $p_1^1$, can be defined as

27. For example, property taxes are associated with the use of housing services and hence should be included in the user cost formula; see section 12.8.2. As Katz (1983, 418) noted, taxation issues also impact the choice of the interest rate: "Should the rate of return be a before or after tax rate?" From the viewpoint of a household that is not borrowing to finance the purchase of the durable, an after-tax rate of return seems appropriate, but from the point of a leasing firm, a before-tax rate of return seems appropriate. This difference helps to explain why rental equivalence prices for the durable might be higher than user cost prices; see also section 12.9.4.

(11) $$p_1^1 \equiv (1 + r^1)P_1^1 - (1 - \delta_1)(1 + i^1)P_1^1,$$

where $P_1^1$ is the beginning-of-period 1 price for the house that is now one period old, $r^1$ is the nominal opportunity cost of capital that the household faces in period 1, $i^1$ is the anticipated period 1 inflation rate for the durable good, and $\delta_1$ is the one-period depreciation rate for a house that is one period old. For a unique durable good, there is no beginning-of-period 1 price for a new unit of the durable, $P^1$, but it is natural to impute this price as the potentially observable market price for the used durable, $P_1^1$, divided by one, minus the period 0 depreciation rate, $\delta_0$; that is, we define an imputed period 1 price for a new unit of the unique durable as follows:

(12) $$P^1 \equiv \frac{P_1^1}{1 - \delta_0}.$$

If equation (12) is solved for $P_1^1$ and the solution is substituted into the user cost defined by equation (11), then the following expression is obtained for $p_1^1$, *the period 1 user cost of a one-period-old unique consumer durable:*

(13) $$p_1^1 \equiv (1 - \delta_0)[(1 + r^1) - (1 - \delta_1)(1 + i^1)]P^1.$$

If it is further assumed that the unique consumer durable follows the geometric model of depreciation, then $\delta_0$ equals $\delta_1$, and setting both of these depreciation rates equal to a common rate, say $\delta$, leads to the following relationship between *the imputed rental cost in period 1 of a new unit of the consumer durable,* $p_0^1$ and *the period 1 user cost of the one-period-old consumer durable,* $p_1^1$:

(14) $$p_1^0 = \frac{p_1^1}{1 - \delta}.$$

Thus, in order to obtain an imputed rental price for the unique consumer durable for period 1, $p_0^1$, that is *comparable* to the period 0 rental price for a new unit of the consumer durable, $p_0^0$, it is necessary to make a *quality adjustment* to the period 1 rental price for the one-period-old durable, $p_1^1$, by dividing this latter price by one, minus the one-period geometric depreciation rate, $\delta$. This observation has implications for the quality adjustment of observed market rents of houses. Without this type of quality adjustment, observed dwelling unit rents will have a *downward bias,* because the observed rents do not adjust for the gradual lowering of the quality of the unit due to depreciation of the unit.[28]

28. There is an exception to this general observation: if housing depreciation is of the one-hoss shay type, then there is no need to quality adjust observed rents for the same unit over time. However, one-hoss shay depreciation is empirically unlikely in the housing market, because renters are generally willing to pay a rent premium for a new unit over an older unit of the same type. For empirical evidence of this age premium, see Malpezzi, Ozanne, and Thibodeau (1987, 378) and Hoffman and Kurz (2002, 19).

Note also that in order to obtain an imputed purchase price for the unique consumer durable for period 1, $P^1$, that is *comparable* to the period 0 purchase price for a new unit of the consumer durable, $P^0$, it is necessary to make a *quality adjustment* to the period 1 used-asset price for the one-period-old durable, $P_1^1$, by dividing this latter price by one, minus the period 0 depreciation rate, $\delta_0$.[29]

This section is concluded with some observations on the difficulties for economic measurement that occur when it is attempted to determine depreciation rates empirically for unique assets. Consider again equation (12), which allows one to express the potentially observable market price of the unique asset at the beginning of period 1, $P_1^1$, as being equal to $(1 - \delta_0)P^1$, where $P^1$ is a hypothetical period 1 price for a new unit of the unique asset. If it is assumed that this hypothetical period 1 new asset price is equal to the period 0-to-1 inflation rate factor $(1 + i^0)$ multiplied by the observable period 0 asset price, $P^0$, then the following relationship between the two observable asset prices is obtained:

$$P_1^1 = (1 - \delta_0)(1 + i^0)P^0. \quad (15)$$

Thus, the potentially observable period 1 used-asset price $P_1^1$ is equal to the period 0 new asset price $P^0$ multiplied by the product of two factors: $(1 - \delta_0)$, *a quality-adjustment factor* that takes into account the effects of aging on the unique asset, and $(1 + i^0)$, a period-to-period *pure price change factor,* holding quality constant. The problem with unique assets is that cross-sectional information on used-asset prices at any point in time is no longer available to enable one to sort out the separate effects of these two factors. Thus, there is a fundamental identification problem with unique assets; without extra information or assumptions, *it will be impossible to distinguish the separate effects of asset deterioration and asset inflation.*[30] In practice, this identification problem is solved by making somewhat arbitrary assumptions about the form of depreciation that the asset is expected to experience. For example, if the unique asset is a painting by a master artist, then the depreciation rate can be assumed to be very close to zero. As a final example of how assumptions replace detailed knowledge about second-hand prices for all vintages of a unique durable good, we could implement a household

29. This type of quality adjustment to the asset prices for unique consumer durables will always be necessary; that is, there is no exception to this rule, as was the case for one-hoss shay depreciation in the context of quality-adjusting rental prices.

30. Special cases of this fundamental identification problem have been noted in the context of various econometric housing models: "For some purposes one might want to adjust the price index for depreciation. Unfortunately, a depreciation adjustment cannot be readily estimated along with the price index using our regression method. . . . In applying our method, therefore, additional information would be needed in order to adjust the price index for depreciation" (Bailey, Muth, and Nourse 1963, 936). "The price index and depreciation are perfectly collinear, so if one cares about the price index, it is necessary to use external information on the geometric depreciation rate of houses" (Palmquist 2006, 43).

retirement survey for these types of unique assets. The survey could ask the following questions:

- When was the asset purchased?
- What was the purchase price?
- When was the asset sold or scrapped?
- If sold, what was the selling price?

The preceding information is not sufficient to determine depreciation rates for the unique asset. In addition to the preceding information, we will have to make some additional assumptions:

- The form of depreciation across periods would have to be determined by assumption; that is, is depreciation of the one-hoss shay, straight line, or geometric type?
- It will be necessary to assume that the price of a hypothetical new unique asset is proportional to a known price index.

Armed with this information, it is possible to determine depreciation rates for the unique asset and hence to form user costs for these assets.

The problems associated with determining user costs for unique assets for businesses are not as severe as the corresponding problems for households. For example, if we want to construct user costs for business structures, this can be done, because businesses normally have *asset registers* and have information on the time of purchase and sale along with the purchase and sale price. This information could be accessed in investment surveys that also ask questions about asset sales and retirements. Canada,[31] the Netherlands,[32] and New Zealand ask such questions on retirements in their investment surveys, and Japan is following suit.[33] Diewert and Wykoff (2007) indicate how this type of survey can be used to obtain estimates for depreciation rates.

*Housing* is the primary example of a unique asset. In addition to the problems outlined in this section, there are other major problems associated with this particular form of unique asset. These problems will be discussed in the following sections.

## 12.6 The User Cost of Owner-Occupied Housing

*Owner-occupied housing* is typically an example of a *unique* consumer durable, so the material on the quality adjustment of both stock and rental

31. For a description and further references to the Canadian program on estimating depreciation rates, see Baldwin et al. (2005) and Statistics Canada (2007).

32. Actually, since 1991, the Dutch have a separate (mail) survey for enterprises with more than one hundred employees to collect information on discards and retirements, called the Survey on Discards; see Bergen et al. (2005, 8) for a description of the Dutch methods.

33. The Economic and Social Research Institute (ESRI), Cabinet Office of Japan, with the help of Koji Nomura, has implemented a new investment survey that asks questions on retirements.

prices developed in the previous section applies to this commodity. However, owner-occupied housing is also an example of a *composite* good; that is, two distinct commodities are bundled together and sold (or rented) at a single price. The two distinct commodities are the structure and the land that the structure sits on.

The decomposition of housing into structures and land components is important for the SNA, because these two components are treated very differently in the SNA. To model this composite-good situation, consider a particular newly constructed dwelling unit that is purchased at the beginning of period 0. Suppose that the purchase price is $V^0$. This value can be regarded as the sum of (a) a cost of producing the structure, $P_S^0 Q_S^0$, where $Q_S^0$ is the number of square meters of floor space in the structure, and $P_S^0$ is the beginning-of-period 0 price of construction per square meter; and (b) the cost of the land, $P_L^0 Q_L^0$, where $Q_L^0$ is the number of square meters of the land that the structure sits on and the associated yard, and $P_L^0$ is the beginning-of-period 0 price of the land per square meter.[34] Thus, at the beginning of period 0, *the value of the dwelling unit* is $V^0$, defined as follows:

$$V^0 = P_S^0 Q_S^0 + P_L^0 Q_L^0. \tag{16}$$

Suppose that the anticipated price of a unit of a new structure at the beginning of period 1 is $P_S^{1a}$ and that the anticipated price of a unit of land at the beginning of period 1 is $P_L^{1a}$. We define the *period 0 anticipated inflation rates for new structures and land,* $i_s^0$ and $i_L^0$, respectively, as follows:

$$1 + i_S^0 \equiv \frac{P_S^{1a}}{P_S^0}; \tag{17}$$

$$1 + i_L^0 \equiv \frac{P_L^{1a}}{P_L^0}. \tag{18}$$

Let $\delta_0$ be the period 0 depreciation rate for the structure. Then, the anticipated beginning-of-period 1 value for the structure and the associated land is equal to

$$V^{1a} = P_S^{1a}(1 - \delta_0)Q_S^0 + P_L^{1a} Q_L^0. \tag{19}$$

Note the presence of the depreciation term $(1 - \delta_0)$ on the right-hand side of equation (19). Should this term be associated with the expected beginning-of-period 1 price for a new unit of structures $P_S^{1a}$ or with the structures quantity term $Q_S^0$? On the principle that like should be compared to like for prices, it seems preferable to associate $(1 - \delta_0)$ with the quantity term $Q_S^0$. This is consistent with the treatment of unique assets that was suggested in the previous section; that is, the initial quantity of structures

34. If the dwelling unit is part of a multiple-unit structure, then the land associated with it will be the appropriate share of the total land space.

$Q_S^0$ should be quality adjusted downward to the amount $(1 - \delta_0)\, Q_S^0$ at the beginning of period 1.

Now, we calculate the cost (including the imputed opportunity cost of capital $r^0$) of buying the dwelling unit at the beginning of period 0 and (hypothetically) selling it at the end of period 0. The following *end-of-period 0 user cost or imputed rental cost* $R^0$ for the dwelling unit is obtained using equations (16) through (19):

$$(20)\quad R^0 \equiv V^0(1 + r^0) - V^{1a}$$
$$= [P_S^0 Q_S^0 + P_L^0 Q_L^0](1 + r^0) - [P_S^{1a}(1 - \delta_0)Q_S^0 + P_L^{1a} Q_L^0]$$
$$= [P_S^0 Q_S^0 + P_L^0 Q_L^0](1 + r^0) - [P_S^0(1 + i_S^0)(1 - \delta_0)Q_S^0 + P_L^0(1 + i_L^0)Q_L^0]$$
$$= p_S^0 Q_S^0 + p_L^0 Q_L^0,$$

where separate period 0 *user costs of structures and land,* $p_S^0$ and $p_L^0$, are defined as follows:

$$(21)\quad p_S^0 = [(1 + r^0) - (1 + i_S^0)(1 - \delta_0)]P_S^0 = [r^0 - i_S^0 + \delta_0(1 + i_S^0)]P_S^0;$$

$$(22)\quad p_L^0 = [(1 + r^0) - (1 + i_L^0)]P_L^0 = [r^0 - i_L^0]P_L^0.$$

Note that the preceding algebra indicates some of the major determinants of market rents for rental properties.[35] The user cost formulae defined by equations (21) and (22) can be further simplified if the same approximations that were made in section 12.4 are made here (recall equation [9]); that is, assume that the terms $r^0 - i_S^0$ and $r^0 - i_L^0$ can be approximated by a real interest rate $r^{0*}$, and neglect the small term $\delta_0$ multiplied by $i_S^0$ in equation (21). Then, the user costs defined by equations (21) and (22) simplify to:

$$(23)\quad p_S^0 = [(r^{0*} + \delta_0)]P_S^0;$$

$$(24)\quad p_L^0 = r^{0*}\, P_L^0.$$

Thus, *the imputed rent for an owner-occupied dwelling unit* is made up of three main costs:

- The real opportunity cost of the financial capital tied up in the structure
- The real opportunity cost of the financial capital tied up in the land
- The depreciation cost of the structure

This simplified approach to the user cost of housing can be even further simplified by assuming that the ratio of the quantity of land to structures is fixed, so the aggregate user cost of housing is equal to $[r^{0*} + \delta]P_H^0$, where $P_H$ is a quality-adjusted housing price index that is based on all properties sold

35. Looking at equation (22), it can be seen that the land user cost defined by this equation could be negative if the anticipated rate of land price appreciation, $i_L^0$, is greater than the beginning of the period opportunity cost of capital, $r^0$. We will discuss possible solutions to this complication in section 12.11.

in the country to households during the period under consideration, and $\delta$ is a geometric depreciation rate that applies to the composite of household structures and land. This super-simplified approach is used by Iceland (see Gudnason [2003, 28–29] and Gudnason and Jónsdóttir [2009]).[36] A variant of this approach is used by the BEA: Lebow and Rudd (2003, 168) note that the U.S. national accounts imputation for the services of owner-occupied housing is obtained by applying rent-to-value ratios for tenant-occupied housing to the stock of owner-occupied housing. The rent-to-value ratio can be regarded as an estimate of the applicable real interest rate plus the depreciation rate.

Now, we can calculate the cost (including the imputed opportunity cost of capital $r^1$) of buying the used dwelling unit at the beginning of period 1 and (hypothetically) selling it at the end of period 1. Thus, at the beginning of period 1, the value of the depreciated dwelling unit is $V^1$, defined as

$$V^1 = P_S^1(1 - \delta_0)Q_S^0 + P_L^1 Q_L^0, \tag{25}$$

where $P_S^1$ is the beginning-of-period 1 construction price for building a new dwelling unit of the same type, and $P_L^1$ is the beginning-of-period 1 price of land for the dwelling unit. Note that equation (25) is an *end-of-period 0 ex post or actual value* of the dwelling unit, whereas the similar expression in equation (19) defined a *beginning-of-period 0 ex ante or anticipated value* of the dwelling unit at the end of period 0 or the beginning of period 1.

Suppose that the anticipated price of a unit of a new structure at the beginning of period 2 is $P_S^{2a}$ and that the anticipated price of a unit of land at the beginning of period 2 is $P_L^{2a}$. We define *the period 1 anticipated inflation rates for new structures and land,* $i_S^1$ and $i_L^1$, respectively, as follows:

$$1 + i_S^1 \equiv \frac{P_S^{2a}}{P_S^1}; \tag{26}$$

$$1 + i_L^1 \equiv \frac{P_L^{2a}}{P_L^1}. \tag{27}$$

Let $\delta_1$ be the period 1 depreciation rate for the structure. Then, *the anticipated beginning-of-period 2 value for the structure and the associated land* is equal to

$$V^{2a} = P_S^{2a}(1 - \delta_0)(1 - \delta_1)Q_S^0 + P_L^{2a}Q_L^0. \tag{28}$$

36. The real interest rate that is used is approximately 4 percent per year, and the combined depreciation rate for land and structures is assumed to equal 1.25 percent per year. The depreciation rate for structures alone is estimated to be 1.5 percent per year. Property taxes are accounted for separately in the Icelandic CPI. Housing price information is provided by the State Evaluation Board (SEB) based on property sales data of both new and old housing. The SEB also estimates the value of the housing stock and land in Iceland, using a hedonic regression model based on property sales data. The value of each household's dwelling is collected in the Household Budget Survey.

The following end-of-period 1 *user cost or imputed rental cost $R_1^1$ for a one-period-old dwelling unit* is obtained using equations (25) through (28):

$$
\begin{aligned}
(29)\qquad R_1^1 &\equiv V^1(1+r^1) - V^{2a} \\
&= [P_S^1(1-\delta_0)Q_S^0 + P_L^1 Q_L^0](1+r^1) \\
&\quad - [P_S^{2a}(1-\delta_0)(1-\delta_1)Q_S^0 + P_L^{2a}Q_L^0] \\
&= [P_S^1(1-\delta_0)Q_S^0 + P_L^1 Q_L^0](1+r^1) \\
&\quad - [P_S^1(1+i_S^1)(1-\delta_0)(1-\delta_1)Q_S^0 + P_L^1(1+i_L^1)Q_L^0] \\
&= p_S^1(1-\delta_0)Q_S^0 + p_L^1 Q_L^0,
\end{aligned}
$$

where the period 1 *user costs of one-period-old structures and land,* $p_{S1}^1$ and $p_L^1$, are defined as follows:

$$(30)\qquad p_S^1 = [(1+r^1) - (1+i_S^1)(1-\delta_1)]P_S^1 = [r^1 - i_S^1 + \delta_1(1+i_S^1)]P_S^1;$$

$$(31)\qquad p_L^1 = [(1+r^1) - (1+i_L^1)]P_L^1 = [r^1 - i_L^1]P_L^1.$$

Now compare the end-of-period 0 imputed rent $R^0$ for the structure and the underlying land, defined by equation (20), and the associated period 0 user costs of structures and land ($p_S^0$ and $p_L^0$, defined by equations [21] and [22]), with the corresponding end-of-period 1 imputed rent $R_1^1$ for the one period older structure and the underlying land, defined by equation (29), and the associated period 1 user costs of structures and land ($p_S^1$ and $p_L^1$, defined by equations [30] and [31]). These period 0 and period 1 user costs are comparable and can be used in price indexes. Also, the period 0 and period 1 quantity of land is the constant amount of land, $Q_L^0$, and this is also comparable and can be used as a weighting factor for the user cost of land in a price index. The only tricky aspect to note is that in order to make the structures quantity comparable for price index purposes, the period 1 quantity of structures associated with the dwelling unit under consideration should be set equal to $(1-\delta_0)Q_S^0$, rather than leaving it at the period 0 level, $Q_S^0$. This is the same point that was made in the previous section, but in this section, the complications due to the fact that housing services are a *mixture* of structure and land services are taken into account.

It is evident that the main drivers for the user costs of structures and land are a price index for new dwelling construction, $P_S^t$, and a price index for residential land, $P_L^t$. Most statistical agencies have a constant-quality price index for new residential structures, because this index is required in the national accounts in order to deflate investment expenditures on residential structures. This index could be used as an approximation to $P_S^t$.[37] The national accounts also require an imputation for the services of owner-occupied housing, and thus the constant-quality price component of this

37. This index may only be an approximation, because it covers the construction of rental properties as well as owner-occupied dwellings.

imputation may be suitable for Consumer Price Index purposes.[38] If the national accounts division also computes quarterly real balance sheets for the economy, then a price index for residential land may be available to the prices division. However, even if this is the case, there will be problems in producing this price index for land on a timely basis and at a monthly frequency.[39] Another possible source of information on land prices may be found in land title registry offices and in the records of real estate firms.

In the following section, the problems involved in obtaining a constant-quality price index for the asset value (or stock value) of a housing unit are examined in a bit more detail. Recall that this type of index is required for both the acquisitions and user cost approaches (and it may be required for the rental equivalence approach as well, if imputed rents are constructed using the rent-to-value ratio method used by the BEA).

## 12.7 The Empirical Estimation of Housing Price Indexes

There are three broad approaches[40] to constructing constant-quality price indexes for the *purchase price* of a housing unit: the repeat sales approach, the stratification approach, and the hedonic regression approach.

These approaches will be discussed next. The hedonic regression approach can also be applied to the problem of constructing constant-quality indexes of rent.

### 12.7.1 The Repeat Sales Approach

The *repeat sales approach* is due to Bailey, Muth, and Nourse (1963), who saw their procedure as a generalization of the *chained matched-model methodology* that was used by the early pioneers in the construction of real estate price indexes, such as Wyngarden (1927) and Wenzlick (1952). We will not describe the technical details of the method, but note that the method uses information on properties that trade on the market more than once over the sample period.[41] By utilizing information on identical properties that trade

38. However, the national accounts imputation for the services of OOH will only be produced on a quarterly basis, so some additional work will be required to produce a price deflator on a monthly basis. Also, even though the SNA recommends that the imputation for the services of OOH be based on the rental equivalent method, it may be the case that the imputation covers only the imputed depreciation on the structures part of OOH. As was pointed out earlier, there are two other important additional components that should also be included in OOH services: namely, the imputed real interest on the structures and the land on which the structures sit. These latter two components of imputed expenditures are likely to be considerably larger than the depreciation component.

39. Another source of information on the value of residential land may be available from the local property tax authorities, particularly if properties are assessed at market values.

40. These approaches are discussed in more detail in Diewert (2009).

41. See Case and Shiller (1989) and Diewert (2003c, 31–39) for detailed technical descriptions of the method. Diewert showed how the repeat sales method is related to Summers' (1973) country product dummy model used in international price comparisons and the product dummy variable hedonic regression model proposed by Aizcorbe, Corrado, and Doms (2001).

more than one period, the repeat sales method attempts to hold the quality of the properties constant over time.

We now discuss some of the advantages and disadvantages of the repeat sales method.[42] The *main advantages* of the repeat sales model are as follows:

- Source data is available from administrative records on the resale of the same property, so no imputations are involved.
- The results are reproducible; that is, different statisticians who are given the same data on the sales of housing units will come up with the same estimate of quality-adjusted price change.[43]

The *main disadvantages* of the repeat sales model are as follows:

- It does not use all of the available information on property sales; it uses only information on units that have sold more than once during the sample period.
- It cannot deal adequately with depreciation of the dwelling unit or structure.
- It cannot deal adequately with units that have undergone major repairs or renovations.[44] Conversely, a general hedonic regression model for housing or structures can adjust for the effects of renovations and extensions if (real) expenditures on renovations and extensions are known at the time of sale (or rental).[45]

42. Throughout this section, we will discuss the relative merits of the different methods that have been suggested for constructing property price indexes. For a similar discussion, see Hoffmann and Lorenz (2006, 2–6).

43. Hedonic regression models suffer from a reproducibility problem; that is, different statisticians will use different characteristics variables, will use different functional forms, and will make different stochastic specifications, possibly leading to quite different results. However, the repeat sales model is not as reproducible in practice as indicated in the main text, because in some variants of the method, houses that are flipped (sold very rapidly) and houses that have not sold for long periods are excluded from the regressions. The exact method for excluding these observations may vary from time to time, leading to a lack of reproducibility.

44. Case and Shiller (1989) used a variant of the repeat sales method using U.S. data on house sales in four major cities over the years 1970 to 1986. They attempted to deal with the depreciation and renovation problems as follows: "The tapes contain actual sales prices and other information about the homes. We extracted from the tapes for each city a file of data on houses sold twice for which there was no apparent quality change and for which conventional mortgages applied" (Case and Shiller 1989, 125–6). It is sometimes argued that renovations are approximately equal to depreciation. While this may be true in the aggregate, it certainly is not true for individual dwelling units, because over time, many units are demolished.

45. However, usually information on maintenance and renovation expenditures is not available in the context of estimating a hedonic regression model for housing. Malpezzi, Ozanne, and Thibodeau (1987, 375–6) comment on this problem as follows: "If all units are identically constructed, inflation is absent, and the rate of maintenance and repair expenditures is the same for all units, then precise measurement of the rate of depreciation is possible by observing the value or rent of two or more units of different ages. . . . To accurately estimate the effects of aging on values and rents, it is necessary to control for inflation, quality differences in housing

- The method cannot be used if indexes are required for very fine classifications of the type of property due to a lack of observations. In particular, if monthly property price indexes are required, the method may fail due to a lack of market sales for smaller categories of property.
- In principle, estimates for past price change obtained by the repeat sales method should be updated as new transaction information becomes available. Thus, the repeat sales property price index may be subject to never-ending revision.

We turn now to another class of methods used to form constant-quality property price indexes.

### 12.7.2 Stratification Methods

Possibly the simplest approach to the construction of a property price index is to *stratify* or decompose the market into separate types of property, calculate the mean (or more commonly, the median) price for all properties transacted in that cell for the current period and the base period, and then use the ratio of the means as a real estate price index.

The problem with this method can be explained as follows: if there are too many cells in the stratification, then there may not be a sufficient number of transactions in any given period in order to form an accurate cell average price, but if there are too few cells in the stratification, then the resulting cell averages will suffer from *unit-value bias;* that is, the mix of properties sold in each period within each cell may change dramatically from period to period, and thus the resulting stratified indexes do not hold quality constant.

The stratification method can work well; for example, see Gudnason and Jónsdóttir (2007, 3–5), where they note that they work with some eight thousand to ten thousand real estate transactions per year in Iceland, which is a sufficient number of observations to be able to produce thirty monthly subindexes.

The Australian Bureau of Statistics[46] (ABS) is also experimenting with stratification techniques in order to produce constant-quality housing price indexes. The ABS clustering procedures are very interesting and novel, but one must be a bit cautious in interpreting the resulting price changes, because any individual suburb might contain a mixture of properties, and thus the resulting indexes may be subject to a certain amount of unit-value bias.[47] The *main advantages* of the stratification method are as follows:

units, and location. The hedonic technique controls for differences in dwelling quality and inflation rates but cannot control for most differences in maintenance (except to the extent that they are correlated with location)."

46. See Branson (2006).

47. However, Prasad and Richards (2006) show that the stratification method applied to Australian house price data gave virtually the same results as a hedonic model that had locational explanatory variables.

- The method is conceptually acceptable, but it depends crucially on the choice of stratification variables.
- The method is reproducible, conditional on an agreed list of stratification variables.
- Housing price indexes can be constructed for different types and locations of housing.
- The method is relatively easy to explain to users.

The *main disadvantages* of the stratification method are as follows:

- The method cannot deal adequately with depreciation of the dwelling units or structures.
- The method cannot deal adequately with units that have undergone major repairs or renovations.
- The method requires some information on housing characteristics, so sales transactions can be allocated to the correct cell in the classification scheme.[48]
- If the classification scheme is very coarse, then there may be some unit-value bias in the indexes.
- If the classification scheme is very fine, the detailed cell indexes may be subject to a considerable amount of sampling variability due to small sample sizes.
- The method cannot decompose a property price index into structure and land components.

My overall evaluation of the stratification method is that it can be quite satisfactory, if an appropriate level of detail is chosen for the number of cells, the index is adjusted using other information for depreciation and renovations bias, and a decomposition of the index into structure and land components is not required.

It is well known that stratification methods can be regarded as special cases of general hedonic regressions,[49] so we now turn to this more general technique.

### 12.7.3 Hedonic Methods

Although there are several variants of the hedonic regression technique, the basic model regresses the logarithm of the sale price of the property on the price-determining characteristics of the property, and a time dummy variable is added for each period in the regression (except the base period).[50]

48. If no information on housing characteristics is used, then the method is subject to tremendous unit-value bias.

49. See Diewert (2003a), who showed that stratification techniques or the use of dummy variables can be viewed as a nonparametric regression technique.

50. The main features of a general hedonic regression model were laid out in Court (1939). This publication was not readily available to researchers, so the technique was not used widely until the work of Griliches (1971a, 1971b) popularized the technique. For a recent survey of

Once the estimation has been completed, these time dummy coefficients can be exponentiated and turned into an index.[51]

Because the method assumes that information on the characteristics of the properties sold is available, the data can be stratified, and a separate regression can be run for each important class of property. Thus, the hedonic regression method can be used to produce a family of indexes.[52]

The issues associated with running *weighted* hedonic regressions are rather subtle, and the recent literature on this topic will not be reviewed here.[53]

However, one main advantage of the hedonic regression approach to constructing constant-quality price indexes for housing is that it can, in principle, tease out the separate contributions of the structure and of the land under the structure to the composite rental price or purchase price for the property. We will now explain how this can be done for purchase price indexes, but the rental price case is similar.[54]

If we momentarily think like a property developer who is planning to build a structure on a particular property, the total cost of the property after the structure is completed will be equal to the floor space area of the structure, say $A$ square feet, multiplied by the building cost per square foot, say $\alpha$, plus the cost of the land, which will be equal to the cost per square foot, say $\beta$, multiplied by the area of the land site, $B$. Now think of a sample of properties of the same general type, which have prices $p_n^0$ in period 0 and structure areas $A_n^0$ and land areas $B_n^0$ for $n = 1, \ldots, N(0)$, and these prices

the hedonic regression technique for making quality adjustments, see Triplett (2004). For some recent examples of hedonic regressions for housing, see Gouriéroux and Laferrère (2006) and Li, Prud'homme, and Yu (2006).

51. An alternative approach to the hedonic method is to estimate separate hedonic regressions for both of the periods compared (i.e., for the base and current period). Predicted prices can then be generated in each period using the estimated hedonic regressions based on a constant characteristics set—say, the characteristics of the base period. A ratio of the geometric means of the estimated prices in each period would yield a pure price comparison based on a constant base-period set of characteristics. A hedonic index based on a constant current-period characteristic could also be compiled, as could such indexes based on a symmetric use of base- and current-period information. Heravi and Silver (2007) outline alternative formulations, and Silver and Heravi (2007) provide a formal analysis of the difference between this approach and that of the time dummy method for the case of one characteristic. Diewert, Heravi, and Silver (see chapter 4 of this volume) provide a generalization to an arbitrary number of characteristics.

52. This property of the hedonic regression method also applies to the stratification method. The main difference between the two methods is that continuous variables can appear in hedonic regressions (like the area of the structure and the area of the lot size), whereas the stratification method can only work with discrete ranges for the independent variables in the regression.

53. Basically, this recent literature makes connections between weighted hedonic regressions and traditional index number formulae that use weights; see Diewert (2003b, 2005b, 2006), de Haan (2003, 2004), and Silver and Heravi (2003, 2007). It is worth noting that a perceived advantage of the stratification method is that *median* price changes can be measured, as opposed to *arithmetic mean* ones that are implicit in, say, an ordinary least squares estimator. However, regression estimates can also be derived from robust estimators from which the parameter estimates for the price change will be similar to a median.

54. The following exposition is based on Diewert (2009).

are equal to costs of the type just described, multiplied by error terms $\eta_n^0$, which we assume have mean 1. This leads to the following hedonic regression model for period 0, where $\alpha$ and $\beta$ are the parameters to be estimated in the regression:[55]

$$(32) \qquad p_n^0 = [\alpha A_n^0 + \beta B_n^0]\eta_n^0;$$
$$n = 1, \ldots, N(0).$$

Taking logarithms of both sides of equation (32) leads to the following traditional additive errors regression model:[56]

$$(33) \qquad \ln p_n^0 = \ln[\alpha A_n^0 + \beta B_n^0] + \varepsilon_n^0;$$
$$n = 1, \ldots, N(0),$$

where the new error terms are defined as $\varepsilon_n^0 \equiv \ln \eta_n^0$ for $n = 1, \ldots, N(0)$ and are assumed to have 0 means and constant variances.

Now, consider the situation in a subsequent period $t$. The price per square meter of this type of structure will have changed from $\alpha$ to $\alpha\gamma^t$, and the land cost per square meter will have changed from $\beta$ to $\beta\delta^t$, where we interpret $\gamma^t$ as the *period 0 to period t price index for the type of structure* and $\delta^t$ as the *period 0 to period t price index for the land that is associated with this type of structure.* The period $t$ counterparts to equations (32) and (33) are:

$$(34) \qquad p_n^t = [\alpha\gamma^t A_n^t + \beta\delta^t B_n^t]\eta_n^t;$$
$$n = 1, \ldots, N(t);$$

$$(35) \qquad \ln p_n^t = \ln[\alpha\gamma^t A_n^t + \beta\delta^t B_n^t] + \varepsilon_n^t;$$
$$n = 1, \ldots, N(t),$$

where $\varepsilon_n^t \equiv \ln \eta_n^t$ for $n = 1, \ldots, N(t)$, the period $t$ property prices are $p_n^t$, and the corresponding structure and land areas are $A_n^t$ and $B_n^t$ for $n = 1, \ldots, N(t)$.

Equations (33) and (35) can be run as a system of nonlinear hedonic regressions, and estimates can be obtained for the four parameters, $\alpha$, $\beta$, $\gamma^t$, and $\delta^t$. The main parameters of interest are of course $\gamma^t$ and $\delta^t$, which can be interpreted as price indexes for the price of a square meter of this type of structure and for the price per meter squared of the underlying land, respectively.

This very basic nonlinear hedonic regression framework can be generalized to encompass the traditional array of characteristics that are used in

55. Multiplicative errors with constant variances are more plausible than additive errors with constant variances; that is, it is more likely that expensive properties have relatively large absolute errors compared to very inexpensive properties. The multiplicative specification for the errors will be consistent with this phenomenon.

56. However, note that this model is not linear in the unknown parameters to be estimated.

real estate hedonic regressions. Thus, suppose that we can associate with each property $n$ that is transacted in each period $t$ a list of $K$ characteristics $X^t_{n1}, X^t_{n2}, \ldots, X^t_{nK}$ that are price-determining characteristics for the structure and a similar list of $M$ characteristics $Y^t_{n1}, Y^t_{n2}, \ldots, Y^t_{nM}$ that are price-determining characteristics for the type of land that sits underneath the structure. The equations that generalize equations (33) and (35) to the present setup are the following ones:

$$(36)\quad \ln p^0_n = \ln\left\{\left[\alpha_0 + \sum_{k=1}^{K} X^0_{nk}\alpha_k\right]A^0_n + \left[\beta_0 + \sum_{m=1}^{M} Y^0_{nm}\beta_m\right]B^0_n\right\} + \varepsilon^0_n;\quad n = 1, \ldots, N(0);$$

$$(37)\quad \ln p^t_n = \ln\left\{\gamma^t\left[\alpha_0 + \sum_{k=1}^{K} X^t_{nk}\alpha_k\right]A^t_n + \delta^t\left[\beta_0 + \sum_{m=1}^{M} Y^t_{nm}\beta_m\right]B^t_n\right\} + \varepsilon^t_n;\quad n = 1, \ldots, N(t),$$

where the parameters to be estimated are now the $K + 1$ quality of structure parameters, $\alpha_0, \alpha_1, \ldots, \alpha_K$, the $M + 1$ quality of land parameters, $\beta_0, \beta_1, \ldots, \beta_M$, the period $t$ price index for structures parameter $\gamma^t$, and the period $t$ price index for the land underlying the structures parameter $\delta^t$. Note that $[\alpha_0 + \sum_{k=1}^{K} X^0_{nk}\alpha_k]$ in equations (36) and (37) replaces the single structures quality parameter $\alpha$ in equations (33) and (35), and $[\beta_0 + \sum_{m=1}^{M} Y^0_{nm}\beta_m]$ in equations (35) and (37) replaces the single land quality parameter $\beta$ in equations (31) and (33).

In order to illustrate how $X$ and $Y$ variables can be formed, we consider the list of exogenous variables in the hedonic housing regression model reported by Li, Prud'homme, and Yu (2006, 23). The following variables in their list of exogenous variables can be regarded as variables that affect structure quality; that is, they are $X$-type variables: number of reported bedrooms, number of reported bathrooms, number of garages, number of fireplaces, age of the unit, age squared of the unit, exterior finish is brick or not, dummy variable for new units, unit has hardwood floors or not, heating fuel is natural gas or not, unit has a patio or not, unit has a central built-in vacuum-cleaning system or not, unit has an indoor or outdoor swimming pool or not, unit has a hot tub unit or not, unit has a sauna or not, and unit has air-conditioning or not. The following variables can be regarded as variables that affect the quality of the land; that is, they are $Y$-type location variables: unit is at the intersection of two streets or not (corner lot or not), unit is at a cul-de-sac or not, shopping center is nearby or not, and various suburb location dummy variables.[57]

57. Of course, in practice, some of the land or location variables could act as proxies for unobserved structure quality variables. There are also some interesting conceptual problems associated with the treatment of rental apartments and owner-occupied apartments or condominiums. Obviously, separate hedonic regressions would be appropriate for apartments, because their structural characteristics are quite different from detached housing. For rental apartments, the sale price of the apartment can be the dependent variable, and there will be associated amounts of structure area and land area. For a condo sale, the price of the single

The nonlinear hedonic regression model defined by equations (36) and (37) is very flexible and can accomplish what none of the other approaches to obtaining constant-quality purchase price indexes for housing were able to accomplish: namely, a decomposition of a property price index into structures and land components. However, this model has a cost compared to the usual hedonic regression model that appears in the housing literature: these models are generally linear in the unknown parameters to be estimated, whereas the model defined by equations (36) and (37) is nonlinear. It remains to be seen whether such a nonlinear model can be estimated successfully for a large data set.[58]

It is useful to discuss the merits of the hedonic regression method compared to other methods for purchase price indexes for housing.

The *main advantages* of the hedonic regression method are as follows:

- Property price indexes can be constructed for different types and locations of the property class under consideration.
- The method is probably the most efficient method for making use of the available data; that is, the method uses *all* of the information on housing sales in each sample period in a nontrivial way, whereas the repeat sales model does not use any information at all on isolated sales that take place in only one of the sample periods.
- The method can be modified to give a decomposition of property prices into land and structures components; none of the other methods previously described can do this.
- If the list of property characteristics is sufficiently detailed so that, for example, it can be determined whether major maintenance projects have been undertaken and when they were done (such as a new roof), then it is possible to deal adequately with the *depreciation and renovations problem,* and a byproduct of the hedonic regression method would be fairly accurate depreciation rates for housing structures.

If the age of the structure was a characteristic in the hedonic regression and if there were no renovations made to the structure since its birth, then it would be straightforward to use the results of the hedonic regression in order to obtain scientific- or evidence-based estimates of structure depreciation rates by type of housing. However, as noted earlier, the econometrician will not have information on additions and renovations on each property at his or her disposal. Thus, hedonic regressions that have age as a character-

unit is the dependent variable, while the dependent variables in the bare-bones model would be the structure area of the apartment, plus the apartment's share of commonly owned facilities, plus the apartment's share of the lot area. In the end, we want to be able to impute the value of the property into land and structure components, so the hedonic regression should be set up to accomplish this task.

58. Of course, large data sets can be transformed into smaller data sets if we run separate hedonic regressions for various property strata!

istic frequently find that the value of the property increases once a certain age is reached. This phenomenon is likely due to the effects of renovations and remodeling,[59] and because these renovation expenditures are generally unknown and hence cannot be entered as an explanatory variable for the hedonic regression, hedonic regression estimates of depreciation may be severely biased downward. A related problem is due to the fact that some homeowners will not undertake normal maintenance expenditures[60] on their property, and as a result, depreciation will be abnormal on their properties. We term these effects the *depreciation and renovations problem* that causes problems for all approaches to the construction of constant-quality housing price indexes. However, the most promising method for overcoming these problems is the hedonic regression approach with renovation and maintenance expenditures as explanatory variables. We will pursue this approach a bit further in section 12.8.4.

The *main disadvantages* of the hedonic method are as follows:

- The method is data intensive (i.e., it requires information on property characteristics), and thus it is relatively expensive to implement.
- The method is not entirely reproducible; that is, different statisticians will enter different property characteristics into the regression,[61] will assume different functional forms for the regression equation,[62] will make different stochastic specifications, and perhaps will choose different transformations of the dependent variable,[63] all of which may lead to different estimates of the amount of overall price change.
- The method is not easy to explain to users.

Our conclusion at this point is that there is no completely satisfactory solution to the problems involved in constructing constant-quality price indexes for the stock of owner-occupied housing. The hedonic regression approach seems to be superior in principle to the repeat sales approach, because the latter approach cannot deal adequately with depreciation and renovations to the structure of a housing unit. However, in practice, the hedonic regression approach has limitations due to its lack of reproduc-

59. If a very old dwelling unit is not renovated, then it will be demolished. Thus, very long-lived housing structures will generally have extensive renovations made to them.

60. "In following this sequence, it may appear as though there are many separate and distinct entities called 'capital.' However, a comparison of each case reveals the following unity: all aspects of capital ultimately are derived from the decision to defer current consumption in order to enhance or maintain expected future consumption" (Hulten 2006, 195). Following Hulten, it would be conceptually correct to capitalize all home maintenance expenditures. However, national income accountants capitalize only above-normal maintenance expenditures.

61. Note that the same criticism can be applied to stratification methods; that is, different analysts will come up with different stratifications.

62. Functional form problems for hedonic regressions are discussed in Diewert (2003a, 2003b).

63. For example, the dependent variable could be the sales price of the property, its logarithm, or the sales price divided by the area of the structure, and so on.

ibility and the lack of information on repairs and renovations. But despite these limitations, the hedonic regression method is probably the best method that could be used in order to construct constant-quality price indexes for various types of property.[64]

Hedonic regression analysis can also be applied to the construction of constant-quality indexes of market rents for owner-occupied structures. Crone, Nakamura, and Voith (2000) have written a very useful paper using hedonic techniques to estimate both a rent index and a selling-price index for housing in the United States. They follow the BEA methodology for rental equivalence by suggesting that *capitalization rates* (i.e., the ratio of the market rent of a housing property to its selling price) can be applied to an index of housing selling prices in order to obtain an imputed rent index for OOH. Note that equation (8) (after dividing both sides of the equation by the asset price of the house) provides a theoretical foundation for this methodological approach; the transformed equation shows that the capitalization rate is a function of the nominal interest rate, the depreciation rate, and the expected asset inflation over the period. If these factors are relatively constant over time, then the BEA methodological approach is justified.

There are many other difficulties associated with measuring the price and quantity of OOH services. The following section discusses some of the problems involved in modeling the costs of certain expenditures that are tied to the ownership of a home.

## 12.8 The Treatment of Costs Tied to Owner-Occupied Housing

There are many costs that are quite directly tied to home ownership. However, it is not always clear how these costs can be decomposed into price and quantity components. Several of these cost components are listed next, and some suggestions for forming their associated prices are suggested.

### 12.8.1 The Treatment of Mortgage Interest Costs

The derivation of the user cost or expected rental price that an owner of a home should charge for the use of the dwelling unit for one period implicitly assumed that the owner had no mortgage interest costs, so the interest rate $r^0$ referred to the owner's opportunity cost of equity capital. In this section, the case where the owner has a mortgage on the property is considered.

Recall the notation in section 12.6 where the user cost or imputed rental cost, $R^0$, for an equity-financed dwelling unit was obtained (see equation [20]). Suppose now that the property purchase is partly financed by a mortgage of $M^0$ dollars at the beginning of period 0. Let $f^0$ be the fraction of

64. This evaluation agrees with that of Hoffmann and Lorenz: "As far as quality adjustment is concerned, the future will certainly belong to hedonic method" (2006, 15).

the beginning-of-period 0 market value of the property that is financed by the mortgage, so that

(38) $$M^0 = f^0V^0 = f^0[P_S^0Q_S^0 + P_L^0Q_L^0].$$

Let the one-period nominal mortgage interest rate be $r_M^0$. The owner's period 0 benefits of owning the dwelling unit remain the same as in section 12.6 and are equal to $V^{1a}$, defined by equation (19). However, the period 0 costs are now made up of an explicit mortgage interest cost equal to $M^0(1 + r_M^0)$, plus an imputed equity cost equal to $(1 - f^0)V^0(1 + r^0)$. Thus, the new imputed opportunity cost for using the property during period 0 is now

(39) $$\begin{aligned} R^0 &\equiv (1 - f^0)V^0(1 + r^0) + M^0(1 + r_M^0) - V^{1a} \\ &= (1 - f^0)[P_S^0Q_S^0 + P_L^0Q_L^0](1 + r^0) + f^0[P_S^0Q_S^0 + P_L^0Q_L^0](1 + r_M^0) \\ &\quad - [P_S^{1a}(1 - \delta_0)Q_S^0 + P_L^{1a}Q_L^0] \\ &= p_S^{0*}Q_S^0 + p_L^{0*}Q_L^0, \end{aligned}$$

where the new mortgage interest-adjusted period 0 *user costs of structures and land,* $p_S{}^{0*}$ and $p_L{}^{0*}$, are defined as follows:

(40) $$\begin{aligned} p_S^{0*} &\equiv [(1 + r^0)(1 - f^0) + (1 + r_M^0)f^0 - (1 + i_S^0)(1 - \delta_0)]P_S^0 \\ &= [(r^0 - i_S^0)(1 - f^0) + (r_M^0 - i_S^0)f^0 + \delta_0(1 + i_S^0)]P_S^0; \end{aligned}$$

(41) $$\begin{aligned} p_L^{0*} &\equiv [(1 + r^0)(1 - f^0) + (1 + r_M^0)f^0 - (1 + i_L^0)]P_S^0 \\ &= [(r^0 - i_L^0)(1 - f^0) + (r_M^0 - i_L^0)f^0]P_S^0. \end{aligned}$$

Comparing the new user costs for structures and land defined by equations (40) and (41) to the corresponding equity-financed user costs defined by equations (21) and (22) in section 12.6, it can be seen that the old equity opportunity cost of capital $r^0$ is now replaced by a weighted average of this equity opportunity cost and the mortgage interest rate, $r^0(1 - f^0) + r_M^0f^0$, where $f^0$ is the fraction of the beginning-of-period 0 value of the dwelling unit that is financed by the mortgage.

Central bankers often object to the inclusion of mortgage interest in a consumer price index. However, examination of the last equation in equations (40) and in (41) shows that the *nominal* mortgage interest rate $r_M^0$ is offset by *anticipated price inflation* in the price of structures—$i_S^0$ in equation (40)—and in the price of land—$i_L^0$ in equation (41)—so as usual, what counts in these user cost formulae are *real* interest costs rather than *nominal* ones.

### 12.8.2 The Treatment of Property Taxes

Recall the user costs of structures and land defined by equations (21) and (22) in section 12.6. It is now supposed that the owner of the housing unit must pay the property taxes $T_S^0$ and $T_L^0$ for the use of the structure and land, respectively, during period 0.[65] We define *the period 0 structures tax rate* $\tau_S^0$ and *land tax rate* $\tau_L^0$ as follows:

$$\tau_S^0 \equiv \frac{T_S^0}{P_S^0 Q_S^0}; \tag{42}$$

$$\tau_L^0 \equiv \frac{T_L^0}{P_L^0 Q_L^0}. \tag{43}$$

The *new imputed rent for using the property during period* 0, $R^0$, including the property tax costs, is defined as follows:

$$\begin{aligned} R^0 &\equiv V^0(1 + r^0) + T_S^0 + T_L^0 - V^{1a} \\ &= [P_S^0 Q_S^0 + P_L^0 Q_L^0](1 + r^0) + \tau_S^0 P_S^0 Q_S^0 + \tau_L^0 P_L^0 Q_L^0 \\ &\quad - [P_S^0(1 + i_S^0)(1 - \delta_0)Q_S^0 + P_L^0(1 + i_L^0)Q_L^0] \\ &= p_S^0 Q_S^0 + p_L^0 Q_L^0, \end{aligned} \tag{44}$$

where separate period 0 *tax-adjusted user costs of structures and land,* $p_S{}^0$ and $p_L{}^0$, are defined as follows:

$$\begin{aligned} p_S^0 &\equiv [(1 + r^0) - (1 + i_S^0)(1 - \delta_0) + \tau_S^0]P_S^0 \\ &= [r^0 - i_S^0 + \delta_0(1 + i_S^0) + \tau_S^0]P_S^0; \end{aligned} \tag{45}$$

$$\begin{aligned} p_L^0 &\equiv [(1 + r^0) - (1 + i_L^0) + \tau_L^0]P_L^0 \\ &= [r^0 - i_L^0 + \tau_S^0]P_L^0. \end{aligned} \tag{46}$$

Thus, the property tax rates, $\tau_S{}^0$ and $\tau_L{}^0$ (defined by equations [42] and [43]), enter the user costs of structures and land, $p_S{}^0$ and $p_L{}^0$ (defined by equations [45] and [46]), in a simple additive manner; that is, these terms are additive to the previous depreciation and real interest rate terms.

### 12.8.3 The Treatment of Property Insurance

At first glance, it would seem that *property insurance* could be treated in the same manner as the treatment of property taxes in the previous subsection. Thus, let $C_S{}^0$ be the cost of insuring the structure at the beginning of period 0, and define *the period 0 structures premium rate* $\gamma_S{}^0$ as follows:

$$\gamma_S{}^0 \equiv \frac{C_S^0}{P_S^0 Q_S^0}. \tag{47}$$

The new *imputed rent* for using the property during period 0, $R^0$, including property tax and insurance costs, is defined as follows:

65. If there is no breakdown of the property taxes into structures and land components, then just impute the overall tax into structures and land components based on the beginning-of-period values of both components.

$$(48)\qquad \begin{aligned} R^0 &\equiv V^0(1 + r^0) + T_S^0 + T_L^0 + C_S^0 - V^{1a} \\ &= [P_S^0Q_S^0 + P_L^0Q_L^0](1 + r^0) + \tau_S^0P_S^0Q_S^0 + \tau_L^0P_L^0Q_L^0 + \gamma_S^0P_S^0Q_S^0 \\ &\quad - [P_S^0(1 + i_S^0)(1 - \delta_0)Q_S^0 + P_L^0(1 + i_L^0)Q_L^0] \\ &= p_S^0Q_S^0 + p_L^0Q_L^0, \end{aligned}$$

where separate period 0 *tax- and insurance-adjusted user costs of structures and land,* $p_S^0$ and $p_L^0$, are defined as follows:

$$(49)\qquad \begin{aligned} p_S^0 &\equiv [(1 + r^0) - (1 + i_S^0)(1 - \delta_0) + \tau_S^0 + \gamma_S^0]P_S^0 \\ &= [r^0 - i_S^0 + \delta_0(1 + i_S^0) + \tau_S^0 + \gamma_S^0]P_S^0; \end{aligned}$$

$$(50)\qquad \begin{aligned} p_L^0 &\equiv [(1 + r^0) - (1 + i_L^0) + \tau_L^0]P_L^0 \\ &= [r^0 - i_L^0 + \tau_S^0]P_L^0. \end{aligned}$$

Thus, the insurance premium rate $\gamma_S^0$ appears in the user cost of structures, $p_S^0$ (defined by equation [49]), in an additive manner, analogous to the additive property tax rate term.[66] If it is desired to have a separate CPI price component for insurance, then the corresponding period 0 and period 1 prices can be defined as $\gamma_S^0P_S^0$ and $\gamma_S^1P_S^1$, respectively, while the corresponding period 0 and period 1 expenditures can be defined as $\gamma_S^0P_S^0Q_S^0$ and $\gamma_S^1P_S^1(1 - \delta)Q_S^0$, respectively.[67] Of course, if this separate treatment is implemented, then these terms have to be dropped from the corresponding user costs of structures.

This treatment of property taxation and insurance assumes that the property taxes and the premium payments are made at the *end* of the period under consideration. While this may be an acceptable approximation for the payment of property taxes, it is not acceptable for the payment of insurance premiums: the premium *must* be paid at the *beginning* of the period of protection rather than at the end. When this complication is taken into account, the user cost of structures becomes

$$(51)\qquad \begin{aligned} p_S^0 &\equiv [(1 + r^0) - (1 + i_S^0)(1 - \delta_0) + \tau_S^0 + \gamma_S^0(1 + r^0)]P_S^0 \\ &= [r^0 - i_S^0 + \delta_0(1 + i_S^0) + \tau_S^0 + \gamma_S^0(1 + r^0)]P_S^0. \end{aligned}$$

There are some additional problems associated with the modeling of property insurance:

- The preceding user cost derivations assume that the *risk* of property damage remains constant from period to period. If the risk of damage changes, then an argument can be made for quality adjustment of the

66. This treatment of property insurance dates back to Walras (1954, 268–9).

67. Similarly, if it is desired to have a separate CPI price component for property taxes on structures, then the corresponding period 0 and period 1 prices can be defined as $\tau_S^0P_S^0$ and $\tau_S^1P_S^1$, respectively, while the corresponding period 0 and period 1 expenditures can be defined as $\tau_S^0P_S^0Q_S^0$ and $\tau_S^1P_S^1(1 - \delta)Q_S^0$, respectively.

premium to hold constant the risk so that like can be compared with like.

- The *gross premium approach* to insurance is taken in the previous treatment; that is, it is assumed that dwelling owners pay premiums for property protection services, regardless of whether they have a claim. In the *net premium approach,* payments to settle claims are subtracted from the gross premium payments.
- The property protection may not be complete; that is, the insurance policy may have various limitations on the type of claim that is allowed, and there may be a deductible or damage threshold, below which no claim is allowed. If the deductible changes from period to period, then the price statistician is faced with a rather complex quality-adjustment problem.

Thus, it can be seen that there are some difficult problems that remain to be resolved in this area.

### 12.8.4 The Treatment of Maintenance and Renovation Expenditures

Another problem associated with home ownership is the treatment of *maintenance expenditures, major repair expenditures, and expenditures associated with renovations or additions.*

Empirical evidence suggests that the normal decline in a structure due to the effects of aging and use can be offset by maintenance and renovation expenditures. How exactly should these expenditures be treated in the context of modeling the costs and benefits of home ownership?

A common approach in the national accounts literature is to treat major renovation and repair expenditures as capital formation and to treat smaller routine maintenance and repair expenditures as current expenditures. If this approach is followed in the CPI context, then these smaller routine maintenance expenditures can be treated in the same manner as other nondurable goods and services. The major renovation and repair expenditures do not enter the CPI in the period that they are made; instead, these expenditures are capitalized and added to expenditures on new structures for the period under consideration, so period 0 investment in structures in constant dollars, say $I_S^0$,[68] would include both types of expenditures. Let $Q_S^0$ and $Q_S^1$ be the stocks (in constant-quality units) of owner-occupied structures in the reference population at the beginning of period 0 and period 1, respectively. Then, if the geometric model of depreciation is used so that the constant period-to-period depreciation rate $\delta$ is applicable, then the beginning-of-period 1 stock of owner-occupied structures $Q_S^1$ is related to the beginning-

68. Let $VI_S^0$ be the nominal value of investment in new owner-occupied structures in period 0, plus the value of major renovation expenditures made during period 0. Then, the constant-dollar quantity of investment could be defined as $I_S^0 \equiv VI_S^0/P_S^0$, where $P_S^0$ is the period 0 construction price index for new structures.

of-period 0 stock of structures $Q_S^0$ and to the period 0 investment in structures $I_S^0$, according to the following equation:

$$(52) \qquad Q_S^1 = (1 - \delta)Q_S^0 + I_S^0.$$

Thus, if declining-balance depreciation is assumed for structures, then the treatment of major repair and renovation expenditures does not pose major *conceptual* problems using a conventional capital accumulation model: it is only necessary to have an estimate for the monthly or quarterly depreciation rate $\delta$, a starting value for the stock of owner-occupied structures for some period, information on new purchases of residential housing structures by the household sector, information on expenditures by owners on major repairs and renovations, and a construction price index for new residential structures. With this information on a timely basis, up-to-date CPI weights for the stock of owner-occupied structures could be constructed.[69]

What would a hedonic regression model look like, taking into account the approximate additivity of the value of the housing structure and the value of the land that the structure sits on? If the renovations problem is ignored and geometric depreciation of the structure is assumed, then the value of a housing unit $n$ in period $t$ that is $m$ periods old, $V_n^t$, should be equal to the depreciated value of the structure, plus the value of the land, plus an error term; that is, the following relationship should hold approximately, assuming geometric depreciation of the structure:[70]

$$(53) \qquad V_n^t = P_S^t(1 - \delta)^m Q_{Sn} + P_L^t Q_L; \quad n = 1, \ldots, N,$$

where $\delta$ is the one-period geometric depreciation rate, $Q_{Sn}$ is the number of square meters of floor space of the original structure for housing unit $n$, and $Q_L$ is the number of square meters of land that the housing structure sits on. The variable $P_S{}^t$ is the beginning-of-*period t price level for structures* of this type, and $P_L{}^t$ is the corresponding *price of land* for this class of housing units. As long as there is more than one vintage of structure in the sample (i.e., observations corresponding to different ages $m$ of the structure), then the parameters $P_S^t$, $P_L^t$, and $\delta$ can be identified by running a nonlinear regression model using equation (53), or more appropriately, by taking logarithms of both sides of equation (53) and adding error terms. Why can the price levels be identified in the present hedonic regression model, whereas they could not be identified in section 12.5?[71] The answer is that the hedonic model in equation (53) does *not* assume property-specific quality-adjustment factors

69. However, the *practical* problems involved in obtaining all of this information on a timely basis are not trivial. Variants of this approach were used by Christensen and Jorgenson (1969) and Leigh (1980) in order to construct estimates of the stock of residential structures in the United States.

70. We have omitted the multiplicative error term in equation (53).

71. Recall the discussion around equation (15) in section 12.5.

for *each* housing unit; instead, *all* of the housing units in the class of properties in the sample are assumed to be of comparable quality once prices are adjusted for the age of the unit and the quantity (in square meters) of original structure and the quantity of land.

Unfortunately, many housing structures that may have started their lives as identical structures do not remain the same over time, due to differing standards of maintenance, as well as major renovations and additions to some of the structures. To model this phenomenon, let $R_n{}^t$ be real maintenance, repair, and renovation expenditures on housing unit $n$ during period $t$, and suppose that these real expenditures depreciate at the geometric rate $\delta_R$. It is reasonable to assume that these expenditures *add* to the value of the housing unit, so equation (53) should be replaced by the following equation:

$$(54)\quad V_n^t = P_S^t(1-\delta)^m Q_{Sn} + P_R^t[R_n^t + (1-\delta_R)R_n^{t-1} + (1-\delta_R)^2 R_n^{t-2} + \ldots + (1-\delta_R)^v R_n^{t-v}] + P_L^t Q_L,$$

where $P_R{}^t$ is the period $t$ price level for real maintenance, repair, and renovation expenditures on this class of housing units. If information on these real renovation and repair expenditures, $R_n^t$, $R_n^{t-1}$, $R_n^{t-2}$, . . . , $R_n^{t-v}$, is available for each housing unit in the sample of housing units that sold in period $t$, then the parameters $P_S^t$, $P_L^t$, $P_R^t$, $\delta$, and $\delta_R$ can be identified by taking logarithms of both sides of equation (54) and running a nonlinear regression model.[72]

However, a major practical problem with implementing a hedonic regression model along these lines is that usually, accurate data on renovation and repair expenditures on a particular dwelling unit between the construction of the initial housing unit and the present period are not available. Without accurate data on repairs and renovations, it will be impossible to obtain accurate estimates of the unknown parameters in the hedonic regression model.

A final practical problem with this hedonic regression model will be mentioned. Theoretically, following Hulten (2006, 195), normal maintenance expenditures could be included in the renovation expenditure terms $R_n^t$ in equation (54). If this is done, then including normal maintenance expenditures in $R_n^t$ will have the effect of increasing the estimated depreciation rates $\delta$ and $\delta_R$. Thus, different statistical agencies that have different criteria for deciding where to draw the line between normal maintenance and major repair and renovations will produce different estimated depreciation rates.

It can be seen that here, as was the case for property insurance, there are many unresolved issues in this area: a statistical agency best practice has not yet emerged.

72. Alternatively, if price levels are available for $P_S^t$ and $P_R^t$ from construction price indexes, then these parameters do not have to be estimated.

### 12.8.5 The Treatment of the Transactions Costs of Home Purchase

Another cost of home ownership needs to be discussed. Normally, when a family purchases a dwelling unit, they have to pay certain fees and costs, which can include:

- The commissions of real estate agents who help the family find the right property
- Various transactions taxes that governments can impose on the sale of the property
- Various legal fees that might be associated with the transfer of title for the property

Should these fees be immediately expensed in the period of purchase, or should they simply be regarded as part of the purchase price of the property and hence be depreciated over time in a manner analogous to the treatment of structures in the national accounts?[73]

An argument can be made for either treatment. From the viewpoint of the opportunity cost treatment of purchases of durable goods, the relevant price of the dwelling unit in the periods following the purchase of the property is the after-tax and transactions fees value of the property. This viewpoint suggests that the transactions costs of the purchaser should be immediately expensed in the period of purchase. However, from the viewpoint of a landlord who has just purchased a dwelling unit for rental purposes, it would not be sensible to charge the tenant the full cost of these transactions fees in the first month of rent. The landlord would tend to capitalize these costs and recover them gradually over the time period that the landlord expects to own the property. Thus, either treatment could be justified, and the statistical agency will have to decide which treatment is most convenient from their particular perspective.

## 12.9 User Costs for Landlords versus Owners

In the previous section, the various financial costs associated with home ownership were discussed. Both homeowners and landlords face these costs. Thus, they will be reflected in market rents, and this fact must be kept in mind if the imputed rent approach is used to value the services of OOH. If some or all of these associated costs of OOH are covered elsewhere in the CPI (e.g., home insurance could be separately covered), then the value of imputed rents for OOH must be *reduced* by the amount of these expenditures covered elsewhere.

73. The Australian Bureau of Statistics follows the second alternative and depreciates the transactions costs of purchasing a dwelling unit over the average length of time a property of that type is held.

However, in addition to the financial costs of home ownership that were covered in the previous section, landlords face a number of *additional costs* compared to the homeowner. These additional costs will be reflected in market rents, and thus if market rents are used to impute the services provided by the ownership of a dwelling unit, then these extra costs should also be *removed* from the market rents that are used for imputation purposes, because they will not be relevant for owner occupiers. These additional landlord-specific costs will be discussed in sections 12.9.1 to 12.9.5. We note that these additional costs will be reflected in market rental rates, and thus they belong in a CPI that is applicable for renters. However, if market rental rates are used as an imputed opportunity cost for the use of an owner-occupied dwelling unit, then we are suggesting that the unadjusted market rental rate is not a true opportunity cost; that is, the extra costs to be discussed in sections 12.9.1 to 12.9.5 should be removed to the extent possible in order to reflect a true opportunity cost of consuming the services of an owned home over the reference period. Thus, *adjusted market rents* should be used in place of *actual market rents* for imputation purposes.

### 12.9.1 Damage Costs

Tenants do not have the same incentive to take care of a rental property compared to an owned property, so depreciation costs for a rental property are likely to exceed depreciation rates for comparable owned properties. If these expected damage costs are included in the rent, then they should be subtracted from the rent when forming imputed rent for an owner-occupied dwelling unit. If the expected damage costs are approximately equal to an up-front damage deposit, then the market rent does not have to be adjusted when forming market equivalent rent for an owner-occupied dwelling unit.

### 12.9.2 Nonpayment of Rent and Vacancy Costs

At times, tenants run into financial difficulties and are unable to pay landlords the rent that is owed. Usually, eviction is a long, drawn-out process, so landlords can lose several months of rent before a nonpaying tenant finally leaves. The landlord also incurs extra costs compared to a homeowner when a rental property remains vacant due to lack of demand.[74] These extra costs will be reflected in market rents but should not be reflected in the user costs of OOH.

### 12.9.3 Billing and Maintenance Costs

A (large) landlord may have to rent office space and employ staff to send out monthly bills to tenants and to respond to requests for maintenance. A

74. The demand for rental properties can vary substantially over the business cycle, and this can lead to depressed rents or very high rents compared to the user costs of home ownership. Thus, imputed rents based on market rents of similar properties can differ substantially from the corresponding user costs of OOH over the business cycle.

homeowner who provides his or her time in order to provide maintenance services[75] provides this time at his or her *after-income tax wage rate,* which may be lower than the *before-income tax wage rate* that a landlord must pay his or her employees. The net effect of these factors leads to higher market rents compared to the corresponding owner-occupied user cost.

### 12.9.4 The Opportunity Cost of Capital

The homeowner's *after-tax* opportunity cost of capital that appeared in the various user cost formulae considered earlier in this chapter will typically be *lower* than the landlord's *before-tax* opportunity cost of capital.[76] Put another way, the landlord has an extra income tax cost compared to the homeowner. In addition, the landlord may face a higher risk premium for the use of capital due to the risks of damage and nonpayment of rent. However, care must be taken so that these additional landlord costs are not counted twice (i.e., in the present subsection, as well as in subsections 12.9.1 and 12.9.2).

### 12.9.5 The Supply of Additional Services for Rental Properties

Often, rental properties will contain some major consumer durables that homeowners have to provide themselves, such as refrigerators, stoves, washing machines, dryers, and air-conditioning units. In addition, landlords may pay for electricity or fuel in some rental apartments. Thus, to make the market rental comparable to an owner-occupied imputed rent, the market rental should be adjusted downward to account for these factors (which will appear elsewhere in the expenditures of owner occupiers).

### 12.9.6 Which Approach Will Give the Highest Expenditure Weight?

The factors just listed will tend to make observed market rental prices *higher* than the corresponding user cost for an owner occupier of a property of the same quality. Thus, if the imputed rental approach is used to value the services of OOH, then these market-based rents should be adjusted downward to account for those factors.

Although all of the factors will tend to lead to an *upward* bias if unadjusted market rental rates are used to impute the services of OOH, there is another factor not discussed thus far that could lead to a large *downward* bias. That factor is *rent controls.*

The previous discussion suggests that under normal conditions, where rent controls are not a factor, the acquisitions approach to the treatment of

75. Typically, these imputed maintenance costs will not appear in the CPI, but if the user cost of an owned dwelling unit is to be comparable with the market rent of a similar property, these imputed labor costs should be included.

76. Due to the complexity of the topic, we have not modeled the implications of the treatment of housing in the system of personal and business income taxation that is relevant for a particular housing unit.

OOH will give rise to the smallest expenditures, the user cost approach will give rise to the next-highest level of expenditures, and the use of imputed market rentals will give the largest level of expenditures for owner-occupied housing. However, these conclusions depend on the assumption that market rents for expensive dwelling units are formed using the same user cost considerations that are used in forming market rents for inexpensive dwelling units, and this assumption does not appear to be satisfied. The problem is this: Garner and Short (2001) and Heston and Nakamura (2009) present substantial evidence that rent-to-value ratios decline as the value of the dwelling unit increases.[77] This cross-sectional decline is simply too large to be reconciled with rents for all types of housing based on user cost considerations. Thus, if we take equation (9) as an approximate guide to the formation of the market rent of a housing asset relative to its starting stock value, the rent-to-value ratio should be equal to $r^0 - i^0 + \delta$, where $r^0$ is defined as the nominal interest rate or opportunity cost of financial capital, $i^0$ is the anticipated asset inflation rate, and $\delta$ is the depreciation rate. There is no reason for the opportunity cost of capital or for the expected asset inflation rate to change substantially as we move from cheaper to more expensive dwelling units. If the land component of more expensive housing becomes larger, then we could expect a drop in the combined depreciation rate for the structure and land components as we move toward more expensive properties, but because structure depreciation rates are quite small, a drop in a small number cannot explain the huge drop in the rent-to-asset value ratio as the dwelling unit asset value increases. Thus, it seems that the user cost approach to pricing the services of owner-occupied housing will *probably* give a higher expenditure share to OOH than the rental equivalence approach will give, even over long periods of time.[78]

The preceding discussion suggests that while the acquisitions approach to the treatment of OOH will give rise to the smallest expenditures, it is not certain whether the user cost or rental equivalence approach will give rise to the next-highest level of expenditures.

77. Heston and Nakamura (2009, 121) summarize the BEA evidence as follows: "The rent to value ratios reported are about 17 percent for dwellings under $20,000 and 6 percent for dwellings in the $200,000–300,000 class in the early 1990s." Heston and Nakamura (2009, 121) present their own evidence for U.S. and Caribbean locations that the ratio of rent to the value of a house falls dramatically as the house value increases; they find that the rent-to-value ratio for expensive houses is about one-half the corresponding ratio for inexpensive houses.

78. It is well known that capitalization rates (the ratio of rent to asset value) for housing vary substantially *over time* due to changes in nominal interest rates, depreciation rates, and expected housing inflation rates; for example, see Crone, Nakamura, and Voith (2000), Verbrugge (2006), Girouard et al. (2006), Garner and Verbrugge (2009), and Heston and Nakamura (2009). However, this time-series variation in capitalization rates could perhaps be explained by variations in nominal interest rates and variations in expected housing inflation rates (although Verbrugge [2006] and Garner and Verbrugge [2009] show that this is unlikely). However, the fact that capitalization rates are not approximately constant in the cross-sectional context means that the user cost and rental equivalence approaches to OOH can give very different answers, even in the long run.

In the following section, we review the three main approaches to the treatment of owner-occupied housing in a CPI and discuss some of the difficulties associated with implementing each approach.

## 12.10 Alternative Approaches for Pricing Owner-Occupied Housing

For consumer durables that have long useful lives, the usual acquisitions approach will not be adequate for CPI users who desire prices that measure the service flows that consumer durables generate. This is particularly true for owner-occupied housing. Hence, it will be useful to many users if in addition to the acquisitions approach, the statistical agency implements both the rental equivalence approach and the user cost approach for long-lived consumer durables and for owner-occupied housing, in particular.[79] Users can then decide which approach best suits their purposes. Any one of the three main approaches could be chosen as the approach that would be used in the headline CPI. The other two approaches should be made available to users as analytic tables.[80]

We conclude this section by outlining some of the problems involved in implementing the three main approaches to the measurement of price change for OOH.

### 12.10.1 The Acquisitions Approach

In order to implement the acquisitions approach, a constant-quality price index for the sales of new residential housing units will be required. The hedonic regression approach to such price indexes outlined in section 12.7.3 seems to be the best approach to constructing such a constant-quality index.

### 12.10.2 The Rental Equivalence Approach

*Option 1: Using Homeowner's Estimates of Rents*

In this option, homeowners would be surveyed and asked to estimate a rental price for their housing unit. Problems with this approach are as follows:

- Homeowners may not be able to provide very accurate estimates for the rental value of their dwelling unit.
- The statistical agency should make an adjustment to these estimated rents over time in order to take into account the effects of depreciation,

79. Because the user cost and rental equivalence approaches will usually be quite different, users should be given the option of using either approach.

80. In section 12.11, we will suggest a fourth approach: the opportunity cost approach. This approach should also be made available to users in an analytical table.

which cause the quality of the unit to slowly decline over time (unless this effect is offset by renovation and repair expenditures).[81]

- Care must be taken to determine exactly what extra services are included in the homeowner's estimated rent; that is, does the rent include insurance, electricity, fuel, or the use of various consumer durables in addition to the structure? If so, these extra services should be stripped out of the rent, because they are covered elsewhere in the CPI.[82]

*Option 2: Using a Hedonic Regression Model of the Rental Market to Impute Rents*

In this option, the statistical agency would collect data on rental properties and their characteristics and then use this information to construct a hedonic regression model for the housing rental market.[83] Then, this model would be used to impute prices for owner-occupied properties. Problems with this approach are as follows:

- It is information intensive; in addition to requiring information on the rents and characteristics of rental properties, information on the characteristics of owner-occupied properties would also be required.
- The characteristics of the owner-occupied population could be quite different from the characteristics of the rental population. In particular, if the rental market for housing is subject to rent controls, this approach is definitely not recommended.
- Hedonic regression models suffer from a lack of reproducibility, in that different researchers will have different characteristics in the model and will use different functional forms.
- From the discussion in section 12.9, it was seen that market rents may contain costs that are not relevant to homeowners, such as higher depreciation rates, billing costs, or higher opportunity costs of capital, and hence using market rents to impute rents for owner occupiers may lead to rents that are too high.[84]

81. Recall the discussion in section 12.8.4.

82. However, it could be argued that these extra services that might be included in the rent are mainly a weighting issue; that is, it could be argued that the *trend* in the homeowner's estimated rent would be a reasonably accurate estimate of the trend in the rents after adjusting for the extra services included in the rent.

83. See Crone, Nakamura, and Voith (2000, 2004) and Hoffmann and Kurz (2002) for examples of such hedonic models that try to cope with the heterogeneity in the rental market. Note that the U.S. Bureau of Labor Statistics selects a panel of rental units (drawn to match the corresponding owner stocks at a particular point in time), and then it computes a monthly rental equivalence index for the owner-occupied stock by aggregating up the price indexes for the chosen rental units; see Ptacek and Baskin (1996) for the details. This can be viewed as a simplified hedonic regression approach, where the characteristics of the owner-occupied stock of houses are rather roughly matched to corresponding rental units.

84. Again, it could argued that this is mainly a weighting issue; that is, it could be argued that the *trend* in market rents would be a reasonably accurate estimate for the trend in homeowners' opportunity costs.

- There is some evidence that depreciation is somewhat different for rental units compared to owner-occupied housing units.[85] If this is so, then the imputation procedure will be somewhat incorrect. However, all studies that estimate depreciation for owner-occupied housing suffer from biases due to the inadequate treatment of land and to the lack of information on repair, renovation, and maintenance expenditures over the life of the dwelling unit. Hence, it is not certain that depreciation for rental units is significantly different than that for owner-occupied units.

### 12.10.3 The User Cost Approach

It is first necessary to decide whether an ex ante or ex post user cost of housing is to be calculated. It seems that the ex ante approach is the more useful one for CPI purposes; these are the prices that should appear in economic models of consumer choice. Moreover, the ex post approach will lead to user costs that fluctuate too much to suit the needs of most users. Of course, the problem with the ex ante approach is that it will be difficult to estimate anticipated inflation rates for house prices.

*Option 3: The Rent-to-Value Approach*

In this option, the statistical agency collects information on market rents paid for a sample of rental properties, but it also collects information on the sales price of these rental properties when they are sold. Using these two pieces of information, the statistical agency can form an estimated *rent-to-value ratio* for rental properties of various types. As was discussed in earlier sections, this rent-to-value ratio represents an estimate of all the terms that go into an ex ante user cost formula, except the asset price of the property; that is, the rent-to-value ratio for a particular property can be regarded as an estimate of the interest rate, less anticipated housing inflation, plus the depreciation rate, plus the other miscellaneous rates that were discussed in section 12.8, such as insurance and property tax rates. Under the assumptions that (a) these rates remain reasonably constant over the short run and (b) these rates are applicable to owner-occupied housing units, then an imputed rent for OOH is equal to the applicable rent-to-value ratio multiplied by the price of the owner-occupied unit. Thus, this approach can be implemented if a constant-quality price index for the stock value of owner-occupied housing can be developed. It may be decided to approximate the comprehensive price index for owner-occupied housing by a new housing price index, and if this is done, the approach essentially reduces down to

85. "The average depreciation rate for rental property is remarkably constant, ranging from 0.58 percent to 0.60 percent over the 25 year period. Depreciation rates for owner occupied units show more variation than the estimated rates for renter occupied units. The average depreciation rate for owner occupied housing ranges from 0.9 percent in year 1 to 0.28 percent in year 20" (Malpezzi, Ozanne, and Thibodeau 1987, 382).

the acquisitions approach, except that the weights will generally be larger using this user cost approach than those obtained using the acquisitions approach.[86] Problems with this approach include the following:

- It will require a considerable amount of resources to construct a constant-quality price index for the stock of owner-occupied housing units. If a hedonic regression model is used, there are problems associated with the reproducibility of the results.
- Rent-to-value ratios can change considerably over time. Hence, it will be necessary to collect information on rents and selling prices of rental properties on an ongoing basis.
- As was noted in section 12.9, the user cost structure of rental properties can be quite different from the corresponding user cost structure of owner-occupied properties. Hence, the use of rent-to-value ratios for rented dwellings can give misleading results when applied to owned structures.[87]

*Option 4: The Simplified User Cost Approach*

This approach is similar to that of Option 3, but instead of using the rent-to-value ratio to estimate the sum of the various rates in the user cost formula, direct estimates are made of these rates. If the simplified Icelandic user cost approach discussed in section 12.6 is used, all that is required is a constant-quality owner-occupied housing price index, an estimated real interest rate, and an estimated composite depreciation rate on the structure and land together. Problems with this approach are as follows:

- As was the case with Option 3, it will require a considerable amount of resources to construct a constant-quality price index for the stock of owner-occupied housing units. If a hedonic regression model is used, there are problems associated with the reproducibility of the results.
- It is not known with any degree of certainty what the appropriate real interest rate should be.
- Similarly, it is difficult to determine what the correct depreciation rate should be.[88] Moreover, this problem is complicated by the fact that over time, the price of land tends to increase faster than the price of building a residential structure, so the land price component of an owner-occupied housing unit will tend to increase in importance, which in turn will tend to decrease the composite depreciation rate.

86. See Diewert (2002, 618–9) on this point.

87. However, this is primarily a weighting issue, so the trend in the constant-quality stock of owner-occupied housing price index should be an adequate approximation to the trend in owner-occupied user costs.

88. Due to the lack of information on repairs and renovations, estimated housing depreciation rates vary widely: "One striking feature with the results of all three approaches used in these and related studies is their variability: estimates range from about a half percent per year to two and a half percent" (Malpezzi, Ozanne, and Thibodeau 1987, 373–5).

*Option 5: A National Accounting Approach*

This approach makes use of the fact that the national accounts division of the statistical agency will usually collect data on investment in residential housing, as well as on repair and renovation expenditures on housing. In addition, many statistical agencies will also construct estimates for the stock of residential dwelling units, so estimates for the structures depreciation rates are available. Finally, if the statistical agency also constructs a national balance sheet, then estimates for the value of residential land will also be available. Thus, all of the basic ingredients that are necessary to construct stocks for residential structures and the associated land stocks are available. If in addition, assumptions about the appropriate nominal interest rate and about expected prices for structures and land are made,[89] then aggregate user costs of residential structures and residential land can be constructed. The proportion of these stocks that is rented can be deducted, and estimates for the user costs and corresponding values for owner-occupied residential land and structures can be made. Of course, it would be almost impossible to do all of this on a current basis, but all of the previous computations can be done for a base period in order to obtain appropriate weights for owner-occupied structures and land. Then, it can be seen that the main drivers for the monthly user costs are the price of a new structure and the price of residential land. Hence, if timely monthly indicators for these two prices can be developed, the entire procedure is feasible. Problems with this approach include the following:

- As was the case with Option 4, it will be difficult to determine what the correct depreciation rates and real interest rates are.[90]
- It will be difficult to construct a monthly price of residential land index.
- It may be difficult to convert the residential housing investment price deflator from a quarterly to a monthly basis.

All of the preceding five options for implementing a rental equivalence or user cost approach to modeling the cost of consuming the services of OOH have their advantages and disadvantages; there does not appear to be a clear winning option.[91] Thus, each statistical agency will have to decide whether they have the resources to implement any of these five options in addition to the usual acquisitions approach to the treatment of owner-occupied housing. From the viewpoint of the cost-of-living approach to the CPI, any one

89. Alternatively, an appropriate real interest rate can be assumed.

90. However, as usual, it can be argued that errors in estimating these parameters will mainly affect the weights used in the price index.

91. For consumer durables that do not change in quality over time, Option 5 will probably suffice. Note that none of the five options includes the acquisitions approach, which is not a suitable approach for pricing the *services* of a long-lived durable good.

of the five options would be an adequate approximation to the ideal treatment from the perspective of measuring the flow of consumption services in each period.

There is yet another approach to the treatment of OOH, which we have not mentioned up to this point, because it is somewhat controversial and untried: the *opportunity cost approach.*[92] This final approach does not involve any new concepts and will be explained in the following section.

## 12.11 The Opportunity Cost Approach to Owner-Occupied Housing

Before presenting the opportunity cost approach to the treatment of OOH in a CPI, it will be useful to review Verbrugge's very interesting attack on the user cost approach to OOH. His work also explains why user costs can diverge markedly from their corresponding market equivalent rents. He summarized his recent research as follows:[93]

> I construct several estimates of *ex ante* user costs for US homeowners, and compare these to rents. There are three novel findings. First, a significant volatility divergence remains even for *ex ante* user cost measures which have been smoothed to mimic the implicit smoothing in the rent data. Indeed, the volatility of smoothed quarterly aggregate *ex ante* user cost growth is about 10 times greater than that of aggregate rent growth. This large volatility probably rules out the use of *ex ante* user costs as a measure of the costs of homeownership. . . . The second novel finding is perhaps more surprising: not only do rents and user costs diverge in the short run, but the gaps persist over extended periods of time. . . . The divergence between rents and user costs highlights a puzzle, explored in greater depth below: rents do not appear to respond very strongly to their theoretical determinants. . . . Despite this divergence, the third novel finding is that there were evidently no unexploited profit opportunities. While the detached unit rental market is surprisingly thick, and detached housing is readily moved between owner and renter markets . . . the large costs associated with real estate transactions would have prevented risk neutral investors from earning expected profits by using the transaction sequence *buy, earn rent on property, sell,* and would have prevented risk neutral homeowners from earning expected profits by using the transaction sequence *sell, rent for one year, repurchase.* (Verbrugge 2006, 3)

How did Verbrugge arrive at these conclusions? He started off with the following expression for the user cost $u_i^t$ of home $i$:[94]

$$u_i^t = P_i^t(i^t + \delta - E\pi_i^t), \tag{55}$$

92. This approach was first suggested by Diewert (2009, 113).

93. Verbrugge's initial research has recently been updated in Garner and Verbrugge (2009), but this updated research did not change the conclusions listed in his original study.

94. See equation (1) in Verbrugge (2006, 11). Note that this formula is a counterpart to equation (9) in this chapter.

where $P_i^t$ is the price of home $i$ in period $t$; $i^t$ is a nominal interest rate;[95] $\delta$ is the sum of annual depreciation, maintenance and repair, insurance, property taxes, and a potential risk premium;[96] and $E\pi_i^t$ represents the expected annual constant-quality home appreciation rate for home $i$ at period $t$.[97] Thus, the resulting user cost can be viewed as an opportunity cost measure for the annual cost of owning a home, starting at the beginning of the quarter indexed by time $t$. As was noted earlier in this chapter, when landlords set an annual rent for a dwelling unit, they would use a formula similar to equation (55) in order to determine the rent for a tenant.[98] So far, there is nothing particularly controversial about Verbrugge's analysis. What is controversial is Verbrugge's determination of the expected house price appreciation term, $E\pi_i^t$.

> Rather than using a crude proxy, I will construct a *forecast* for $E\pi_i^t$, as described below. This choice is crucial, for four reasons. First, expected home price appreciation is extremely volatile; setting this term to a constant is strongly at odds with the data, and its level of volatility will be central to this study. Second, this term varies considerably across cities, and its temporal dynamics might well vary across cities as well. Third, the properties of $(i^t - E\pi_i^t)$ are central to user cost dynamics, yet these properties are unknown (or at least, not documented); again, setting $E\pi_i^t$ to a constant (or even to a long moving average) would be inappropriate for this study, since this choice obviously suppresses the correlation between $i^t$ and $E\pi_i^t$. Finally, the recent surge in $E\pi_i^t$ is well above its 15 year average, and implies that the user cost/rent ratio has fallen dramatically. A *single* year appreciation rate is used since we are considering the *one year* user cost, in order to remain comparable to the typical rental contract. (Verbrugge 2006, 12)

Verbrugge (2006, 13) went on to use various econometric forecasting techniques to forecast expected price appreciation for his one-year horizon; he inserted these forecasts into the user cost formula in equation (55) and obtained tremendously volatile ex ante user costs. The rest of his conclusions followed.

However, it is unlikely that landlords use econometric forecasts of housing price appreciation one year away and adjust rents for their tenants every year based on these forecasts. Tenants do not like tremendous volatility in

95. Verbrugge (2006, 11) used either the current thirty-year mortgage rate or the average one-year Treasury bill rate and noted that the choice of interest rate turned out to be inconsequential for his analysis.

96. Verbrugge (2006, 13) assumed that $\delta$ was approximately equal to 7 percent. Note that the higher the volatility in house prices is, the higher the risk premium would be for a risk-averse consumer.

97. The variable $\pi_i^t$ is the actual four-quarter (constant-quality) home price appreciation between the beginning of period $t$ and one year from this period.

98. As was noted in sections 12.8 and 12.9, there are some differences between a user cost formula for an owner occupier as compared to a landlord, but these differences are not important for Verbrugge's analysis.

their rents, and any landlord that attempted to set such volatile rents would soon have very high vacancy rates on his or her properties. However, it is possible that landlords may have some idea of the long-run average rate of property inflation for the type of property that they manage, and this long-run average annual rate of price appreciation could be inserted into the user cost formula in equation (55).[99]

Looking at the opportunity costs of owning a house from the viewpoint of an owner occupier, the relevant time horizon to consider for working out an annualized average rate of expected price appreciation is the expected time that the owner expects to use the dwelling before reselling it. This time horizon is typically some number between six and twelve years, so again, it does not seem appropriate to stick annual forecasts of expected price inflation into the user cost formula. Once we use annualized forecasts of expected price inflation over longer time horizons, the volatility in the ex ante user cost formula will vanish, or at least will be much diminished.[100]

Another method for reducing the volatility in the user cost formula is to replace the nominal interest rate, less expected price appreciation term ($i^t - E\pi_i^t$), by a constant or slowly changing long-run average *real interest rate,* say $r^t$. This is what was done in Iceland, as noted in section 12.6, and the resulting user cost seems to be acceptable to the population (and it is not overly volatile).

Verbrugge had an interesting section in his paper that helps to explain why user costs and market rentals can diverge so much over the short run. The answer is that high transactions costs involved in selling or purchasing real estate properties prevent arbitrage opportunities:[101]

> The first question is thus answered: there is no evidence of unexploited profits for prospective landlords. How about the second: was there ever a period of time in any city during which a "median" homeowner should have sold his house, rented for a year, and repurchased his house a year later?. . . . In this case, it appears that for Los Angeles, there was a single year, 1994, during which a homeowner should have sold her house, rented for a year, and repurchased her house. For every other time period, and for the entire period for the other four cities, a homeowner was always better off remaining in his house. (Verbrugge 2006, 36)

99. The paper by Girouard et al. nicely documents the length of housing booms and busts: "To qualify as a major cycle, the appreciation had to feature a cumulative real price increase equaling or exceeding 15 percent. This criterion identified 37 such episodes, corresponding to about two large upswings on average per 35 years for English speaking and Nordic countries and to 11/2 for the continental European countries" (2006, 6). Thus, one could justify taking ten- to twenty-year (annualized) average rates of property price inflation in the user cost formula rather than one-year rates.

100. Garner and Verbrugge (2009, 139) noted that volatility in their forecasted user costs dropped to about one-fifth of the previous level when one-year forecasts of expected house price inflation were replaced by five-year forecasts.

101. Verbrugge (2006, 35) assumed that the transactions costs in the United States were approximately 8 to 10 percent of the sales price.

Because high real estate transactions costs prevent the exploitation of arbitrage opportunities between owning and renting a property, user costs can differ considerably over the corresponding rental equivalence measures over the lifetime of a property cycle.

There is another puzzle in the behavior of user costs versus market rental prices that Verbrugge (2006) and Garner and Verbrugge (2009) did not comment on—the puzzling decrease in the ratio of market rents to housing price as the house price increases, as noted in section 12.9. This phenomenon seems to indicate that the rental market for housing for relatively inexpensive housing is at least somewhat segmented from the higher-end rental market. This segmentation could be explained as follows: as family income grows, people tend to want to own their own home, because this provides more security of tenure compared to renting.[102] Thus, the active rental market for housing is mostly geared toward low-income families. On the other hand, if an owner of an expensive unit wishes to rent the unit to someone else (perhaps for temporary purposes or to simply have someone reliable to occupy the property), the rental rate must be relatively low in order to induce a relatively low-income renter to occupy the property. In any case, it seems clear that user costs do not always equal the corresponding market rental rates.

Note that the user cost and the market equivalent rent that an owner-occupied house can generate are both *opportunity costs* that can be associated with that housing unit: the user cost is a somewhat indirect financial capital opportunity cost, whereas the market equivalent rent is a more direct opportunity cost. But the true opportunity cost of housing for an owner occupier is not his or her internal user cost or the market equivalent rent but instead is the *maximum* of the internal user cost and what the property could rent for on the rental market.[103] After all, the concept of opportunity cost is supposed to represent the *maximum sacrifice* that one makes in order to consume or use some object, so this point would seem to follow. If this point of view is accepted, then at certain points in the property cycle, user costs would replace market rents as the correct pricing concept for owner-occupied housing,[104] which would dramatically affect CPIs and the conduct of monetary policy. This point also indicates the need for statistical agencies to produce *both* user costs and equivalent rent price series for their CPI users. This *opportunity cost approach to pricing the services of durable assets* could also be used in production and productivity accounts, and this treatment would eliminate the problem of negative user costs, because market rents would always be nonnegative.

In conclusion, we suggest that the best pricing concept for the services of

102. There are typically tax advantages to owning over renting, as well.

103. See Diewert (2009, 113).

104. Garner and Verbrugge (2009) look at the levels of user costs and market rents in five U.S. cities and find that user costs are sometimes above and sometimes below their corresponding estimates of market rents.

OOH is the opportunity cost approach, which is equal to the maximum of the market rental and the ex ante user cost for any particular property.

## References


Aizcorbe, A., C. Corrado, and M. Doms. 2001. Constructing price and quantity indexes for high technology goods. Industrial Output Section, Division of Research and Statistics. Washington, DC: Board of Governors of the Federal Reserve System, July.

Bailey, M. J., R. F. Muth, and H. O. Nourse. 1963. A regression method for real estate price construction. *Journal of the American Statistical Association* 58:933–42.

Baldwin, J., G. Gellatly, M. Tanguay, and A. Patry. 2005. Estimating depreciation rates for the productivity accounts. Paper presented at the Organization for Economic Cooperation and Development (OECD) Workshop on Productivity Measurement. 17–19 October, Madrid, Spain.

Beidelman, C. R. 1973. *Valuation of used capital assets.* Sarasota, FL: American Accounting Association.

———. 1976. Economic depreciation in a capital goods industry. *National Tax Journal* 29 (4): 379–90.

Boskin, M. J., E. Dulberger, R. Gordon, Z. Griliches, and D. W. Jorgenson. 1996. Toward a more accurate measure of the cost of living. Final Report to the Senate Finance Committee from the Advisory Committee to Study the Consumer Price Index. Washington, DC: Government Printing Office, December.

Branson, M. 2006. The Australian experience in developing an established house price index. Paper presented at the OECD and International Monetary Fund (IMF) Workshop on Real Estate Price Indexes. 6–7 November, Paris.

Case, K. E., and R. J. Shiller. 1989. The efficiency of the market for single family homes. *American Economic Review* 79 (1): 125–37.

Christensen, L. R., and D. W. Jorgenson. 1969. The measurement of U.S. real capital input, 1929–1967. *Review of Income and Wealth* 15 (4): 293–320.

Court, A. T. 1939. Hedonic price indexes with automotive examples. In *The dynamics of automobile demand,* 98–117. New York: General Motors Corporation.

Crone, T. M., L. I. Nakamura, and R. Voith. 2000. Measuring housing services inflation. *Journal of Economic and Social Measurement* 26 (3/4): 153–71.

———. 2004. Hedonic estimates of the cost of housing services: Rental and owner-occupied units. Working Paper no. 04-22. Federal Reserve Bank of Philadelphia, Research Department.

de Haan, J. 2003. Time dummy approaches to hedonic price measurement. Paper presented at the Seventh Ottawa Group Meeting on Price Indices. 27–29, May, Paris. Available at: http://www.insee.fr/en/nom_def_met/colloques/ottawa/ottawa_papers.htm.

———. 2004. Hedonic regressions: The time dummy index as a special case of the Törnqvist Index, time dummy approaches to hedonic price measurement. Paper presented at the Statistics Finland Eighth Meeting of the International Working Group on Price Indices. 23–25 August, Helsinki, Finland.

Diewert, W. E. 1974. Intertemporal consumer theory and the demand for durables. *Econometrica* 42 (3): 497–516.

———. 1980. Aggregation problems in the measurement of capital. In *The measurement of capital,* ed. D. Usher, 433–528. Chicago: University of Chicago Press.

———. 2002. Harmonized indexes of consumer prices: Their conceptual foundations. *Swiss Journal of Economics and Statistics* 138 (4): 547–637.

———. 2003a. Hedonic regressions: A consumer theory approach. In *Studies in income and wealth,* vol. 64, *Scanner data and price indexes,* ed. R. C. Feenstra and M. D. Shapiro, 317–48. Chicago: University of Chicago Press.

———. 2003b. Hedonic regressions: A review of some unresolved issues. Paper presented at the Seventh Ottawa Group Meeting on Price Indices. 27–29 May, Paris. Available at http://www.insee.fr/en/av_service/colloques/ottawa/ottawa_papers.htm.

———. 2003c. The treatment of owner occupied housing and other durables in a consumer price index. Discussion Paper no. 03-08. University of British Columbia, Department of Economics.

———. 2005a. Issues in the measurement of capital services, depreciation, asset price changes and interest rates. In *Measuring capital in the new economy,* ed. C. Corrado, J. Haltiwanger, and D. Sichel, 479–542. Chicago: University of Chicago Press.

———. 2005b. Weighted country product dummy variable regressions and index number formulae. *Review of Income and Wealth* 51 (4): 561–71.

———. 2006. Adjacent period dummy variable hedonic regressions and bilateral index number theory. *Annales d'économie et de statistique,* no. 79/80, 1–28.

———. 2009. The Paris OECD-IMF Workshop on real estate price indexes: Conclusions and future directions. In *Price and productivity measurement,* vol. 1, *Housing,* ed. W. E. Diewert, B. M. Balk, D. Fixler, K. J. Fox and A. O. Nakamura, 87–116. Victoria, B.C.: Trafford Press. Available at: www.vancouvervolumes.com.

Diewert, W. E., and D. A. Lawrence. 2000. Progress in measuring the price and quantity of capital. In *Econometrics,* vol. 2, *Econometrics and the cost of capital: Essays in honor of Dale W. Jorgenson,* ed. L. J. Lau, 273–326. Cambridge, MA: MIT Press.

Diewert, W. E., and F. C. Wykoff. 2007. Depreciation, deterioration and obsolescence when there is embodied or disembodied technical change. University of British Columbia, Department of Economics. Working Paper. Available at http://www.econ.ubc.ca/diewert/dp0602.pdf.

Eurostat, World Bank, International Monetary Fund, Organization for Economic Cooperation and Development, and United Nations. 1993. *System of National Accounts, 1993.* New York: United Nations.

Eurostat. 2001. *Handbook on price and volume measures in national accounts.* Luxembourg: European Commission.

Garner, T. I., G. Janini, W. Passero, L. Paszkiewicz, and M. Vendemia. 2003. The consumer expenditure survey in comparison: Focus on personal consumption expenditures. Paper presented at the meeting of the BLS Federal Economic Statistics Advisory Committee. 21 March, Washington, DC. Available at http://www.bls.gov/bls/fesacp1032103.pdf.

Garner, T. I., and K. Short. 2001. Owner-occupied shelter in experimental poverty measurement with a "look" at inequality and poverty rates. Paper presented at the annual meeting of the Southern Economics Association. November, Tampa, FL.

Garner, T. I., and R. Verbrugge. 2009. The puzzling divergence of rents and user costs, 1980–2004: Summary and extensions. In *Price and productivity measurement,* Vol. 1, *Housing,* ed. W. E. Diewert, B. M. Balk, D. Fixler, K. J. Fox, and A. O. Nakamura, 125–46. Victoria, B.C.: Trafford Press. Available at: http://www.vancouvervolumes.com.

Gilman, S. 1939. *Accounting concepts of profit.* New York: Rolland Press.

Girouard, N., M. Kennedy, P. van den Noord, and C. André. 2006. Recent house price developments: The role of fundamentals. Paper presented at the OECD-IMF

Workshop on Real Estate Price Indexes. 6–7 November, Paris. Available at: http://www.oecd.org/dataoecd/3/6/37583208.pdf
Goodhart, C. 2001. What weights should be given to asset prices in the measurement of inflation? *Economic Journal* 111 (June): F335–F356.
Gouriéroux, C., and A. Laferrère. 2006. Managing hedonic housing price indexes: The French experience. Paper presented at the OECD-IMF Workshop on Real Estate Price Indexes. 6–7 November, Paris. Available at: http://www.oecd.org/dataoecd/2/24/37583497.pdf.
Griliches, Z. 1971a. Hedonic price indexes for automobiles: An econometric analysis of quality change. In *Price indexes and quality change,* ed. Z. Griliches, 55–87. Cambridge, MA: Harvard University Press.
———. 1971b. Introduction: Hedonic price indexes revisited. In *Price indexes and quality change,* ed. Z. Griliches, 3–15. Cambridge, MA: Harvard University Press.
Gudnason, R. 2003. How do we measure inflation? Some measurement problems. Paper presented at the Seventh Ottawa Group Meeting on Price Indices. 27–29 May, Paris. Available at: http://www.insee.fr/en/av_service/colloques/ottawa/ottawa_papers.htm.
Gudnason, R., and G. R. Jónsdóttir. 2009. Owner occupied housing in the Icelandic CPI. In *Price and productivity measurement,* vol. 1, *Housing,* ed. W. E. Diewert, B. M. Balk, D. Fixler, K. J. Fox, and A. O. Nakamura, 147–50. Victoria, B.C.: Trafford Press. Available at: www.vancouvervolumes.com.
Hall, R. E. 1971. The measurement of quality change from vintage price data. In *Price indexes and quality change,* ed. Z. Griliches, 240–71. Cambridge, MA: Harvard University Press.
Harper, M. J., E. R. Berndt, and D. O. Wood. 1989. Rates of return and capital aggregation using alternative rental prices. In *Technology and capital formation,* ed. D. W. Jorgenson and R. Landau, 331–72. Cambridge, MA: MIT Press.
Heravi, S., and M. Silver. 2007. Different approaches to estimating hedonic indexes. In *Studies in Income and Wealth,* vol. 67, *Hard-to-measure goods and services: Essays in honor of Zvi Griliches,* ed. E. R. Berndt and C. Hulten, 235–69. Chicago: University of Chicago Press.
Heston, A., and A. Nakamura. 2009. Reported prices and rents of housing: Reflections of costs, amenities or both? In *Price and productivity measurement,* Vol. 1, *Housing,* ed. W. E. Diewert, B. M. Balk, D. Fixler, K. J. Fox, and A. O. Nakamura, 117–24. Victoria, B.C.: Trafford Press. Available at: www.vancouvervolumes.com.
Hicks, J. R. 1946. *Value and capital.* 2nd ed. Oxford: Clarendon Press.
Hoffmann, J., and C. Kurz. 2002. Rent indices for housing in West Germany: 1985 to 1998. Discussion Paper no. 01/02. Deutsche Bundesbank, Economic Research Center.
Hoffmann, J., and A. Lorenz. 2006. Real estate price indices for Germany: Past, present and future. Paper presented at the OECD-IMF Workshop on Real Estate Price Indexes, 6–7 November, Paris. Available at: http://www.oecd.org/dataoecd/31/20/37625451.pdf.
Hulten, C. R. 1990. The measurement of capital. In *Fifty years of economic measurement,* ed. E. R. Berndt and J. E. Triplett, 119–58. Chicago: University of Chicago Press.
———. 1996. Capital and wealth in the revised SNA. In *The New System of National Accounts,* ed. J. W. Kendrick, 149–81. New York: Kluwer Academic Publishers.
———. 2006. The "architecture" of capital accounting: Basic design principles. In *Studies in income and wealth,* vol. 66, *A new architecture for the U.S. national*

*accounts,* ed. D. W. Jorgenson, J. S. Landefeld, and W. E. Nordhaus, 193–214. Chicago: University of Chicago Press.
Hulten, C. R., and F. C. Wykoff. 1981a. The estimation of economic depreciation using vintage asset prices. *Journal of Econometrics* 15 (3): 367–96.
———. 1981b. The measurement of economic depreciation. In *Depreciation, inflation and the taxation of income from capital,* ed. C. R. Hulten, 81–125. Washington, DC: Urban Institute Press.
———. 1996. Issues in the measurement of economic depreciation: Introductory remarks. *Economic Inquiry* 34 (1): 10–23.
International Labor Organization (ILO), in collaboration with the IMF, OECD, United Nations Economic Commission for Europe (UNECE), Eurostat, and the World Bank. 2004. *Consumer Price Index manual: Theory and practice.* Geneva: ILO.
Jorgenson, D. W. 1973. The economic theory of replacement and depreciation. In *Econometrics and economic theory,* ed. W. Sellekaerts, 189–221. New York: Macmillan.
———. 1989. Capital as a factor of production. In *Technology and capital formation,* ed. D. W. Jorgenson and R. Landau, 1–35. Cambridge, MA: MIT Press.
———. 1996. Empirical studies of depreciation. *Economic Inquiry* 34 (1): 24–42.
Katz, A. J. 1983. Valuing the services of consumer durables. *Review of Income and Wealth* 29 (4): 405–27.
Lebow, D. E., and J. B. Rudd. 2003. Measurement error in the Consumer Price Index: Where do we stand? *Journal of Economic Literature* 41 (1): 159–201.
Leigh, W. A. 1980. Economic depreciation of the residential housing stock of the United States, 1950–1970. *Review of Economics and Statistics* 62 (2): 200–6.
Li, W., M. Prud'homme, and K. Yu. 2006. Studies in hedonic resale housing price indexes. Paper presented at the OECD-IMF Workshop on Real Estate Price Indexes. 6–7 November, Paris. Available at: http://www.oecd.org/dataoecd/2/25/37583404.pdf.
Malpezzi, S., L. Ozanne, and T. Thibodeau. 1987. Microeconomic estimates of housing depreciation. *Land Economics* 63 (4): 372–85.
Marshall, A. 1898. *Principles of economics.* 4th ed. London: Macmillan.
Palmquist, R. B. 2006. Property value models. In *Handbook of environmental economics,* vol. 2, ed. K. -G. Mäler and J. Vincent, 763–819. Amsterdam: North-Holland.
Prasad, N., and A. Richards. 2006. Measuring aggregate house prices in Australian capital cities: A review of RBA research. Paper presented at the Economic Measurement Group Workshop. 13–15 December, Coogee, Australia. Available at: http://www.sam.sdu.dk/parn/EMG%20Workshop%20′06%20program.pdf.
Ptacek, F., and R. M. Baskin. 1996. Revision of the CPI housing sample and estimators. *Monthly Labor Review* 119 (12): 31–39.
Silver, M., and S. Heravi. 2003. The measurement of quality adjusted price changes. In *Studies in income and wealth,* vol. 64, *Scanner data and price indexes,* ed. R. C. Feenstra and M. D. Shapiro, 277–316. Chicago: University of Chicago Press.
———. 2007. The difference between hedonic imputation indexes and time dummy hedonic indexes. *Journal of Business and Economic Statistics* 25 (2): 239–46.
Solomons, D. 1961. Economic and accounting concepts of income. *Accounting Review* 36 (4): 374–83.
Statistics Canada. 2007. Depreciation rates for the productivity accounts. *Canadian Productivity Review,* no. 005, catalog no. 15-206-XIE. Microeconomics Analysis Division, Statistics Canada. Available at: http://www.statcan.gc.ca/pub/15-206-x/15-206-x2007005-eng.pdf.

Summers, R. 1973. International comparisons with incomplete data. *Review of Income and Wealth* 29 (1): 1–16.
Triplett, J. 2004. Handbook on hedonic indexes and quality adjustments in price indexes: Special application to information technology products. STI Working Paper no. 2004/9. OECD Directorate for Science, Technology and Industry. Available at: http://www.oecd.org.dataoecd/37/31/33789552.pdf.
U.S. Department of Labor, Bureau of Labor Statistics (BLS). 1983. Changing the home ownership component of the Consumer Price Index to rental equivalence. *CPI detailed report,* January: 7–13.
van den Bergen, D., M. de Haan, R. de Heij, and M. Horsten. 2005. Measuring capital in the Netherlands. Paper presented at the Meeting of the OECD Working Party on National Accounts. 11–14 October, Paris.
Verbrugge, R. 2006. The puzzling divergence of rents and user costs, 1980–2004. Paper presented at the OECD-IMF Workshop on Real Estate Price Indexes. 6–7 November, Paris. Available at: http://www.oecd.org/dataoecd/42/57/37612870.pdf.
Walras, L. 1954. *Elements of pure economics.* Trans. W. Jaffe. London: George Allen and Unwin. (orig.pub. 1874.)
Wenzlick, R. 1952. As I see the fluctuations in the selling prices of single family residences. *Real Estate Analyst* 21 (December 24): 541–8.
Woolford, K. 1999. Measuring inflation: A framework based on domestic final purchases. In *Proceedings of the Measurement of Inflation Conference,* ed. M. Silver and D. Fenwick, 534–43. Wales, U.K.: Cardiff University.
Wyngarden, H. 1927. *An index of local real estate prices.* Vol. 1, no. 2 of *Michigan business studies.* Ann Arbor: University of Michigan.

## Comments Alan Heston

Diewert brings to this chapter on the valuation of services flowing from durable assets a strong background rooted in academic conferences, the development of Organization for Economic Cooperation and Development (OECD) manuals, and hands-on experience with country methods. More recently, Diewert has been involved in contributing to manuals on national and international consumer price indexes and with advising governments on the subject of chapter 12 in this volume: the treatment of time-to-time indexes of owner-occupied housing (OOH). The chapter is long and rich in detail, providing a significant conceptual discussion and a panoramic view of how price statisticians have dealt in practice with measuring rental service flows for what is now the largest component of consumer expenditures in middle-, high-, and many low-income countries. Diewert has long advocated the user cost approach in most estimates of service flows from durables, and not surprisingly, compared to the net acquisitions and rental equivalence approaches, he devotes more space to user cost in his conceptual discussion of OOH.

Alan Heston was formerly professor of economics at the University of Pennsylvania.

## Treatment of Land

The reader is rewarded in Diewert's conceptual discussion of user cost with a very interesting section on unique durable goods, such as housing. In this section, Diewert makes an important point that is generally ignored: namely that an OOH index should include both land and structure, and separate accounts for the two should be kept in building up user cost. The reason for this is clear when one is considering the value measure—namely that of structures—that requires depreciation when estimating user cost.

In reviewing the acquisitions cost approach, an early method that remains in use in several countries, Diewert makes clear a number of its limitations, including the fact that it does not allow for land values. Turning to rental equivalence, one common approach is to use rental surveys to impute the flow of rents to OOH by type, size, location, and other stratifications. This is practiced in a number of OECD countries, and it implicitly reflects the rental value of residential land. An alternative approach that is used in many countries without rental surveys is to impute rental equivalence on the basis of the cost or replacement value of structures. Typically, the opportunity cost of the value of the land is ignored in this approach. In fact, many governments that impose a real property tax keep separate current values for both land and structure, so the task of keeping separate accounts may not be that difficult to implement.

In addition to the treatment of structures versus land, Diewert notes that the effect of age of structure on depreciation is closely tied to the amount of maintenance expenditures on the structure. Structures that are not maintained drop out of the housing stock as they age, whereas structures that are maintained often take on increased value after a certain age, both because of their vintage value and the land value. In the work reported in Heston and Nakamura (2009), it is found that in hedonic regressions on observed rents, if age and age squared are used as variables, then they respectively have negative and positive coefficients for Washington, DC, where the vintage effects sets in at about eighty years of age. This result, then, is quite consistent with the story abandonment versus maintenance that Diewert notes.

## User Cost and Rental Equivalence

User costs require an estimate of the flow of shelter services from the housing stock in current prices, which in turn requires a constant-quality corrected index of housing costs, service-life estimates, and a real interest rate that takes into account expected depreciation. Not surprisingly, few countries can provide good estimates of these variables. Unfortunately, empirical studies do not even find that current housing prices bear a relationship with current rents that is consistent with reasonable estimates of interest rates, expected appreciation, and service lives. Further, there are large differences in the rent-house price ratio across space in the same country and over time for the same location. Existing empirical findings simply do not support the application of user cost to estimate rent indexes or the opposite.[1] However, the message is certainly not to abandon user cost, but rather to devote more research to finding out more about the relationship between market rents and user costs.

The last part of Diewert's chapter takes on this task, concluding with a proposal in applications to take neither user cost nor market rents exclusively as the price of housing. The remaining discussion will consider: first, the weight of OOH in the Bureau of Labor Statistics (BLS) Consumer Price Index (CPI); second, the differences between user costs of landlords versus homeowners and the implication for CPIs in general; third, the observed divergences of rents and user cost; and finally, Diewert's proposal on how to deal with rent and user cost differences.

## The Expenditure Weight of Owner-Occupied Housing

The share of OOH shelter expenditures was 13.4 percent of the CPI weight based on the 2002 BLS Consumer Expenditure Survey (CES), larger than motor vehicles at 8.9 percent or food at 7.9 percent. While the BLS in the United States has experimented with alternative ways to derive this estimate, it presently relies on the response to the following question in the CES:

*If someone were to rent your home today, how much do you think it would rent for monthly, unfurnished and without utilities?*

Taking this response, the location, some characteristics of the dwelling, and the sampling frame of the CES, it is possible to estimate an OOH weight to apply to the temporal index of rents from the CPI survey.

Some research based on a special survey described in Heston and Nakamura (2009) had an estimate of rent by owners with characteristics that were part of the sample that also included renters. So, it was possible in several, quite different geographical areas of the United States to hold constant floor area, bathrooms, and other measurable characteristics and to see if owners typically would impute their rent the same as the market. In the four survey areas considered, it was found that owners estimated their market rent as 14 percent, 19 percent, 9 percent, and 21 percent higher than in a comparable rented dwelling.

It is likely that owners value characteristics of their houses higher than the market does, but it is also plausible that it may be due to asymmetry of information available to rental agents and potential renters versus the owner. The argument would be that the homeowner possesses much more knowledge of the unmeasured quality features of his or her dwelling than

1. See the paper of Garner and Verbrugge (2009) and earlier work of Verbrugge cited there.

do others. In any event, if this result is totally due to unmeasured quality differences, it would mean that the weight of OOH is moving in the right direction. However, to the extent it is hubris on the part of owners, then it operates to overstate the share of OOH in consumer expenditures.

### User Costs of Landlords versus Owners

Diewert provides a thorough discussion of issues involved in treating financial costs of landlords versus owners. Typically, homeowners insurance is a financial cost that is usually a separate category of consumer expenditures, as is insurance for movable property of renters. Property taxes appear to affect rented housing and OOH similarly, while transactions costs involved in the purchase of a home for a landlord and a homeowner are less clear. And country practice with respect to the line to be drawn between routine maintenance and renovations that should be capitalized has yet to be harmonized.

Diewert considers other differences that may exist between the user cost of landlords versus owners, where the direction of divergence is clearer. These include damage costs, vacancy and default on rent costs, billing costs, and tax advantages of homeownership, at least in the United States. Usually, adjustments are made to surveyed rents for another landlord cost—namely, any included extras, such as appliances and utilities. All of these factors operate to make surveyed rents higher than the user cost of OOH. So, simple application of market rents, stratified by size, location, or other features, to estimate the share of OOH would appear to produce too large a share. Note that this can result in an effect similar in direction to that when owners are asked to estimate the rent their dwelling would get on the market.

### Observed Differences Between User Cost, Rent Proposal, and Rent-Price Ratios

Diewert considers a number of ways to measure user costs. He notes that the key ingredient of user cost is the real interest rate—namely, the interest cost, less expected appreciation on the dwelling and land. As Diewert points out, use of ex post appreciation often produces highly volatile results and sometimes even negative user costs. This is hardly the practical measure anyone would want to use, except perhaps to disparage the user cost approach. However, even use of a less volatile ex ante appreciation rate appears in application to produce more fluctuations than market rents. Garner and Verbrugge (2009) construct ex ante appreciation rates and estimate market rents for median structures for five U.S. cities over the period 1982 to 2002. This permits a comparison of user costs and rents with some common and idiosyncratic behaviors across cities.

The striking results are that annual user costs move from nearly zero to over $30,000 a year for median structures in Los Angeles and New York City over the period, while in Chicago, they varied within the $5,000 to $10,000 range and were usually below predicted rents. Garner and Verbrugge (2009) also examine price-to-rent ratios across the cities, and these are about nine on average in Houston, compared to thirteen in Los Angeles and New York City and twelve in Chicago and Philadelphia. The pattern over the 1982 to 2002 period displays wide fluctuations and is not very similar from year to year across the cities.

Heston and Nakamura (2009) pick up on another aspect of the price-to-rent ratios—namely that they appear to systematically rise with the price of a house within cities. Diewert has a nice life cycle explanation of this finding—namely that there is market segmentation. Young families are actively in the rental market until their increased income allows them to move to larger and more expensive accommodation. Typically, there is relatively little supply and relatively even less demand for more expensive accommodation, so price-to-rent ratios are higher. This story is also consistent with the fact that land values enter into the total price of housing; renters of larger housing are unlikely to want to pay the user cost of the land associated with such housing, hence a rising price-to-rent ratio. Whatever the explanation, if there is such market segmentation, then it is important to understand how this might affect time-to-time indexes as typically constructed by both price and national income statisticians.

### Diewert's Proposal

Diewert concludes, "We suggest that the best pricing concept for the services of OOH is the opportunity cost approach, which is equal to the maximum of the market rental and the ex ante user cost for any particular property" (see chapter 12 of this volume).

Market rents certainly are a more stable series and are not subject to the substantial plummets of user cost that characterize national experience in the United States or the experience of Los Angeles and New York City, as shown in the previously cited results. However, Diewert's conclusion is unlikely to be adapted soon by national statistical offices if they simply look at the five city results of Garner and Verbrugge. This is because in those years when user costs exceed market rents, their substitution for rents would lead to a more than doubling of the rent index in some cities, with equivalent drops when user costs went below rent.

However, Diewert's proposal is clearly more attractive if one argues that the appropriate internal user cost to an owner is not the annual fluctuation in user cost but some average of several years to cover the substantial transactions costs associated with property exchanges. As Diewert notes, often user cost may exceed market rents by a fairly stable factor for a number of years, which has been the case in Chicago. Thus, I would end up endorsing very strongly Diewert when he says there is a "need for statistical agencies to produce *both* user costs and equivalent rent price series for their CPI users. This *opportunity cost approach to pricing the services of durable assets* could also be used in production and productivity accounts, and this treatment would eliminate the problem of negative user costs, because market rents would always be nonnegative" (see chapter 12 of this volume).

Once statistical offices develop more measures of user costs for housing, it is likely to lead to satisfactory ways of implementing Diewert's proposal. So, not only has Diewert provided us with a definitive discussion of the theoretical and practical issues surrounding the treatment durables and owner-occupied housing, but he has also provided us with an important insight into further improving practice. Rather than go for any of the existing methods, he recommends opportunity cost to homeowners as the unifying concept, which in turn leads to a new treatment of OOH that, with some fine-tuning, seems practical to implement—not a small achievement.

## References

Garner, T. I., and R. Verbrugge. 2009. The puzzling divergence of rents and user costs, 1980–2004: Summary and extensions. In *Price and productivity measurement,* Vol. 1, *Housing*, ed. W. E. Diewert, B. M. Balk, D. Fixler, K. J. Fox, and A. O. Nakamura, 125–46. Victoria, B.C.: Trafford Press.

Heston, A., and A. Nakamura. 2009. Reported prices and rents of housing: Reflections of costs, amenities or both? In *Price and productivity measurement*, Vol. 1, *Housing,* ed. W. E. Diewert, B. M. Balk, D. Fixler, K. J. Fox, and A. O. Nakamura, 117–24. Victoria, B.C.: Trafford Press.

# Contributors

Susanto Basu
Department of Economics
Boston College
140 Commonwealth Avenue
Chestnut Hill, MA 02467

Ernst R. Berndt
Sloan School of Management
Massachusetts Institute of Technology, Room E52-452
50 Memorial Drive
Cambridge, MA 02142

Ralph Bradley
Division of Price and Index Number Research
Bureau of Labor Statistics
2 Massachusetts Avenue, NE Suite 3105
Washington, D.C. 20212

Jonathan E. Conklin
Thomson Reuters
5425 Hollister Avenue, Suite 140
Santa Barbara, CA 93111

Jan de Haan
Statistics Netherlands
P.O. Box 24500
2490 HA The Hague
The Netherlands

W. Erwin Diewert
Department of Economics
University of British Columbia
#997-1873 East Mall
Vancouver, B.C. V6T 1Z1
Canada

Robert C. Feenstra
Department of Economics
University of California, Davis
One Shields Avenue
Davis, CA 95616

John G. Fernald
Research Department, Mail Stop 1130
Federal Reserve Bank of San Francisco
101 Market Street
San Francisco, CA 94105

Dennis Fixler
Bureau of Economic Analysis
1441 L Street, NW
Washington, D.C. 20230

Barbara M. Fraumeni
Muskie School of Public Service
University of Southern Maine
P.O. Box 9300
34 Bedford Street
Portland, ME 04104

Robert J. Gordon
Department of Economics
Northwestern University
Evanston, IL 60208

John Greenlees
Division of Price and Index Number Research
Bureau of Labor Statistics
2 Massachusetts Avenue, NE Suite 3105
Washington, D.C. 20212

Jerry Hausman
Department of Economics
Massachusetts Institute of Technology, Room E52-271A
50 Memorial Drive
Cambridge, MA 02139

Saeed Heravi
Cardiff Business School
Cardiff University
Colum Drive
Cardiff, CF10 3EU
United Kingdom

Alan Heston
Department of Economics
University of Pennsylvania
3718 Locust Walk
Philadelphia, PA 19104

Peter Hill
Broadwater
The Street
Flordon
Norwich NR15 1RN
United Kingdom

Robert Houchens
Thomson Reuters
5425 Hollister Avenue, Suite 140
Santa Barbara, CA 93111

Charles Hulten
Department of Economics
University of Maryland
Tydings Hall, Room 3105
College Park, MD 20742

Christopher R. Knittel
University of California, Davis
Department of Economics
One Shields Avenue
Davis, CA 95616

Ephraim Leibtag
Economic Research Service
U.S. Department of Agriculture, Room N2124
1800 M Street, NW
Washington, D.C. 20036

William D. Marder
Thomson Reuters
150 Cambridge Park Drive, second floor
Cambridge, MA 02140

Marshall Reinsdorf
Bureau of Economic Analysis
1441 L Street, NW
Washington, D.C. 20230

Brooks B. Robinson
Economic Advisor, U.S. Pacific Command HQ, USPACOM J01E/J5ECON
Box 64015
Camp H. M. Smith, HI 96861

Paul Schreyer
Organization for Economic Cooperation and Development
2, rue André Pascal
F-75775 Paris Cedex 16
France

Mick Silver
International Monetary Fund
HQ2 Room 10A 641
700 19th Street, NW
Washington, D.C. 20431

Xue Song
Thomson Reuters
150 Cambridge Park Drive, second floor
Cambridge, MA 02140

Jack E. Triplett
The Brookings Institution
1775 Massachusetts Avenue, NW
Washington, D.C. 20036

J. Christina Wang
Federal Reserve Bank of Boston
600 Atlantic Avenue
Boston, MA 02210

Alan G. White
Analysis Group, Inc.
111 Huntington Avenue, tenth floor
Boston, MA 02199

Matthew P. Williams
Bureau of Economic Analysis
1441 L Street, NW
Washington, D.C. 20230

Kam Yu
Department of Economics
Lakehead University
Room RC 3016 B
Thunder Bay, Ontario
Canada P7B 5E1

# Author Index

# Subject Index